JUST IMAGINE...

DAI

METROPOLITAN NEW PER

TOGETHER AGAIN FOR TH FIRST TI

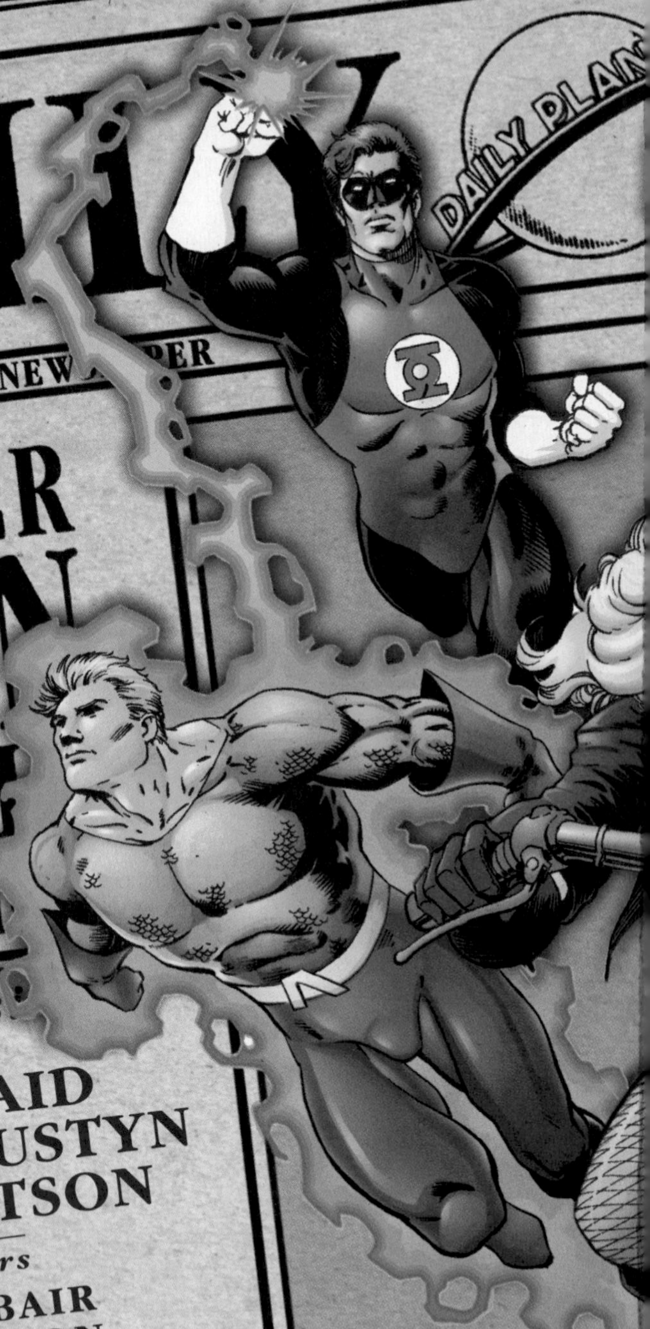

DAILY PLAN

Exclusive Ins

MARK WAID
BRIAN AUGUSTYN
BARRY KITSON

Storytellers

MICHAEL BAIR
BARRY KITSON
MARK PROPST
JOHN STOKES

Inkers

PAT GARRAHY

Colorist

KEN LOPEZ

Letterer

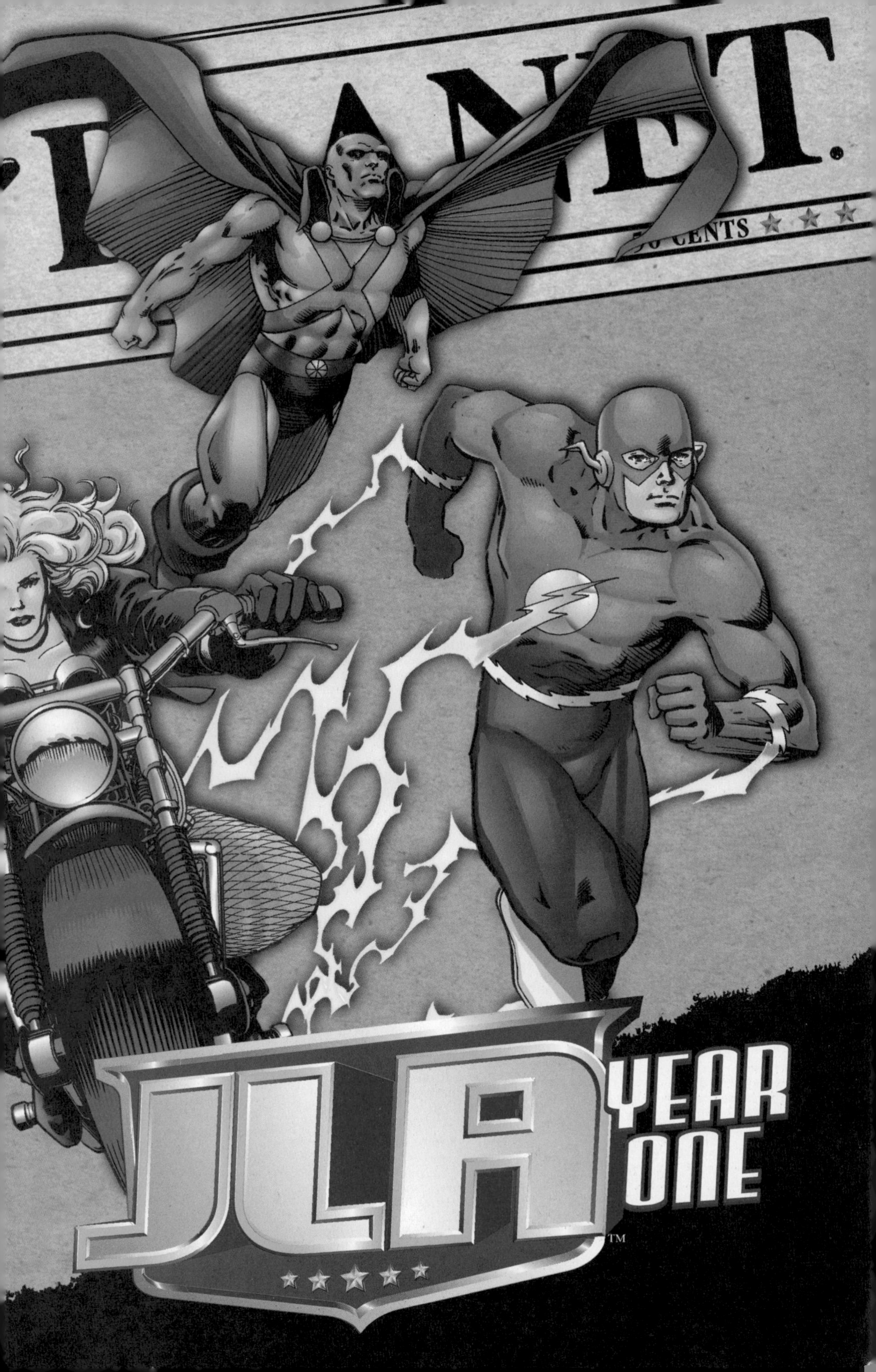
CENTS
JLA
YEAR
ONE
TM

An Introduction to JLA Year One

TOGETHER AGAIN FOR THE FIRST TIME

★★★ DAILY PLANET ★★★

The Justice League. The world's greatest super-heroes — an alliance of solo superstars, each impressive on his or her own, coming together to battle threats too large for any one hero. Famous. Storied. Experienced.

Sounds about right? Okay, now try this:

The Justice League. Two young champions — one a cocky extrovert, one an analytical introvert — one second-generation vigilante out to prove something to her mother, and two outsiders — one an angry loner, the other a cautious philosopher, intentionally distanced from the world around him. New. Raw. Nervous with one another and their new roles.

Not quite the same thing, eh? At least, not until now...

It's always dangerous to mess around with the past — and I've had a little experience with that here and there, so trust me on that. And it's even trickier to mess around with the past of the DC Universe, where time is often subject to revision, and crises and zero hours have a habit of changing everything retroactively, without warning and, on occasion, without a clear plan as to how the new reality fits together, now that the old one's been overturned.

Case in point — the Justice League. Originally, when the origin of the League was told, back in JUSTICE LEAGUE OF AMERICA #9, it was pretty straightforward. Seven alien beings were sent to Earth to battle it out among themselves for the throne of their homeworld. Once there, they clashed with seven of Earth's super-champions — Superman, Batman, Wonder Woman, Flash, Green Lantern, Aquaman and the Martian Manhunter — who wound up banding together after their victory, in anticipation of the never-ending parade of threats it would take a team to triumph over.

Along the way, they inducted more members — including, at one point, Black Canary, who transferred to the JLA's world from Earth-Two, a parallel Earth that was home to the super-heroes of the 1940s.

And then, well, things changed.

As time rolled on, the age difference between the Justice Leaguers (who remained young, their pasts rolling up behind them in the manner of serial-fiction heroes) and the heroes of Earth-Two (who remained tied to the 1940s), became great enough that we learned an untold secret — the Black Canary who'd joined the League was actually the daughter of the one who'd fought crime during World War II.

CRISIS ON INFINITE EARTHS, the smash hit maxiseries that reorganized DC's realities in the 1980s, did away with the parallel Earths, so that those Earth-Two heroes suddenly became the heroes of Earth's past. And in the wake of Crisis, Wonder Woman's history was altered, so that she wasn't around when the JLA was formed. So in the next retelling of the JLA's origin, Black-Canary-the-second, who had now always been around, stepped into Wonder Woman's role.

Superman and Batman, who'd stayed in relatively minor roles anyway during the first pass through the JLA's early days, became more aloof as their own histories were tweaked and revised — and then the ZERO HOUR miniseries passed over the DC Universe, and in its wake, Batman had become an urban myth, rumored to exist without any hard proof, and not someone who could play the open, smiling part he did in JLA history.

And along the way, the Martian Manhunter's past was expanded and rewoven, Aquaman got a new origin, Green Lantern got a DWI and did time, and...

But it's okay. These things happen. They're super-heroes — they can take it.

The point is, JLA history had become something of a tangle, with changes overlaying revisions overlaying alterations, and more. So how to revisit that era and build something out of it to reintroduce the JLA's roots to a new generation of fans?

Simple — get Mark Waid and Brian Augustyn.

As Mark and Brian have proved time and again, in their years on THE FLASH, as writer and editor respectively, and then as co-writers, they understand the DC pantheon's rich heritage, and can explore it and build on it without their stories seeming in the least "old-fashioned" or their plots crumbling under the weight of all that has gone before. And for good measure, bring in Barry Kitson on the art — a rare talent who combines clear, straightforward storytelling with a thoroughly modern gloss.

And here you have the result — JLA YEAR ONE — and what a result it is! Not content to simply retell old stories with new players, or throw out the past wholesale, as many "Year One" projects have, Mark, Brian and Barry chose to weave an entirely new story through, between and around existing JLA history, preserving as much of the work of their predecessors as they could, while exploring that history, and those characters, in a new way.

And along the way, the creative team found considerable new ground to tread. The original JLA tales, for all that they're crisply drawn, deftly plotted and full of inventive twists and turns, were creations of their time — and it was a time that emphasized plot over characterization. The original JLAers came together because of their common bonds as super-heroes, and as the rational, mature, stable adults they were, they worked together as a team right away. But time rolls along, and things change, even in a world where the past stays relatively put, and comics have changed as well. Today's readers want their plot-twists and bold heroes — but along with that, they also want to get to know their heroes, to see what makes them tick, what goes on beneath the heroic facades.

So while Mark, Brian and Barry spun their tale of alien invasion and conspiracy, they looked beyond the JLAers' common bonds, looking for what made their heroes different, not the same. And they found plenty — Green Lantern's fearless confidence contrasting with the Martian Manhunter's ingrained reticence and secretiveness, the Flash's quiet awe of his heroic predecessors contrasting with Black Canary's assertive familiarity with her mother's generation, and Aquaman's confusion at his natural abilities causing him to be thought of as a "super-hero" at all. And they told the story we missed back then — of a group of young individuals, just starting their careers, finding their way into teamwork, into mutual trust and respect, as they built the foundations of the rich heritage that would follow.

And the end result? An absolutely contemporary take on a grand tradition, an epic that resonates with the atmosphere of the tales that made Mark, Brian and Barry fans of this material in the first place, while bringing a fresh viewpoint and a vivid sense of character to the proceedings.

So if you're a newcomer to the JLA, be confident — you're in for a treat, as you learn where the League of today came from. And if you're a longtime fan, you're in luck as well — since you'll get to see the legend you love fleshed out with skill, respect and new depth, as you see the formation of bonds you could only imagine before.

Lucky you, whoever you are.

Kurt Busiek, the award-winning writer of Astro City *and* Avengers, *hasn't had much opportunity to root about in DC's past (though he did take part in the revamp/reboot of the* Legion of Super-Heroes *in "End of an Era"), but he has played around extensively with the early days of Marvel's universe, in such series as* Marvels, Untold Tales of Spider-Man *and* Iron Man: The Iron Age.

★ ★ ★ DAILY PLANET ★ ★ ★

By Clark Kent

INVASION ROUTED!

Appellaxian Alien Defeated in JLA's Inaugural Case

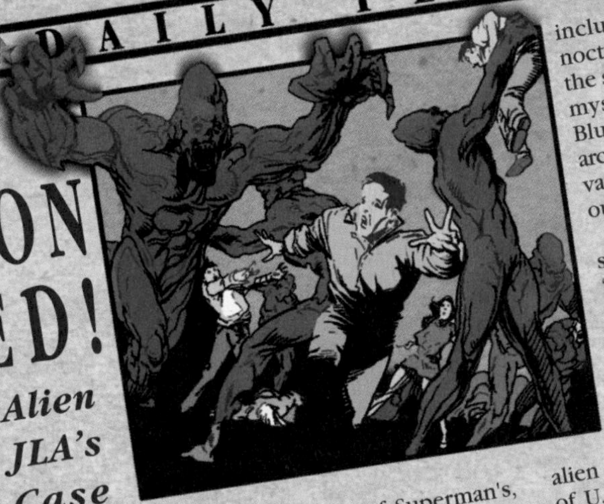

GOTHAM CITY—Earth owes its freedom to the JLA, a name sure to make headlines in coming days. Last Thursday, an apparent invasion of alien beings from the planet Appellax, a world orbiting the distant star Andromache, was routed by a small group of fledgling "super-heroes" from five separate American cities who have since united to call themselves the Justice League of America. In the grand tradition of the Justice Society of America and latter-day contemporaries such as the recently active Doom Patrol and the stalwart Challengers of the Unknown, the JLA promises to stand as the United States' and Earth's first line of defense against evil threats.

"Just like the Justice Society of old, we've marshaled our abilities to serve America and the world in time of need," said the Black Canary, costumed adventurer of Star City. "Get used to us."

While the Canary shattered a glass creature transforming Star City citizens into crystalline statues with her "Canary Cry," four of her comrades-in-arms defeated powerful aliens across the globe. The Flash, the "Fastest Man Alive" and champion of Central City, Kansas, defeated a being composed of fire in the British hamlet of Croydon. Coast City's Green Lantern used his miraculous power ring to prevent a giant golden avian alien from transforming wildlife of the African veldt into creatures resembling itself. In Middleton, Colorado, the so-called Martian Manhunter, an admitted extraterrestrial himself with powers rivalling those of Superman's, thwarted a colossal rocky giant which rumbled through the streets turning ordinary citizens to stone. Finally, it was reported that the maritime adventurer the press has dubbed "Aquaman" prevented an alien composed of mercury from poisoning the Atlantic Ocean by transmuting sealife into the same toxic element.

"I've seen worse dumped by surface-dwellers," said the taciturn amphibious hero.

Operating in tandem, the five super-powered defenders were able to defeat a sixth alien, a monstrosity of wood, in the Florida Everglades. Metropolis's own Superman beat the newly formed JLA to the punch in Antarctica, fending off a seventh and final invader, an alien whose body was literally composed of ice. Though rumored to have been offered a seat in the fledgling JLA, Superman has declined membership.

"I'm honored to have been asked," said Superman in an exclusive to *The Daily Planet*, "but my duties to the world take precedence. Perhaps someday I'll find a place in their remarkable ranks. Now just isn't the time."

While the JLA's roster stands at five core members, the team does not rule out the possibility that other costumed adventurers, including Gotham City's nocturnal avenger Batman, the size-reducing Atom, the mystical scarab-charged Blue Beetle, the emerald archer Green Arrow and various others were not out of consideration.

"I wouldn't pay to join," said the Green Arrow. "Now, if the pretty bird Canary said 'please,' I'd have to seriously think about it."

The Batman was unavailable for comment.

Though the defeated alien creatures, now in the custody of U.S. Army tactical forces under the command of General Wade Eiling, were all very much physically diverse, the JLA attest that all were part of a bizarre contest to lead the planet Appellax, using Earth as battleground for the vying candidates.

"The aliens' minds were transported to Earth in the various 'battle forms' my compatriots and I encountered," said the Martian Manhunter, who would not divulge the source of his startling revelations. "Rather than decimate their own world during thei 'contest'—as they have done i the past—the Appellaxians chos Earth, which they believed w beneath their concern and unc fended. I remain concerned th the Appellaxians were part o larger advance force of invader

DAILY PLANET
AILY
50 CENTS
METROPOLITAN NEWSPAPER
WORLD'S GREATEST
THE BALD AND THE BEAUTIFUL
VES TOWN
TO THE RESCUE

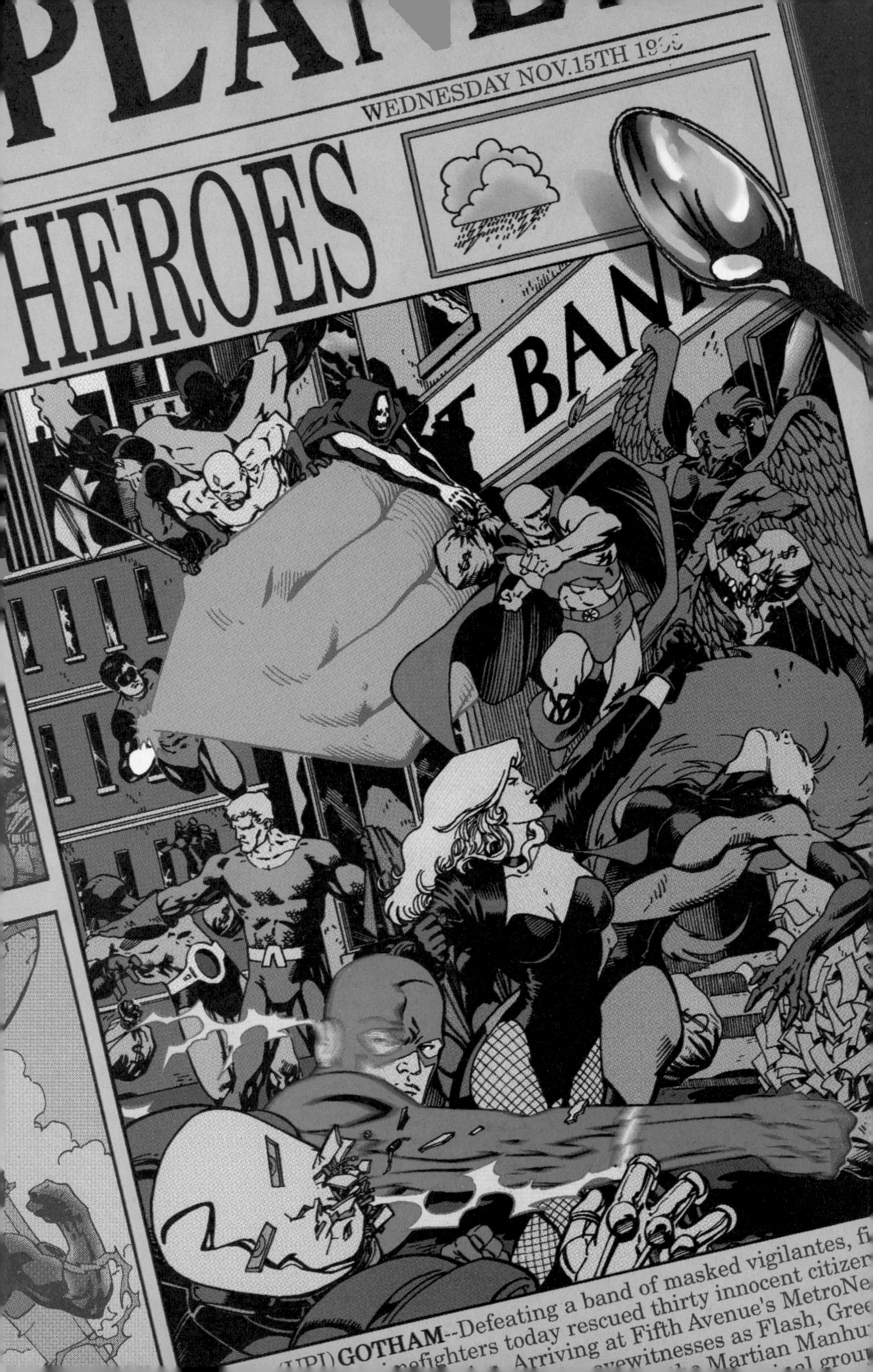
PLA
WEDNESDAY NOV.15TH 19
HEROES
BAN
(UPI) GOTHAM--Defeating a band of masked vigilantes,
today rescued thirty innocent
Arriving at Fifth Avenue's
as Flash,
Martian

CLASSIFIEDS

Savages at the Gate
Vandal Savage: Mogul or Myth?

And you thought Howard Hughes was quirky.

If you subscribe to the rumors circulating like legend through Manhattan's most exclusive men's clubs, the last bastions of misogyny where leather and mahogany are infused with the indelible smells of Havanas and Kentucky bourbon, then you'll know: Hughes's eccentricities were pitiable compared to what we know of the entrepreneur Vandal Savage. That, of course, is assuming that "Vandal Savage" is his real name.

Whispered about among bankers and corporate giants on Wall Street, Savage is a man with whom it seems every mover and shaker of note has done business, but whom no one has been able to boast of having met in person. Those who have spoken to Savage (and always over the telephone from what one imagines to be Savage's hidden opulent Xanadu fortress), describe an intelligent, almost commanding voice, though a bit on the gravelly side—as if only a few evolutionary steps removed from grunting. One commodities trader, who asked to remain anonymous, said Savage "speaks as if some dark, evil thing is ready to crawl up out of his throat and eat out your eyes."

Indeed.

Despite his interests in pharmaceuticals, medical and technological research,

as well as a dozen global philanthropies, Vandal Savage's myth colors an otherwise unquestionably giving soul.

Quite conversely, in the art world, Savage is an aficionado whose collection is the envy of museums and monarchs. But, in keeping with his dichotomous nature, Savage's tastes seem to vacillate between ancient Egyptian artifacts and Renaissance art. In fact, Savage once offered a blank check for the

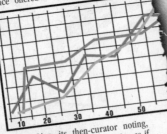

Mona Lisa, its then-curator noting, "Mr. Savage spoke of the painting as if he had known the subject affectionately. It was…*unsettling.*" Adding more kindling to Vandal Savage's fiery reputation, Egypt's Ministry of Antiquities has accused Savage of "leading expeditions to raid the tombs of at least two pharaohs of the fourth dynasty," a crime punishable by hang-

Continued on page following

CHICKEN MAN VS. THE EVIL EGG
The conundrum of metahuman heroes as cause or cure of super-villain psychosis
By Dr. Roger Huntoon, Ph.D.

Since the wartime Justice Society first donned colorful skintight costumes and banded together to keep America's shores safe from Axis spies and profiteers, our country has seen the threat of super-villains—super-heroes' opposite numbers dressed as garishly and wielding similarly destructive metahuman abilities.

In recent days, since the inheritors of the JSA's legacy, the similarly named Justice League of America, have declared their union, America has seen a dramatic spike in super-villain activity.

Consider the attacks of Eclipso, whose ebon gem has wrought havoc on several cities, turning its citizens to their very worst "dark sides." Or Thorn, once a foe of the original Green Lantern, who has threatened life and limb with her fast-growing spiked vines. Or Clayface (upon whom I have had the liberty to effect treatment while on staff at Gotham City's Arkham Asylum for the Criminally Insane), the tortured soul

Matthew Hagen, whose body has been irrevocably transformed into a gooey mud which can replicate anything or anyone Hagen imagines. And what of Solomon Grundy, a soulless monstrosity borne out of a swamp, whose desires to kill the Justice Society have always fueled his single-minded fury? The Invisible Destroyer, Xotar the Weapons Master, the Brotherhood of Evil—names right out of pulp novels—have dotted the media, very nearly making the public forget the latest government election and "normal" everyday life. This rash of super-villain activity threatens the very fabric of human existence and begs the question: Which came first, the hero or the villain?

Though many self-proclaimed super-heroes declare their exploits "reactive" to diabolical foes, I and quite a few of my colleagues assert that the heroes themselves spawn the very grim and gritty environment which fosters—and, dare I say, promotes—the rise of super-villainy. Look at the photographs. Doesn't Green Lantern fairly

beam with pleasure —more so than his customary emerald glow— after bashing the malformed genius Hector Hammond? It it his hyperspeed or infectious

glee that fuels the Flash when he makes a monkey out of the misunderstood evolutionary wonder Gorilla Grodd? Is being bitten by a radioactive some-such and granted miraculous powers with which to grind one's axe the genesis of super-villain behavior? Or is it the latent fear of being dominated by the beautiful Nietzschean men and women who fly above us and crowd out the sun? As a licensed psychotherapist and author, I've seen my fill of muta-

Continued on Page 325

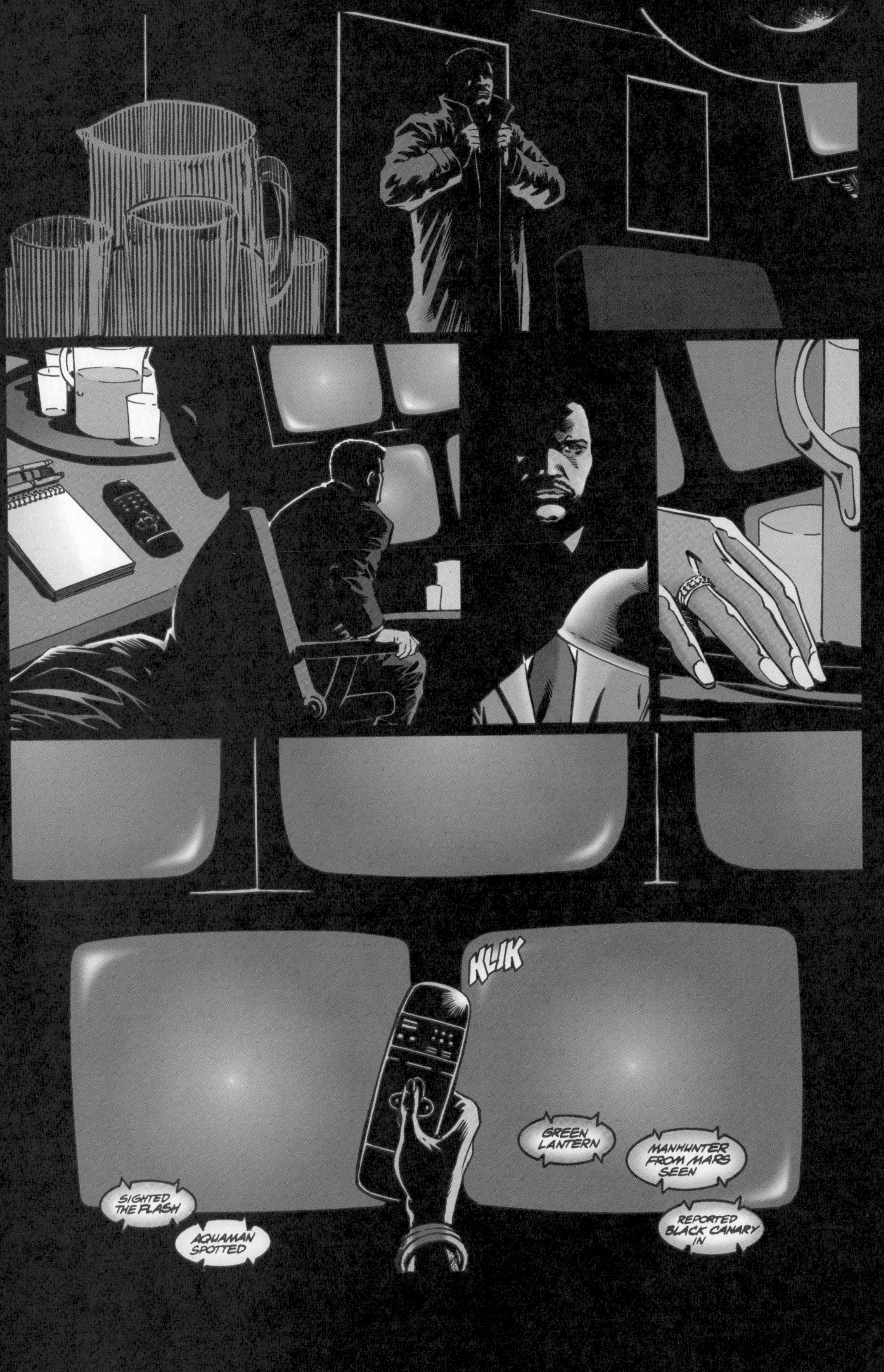
KLIK
SIGHTED THE FLASH
AQUAMAN SPOTTED
GREEN LANTERN
MANHUNTER FROM MARS SEEN
REPORTED BLACK CANARY IN

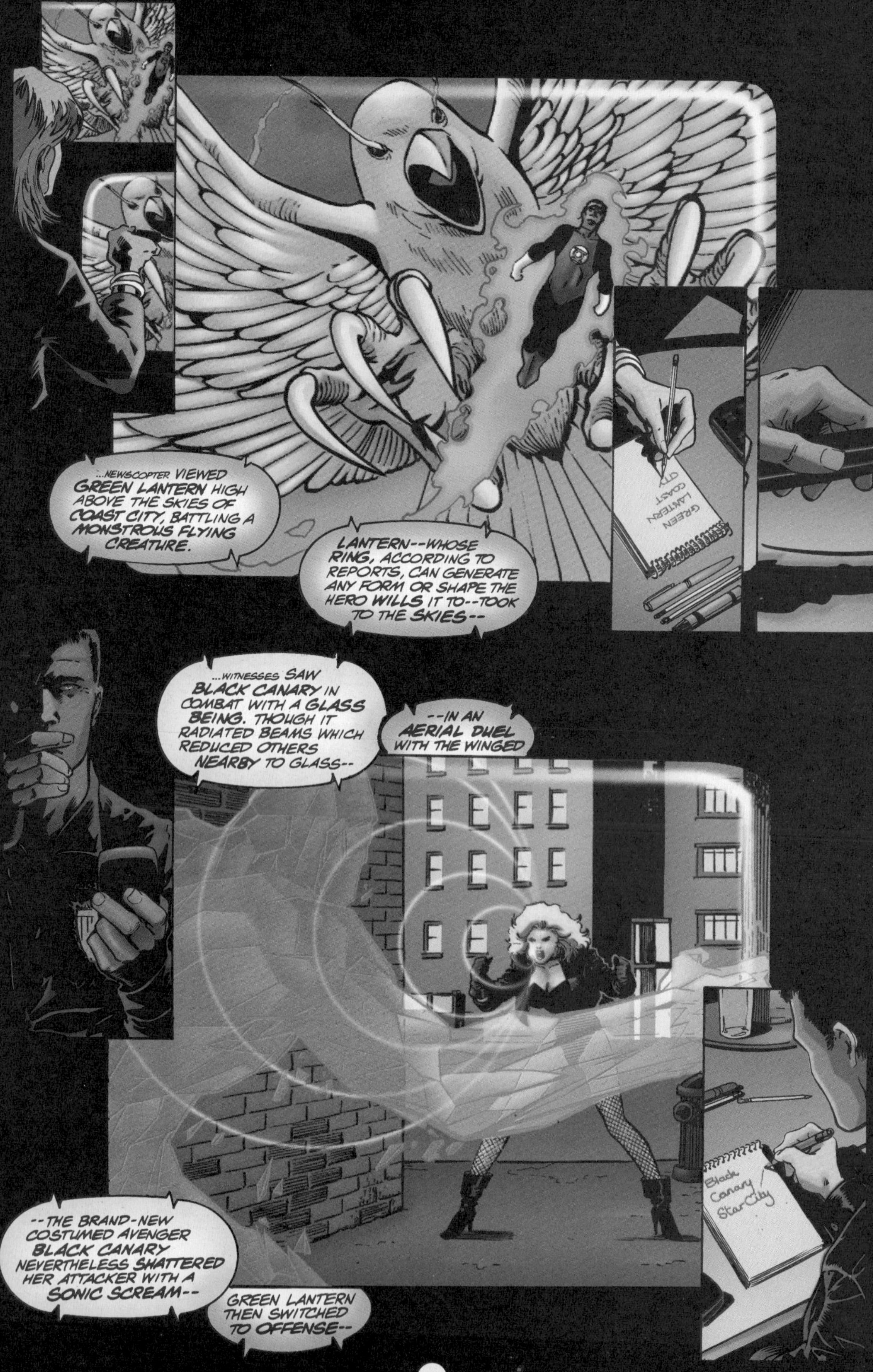
...NEWSCOPTER VIEWED GREEN LANTERN HIGH ABOVE THE SKIES OF COAST CITY, BATTLING A MONSTROUS FLYING CREATURE.
LANTERN--WHOSE RING, ACCORDING TO REPORTS, CAN GENERATE ANY FORM OR SHAPE THE HERO WILLS IT TO--TOOK TO THE SKIES--
GREEN LANTERN COAST CITY
...WITNESSES SAW BLACK CANARY IN COMBAT WITH A GLASS BEING. THOUGH IT RADIATED BEAMS WHICH REDUCED OTHERS NEARBY TO GLASS--
--IN AN AERIAL DUEL WITH THE WINGED
--THE BRAND-NEW COSTUMED AVENGER BLACK CANARY NEVERTHELESS SHATTERED HER ATTACKER WITH A SONIC SCREAM--
GREEN LANTERN THEN SWITCHED TO OFFENSE--
Black Canary Star City

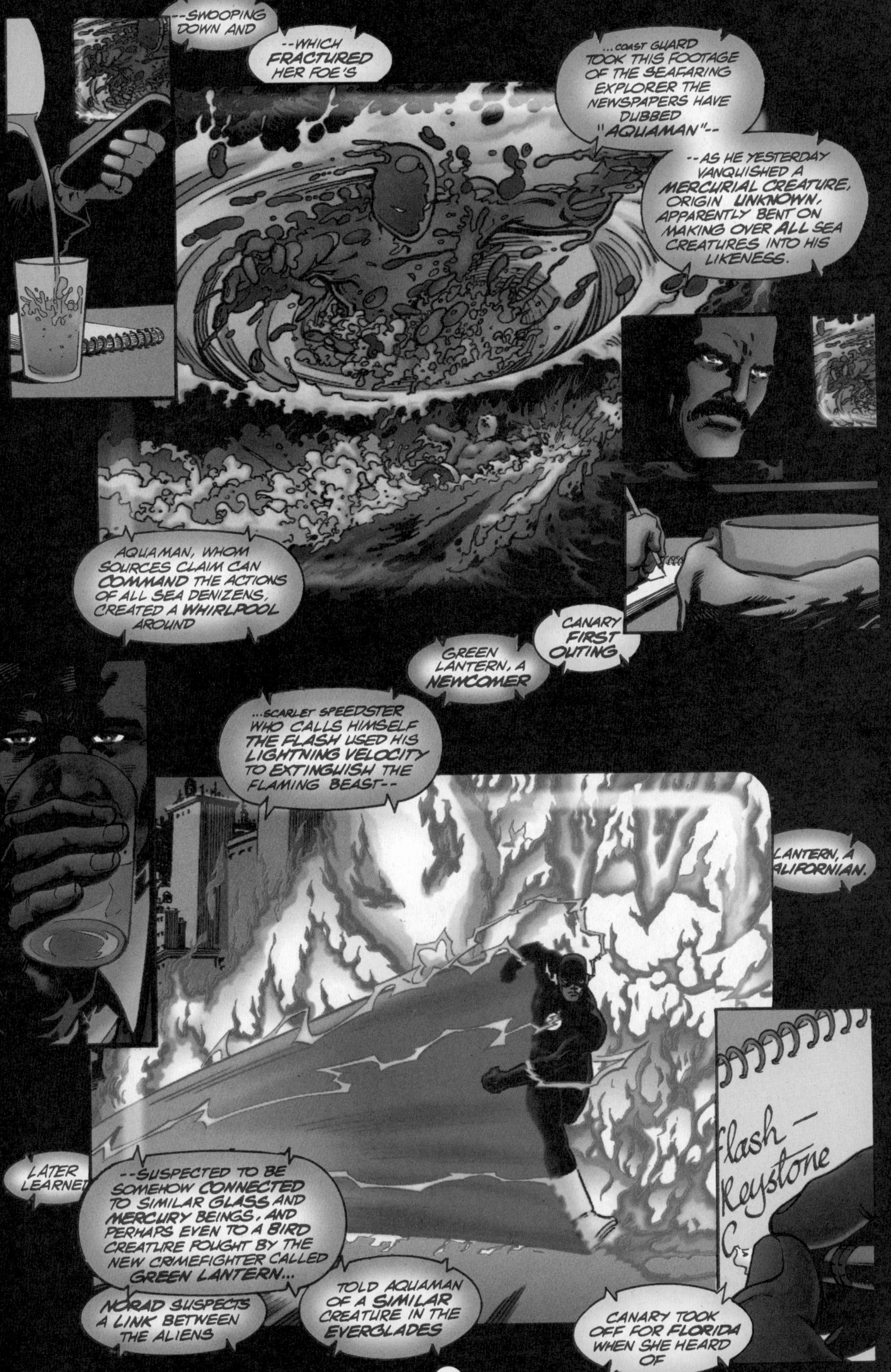

--SWOOPING DOWN AND
--WHICH FRACTURED HER FOE'S
...COAST GUARD TOOK THIS FOOTAGE OF THE SEAFARING EXPLORER THE NEWSPAPERS HAVE DUBBED "AQUAMAN"--
--AS HE YESTERDAY VANQUISHED A MERCURIAL CREATURE, ORIGIN UNKNOWN, APPARENTLY BENT ON MAKING OVER ALL SEA CREATURES INTO HIS LIKENESS.
AQUAMAN, WHOM SOURCES CLAIM CAN COMMAND THE ACTIONS OF ALL SEA DENIZENS, CREATED A WHIRLPOOL AROUND
CANARY FIRST OUTING
GREEN LANTERN, A NEWCOMER
...SCARLET SPEEDSTER WHO CALLS HIMSELF THE FLASH USED HIS LIGHTNING VELOCITY TO EXTINGUISH THE FLAMING BEAST--
LANTERN, A ALIFORNIAN.
flash - Keystone C
LATER LEARNED
--SUSPECTED TO BE SOMEHOW CONNECTED TO SIMILAR GLASS AND MERCURY BEINGS, AND PERHAPS EVEN TO A BIRD CREATURE FOUGHT BY THE NEW CRIMEFIGHTER CALLED GREEN LANTERN...
NORAD SUSPECTS A LINK BETWEEN THE ALIENS
TOLD AQUAMAN OF A SIMILAR CREATURE IN THE EVERGLADES
CANARY TOOK OFF FOR FLORIDA WHEN SHE HEARD OF

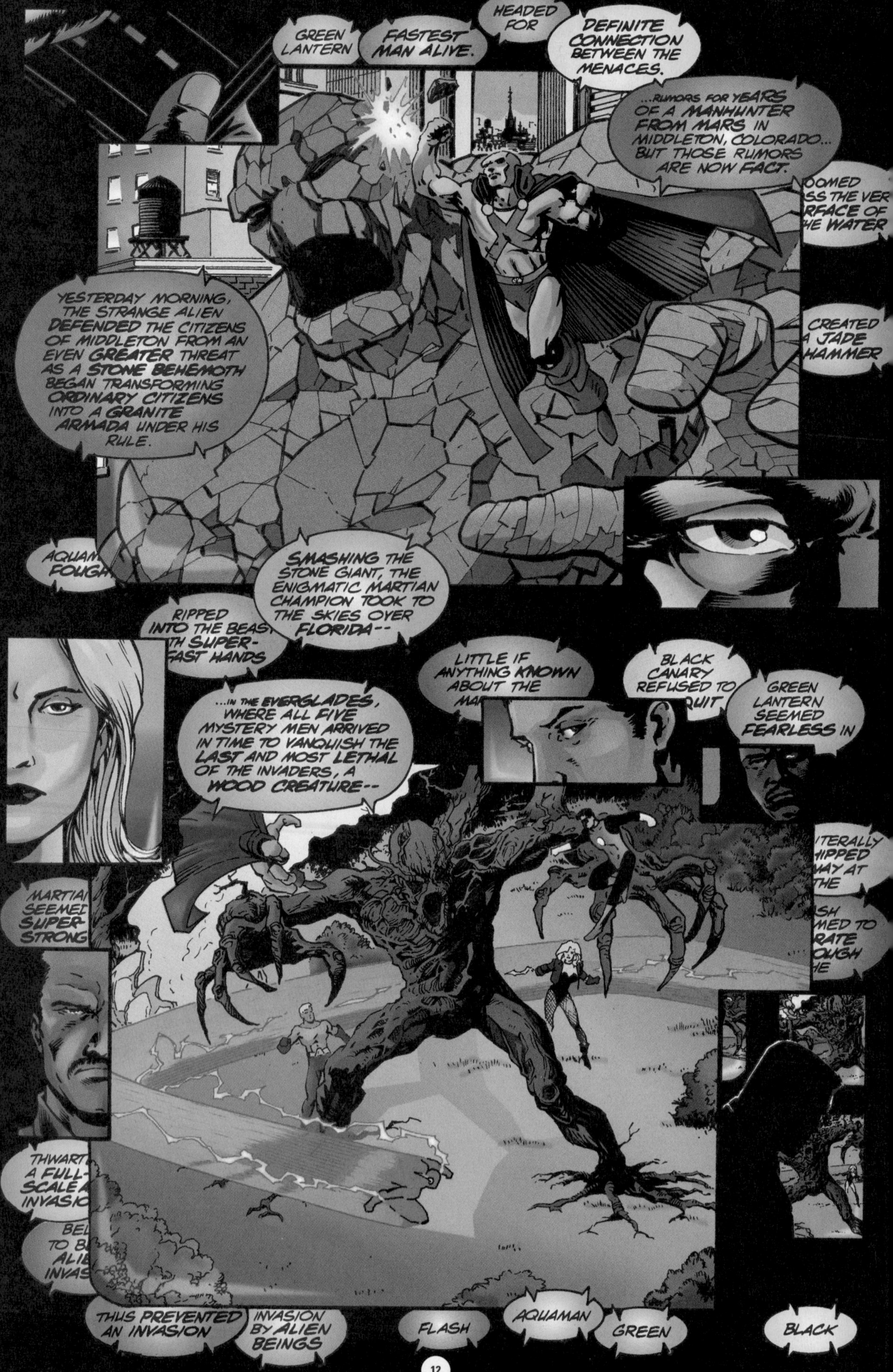

GREEN LANTERN
FASTEST MAN ALIVE.
HEADED FOR
DEFINITE CONNECTION BETWEEN THE MENACES.
...RUMORS FOR YEARS OF A MANHUNTER FROM MARS IN MIDDLETON, COLORADO... BUT THOSE RUMORS ARE NOW FACT.
OOMED
SS THE VER
RFACE OF
HE WATER
YESTERDAY MORNING, THE STRANGE ALIEN DEFENDED THE CITIZENS OF MIDDLETON FROM AN EVEN GREATER THREAT AS A STONE BEHEMOTH BEGAN TRANSFORMING ORDINARY CITIZENS INTO A GRANITE ARMADA UNDER HIS RULE.
CREATED A JADE HAMMER
AQUAM
FOUGH
SMASHING THE STONE GIANT, THE ENIGMATIC MARTIAN CHAMPION TOOK TO THE SKIES OVER FLORIDA--
RIPPED INTO THE BEAST
TH SUPER-FAST HANDS
LITTLE IF ANYTHING KNOWN ABOUT THE
BLACK CANARY REFUSED TO QUIT
GREEN LANTERN SEEMED FEARLESS IN
...IN THE EVERGLADES, WHERE ALL FIVE MYSTERY MEN ARRIVED IN TIME TO VANQUISH THE LAST AND MOST LETHAL OF THE INVADERS, A WOOD CREATURE--
ITERALLY
HIPPED
MAY AT
THE
MARTIA
SEEMED
SUPER-
STRONG
SH
MED TO
RATE
OUGH
HE
THWART
A FULL-
SCALE
INVASIO
BE
TO B
ALIE
INVAS
THUS PREVENTED AN INVASION
INVASION BY ALIEN BEINGS
FLASH
AQUAMAN
GREEN
BLACK

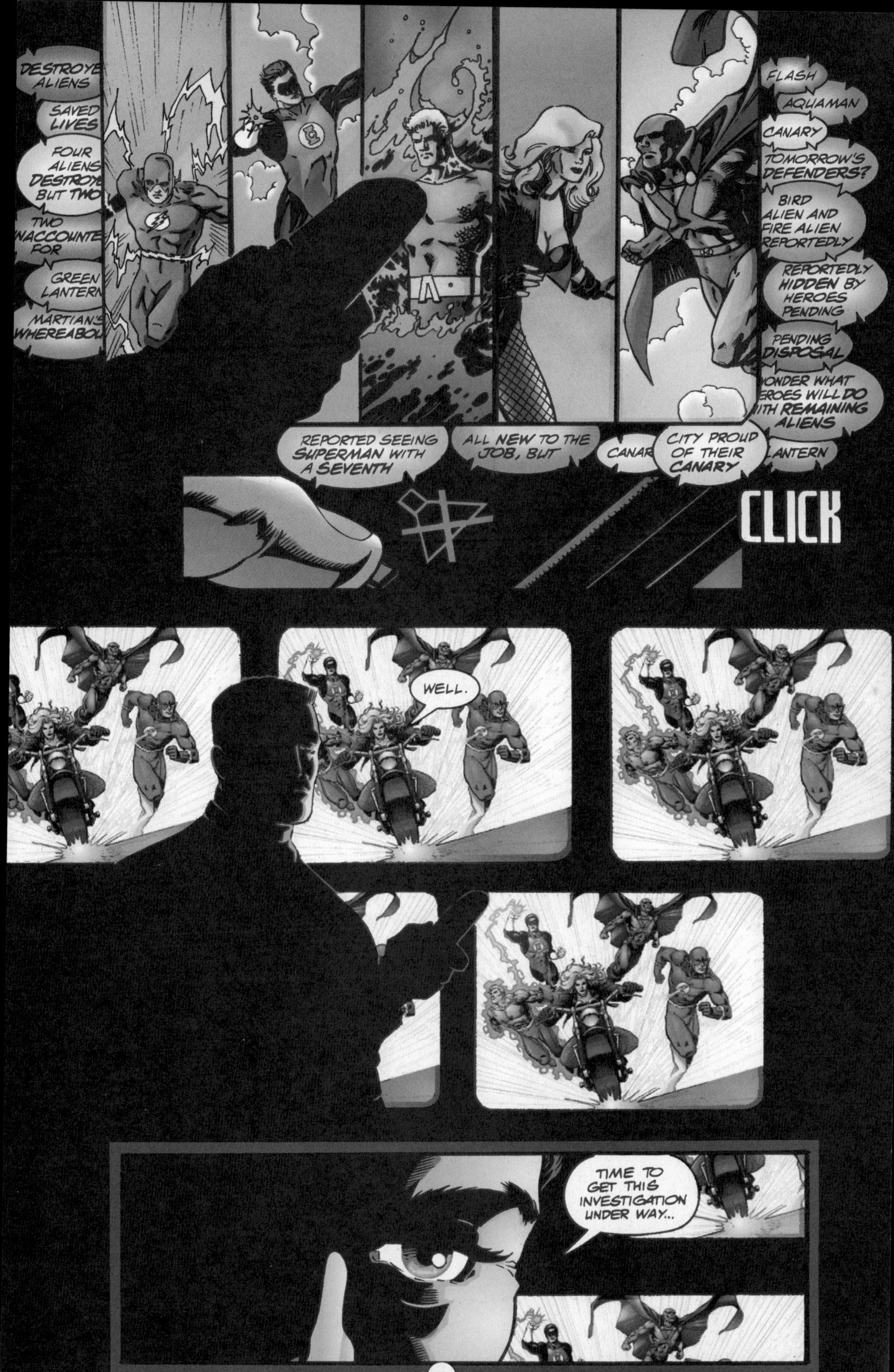
DESTROYE ALIENS
SAVED LIVES
FOUR ALIENS DESTROYE BUT TWO
TWO NACCOUNTE FOR
GREEN LANTERN
MARTIAN'S WHEREABOU
FLASH
AQUAMAN
CANARY
TOMORROW'S DEFENDERS?
BIRD ALIEN AND FIRE ALIEN REPORTEDLY
REPORTEDLY HIDDEN BY HEROES PENDING
PENDING DISPOSAL
WONDER WHAT HEROES WILL DO WITH REMAINING ALIENS
REPORTED SEEING SUPERMAN WITH A SEVENTH
ALL NEW TO THE JOB, BUT
CANAR
CITY PROUD OF THEIR CANARY
LANTERN
CLICK
WELL.
TIME TO GET THIS INVESTIGATION UNDER WAY...

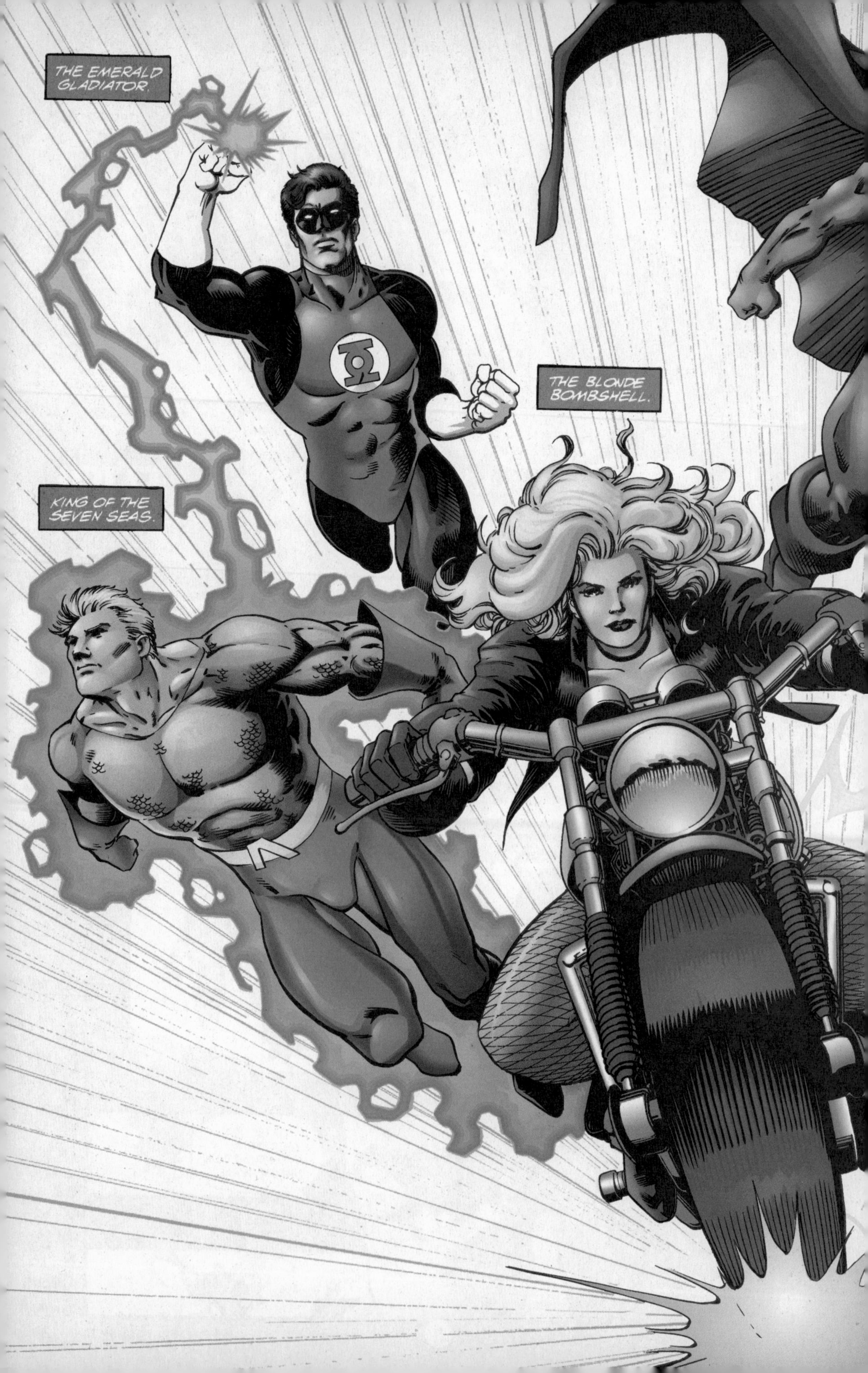
THE EMERALD GLADIATOR.
THE BLONDE BOMBSHELL.
KING OF THE SEVEN SEAS.

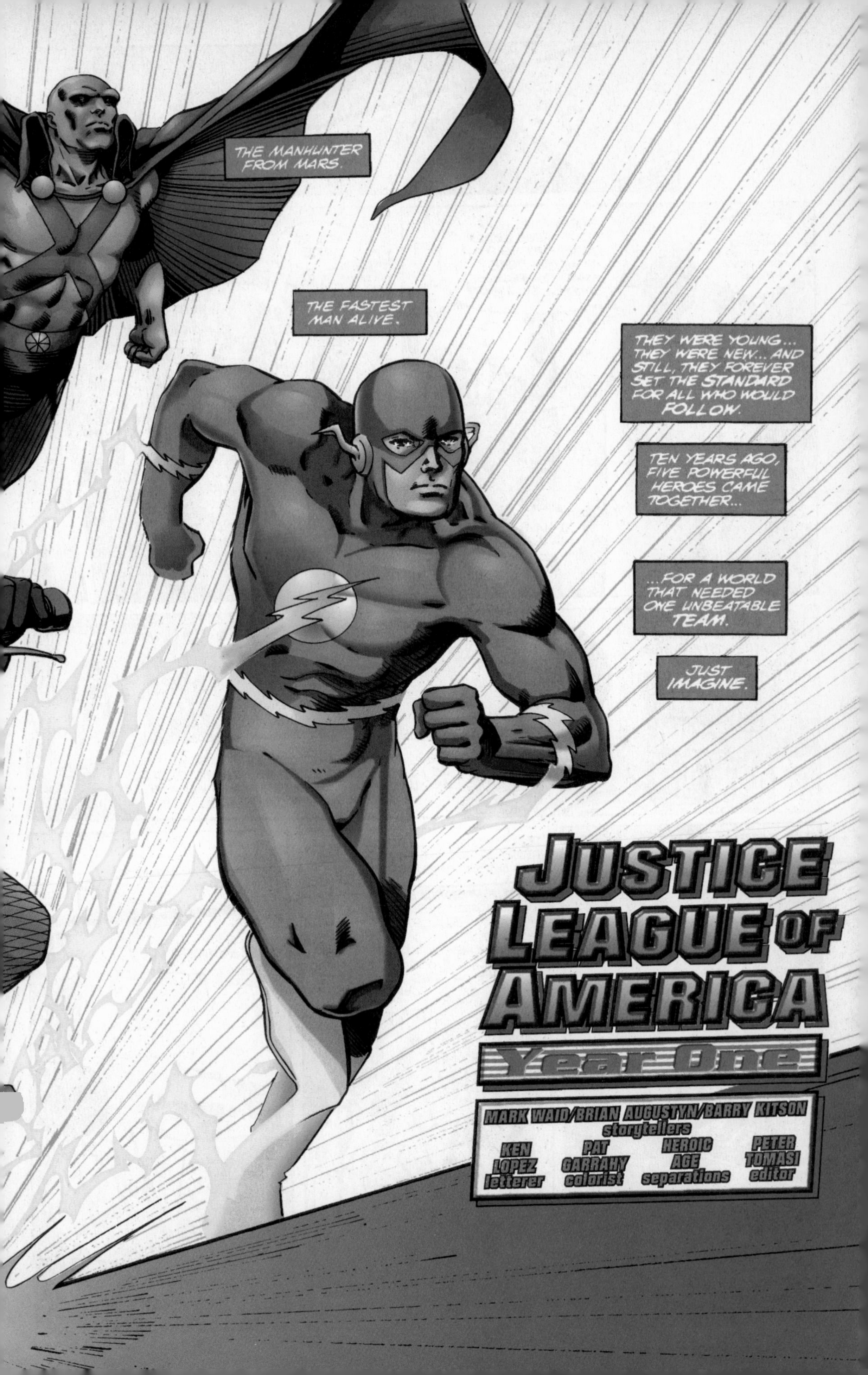
THE MANHUNTER FROM MARS.
THE FASTEST MAN ALIVE.
THEY WERE YOUNG... THEY WERE NEW... AND STILL, THEY FOREVER SET THE STANDARD FOR ALL WHO WOULD FOLLOW.
TEN YEARS AGO, FIVE POWERFUL HEROES CAME TOGETHER...
...FOR A WORLD THAT NEEDED ONE UNBEATABLE TEAM.
JUST IMAGINE.
JUSTICE LEAGUE OF AMERICA
Year One
MARK WAID/BRIAN AUGUSTYN/BARRY KITSON storytellers
KEN LOPEZ letterer
PAT GARRAHY colorist
HEROIC AGE separations
PETER TOMASI editor

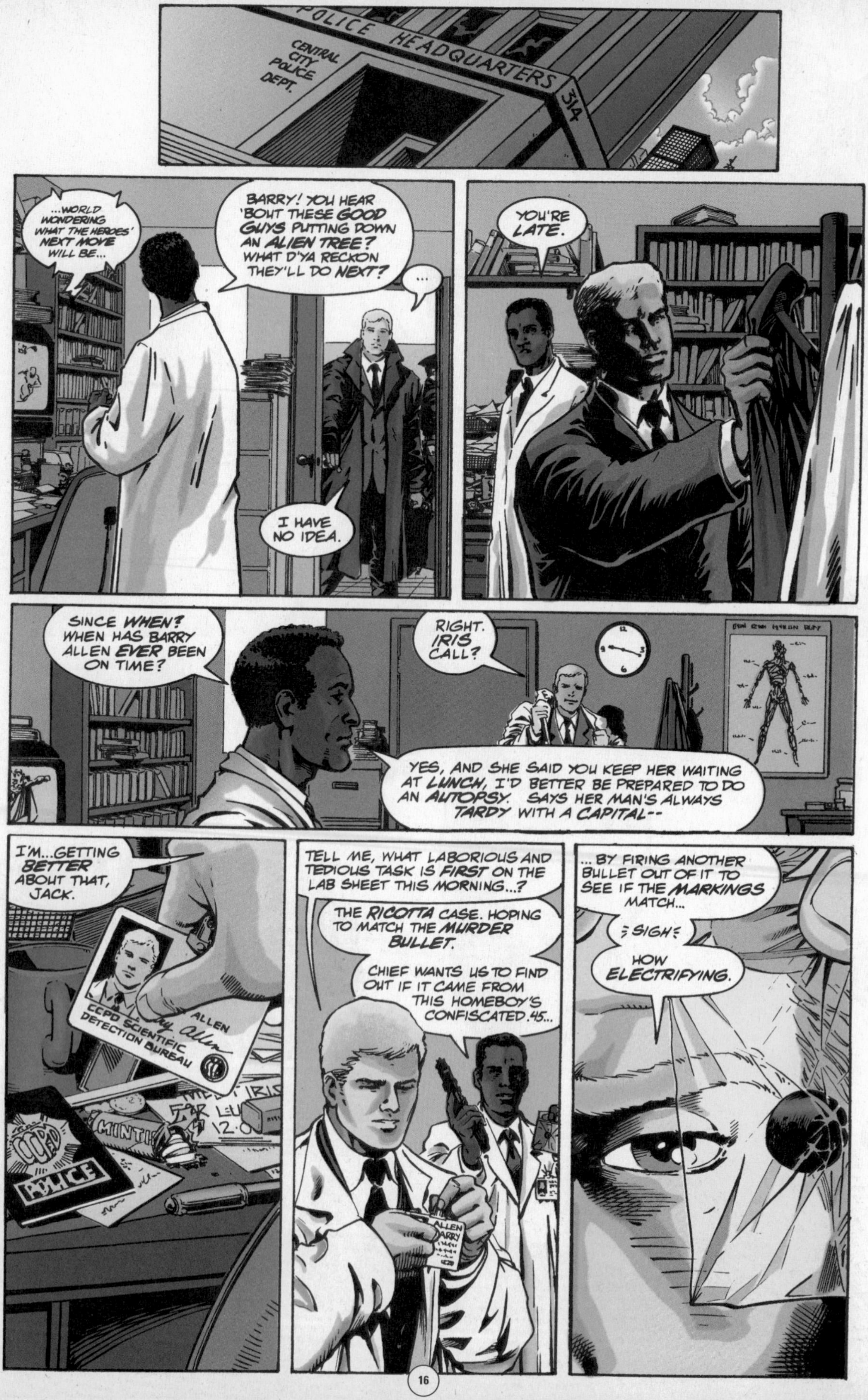
POLICE HEADQUARTERS
CENTRAL CITY POLICE DEPT.
314
...WORLD WONDERING WHAT THE HEROES' NEXT MOVE WILL BE...
BARRY! YOU HEAR 'BOUT THESE GOOD GUYS PUTTING DOWN AN ALIEN TREE? WHAT D'YA RECKON THEY'LL DO NEXT?
...
I HAVE NO IDEA.
YOU'RE LATE.
SINCE WHEN? WHEN HAS BARRY ALLEN EVER BEEN ON TIME?
RIGHT. IRIS CALL?
YES, AND SHE SAID YOU KEEP HER WAITING AT LUNCH, I'D BETTER BE PREPARED TO DO AN AUTOPSY. SAYS HER MAN'S ALWAYS TARDY WITH A CAPITAL--
I'M...GETTING BETTER ABOUT THAT, JACK.
ALLEN
CCPD SCIENTIFIC DETECTION BUREAU
CCPD
POLICE
TELL ME, WHAT LABORIOUS AND TEDIOUS TASK IS FIRST ON THE LAB SHEET THIS MORNING...?
THE RICOTTA CASE. HOPING TO MATCH THE MURDER BULLET.
CHIEF WANTS US TO FIND OUT IF IT CAME FROM THIS HOMEBOY'S CONFISCATED .45...
ALLEN BARRY
... BY FIRING ANOTHER BULLET OUT OF IT TO SEE IF THE MARKINGS MATCH...
SIGH
HOW ELECTRIFYING.

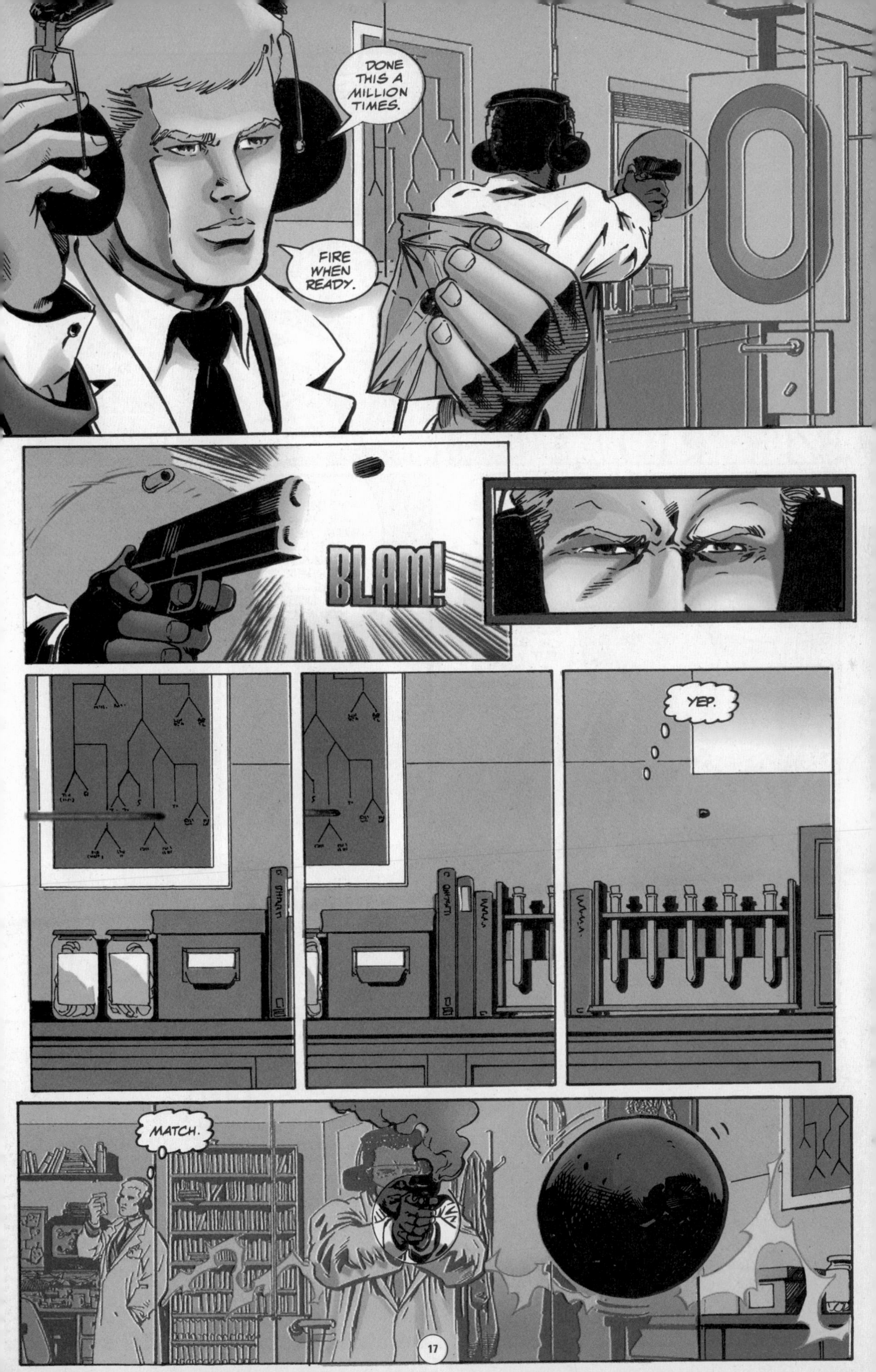
DONE THIS A MILLION TIMES.
FIRE WHEN READY.
BLAM!
YEP.
MATCH.

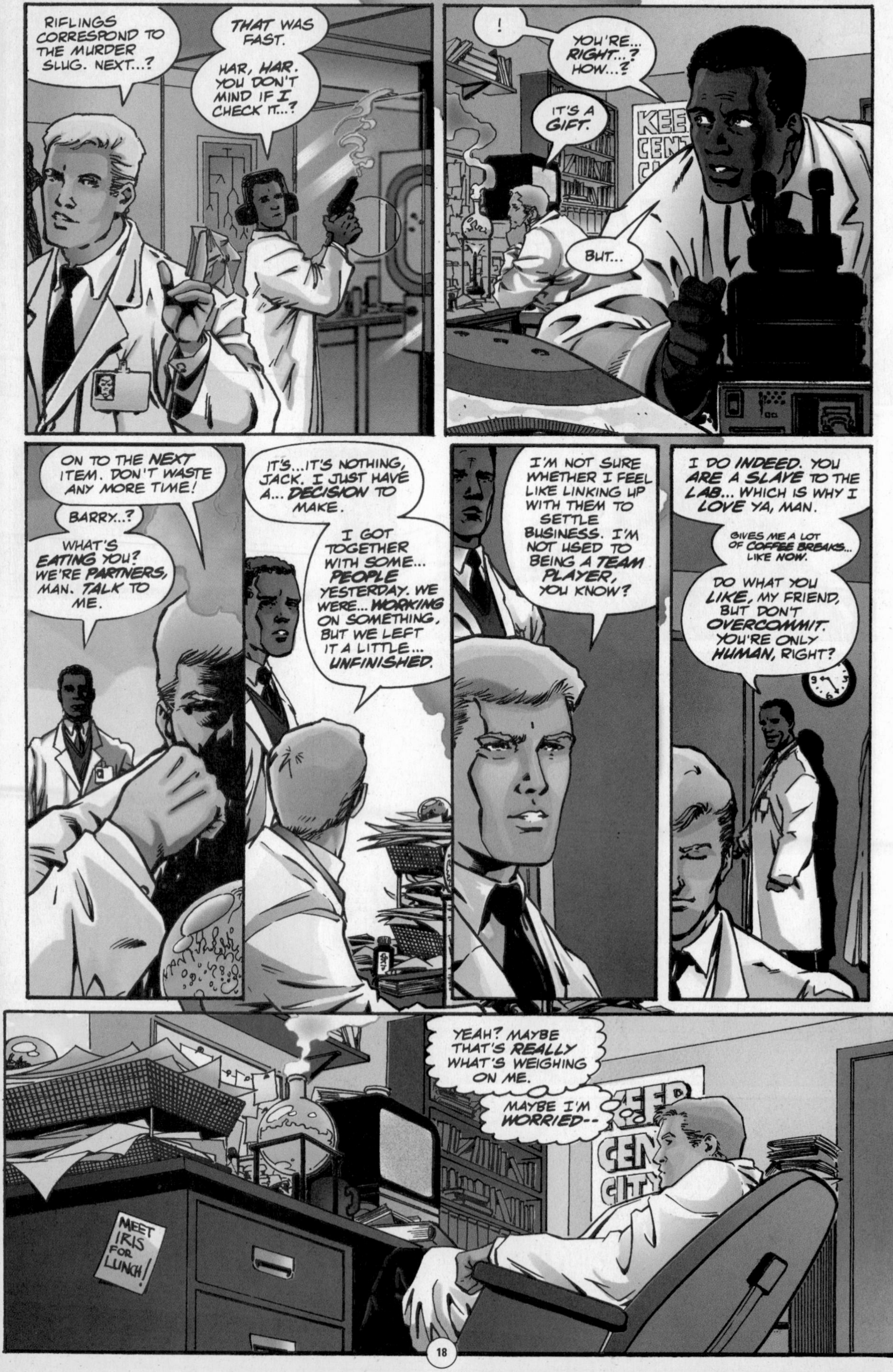
RIFLINGS CORRESPOND TO THE MURDER SLUG. NEXT...?
THAT WAS FAST.
HAR, HAR. YOU DON'T MIND IF I CHECK IT...?
!
YOU'RE... RIGHT...? HOW...?
IT'S A GIFT.
KEE
CENT
C
BUT...
ON TO THE NEXT ITEM. DON'T WASTE ANY MORE TIME!
BARRY...?
WHAT'S EATING YOU? WE'RE PARTNERS, MAN. TALK TO ME.
IT'S...IT'S NOTHING, JACK. I JUST HAVE A... DECISION TO MAKE.
I GOT TOGETHER WITH SOME... PEOPLE YESTERDAY. WE WERE... WORKING ON SOMETHING, BUT WE LEFT IT A LITTLE... UNFINISHED.
I'M NOT SURE WHETHER I FEEL LIKE LINKING UP WITH THEM TO SETTLE BUSINESS. I'M NOT USED TO BEING A TEAM PLAYER, YOU KNOW?
I DO INDEED. YOU ARE A SLAVE TO THE LAB... WHICH IS WHY I LOVE YA, MAN.
GIVES ME A LOT OF COFFEE BREAKS... LIKE NOW.
DO WHAT YOU LIKE, MY FRIEND, BUT DON'T OVERCOMMIT. YOU'RE ONLY HUMAN, RIGHT?
YEAH? MAYBE THAT'S REALLY WHAT'S WEIGHING ON ME.
MAYBE I'M WORRIED--
KEEP
CEN
CITY
MEET IRIS FOR LUNCH!

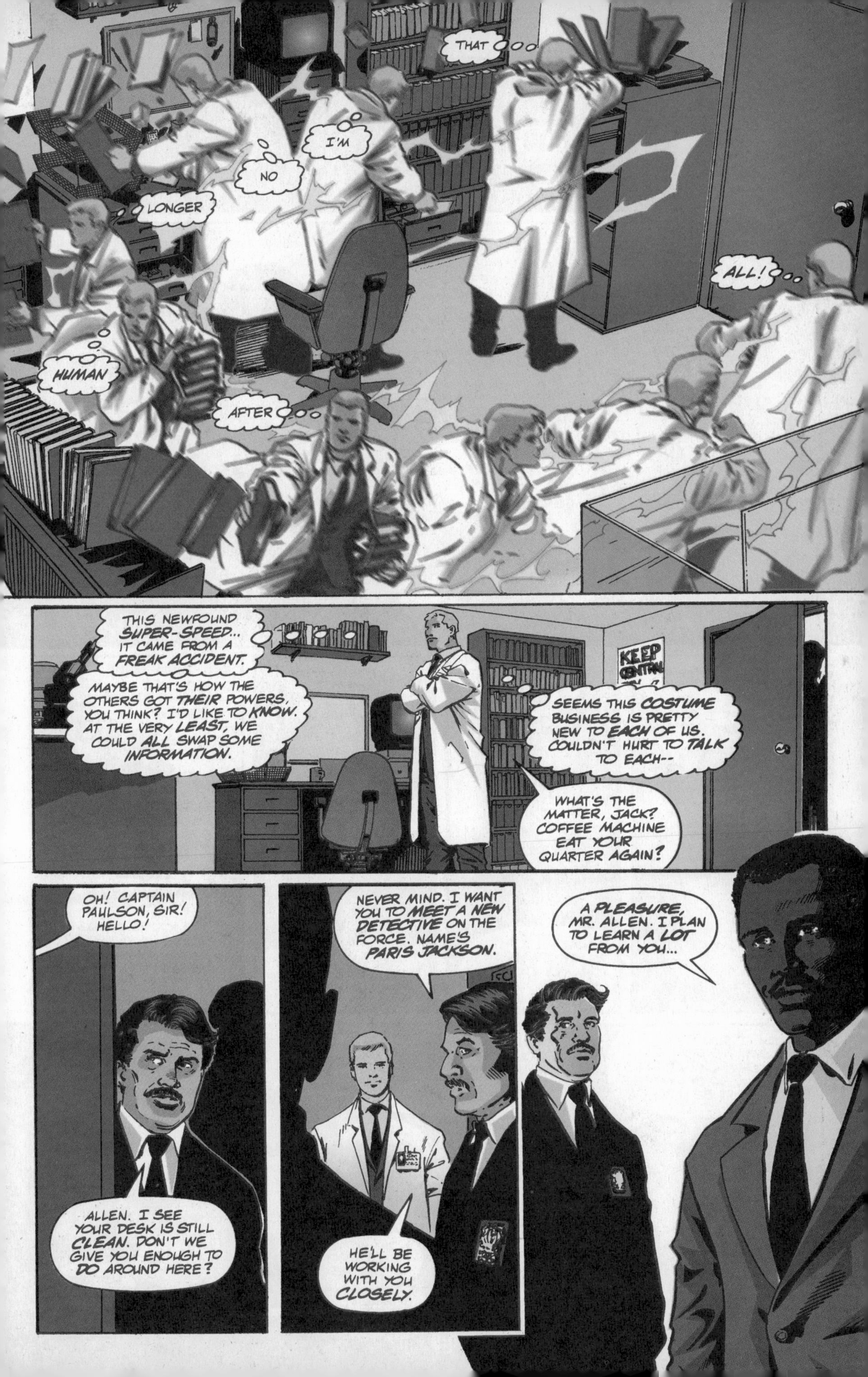

THAT
I'M
NO
LONGER
HUMAN
AFTER
ALL!
THIS NEWFOUND SUPER-SPEED... IT CAME FROM A FREAK ACCIDENT.
MAYBE THAT'S HOW THE OTHERS GOT THEIR POWERS, YOU THINK? I'D LIKE TO KNOW. AT THE VERY LEAST, WE COULD ALL SWAP SOME INFORMATION.
SEEMS THIS COSTUME BUSINESS IS PRETTY NEW TO EACH OF US. COULDN'T HURT TO TALK TO EACH--
WHAT'S THE MATTER, JACK? COFFEE MACHINE EAT YOUR QUARTER AGAIN?
OH! CAPTAIN PAULSON, SIR! HELLO!
ALLEN. I SEE YOUR DESK IS STILL CLEAN. DON'T WE GIVE YOU ENOUGH TO DO AROUND HERE?
NEVER MIND. I WANT YOU TO MEET A NEW DETECTIVE ON THE FORCE. NAME'S PARIS JACKSON.
HE'LL BE WORKING WITH YOU CLOSELY.
A PLEASURE, MR. ALLEN. I PLAN TO LEARN A LOT FROM YOU...

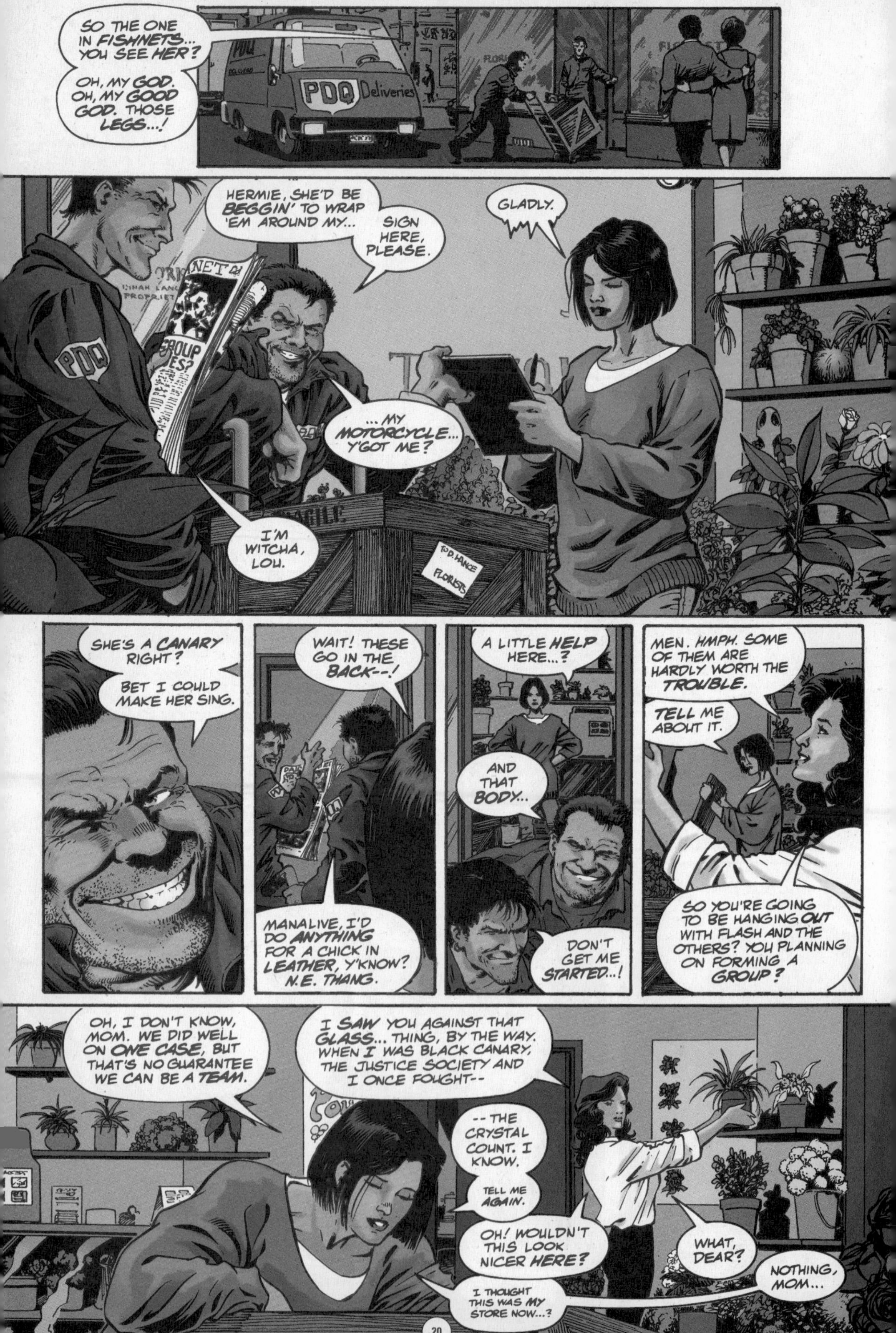
SO THE ONE IN FISHNETS... YOU SEE HER?
OH, MY GOD. OH, MY GOOD GOD. THOSE LEGS...!
PDQ Deliveries
HERMIE, SHE'D BE BEGGIN' TO WRAP 'EM AROUND MY...
SIGN HERE, PLEASE.
GLADLY.
... MY MOTORCYCLE... Y'GOT ME?
I'M WITCHA, LOU.
FRAGILE
TO D. LANCE FLORISTS
SHE'S A CANARY RIGHT?
BET I COULD MAKE HER SING.
WAIT! THESE GO IN THE BACK--!
MANALIVE, I'D DO ANYTHING FOR A CHICK IN LEATHER, Y'KNOW? N.E. THANG.
A LITTLE HELP HERE...?
AND THAT BODY..
DON'T GET ME STARTED...!
MEN. HMPH. SOME OF THEM ARE HARDLY WORTH THE TROUBLE.
TELL ME ABOUT IT.
SO YOU'RE GOING TO BE HANGING OUT WITH FLASH AND THE OTHERS? YOU PLANNING ON FORMING A GROUP?
OH, I DON'T KNOW, MOM. WE DID WELL ON ONE CASE, BUT THAT'S NO GUARANTEE WE CAN BE A TEAM.
I SAW YOU AGAINST THAT GLASS... THING, BY THE WAY. WHEN I WAS BLACK CANARY, THE JUSTICE SOCIETY AND I ONCE FOUGHT--
-- THE CRYSTAL COUNT. I KNOW.
TELL ME AGAIN.
OH! WOULDN'T THIS LOOK NICER HERE?
WHAT, DEAR?
I THOUGHT THIS WAS MY STORE NOW...?
NOTHING, MOM...

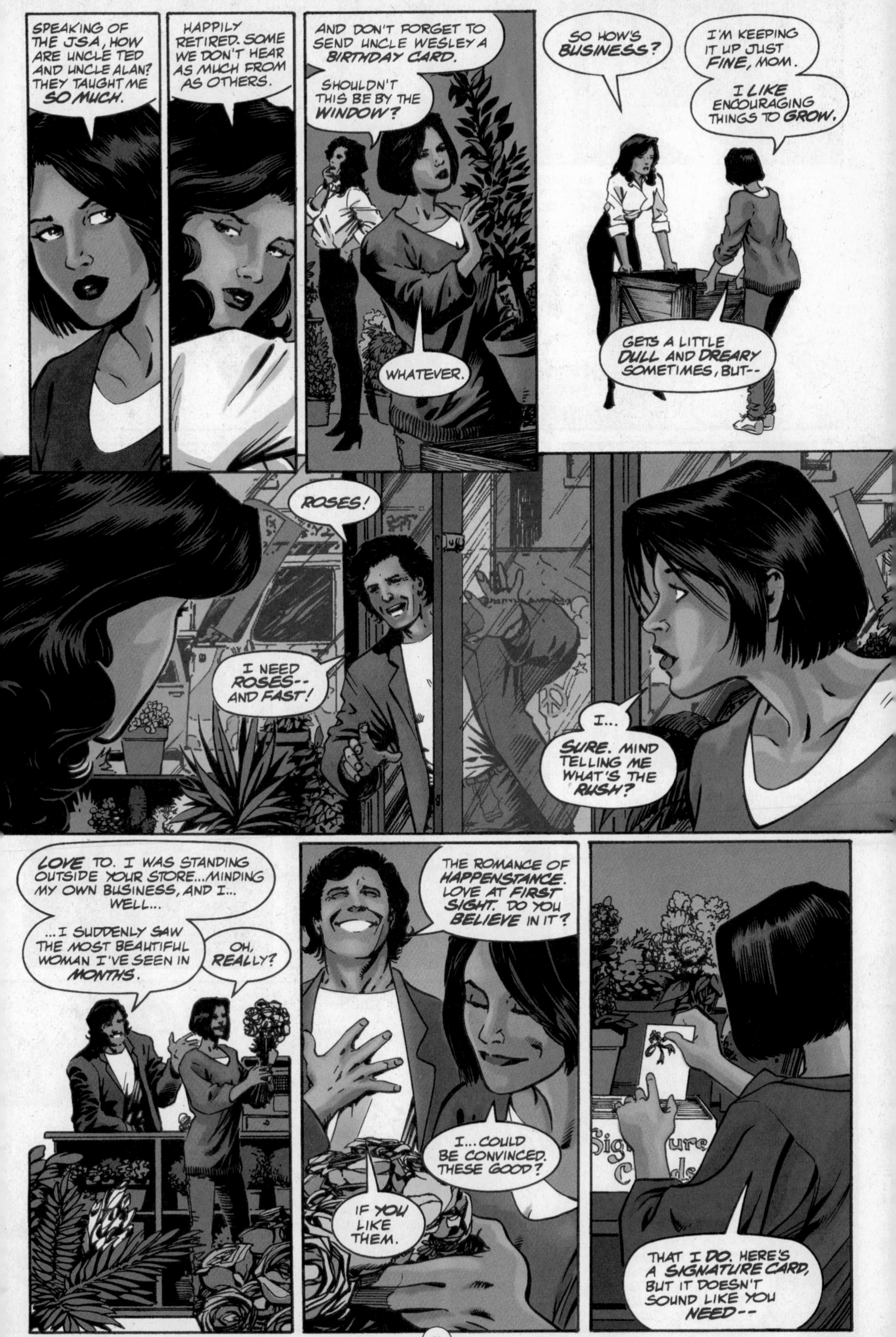
SPEAKING OF THE JSA, HOW ARE UNCLE TED AND UNCLE ALAN? THEY TAUGHT ME SO MUCH.
HAPPILY RETIRED. SOME WE DON'T HEAR AS MUCH FROM AS OTHERS.
AND DON'T FORGET TO SEND UNCLE WESLEY A BIRTHDAY CARD.
SHOULDN'T THIS BE BY THE WINDOW?
WHATEVER.
SO HOW'S BUSINESS?
I'M KEEPING IT UP JUST FINE, MOM.
I LIKE ENCOURAGING THINGS TO GROW.
GETS A LITTLE DULL AND DREARY SOMETIMES, BUT--
ROSES!
I NEED ROSES-- AND FAST!
I...
SURE. MIND TELLING ME WHAT'S THE RUSH?
LOVE TO. I WAS STANDING OUTSIDE YOUR STORE...MINDING MY OWN BUSINESS, AND I... WELL...
...I SUDDENLY SAW THE MOST BEAUTIFUL WOMAN I'VE SEEN IN MONTHS.
OH, REALLY?
THE ROMANCE OF HAPPENSTANCE. LOVE AT FIRST SIGHT. DO YOU BELIEVE IN IT?
I...COULD BE CONVINCED. THESE GOOD?
IF YOU LIKE THEM.
THAT I DO. HERE'S A SIGNATURE CARD, BUT IT DOESN'T SOUND LIKE YOU NEED--

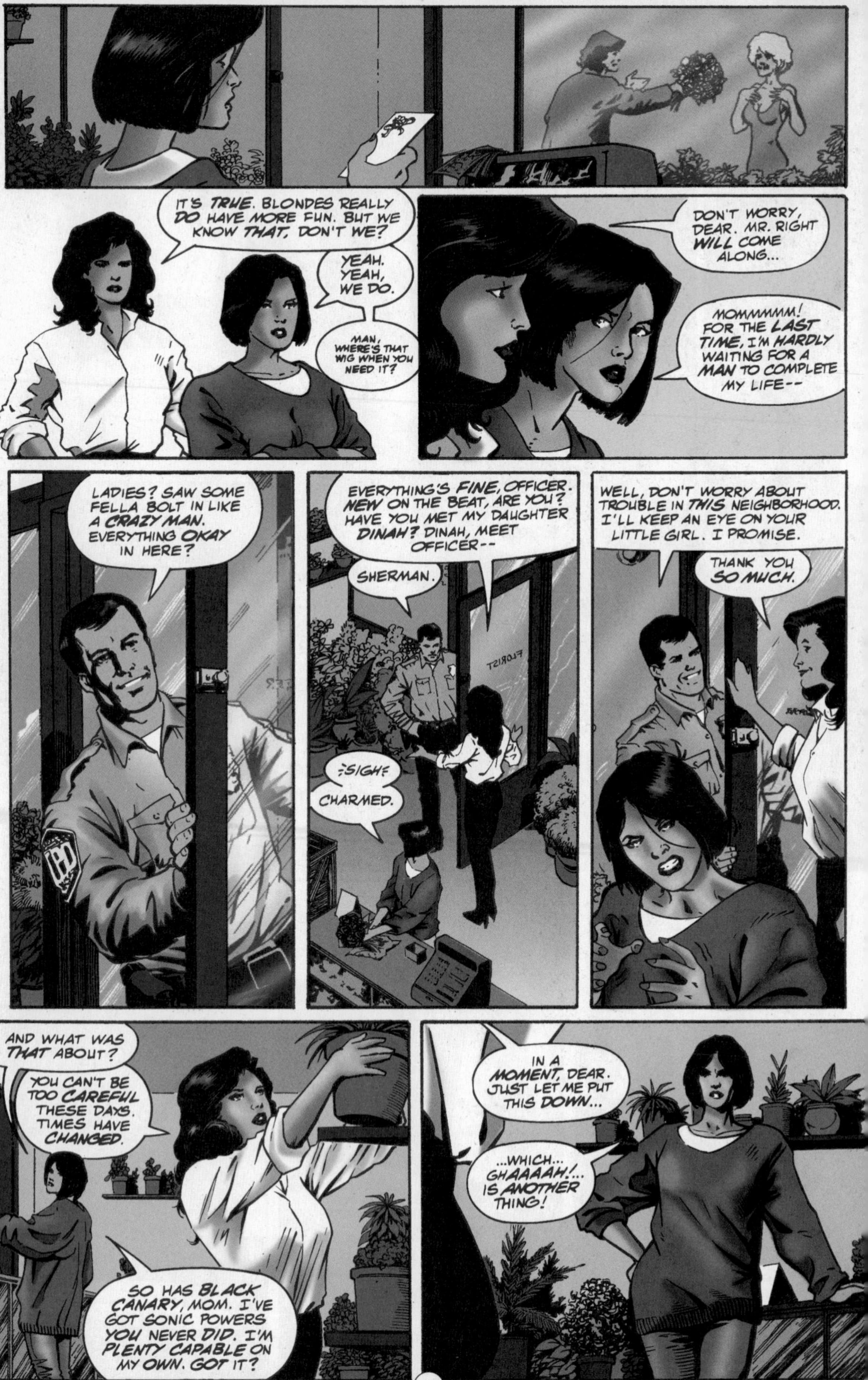

IT'S TRUE. BLONDES REALLY DO HAVE MORE FUN. BUT WE KNOW THAT, DON'T WE?
YEAH. YEAH, WE DO.
MAN, WHERE'S THAT WIG WHEN YOU NEED IT?
DON'T WORRY, DEAR. MR. RIGHT WILL COME ALONG...
MOMMMMM! FOR THE LAST TIME, I'M HARDLY WAITING FOR A MAN TO COMPLETE MY LIFE--
LADIES? SAW SOME FELLA BOLT IN LIKE A CRAZY MAN. EVERYTHING OKAY IN HERE?
EVERYTHING'S FINE, OFFICER. NEW ON THE BEAT, ARE YOU? HAVE YOU MET MY DAUGHTER DINAH? DINAH, MEET OFFICER--
SHERMAN.
SIGH
CHARMED.
WELL, DON'T WORRY ABOUT TROUBLE IN THIS NEIGHBORHOOD. I'LL KEEP AN EYE ON YOUR LITTLE GIRL. I PROMISE.
THANK YOU SO MUCH.
AND WHAT WAS THAT ABOUT?
YOU CAN'T BE TOO CAREFUL THESE DAYS. TIMES HAVE CHANGED.
SO HAS BLACK CANARY, MOM. I'VE GOT SONIC POWERS YOU NEVER DID. I'M PLENTY CAPABLE ON MY OWN. GOT IT?
IN A MOMENT, DEAR. JUST LET ME PUT THIS DOWN...
...WHICH... GHAAAAH!... IS ANOTHER THING!

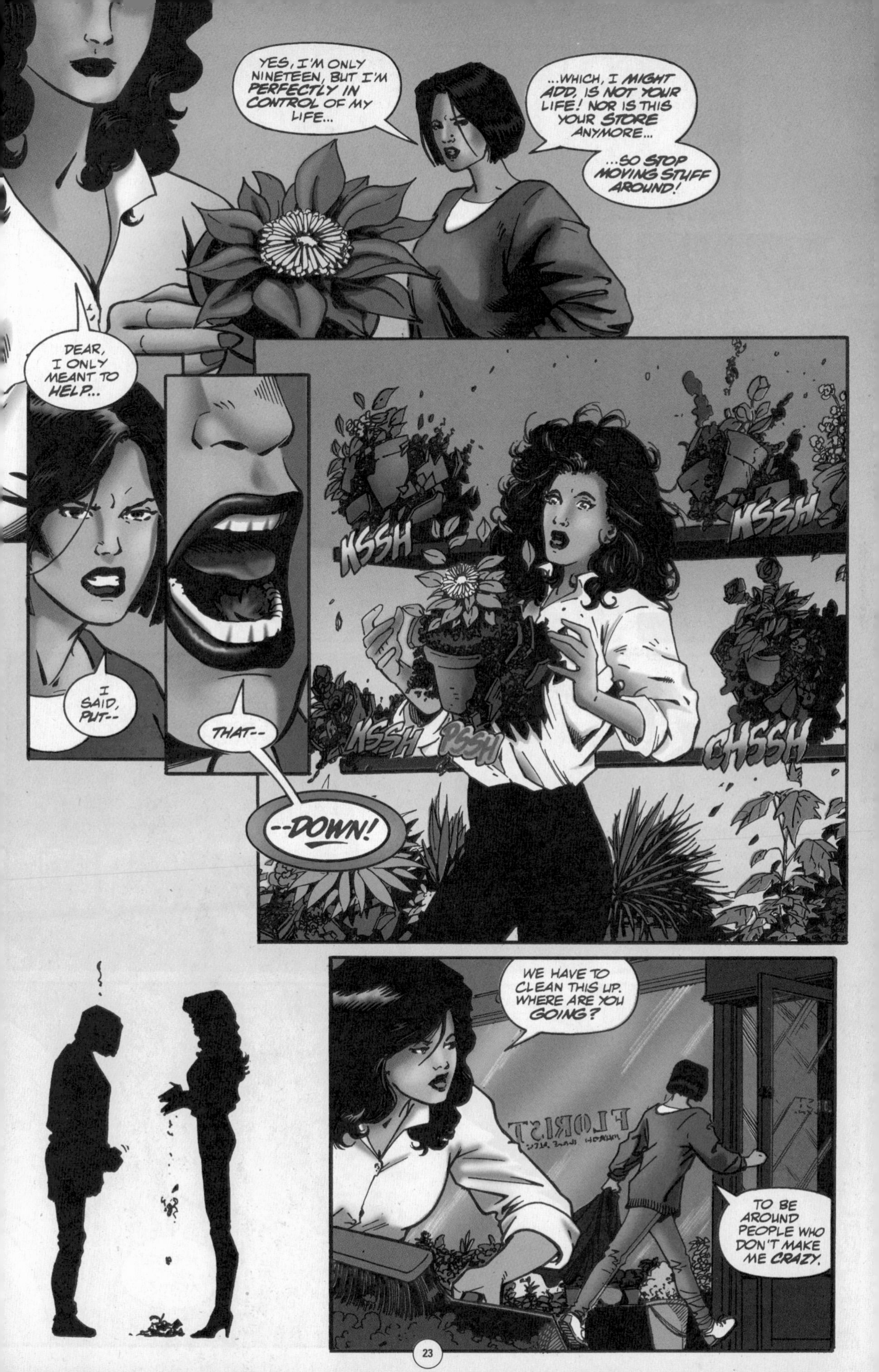
YES, I'M ONLY NINETEEN, BUT I'M PERFECTLY IN CONTROL OF MY LIFE...
...WHICH, I MIGHT ADD, IS NOT YOUR LIFE! NOR IS THIS YOUR STORE ANYMORE...
...SO STOP MOVING STUFF AROUND!
DEAR, I ONLY MEANT TO HELP...
I SAID, PUT--
THAT--
--DOWN!
KSSH
KSSH
KSSH
POSH
CHSSH
WE HAVE TO CLEAN THIS UP. WHERE ARE YOU GOING?
FLORIST
TO BE AROUND PEOPLE WHO DON'T MAKE ME CRAZY.

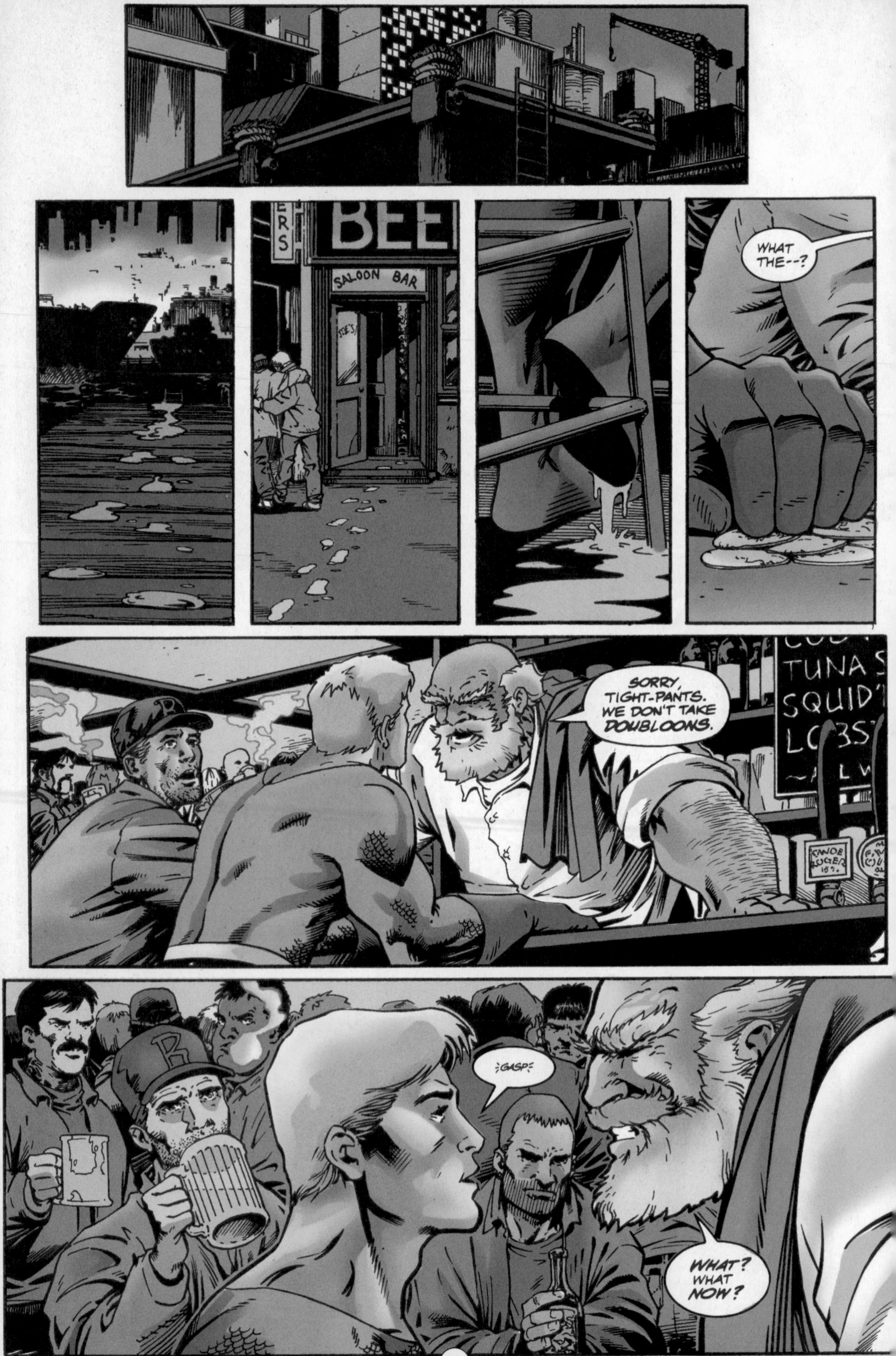
BEE
SALOON BAR
JOE'S
WHAT THE--?
SORRY, TIGHT-PANTS. WE DON'T TAKE DOUBLOONS.
TUNA
SQUID
GASP
WHAT? WHAT NOW?

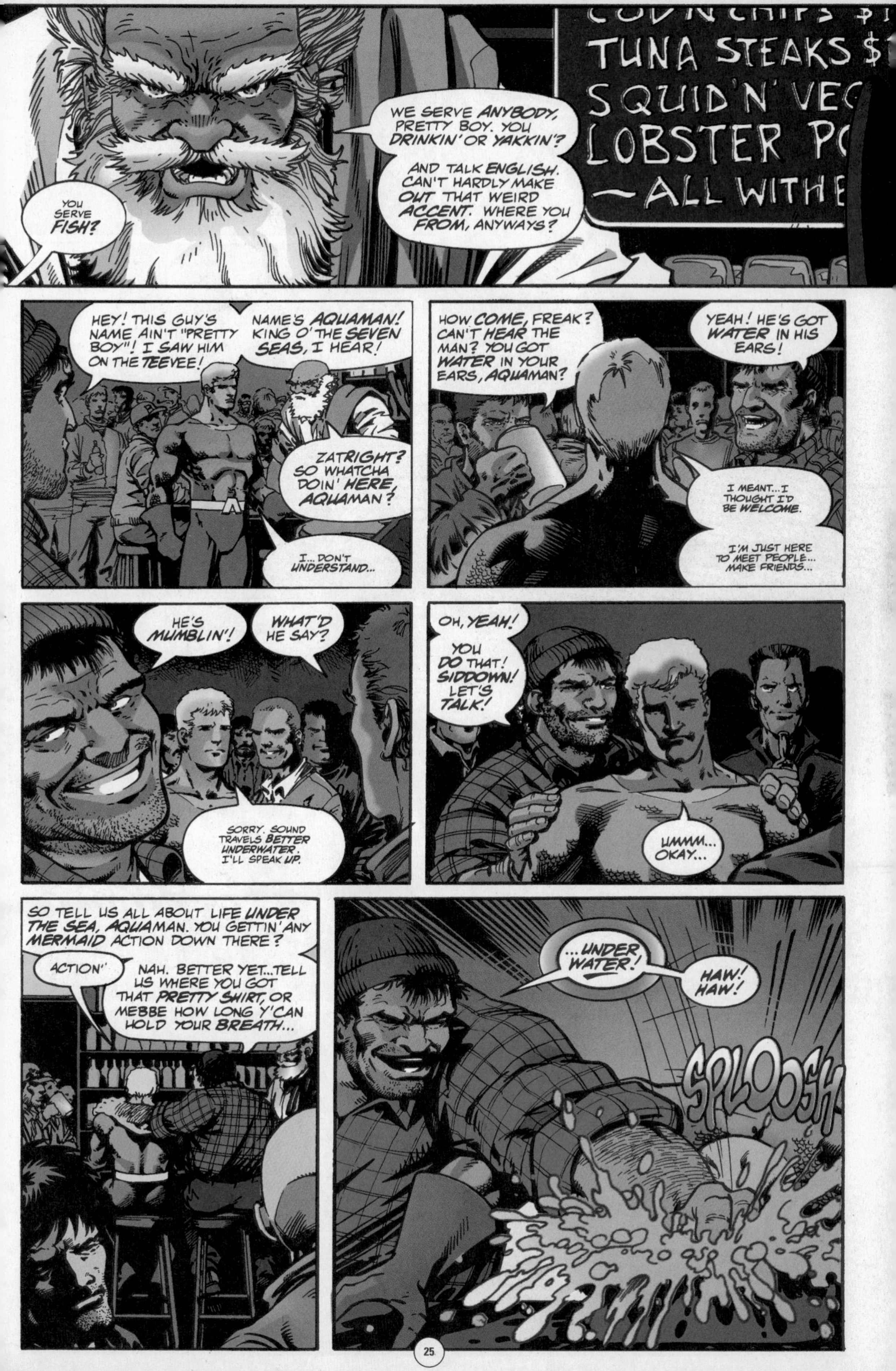
COD N CHIPS $1
TUNA STEAKS $
SQUID 'N' VEG
LOBSTER PO
—ALL WITH E
YOU SERVE FISH?
WE SERVE ANYBODY, PRETTY BOY. YOU DRINKIN' OR YAKKIN'?
AND TALK ENGLISH. CAN'T HARDLY MAKE OUT THAT WEIRD ACCENT. WHERE YOU FROM, ANYWAYS?
HEY! THIS GUY'S NAME AIN'T "PRETTY BOY"! I SAW HIM ON THE TEEVEE!
NAME'S AQUAMAN! KING O' THE SEVEN SEAS, I HEAR!
ZATRIGHT? SO WHATCHA DOIN' HERE, AQUAMAN?
I... DON'T UNDERSTAND...
HOW COME, FREAK? CAN'T HEAR THE MAN? YOU GOT WATER IN YOUR EARS, AQUAMAN?
YEAH! HE'S GOT WATER IN HIS EARS!
I MEANT... I THOUGHT I'D BE WELCOME.
I'M JUST HERE TO MEET PEOPLE... MAKE FRIENDS...
HE'S MUMBLIN'!
WHAT'D HE SAY?
SORRY. SOUND TRAVELS BETTER UNDERWATER. I'LL SPEAK UP.
OH, YEAH!
YOU DO THAT! SIDDOWN! LET'S TALK!
UMMM... OKAY...
SO TELL US ALL ABOUT LIFE UNDER THE SEA, AQUAMAN. YOU GETTIN' ANY MERMAID ACTION DOWN THERE?
ACTION''
NAH. BETTER YET...TELL US WHERE YOU GOT THAT PRETTY SHIRT, OR MEBBE HOW LONG Y'CAN HOLD YOUR BREATH...
...UNDER WATER!
HAW! HAW!
SPLOOSH

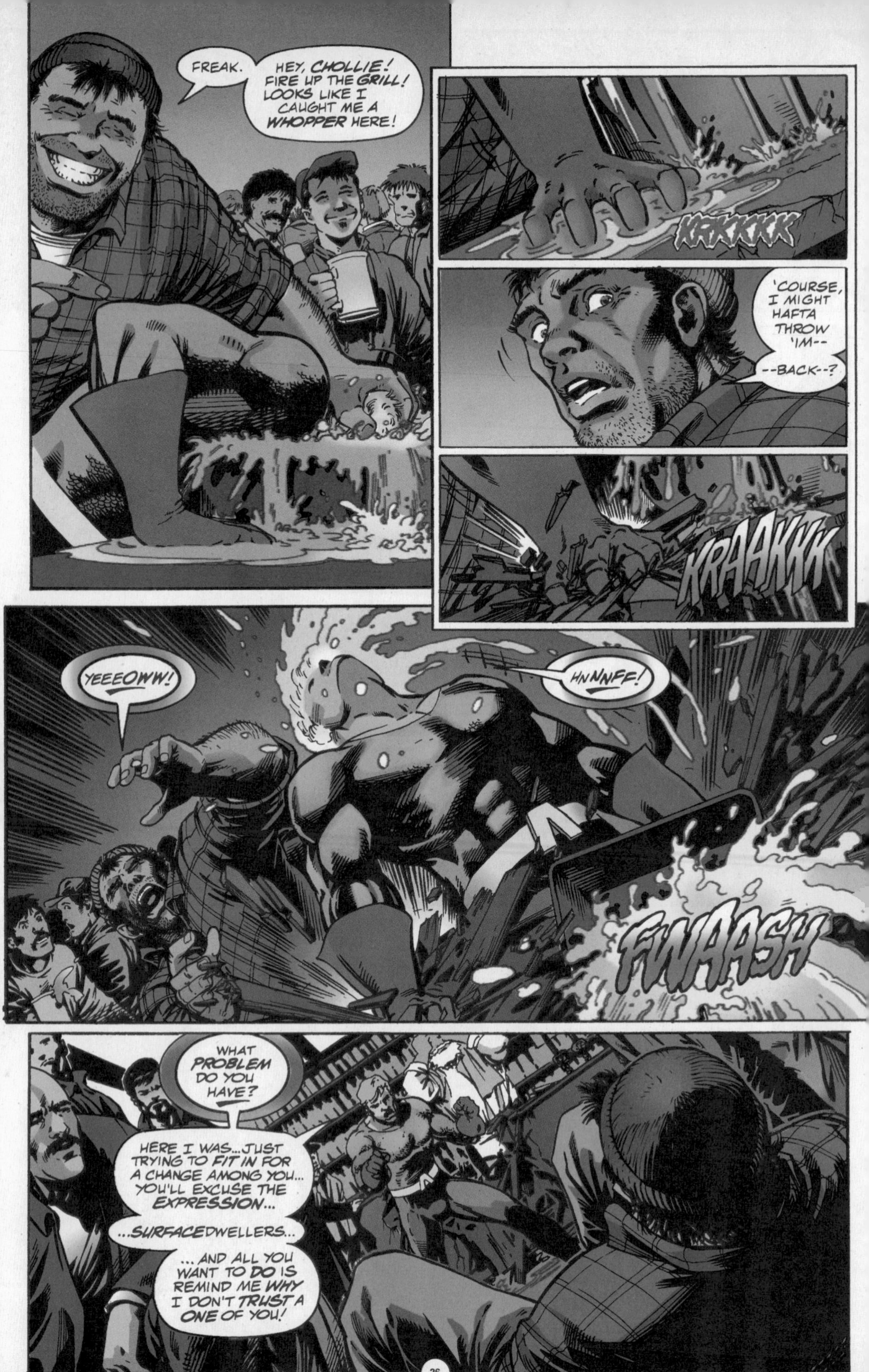
FREAK.
HEY, CHOLLIE! FIRE UP THE GRILL! LOOKS LIKE I CAUGHT ME A WHOPPER HERE!
KRKKKK
'COURSE, I MIGHT HAFTA THROW 'IM--
--BACK--?
KRAAKKK
YEEEOWW!
HNNNFF!
FWAASH
WHAT PROBLEM DO YOU HAVE?
HERE I WAS...JUST TRYING TO FIT IN FOR A CHANGE AMONG YOU... YOU'LL EXCUSE THE EXPRESSION...
...SURFACE DWELLERS...
...AND ALL YOU WANT TO DO IS REMIND ME WHY I DON'T TRUST A ONE OF YOU!

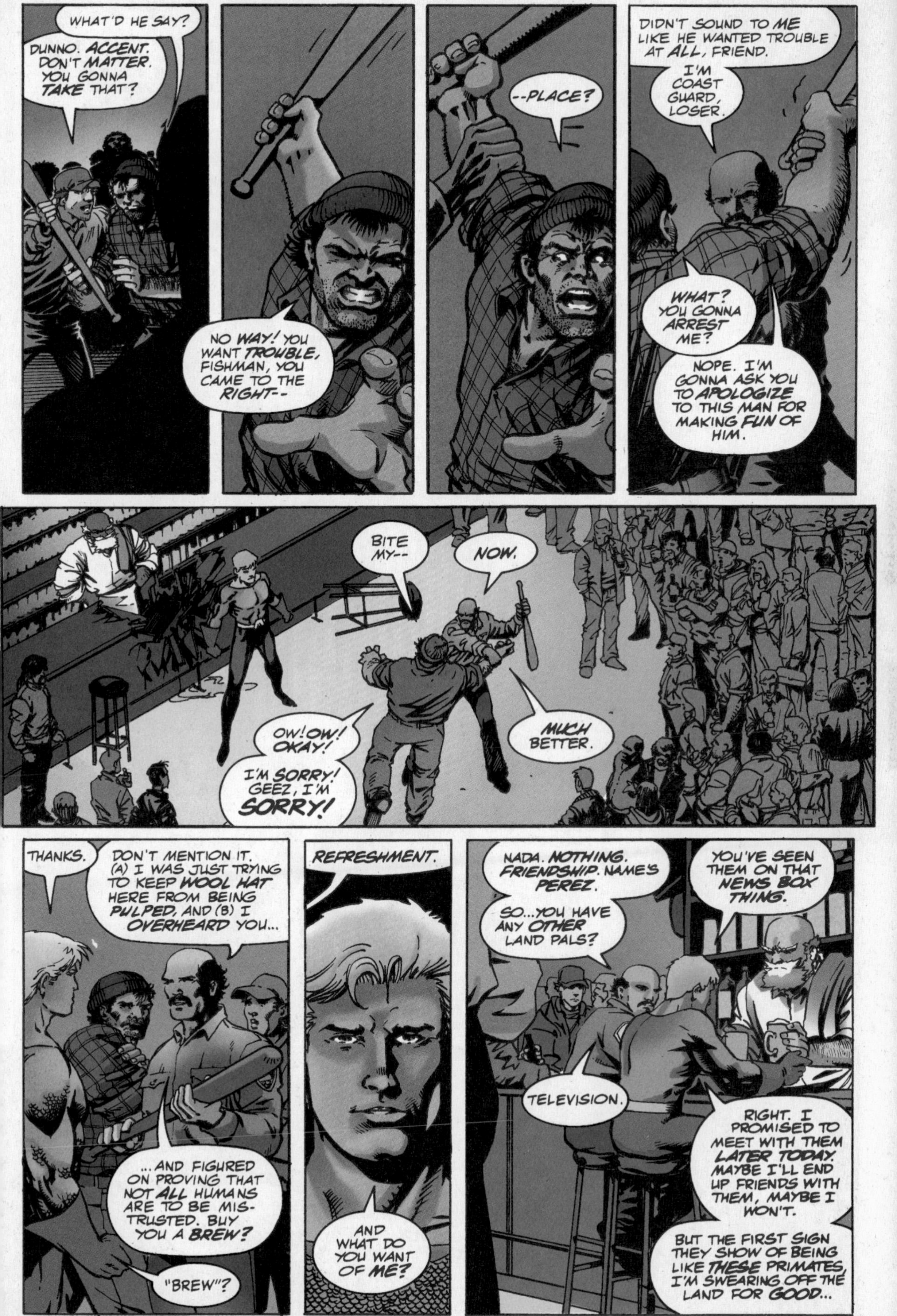

WHAT'D HE SAY?
DUNNO. ACCENT. DON'T MATTER. YOU GONNA TAKE THAT?
NO WAY! YOU WANT TROUBLE, FISHMAN, YOU CAME TO THE RIGHT--
--PLACE?
DIDN'T SOUND TO ME LIKE HE WANTED TROUBLE AT ALL, FRIEND.
I'M COAST GUARD, LOSER.
WHAT? YOU GONNA ARREST ME?
NOPE. I'M GONNA ASK YOU TO APOLOGIZE TO THIS MAN FOR MAKING FUN OF HIM.
BITE MY--
NOW.
OW! OW! OKAY!
I'M SORRY! GEEZ, I'M SORRY!
MUCH BETTER.
THANKS.
DON'T MENTION IT. (A) I WAS JUST TRYING TO KEEP WOOL HAT HERE FROM BEING PULPED, AND (B) I OVERHEARD YOU...
...AND FIGURED ON PROVING THAT NOT ALL HUMANS ARE TO BE MIS-TRUSTED. BUY YOU A BREW?
"BREW"?
REFRESHMENT.
AND WHAT DO YOU WANT OF ME?
NADA. NOTHING. FRIENDSHIP. NAME'S PEREZ.
SO...YOU HAVE ANY OTHER LAND PALS?
YOU'VE SEEN THEM ON THAT NEWS BOX THING.
TELEVISION.
RIGHT. I PROMISED TO MEET WITH THEM LATER TODAY. MAYBE I'LL END UP FRIENDS WITH THEM, MAYBE I WON'T.
BUT THE FIRST SIGN THEY SHOW OF BEING LIKE THESE PRIMATES, I'M SWEARING OFF THE LAND FOR GOOD...

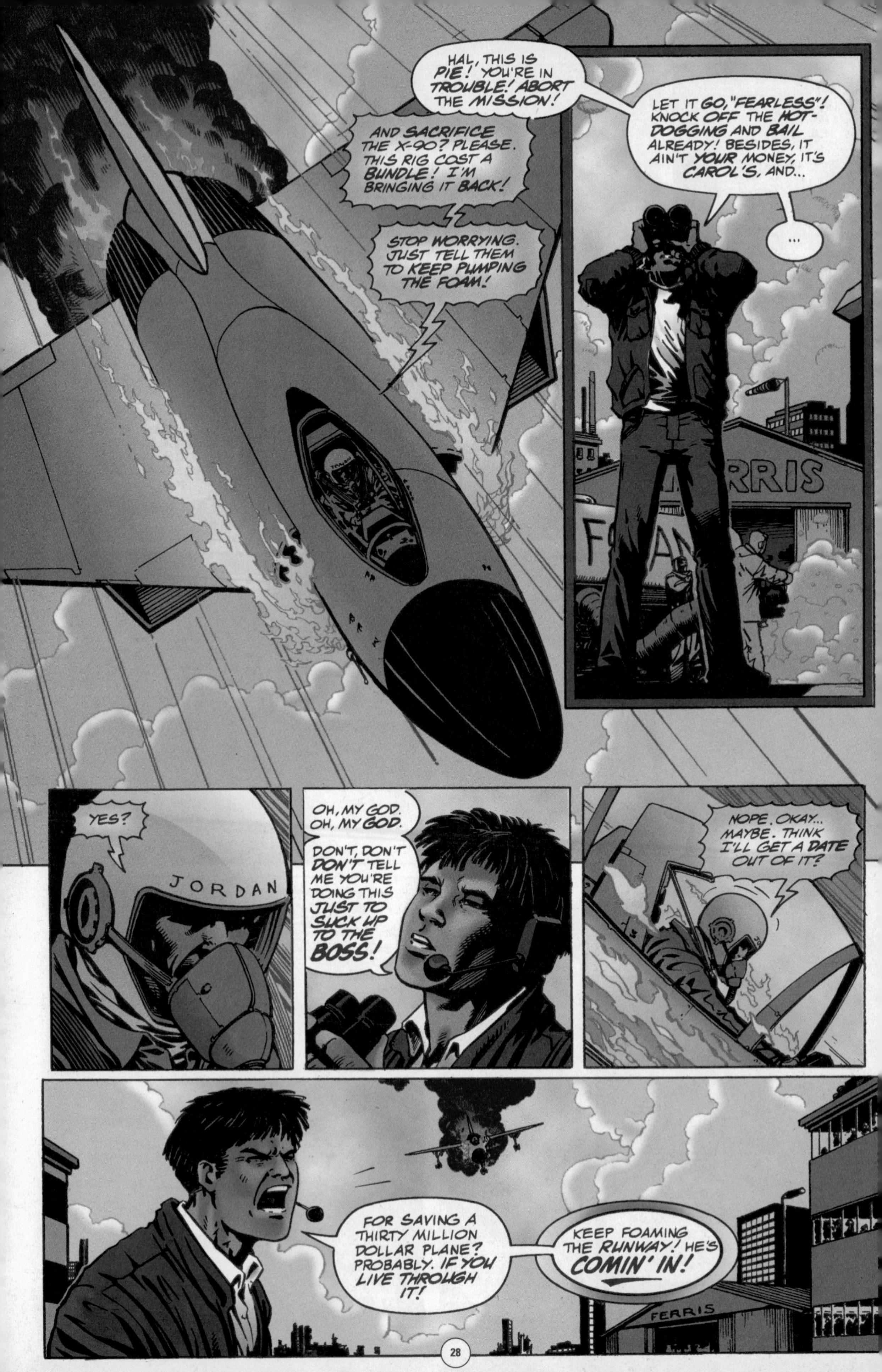
HAL, THIS IS PIE! YOU'RE IN TROUBLE! ABORT THE MISSION!
AND SACRIFICE THE X-90? PLEASE. THIS RIG COST A BUNDLE! I'M BRINGING IT BACK!
STOP WORRYING. JUST TELL THEM TO KEEP PUMPING THE FOAM!
LET IT GO, "FEARLESS"! KNOCK OFF THE HOT-DOGGING AND BAIL ALREADY! BESIDES, IT AIN'T YOUR MONEY, IT'S CAROL'S, AND...
...
FERRIS
YES?
JORDAN
OH, MY GOD. OH, MY GOD.
DON'T, DON'T DON'T TELL ME YOU'RE DOING THIS JUST TO SUCK UP TO THE BOSS!
NOPE. OKAY... MAYBE. THINK I'LL GET A DATE OUT OF IT?
FOR SAVING A THIRTY MILLION DOLLAR PLANE? PROBABLY. IF YOU LIVE THROUGH IT!
KEEP FOAMING THE RUNWAY! HE'S COMIN' IN!
FERRIS

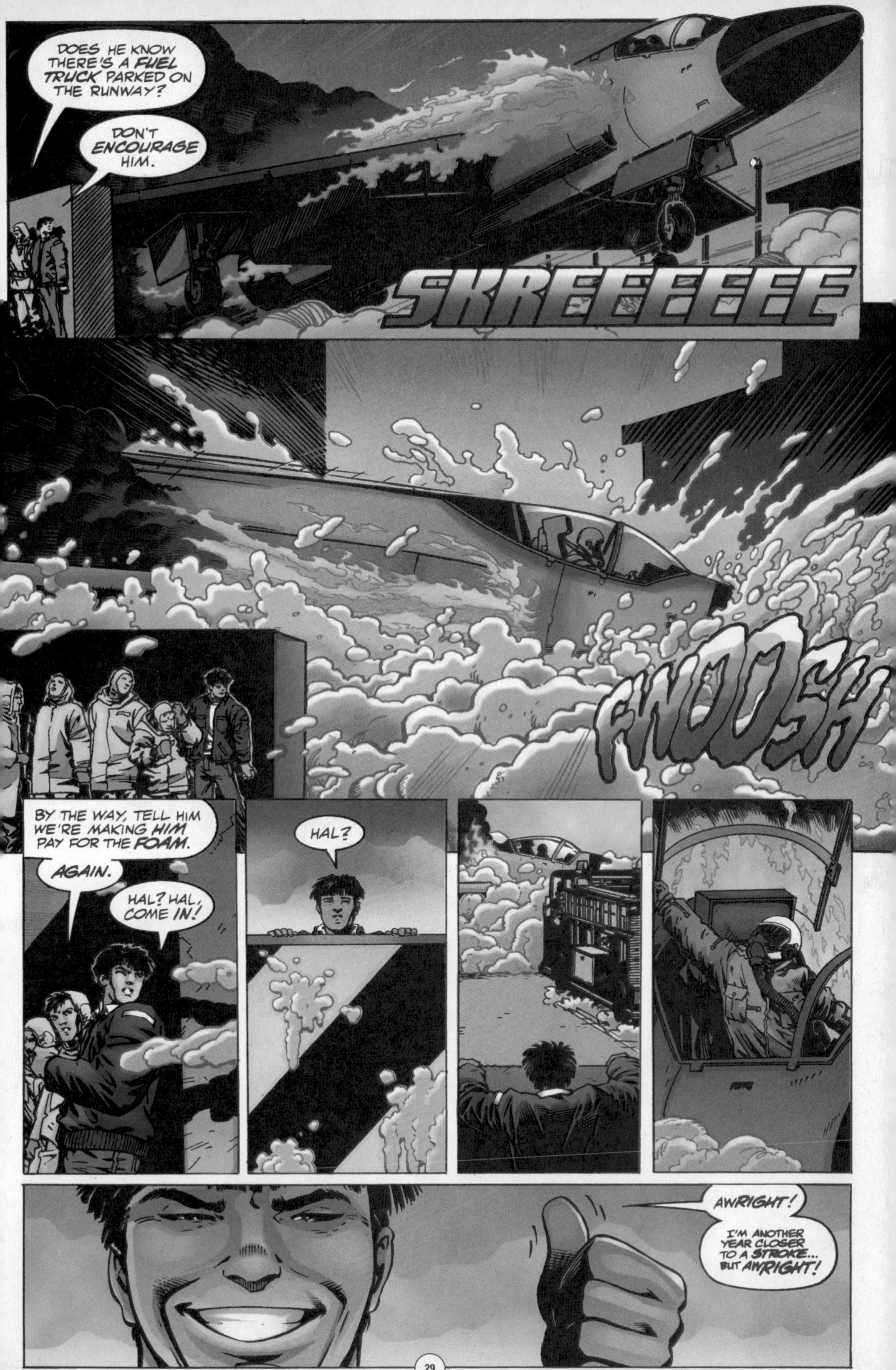
DOES HE KNOW THERE'S A FUEL TRUCK PARKED ON THE RUNWAY?
DON'T ENCOURAGE HIM.
SKREEEEEEE
FWOOSH
BY THE WAY, TELL HIM WE'RE MAKING HIM PAY FOR THE FOAM.
AGAIN.
HAL? HAL, COME IN!
HAL?
AWRIGHT!
I'M ANOTHER YEAR CLOSER TO A STROKE... BUT AWRIGHT!

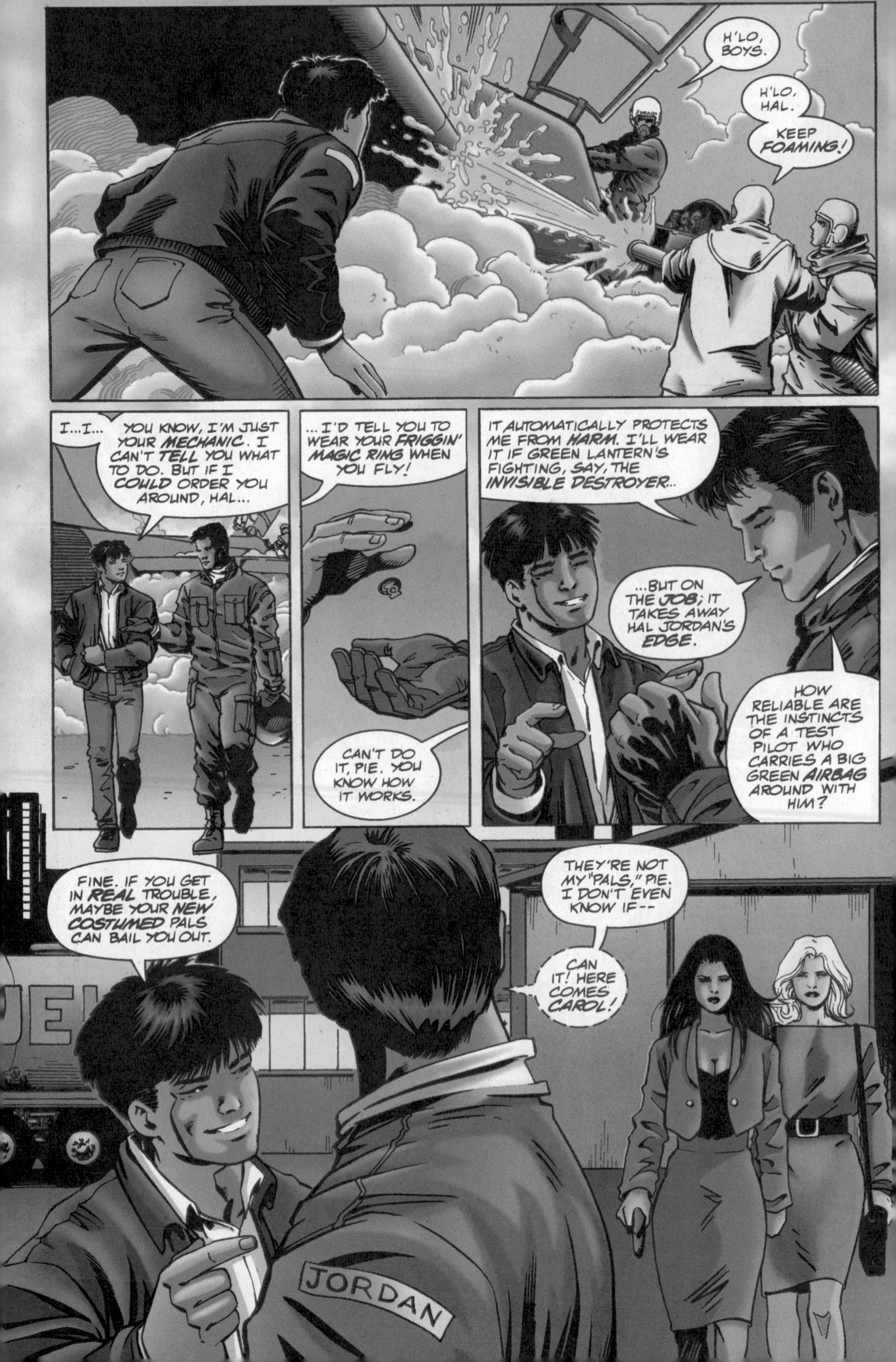
H'LO, BOYS.
H'LO, HAL.
KEEP FOAMING!
I...I...
YOU KNOW, I'M JUST YOUR MECHANIC. I CAN'T TELL YOU WHAT TO DO. BUT IF I COULD ORDER YOU AROUND, HAL...
...I'D TELL YOU TO WEAR YOUR FRIGGIN' MAGIC RING WHEN YOU FLY!
CAN'T DO IT, PIE. YOU KNOW HOW IT WORKS.
IT AUTOMATICALLY PROTECTS ME FROM HARM. I'LL WEAR IT IF GREEN LANTERN'S FIGHTING, SAY, THE INVISIBLE DESTROYER...
...BUT ON THE JOB; IT TAKES AWAY HAL JORDAN'S EDGE.
HOW RELIABLE ARE THE INSTINCTS OF A TEST PILOT WHO CARRIES A BIG GREEN AIRBAG AROUND WITH HIM?
FINE. IF YOU GET IN REAL TROUBLE, MAYBE YOUR NEW COSTUMED PALS CAN BAIL YOU OUT.
THEY'RE NOT MY "PALS," PIE. I DON'T EVEN KNOW IF--
CAN IT! HERE COMES CAROL!
JORDAN

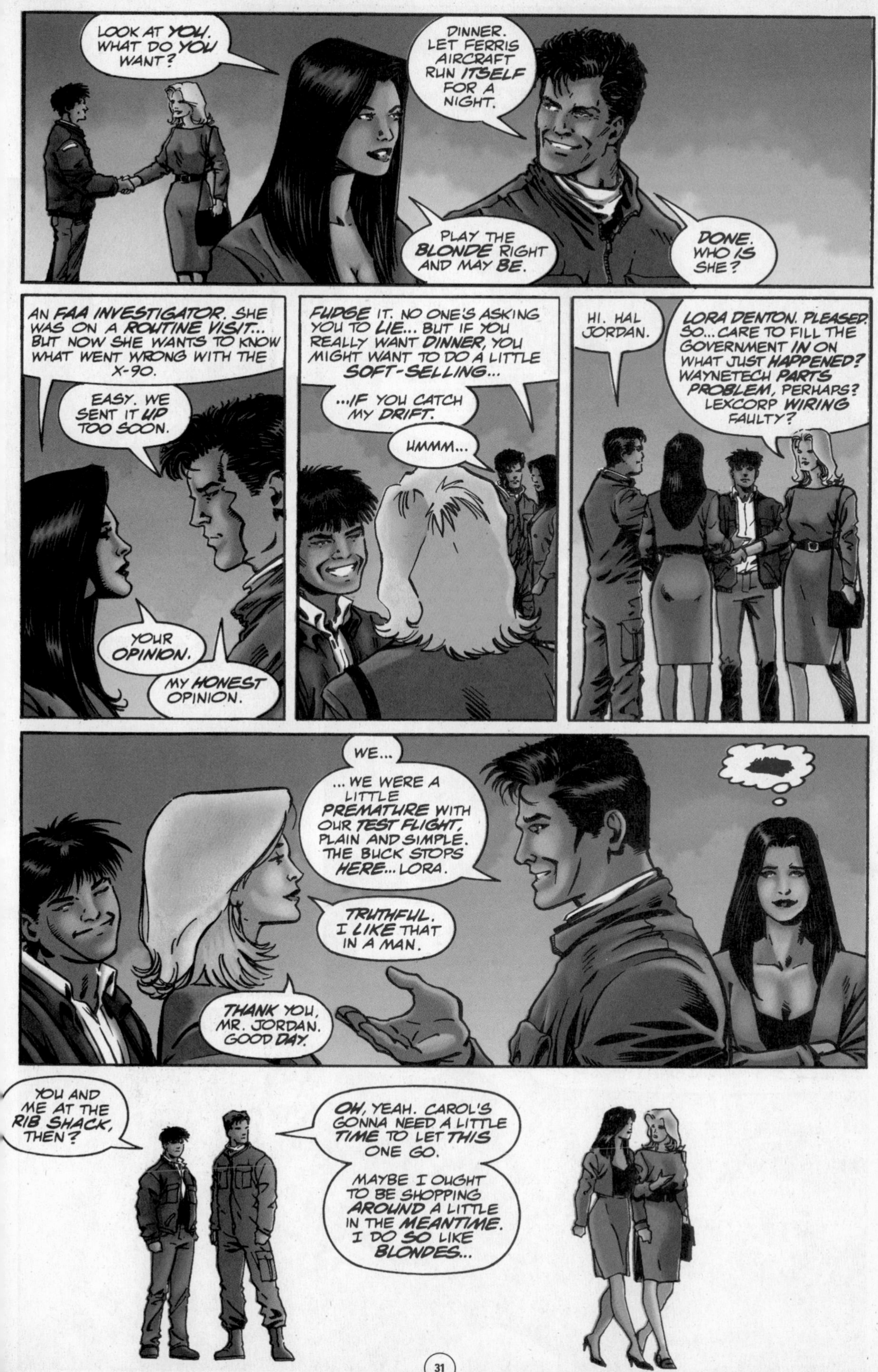
LOOK AT YOU. WHAT DO YOU WANT?
DINNER. LET FERRIS AIRCRAFT RUN ITSELF FOR A NIGHT.
PLAY THE BLONDE RIGHT AND MAY BE.
DONE. WHO IS SHE?
AN FAA INVESTIGATOR. SHE WAS ON A ROUTINE VISIT... BUT NOW SHE WANTS TO KNOW WHAT WENT WRONG WITH THE X-90.
EASY. WE SENT IT UP TOO SOON.
YOUR OPINION.
MY HONEST OPINION.
FUDGE IT. NO ONE'S ASKING YOU TO LIE... BUT IF YOU REALLY WANT DINNER, YOU MIGHT WANT TO DO A LITTLE SOFT-SELLING...
...IF YOU CATCH MY DRIFT.
UMMM...
HI. HAL JORDAN.
LORA DENTON. PLEASED. SO... CARE TO FILL THE GOVERNMENT IN ON WHAT JUST HAPPENED? WAYNETECH PARTS PROBLEM, PERHAPS? LEXCORP WIRING FAULTY?
WE...
...WE WERE A LITTLE PREMATURE WITH OUR TEST FLIGHT, PLAIN AND SIMPLE. THE BUCK STOPS HERE... LORA.
TRUTHFUL. I LIKE THAT IN A MAN.
THANK YOU, MR. JORDAN. GOOD DAY.
YOU AND ME AT THE RIB SHACK, THEN?
OH, YEAH. CAROL'S GONNA NEED A LITTLE TIME TO LET THIS ONE GO.
MAYBE I OUGHT TO BE SHOPPING AROUND A LITTLE IN THE MEANTIME. I DO SO LIKE BLONDES...

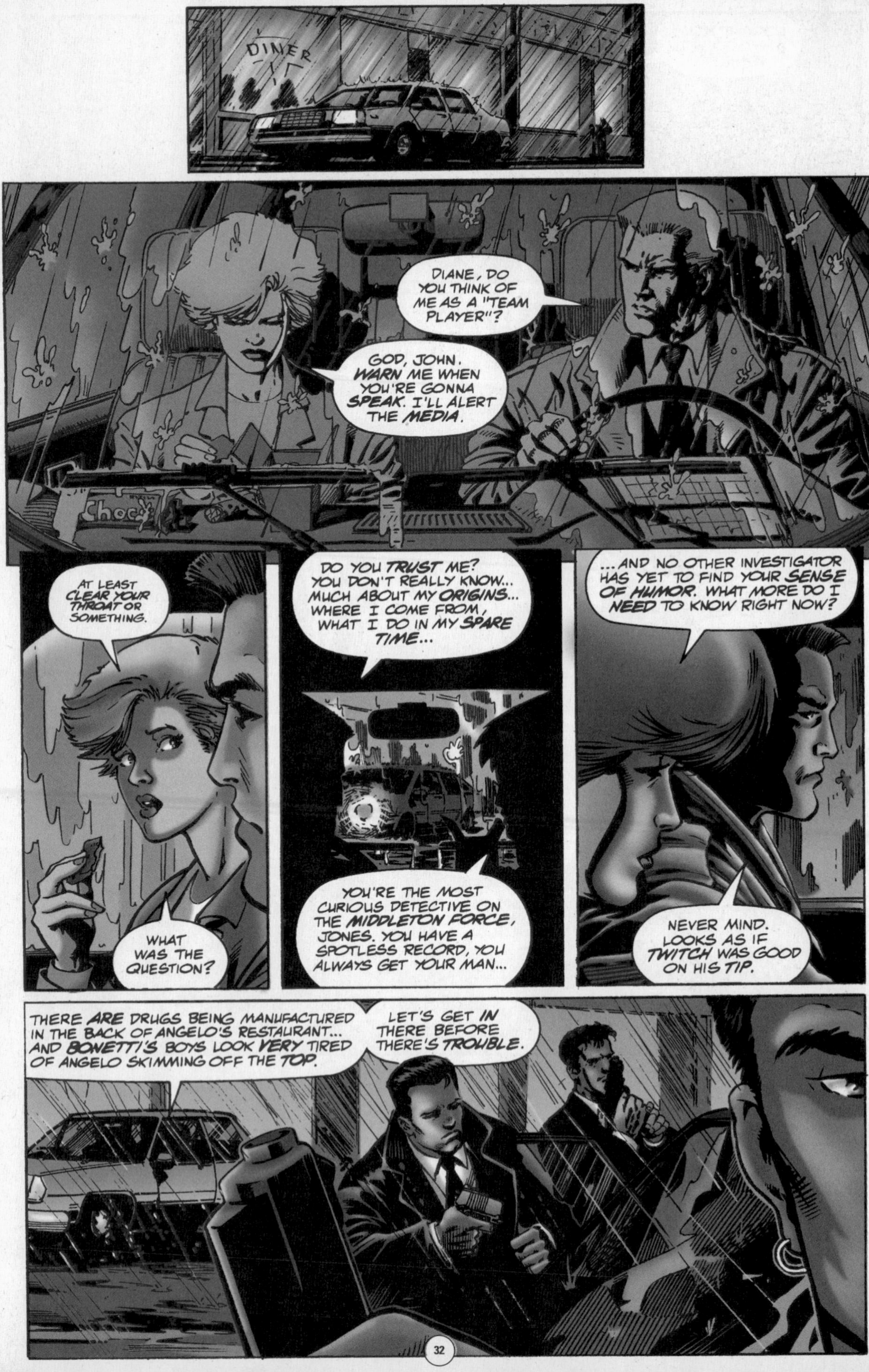
DINER
DIANE, DO YOU THINK OF ME AS A "TEAM PLAYER"?
GOD, JOHN. WARN ME WHEN YOU'RE GONNA SPEAK. I'LL ALERT THE MEDIA.
Choc
AT LEAST CLEAR YOUR THROAT OR SOMETHING.
WHAT WAS THE QUESTION?
DO YOU TRUST ME? YOU DON'T REALLY KNOW... MUCH ABOUT MY ORIGINS... WHERE I COME FROM, WHAT I DO IN MY SPARE TIME...
YOU'RE THE MOST CURIOUS DETECTIVE ON THE MIDDLETON FORCE, JONES. YOU HAVE A SPOTLESS RECORD, YOU ALWAYS GET YOUR MAN...
...AND NO OTHER INVESTIGATOR HAS YET TO FIND YOUR SENSE OF HUMOR. WHAT MORE DO I NEED TO KNOW RIGHT NOW?
NEVER MIND. LOOKS AS IF TWITCH WAS GOOD ON HIS TIP.
THERE ARE DRUGS BEING MANUFACTURED IN THE BACK OF ANGELO'S RESTAURANT... AND BONETTI'S BOYS LOOK VERY TIRED OF ANGELO SKIMMING OFF THE TOP.
LET'S GET IN THERE BEFORE THERE'S TROUBLE.

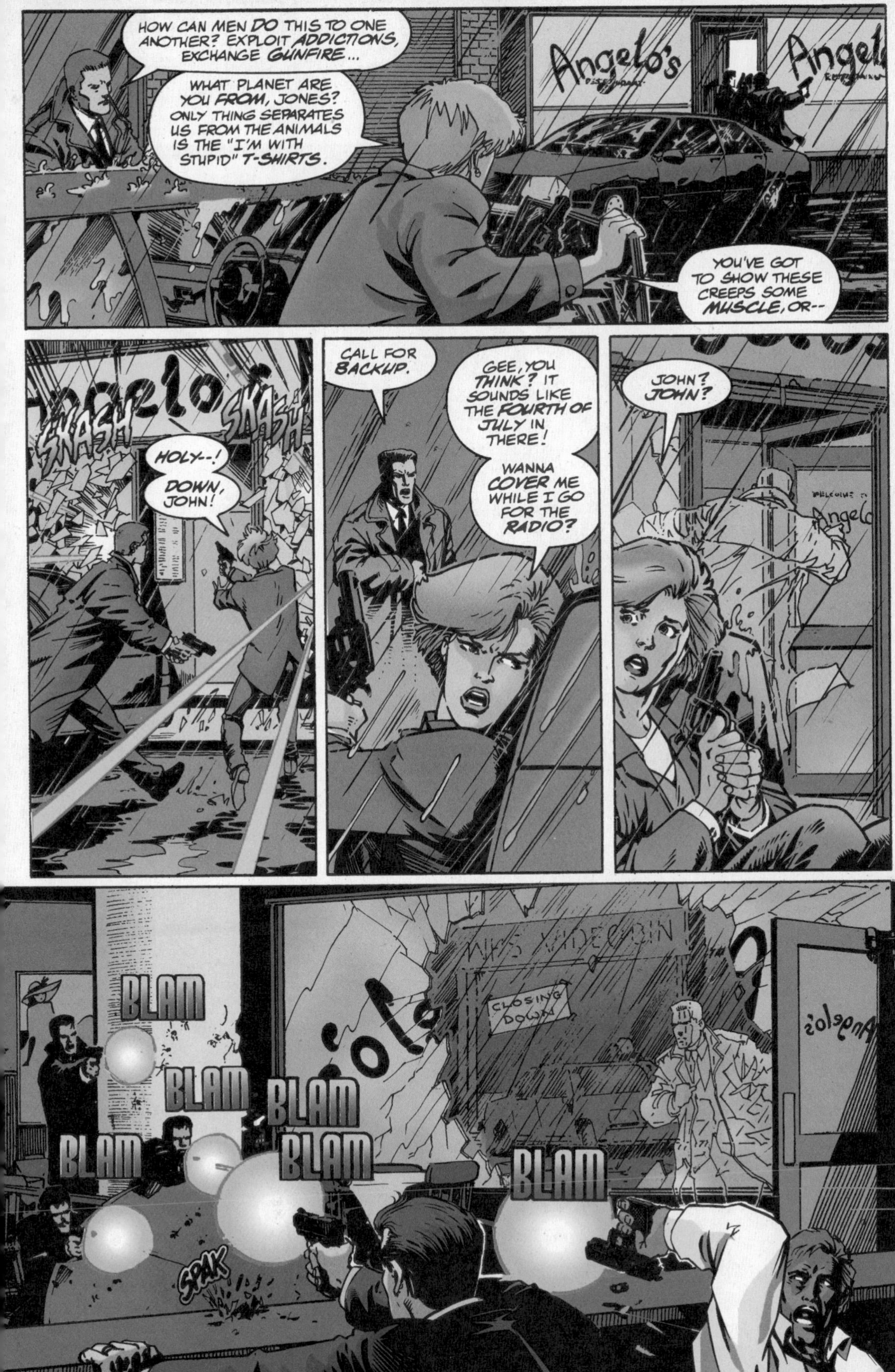
HOW CAN MEN DO THIS TO ONE ANOTHER? EXPLOIT ADDICTIONS, EXCHANGE GUNFIRE...
WHAT PLANET ARE YOU FROM, JONES? ONLY THING SEPARATES US FROM THE ANIMALS IS THE "I'M WITH STUPID" T-SHIRTS.
Angelo's
Angelo's
YOU'VE GOT TO SHOW THESE CREEPS SOME MUSCLE, OR--
SKASH
SKASH
HOLY--!
DOWN, JOHN!
CALL FOR BACKUP.
GEE, YOU THINK? IT SOUNDS LIKE THE FOURTH OF JULY IN THERE!
WANNA COVER ME WHILE I GO FOR THE RADIO?
JOHN? JOHN?
CLOSING DOWN
BLAM
BLAM
BLAM
BLAM
BLAM
BLAM
SPAK

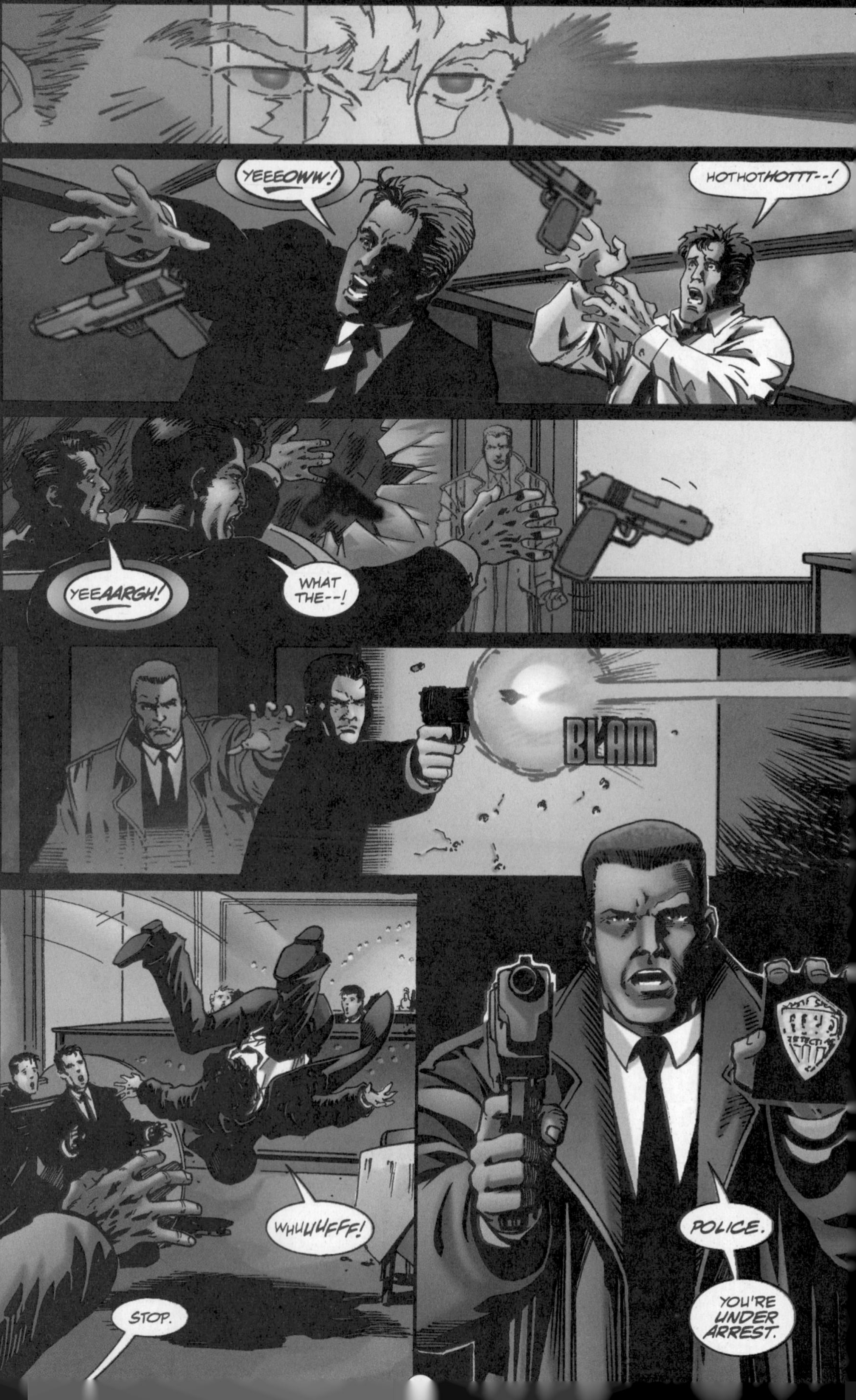
YEEEOWW!
HOTHOTHOTTT--!
YEEAARGH!
WHAT THE--!
BLAM
WHUUUFFF!
STOP.
POLICE.
YOU'RE UNDER ARREST.

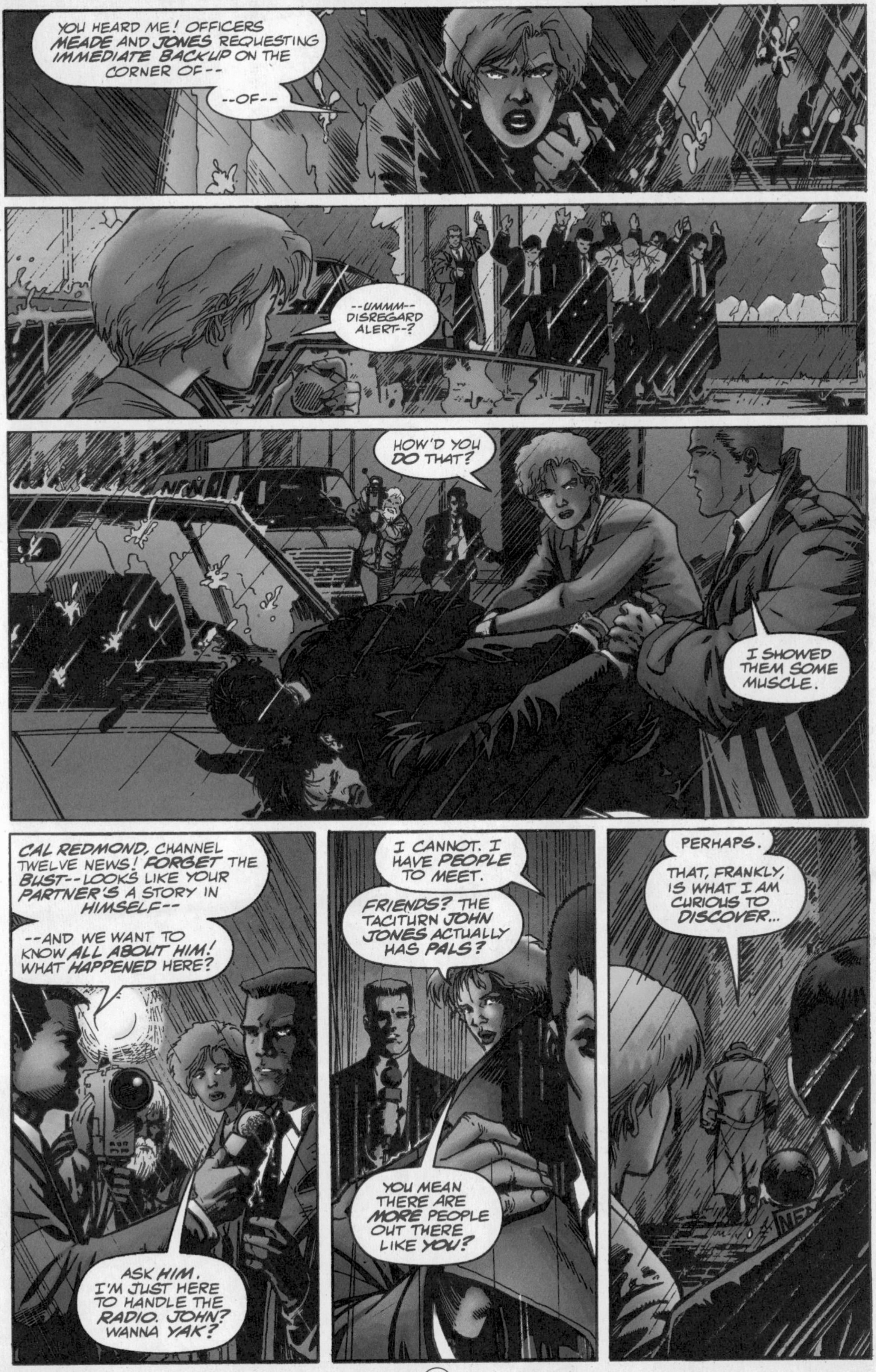
YOU HEARD ME! OFFICERS MEADE AND JONES REQUESTING IMMEDIATE BACKUP ON THE CORNER OF--
--OF--
--UMMM-- DISREGARD ALERT--?
HOW'D YOU DO THAT?
I SHOWED THEM SOME MUSCLE.
CAL REDMOND, CHANNEL TWELVE NEWS! FORGET THE BUST--LOOKS LIKE YOUR PARTNER'S A STORY IN HIMSELF--
--AND WE WANT TO KNOW ALL ABOUT HIM! WHAT HAPPENED HERE?
ASK HIM. I'M JUST HERE TO HANDLE THE RADIO. JOHN? WANNA YAK?
I CANNOT. I HAVE PEOPLE TO MEET.
FRIENDS? THE TACITURN JOHN JONES ACTUALLY HAS PALS?
YOU MEAN THERE ARE MORE PEOPLE OUT THERE LIKE YOU?
PERHAPS.
THAT, FRANKLY, IS WHAT I AM CURIOUS TO DISCOVER...

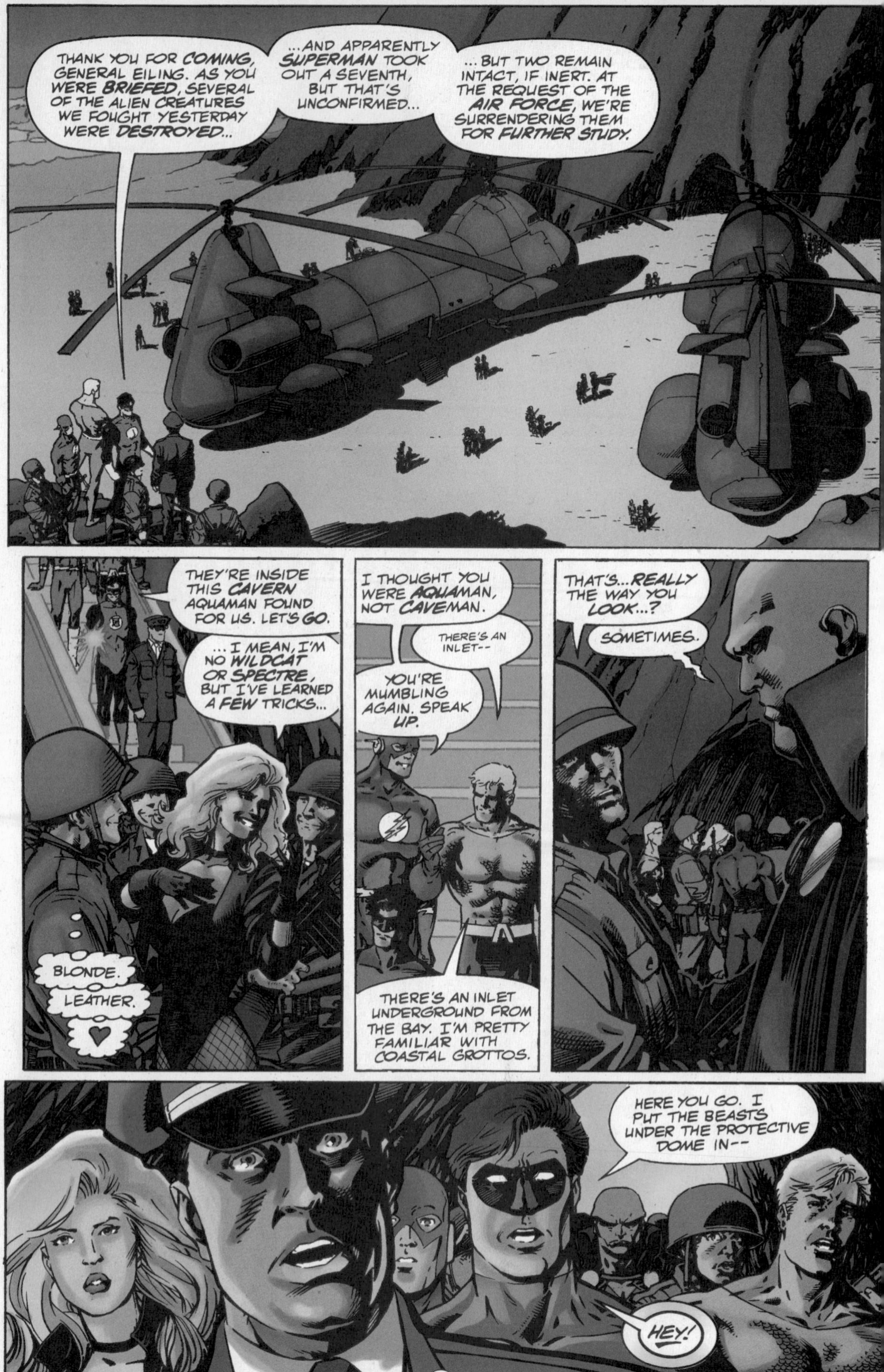

THANK YOU FOR COMING, GENERAL EILING. AS YOU WERE BRIEFED, SEVERAL OF THE ALIEN CREATURES WE FOUGHT YESTERDAY WERE DESTROYED...
...AND APPARENTLY SUPERMAN TOOK OUT A SEVENTH, BUT THAT'S UNCONFIRMED...
...BUT TWO REMAIN INTACT, IF INERT. AT THE REQUEST OF THE AIR FORCE, WE'RE SURRENDERING THEM FOR FURTHER STUDY.
THEY'RE INSIDE THIS CAVERN AQUAMAN FOUND FOR US. LET'S GO.
...I MEAN, I'M NO WILDCAT OR SPECTRE, BUT I'VE LEARNED A FEW TRICKS...
BLONDE.
LEATHER.
I THOUGHT YOU WERE AQUAMAN, NOT CAVEMAN.
THERE'S AN INLET--
YOU'RE MUMBLING AGAIN. SPEAK UP.
THERE'S AN INLET UNDERGROUND FROM THE BAY. I'M PRETTY FAMILIAR WITH COASTAL GROTTOS.
THAT'S...REALLY THE WAY YOU LOOK...?
SOMETIMES.
HERE YOU GO. I PUT THE BEASTS UNDER THE PROTECTIVE DOME IN--
HEY!

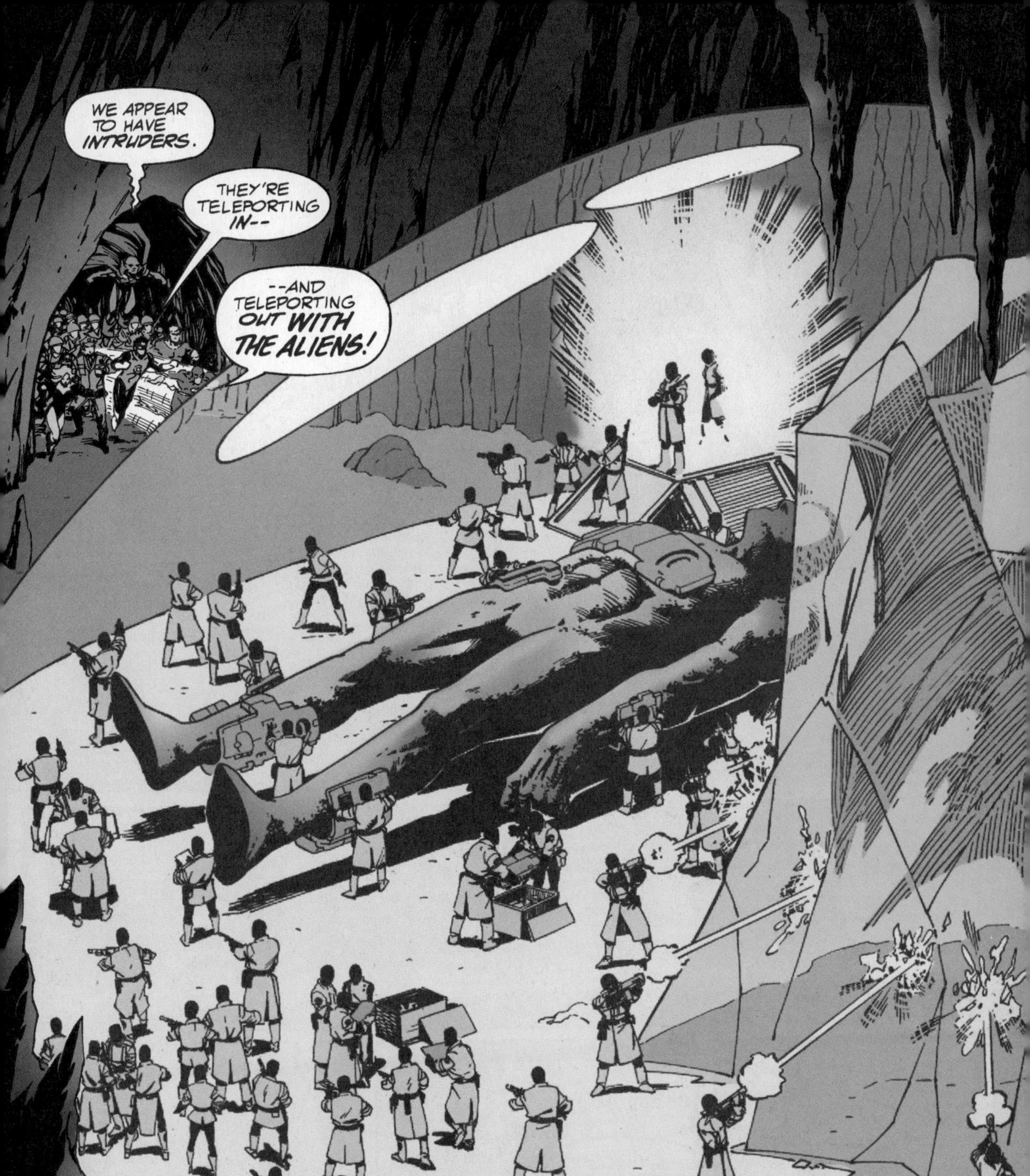
WE APPEAR TO HAVE INTRUDERS.
THEY'RE TELEPORTING IN--
--AND TELEPORTING OUT WITH THE ALIENS!

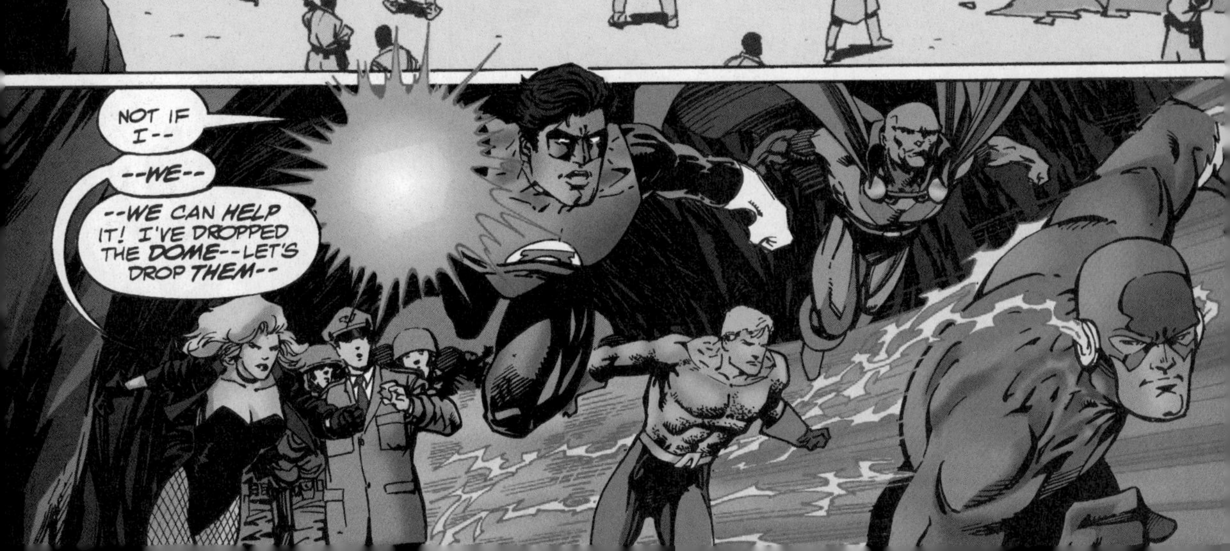
NOT IF I--
--WE--
--WE CAN HELP IT! I'VE DROPPED THE DOME--LET'S DROP THEM--

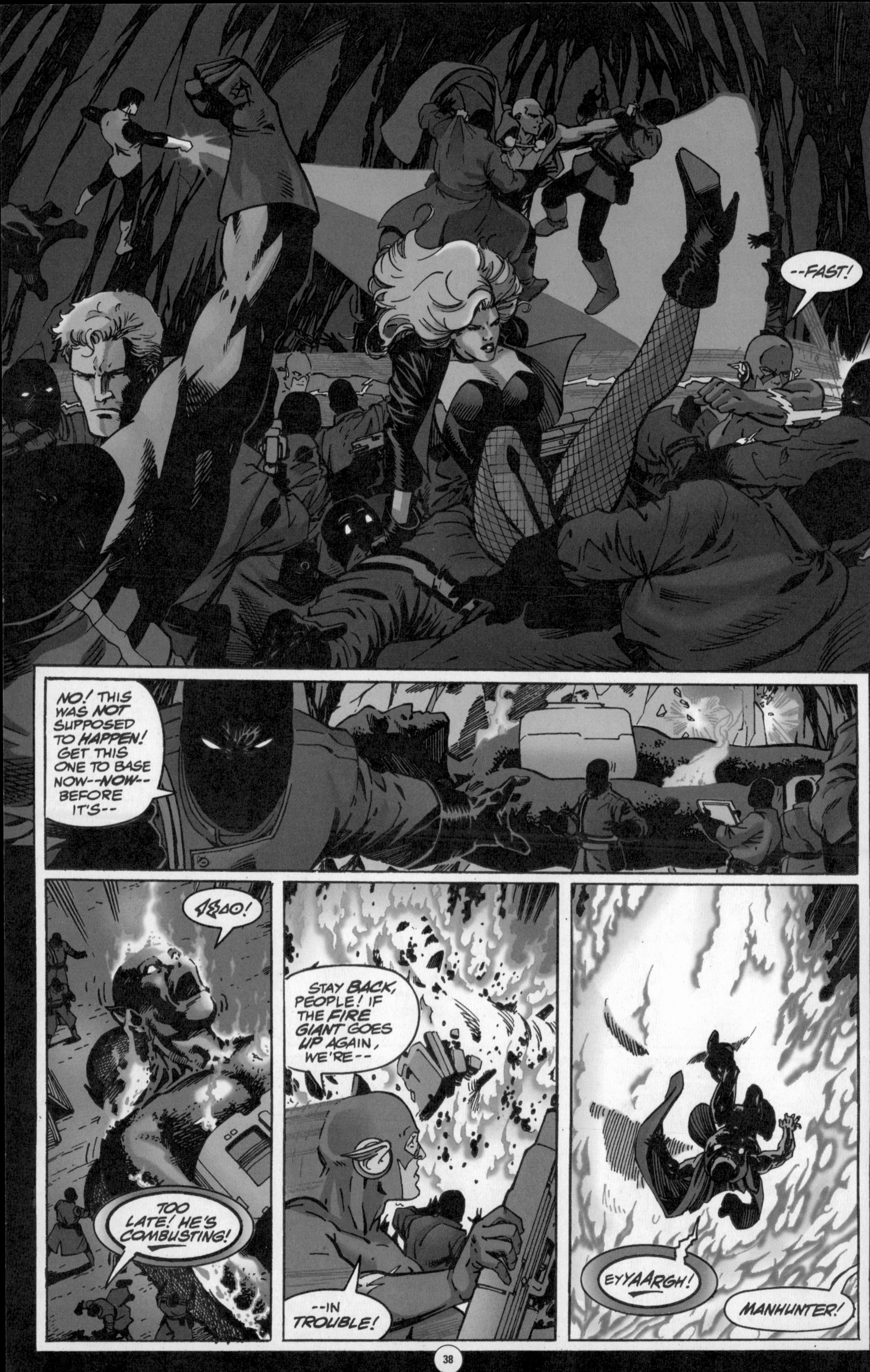
--FAST!
NO! THIS WAS NOT SUPPOSED TO HAPPEN! GET THIS ONE TO BASE NOW--NOW--BEFORE IT'S--
TOO LATE! HE'S COMBUSTING!
STAY BACK, PEOPLE! IF THE FIRE GIANT GOES UP AGAIN, WE'RE--
--IN TROUBLE!
EYYAARGH!
MANHUNTER!

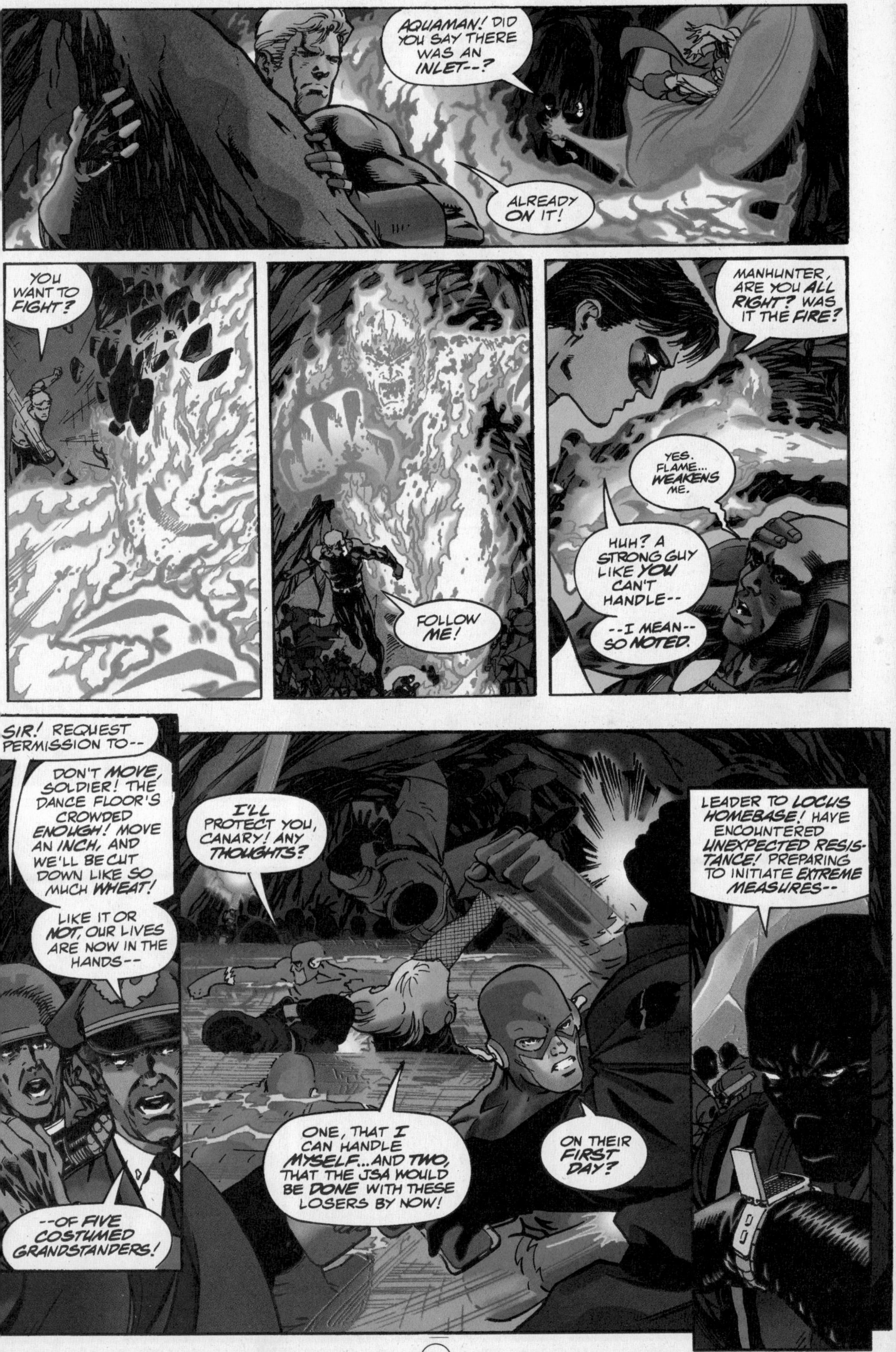
AQUAMAN! DID YOU SAY THERE WAS AN INLET--?
ALREADY ON IT!
YOU WANT TO FIGHT?
FOLLOW ME!
MANHUNTER, ARE YOU ALL RIGHT? WAS IT THE FIRE?
YES. FLAME... WEAKENS ME.
HUH? A STRONG GUY LIKE YOU CAN'T HANDLE--
--I MEAN-- SO NOTED.
SIR! REQUEST PERMISSION TO--
DON'T MOVE, SOLDIER! THE DANCE FLOOR'S CROWDED ENOUGH! MOVE AN INCH, AND WE'LL BE CUT DOWN LIKE SO MUCH WHEAT!
LIKE IT OR NOT, OUR LIVES ARE NOW IN THE HANDS--
--OF FIVE COSTUMED GRANDSTANDERS!
I'LL PROTECT YOU, CANARY! ANY THOUGHTS?
ONE, THAT I CAN HANDLE MYSELF... AND TWO, THAT THE JSA WOULD BE DONE WITH THESE LOSERS BY NOW!
ON THEIR FIRST DAY?
LEADER TO LOCUS HOMEBASE! HAVE ENCOUNTERED UNEXPECTED RESISTANCE! PREPARING TO INITIATE EXTREME MEASURES--

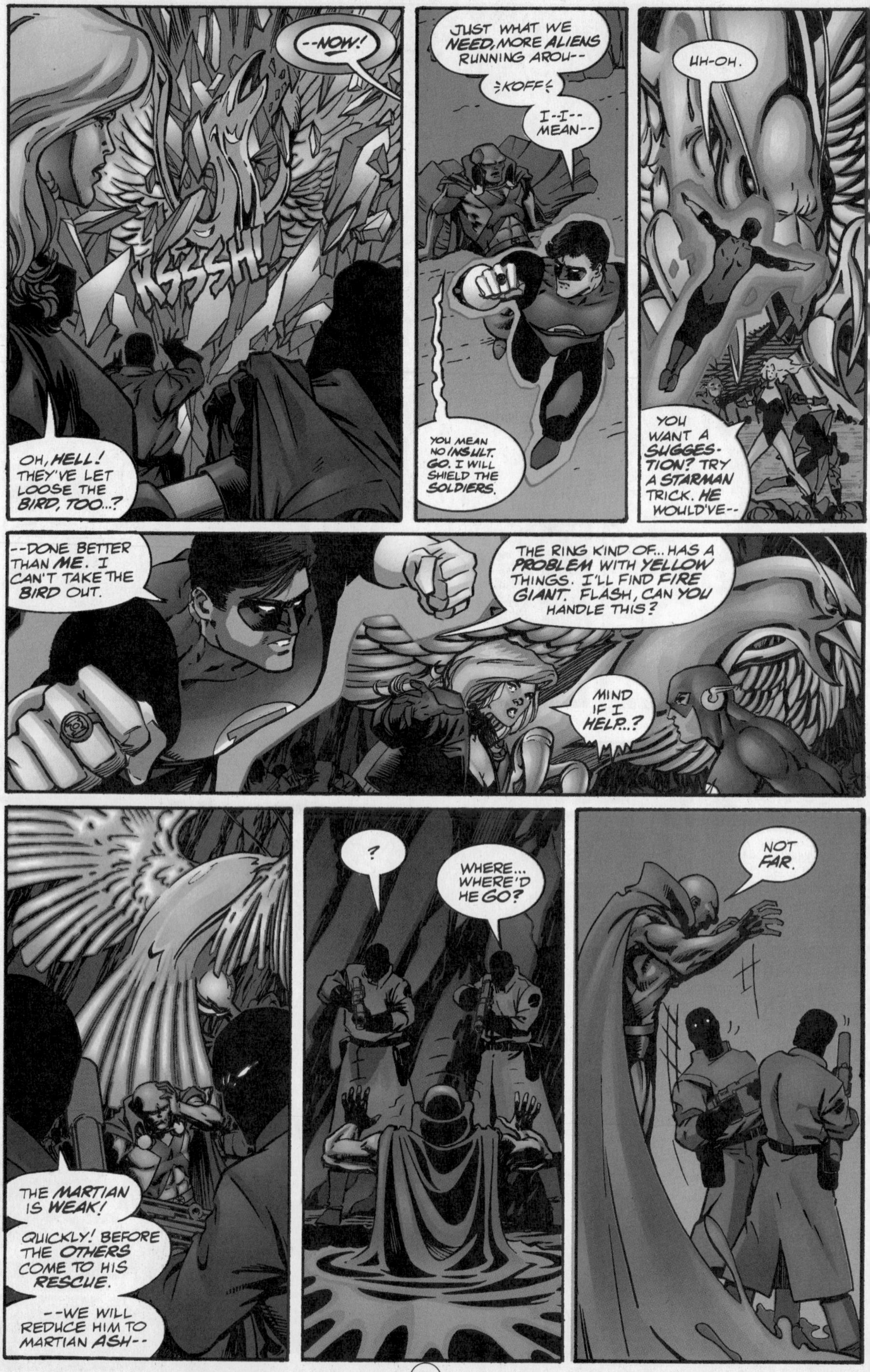
--NOW!
KSSSH!
OH, HELL! THEY'VE LET LOOSE THE BIRD, TOO...?
JUST WHAT WE NEED, MORE ALIENS RUNNING AROU--
KOFF
I--I-- MEAN--
YOU MEAN NO INSULT. GO. I WILL SHIELD THE SOLDIERS.
UH-OH.
YOU WANT A SUGGES-TION? TRY A STARMAN TRICK. HE WOULD'VE--
--DONE BETTER THAN ME. I CAN'T TAKE THE BIRD OUT.
THE RING KIND OF... HAS A PROBLEM WITH YELLOW THINGS. I'LL FIND FIRE GIANT. FLASH, CAN YOU HANDLE THIS?
MIND IF I HELP...?
THE MARTIAN IS WEAK!
QUICKLY! BEFORE THE OTHERS COME TO HIS RESCUE.
--WE WILL REDUCE HIM TO MARTIAN ASH--
?
WHERE... WHERE'D HE GO?
NOT FAR.

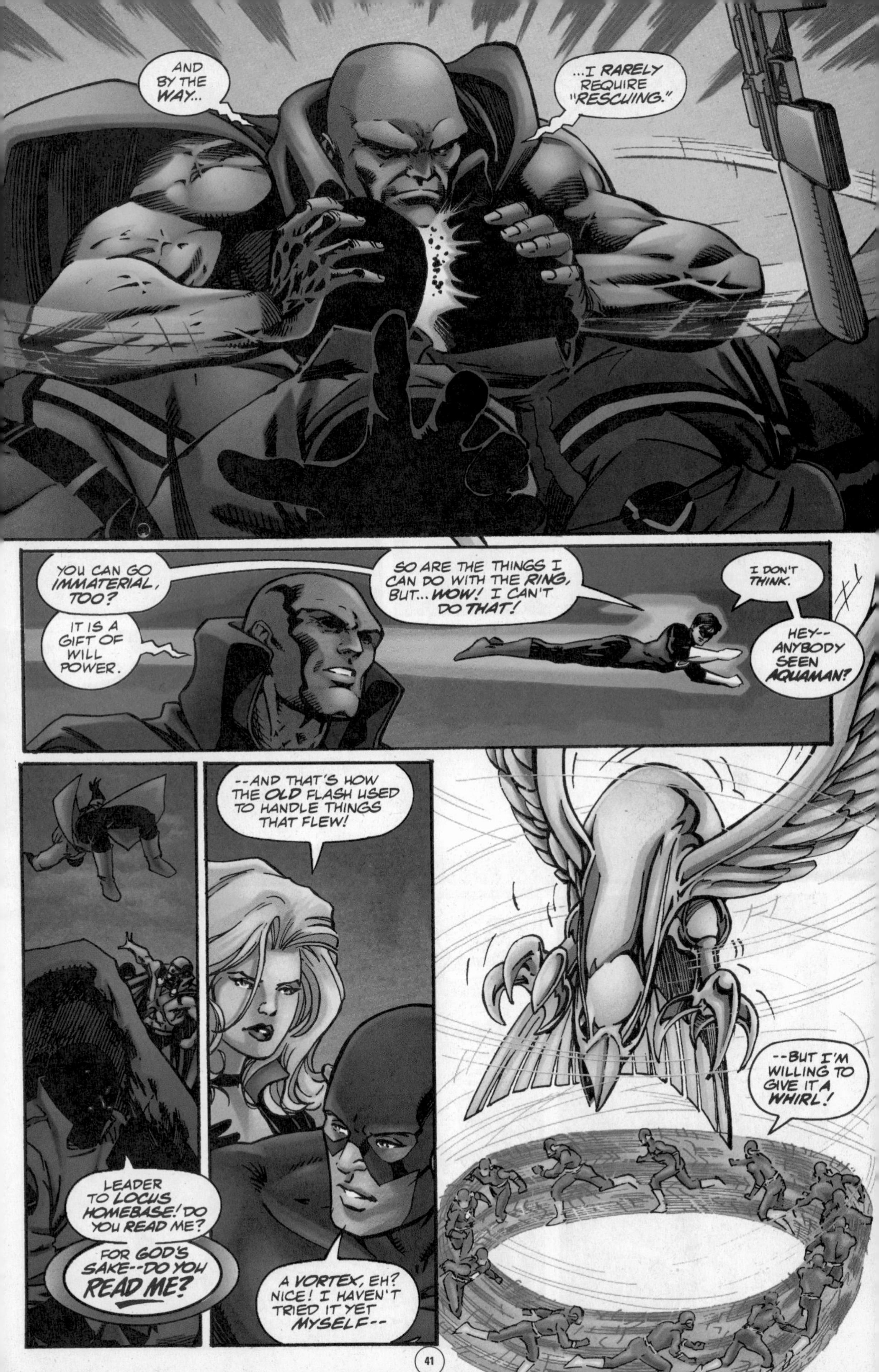

AND BY THE WAY...
...I RARELY REQUIRE "RESCUING."
YOU CAN GO IMMATERIAL, TOO?
IT IS A GIFT OF WILL POWER.
SO ARE THE THINGS I CAN DO WITH THE RING, BUT... WOW! I CAN'T DO THAT!
I DON'T THINK.
HEY-- ANYBODY SEEN AQUAMAN?
--AND THAT'S HOW THE OLD FLASH USED TO HANDLE THINGS THAT FLEW!
LEADER TO LOCUS HOMEBASE! DO YOU READ ME?
FOR GOD'S SAKE--DO YOU READ ME?
A VORTEX, EH? NICE! I HAVEN'T TRIED IT YET MYSELF--
--BUT I'M WILLING TO GIVE IT A WHIRL!

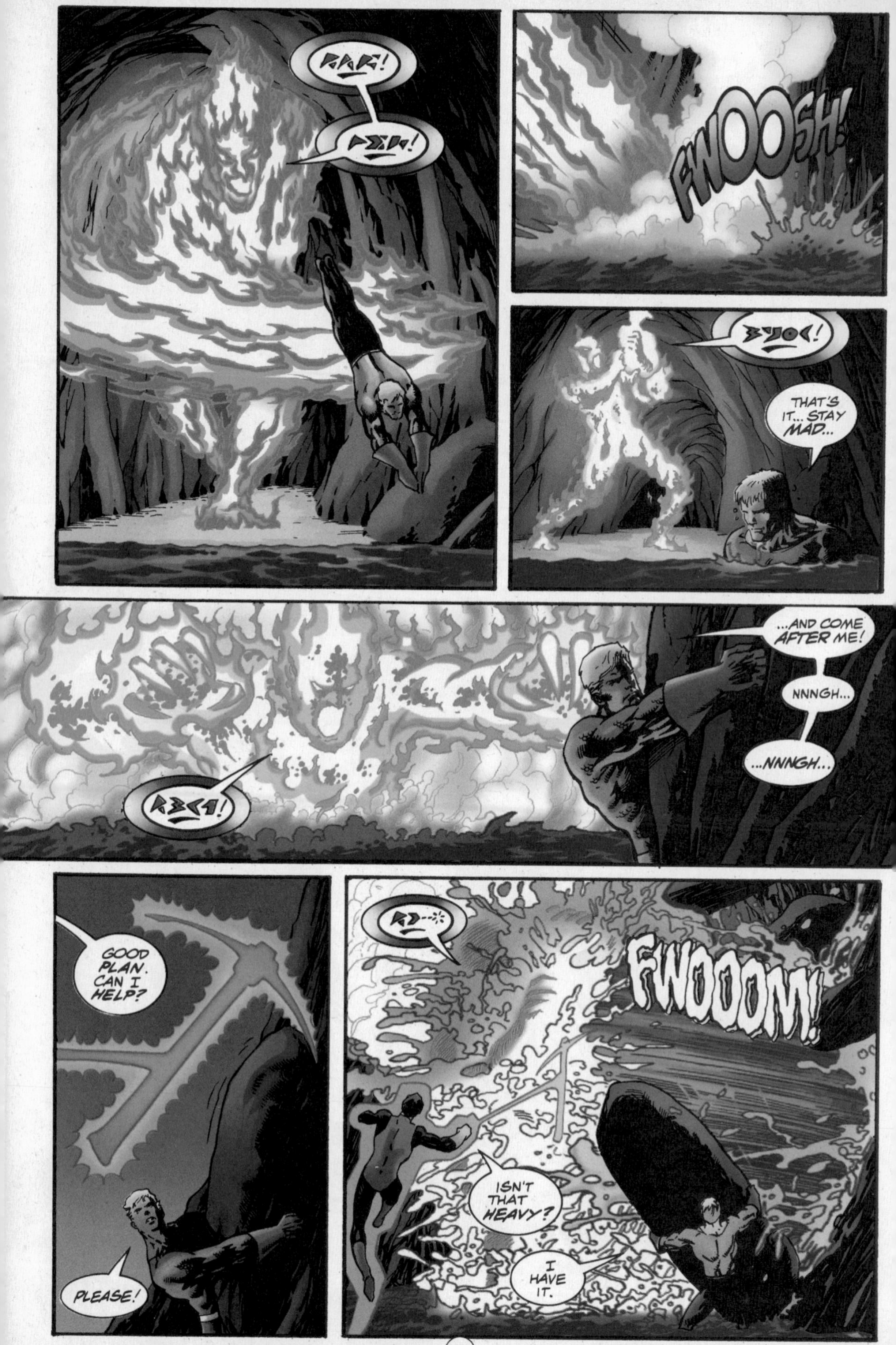
FWOOSH!
THAT'S IT... STAY MAD...
...AND COME AFTER ME!
NNNGH...
...NNNGH...
GOOD PLAN. CAN I HELP?
PLEASE!
FWOOOM!
ISN'T THAT HEAVY?
I HAVE IT.

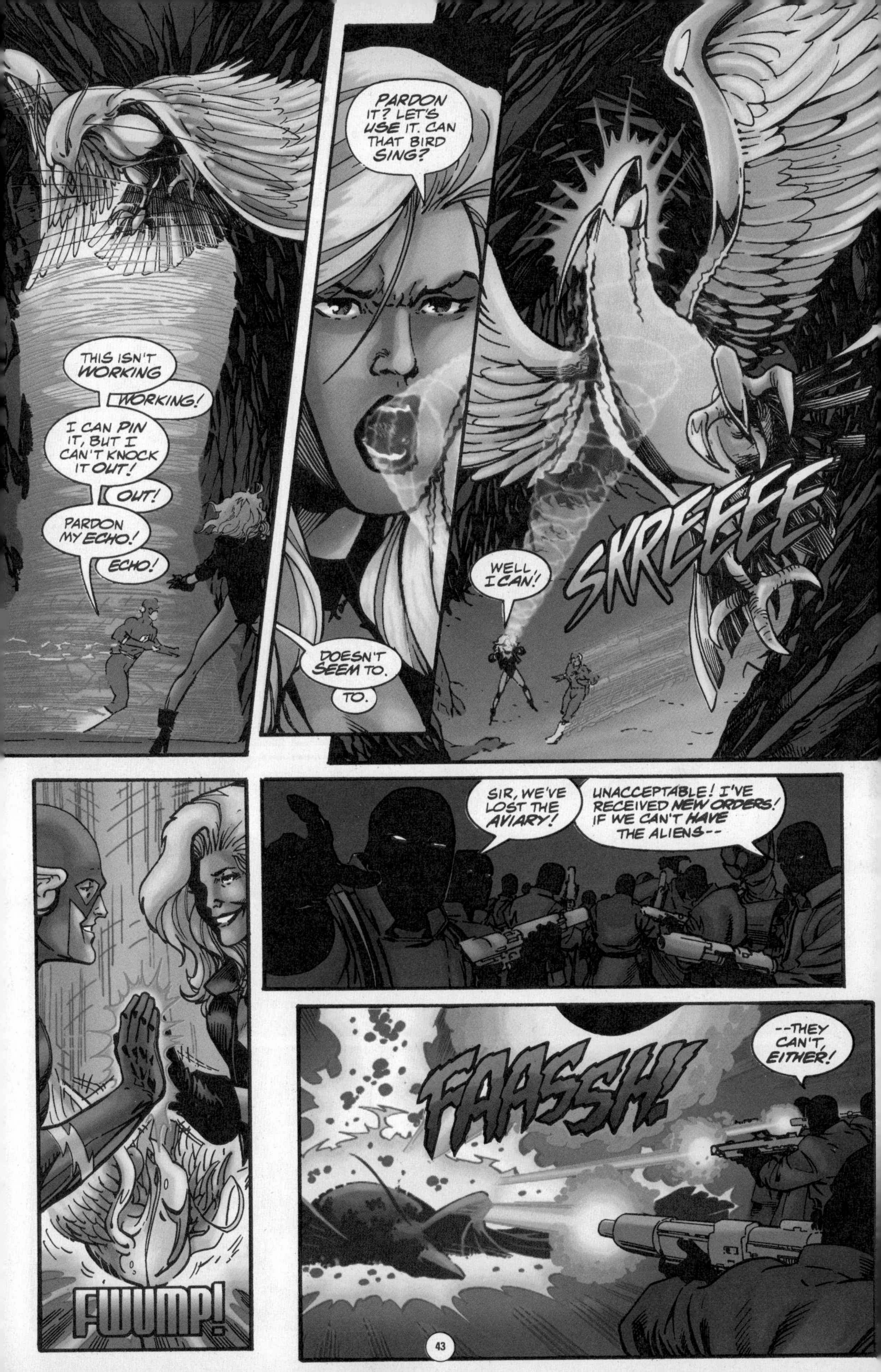
THIS ISN'T WORKING
WORKING!
I CAN PIN IT, BUT I CAN'T KNOCK IT OUT!
OUT!
PARDON MY ECHO!
ECHO!
PARDON IT? LET'S USE IT. CAN THAT BIRD SING?
DOESN'T SEEM TO.
TO.
WELL I CAN!
SKREEEEE
FWUMP!
SIR, WE'VE LOST THE AVIARY!
UNACCEPTABLE! I'VE RECEIVED NEW ORDERS! IF WE CAN'T HAVE THE ALIENS--
FAASSH!
--THEY CAN'T, EITHER!

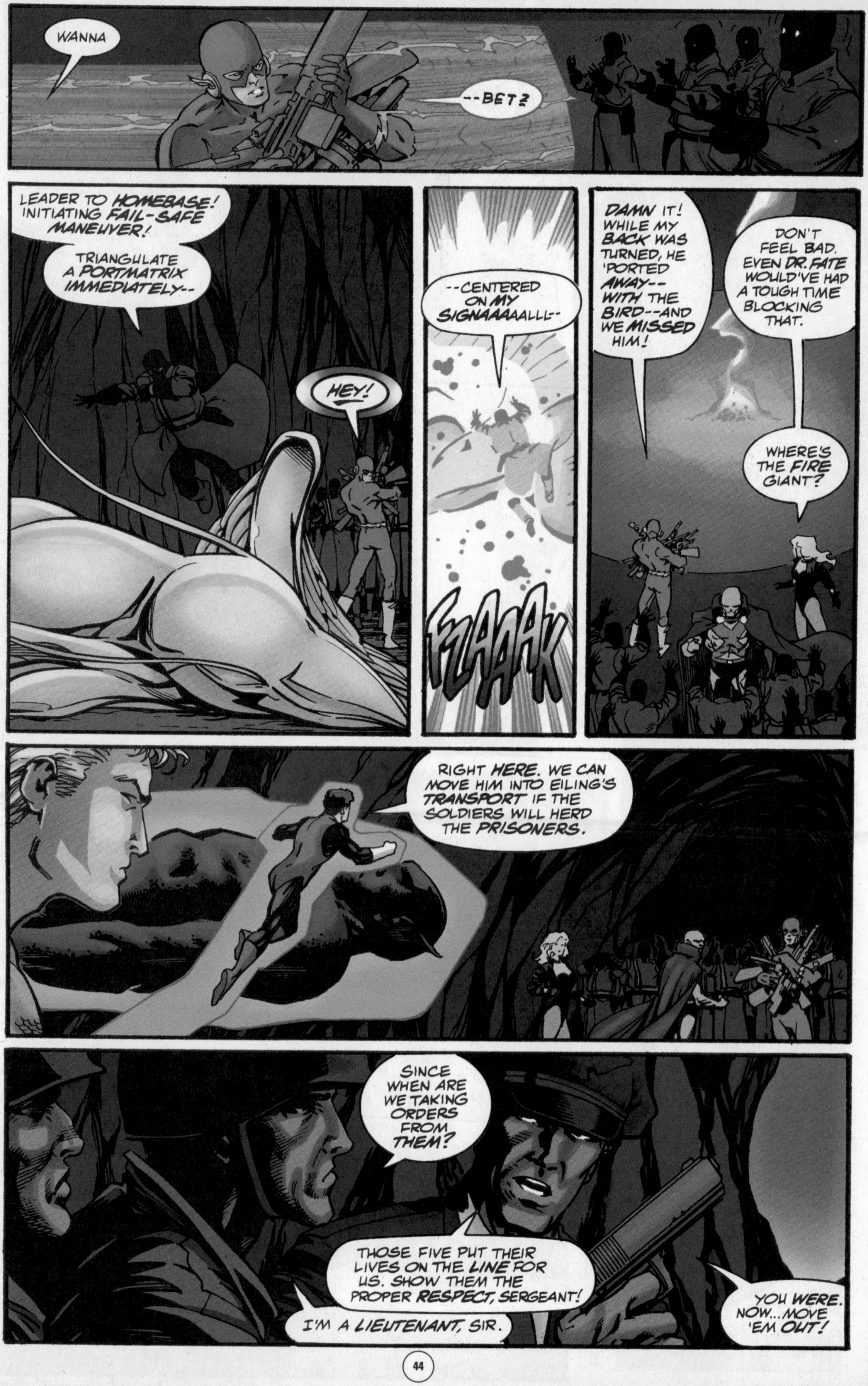
WANNA
--BET?
LEADER TO HOMEBASE! INITIATING FAIL-SAFE MANEUVER!
TRIANGULATE A PORTMATRIX IMMEDIATELY--
HEY!
--CENTERED ON MY SIGNAAAAALLL--
FZAAAK
DAMN IT! WHILE MY BACK WAS TURNED, HE 'PORTED AWAY--WITH THE BIRD--AND WE MISSED HIM!
DON'T FEEL BAD. EVEN DR. FATE WOULD'VE HAD A TOUGH TIME BLOCKING THAT.
WHERE'S THE FIRE GIANT?
RIGHT HERE. WE CAN MOVE HIM INTO EILING'S TRANSPORT IF THE SOLDIERS WILL HERD THE PRISONERS.
SINCE WHEN ARE WE TAKING ORDERS FROM THEM?
THOSE FIVE PUT THEIR LIVES ON THE LINE FOR US. SHOW THEM THE PROPER RESPECT, SERGEANT!
I'M A LIEUTENANT, SIR.
YOU WERE. NOW...MOVE 'EM OUT!

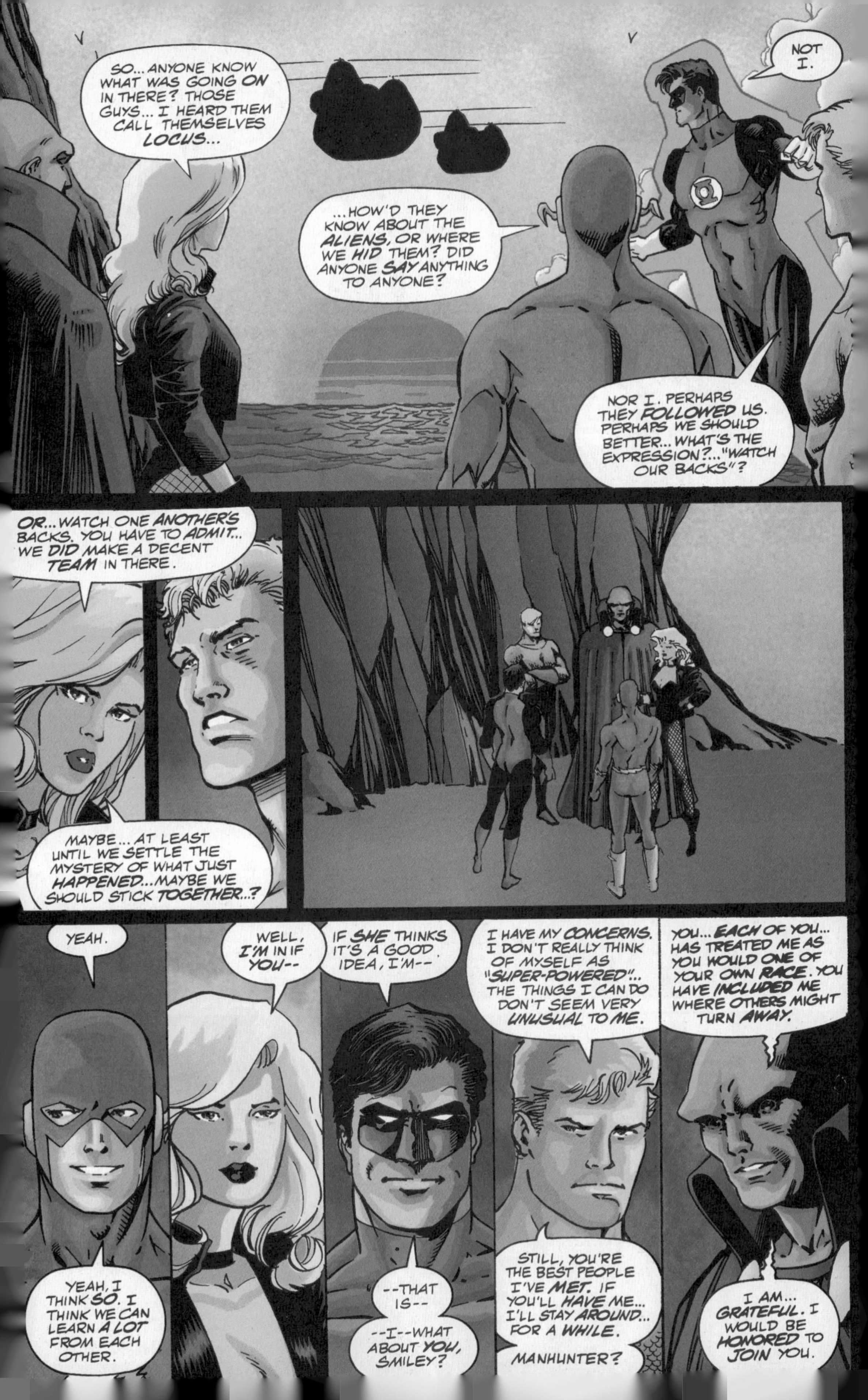
SO... ANYONE KNOW WHAT WAS GOING ON IN THERE? THOSE GUYS... I HEARD THEM CALL THEMSELVES LOCUS...
...HOW'D THEY KNOW ABOUT THE ALIENS, OR WHERE WE HID THEM? DID ANYONE SAY ANYTHING TO ANYONE?
NOT I.
NOR I. PERHAPS THEY FOLLOWED US. PERHAPS WE SHOULD BETTER... WHAT'S THE EXPRESSION?... "WATCH OUR BACKS"?
OR... WATCH ONE ANOTHER'S BACKS. YOU HAVE TO ADMIT... WE DID MAKE A DECENT TEAM IN THERE.
MAYBE... AT LEAST UNTIL WE SETTLE THE MYSTERY OF WHAT JUST HAPPENED... MAYBE WE SHOULD STICK TOGETHER..?
YEAH.
YEAH, I THINK SO. I THINK WE CAN LEARN A LOT FROM EACH OTHER.
WELL, I'M IN IF YOU--
IF SHE THINKS IT'S A GOOD IDEA, I'M--
--THAT IS--
--I--WHAT ABOUT YOU, SMILEY?
I HAVE MY CONCERNS. I DON'T REALLY THINK OF MYSELF AS "SUPER-POWERED"... THE THINGS I CAN DO DON'T SEEM VERY UNUSUAL TO ME.
STILL, YOU'RE THE BEST PEOPLE I'VE MET. IF YOU'LL HAVE ME... I'LL STAY AROUND... FOR A WHILE.
MANHUNTER?
YOU... EACH OF YOU... HAS TREATED ME AS YOU WOULD ONE OF YOUR OWN RACE. YOU HAVE INCLUDED ME WHERE OTHERS MIGHT TURN AWAY.
I AM... GRATEFUL. I WOULD BE HONORED TO JOIN YOU.

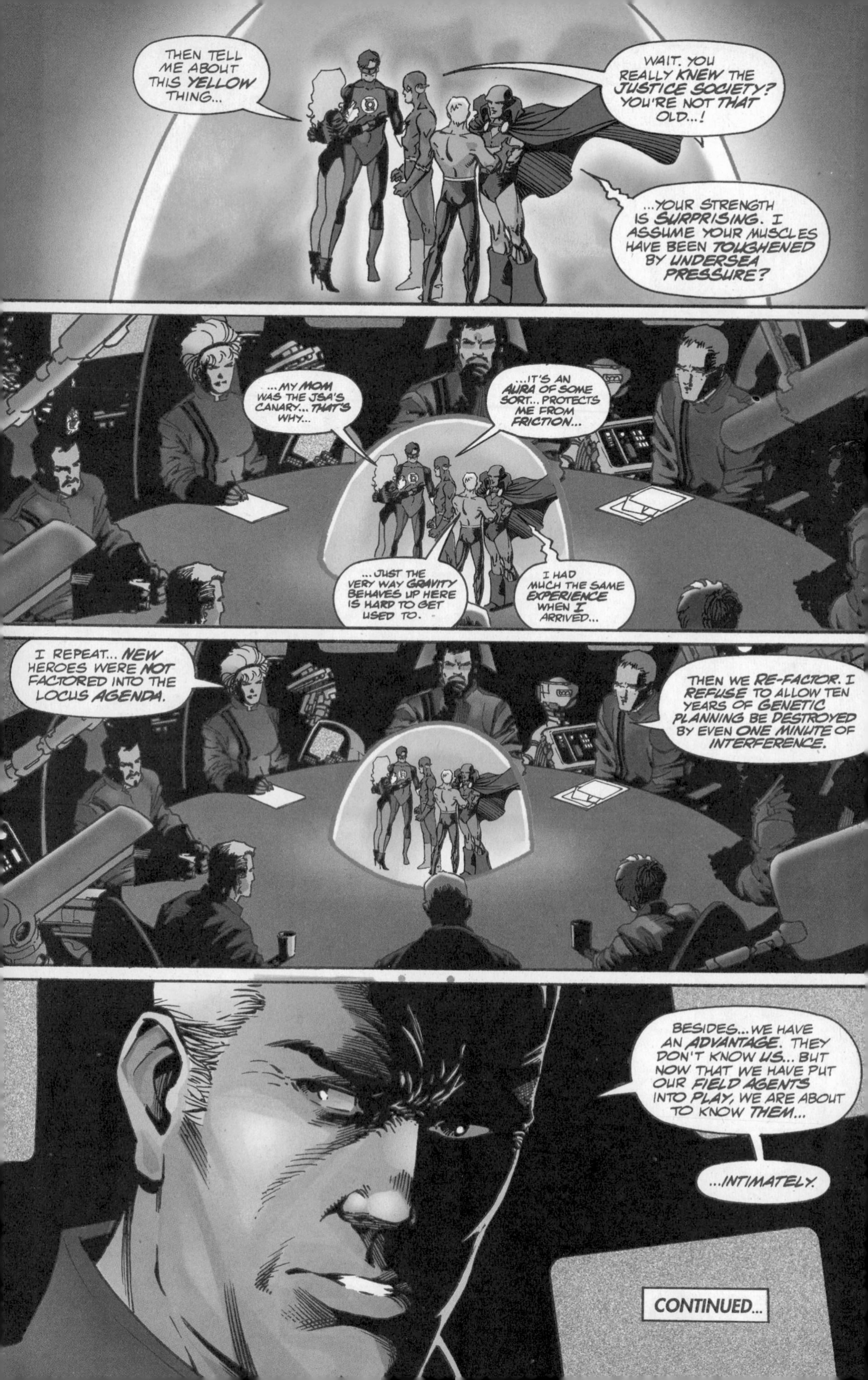
THEN TELL ME ABOUT THIS YELLOW THING...
WAIT. YOU REALLY KNEW THE JUSTICE SOCIETY? YOU'RE NOT THAT OLD...!
...YOUR STRENGTH IS SURPRISING. I ASSUME YOUR MUSCLES HAVE BEEN TOUGHENED BY UNDERSEA PRESSURE?
...MY MOM WAS THE JSA'S CANARY... THAT'S WHY...
...IT'S AN AURA OF SOME SORT... PROTECTS ME FROM FRICTION...
...JUST THE VERY WAY GRAVITY BEHAVES UP HERE IS HARD TO GET USED TO.
I HAD MUCH THE SAME EXPERIENCE WHEN I ARRIVED...
I REPEAT... NEW HEROES WERE NOT FACTORED INTO THE LOCUS AGENDA.
THEN WE RE-FACTOR. I REFUSE TO ALLOW TEN YEARS OF GENETIC PLANNING BE DESTROYED BY EVEN ONE MINUTE OF INTERFERENCE.
BESIDES... WE HAVE AN ADVANTAGE. THEY DON'T KNOW US... BUT NOW THAT WE HAVE PUT OUR FIELD AGENTS INTO PLAY, WE ARE ABOUT TO KNOW THEM...
...INTIMATELY.
CONTINUED...

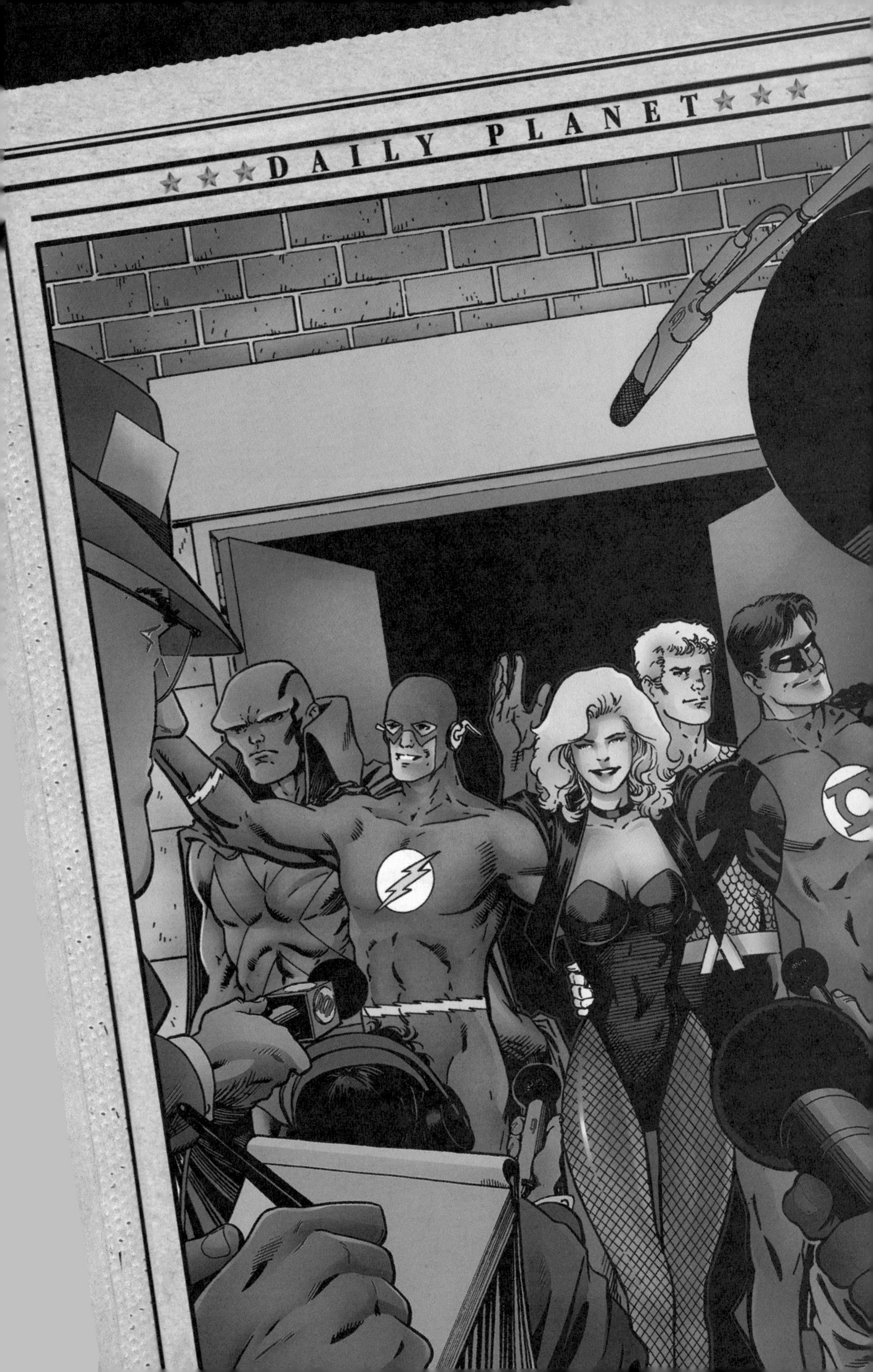
DAILY PLANET

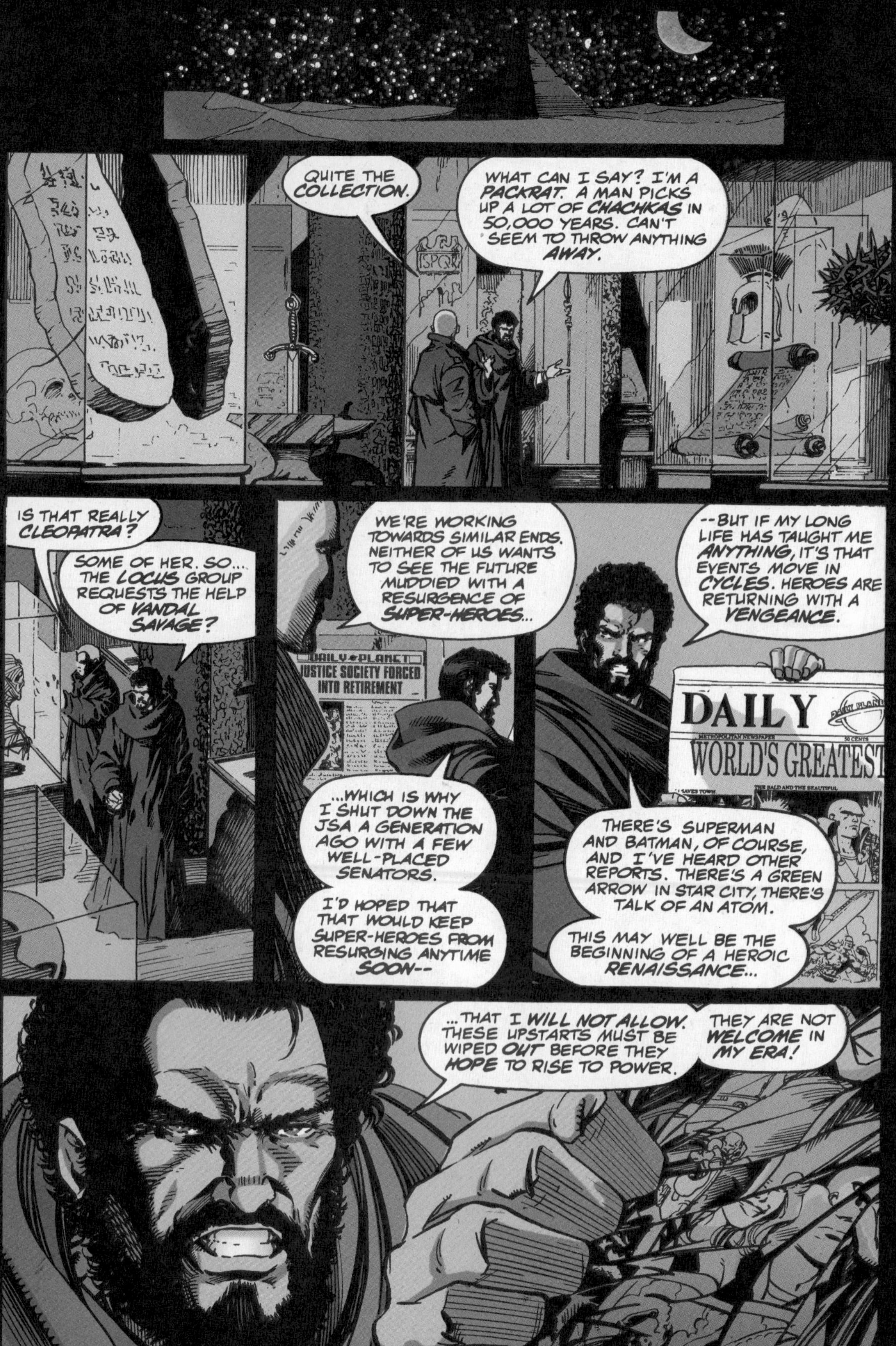
QUITE THE COLLECTION.
WHAT CAN I SAY? I'M A PACKRAT. A MAN PICKS UP A LOT OF CHACHKAS IN 50,000 YEARS. CAN'T SEEM TO THROW ANYTHING AWAY.
SPQR
IS THAT REALLY CLEOPATRA?
SOME OF HER. SO... THE LOCUS GROUP REQUESTS THE HELP OF VANDAL SAVAGE?
WE'RE WORKING TOWARDS SIMILAR ENDS. NEITHER OF US WANTS TO SEE THE FUTURE MUDDIED WITH A RESURGENCE OF SUPER-HEROES...
DAILY PLANET
JUSTICE SOCIETY FORCED INTO RETIREMENT
...WHICH IS WHY I SHUT DOWN THE JSA A GENERATION AGO WITH A FEW WELL-PLACED SENATORS.
I'D HOPED THAT THAT WOULD KEEP SUPER-HEROES FROM RESURGING ANYTIME SOON--
--BUT IF MY LONG LIFE HAS TAUGHT ME ANYTHING, IT'S THAT EVENTS MOVE IN CYCLES. HEROES ARE RETURNING WITH A VENGEANCE.
DAILY
METROPOLITAN NEWSPAPER
50 CENTS
WORLD'S GREATEST
THE BALD AND THE BEAUTIFUL
THERE'S SUPERMAN AND BATMAN, OF COURSE, AND I'VE HEARD OTHER REPORTS. THERE'S A GREEN ARROW IN STAR CITY, THERE'S TALK OF AN ATOM.
THIS MAY WELL BE THE BEGINNING OF A HEROIC RENAISSANCE...
...THAT I WILL NOT ALLOW. THESE UPSTARTS MUST BE WIPED OUT BEFORE THEY HOPE TO RISE TO POWER.
THEY ARE NOT WELCOME IN MY ERA!

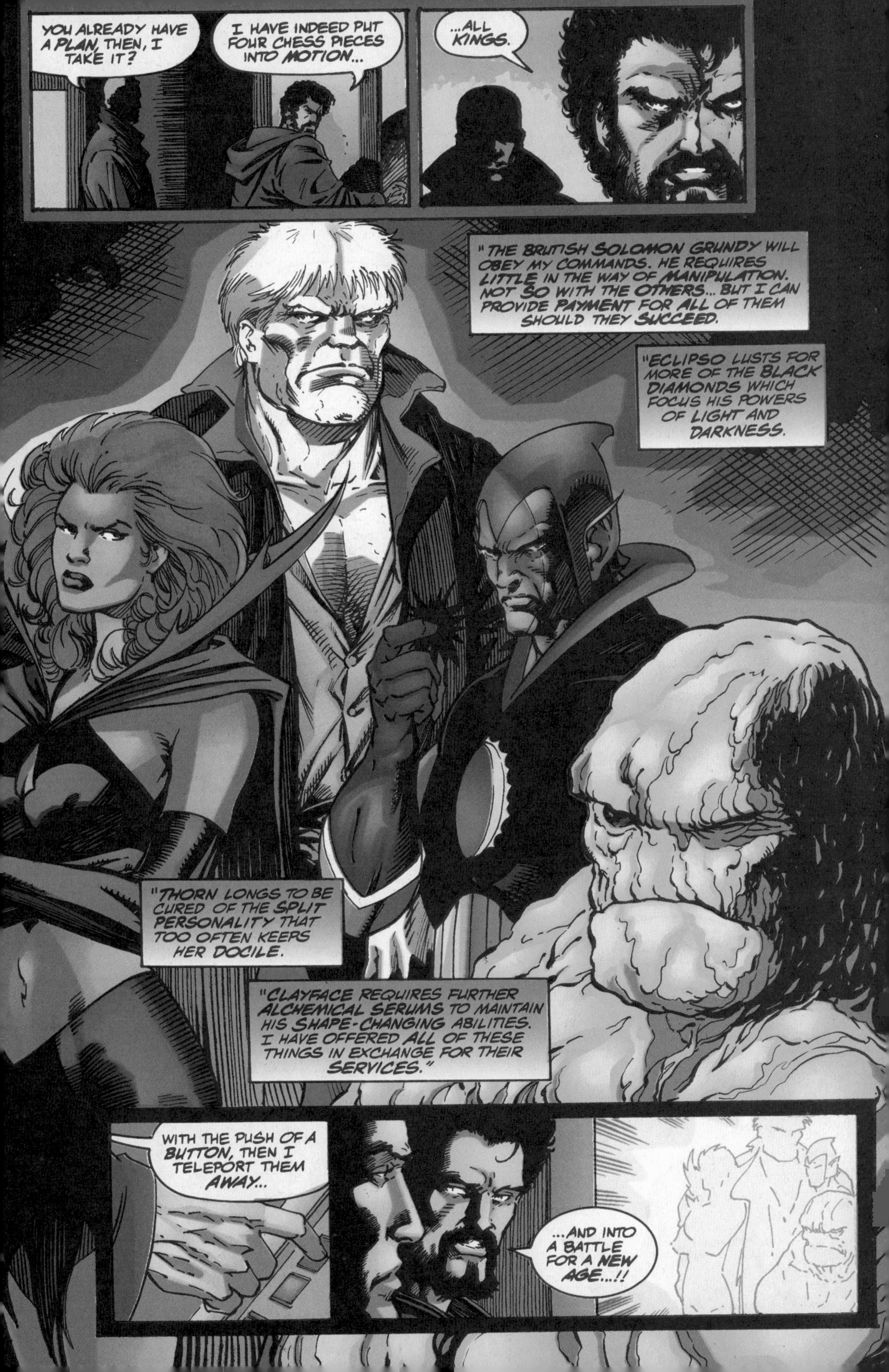
YOU ALREADY HAVE A PLAN, THEN, I TAKE IT?
I HAVE INDEED PUT FOUR CHESS PIECES INTO MOTION...
...ALL KINGS.
"THE BRITISH SOLOMON GRUNDY WILL OBEY MY COMMANDS. HE REQUIRES LITTLE IN THE WAY OF MANIPULATION. NOT SO WITH THE OTHERS... BUT I CAN PROVIDE PAYMENT FOR ALL OF THEM SHOULD THEY SUCCEED.
"ECLIPSO LUSTS FOR MORE OF THE BLACK DIAMONDS WHICH FOCUS HIS POWERS OF LIGHT AND DARKNESS.
"THORN LONGS TO BE CURED OF THE SPLIT PERSONALITY THAT TOO OFTEN KEEPS HER DOCILE.
"CLAYFACE REQUIRES FURTHER ALCHEMICAL SERUMS TO MAINTAIN HIS SHAPE-CHANGING ABILITIES. I HAVE OFFERED ALL OF THESE THINGS IN EXCHANGE FOR THEIR SERVICES."
WITH THE PUSH OF A BUTTON, THEN I TELEPORT THEM AWAY...
...AND INTO A BATTLE FOR A NEW AGE...!!

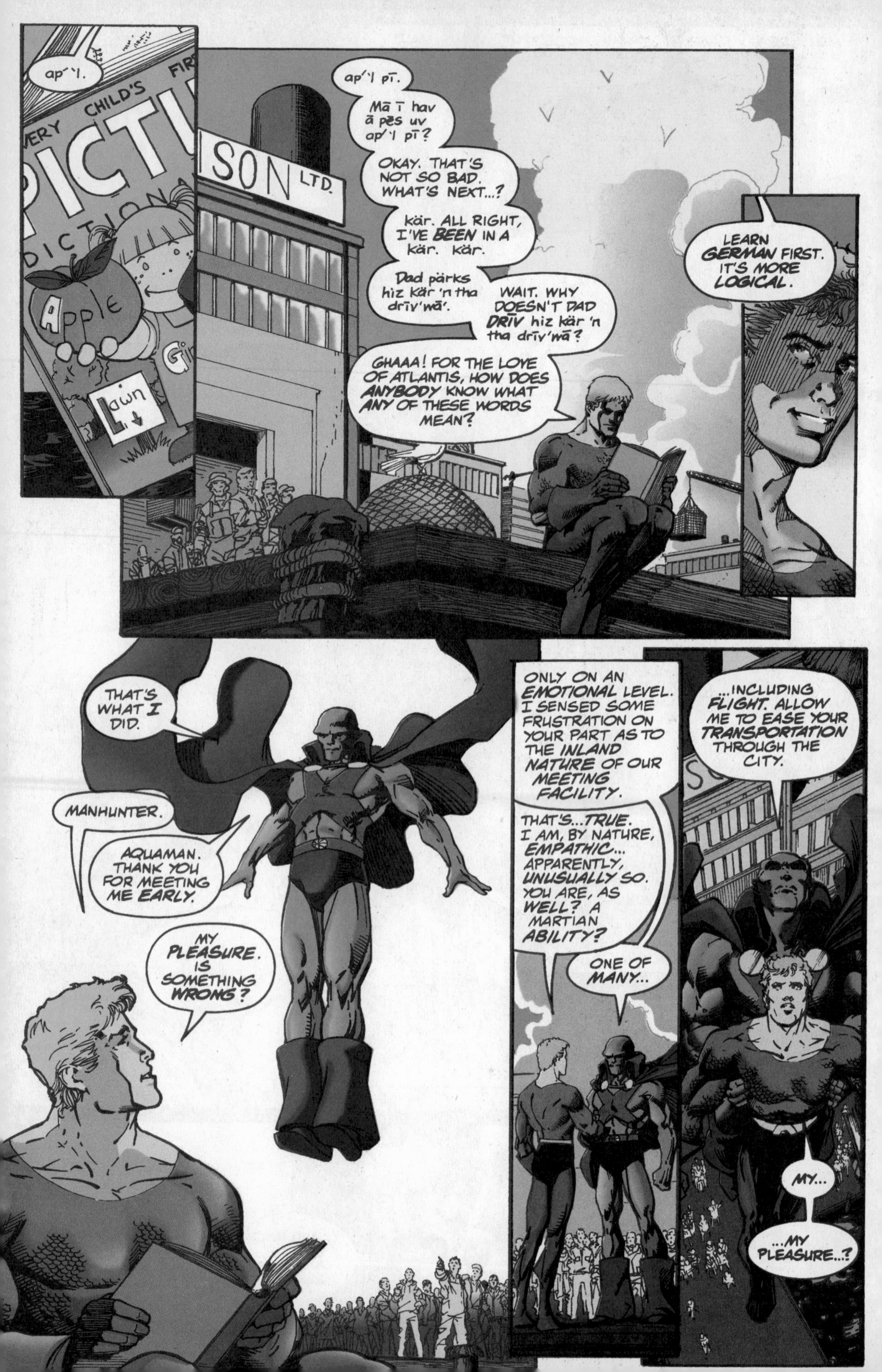
ap´'l.
ap´'l pī.
Mā ī hav ā pēs uv ap´'l pī?
OKAY. THAT'S NOT SO BAD. WHAT'S NEXT...?
kär. ALL RIGHT, I'VE BEEN IN A kär. kär.
Dad pärks hiz kär 'n tha drīv'wā'.
WAIT. WHY DOESN'T DAD DRIV hiz kär 'n tha drīv'wā?
GHAAA! FOR THE LOVE OF ATLANTIS, HOW DOES ANYBODY KNOW WHAT ANY OF THESE WORDS MEAN?
LEARN GERMAN FIRST. IT'S MORE LOGICAL.
THAT'S WHAT I DID.
MANHUNTER.
AQUAMAN. THANK YOU FOR MEETING ME EARLY.
MY PLEASURE. IS SOMETHING WRONG?
ONLY ON AN EMOTIONAL LEVEL. I SENSED SOME FRUSTRATION ON YOUR PART AS TO THE INLAND NATURE OF OUR MEETING FACILITY.
THAT'S...TRUE. I AM, BY NATURE, EMPATHIC... APPARENTLY, UNUSUALLY SO. YOU ARE, AS WELL? A MARTIAN ABILITY?
ONE OF MANY...
...INCLUDING FLIGHT. ALLOW ME TO EASE YOUR TRANSPORTATION THROUGH THE CITY.
MY...
...MY PLEASURE...?

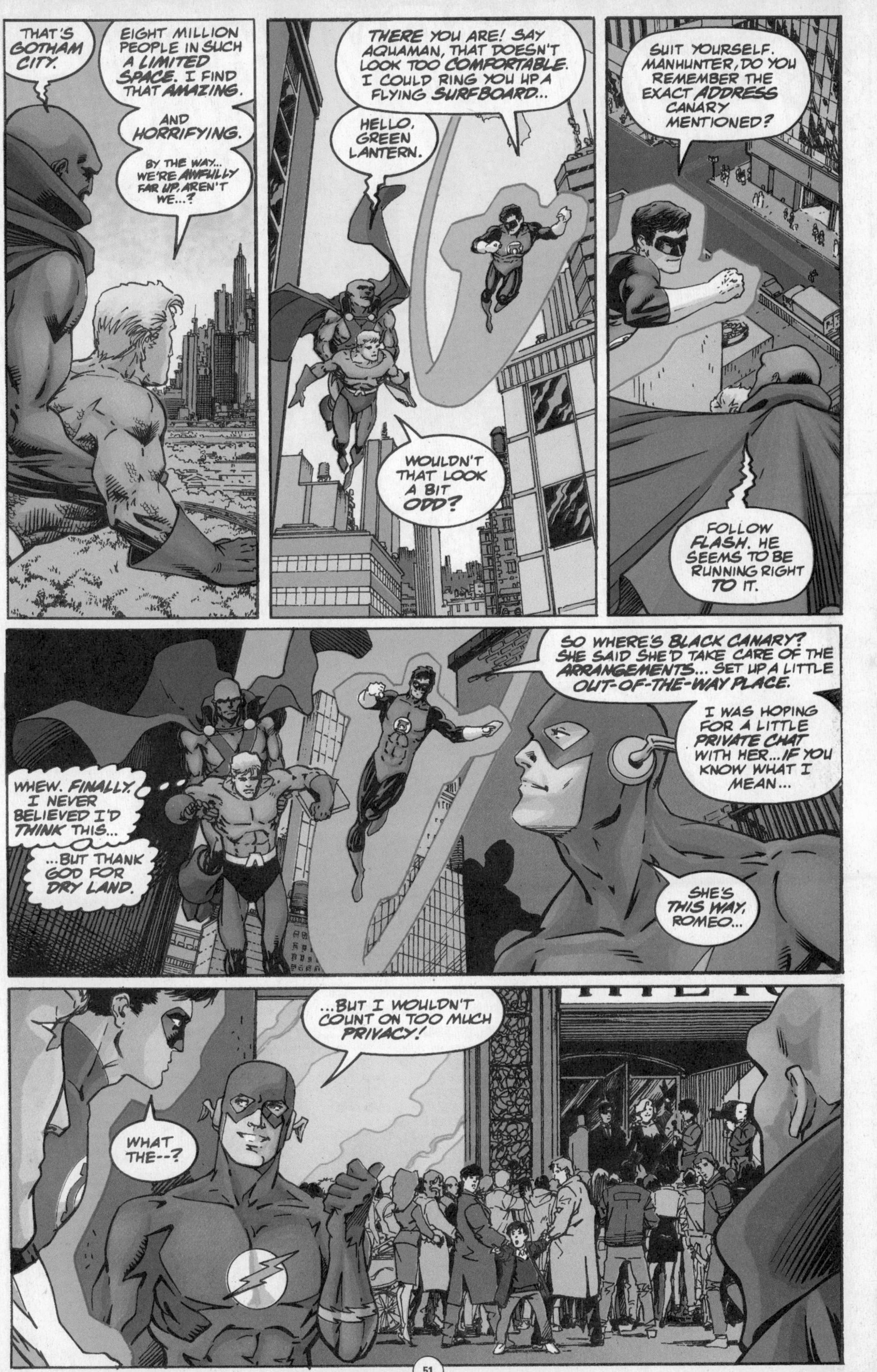
THAT'S GOTHAM CITY.
EIGHT MILLION PEOPLE IN SUCH A LIMITED SPACE. I FIND THAT AMAZING.
AND HORRIFYING.
BY THE WAY... WE'RE AWFULLY FAR UP, AREN'T WE...?
THERE YOU ARE! SAY AQUAMAN, THAT DOESN'T LOOK TOO COMFORTABLE. I COULD RING YOU UP A FLYING SURFBOARD...
HELLO, GREEN LANTERN.
WOULDN'T THAT LOOK A BIT ODD?
SUIT YOURSELF. MANHUNTER, DO YOU REMEMBER THE EXACT ADDRESS CANARY MENTIONED?
FOLLOW FLASH. HE SEEMS TO BE RUNNING RIGHT TO IT.
WHEW. FINALLY. I NEVER BELIEVED I'D THINK THIS...
...BUT THANK GOD FOR DRY LAND.
SO WHERE'S BLACK CANARY? SHE SAID SHE'D TAKE CARE OF THE ARRANGEMENTS... SET UP A LITTLE OUT-OF-THE-WAY PLACE.
I WAS HOPING FOR A LITTLE PRIVATE CHAT WITH HER... IF YOU KNOW WHAT I MEAN...
SHE'S THIS WAY, ROMEO...
...BUT I WOULDN'T COUNT ON TOO MUCH PRIVACY!
WHAT THE--?

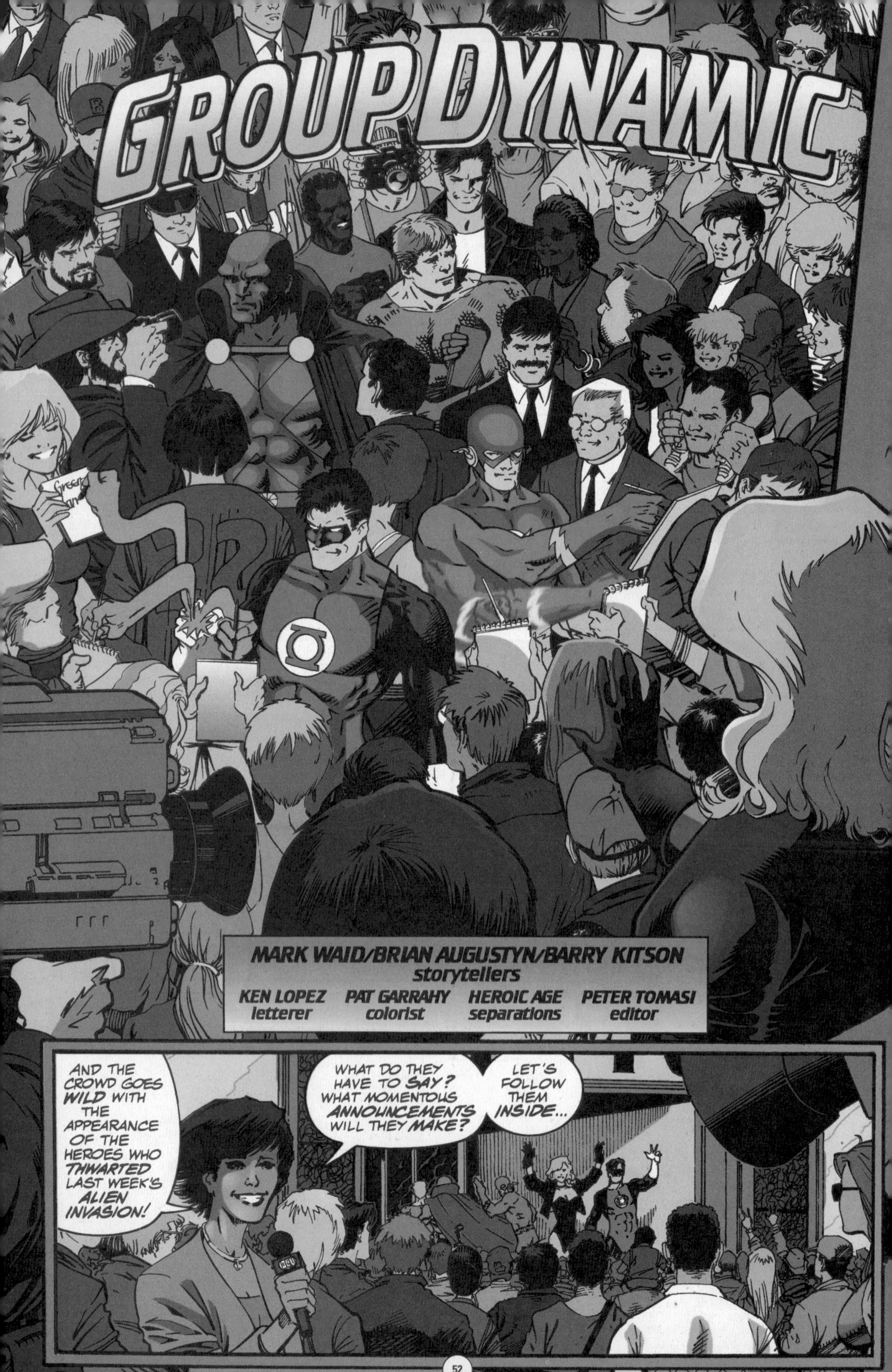
GROUP DYNAMIC
MARK WAID/BRIAN AUGUSTYN/BARRY KITSON
storytellers
KEN LOPEZ letterer
PAT GARRAHY colorist
HEROIC AGE separations
PETER TOMASI editor
AND THE CROWD GOES WILD WITH THE APPEARANCE OF THE HEROES WHO THWARTED LAST WEEK'S ALIEN INVASION!
WHAT DO THEY HAVE TO SAY? WHAT MOMENTOUS ANNOUNCEMENTS WILL THEY MAKE?
LET'S FOLLOW THEM INSIDE...

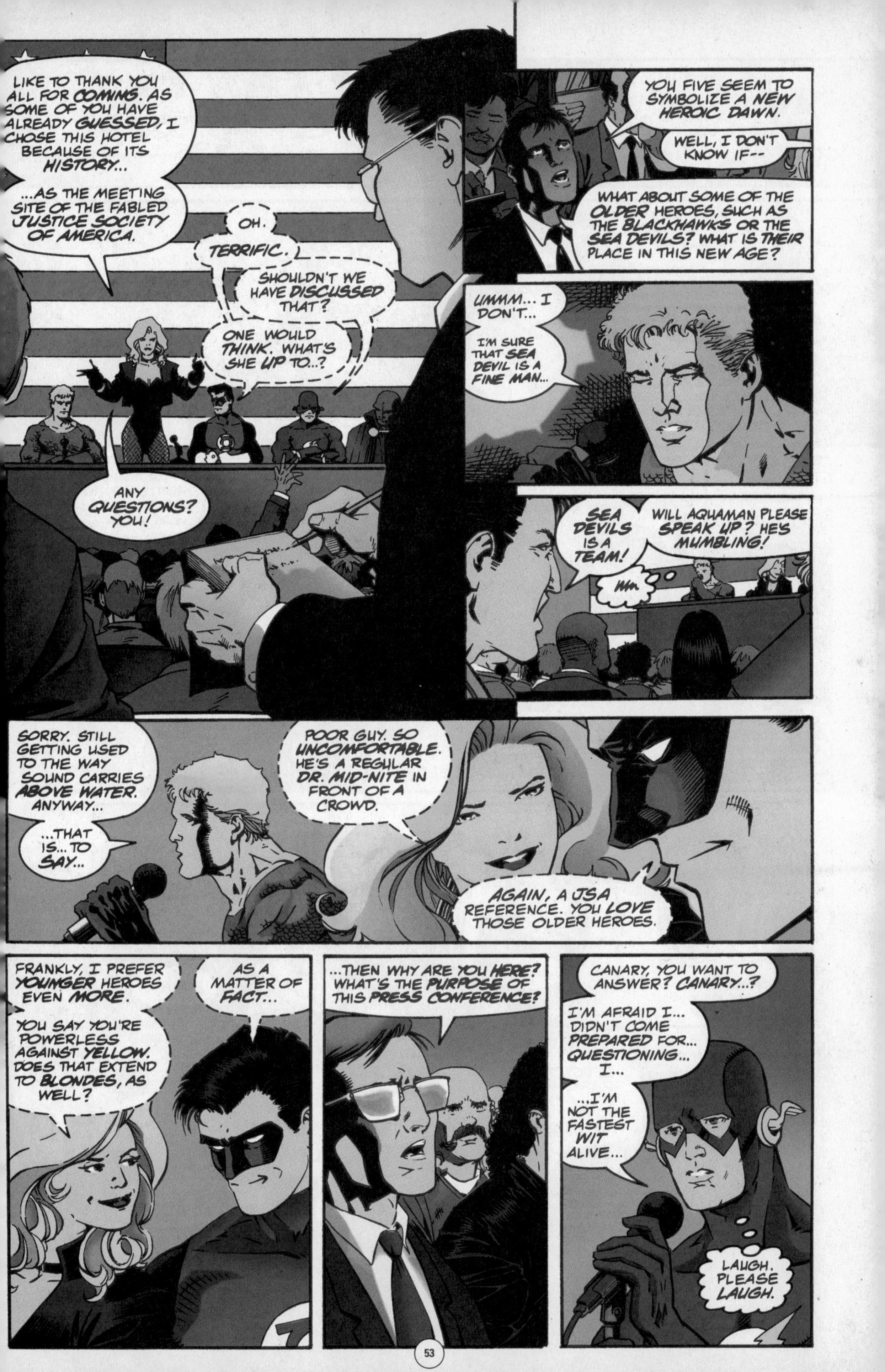

LIKE TO THANK YOU ALL FOR COMING. AS SOME OF YOU HAVE ALREADY GUESSED, I CHOSE THIS HOTEL BECAUSE OF ITS HISTORY...
...AS THE MEETING SITE OF THE FABLED JUSTICE SOCIETY OF AMERICA.
OH.
TERRIFIC.
SHOULDN'T WE HAVE DISCUSSED THAT?
ONE WOULD THINK. WHAT'S SHE UP TO...?
ANY QUESTIONS? YOU!
YOU FIVE SEEM TO SYMBOLIZE A NEW HEROIC DAWN.
WELL, I DON'T KNOW IF--
WHAT ABOUT SOME OF THE OLDER HEROES, SUCH AS THE BLACKHAWKS OR THE SEA DEVILS? WHAT IS THEIR PLACE IN THIS NEW AGE?
UMMM... I DON'T...
I'M SURE THAT SEA DEVIL IS A FINE MAN...
SEA DEVILS IS A TEAM!
WILL AQUAMAN PLEASE SPEAK UP? HE'S MUMBLING!
Mm
SORRY. STILL GETTING USED TO THE WAY SOUND CARRIES ABOVE WATER. ANYWAY...
...THAT IS...TO SAY...
POOR GUY. SO UNCOMFORTABLE. HE'S A REGULAR DR. MID-NITE IN FRONT OF A CROWD.
AGAIN, A JSA REFERENCE. YOU LOVE THOSE OLDER HEROES.
FRANKLY, I PREFER YOUNGER HEROES EVEN MORE.
AS A MATTER OF FACT...
YOU SAY YOU'RE POWERLESS AGAINST YELLOW. DOES THAT EXTEND TO BLONDES, AS WELL?
...THEN WHY ARE YOU HERE? WHAT'S THE PURPOSE OF THIS PRESS CONFERENCE?
CANARY, YOU WANT TO ANSWER? CANARY...?
I'M AFRAID I... DIDN'T COME PREPARED FOR... QUESTIONING... I...
...I'M NOT THE FASTEST WIT ALIVE...
LAUGH. PLEASE LAUGH.

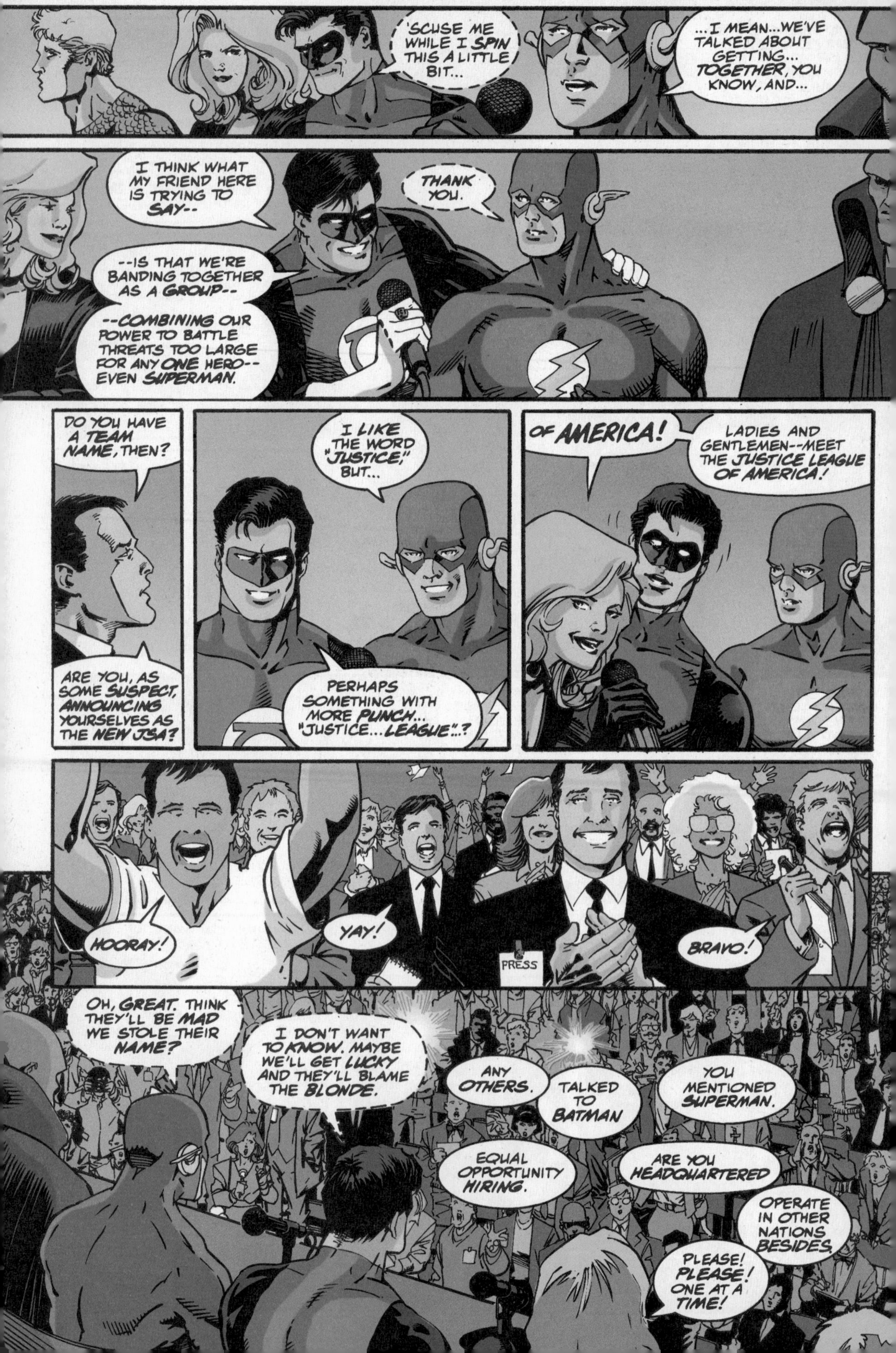
'SCUSE ME WHILE I SPIN THIS A LITTLE BIT...
...I MEAN...WE'VE TALKED ABOUT GETTING... TOGETHER, YOU KNOW, AND...
I THINK WHAT MY FRIEND HERE IS TRYING TO SAY--
THANK YOU.
--IS THAT WE'RE BANDING TOGETHER AS A GROUP--
--COMBINING OUR POWER TO BATTLE THREATS TOO LARGE FOR ANY ONE HERO-- EVEN SUPERMAN.
DO YOU HAVE A TEAM NAME, THEN?
ARE YOU, AS SOME SUSPECT, ANNOUNCING YOURSELVES AS THE NEW JSA?
I LIKE THE WORD "JUSTICE," BUT...
PERHAPS SOMETHING WITH MORE PUNCH... "JUSTICE...LEAGUE"...?
LADIES AND GENTLEMEN--MEET THE JUSTICE LEAGUE OF AMERICA!
OF AMERICA!
HOORAY!
YAY!
PRESS
BRAVO!
OH, GREAT. THINK THEY'LL BE MAD WE STOLE THEIR NAME?
I DON'T WANT TO KNOW. MAYBE WE'LL GET LUCKY AND THEY'LL BLAME THE BLONDE.
ANY OTHERS.
TALKED TO BATMAN
YOU MENTIONED SUPERMAN.
EQUAL OPPORTUNITY HIRING.
ARE YOU HEADQUARTERED
OPERATE IN OTHER NATIONS BESIDES
PLEASE! PLEASE! ONE AT A TIME!

LOIS LANE, DAILY PLANET! GREEN LANTERN, WHAT HOLDS YOU FIVE *TOGETHER?*

THE *AIR FORCE* REPORTS SOMETHING ABOUT A CRIMINAL GROUP NAMED *LOCUS...?*

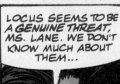

LOCUS SEEMS TO BE A *GENUINE* THREAT, MS. LANE. WE DON'T KNOW MUCH ABOUT THEM...

AS TO WHAT HOLDS US *TOGETHER...* I'D HAVE TO SAY SPANDEX.

HAHAHAHA!

NEXT? THE *REDHEAD?*

VICKI VALE, GOTHAM GAZETTE! GREEN LANTERN, AS ALL GOTHAMITES KNOW, THE WORLD'S A MUCH DARKER PLACE THAN WHEN THE JSA WAS AROUND.

WHAT MAKES YOU THINK THIS *NEW LEAGUE* CAN CONQUER TODAY'S PROBLEMS?

IN MY EXPERIENCE, POWER AND COURAGE GO A *LONG WAY* TOWARDS--

--AND WHAT'S YOUR ROLE IN DEALING WITH *SOCIOLOGICAL* CHALLENGES?

WE HAVEN'T REALLY TALKED ABOUT--

BY INCORPORATING "*AMERICA*" INTO YOUR NAME, ARE YOU ADVOCATING *NATIONALISM?*

HOW DOES YOUR EXISTENCE AFFECT THE BALANCE OF *WORLD POWER?*

IF ASKED, WILL YOU PLACE *AMERICA'S* INTERESTS ABOVE THOSE OF *OTHER*

WHAT, IF ANY ARE YOUR TIES TO THE *REPUBLICAN* ADMINISTRATION?

DO YOU ADVOCATE ANY *POLITICAL* AFFILIATION?

CONNECTED TO U.N.

HOW DOES A *MARTIAN* FIGURE INTO

MS. CANARY, ARE YOU THE *YOUNGEST*

ADDRESS THE PLIGHT OF *THIRD WORLD*

TAKE A STANCE ON THE *ARMS RACE*

FAAAAASSH

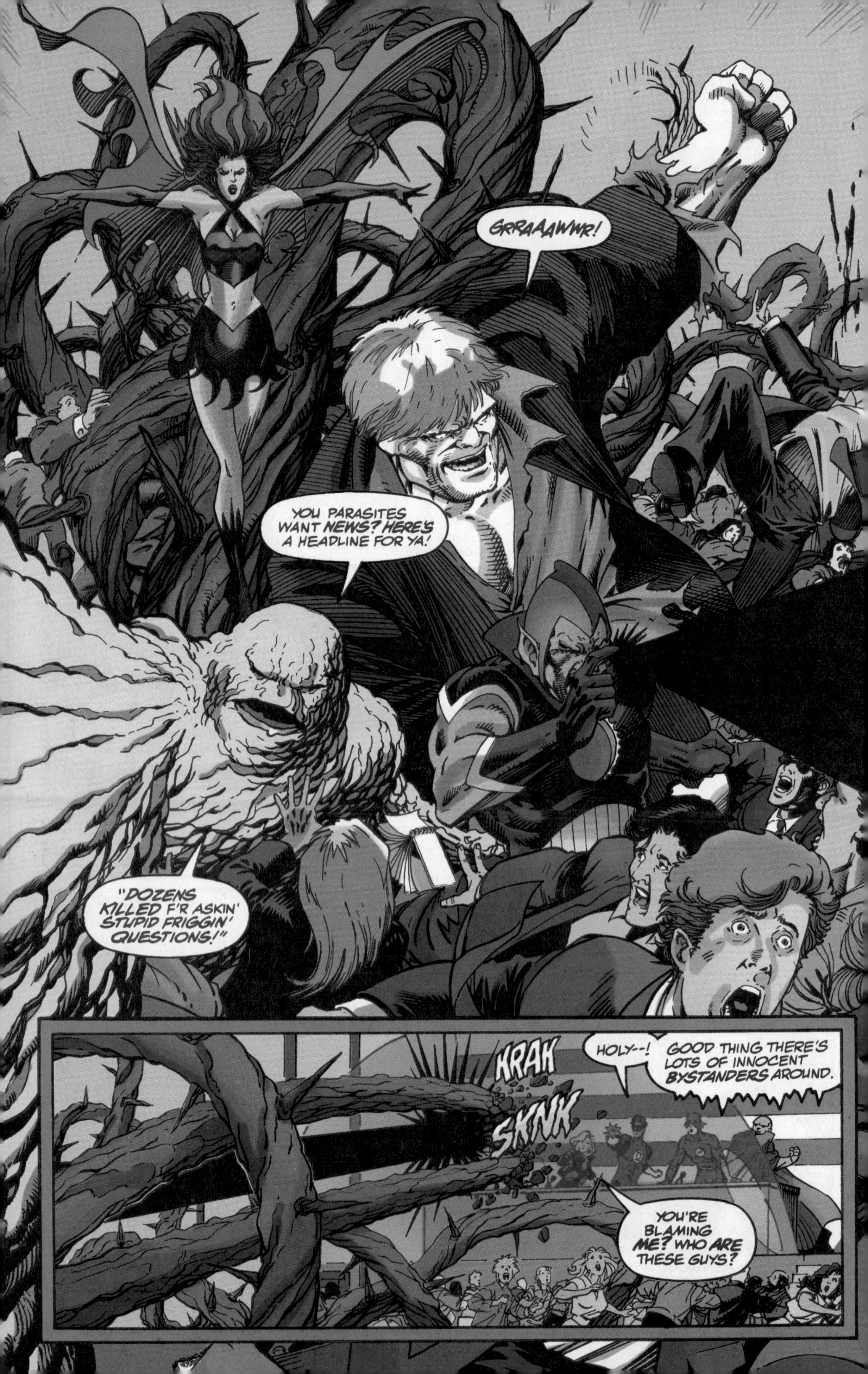
GRRAAAWWR!
YOU PARASITES WANT NEWS? HERE'S A HEADLINE FOR YA!
"DOZENS KILLED F'R ASKIN' STUPID FRIGGIN' QUESTIONS!"
KRAK
SKNK
HOLY--!
GOOD THING THERE'S LOTS OF INNOCENT BYSTANDERS AROUND.
YOU'RE BLAMING ME? WHO ARE THESE GUYS?

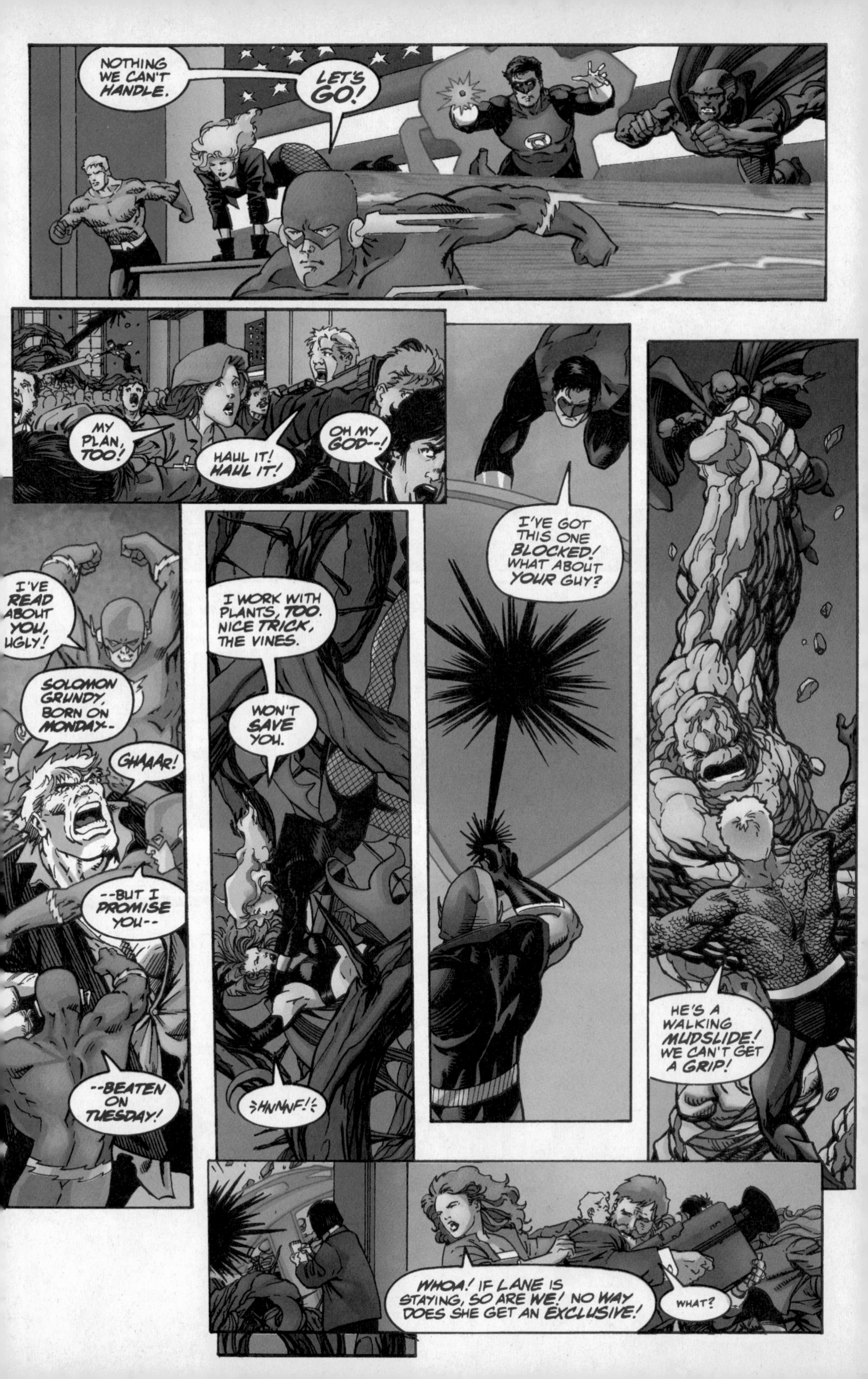
NOTHING WE CAN'T HANDLE.
LET'S GO!
MY PLAN, TOO!
HAUL IT! HAUL IT!
OH MY GOD--!
I'VE GOT THIS ONE BLOCKED! WHAT ABOUT YOUR GUY?
HE'S A WALKING MUDSLIDE! WE CAN'T GET A GRIP!
I'VE READ ABOUT YOU, UGLY!
SOLOMON GRUNDY, BORN ON MONDAY--
GHAAAR!
--BUT I PROMISE YOU--
--BEATEN ON TUESDAY!
I WORK WITH PLANTS, TOO. NICE TRICK, THE VINES.
WON'T SAVE YOU.
HNNNF!
WHOA! IF LANE IS STAYING, SO ARE WE! NO WAY DOES SHE GET AN EXCLUSIVE!
WHAT?

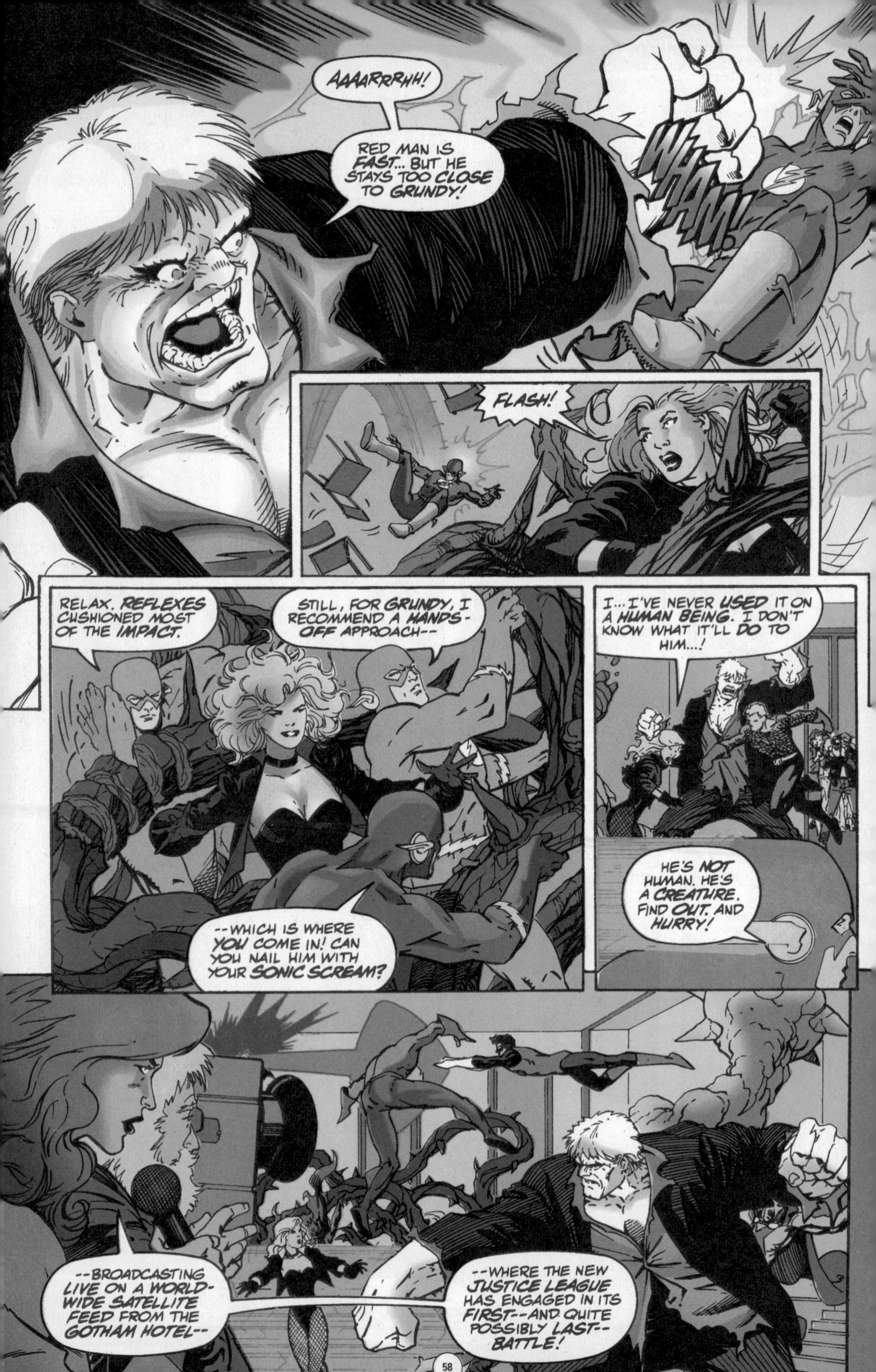
AAAARRRHH!
RED MAN IS FAST... BUT HE STAYS TOO CLOSE TO GRUNDY!
WHAM!
FLASH!
RELAX. REFLEXES CUSHIONED MOST OF THE IMPACT.
STILL, FOR GRUNDY, I RECOMMEND A HANDS-OFF APPROACH--
--WHICH IS WHERE YOU COME IN! CAN YOU NAIL HIM WITH YOUR SONIC SCREAM?
I... I'VE NEVER USED IT ON A HUMAN BEING. I DON'T KNOW WHAT IT'LL DO TO HIM...!
HE'S NOT HUMAN. HE'S A CREATURE. FIND OUT. AND HURRY!
--BROADCASTING LIVE ON A WORLD-WIDE SATELLITE FEED FROM THE GOTHAM HOTEL--
--WHERE THE NEW JUSTICE LEAGUE HAS ENGAGED IN ITS FIRST--AND QUITE POSSIBLY LAST--BATTLE!

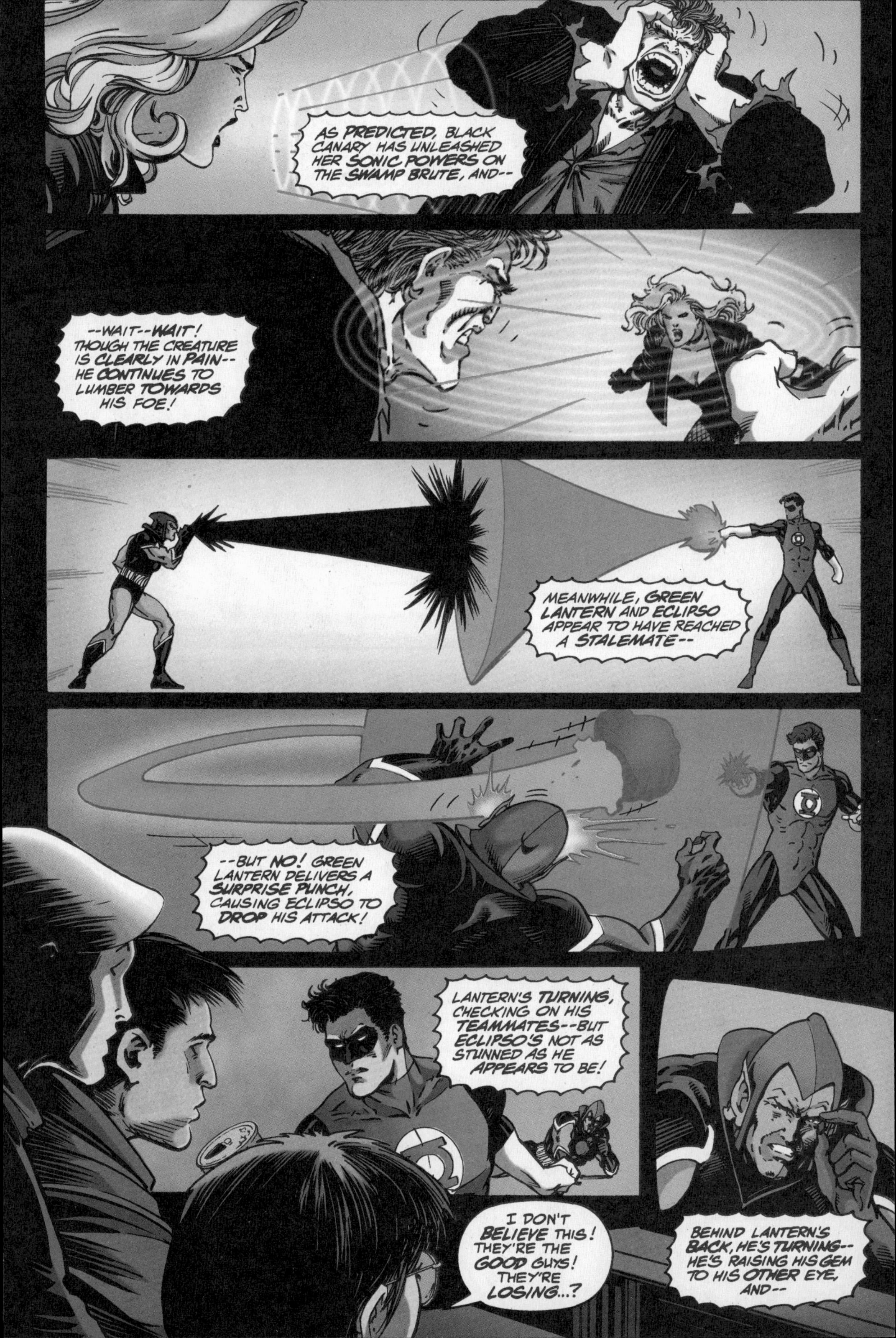
AS PREDICTED, BLACK CANARY HAS UNLEASHED HER SONIC POWERS ON THE SWAMP BRUTE, AND--
--WAIT--WAIT! THOUGH THE CREATURE IS CLEARLY IN PAIN-- HE CONTINUES TO LUMBER TOWARDS HIS FOE!
MEANWHILE, GREEN LANTERN AND ECLIPSO APPEAR TO HAVE REACHED A STALEMATE--
--BUT NO! GREEN LANTERN DELIVERS A SURPRISE PUNCH, CAUSING ECLIPSO TO DROP HIS ATTACK!
LANTERN'S TURNING, CHECKING ON HIS TEAMMATES--BUT ECLIPSO'S NOT AS STUNNED AS HE APPEARS TO BE!
I DON'T BELIEVE THIS! THEY'RE THE GOOD GUYS! THEY'RE LOSING...?
BEHIND LANTERN'S BACK, HE'S TURNING-- HE'S RAISING HIS GEM TO HIS OTHER EYE, AND--

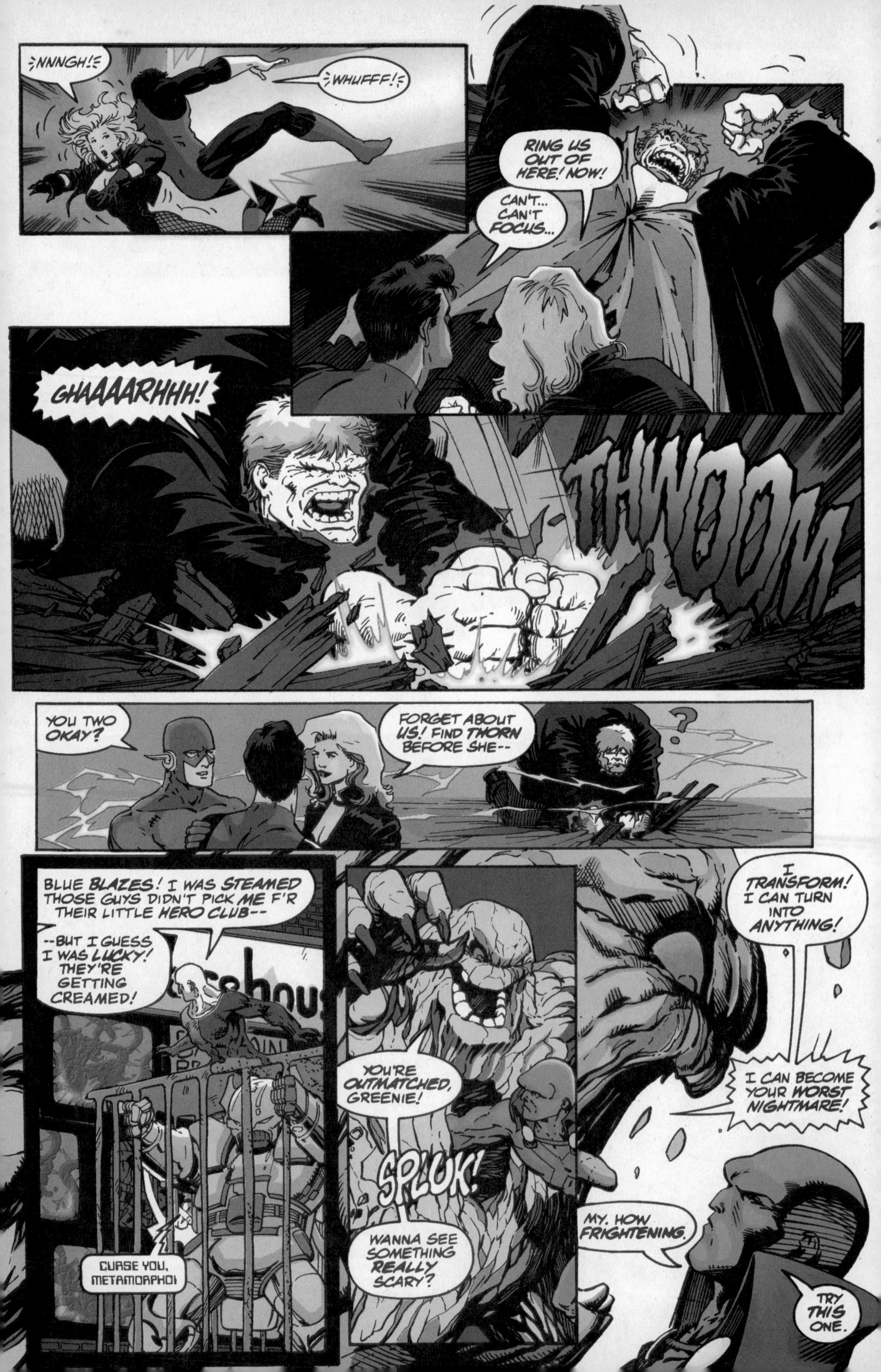

NNNGH!
WHUFFF!
RING US OUT OF HERE! NOW!
CAN'T... CAN'T FOCUS...
GHAAAARHHH!
THWOOM
YOU TWO OKAY?
FORGET ABOUT US! FIND THORN BEFORE SHE--
?
BLUE BLAZES! I WAS STEAMED THOSE GUYS DIDN'T PICK ME F'R THEIR LITTLE HERO CLUB--
--BUT I GUESS I WAS LUCKY! THEY'RE GETTING CREAMED!
CURSE YOU, METAMORPHO!
YOU'RE OUTMATCHED, GREENIE!
SPLUK!
WANNA SEE SOMETHING REALLY SCARY?
I TRANSFORM! I CAN TURN INTO ANYTHING!
I CAN BECOME YOUR WORST NIGHTMARE!
MY. HOW FRIGHTENING.
TRY THIS ONE.

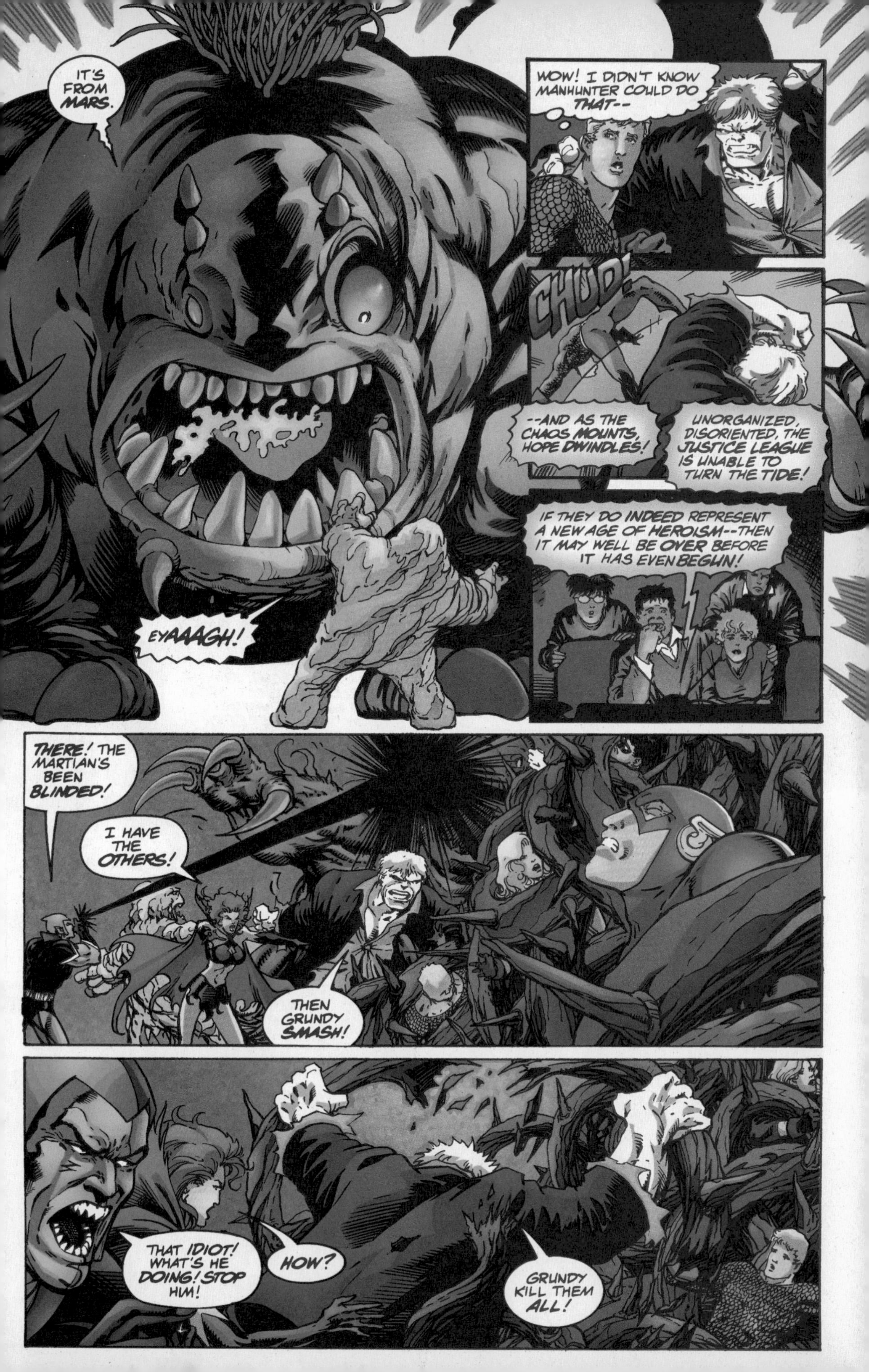
IT'S FROM MARS.
WOW! I DIDN'T KNOW MANHUNTER COULD DO THAT--
CHUD!
EYAAAGH!
--AND AS THE CHAOS MOUNTS, HOPE DWINDLES!
UNORGANIZED, DISORIENTED, THE JUSTICE LEAGUE IS UNABLE TO TURN THE TIDE!
IF THEY DO INDEED REPRESENT A NEW AGE OF HEROISM--THEN IT MAY WELL BE OVER BEFORE IT HAS EVEN BEGUN!
THERE! THE MARTIAN'S BEEN BLINDED!
I HAVE THE OTHERS!
THEN GRUNDY SMASH!
THAT IDIOT! WHAT'S HE DOING! STOP HIM!
HOW?
GRUNDY KILL THEM ALL!

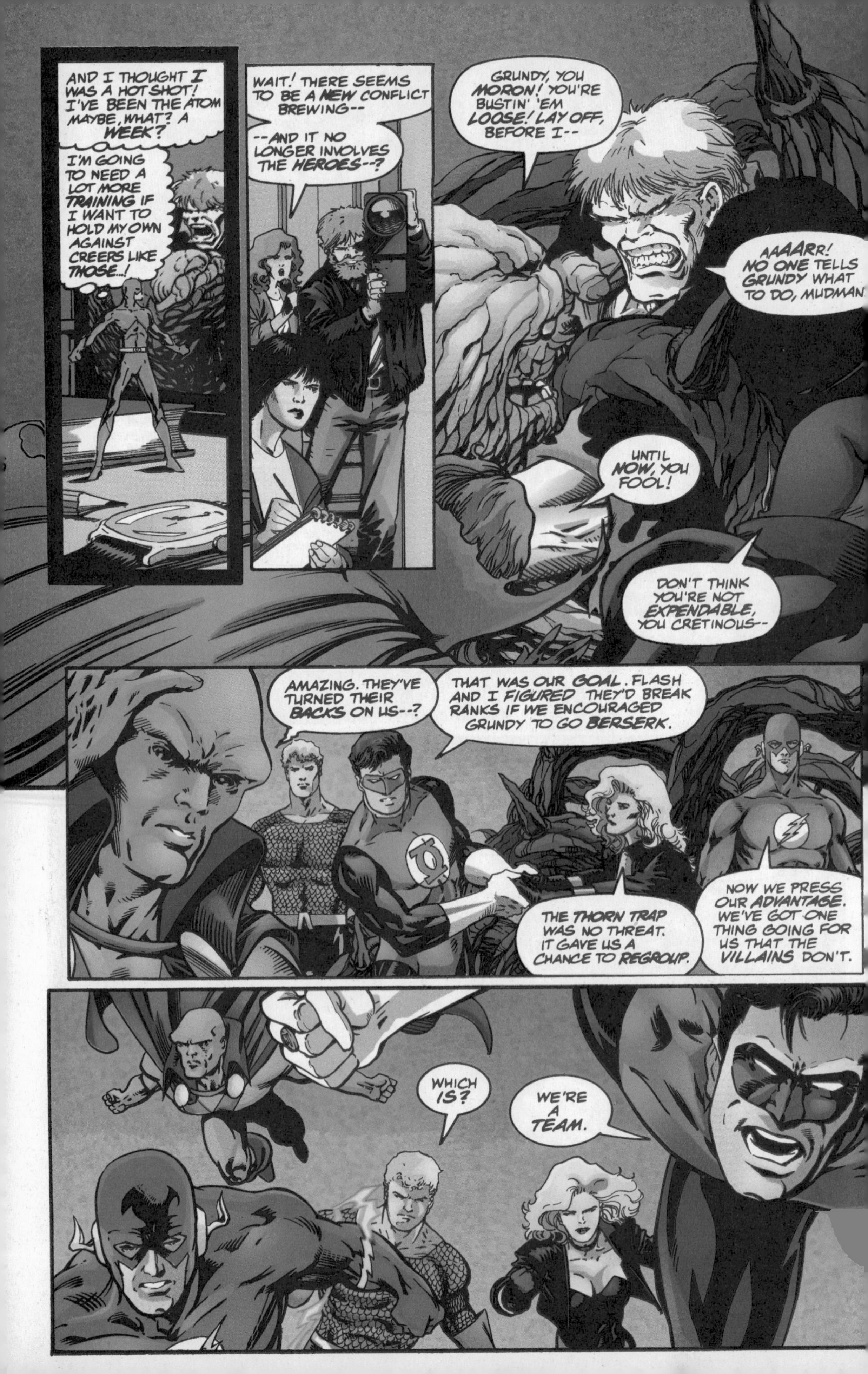
AND I THOUGHT I WAS A HOT SHOT! I'VE BEEN THE ATOM MAYBE, WHAT? A WEEK?
I'M GOING TO NEED A LOT MORE TRAINING IF I WANT TO HOLD MY OWN AGAINST CREEPS LIKE THOSE...!
WAIT! THERE SEEMS TO BE A NEW CONFLICT BREWING--
--AND IT NO LONGER INVOLVES THE HEROES--?
GRUNDY, YOU MORON! YOU'RE BUSTIN' 'EM LOOSE! LAY OFF, BEFORE I--
AAAARR! NO ONE TELLS GRUNDY WHAT TO DO, MUDMAN
UNTIL NOW, YOU FOOL!
DON'T THINK YOU'RE NOT EXPENDABLE, YOU CRETINOUS--
AMAZING. THEY'VE TURNED THEIR BACKS ON US--?
THAT WAS OUR GOAL. FLASH AND I FIGURED THEY'D BREAK RANKS IF WE ENCOURAGED GRUNDY TO GO BERSERK.
THE THORN TRAP WAS NO THREAT. IT GAVE US A CHANCE TO REGROUP.
NOW WE PRESS OUR ADVANTAGE. WE'VE GOT ONE THING GOING FOR US THAT THE VILLAINS DON'T.
WHICH IS?
WE'RE A TEAM.

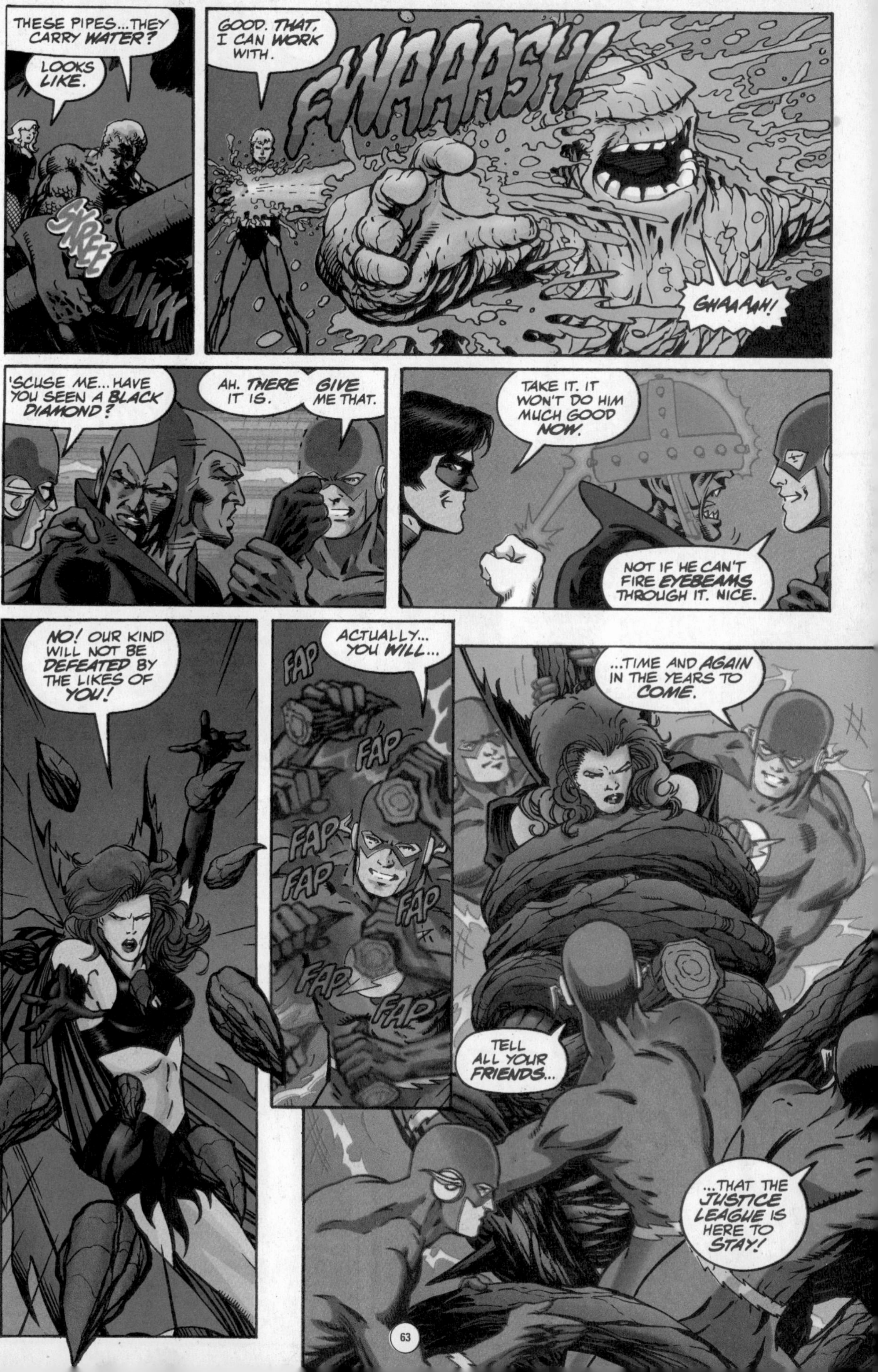
THESE PIPES... THEY CARRY WATER?
LOOKS LIKE.
SKREE
UNKK
GOOD. THAT, I CAN WORK WITH.
FWAAASH!
GHAAAAH!
'SCUSE ME... HAVE YOU SEEN A BLACK DIAMOND?
AH. THERE IT IS.
GIVE ME THAT.
TAKE IT. IT WON'T DO HIM MUCH GOOD NOW.
NOT IF HE CAN'T FIRE EYEBEAMS THROUGH IT. NICE.
NO! OUR KIND WILL NOT BE DEFEATED BY THE LIKES OF YOU!
ACTUALLY... YOU WILL...
FAP
FAP
FAP
FAP
FAP
FAP
FAP
...TIME AND AGAIN IN THE YEARS TO COME.
TELL ALL YOUR FRIENDS...
...THAT THE JUSTICE LEAGUE IS HERE TO STAY!

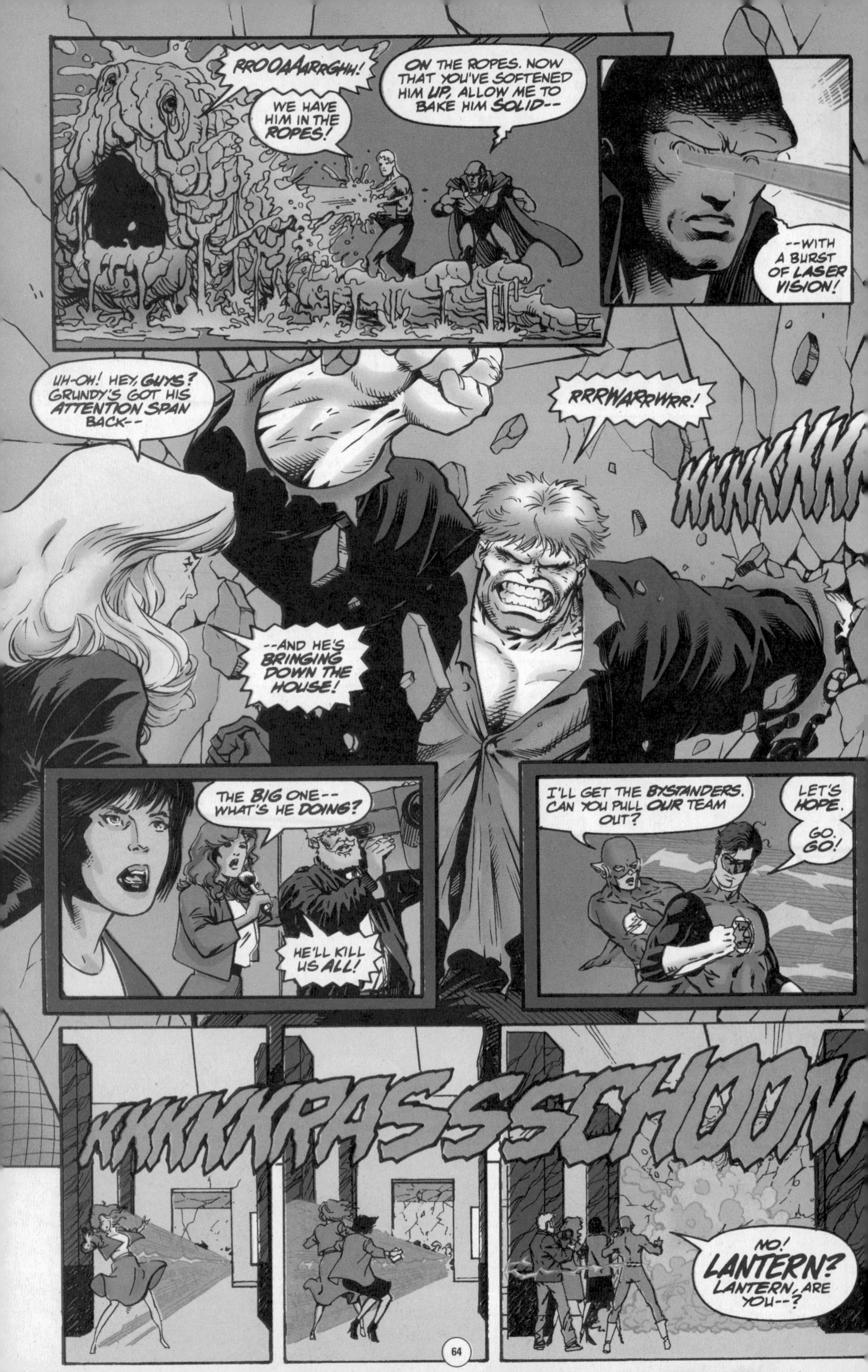
RRROAAARRGHH!
WE HAVE HIM IN THE ROPES!
ON THE ROPES. NOW THAT YOU'VE SOFTENED HIM UP, ALLOW ME TO BAKE HIM SOLID--
--WITH A BURST OF LASER VISION!
UH-OH! HEY, GUYS? GRUNDY'S GOT HIS ATTENTION SPAN BACK--
RRRWARRWRR!
KKKKKKK
--AND HE'S BRINGING DOWN THE HOUSE!
THE BIG ONE-- WHAT'S HE DOING?
HE'LL KILL US ALL!
I'LL GET THE BYSTANDERS. CAN YOU PULL OUR TEAM OUT?
LET'S HOPE.
GO. GO!
KKKKKRASSSCHOOM
NO! LANTERN? LANTERN, ARE YOU--?

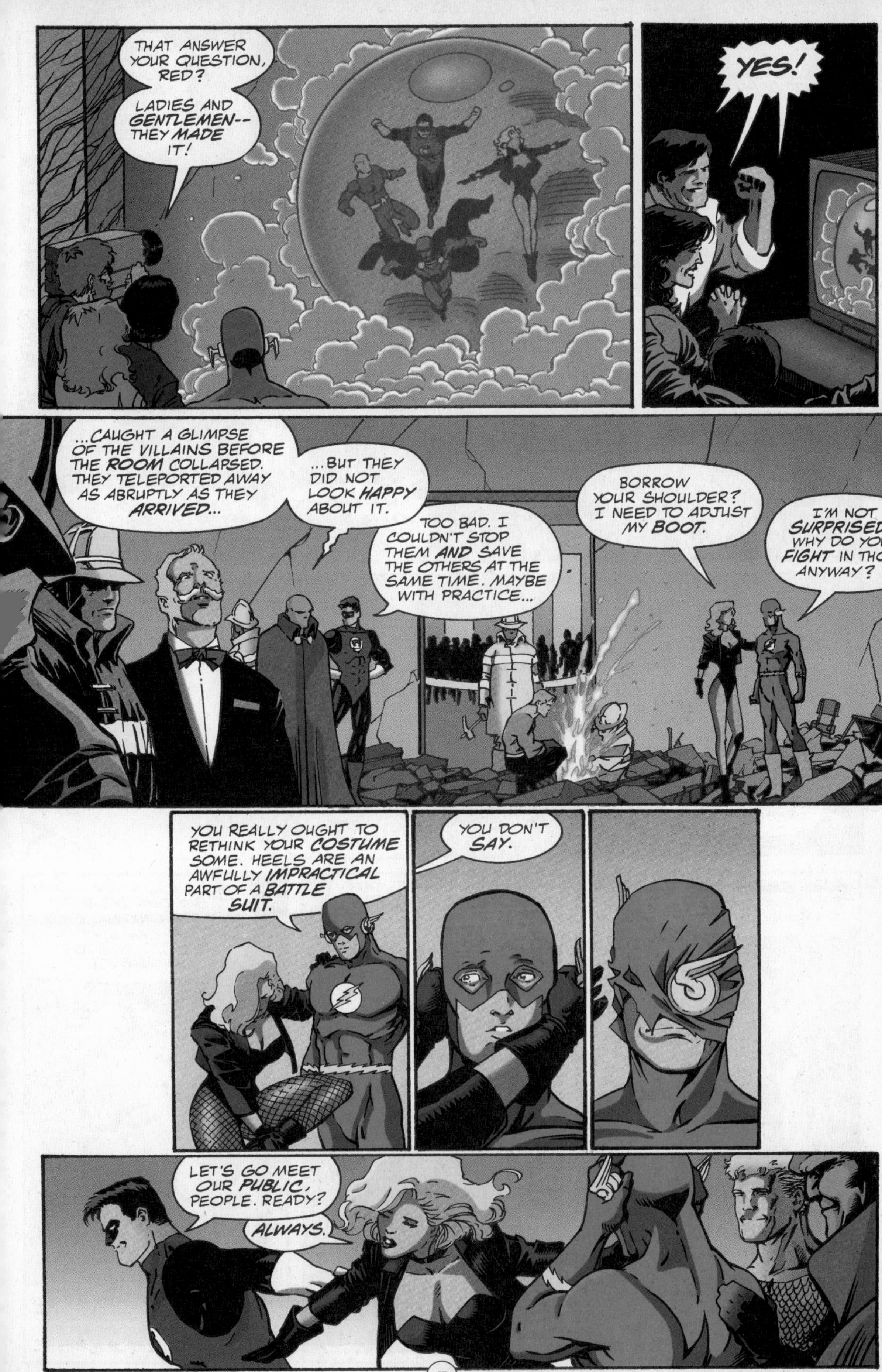

THAT ANSWER YOUR QUESTION, RED?
LADIES AND GENTLEMEN-- THEY MADE IT!
YES!
...CAUGHT A GLIMPSE OF THE VILLAINS BEFORE THE ROOM COLLAPSED. THEY TELEPORTED AWAY AS ABRUPTLY AS THEY ARRIVED...
...BUT THEY DID NOT LOOK HAPPY ABOUT IT.
TOO BAD. I COULDN'T STOP THEM AND SAVE THE OTHERS AT THE SAME TIME. MAYBE WITH PRACTICE...
BORROW YOUR SHOULDER? I NEED TO ADJUST MY BOOT.
I'M NOT SURPRISED. WHY DO YOU FIGHT IN THOSE, ANYWAY?
YOU REALLY OUGHT TO RETHINK YOUR COSTUME SOME. HEELS ARE AN AWFULLY IMPRACTICAL PART OF A BATTLE SUIT.
YOU DON'T SAY.
LET'S GO MEET OUR PUBLIC, PEOPLE. READY?
ALWAYS.

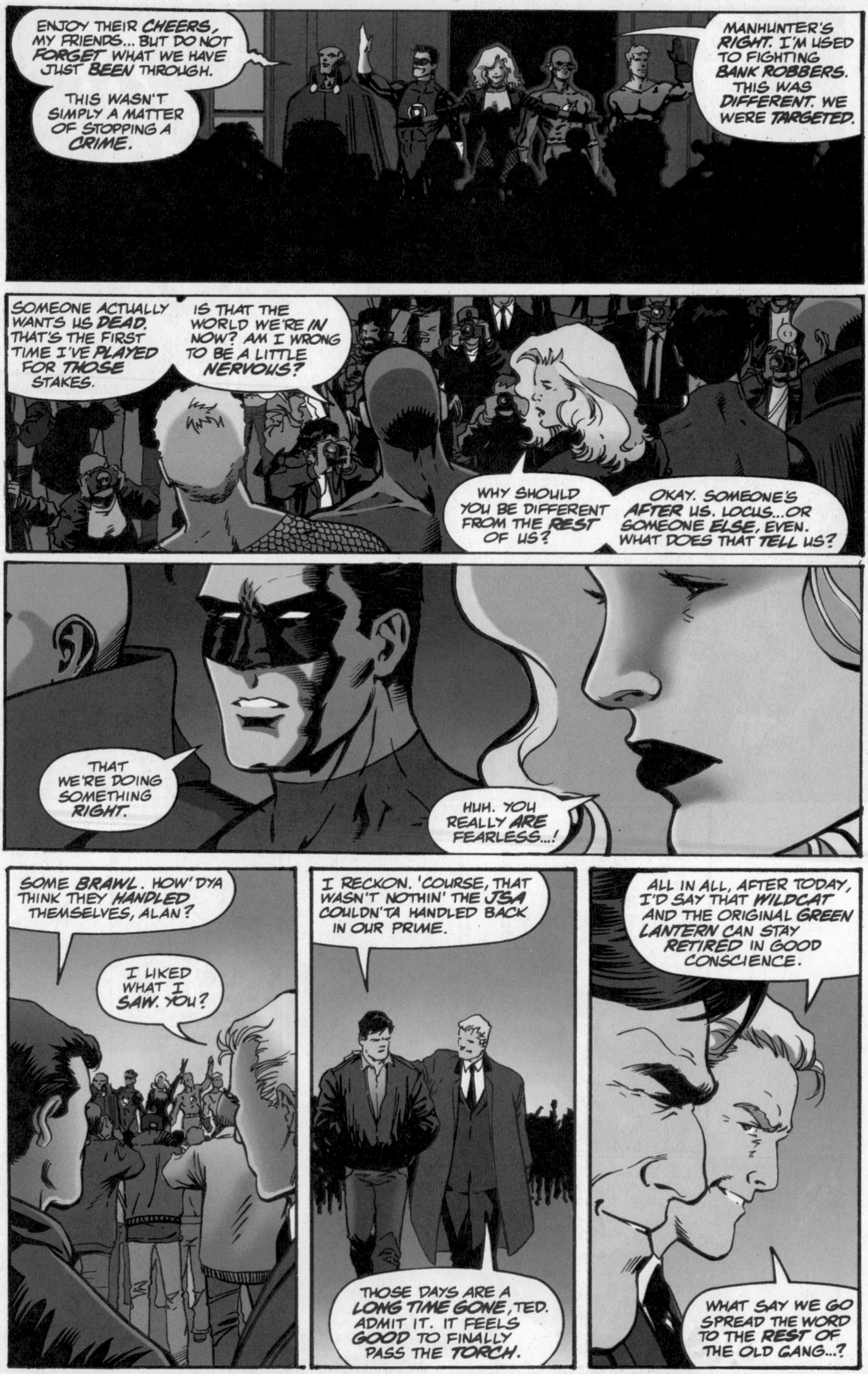
ENJOY THEIR CHEERS, MY FRIENDS... BUT DO NOT FORGET WHAT WE HAVE JUST BEEN THROUGH.
THIS WASN'T SIMPLY A MATTER OF STOPPING A CRIME.
MANHUNTER'S RIGHT. I'M USED TO FIGHTING BANK ROBBERS. THIS WAS DIFFERENT. WE WERE TARGETED.
SOMEONE ACTUALLY WANTS US DEAD. THAT'S THE FIRST TIME I'VE PLAYED FOR THOSE STAKES.
IS THAT THE WORLD WE'RE IN NOW? AM I WRONG TO BE A LITTLE NERVOUS?
WHY SHOULD YOU BE DIFFERENT FROM THE REST OF US?
OKAY. SOMEONE'S AFTER US. LOCUS...OR SOMEONE ELSE, EVEN. WHAT DOES THAT TELL US?
THAT WE'RE DOING SOMETHING RIGHT.
HUH. YOU REALLY ARE FEARLESS...!
SOME BRAWL. HOW'DYA THINK THEY HANDLED THEMSELVES, ALAN?
I LIKED WHAT I SAW. YOU?
I RECKON. 'COURSE, THAT WASN'T NOTHIN' THE JSA COULDN'TA HANDLED BACK IN OUR PRIME.
THOSE DAYS ARE A LONG TIME GONE, TED. ADMIT IT. IT FEELS GOOD TO FINALLY PASS THE TORCH.
ALL IN ALL, AFTER TODAY, I'D SAY THAT WILDCAT AND THE ORIGINAL GREEN LANTERN CAN STAY RETIRED IN GOOD CONSCIENCE.
WHAT SAY WE GO SPREAD THE WORD TO THE REST OF THE OLD GANG...?

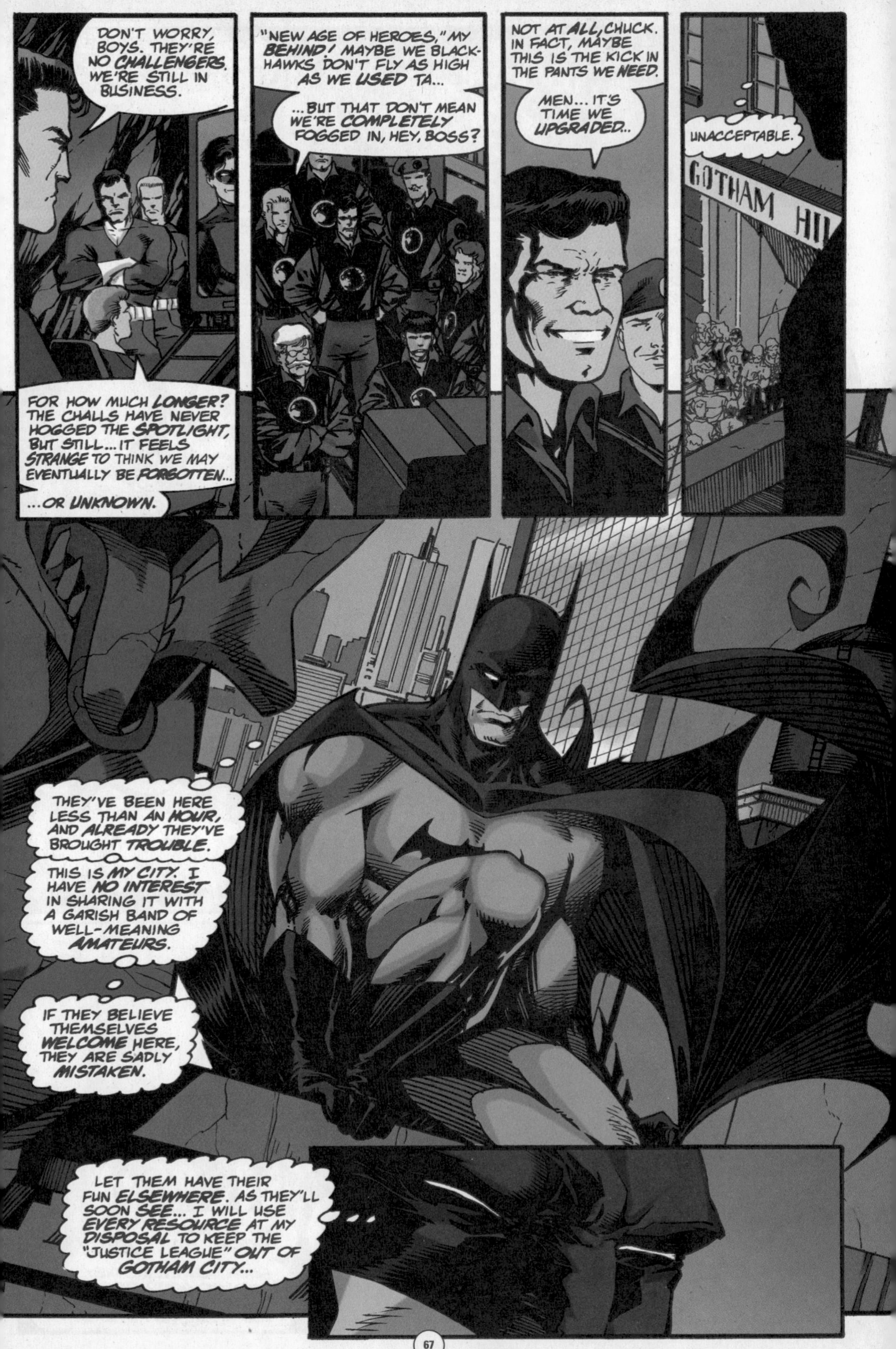
DON'T WORRY, BOYS. THEY'RE NO CHALLENGERS. WE'RE STILL IN BUSINESS.
FOR HOW MUCH LONGER? THE CHALLS HAVE NEVER HOGGED THE SPOTLIGHT, BUT STILL... IT FEELS STRANGE TO THINK WE MAY EVENTUALLY BE FORGOTTEN...
...OR UNKNOWN.
"NEW AGE OF HEROES," MY BEHIND! MAYBE WE BLACK-HAWKS DON'T FLY AS HIGH AS WE USED TA...
...BUT THAT DON'T MEAN WE'RE COMPLETELY FOGGED IN, HEY, BOSS?
NOT AT ALL, CHUCK. IN FACT, MAYBE THIS IS THE KICK IN THE PANTS WE NEED.
MEN... IT'S TIME WE UPGRADED...
UNACCEPTABLE.
GOTHAM HI
THEY'VE BEEN HERE LESS THAN AN HOUR, AND ALREADY THEY'VE BROUGHT TROUBLE.
THIS IS MY CITY. I HAVE NO INTEREST IN SHARING IT WITH A GARISH BAND OF WELL-MEANING AMATEURS.
IF THEY BELIEVE THEMSELVES WELCOME HERE, THEY ARE SADLY MISTAKEN.
LET THEM HAVE THEIR FUN ELSEWHERE. AS THEY'LL SOON SEE... I WILL USE EVERY RESOURCE AT MY DISPOSAL TO KEEP THE "JUSTICE LEAGUE" OUT OF GOTHAM CITY...

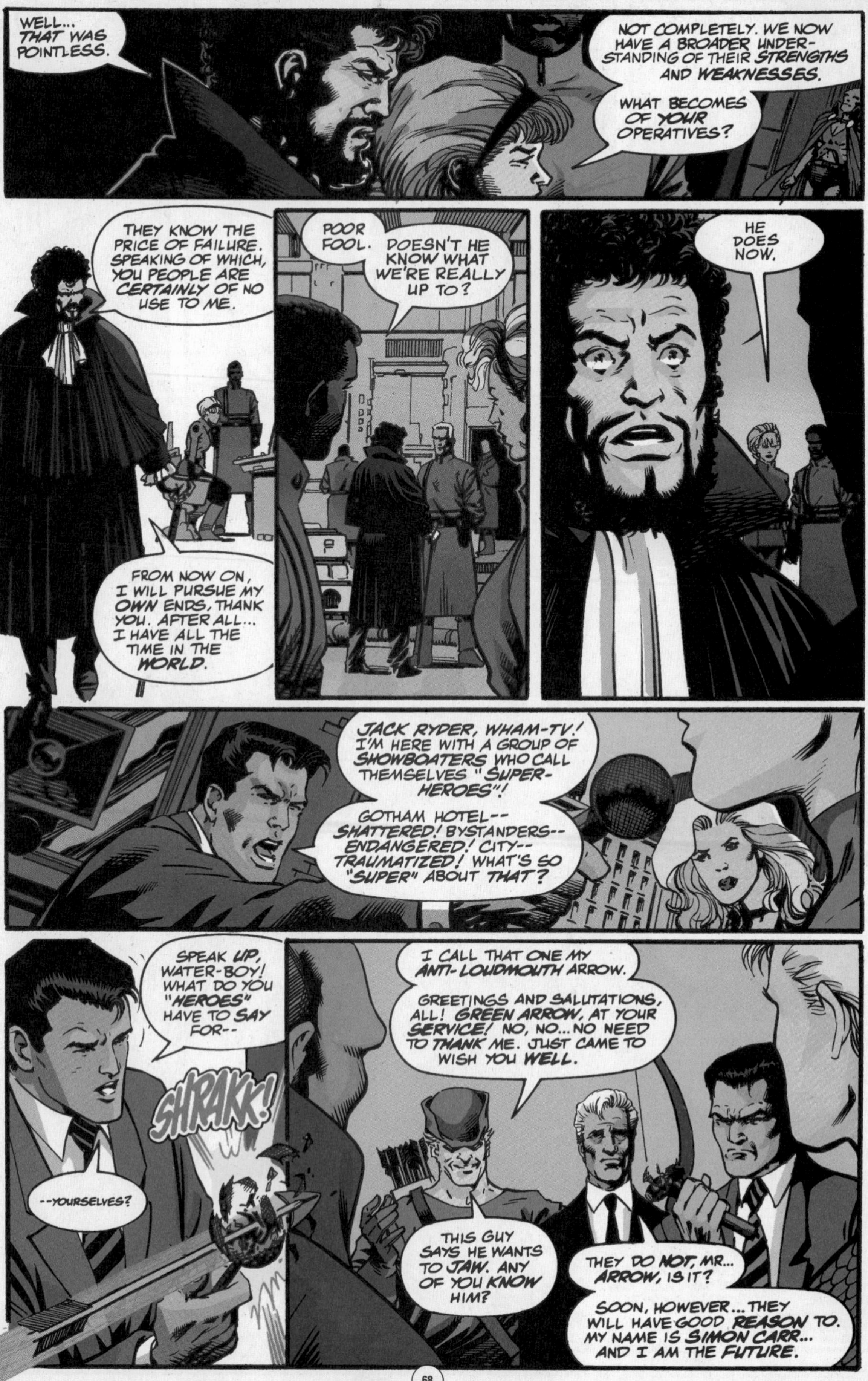
WELL... THAT WAS POINTLESS.
NOT COMPLETELY. WE NOW HAVE A BROADER UNDER-STANDING OF THEIR STRENGTHS AND WEAKNESSES.
WHAT BECOMES OF YOUR OPERATIVES?
THEY KNOW THE PRICE OF FAILURE. SPEAKING OF WHICH, YOU PEOPLE ARE CERTAINLY OF NO USE TO ME.
FROM NOW ON, I WILL PURSUE MY OWN ENDS, THANK YOU. AFTER ALL... I HAVE ALL THE TIME IN THE WORLD.
POOR FOOL.
DOESN'T HE KNOW WHAT WE'RE REALLY UP TO?
HE DOES NOW.
JACK RYDER, WHAM-TV! I'M HERE WITH A GROUP OF SHOWBOATERS WHO CALL THEMSELVES "SUPER-HEROES"!
GOTHAM HOTEL--SHATTERED! BYSTANDERS--ENDANGERED! CITY--TRAUMATIZED! WHAT'S SO "SUPER" ABOUT THAT?
SPEAK UP, WATER-BOY! WHAT DO YOU "HEROES" HAVE TO SAY FOR--
SHRAKK!
--YOURSELVES?
I CALL THAT ONE MY ANTI-LOUDMOUTH ARROW.
GREETINGS AND SALUTATIONS, ALL! GREEN ARROW, AT YOUR SERVICE! NO, NO... NO NEED TO THANK ME. JUST CAME TO WISH YOU WELL.
THIS GUY SAYS HE WANTS TO JAW. ANY OF YOU KNOW HIM?
THEY DO NOT, MR... ARROW, IS IT?
SOON, HOWEVER... THEY WILL HAVE GOOD REASON TO. MY NAME IS SIMON CARR... AND I AM THE FUTURE.

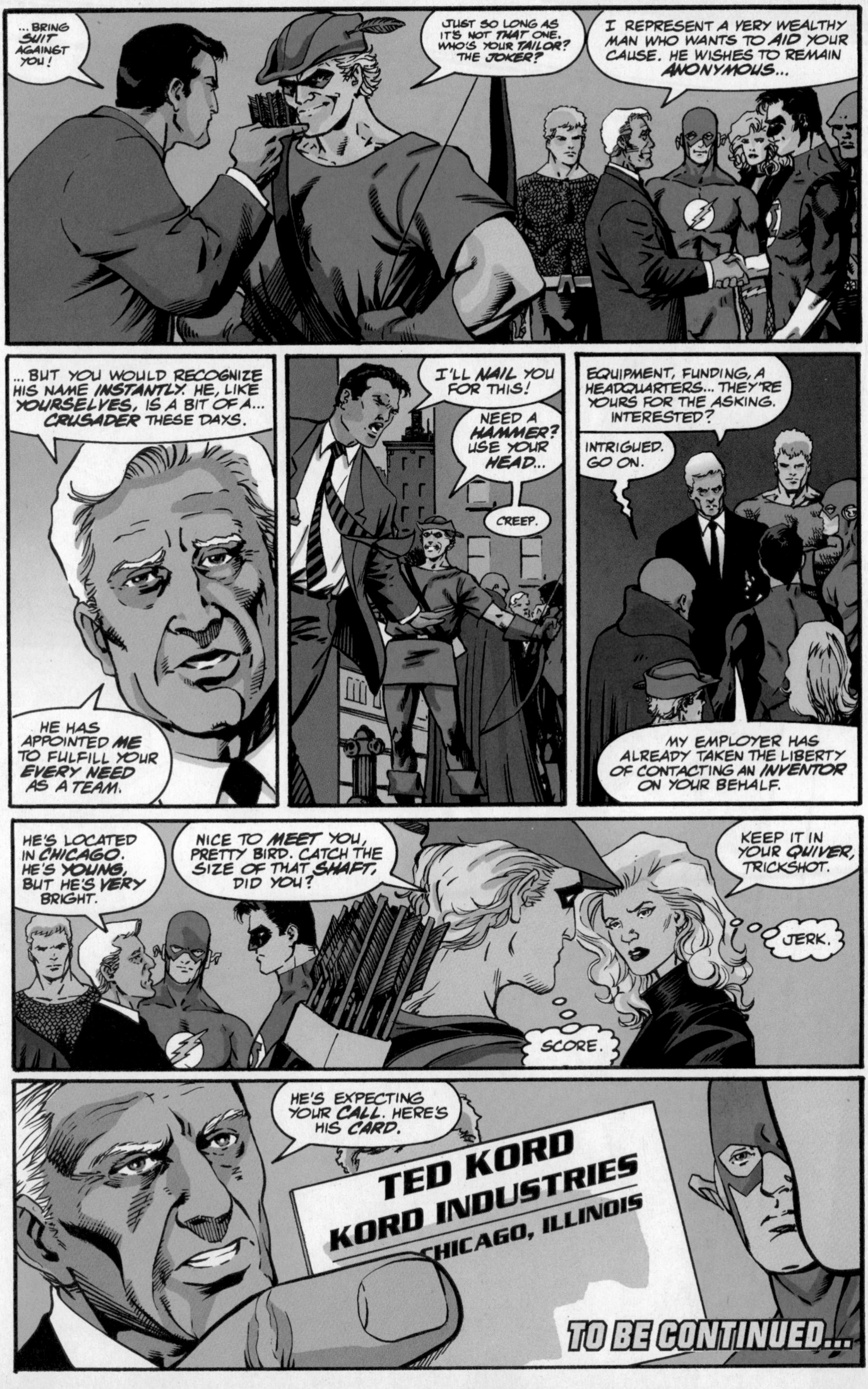
...BRING SUIT AGAINST YOU!
JUST SO LONG AS IT'S NOT THAT ONE. WHO'S YOUR TAILOR? THE JOKER?
I REPRESENT A VERY WEALTHY MAN WHO WANTS TO AID YOUR CAUSE. HE WISHES TO REMAIN ANONYMOUS...
...BUT YOU WOULD RECOGNIZE HIS NAME INSTANTLY. HE, LIKE YOURSELVES, IS A BIT OF A... CRUSADER THESE DAYS.
HE HAS APPOINTED ME TO FULFILL YOUR EVERY NEED AS A TEAM.
I'LL NAIL YOU FOR THIS!
NEED A HAMMER? USE YOUR HEAD...
CREEP.
EQUIPMENT, FUNDING, A HEADQUARTERS... THEY'RE YOURS FOR THE ASKING. INTERESTED?
INTRIGUED. GO ON.
MY EMPLOYER HAS ALREADY TAKEN THE LIBERTY OF CONTACTING AN INVENTOR ON YOUR BEHALF.
HE'S LOCATED IN CHICAGO. HE'S YOUNG, BUT HE'S VERY BRIGHT.
NICE TO MEET YOU, PRETTY BIRD. CATCH THE SIZE OF THAT SHAFT, DID YOU?
KEEP IT IN YOUR QUIVER, TRICKSHOT.
JERK.
SCORE.
HE'S EXPECTING YOUR CALL. HERE'S HIS CARD.
TED KORD
KORD INDUSTRIES
CHICAGO, ILLINOIS
TO BE CONTINUED...

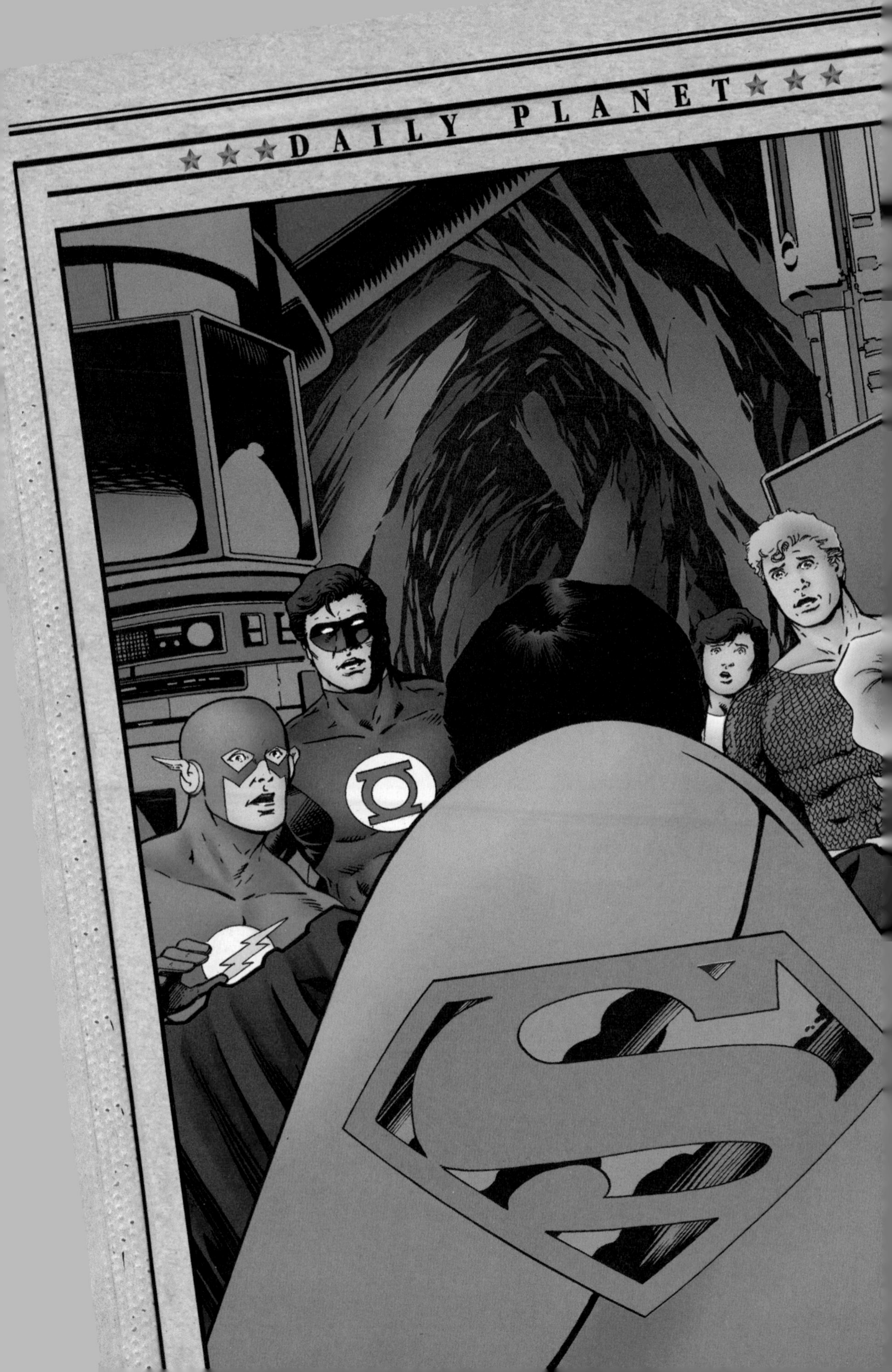
DAILY PLANET

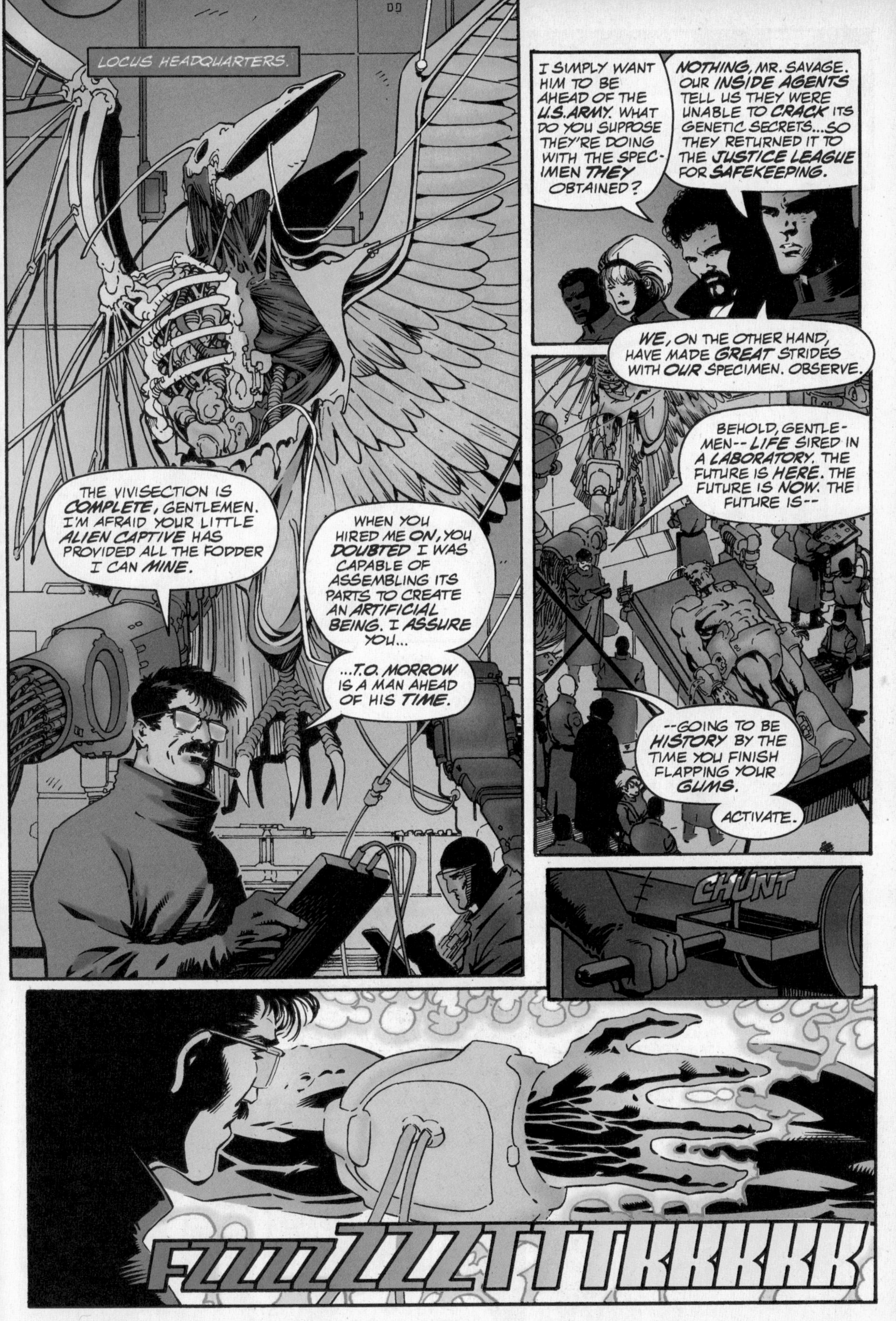
LOCUS HEADQUARTERS.
THE VIVISECTION IS COMPLETE, GENTLEMEN. I'M AFRAID YOUR LITTLE ALIEN CAPTIVE HAS PROVIDED ALL THE FODDER I CAN MINE.
WHEN YOU HIRED ME ON, YOU DOUBTED I WAS CAPABLE OF ASSEMBLING ITS PARTS TO CREATE AN ARTIFICIAL BEING. I ASSURE YOU...
...T.O. MORROW IS A MAN AHEAD OF HIS TIME.
I SIMPLY WANT HIM TO BE AHEAD OF THE U.S. ARMY. WHAT DO YOU SUPPOSE THEY'RE DOING WITH THE SPECIMEN THEY OBTAINED?
NOTHING, MR. SAVAGE. OUR INSIDE AGENTS TELL US THEY WERE UNABLE TO CRACK ITS GENETIC SECRETS...SO THEY RETURNED IT TO THE JUSTICE LEAGUE FOR SAFEKEEPING.
WE, ON THE OTHER HAND, HAVE MADE GREAT STRIDES WITH OUR SPECIMEN. OBSERVE.
BEHOLD, GENTLEMEN--LIFE SIRED IN A LABORATORY. THE FUTURE IS HERE. THE FUTURE IS NOW. THE FUTURE IS--
--GOING TO BE HISTORY BY THE TIME YOU FINISH FLAPPING YOUR GUMS.
ACTIVATE.
CHUNT
FZZZZZZZZTTTTKKKKKK

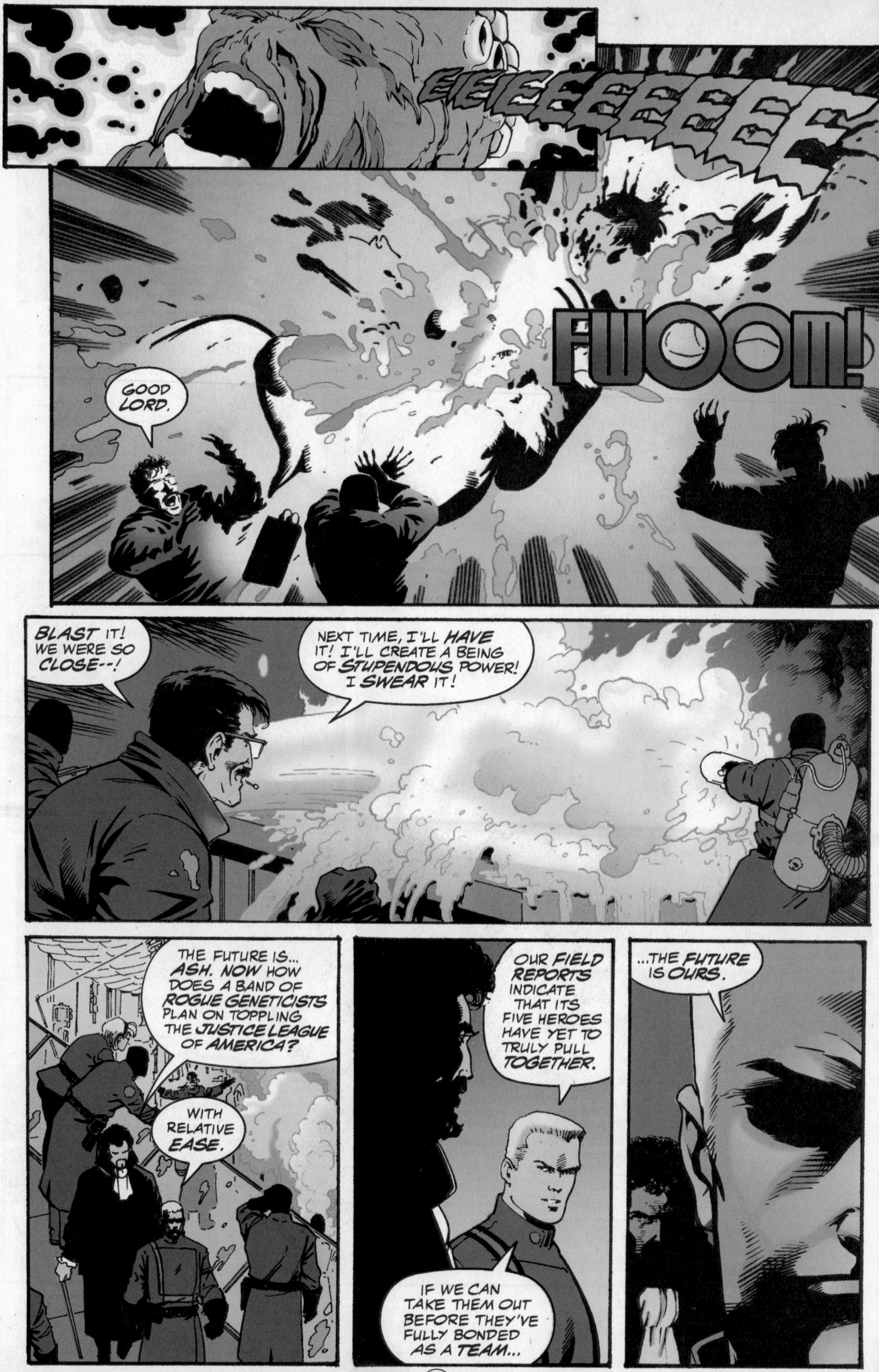
EIEIEEEEEEEEEE
FWOOM!
GOOD LORD.
BLAST IT! WE WERE SO CLOSE--!
NEXT TIME, I'LL HAVE IT! I'LL CREATE A BEING OF STUPENDOUS POWER! I SWEAR IT!
THE FUTURE IS... ASH. NOW HOW DOES A BAND OF ROGUE GENETICISTS PLAN ON TOPPLING THE JUSTICE LEAGUE OF AMERICA?
WITH RELATIVE EASE.
OUR FIELD REPORTS INDICATE THAT ITS FIVE HEROES HAVE YET TO TRULY PULL TOGETHER.
IF WE CAN TAKE THEM OUT BEFORE THEY'VE FULLY BONDED AS A TEAM...
...THE FUTURE IS OURS.

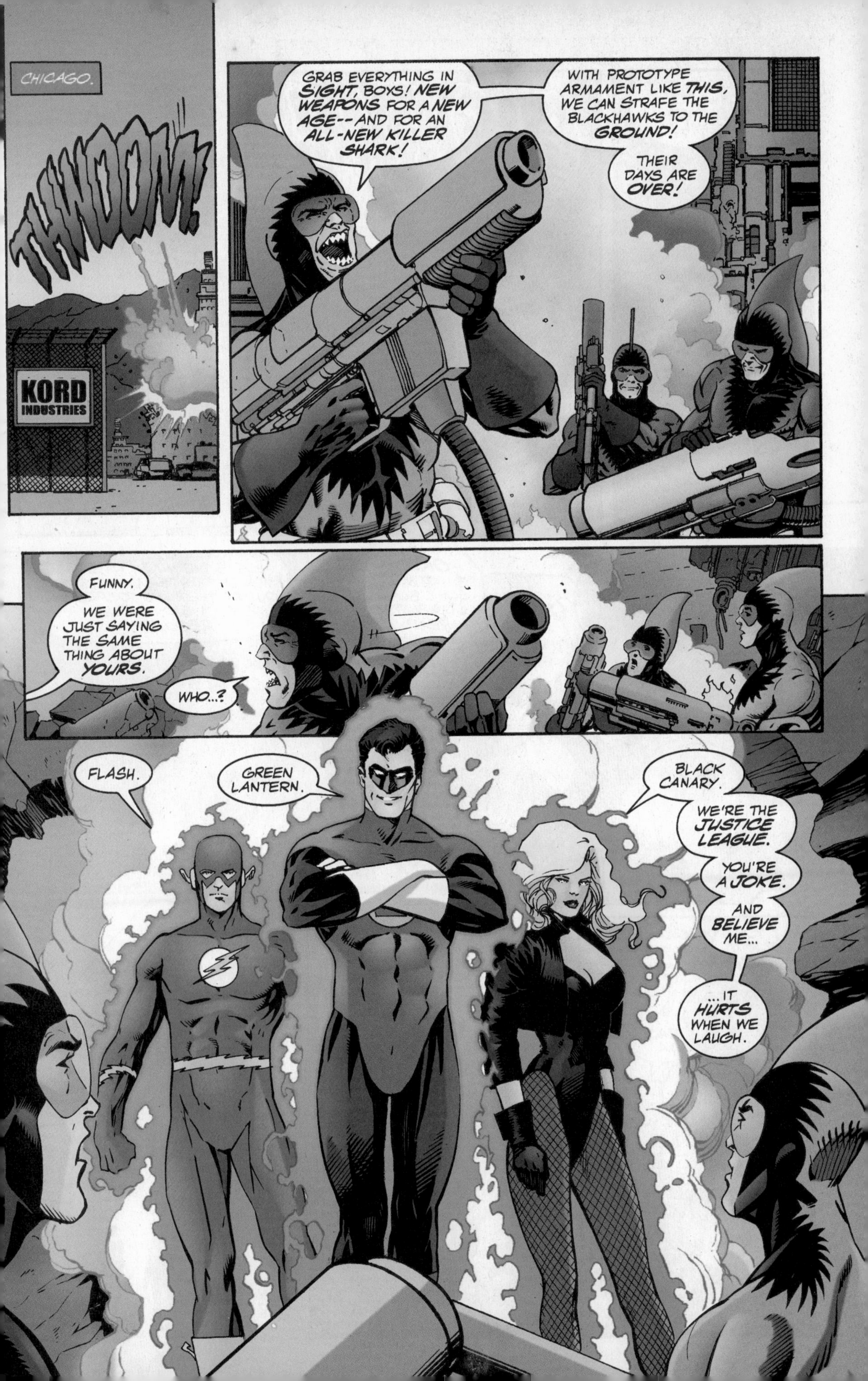
CHICAGO.
THWOOM!
KORD INDUSTRIES
GRAB EVERYTHING IN SIGHT, BOYS! NEW WEAPONS FOR A NEW AGE-- AND FOR AN ALL-NEW KILLER SHARK!
WITH PROTOTYPE ARMAMENT LIKE THIS, WE CAN STRAFE THE BLACKHAWKS TO THE GROUND!
THEIR DAYS ARE OVER!
FUNNY.
WE WERE JUST SAYING THE SAME THING ABOUT YOURS.
WHO...?
FLASH.
GREEN LANTERN.
BLACK CANARY.
WE'RE THE JUSTICE LEAGUE.
YOU'RE A JOKE.
AND BELIEVE ME...
...IT HURTS WHEN WE LAUGH.

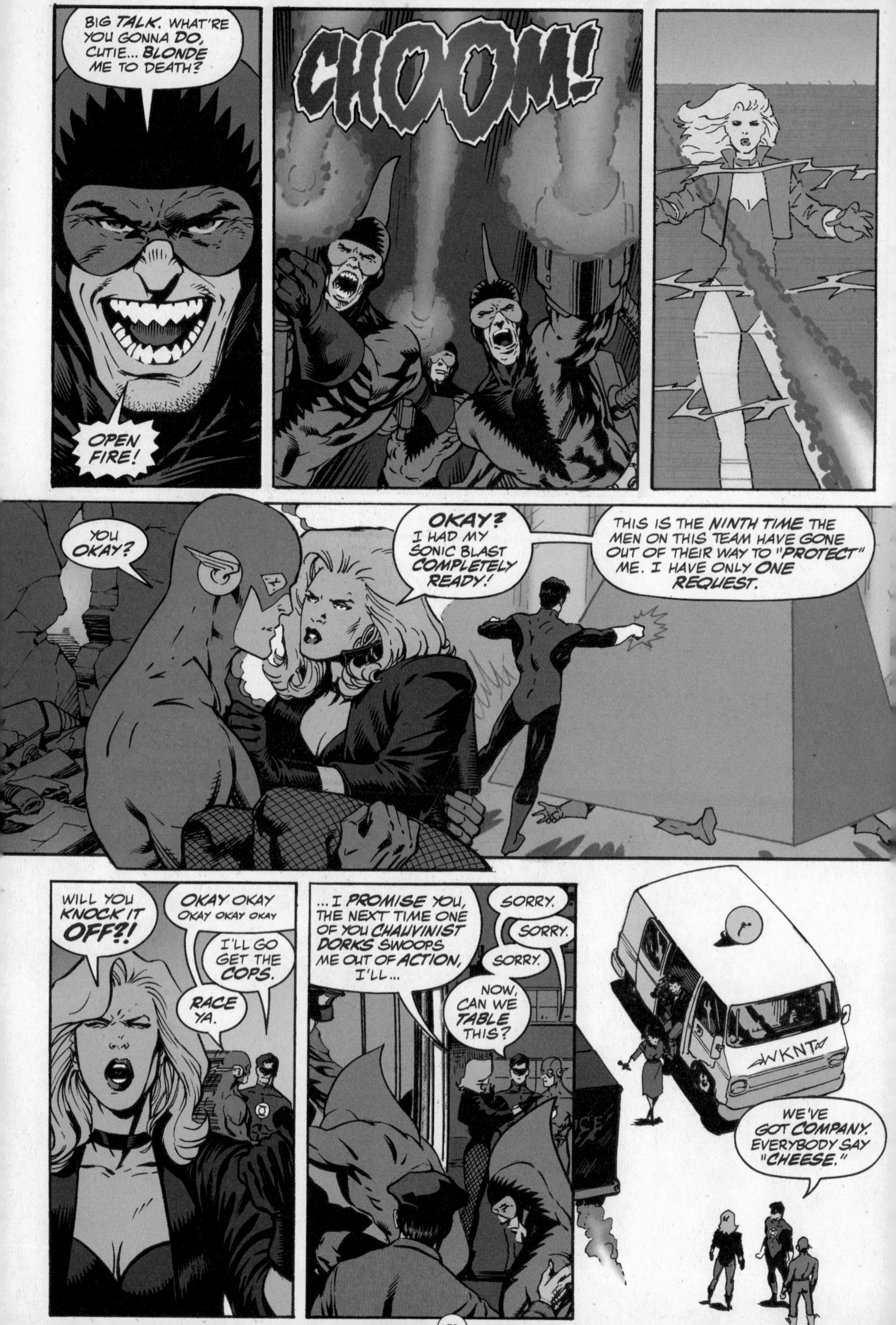
BIG TALK. WHAT'RE YOU GONNA DO, CUTIE... BLONDE ME TO DEATH?
OPEN FIRE!
CHOOM!
YOU OKAY?
OKAY? I HAD MY SONIC BLAST COMPLETELY READY!
THIS IS THE NINTH TIME THE MEN ON THIS TEAM HAVE GONE OUT OF THEIR WAY TO "PROTECT" ME. I HAVE ONLY ONE REQUEST.
WILL YOU KNOCK IT OFF?!
OKAY OKAY OKAY OKAY OKAY
I'LL GO GET THE COPS.
RACE YA.
...I PROMISE YOU, THE NEXT TIME ONE OF YOU CHAUVINIST DORKS SWOOPS ME OUT OF ACTION, I'LL...
SORRY.
SORRY.
SORRY.
NOW, CAN WE TABLE THIS?
WKNT
WE'VE GOT COMPANY. EVERYBODY SAY "CHEESE."

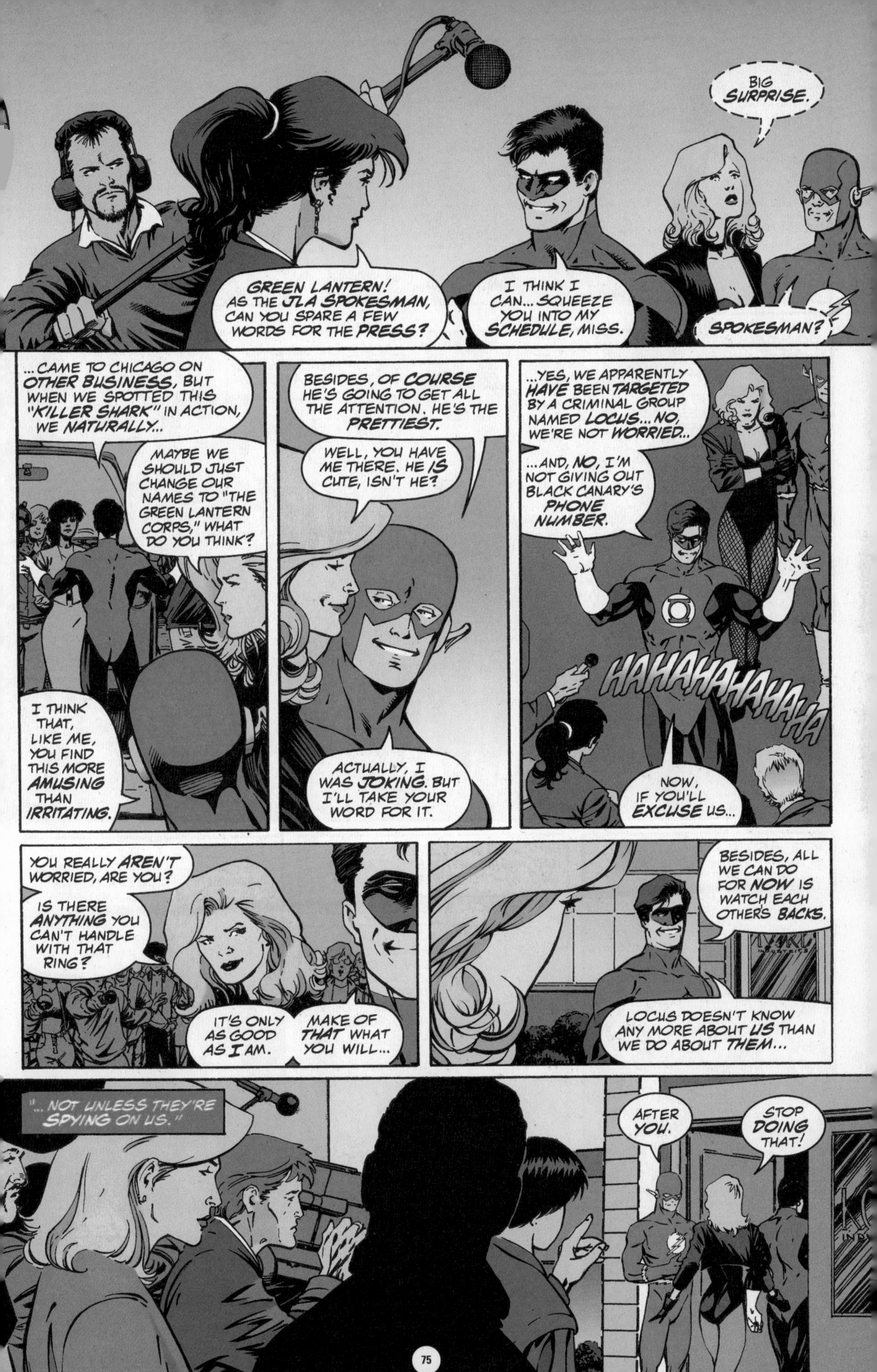
BIG SURPRISE.
GREEN LANTERN! AS THE JLA SPOKESMAN, CAN YOU SPARE A FEW WORDS FOR THE PRESS?
I THINK I CAN... SQUEEZE YOU INTO MY SCHEDULE, MISS.
SPOKESMAN?
...CAME TO CHICAGO ON OTHER BUSINESS, BUT WHEN WE SPOTTED THIS "KILLER SHARK" IN ACTION, WE NATURALLY...
MAYBE WE SHOULD JUST CHANGE OUR NAMES TO "THE GREEN LANTERN CORPS," WHAT DO YOU THINK?
I THINK THAT, LIKE ME, YOU FIND THIS MORE AMUSING THAN IRRITATING.
BESIDES, OF COURSE HE'S GOING TO GET ALL THE ATTENTION. HE'S THE PRETTIEST.
WELL, YOU HAVE ME THERE. HE IS CUTE, ISN'T HE?
ACTUALLY, I WAS JOKING. BUT I'LL TAKE YOUR WORD FOR IT.
...YES, WE APPARENTLY HAVE BEEN TARGETED BY A CRIMINAL GROUP NAMED LOCUS... NO, WE'RE NOT WORRIED...
...AND, NO, I'M NOT GIVING OUT BLACK CANARY'S PHONE NUMBER.
HAHAHAHAHAHAHAHA
NOW, IF YOU'LL EXCUSE US...
YOU REALLY AREN'T WORRIED, ARE YOU?
IS THERE ANYTHING YOU CAN'T HANDLE WITH THAT RING?
IT'S ONLY AS GOOD AS I AM.
MAKE OF THAT WHAT YOU WILL...
BESIDES, ALL WE CAN DO FOR NOW IS WATCH EACH OTHER'S BACKS.
LOCUS DOESN'T KNOW ANY MORE ABOUT US THAN WE DO ABOUT THEM...
"...NOT UNLESS THEY'RE SPYING ON US."
AFTER YOU.
STOP DOING THAT!

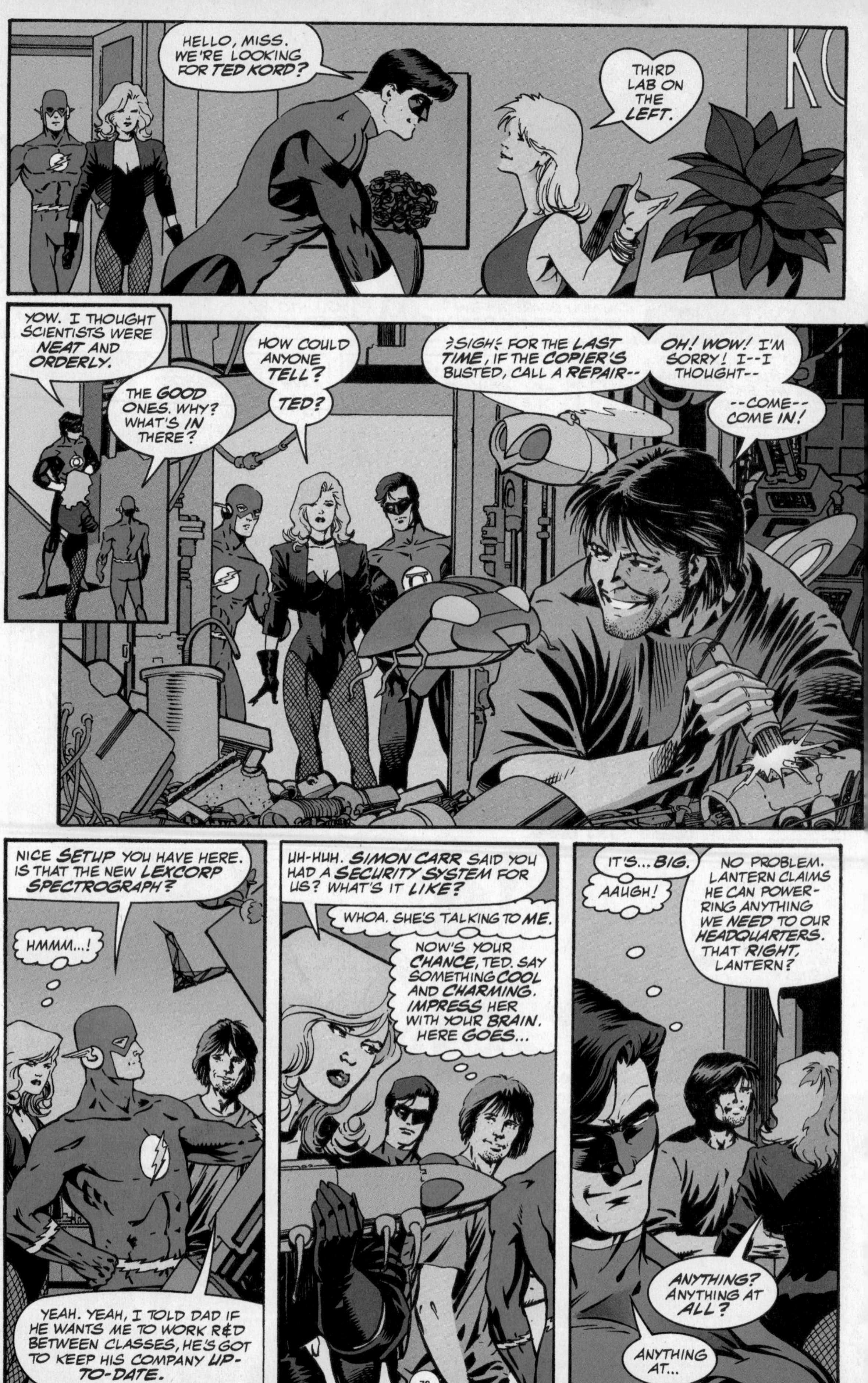
HELLO, MISS. WE'RE LOOKING FOR TED KORD?
THIRD LAB ON THE LEFT.
YOW. I THOUGHT SCIENTISTS WERE NEAT AND ORDERLY.
THE GOOD ONES. WHY? WHAT'S IN THERE?
HOW COULD ANYONE TELL?
TED?
SIGH FOR THE LAST TIME, IF THE COPIER'S BUSTED, CALL A REPAIR--
OH! WOW! I'M SORRY! I--I THOUGHT--
--COME--COME IN!
NICE SETUP YOU HAVE HERE. IS THAT THE NEW LEXCORP SPECTROGRAPH?
HMMM...!
YEAH. YEAH, I TOLD DAD IF HE WANTS ME TO WORK R&D BETWEEN CLASSES, HE'S GOT TO KEEP HIS COMPANY UP-TO-DATE.
UH-HUH. SIMON CARR SAID YOU HAD A SECURITY SYSTEM FOR US? WHAT'S IT LIKE?
WHOA. SHE'S TALKING TO ME.
NOW'S YOUR CHANCE, TED. SAY SOMETHING COOL AND CHARMING. IMPRESS HER WITH YOUR BRAIN. HERE GOES...
IT'S... BIG.
AAUGH!
NO PROBLEM. LANTERN CLAIMS HE CAN POWER-RING ANYTHING WE NEED TO OUR HEADQUARTERS. THAT RIGHT, LANTERN?
ANYTHING? ANYTHING AT ALL?
ANYTHING AT...

...ALL...

IT'S...

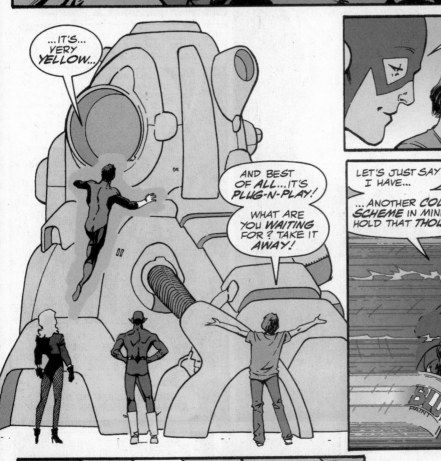

...IT'S... VERY YELLOW...

AND BEST OF ALL...IT'S PLUG-N-PLAY!

WHAT ARE YOU WAITING FOR? TAKE IT AWAY!

TELL ME... DOES IT HAVE TO BE YELLOW?

WELL... NO. WHY?

LET'S JUST SAY I HAVE...

...ANOTHER COLOR SCHEME IN MIND. HOLD THAT THOUGHT...

THANKS FOR THE SAVE.

SO THE RING DOESN'T WORK ON YELLOW THINGS. NO PROBLEM. HAVE PAINTBRUSH, WILL TRAVEL.

WHOA. GEEZ, DAD... SCREW THE FAMILY BUSINESS...

...I WANNA BE ONE OF THOSE GUYS!

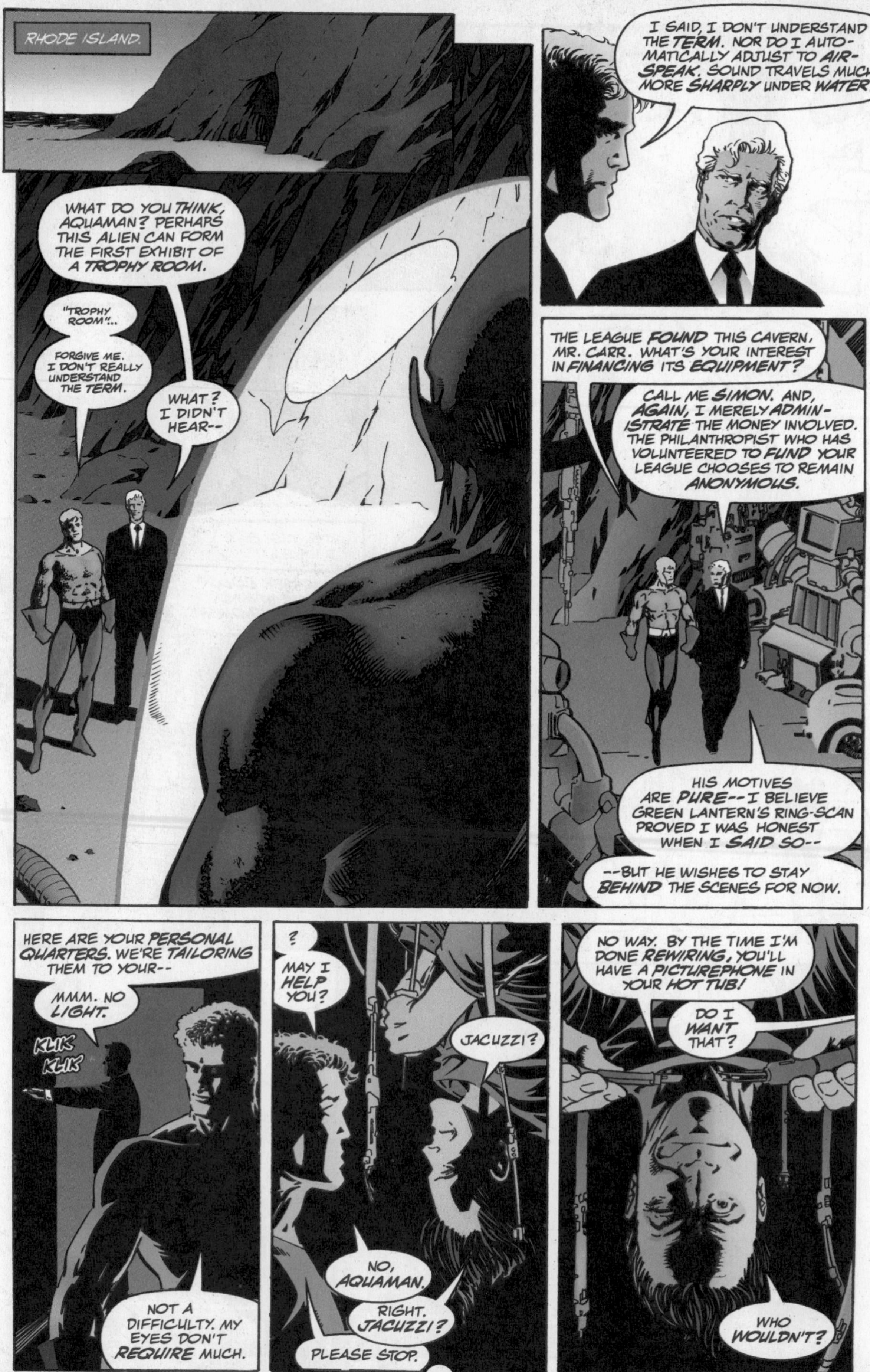
RHODE ISLAND.
WHAT DO YOU THINK, AQUAMAN? PERHAPS THIS ALIEN CAN FORM THE FIRST EXHIBIT OF A TROPHY ROOM.
"TROPHY ROOM"...
FORGIVE ME. I DON'T REALLY UNDERSTAND THE TERM.
WHAT? I DIDN'T HEAR--
I SAID, I DON'T UNDERSTAND THE TERM. NOR DO I AUTOMATICALLY ADJUST TO AIR-SPEAK. SOUND TRAVELS MUCH MORE SHARPLY UNDER WATER.
THE LEAGUE FOUND THIS CAVERN, MR. CARR. WHAT'S YOUR INTEREST IN FINANCING ITS EQUIPMENT?
CALL ME SIMON. AND, AGAIN, I MERELY ADMINISTRATE THE MONEY INVOLVED. THE PHILANTHROPIST WHO HAS VOLUNTEERED TO FUND YOUR LEAGUE CHOOSES TO REMAIN ANONYMOUS.
HIS MOTIVES ARE PURE--I BELIEVE GREEN LANTERN'S RING-SCAN PROVED I WAS HONEST WHEN I SAID SO--
--BUT HE WISHES TO STAY BEHIND THE SCENES FOR NOW.
HERE ARE YOUR PERSONAL QUARTERS. WE'RE TAILORING THEM TO YOUR--
MMM. NO LIGHT.
KLIK KLIK
NOT A DIFFICULTY. MY EYES DON'T REQUIRE MUCH.
?
MAY I HELP YOU?
JACUZZI?
NO, AQUAMAN.
RIGHT. JACUZZI?
PLEASE STOP.
NO WAY. BY THE TIME I'M DONE REWIRING, YOU'LL HAVE A PICTUREPHONE IN YOUR HOT TUB!
DO I WANT THAT?
WHO WOULDN'T?

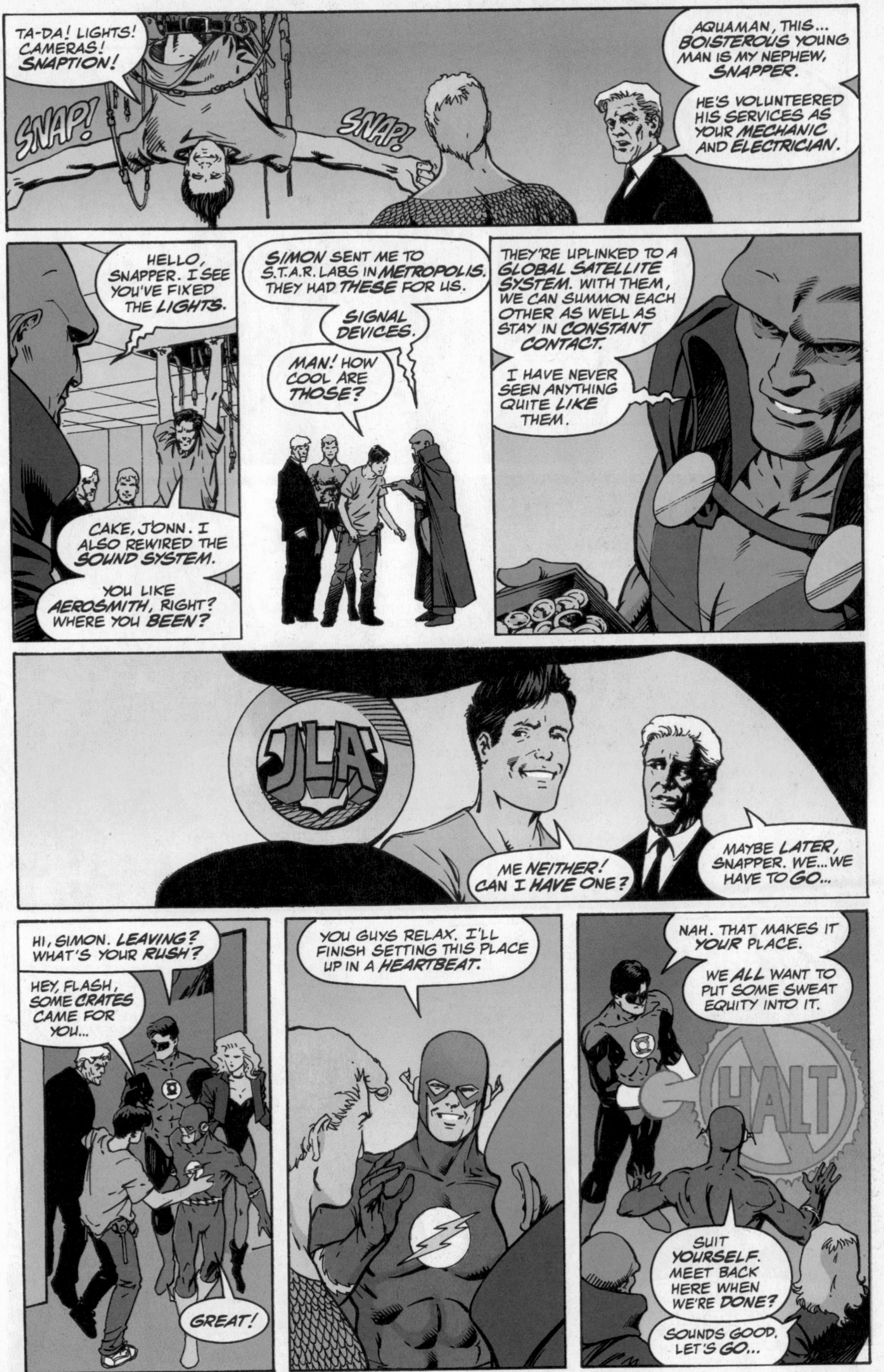
TA-DA! LIGHTS! CAMERAS! SNAPTION!
SNAP!
SNAP!
AQUAMAN, THIS... BOISTEROUS YOUNG MAN IS MY NEPHEW, SNAPPER.
HE'S VOLUNTEERED HIS SERVICES AS YOUR MECHANIC AND ELECTRICIAN.
HELLO, SNAPPER. I SEE YOU'VE FIXED THE LIGHTS.
CAKE, J'ONN. I ALSO REWIRED THE SOUND SYSTEM.
YOU LIKE AEROSMITH, RIGHT? WHERE YOU BEEN?
SIMON SENT ME TO S.T.A.R. LABS IN METROPOLIS. THEY HAD THESE FOR US.
SIGNAL DEVICES.
MAN! HOW COOL ARE THOSE?
THEY'RE UPLINKED TO A GLOBAL SATELLITE SYSTEM. WITH THEM, WE CAN SUMMON EACH OTHER AS WELL AS STAY IN CONSTANT CONTACT.
I HAVE NEVER SEEN ANYTHING QUITE LIKE THEM.
JLA
ME NEITHER! CAN I HAVE ONE?
MAYBE LATER, SNAPPER. WE... WE HAVE TO GO...
HI, SIMON. LEAVING? WHAT'S YOUR RUSH?
HEY, FLASH, SOME CRATES CAME FOR YOU...
GREAT!
YOU GUYS RELAX. I'LL FINISH SETTING THIS PLACE UP IN A HEARTBEAT.
NAH. THAT MAKES IT YOUR PLACE.
WE ALL WANT TO PUT SOME SWEAT EQUITY INTO IT.
HALT
SUIT YOURSELF. MEET BACK HERE WHEN WE'RE DONE?
SOUNDS GOOD. LET'S GO...

GENTLY. I NEVER KNOW MY OWN STRENGTH OUT OF THE WATER.

KSSSHH

WHOOPS.

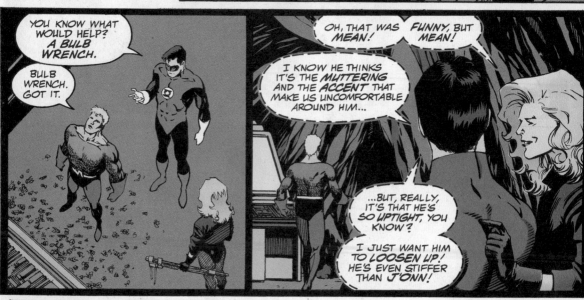

YOU KNOW WHAT WOULD HELP? A *BULB WRENCH.*

BULB WRENCH. GOT IT.

OH, THAT WAS *MEAN!*

FUNNY, BUT *MEAN!*

I KNOW HE THINKS IT'S THE *MUTTERING* AND THE *ACCENT* THAT MAKE US UNCOMFORTABLE AROUND HIM...

...BUT, REALLY, IT'S THAT HE'S *SO UPTIGHT,* YOU KNOW?

I JUST WANT HIM TO *LOOSEN UP!* HE'S EVEN STIFFER THAN *J'ONN!*

C'MON, HE'LL *LAUGH* ONCE HE GETS THE JOKE.

WHICH WE'RE SAFE FROM. UNLESS, OF COURSE, THEY'RE PAINTED *YELLOW.*

YOU JUST DON'T LET GO OF THINGS, DO YOU?

SO WHAT'S THE *STORY* ON THAT RING? WHERE DID IT *COME* FROM? I KNOW WE'RE NOT GIVING OUT *REAL NAMES* HERE... BUT SPILL *SOMETHING.*

HELL, HE'LL PROBABLY RETALIATE WITH AN ARMY OF *LOBSTERS* OR SOMETHING.

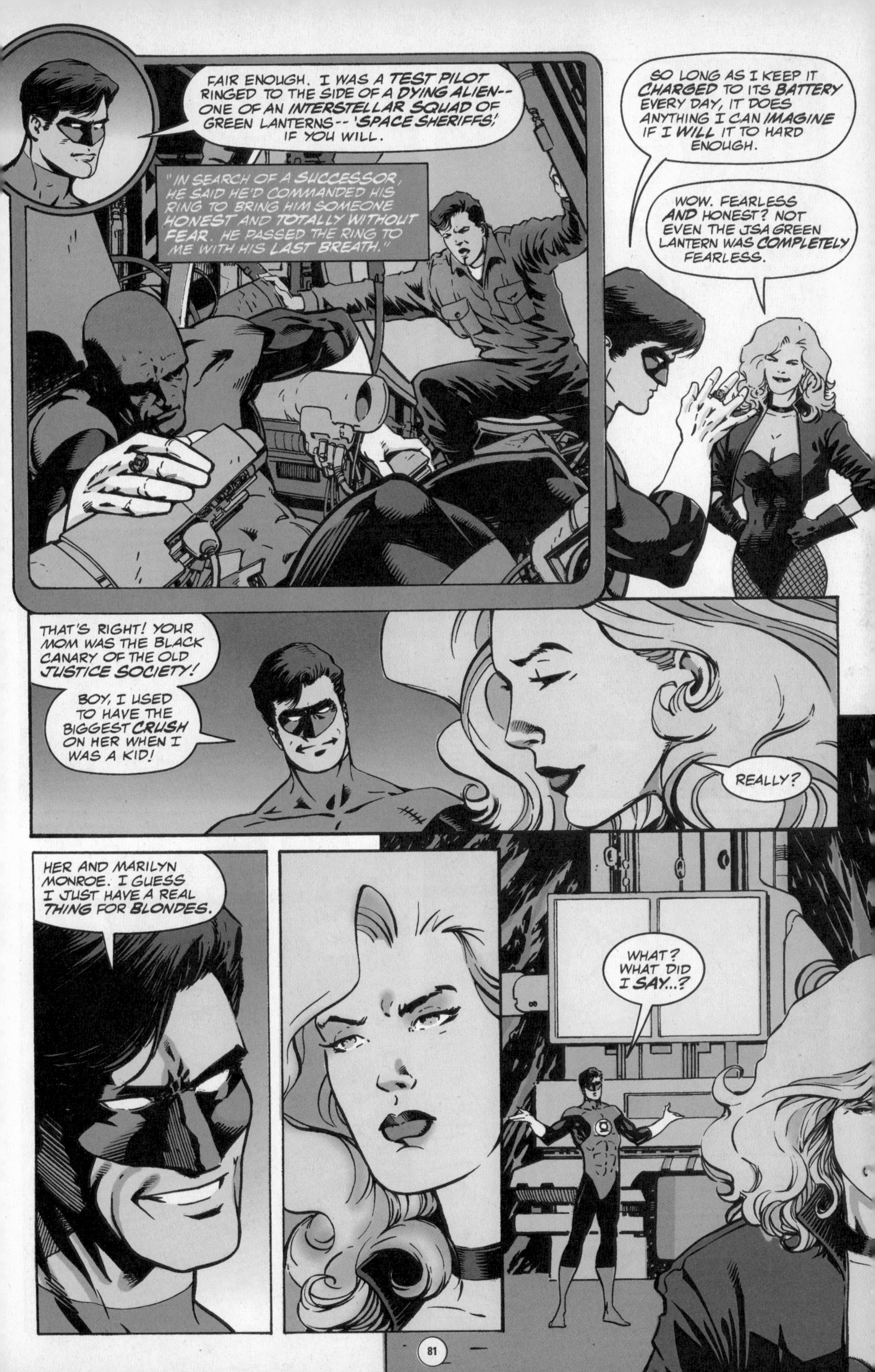
FAIR ENOUGH. I WAS A TEST PILOT RINGED TO THE SIDE OF A DYING ALIEN-- ONE OF AN INTERSTELLAR SQUAD OF GREEN LANTERNS-- 'SPACE SHERIFFS,' IF YOU WILL.
"IN SEARCH OF A SUCCESSOR, HE SAID HE'D COMMANDED HIS RING TO BRING HIM SOMEONE HONEST AND TOTALLY WITHOUT FEAR. HE PASSED THE RING TO ME WITH HIS LAST BREATH."
SO LONG AS I KEEP IT CHARGED TO ITS BATTERY EVERY DAY, IT DOES ANYTHING I CAN IMAGINE IF I WILL IT TO HARD ENOUGH.
WOW. FEARLESS AND HONEST? NOT EVEN THE JSA GREEN LANTERN WAS COMPLETELY FEARLESS.
THAT'S RIGHT! YOUR MOM WAS THE BLACK CANARY OF THE OLD JUSTICE SOCIETY!
BOY, I USED TO HAVE THE BIGGEST CRUSH ON HER WHEN I WAS A KID!
REALLY?
HER AND MARILYN MONROE. I GUESS I JUST HAVE A REAL THING FOR BLONDES.
WHAT? WHAT DID I SAY...?

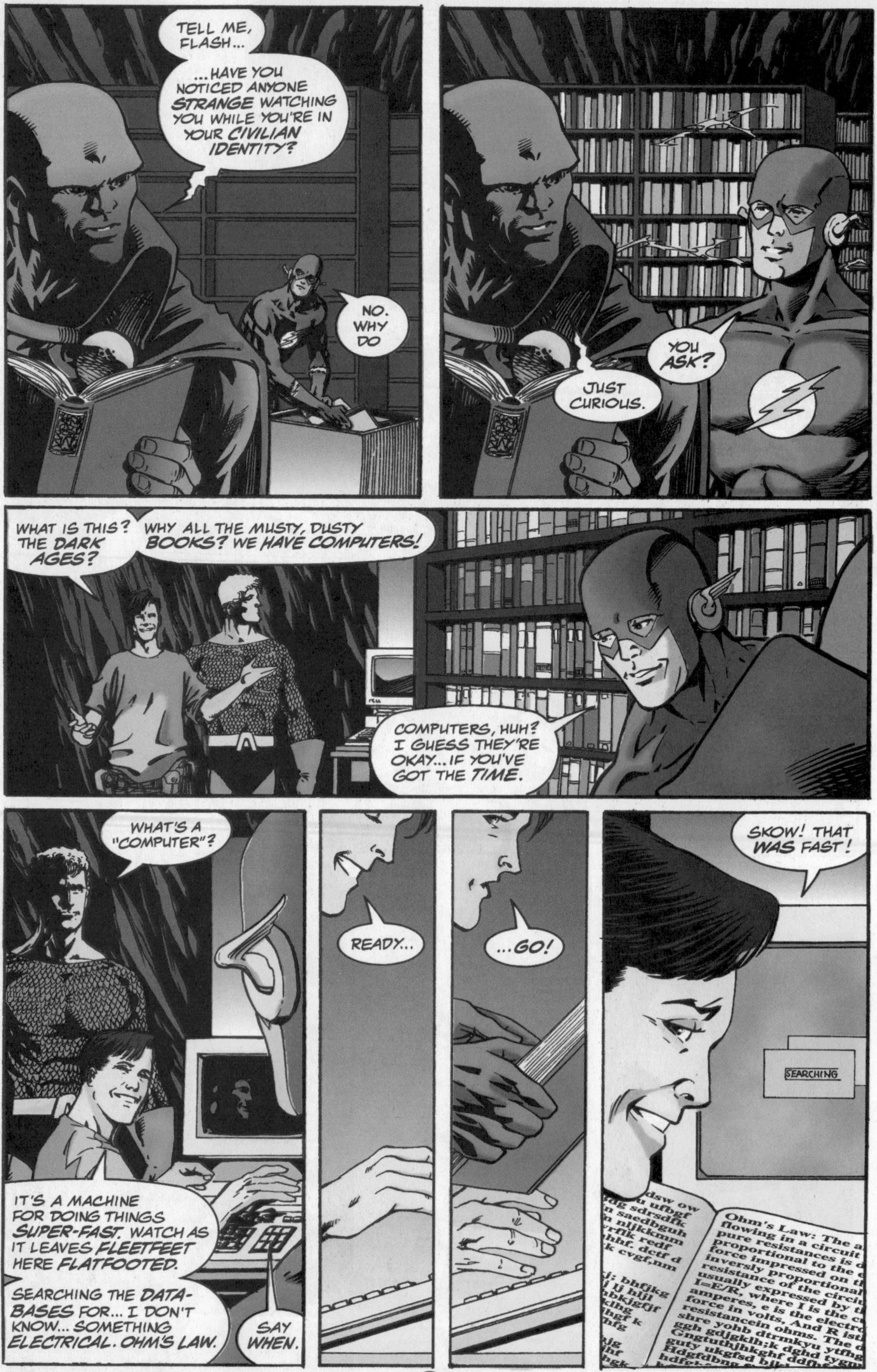
TELL ME, FLASH...
...HAVE YOU NOTICED ANYONE STRANGE WATCHING YOU WHILE YOU'RE IN YOUR CIVILIAN IDENTITY?
NO. WHY DO
YOU ASK?
JUST CURIOUS.
WHAT IS THIS? THE DARK AGES?
WHY ALL THE MUSTY, DUSTY BOOKS? WE HAVE COMPUTERS!
COMPUTERS, HUH? I GUESS THEY'RE OKAY... IF YOU'VE GOT THE TIME.
WHAT'S A "COMPUTER"?
IT'S A MACHINE FOR DOING THINGS SUPER-FAST. WATCH AS IT LEAVES FLEETFEET HERE FLATFOOTED.
SEARCHING THE DATA-BASES FOR... I DON'T KNOW... SOMETHING ELECTRICAL. OHM'S LAW.
SAY WHEN.
READY...
...GO!
SKOW! THAT WAS FAST!
SEARCHING

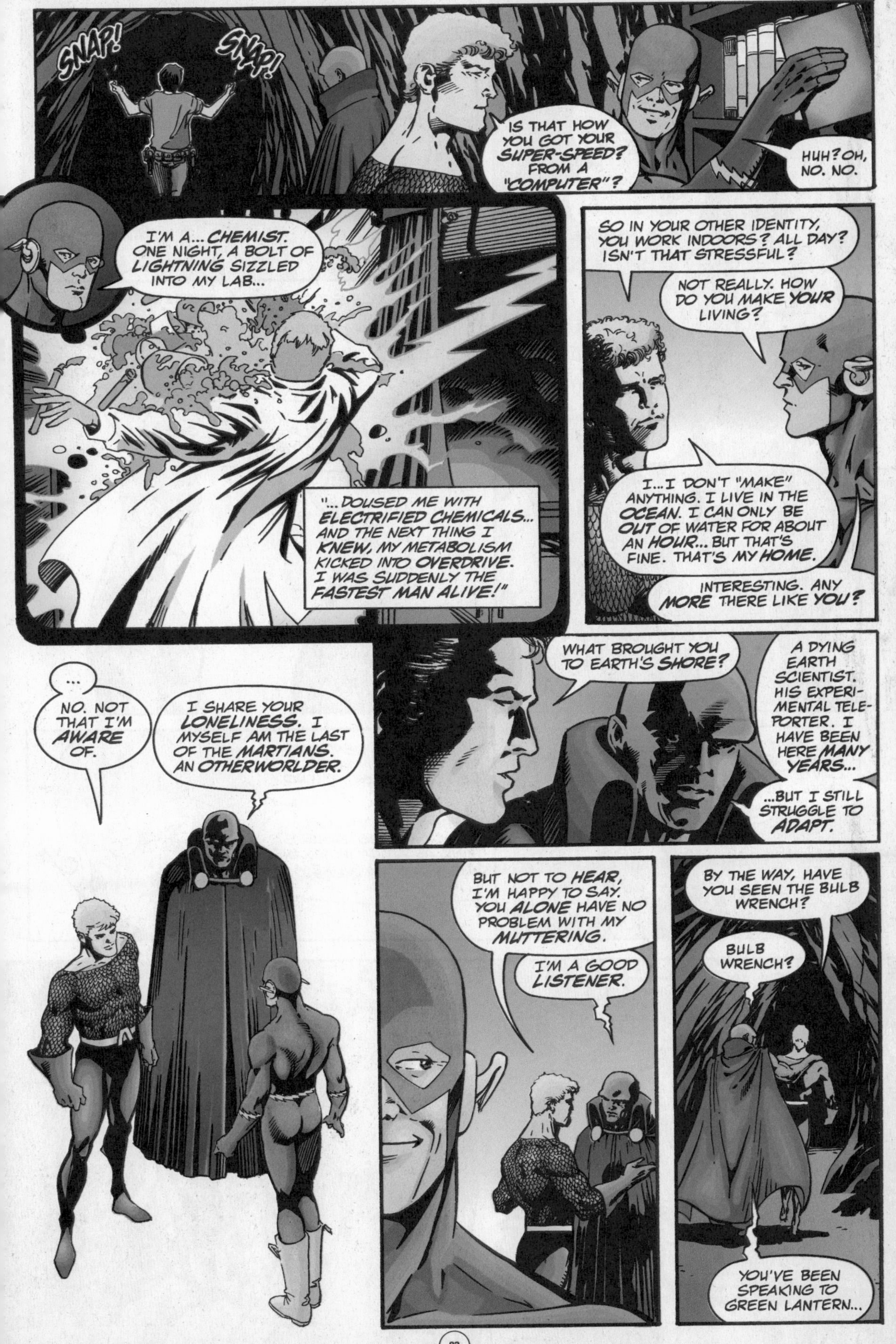

SNAP!
SNAP!
IS THAT HOW YOU GOT YOUR SUPER-SPEED? FROM A "COMPUTER"?
HUH? OH, NO. NO.
I'M A... CHEMIST. ONE NIGHT, A BOLT OF LIGHTNING SIZZLED INTO MY LAB...
"...DOUSED ME WITH ELECTRIFIED CHEMICALS... AND THE NEXT THING I KNEW, MY METABOLISM KICKED INTO OVERDRIVE. I WAS SUDDENLY THE FASTEST MAN ALIVE!"
SO IN YOUR OTHER IDENTITY, YOU WORK INDOORS? ALL DAY? ISN'T THAT STRESSFUL?
NOT REALLY. HOW DO YOU MAKE YOUR LIVING?
I...I DON'T "MAKE" ANYTHING. I LIVE IN THE OCEAN. I CAN ONLY BE OUT OF WATER FOR ABOUT AN HOUR... BUT THAT'S FINE. THAT'S MY HOME.
INTERESTING. ANY MORE THERE LIKE YOU?
...
NO. NOT THAT I'M AWARE OF.
I SHARE YOUR LONELINESS. I MYSELF AM THE LAST OF THE MARTIANS. AN OTHERWORLDER.
WHAT BROUGHT YOU TO EARTH'S SHORE?
A DYING EARTH SCIENTIST. HIS EXPERIMENTAL TELEPORTER. I HAVE BEEN HERE MANY YEARS...
...BUT I STILL STRUGGLE TO ADAPT.
BUT NOT TO HEAR, I'M HAPPY TO SAY. YOU ALONE HAVE NO PROBLEM WITH MY MUTTERING.
I'M A GOOD LISTENER.
BY THE WAY, HAVE YOU SEEN THE BULB WRENCH?
BULB WRENCH?
YOU'VE BEEN SPEAKING TO GREEN LANTERN...

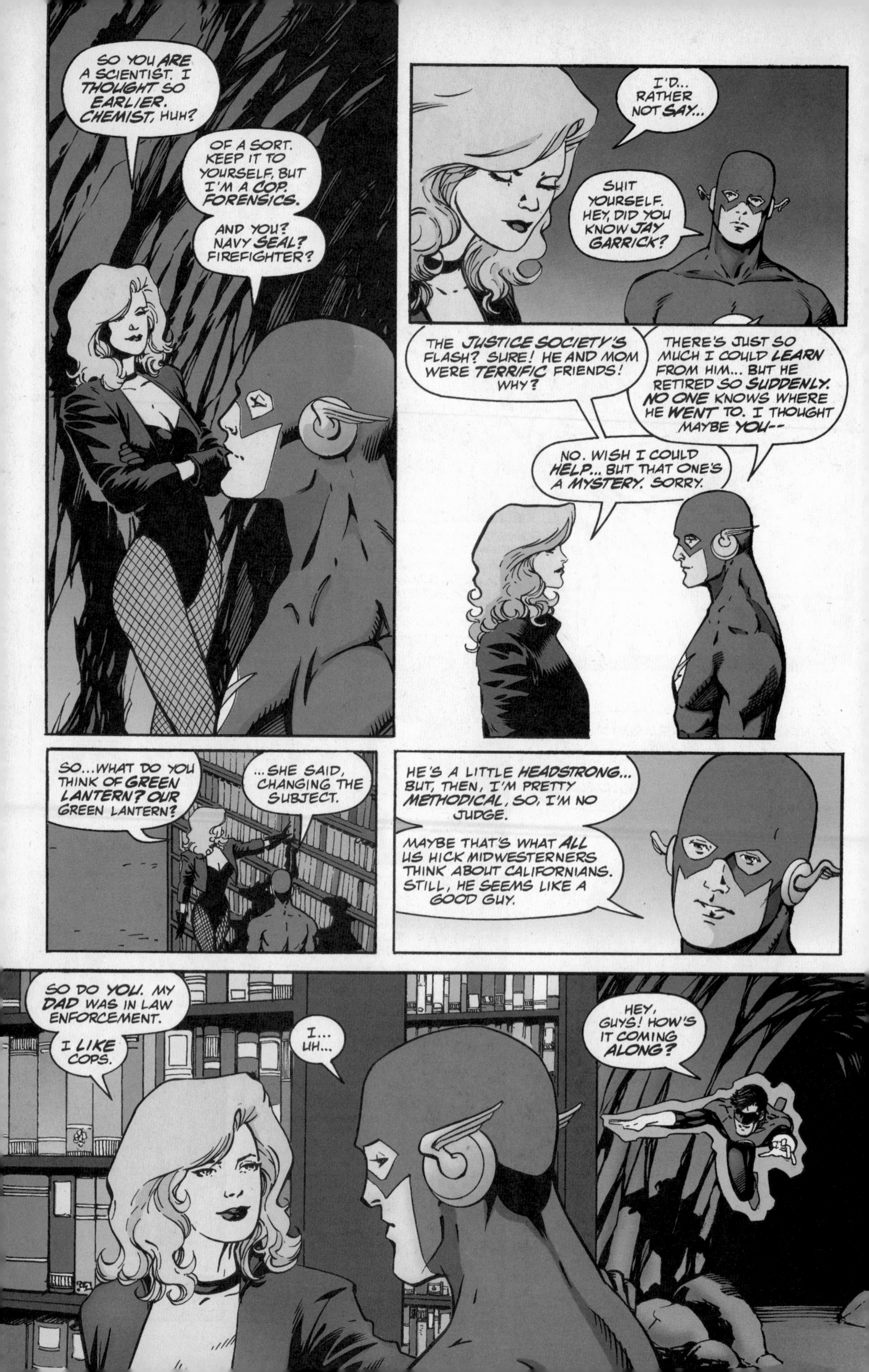
SO YOU ARE A SCIENTIST. I THOUGHT SO EARLIER. CHEMIST, HUH?
OF A SORT. KEEP IT TO YOURSELF, BUT I'M A COP. FORENSICS.
AND YOU? NAVY SEAL? FIREFIGHTER?
I'D... RATHER NOT SAY...
SUIT YOURSELF. HEY, DID YOU KNOW JAY GARRICK?
THE JUSTICE SOCIETY'S FLASH? SURE! HE AND MOM WERE TERRIFIC FRIENDS! WHY?
THERE'S JUST SO MUCH I COULD LEARN FROM HIM... BUT HE RETIRED SO SUDDENLY. NO ONE KNOWS WHERE HE WENT TO. I THOUGHT MAYBE YOU--
NO. WISH I COULD HELP... BUT THAT ONE'S A MYSTERY. SORRY.
SO...WHAT DO YOU THINK OF GREEN LANTERN? OUR GREEN LANTERN?
...SHE SAID, CHANGING THE SUBJECT.
HE'S A LITTLE HEADSTRONG... BUT, THEN, I'M PRETTY METHODICAL, SO, I'M NO JUDGE.
MAYBE THAT'S WHAT ALL US HICK MIDWESTERNERS THINK ABOUT CALIFORNIANS. STILL, HE SEEMS LIKE A GOOD GUY.
SO DO YOU. MY DAD WAS IN LAW ENFORCEMENT.
I LIKE COPS.
I... UH...
HEY, GUYS! HOW'S IT COMING ALONG?

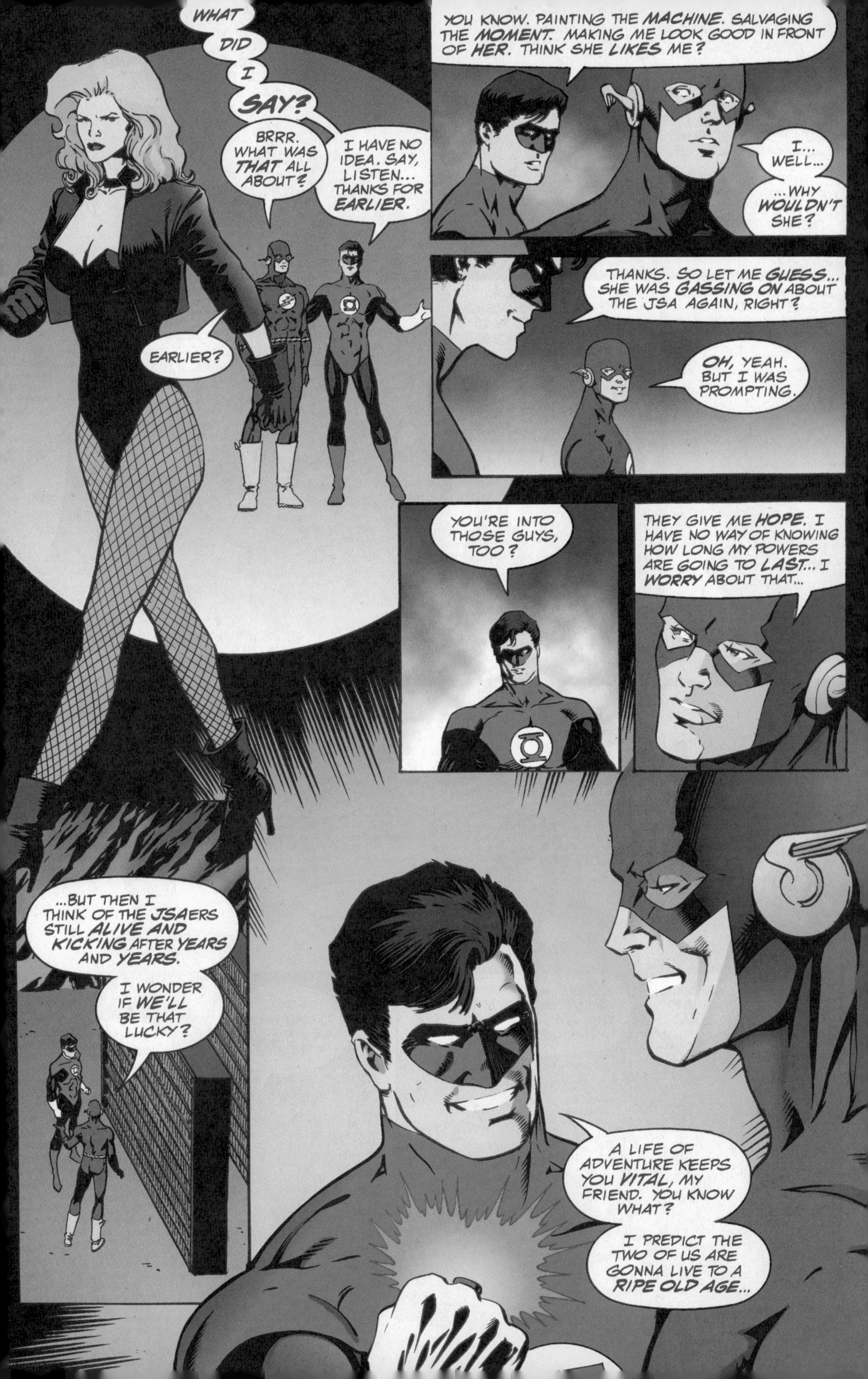
WHAT DID I SAY?
BRRR. WHAT WAS THAT ALL ABOUT?
I HAVE NO IDEA. SAY, LISTEN... THANKS FOR EARLIER.
EARLIER?
YOU KNOW. PAINTING THE MACHINE. SALVAGING THE MOMENT. MAKING ME LOOK GOOD IN FRONT OF HER. THINK SHE LIKES ME?
I... WELL...
...WHY WOULDN'T SHE?
THANKS. SO LET ME GUESS... SHE WAS GASSING ON ABOUT THE JSA AGAIN, RIGHT?
OH, YEAH. BUT I WAS PROMPTING.
YOU'RE INTO THOSE GUYS, TOO?
THEY GIVE ME HOPE. I HAVE NO WAY OF KNOWING HOW LONG MY POWERS ARE GOING TO LAST... I WORRY ABOUT THAT...
...BUT THEN I THINK OF THE JSAERS STILL ALIVE AND KICKING AFTER YEARS AND YEARS.
I WONDER IF WE'LL BE THAT LUCKY?
A LIFE OF ADVENTURE KEEPS YOU VITAL, MY FRIEND. YOU KNOW WHAT?
I PREDICT THE TWO OF US ARE GONNA LIVE TO A RIPE OLD AGE...

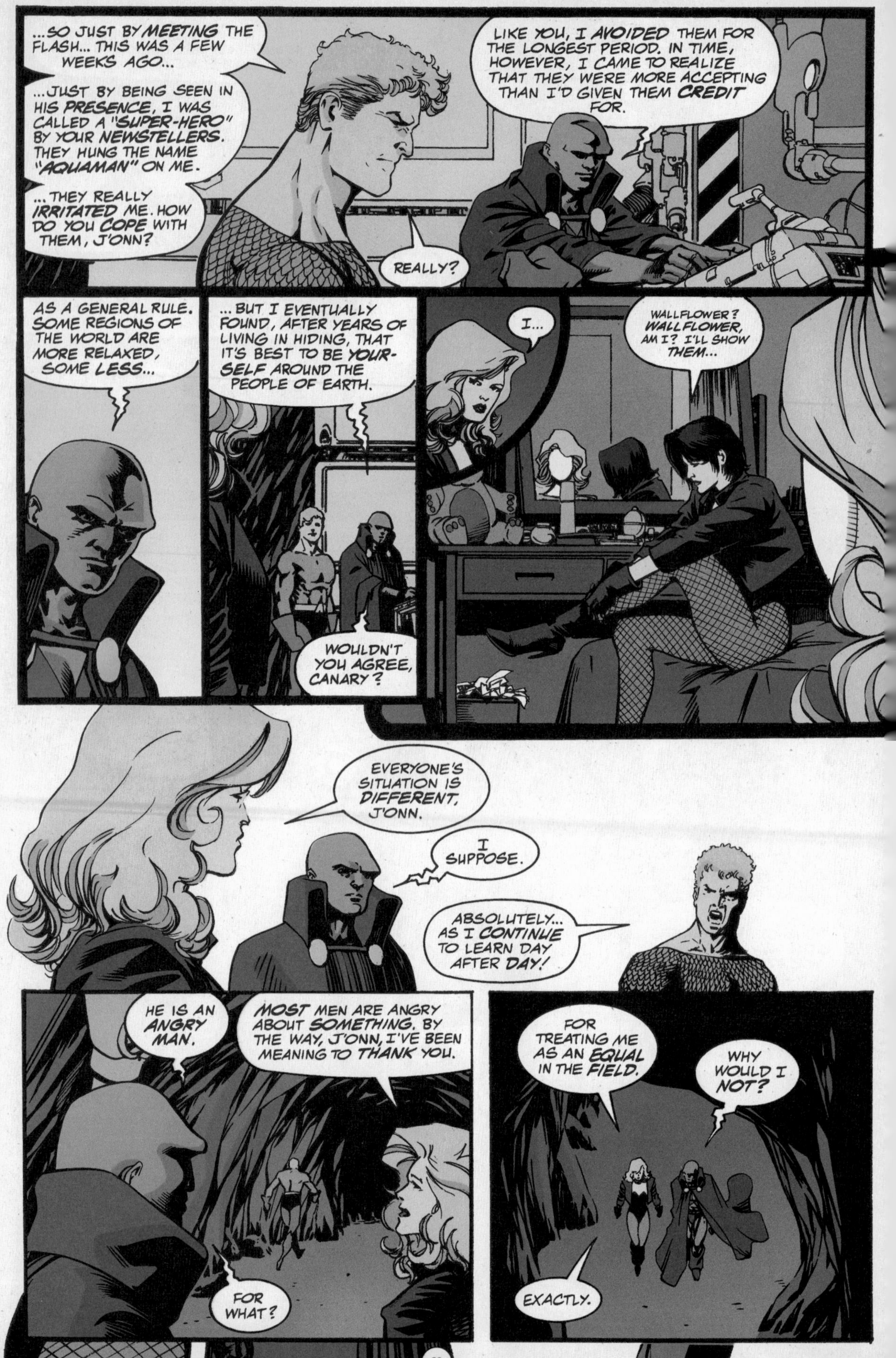

...SO JUST BY MEETING THE FLASH... THIS WAS A FEW WEEKS AGO...
...JUST BY BEING SEEN IN HIS PRESENCE, I WAS CALLED A "SUPER-HERO" BY YOUR NEWSTELLERS. THEY HUNG THE NAME "AQUAMAN" ON ME.
...THEY REALLY IRRITATED ME. HOW DO YOU COPE WITH THEM, J'ONN?
LIKE YOU, I AVOIDED THEM FOR THE LONGEST PERIOD. IN TIME, HOWEVER, I CAME TO REALIZE THAT THEY WERE MORE ACCEPTING THAN I'D GIVEN THEM CREDIT FOR.
REALLY?
AS A GENERAL RULE. SOME REGIONS OF THE WORLD ARE MORE RELAXED, SOME LESS...
...BUT I EVENTUALLY FOUND, AFTER YEARS OF LIVING IN HIDING, THAT IT'S BEST TO BE YOURSELF AROUND THE PEOPLE OF EARTH.
WOULDN'T YOU AGREE, CANARY?
I...
WALLFLOWER? WALLFLOWER, AM I? I'LL SHOW THEM...
EVERYONE'S SITUATION IS DIFFERENT, J'ONN.
I SUPPOSE.
ABSOLUTELY... AS I CONTINUE TO LEARN DAY AFTER DAY!
HE IS AN ANGRY MAN.
MOST MEN ARE ANGRY ABOUT SOMETHING. BY THE WAY, J'ONN, I'VE BEEN MEANING TO THANK YOU.
FOR WHAT?
FOR TREATING ME AS AN EQUAL IN THE FIELD.
WHY WOULD I NOT?
EXACTLY.

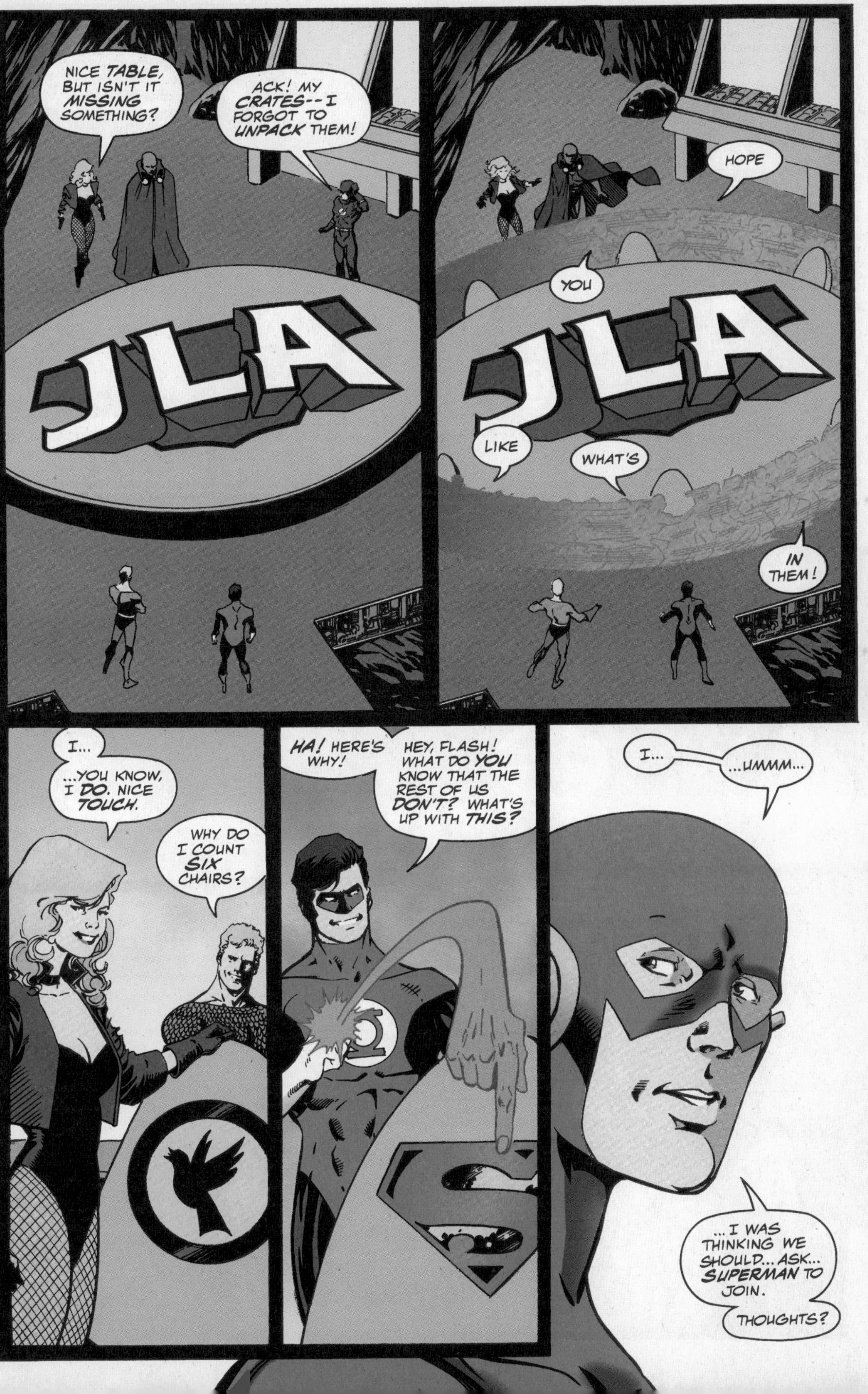
NICE TABLE, BUT ISN'T IT MISSING SOMETHING?
ACK! MY CRATES--I FORGOT TO UNPACK THEM!
HOPE
YOU
LIKE
WHAT'S
IN THEM!
I...
...YOU KNOW, I DO. NICE TOUCH.
WHY DO I COUNT SIX CHAIRS?
HA! HERE'S WHY!
HEY, FLASH! WHAT DO YOU KNOW THAT THE REST OF US DON'T? WHAT'S UP WITH THIS?
I...
...UMMM...
...I WAS THINKING WE SHOULD...ASK...SUPERMAN TO JOIN.
THOUGHTS?

AS OPPOSED, APPARENTLY, TO ASKING ANOTHER WOMAN...

INTERESTING. I DON'T KNOW THAT I'M THAT IMPRESSED BY HIM... I MEAN, I KNOW THE SPECTRE...

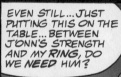

EVEN STILL...JUST PUTTING THIS ON THE TABLE...BETWEEN J'ONN'S STRENGTH AND MY RING, DO WE NEED HIM?

WHY NOT? I MET HIM ONCE. I WAS IMPRESSED, BUT HE SEEMS LIKE A MAN WITH A LOT ON HIS MIND...AND NOT A LOT OF FREE TIME.

YOU KNOW, GUYS...IT'S OKAY TO COME OUT AND SAY THAT YOU'RE NERVOUS ABOUT IT. I AM. I MEAN, HE'S... SUPERMAN.

NOW, WHAT DO YOU REALLY THINK? SHOULD WE TRY TO FIND HIM?

MAYBE.

OR...

...MAYBE HE COULD FIND YOU.

88

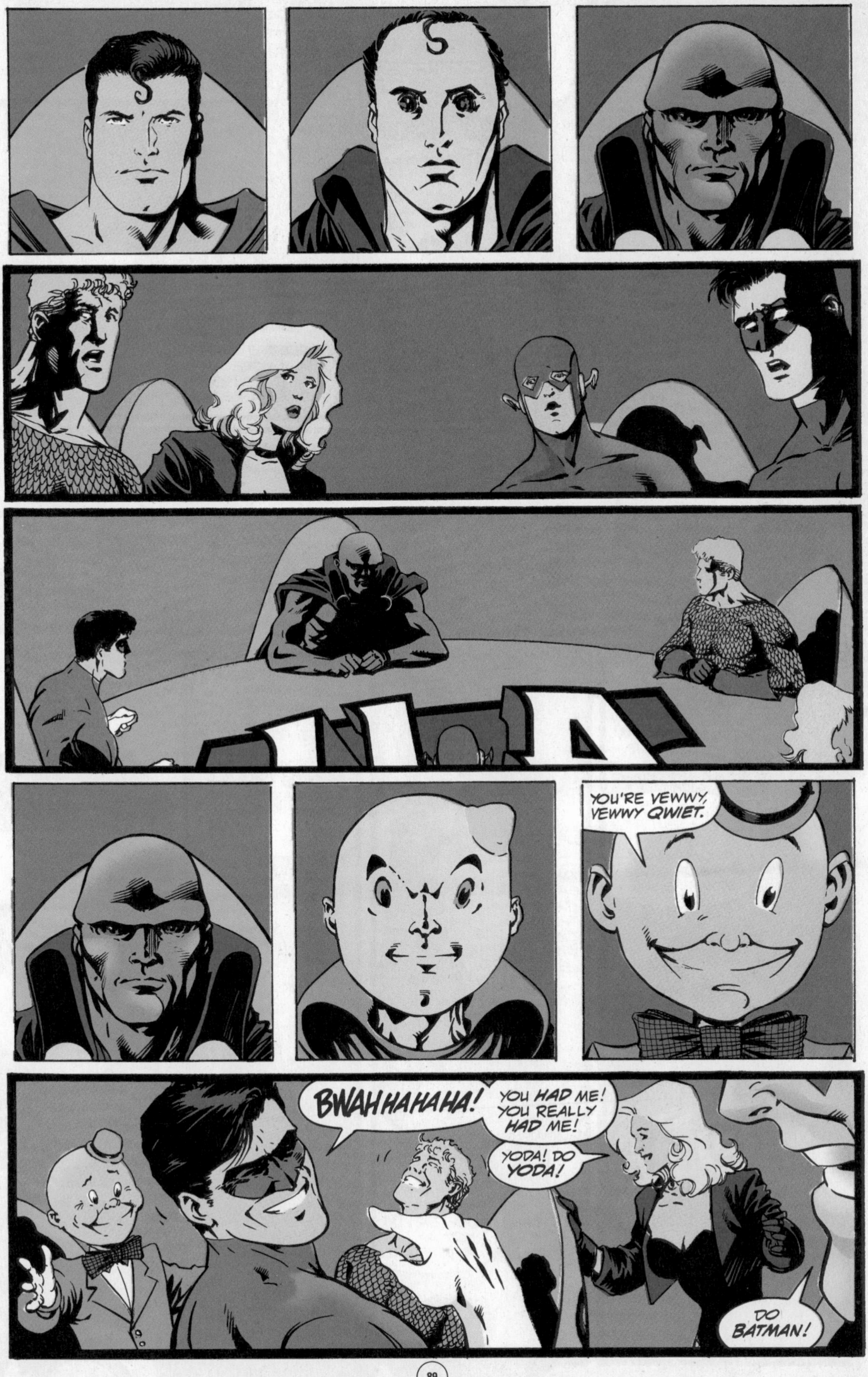
YOU'RE VEWWY, VEWWY QWIET.
BWAHHAHAHA!
YOU HAD ME! YOU REALLY HAD ME!
YODA! DO YODA!
DO BATMAN!

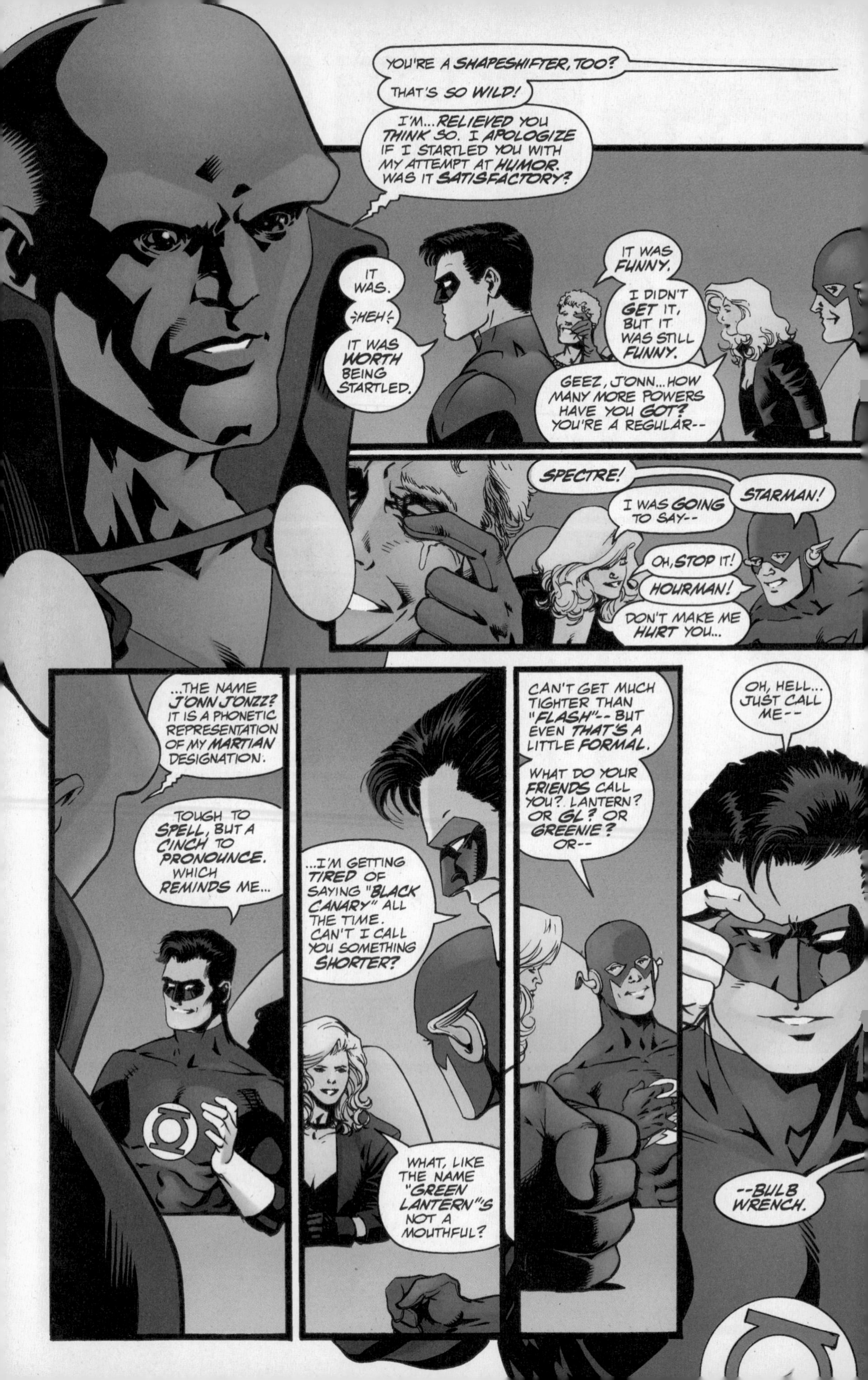

YOU'RE A SHAPESHIFTER, TOO?
THAT'S SO WILD!
I'M...RELIEVED YOU THINK SO. I APOLOGIZE IF I STARTLED YOU WITH MY ATTEMPT AT HUMOR. WAS IT SATISFACTORY?
IT WAS.
HEH
IT WAS WORTH BEING STARTLED.
IT WAS FUNNY.
I DIDN'T GET IT, BUT IT WAS STILL FUNNY.
GEEZ, J'ONN...HOW MANY MORE POWERS HAVE YOU GOT? YOU'RE A REGULAR--
SPECTRE!
STARMAN!
I WAS GOING TO SAY--
OH, STOP IT!
HOURMAN!
DON'T MAKE ME HURT YOU...
...THE NAME J'ONN J'ONZZ? IT IS A PHONETIC REPRESENTATION OF MY MARTIAN DESIGNATION.
TOUGH TO SPELL, BUT A CINCH TO PRONOUNCE. WHICH REMINDS ME...
...I'M GETTING TIRED OF SAYING "BLACK CANARY" ALL THE TIME. CAN'T I CALL YOU SOMETHING SHORTER?
WHAT, LIKE THE NAME "GREEN LANTERN"'S NOT A MOUTHFUL?
CAN'T GET MUCH TIGHTER THAN "FLASH"-- BUT EVEN THAT'S A LITTLE FORMAL.
WHAT DO YOUR FRIENDS CALL YOU? LANTERN? OR GL? OR GREENIE? OR--
OH, HELL... JUST CALL ME--
--BULB WRENCH.

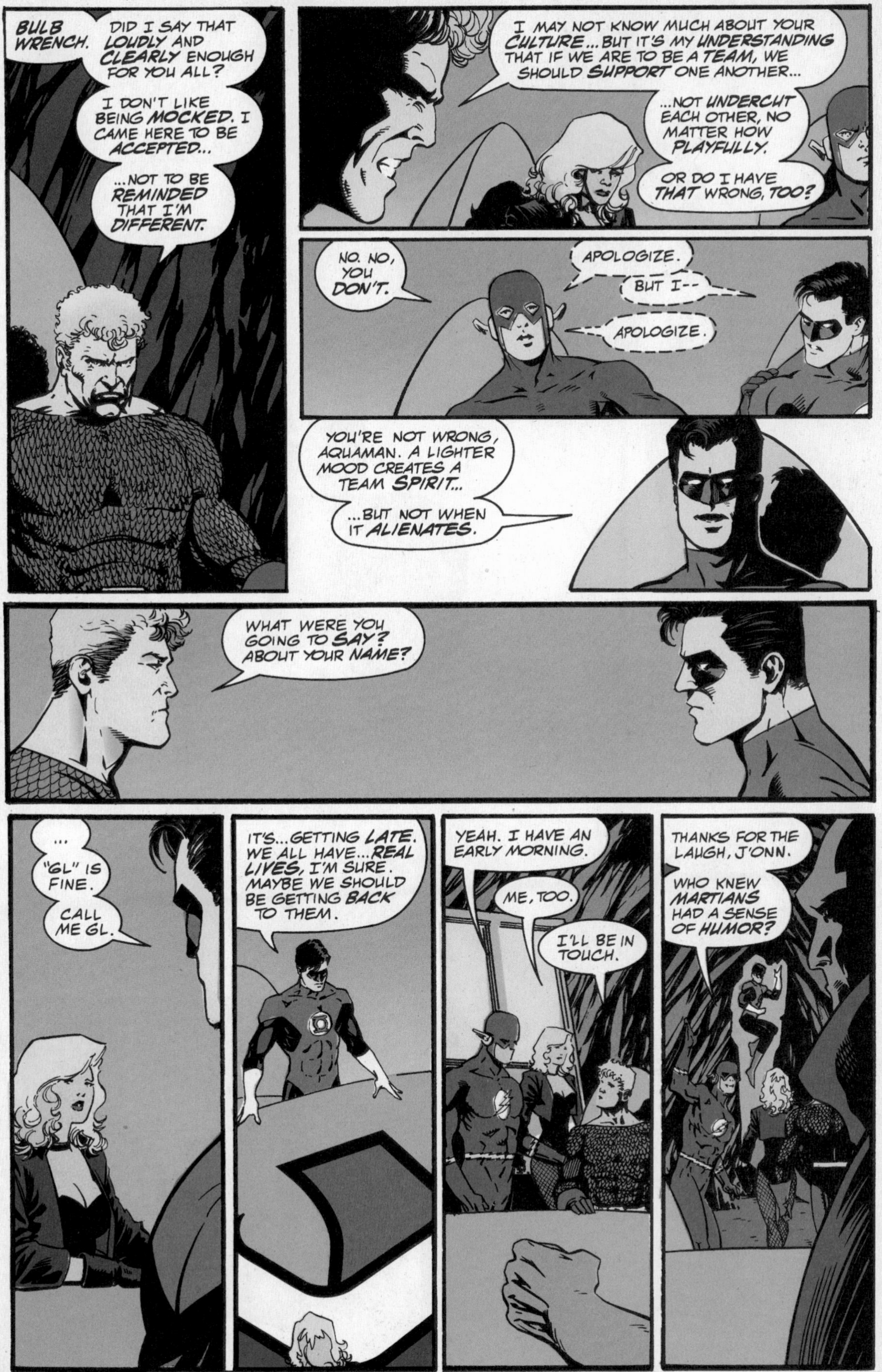
BULB WRENCH.
DID I SAY THAT LOUDLY AND CLEARLY ENOUGH FOR YOU ALL?
I DON'T LIKE BEING MOCKED. I CAME HERE TO BE ACCEPTED...
...NOT TO BE REMINDED THAT I'M DIFFERENT.
I MAY NOT KNOW MUCH ABOUT YOUR CULTURE... BUT IT'S MY UNDERSTANDING THAT IF WE ARE TO BE A TEAM, WE SHOULD SUPPORT ONE ANOTHER...
...NOT UNDERCUT EACH OTHER, NO MATTER HOW PLAYFULLY.
OR DO I HAVE THAT WRONG, TOO?
NO. NO, YOU DON'T.
APOLOGIZE.
BUT I--
APOLOGIZE.
YOU'RE NOT WRONG, AQUAMAN. A LIGHTER MOOD CREATES A TEAM SPIRIT...
...BUT NOT WHEN IT ALIENATES.
WHAT WERE YOU GOING TO SAY? ABOUT YOUR NAME?
...
"GL" IS FINE.
CALL ME GL.
IT'S...GETTING LATE. WE ALL HAVE...REAL LIVES, I'M SURE. MAYBE WE SHOULD BE GETTING BACK TO THEM.
YEAH. I HAVE AN EARLY MORNING.
ME, TOO.
I'LL BE IN TOUCH.
THANKS FOR THE LAUGH, J'ONN.
WHO KNEW MARTIANS HAD A SENSE OF HUMOR?

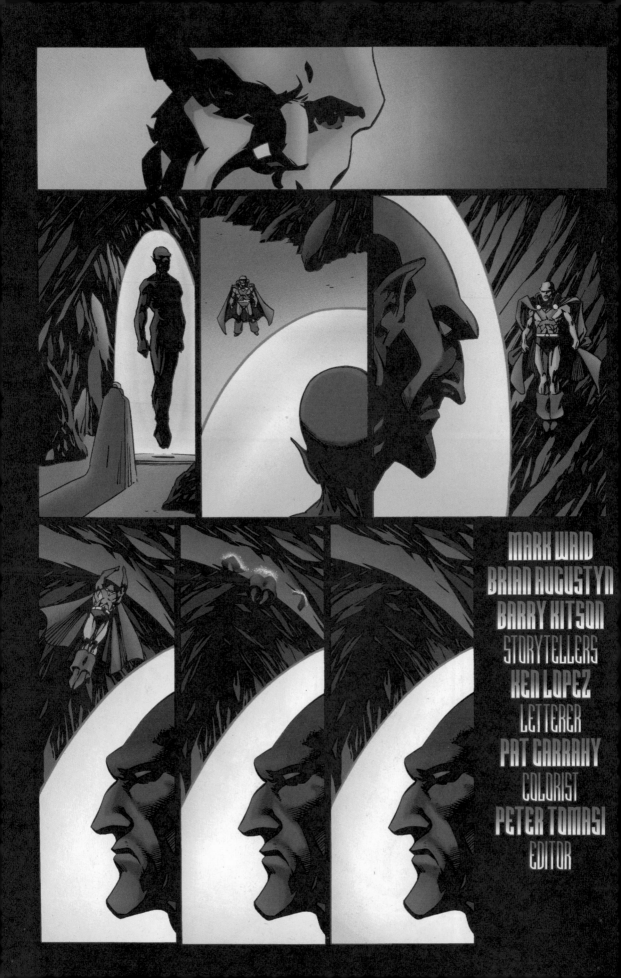

MARK WAID
BRIAN AUGUSTYN
BARRY KITSON
STORYTELLERS
KEN LOPEZ
LETTERER
PAT GARRAHY
COLORIST
PETER TOMASI
EDITOR

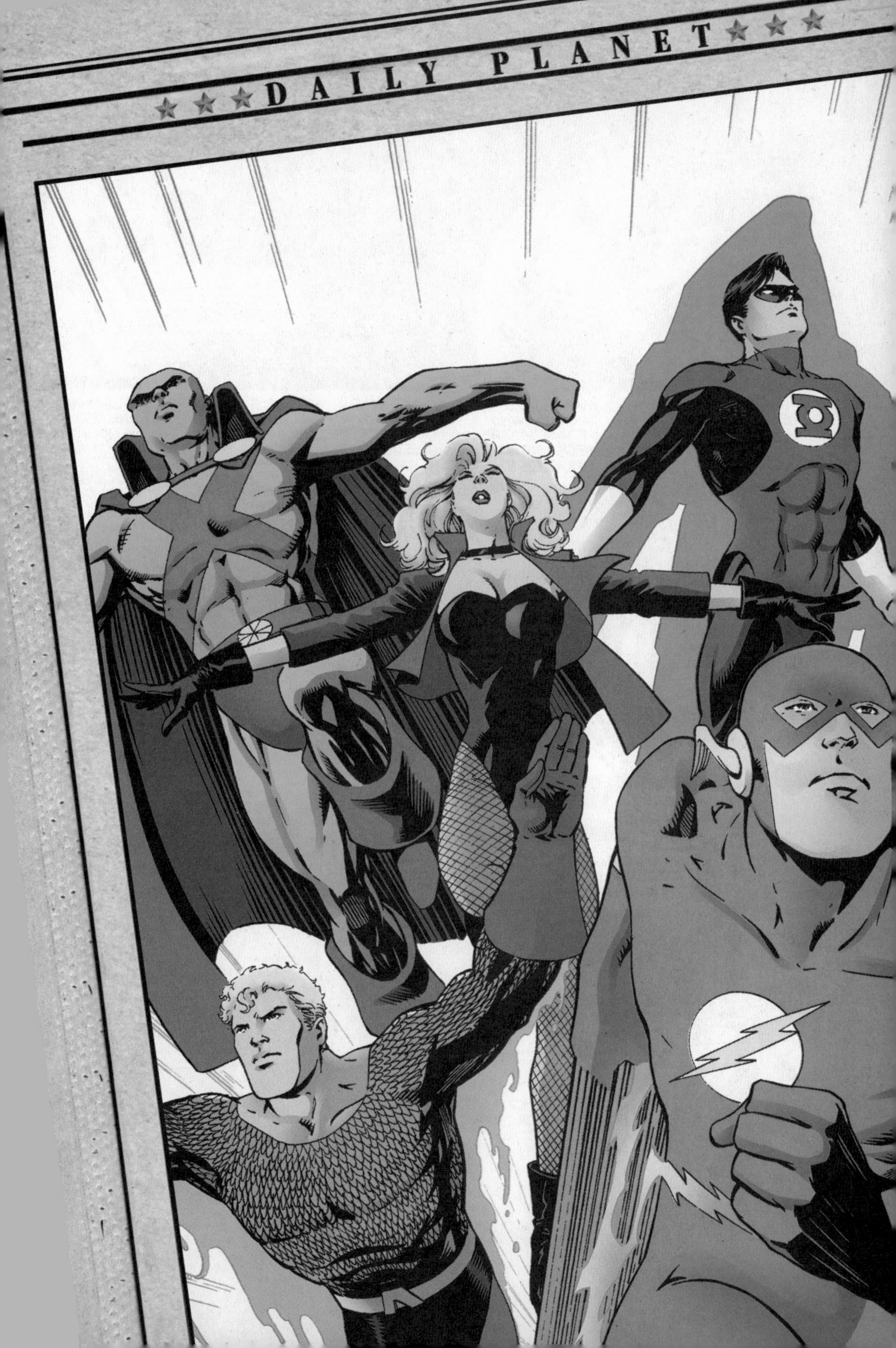
DAILY PLANET

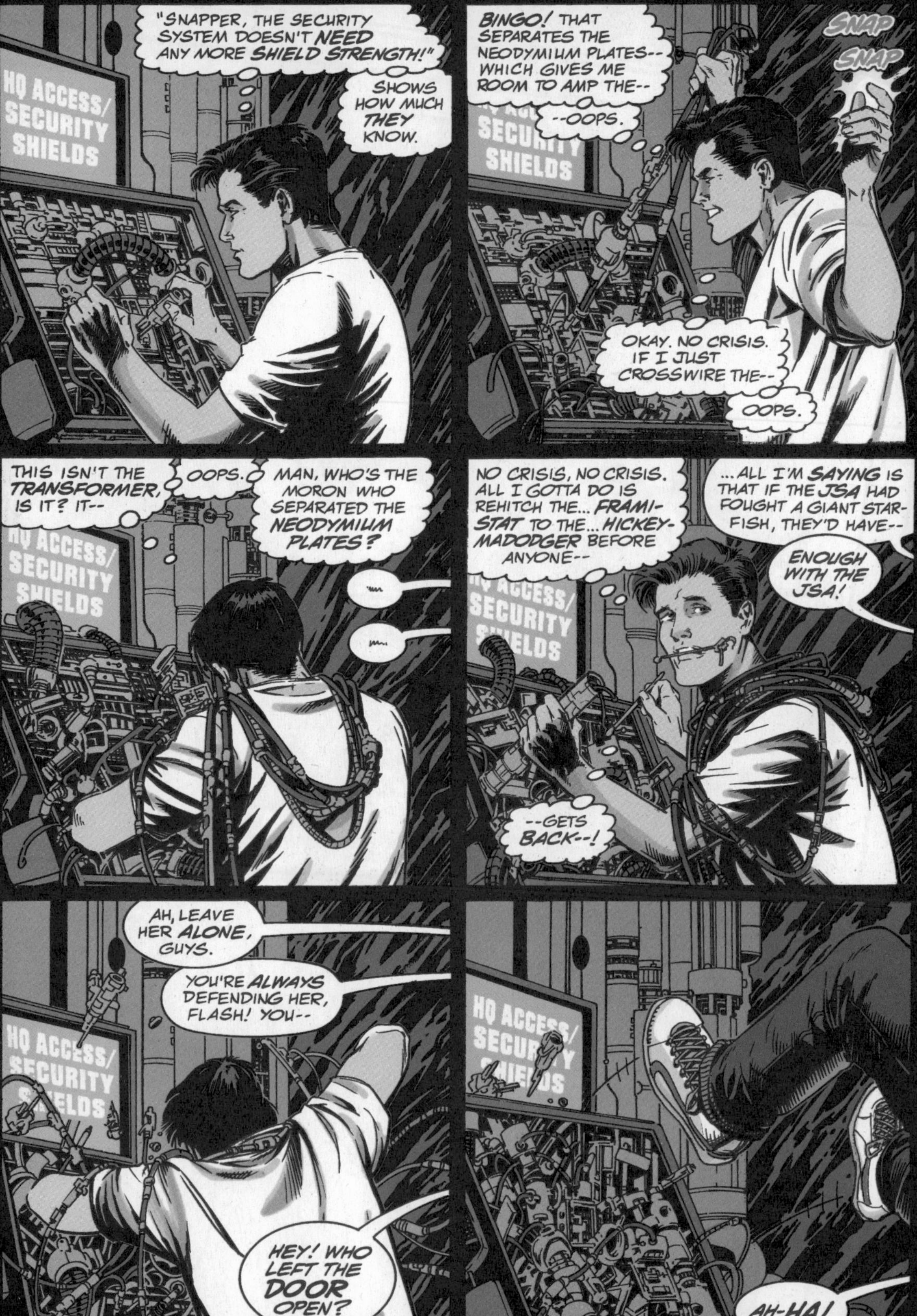
"SNAPPER, THE SECURITY SYSTEM DOESN'T NEED ANY MORE SHIELD STRENGTH!"
SHOWS HOW MUCH THEY KNOW.
HQ ACCESS/ SECURITY SHIELDS
BINGO! THAT SEPARATES THE NEODYMIUM PLATES-- WHICH GIVES ME ROOM TO AMP THE--
--OOPS.
SNAP
SNAP
OKAY. NO CRISIS. IF I JUST CROSSWIRE THE--
OOPS.
THIS ISN'T THE TRANSFORMER, IS IT? IT--
OOPS.
MAN, WHO'S THE MORON WHO SEPARATED THE NEODYMIUM PLATES?
NO CRISIS, NO CRISIS. ALL I GOTTA DO IS REHITCH THE... FRAMI-STAT TO THE... HICKEY-MADODGER BEFORE ANYONE--
...ALL I'M SAYING IS THAT IF THE JSA HAD FOUGHT A GIANT STAR-FISH, THEY'D HAVE--
ENOUGH WITH THE JSA!
--GETS BACK--!
AH, LEAVE HER ALONE, GUYS.
YOU'RE ALWAYS DEFENDING HER, FLASH! YOU--
HEY! WHO LEFT THE DOOR OPEN?
AH-HA!

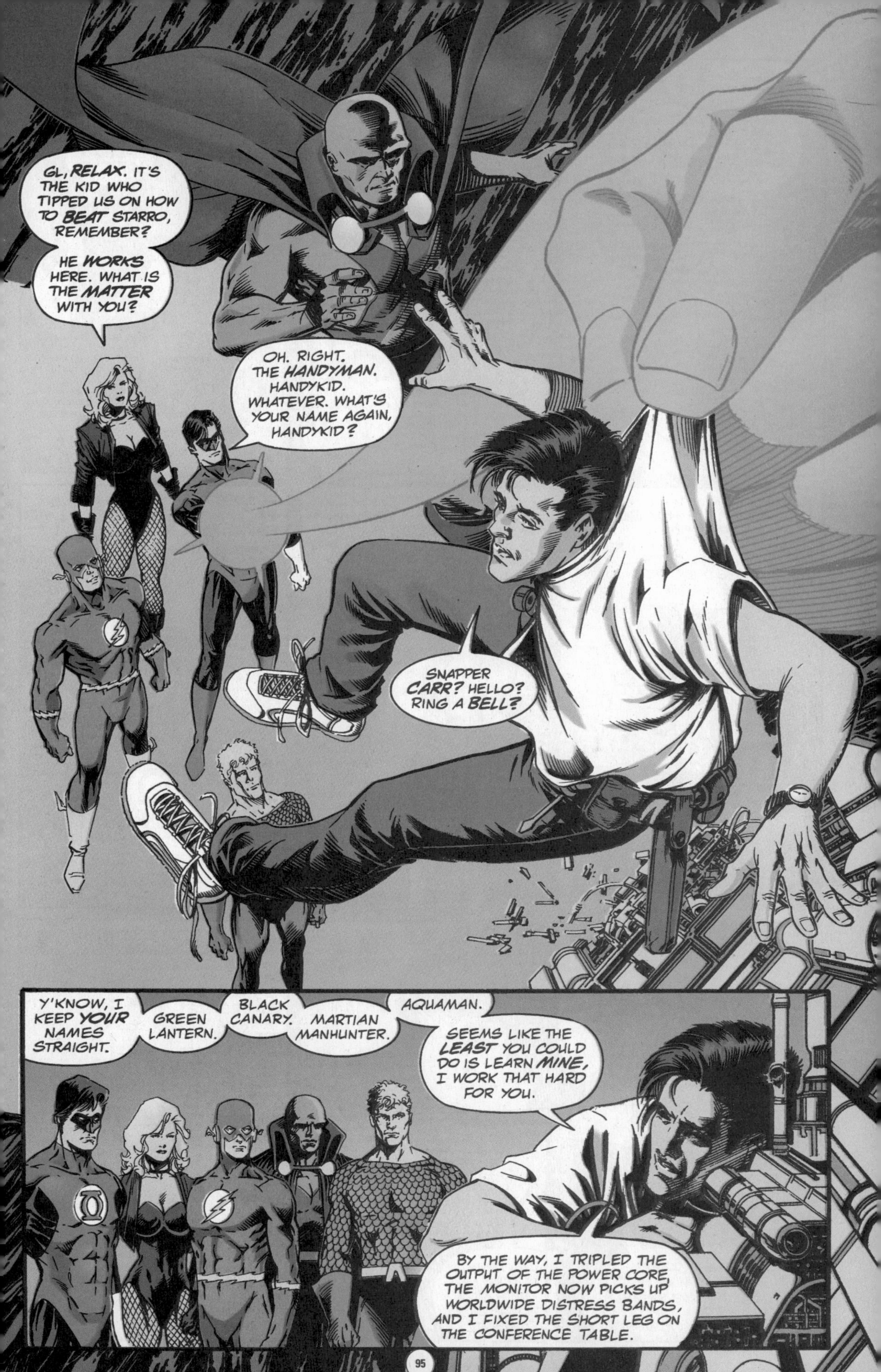
GL, RELAX. IT'S THE KID WHO TIPPED US ON HOW TO BEAT STARRO, REMEMBER?
HE WORKS HERE. WHAT IS THE MATTER WITH YOU?
OH. RIGHT. THE HANDYMAN. HANDYKID. WHATEVER. WHAT'S YOUR NAME AGAIN, HANDYKID?
SNAPPER CARR? HELLO? RING A BELL?
Y'KNOW, I KEEP YOUR NAMES STRAIGHT.
GREEN LANTERN.
BLACK CANARY.
MARTIAN MANHUNTER.
AQUAMAN.
SEEMS LIKE THE LEAST YOU COULD DO IS LEARN MINE, I WORK THAT HARD FOR YOU.
BY THE WAY, I TRIPLED THE OUTPUT OF THE POWER CORE, THE MONITOR NOW PICKS UP WORLDWIDE DISTRESS BANDS, AND I FIXED THE SHORT LEG ON THE CONFERENCE TABLE.

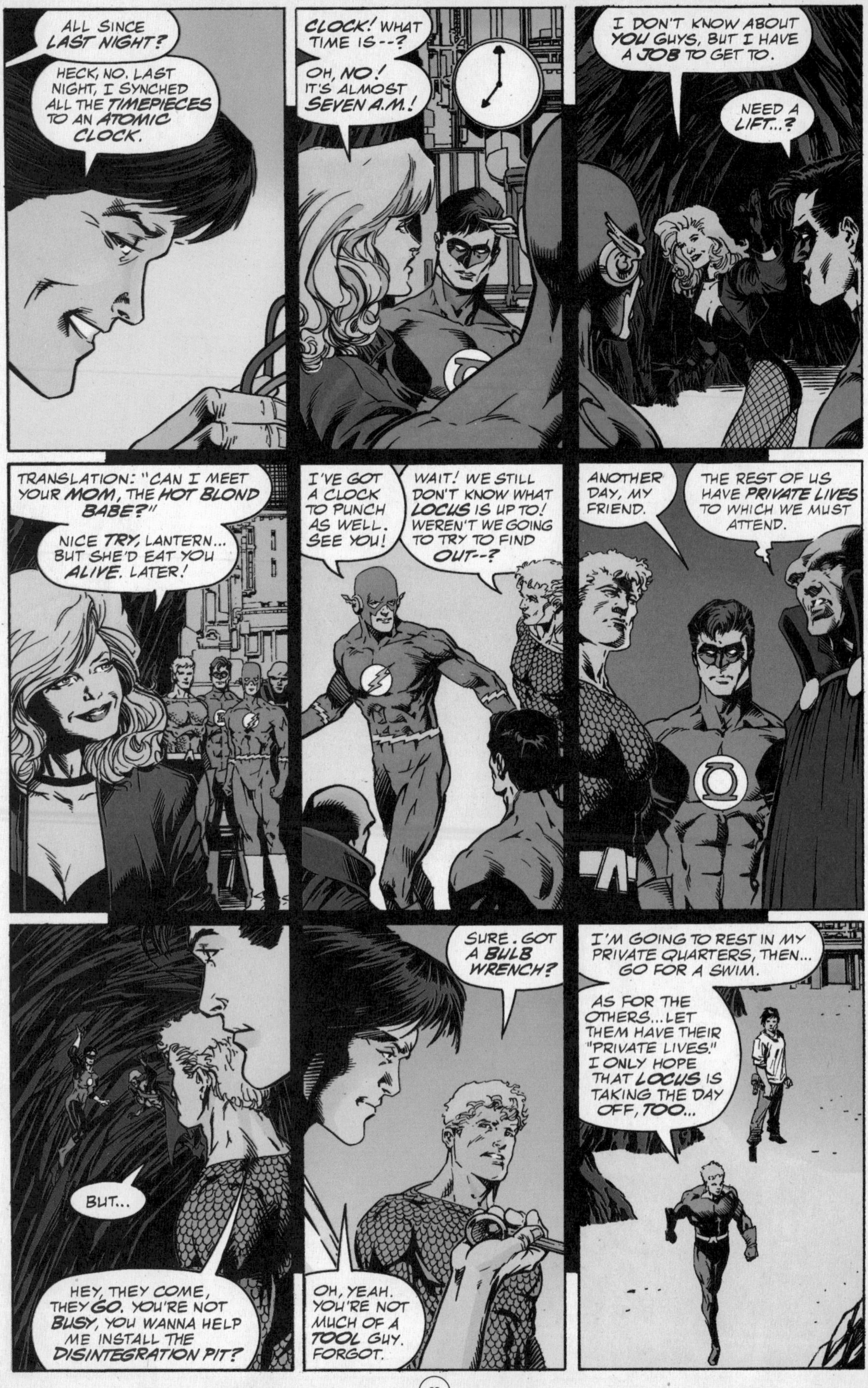
ALL SINCE LAST NIGHT?
HECK, NO. LAST NIGHT, I SYNCHED ALL THE TIMEPIECES TO AN ATOMIC CLOCK.
CLOCK! WHAT TIME IS--?
OH, NO! IT'S ALMOST SEVEN A.M.!
I DON'T KNOW ABOUT YOU GUYS, BUT I HAVE A JOB TO GET TO.
NEED A LIFT...?
TRANSLATION: "CAN I MEET YOUR MOM, THE HOT BLOND BABE?"
NICE TRY, LANTERN... BUT SHE'D EAT YOU ALIVE. LATER!
I'VE GOT A CLOCK TO PUNCH AS WELL. SEE YOU!
WAIT! WE STILL DON'T KNOW WHAT LOCUS IS UP TO! WEREN'T WE GOING TO TRY TO FIND OUT--?
ANOTHER DAY, MY FRIEND.
THE REST OF US HAVE PRIVATE LIVES TO WHICH WE MUST ATTEND.
BUT...
HEY, THEY COME, THEY GO. YOU'RE NOT BUSY, YOU WANNA HELP ME INSTALL THE DISINTEGRATION PIT?
SURE. GOT A BULB WRENCH?
OH, YEAH. YOU'RE NOT MUCH OF A TOOL GUY. FORGOT.
I'M GOING TO REST IN MY PRIVATE QUARTERS, THEN... GO FOR A SWIM.
AS FOR THE OTHERS... LET THEM HAVE THEIR "PRIVATE LIVES." I ONLY HOPE THAT LOCUS IS TAKING THE DAY OFF, TOO...

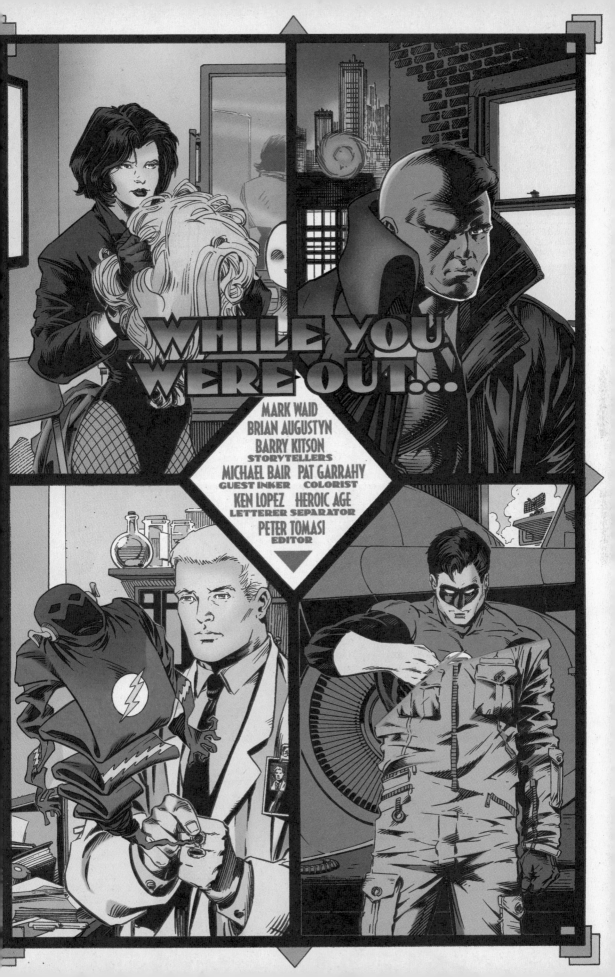

WHILE YOU WERE OUT...!

MARK WAID
BRIAN AUGUSTYN
BARRY KITSON
STORYTELLERS

MICHAEL BAIR   PAT GARRAHY
GUEST INKER   COLORIST

KEN LOPEZ   HEROIC AGE
LETTERER   SEPARATOR

PETER TOMASI
EDITOR

THAT'S THE *STARRO* TENTACLE? PUT IT IN *CRYO*. IT'S GOT *REGENERATIVE* CAPABILITIES.

HOW'S THE *NEW* PROJECT GOING?

LOOK FOR YOURSELF.

I SEE THE ENTRAPMENT DEVICE IS READY. AND THE *RAY PROJECTOR?*

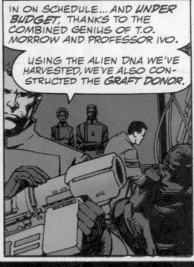

IN ON SCHEDULE... AND *UNDER BUDGET*, THANKS TO THE COMBINED GENIUS OF T.O. MORROW AND PROFESSOR IVO.

USING THE ALIEN DNA WE'VE HARVESTED, WE'VE ALSO CON-STRUCTED THE *GRAFT DONOR.*

NOW ALL WE NEED IS OUR *TEST SUBJECT.* WHO WAS *CHOSEN?*

WE WENT WITH THE *BLUE BEETLE.*

HE'S IN *CUSTODY,* THEN?

"SOON."

NO... GET AWAY...

GET AWAY!

WHAT ABOUT THE *JLA?*

DON'T WORRY. THEY'RE STILL FULLY UNDER INVESTIGATION...

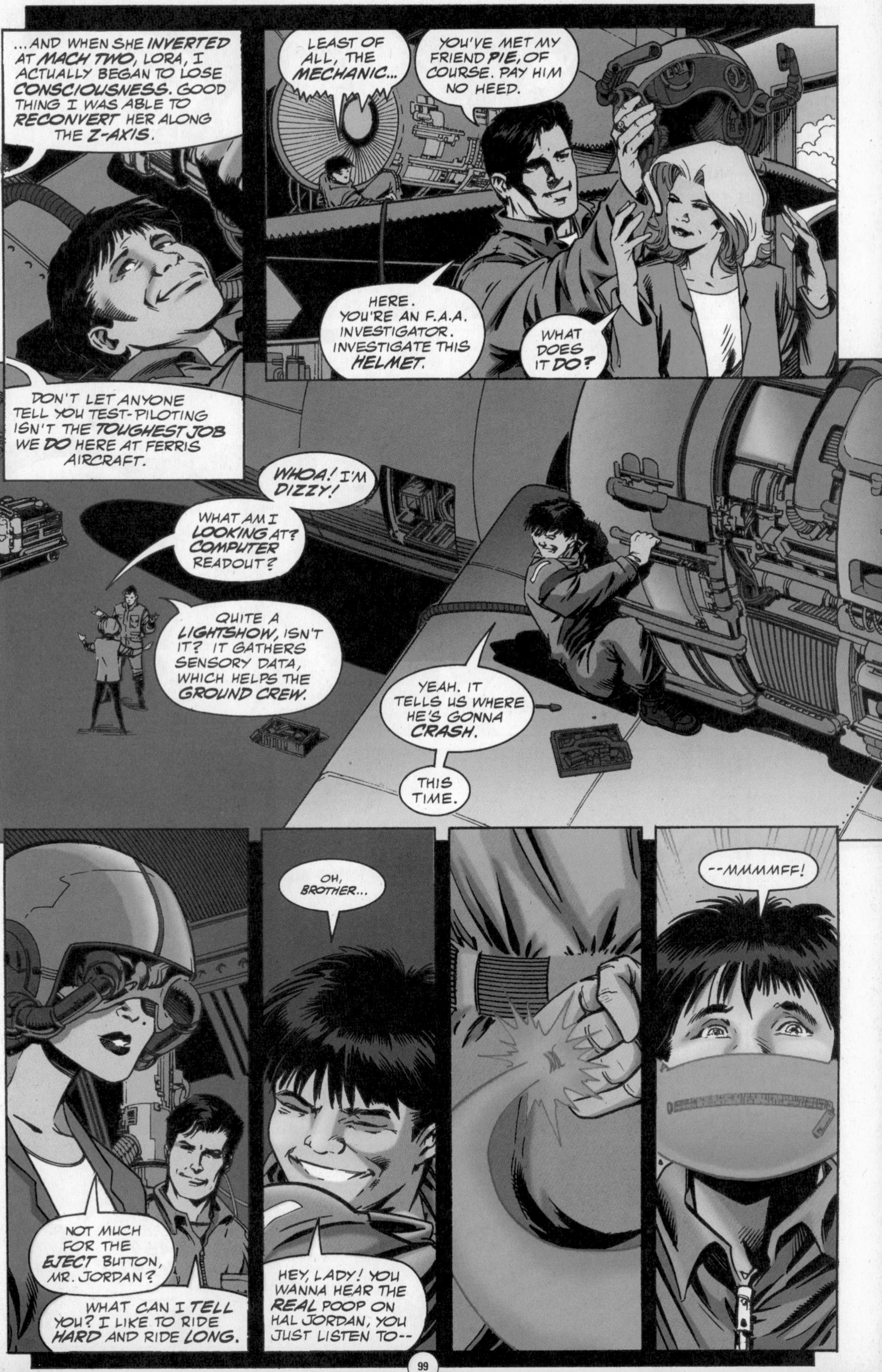
...AND WHEN SHE INVERTED AT MACH TWO, LORA, I ACTUALLY BEGAN TO LOSE CONSCIOUSNESS. GOOD THING I WAS ABLE TO RECONVERT HER ALONG THE Z-AXIS.
LEAST OF ALL, THE MECHANIC...
YOU'VE MET MY FRIEND PIE, OF COURSE. PAY HIM NO HEED.
HERE. YOU'RE AN F.A.A. INVESTIGATOR. INVESTIGATE THIS HELMET.
WHAT DOES IT DO?
DON'T LET ANYONE TELL YOU TEST-PILOTING ISN'T THE TOUGHEST JOB WE DO HERE AT FERRIS AIRCRAFT.
WHOA! I'M DIZZY!
WHAT AM I LOOKING AT? COMPUTER READOUT?
QUITE A LIGHTSHOW, ISN'T IT? IT GATHERS SENSORY DATA, WHICH HELPS THE GROUND CREW.
YEAH. IT TELLS US WHERE HE'S GONNA CRASH.
THIS TIME.
NOT MUCH FOR THE EJECT BUTTON, MR. JORDAN?
WHAT CAN I TELL YOU? I LIKE TO RIDE HARD AND RIDE LONG.
OH, BROTHER...
HEY, LADY! YOU WANNA HEAR THE REAL POOP ON HAL JORDAN, YOU JUST LISTEN TO--
--MMMMFF!

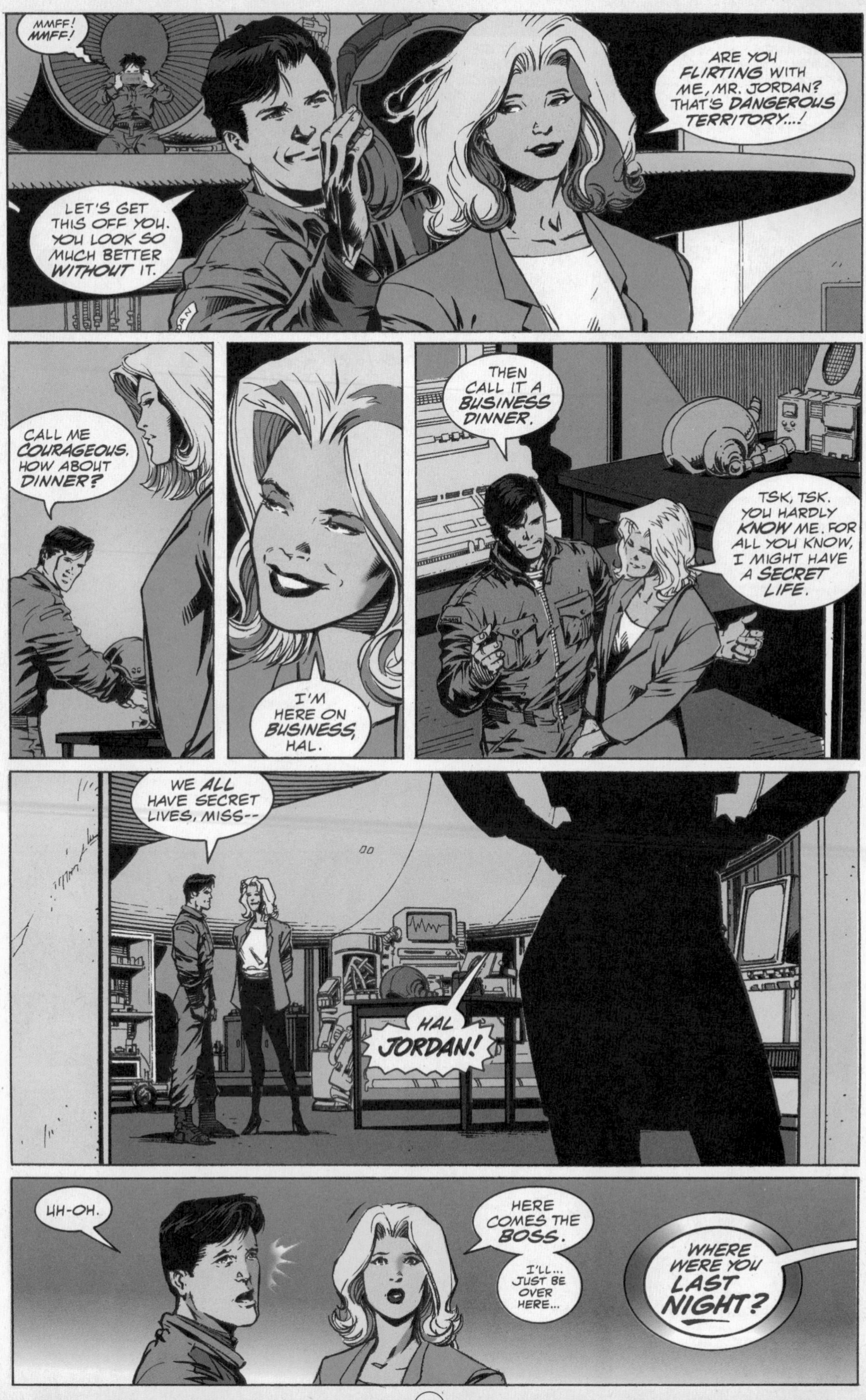
MMFF! MMFF!
ARE YOU FLIRTING WITH ME, MR. JORDAN? THAT'S DANGEROUS TERRITORY...!
LET'S GET THIS OFF YOU. YOU LOOK SO MUCH BETTER WITHOUT IT.
CALL ME COURAGEOUS. HOW ABOUT DINNER?
I'M HERE ON BUSINESS, HAL.
THEN CALL IT A BUSINESS DINNER.
TSK, TSK. YOU HARDLY KNOW ME. FOR ALL YOU KNOW, I MIGHT HAVE A SECRET LIFE.
WE ALL HAVE SECRET LIVES, MISS--
HAL JORDAN!
UH-OH.
HERE COMES THE BOSS.
I'LL... JUST BE OVER HERE...
WHERE WERE YOU LAST NIGHT?

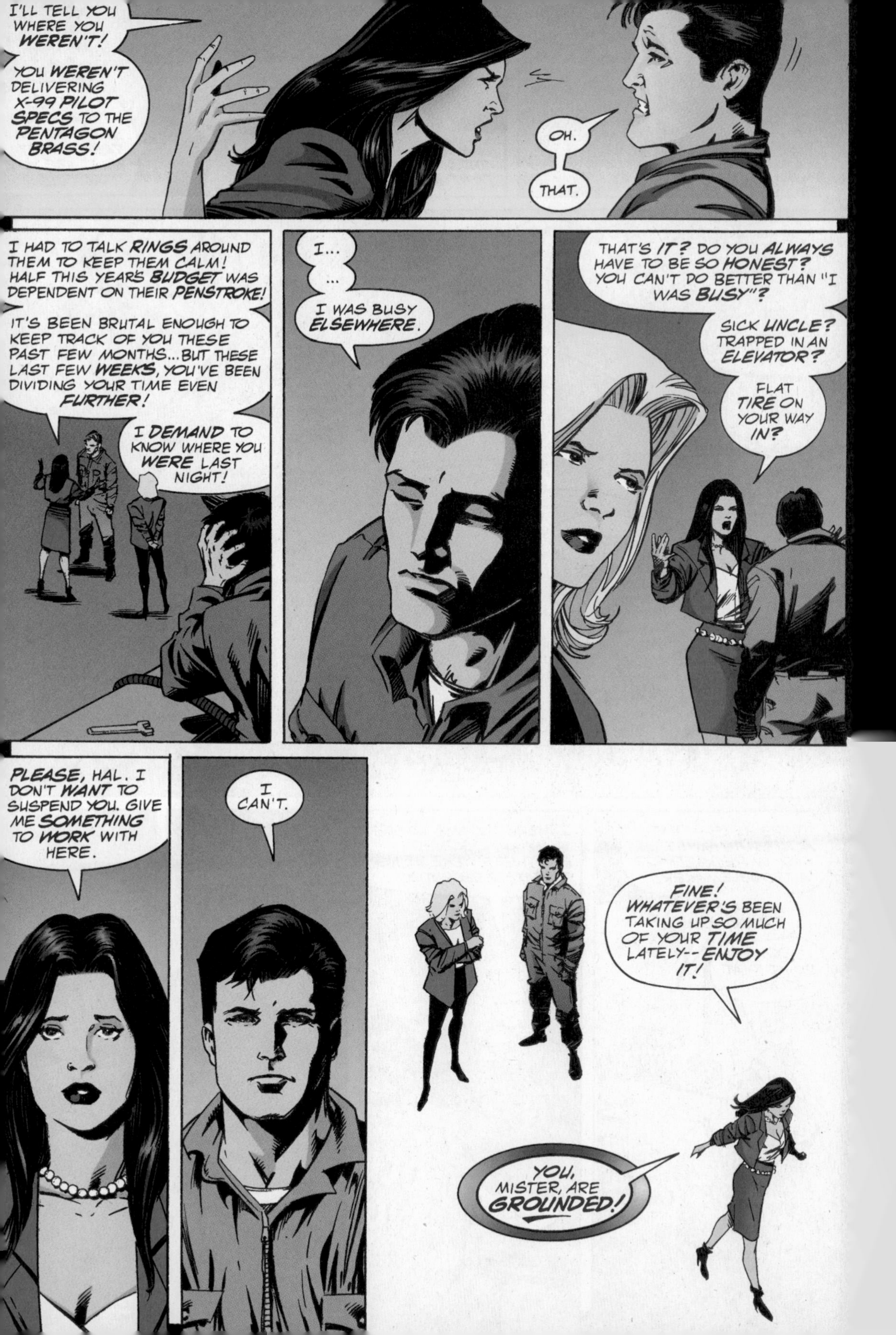
I'LL TELL YOU WHERE YOU WEREN'T!
YOU WEREN'T DELIVERING X-99 PILOT SPECS TO THE PENTAGON BRASS!
OH.
THAT.
I HAD TO TALK RINGS AROUND THEM TO KEEP THEM CALM! HALF THIS YEAR'S BUDGET WAS DEPENDENT ON THEIR PENSTROKE!
IT'S BEEN BRUTAL ENOUGH TO KEEP TRACK OF YOU THESE PAST FEW MONTHS... BUT THESE LAST FEW WEEKS, YOU'VE BEEN DIVIDING YOUR TIME EVEN FURTHER!
I DEMAND TO KNOW WHERE YOU WERE LAST NIGHT!
I...
...
I WAS BUSY ELSEWHERE.
THAT'S IT? DO YOU ALWAYS HAVE TO BE SO HONEST? YOU CAN'T DO BETTER THAN "I WAS BUSY"?
SICK UNCLE? TRAPPED IN AN ELEVATOR?
FLAT TIRE ON YOUR WAY IN?
PLEASE, HAL. I DON'T WANT TO SUSPEND YOU. GIVE ME SOMETHING TO WORK WITH HERE.
I CAN'T.
FINE! WHATEVER'S BEEN TAKING UP SO MUCH OF YOUR TIME LATELY--ENJOY IT!
YOU, MISTER, ARE GROUNDED!

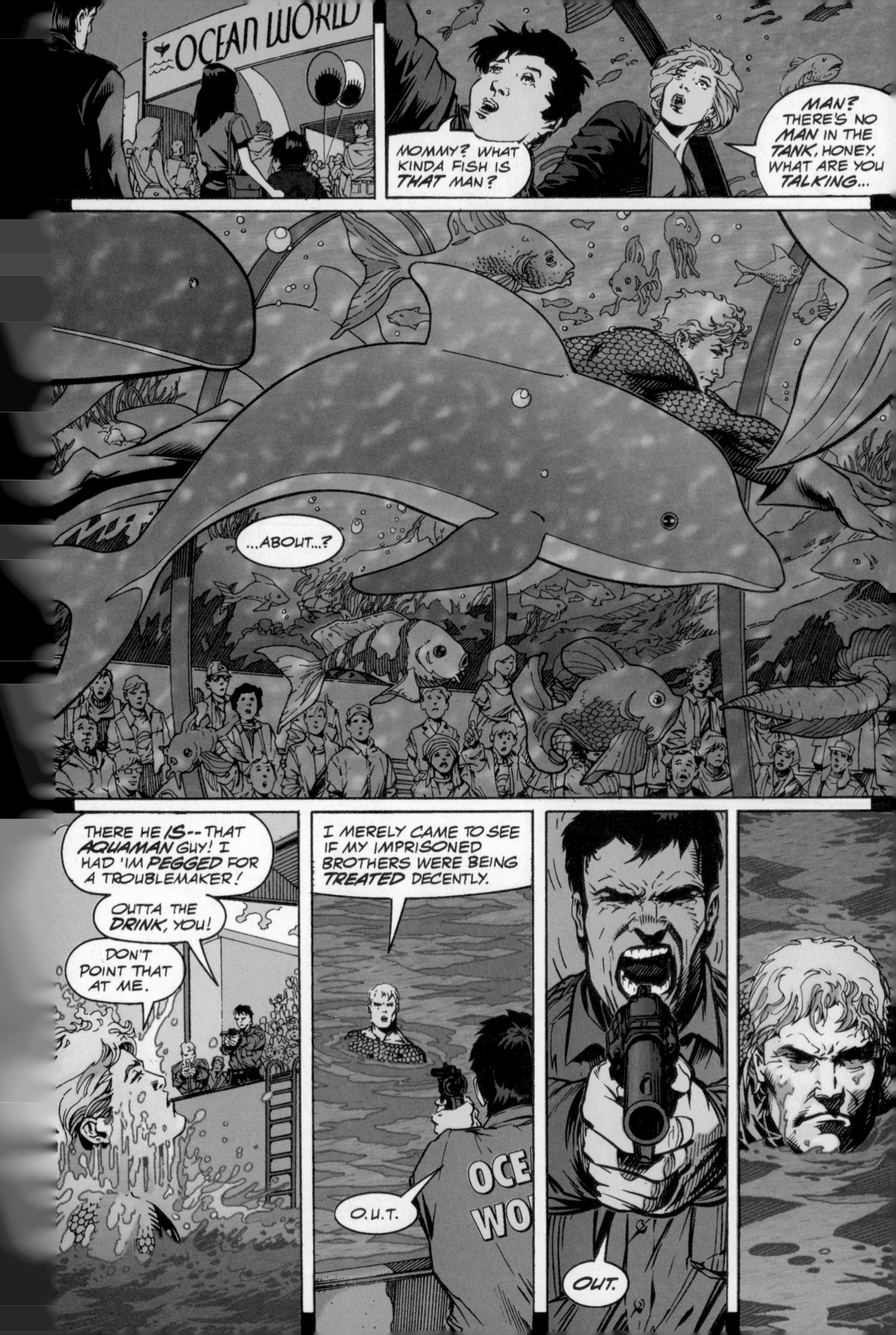
OCEAN WORLD
MOMMY? WHAT KINDA FISH IS THAT MAN?
MAN? THERE'S NO MAN IN THE TANK, HONEY. WHAT ARE YOU TALKING...
...ABOUT...?
THERE HE IS--THAT AQUAMAN GUY! I HAD 'IM PEGGED FOR A TROUBLEMAKER!
OUTTA THE DRINK, YOU!
DON'T POINT THAT AT ME.
I MERELY CAME TO SEE IF MY IMPRISONED BROTHERS WERE BEING TREATED DECENTLY.
O.U.T.
OUT.

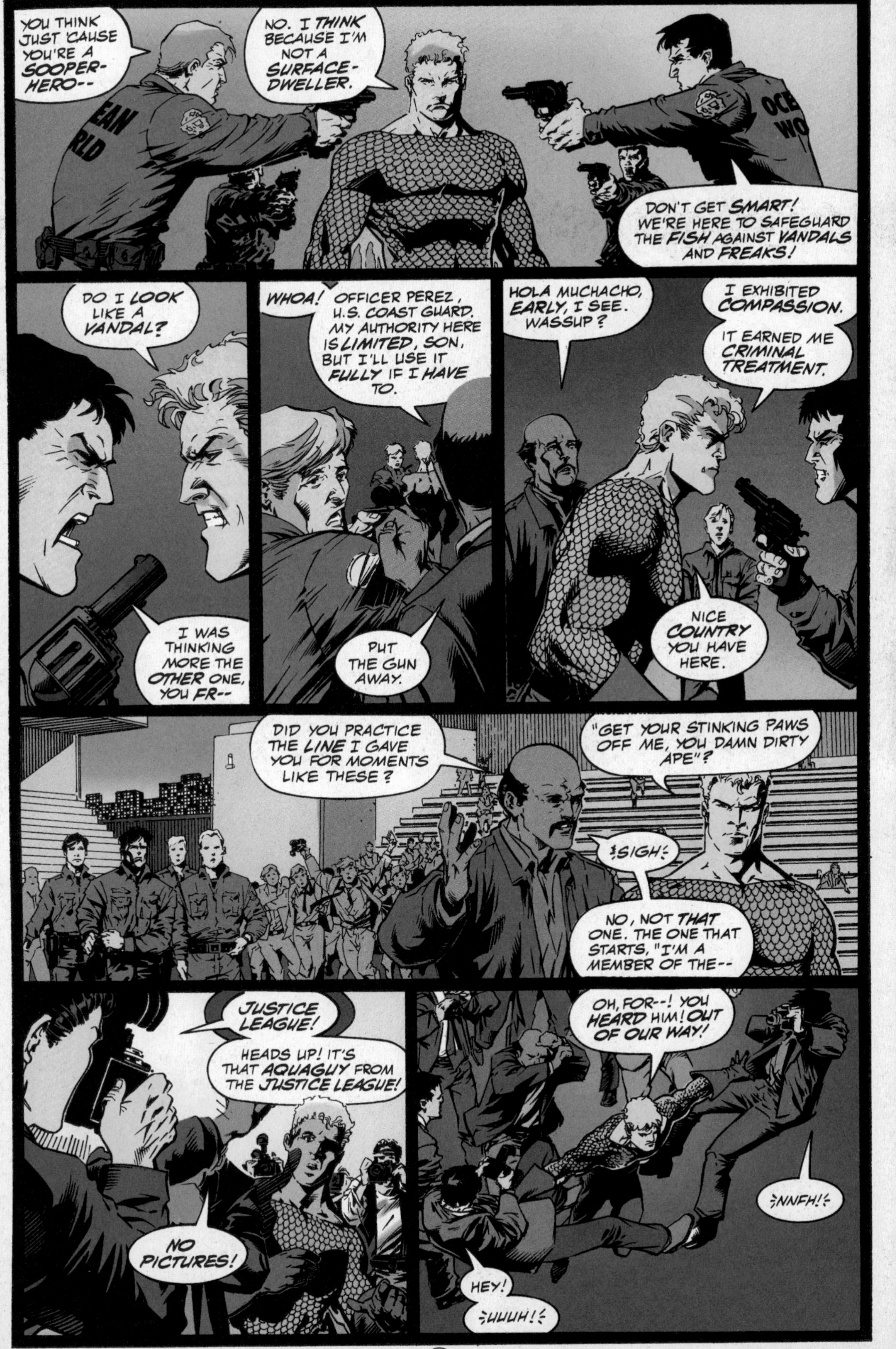
YOU THINK JUST 'CAUSE YOU'RE A SOOPER-HERO--
NO. I THINK BECAUSE I'M NOT A SURFACE-DWELLER.
DON'T GET SMART! WE'RE HERE TO SAFEGUARD THE FISH AGAINST VANDALS AND FREAKS!
DO I LOOK LIKE A VANDAL?
I WAS THINKING MORE THE OTHER ONE, YOU FR--
WHOA!
OFFICER PEREZ, U.S. COAST GUARD. MY AUTHORITY HERE IS LIMITED, SON, BUT I'LL USE IT FULLY IF I HAVE TO.
PUT THE GUN AWAY.
HOLA MUCHACHO, EARLY, I SEE. WASSUP?
I EXHIBITED COMPASSION.
IT EARNED ME CRIMINAL TREATMENT.
NICE COUNTRY YOU HAVE HERE.
DID YOU PRACTICE THE LINE I GAVE YOU FOR MOMENTS LIKE THESE?
"GET YOUR STINKING PAWS OFF ME, YOU DAMN DIRTY APE"?
SIGH
NO, NOT THAT ONE. THE ONE THAT STARTS, "I'M A MEMBER OF THE--
JUSTICE LEAGUE!
HEADS UP! IT'S THAT AQUAGUY FROM THE JUSTICE LEAGUE!
NO PICTURES!
OH, FOR--! YOU HEARD HIM! OUT OF OUR WAY!
NNFH!
HEY!
UUUH!

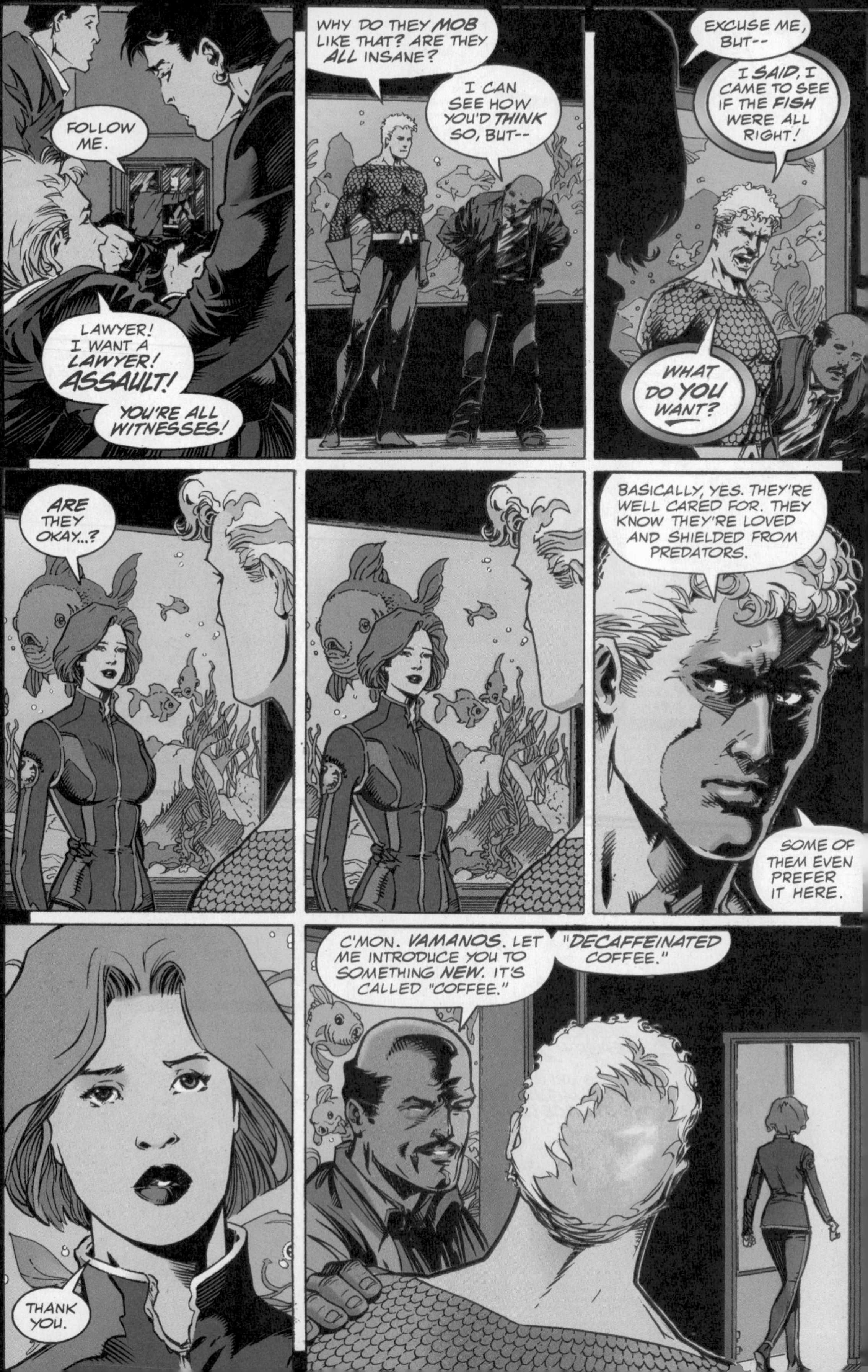
FOLLOW ME.
LAWYER! I WANT A LAWYER! ASSAULT!
YOU'RE ALL WITNESSES!
WHY DO THEY MOB LIKE THAT? ARE THEY ALL INSANE?
I CAN SEE HOW YOU'D THINK SO, BUT--
EXCUSE ME, BUT--
I SAID, I CAME TO SEE IF THE FISH WERE ALL RIGHT!
WHAT DO YOU WANT?
ARE THEY OKAY...?
BASICALLY, YES. THEY'RE WELL CARED FOR. THEY KNOW THEY'RE LOVED AND SHIELDED FROM PREDATORS.
SOME OF THEM EVEN PREFER IT HERE.
THANK YOU.
C'MON. VAMANOS. LET ME INTRODUCE YOU TO SOMETHING NEW. IT'S CALLED "COFFEE."
"DECAFFEINATED COFFEE."

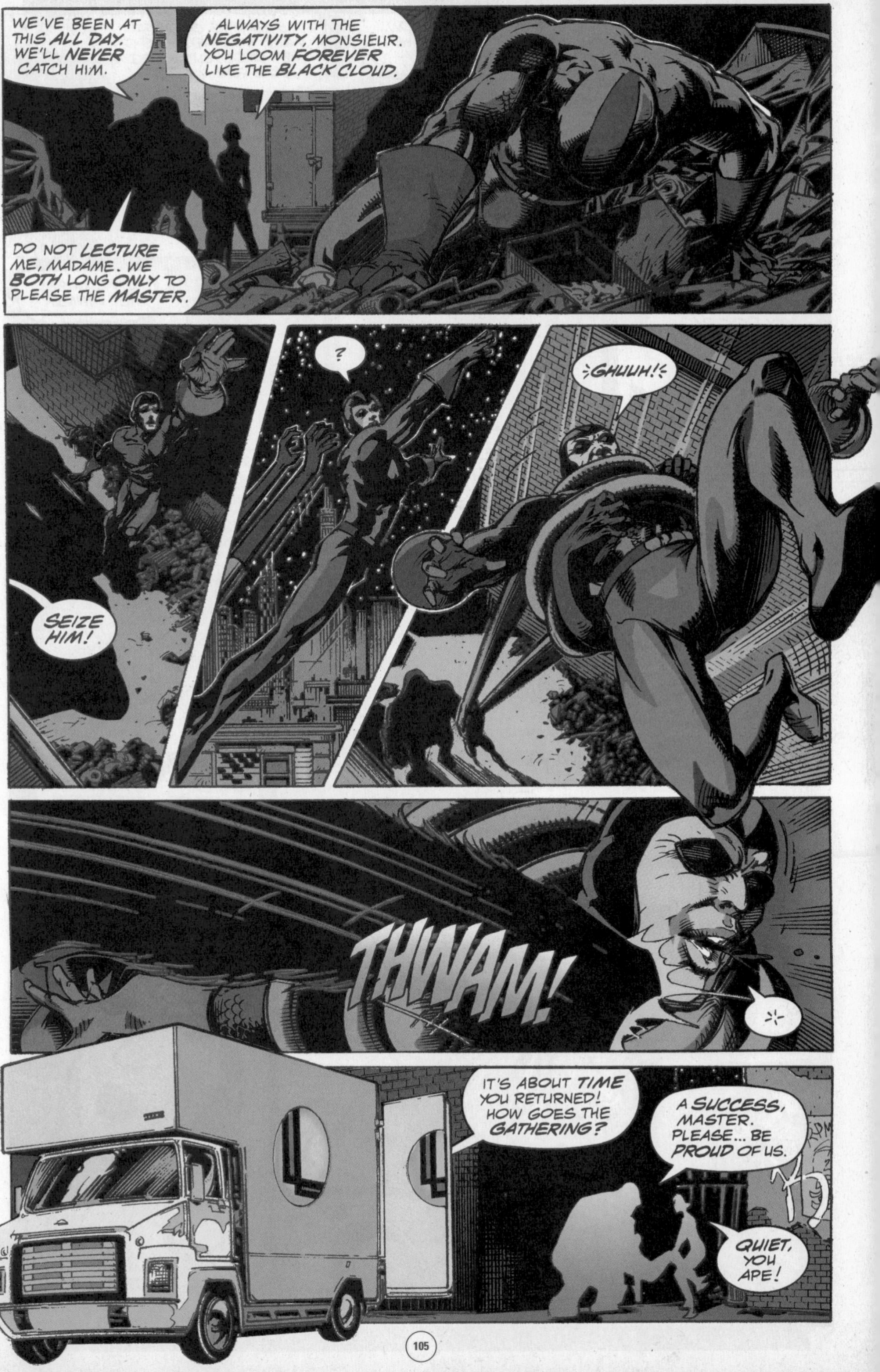
WE'VE BEEN AT THIS ALL DAY. WE'LL NEVER CATCH HIM.
ALWAYS WITH THE NEGATIVITY, MONSIEUR. YOU LOOM FOREVER LIKE THE BLACK CLOUD.
DO NOT LECTURE ME, MADAME. WE BOTH LONG ONLY TO PLEASE THE MASTER.
SEIZE HIM!
?
GHUUH!
THWAM!
IT'S ABOUT TIME YOU RETURNED! HOW GOES THE GATHERING?
A SUCCESS, MASTER. PLEASE... BE PROUD OF US.
QUIET, YOU APE!

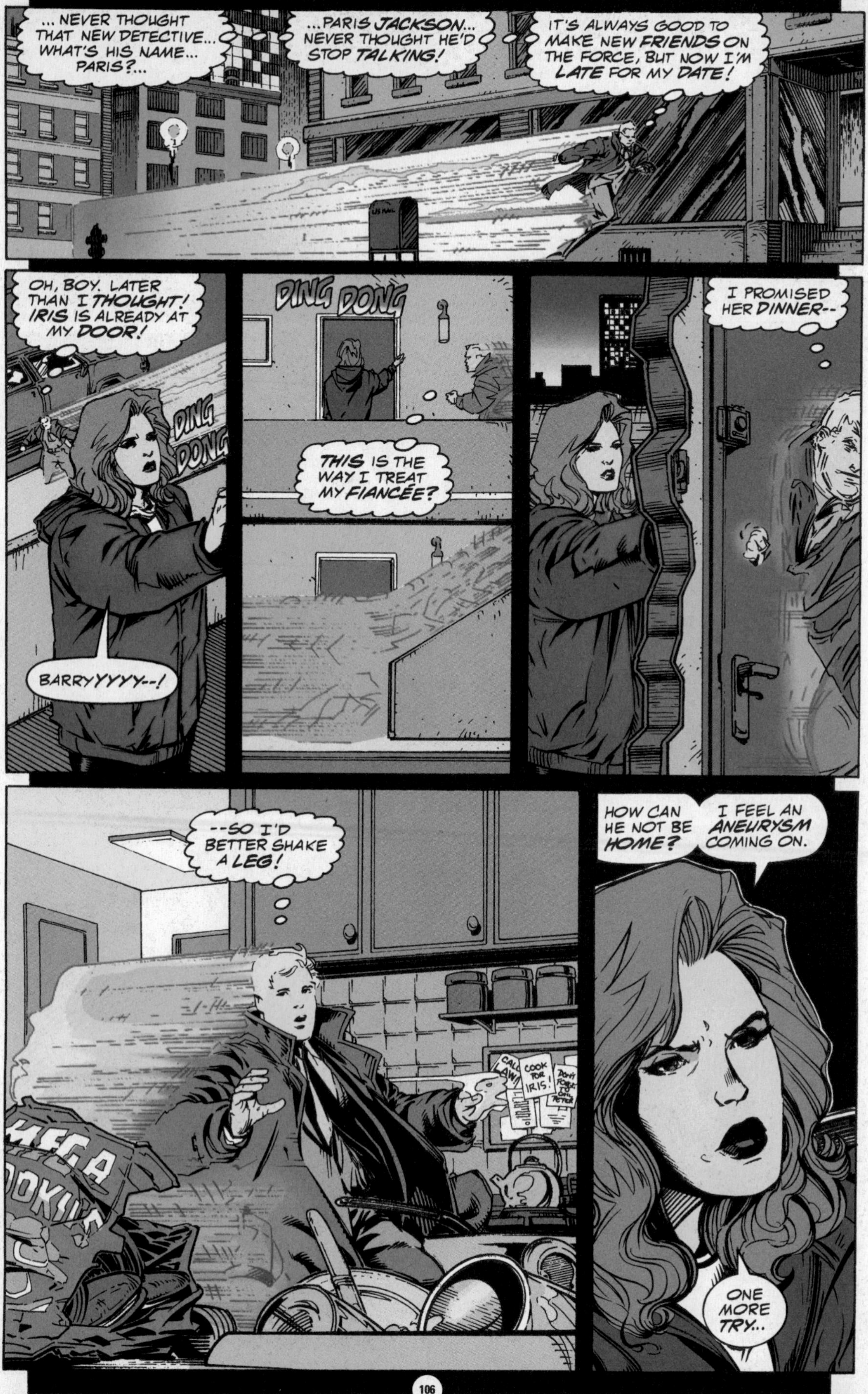
...NEVER THOUGHT THAT NEW DETECTIVE... WHAT'S HIS NAME... PARIS?...
...PARIS JACKSON... NEVER THOUGHT HE'D STOP TALKING!
IT'S ALWAYS GOOD TO MAKE NEW FRIENDS ON THE FORCE, BUT NOW I'M LATE FOR MY DATE!
OH, BOY. LATER THAN I THOUGHT! IRIS IS ALREADY AT MY DOOR!
DING DONG
BARRYYYY--!
DING DONG
THIS IS THE WAY I TREAT MY FIANCÉE?
I PROMISED HER DINNER--
--SO I'D BETTER SHAKE A LEG!
COOK FOR IRIS!
HOW CAN HE NOT BE HOME?
I FEEL AN ANEURYSM COMING ON.
ONE MORE TRY...

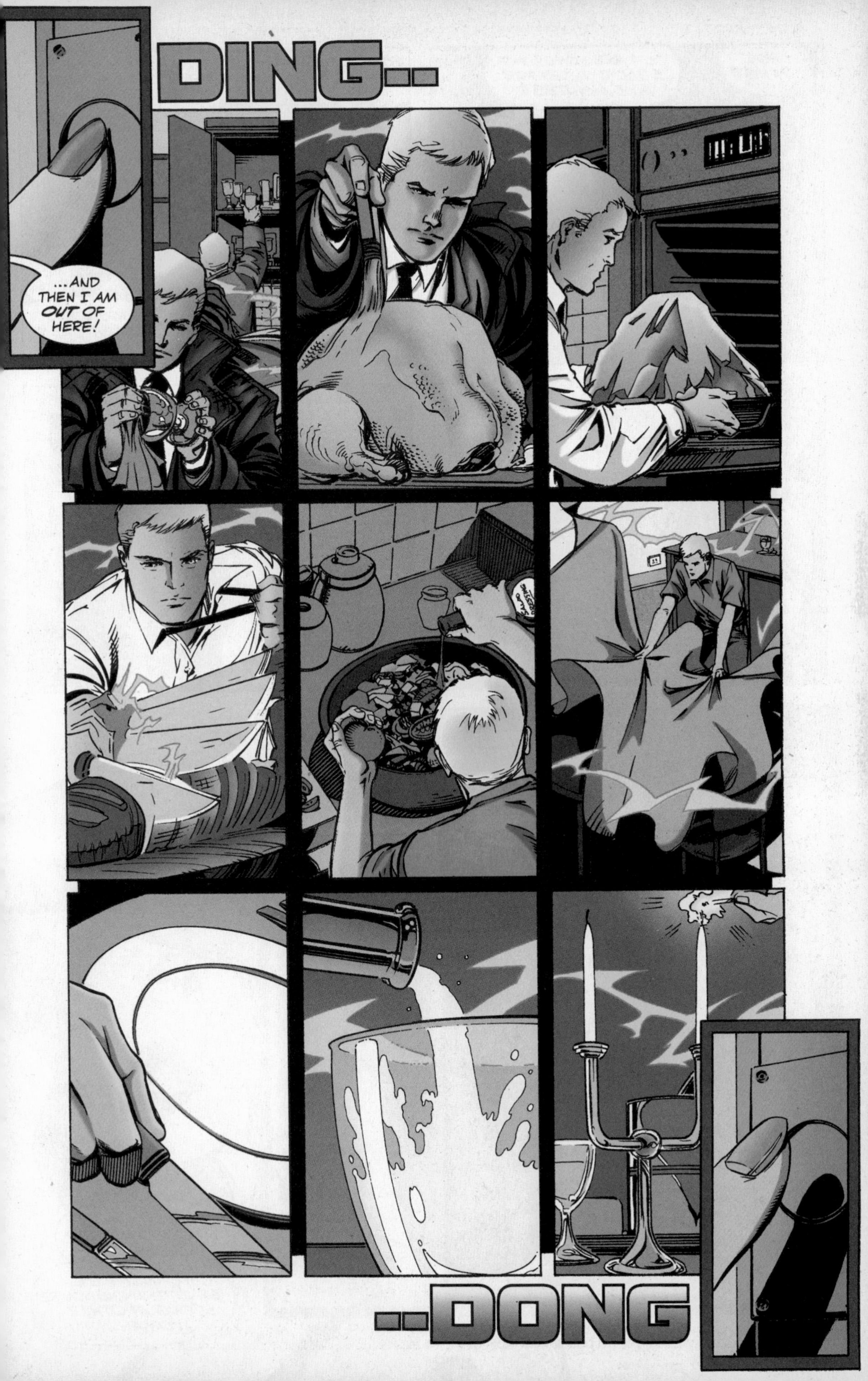

DING--
...AND THEN I AM OUT OF HERE!
--DONG

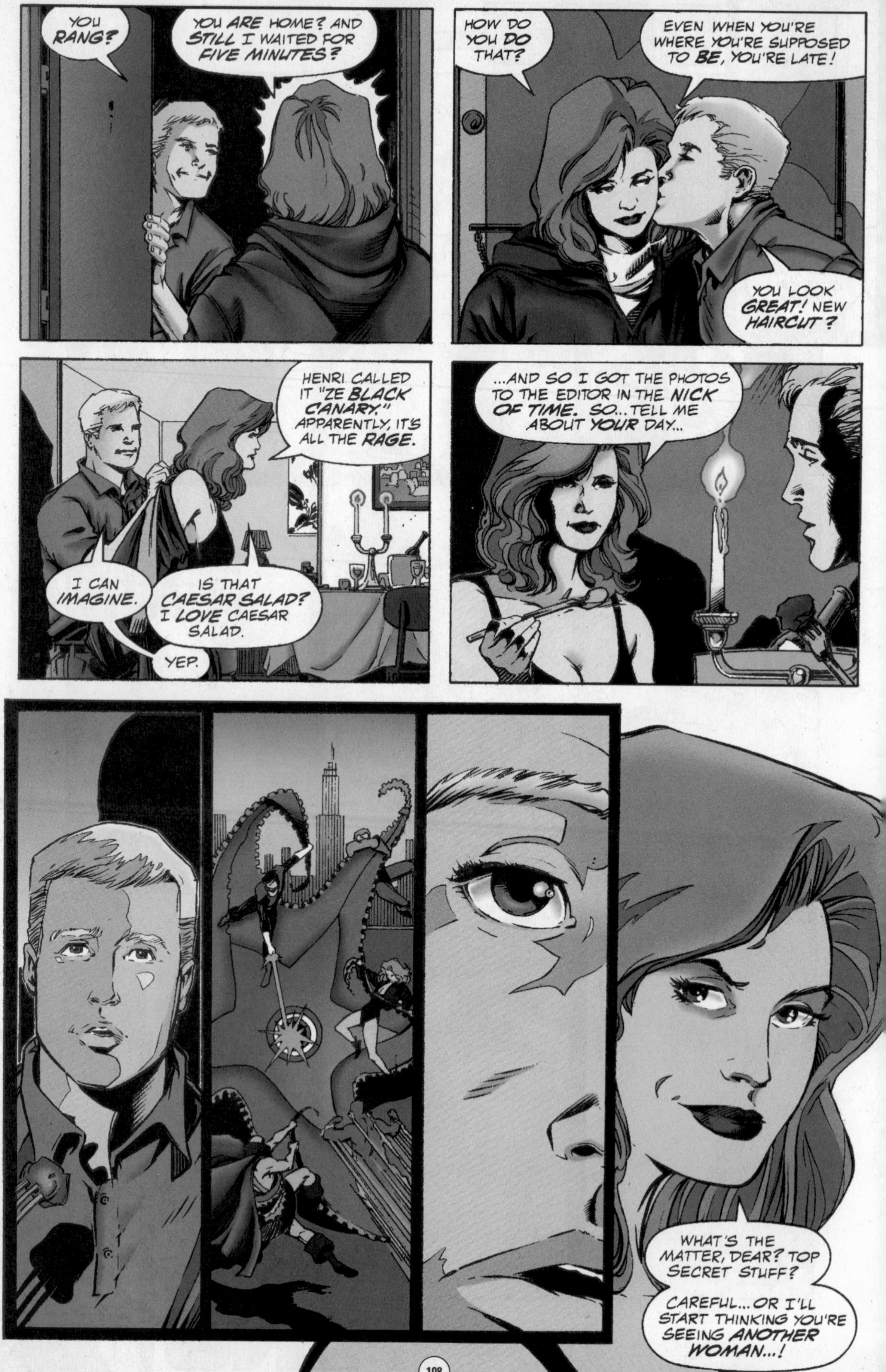
YOU RANG?
YOU ARE HOME? AND STILL I WAITED FOR FIVE MINUTES?
HOW DO YOU DO THAT?
EVEN WHEN YOU'RE WHERE YOU'RE SUPPOSED TO BE, YOU'RE LATE!
YOU LOOK GREAT! NEW HAIRCUT?
HENRI CALLED IT "ZE BLACK CANARY." APPARENTLY, IT'S ALL THE RAGE.
I CAN IMAGINE.
IS THAT CAESAR SALAD? I LOVE CAESAR SALAD.
YEP.
...AND SO I GOT THE PHOTOS TO THE EDITOR IN THE NICK OF TIME. SO...TELL ME ABOUT YOUR DAY...
WHAT'S THE MATTER, DEAR? TOP SECRET STUFF?
CAREFUL...OR I'LL START THINKING YOU'RE SEEING ANOTHER WOMAN...!

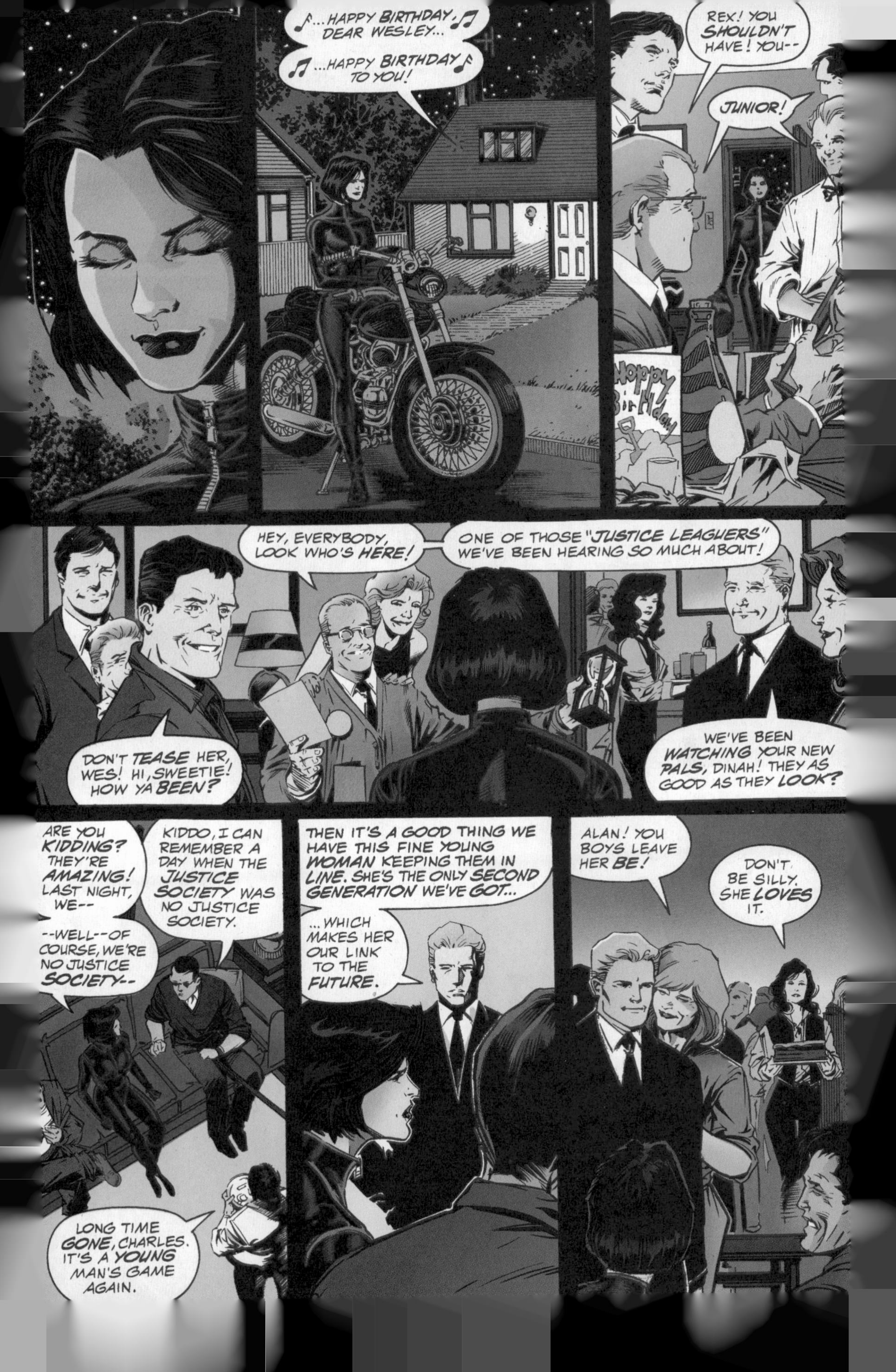
♪...HAPPY BIRTHDAY, DEAR WESLEY...♪
♪...HAPPY BIRTHDAY TO YOU!♪
REX! YOU SHOULDN'T HAVE! YOU--
JUNIOR!
HEY, EVERYBODY, LOOK WHO'S HERE!
ONE OF THOSE "JUSTICE LEAGUERS" WE'VE BEEN HEARING SO MUCH ABOUT!
DON'T TEASE HER, WES! HI, SWEETIE! HOW YA BEEN?
WE'VE BEEN WATCHING YOUR NEW PALS, DINAH! THEY AS GOOD AS THEY LOOK?
ARE YOU KIDDING? THEY'RE AMAZING! LAST NIGHT, WE--
KIDDO, I CAN REMEMBER A DAY WHEN THE JUSTICE SOCIETY WAS NO JUSTICE SOCIETY.
--WELL--OF COURSE, WE'RE NO JUSTICE SOCIETY--
LONG TIME GONE, CHARLES. IT'S A YOUNG MAN'S GAME AGAIN.
THEN IT'S A GOOD THING WE HAVE THIS FINE YOUNG WOMAN KEEPING THEM IN LINE. SHE'S THE ONLY SECOND GENERATION WE'VE GOT...
...WHICH MAKES HER OUR LINK TO THE FUTURE.
ALAN! YOU BOYS LEAVE HER BE!
DON'T BE SILLY. SHE LOVES IT.

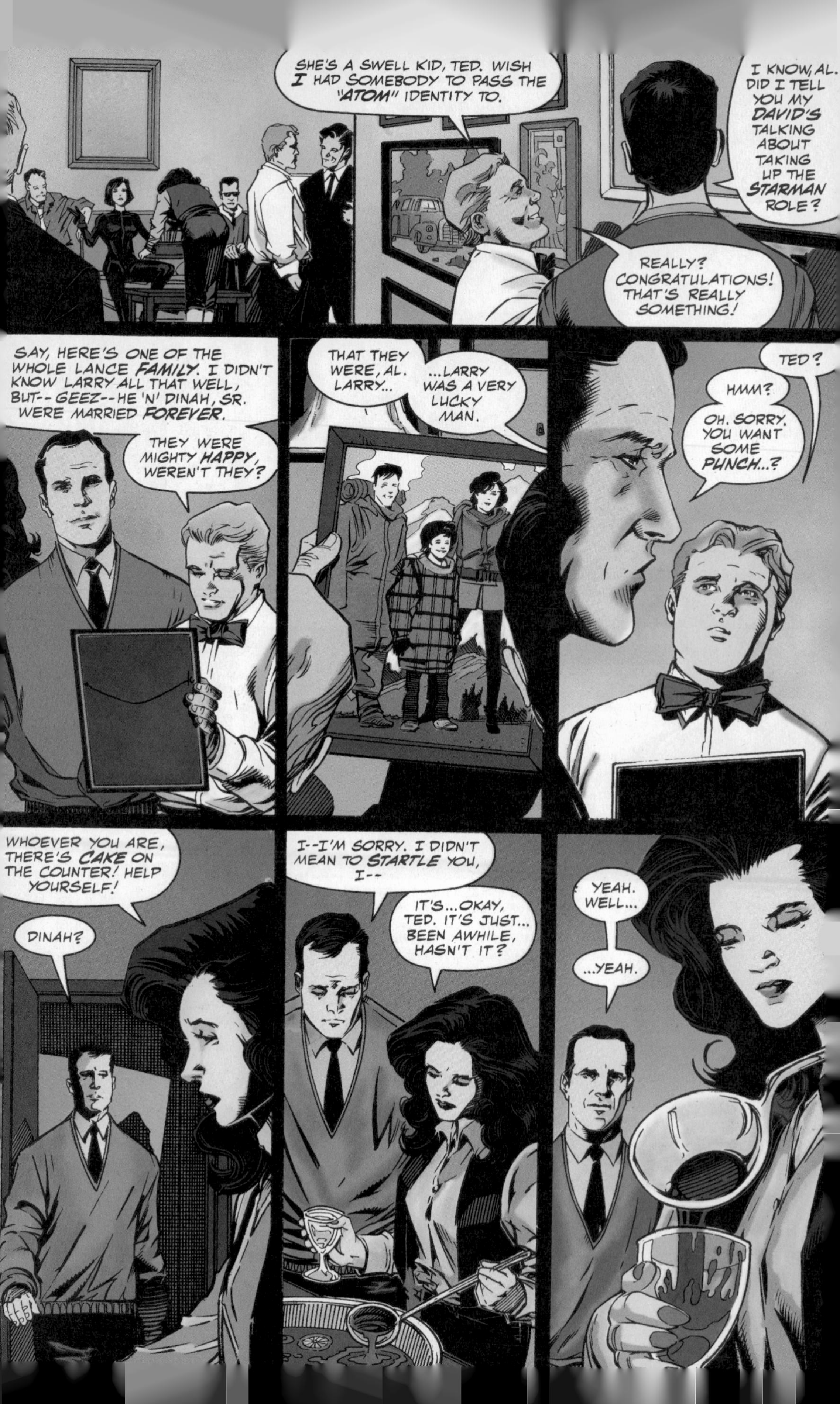
SHE'S A SWELL KID, TED. WISH I HAD SOMEBODY TO PASS THE "ATOM" IDENTITY TO.
I KNOW, AL. DID I TELL YOU MY DAVID'S TALKING ABOUT TAKING UP THE STARMAN ROLE?
REALLY? CONGRATULATIONS! THAT'S REALLY SOMETHING!
SAY, HERE'S ONE OF THE WHOLE LANCE FAMILY. I DIDN'T KNOW LARRY ALL THAT WELL, BUT-- GEEZ--HE 'N' DINAH, SR. WERE MARRIED FOREVER.
THEY WERE MIGHTY HAPPY, WEREN'T THEY?
THAT THEY WERE, AL. LARRY...
...LARRY WAS A VERY LUCKY MAN.
TED?
HMM?
OH. SORRY. YOU WANT SOME PUNCH...?
WHOEVER YOU ARE, THERE'S CAKE ON THE COUNTER! HELP YOURSELF!
DINAH?
I--I'M SORRY. I DIDN'T MEAN TO STARTLE YOU, I--
IT'S...OKAY, TED. IT'S JUST... BEEN AWHILE, HASN'T IT?
YEAH. WELL...
...YEAH.

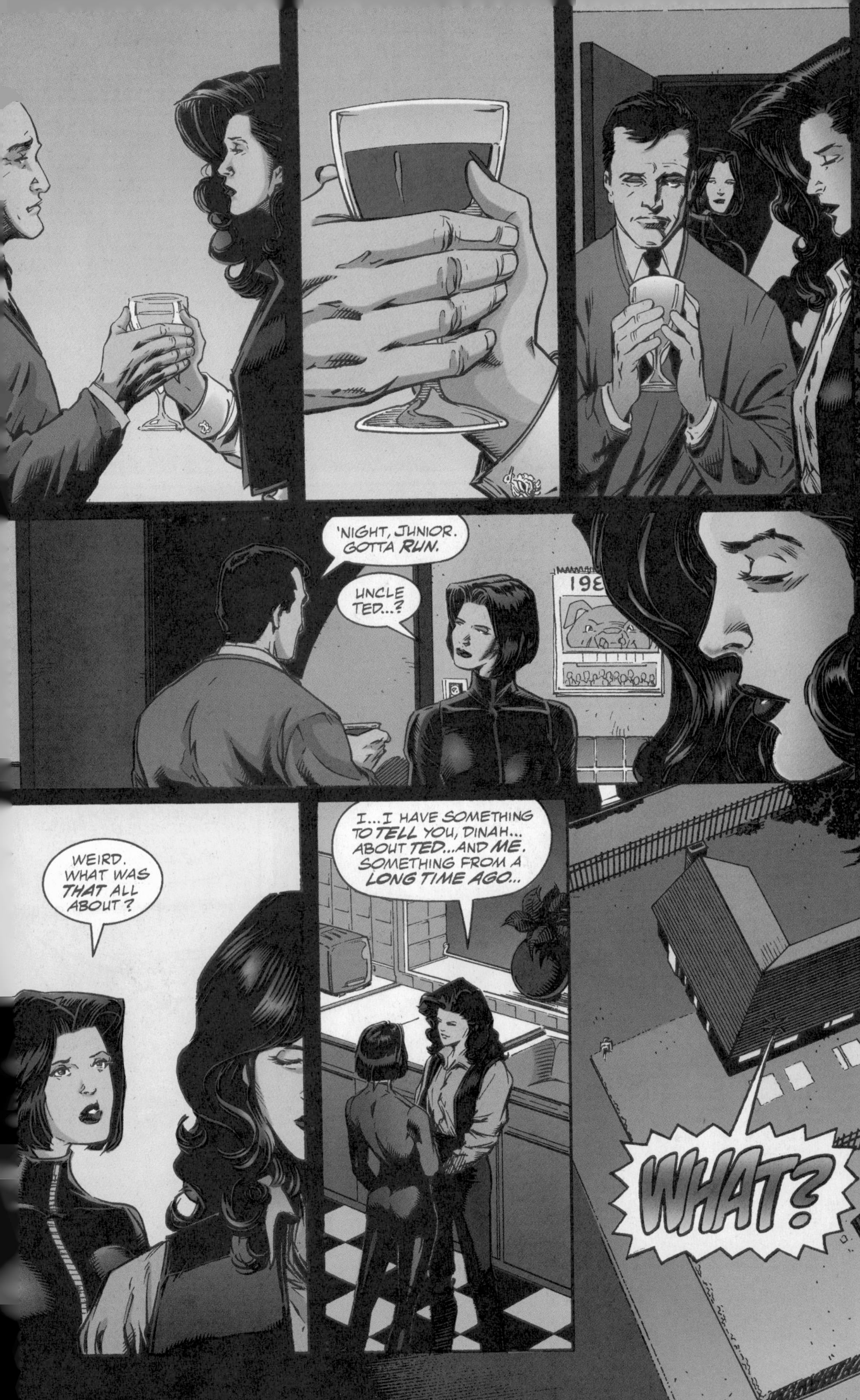
'NIGHT, JUNIOR. GOTTA RUN.
UNCLE TED...?
WEIRD. WHAT WAS THAT ALL ABOUT?
I...I HAVE SOMETHING TO TELL YOU, DINAH... ABOUT TED...AND ME. SOMETHING FROM A LONG TIME AGO...
WHAT?

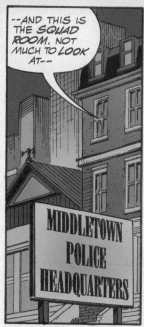

--AND THIS IS THE **SQUAD ROOM.** NOT MUCH TO LOOK AT--

MIDDLETOWN POLICE HEADQUARTERS

...AND THAT WRAPS UP **TODAY'S** INVESTIGATION...

--BUT WE TAKE **PRIDE** IN OUR **CONVICTION RECORD**--

JOHN! I DIDN'T EXPECT TO SEE EVEN **YOU** HERE THIS LATE!

HELLO, DIANE. WHO'S YOUR **FRIEND?**

DETECTIVE VINCE LOGAN, THIS IS MY PARTNER, **JOHN JONES.**

VINCE AND I MET AT **O'HERLIHY'S.** HE SAID HE'S NEVER ATTENDED AN **AUTOPSY.** I CALLED HIM A **WUSS,** AND IT TURNED INTO A **DATE.**

ECTIVE

IS SHE THIS **ROUGH** ON **ALL** OUT-OF-TOWNERS?

HI, JOHN. I KNOW YOU BY **REPUTATION.**

REALLY.

APPARENTLY, YOU'RE QUITE... THE **MANHUNTER.**

I HOPE TO **LEARN** FROM YOU.

WELL?

WELL, **WHAT?**

WELL, WHAT'S YOUR **READING?**

COFFEE Co.

YOU **KNOW** YOU'RE MY **LITMUS TEST** ON GUYS. YOU REALLY HAVE AN **INSTINCT** FOR SNIFFING OUT THE **WINNERS** FROM THE **LOSERS.**

SO?

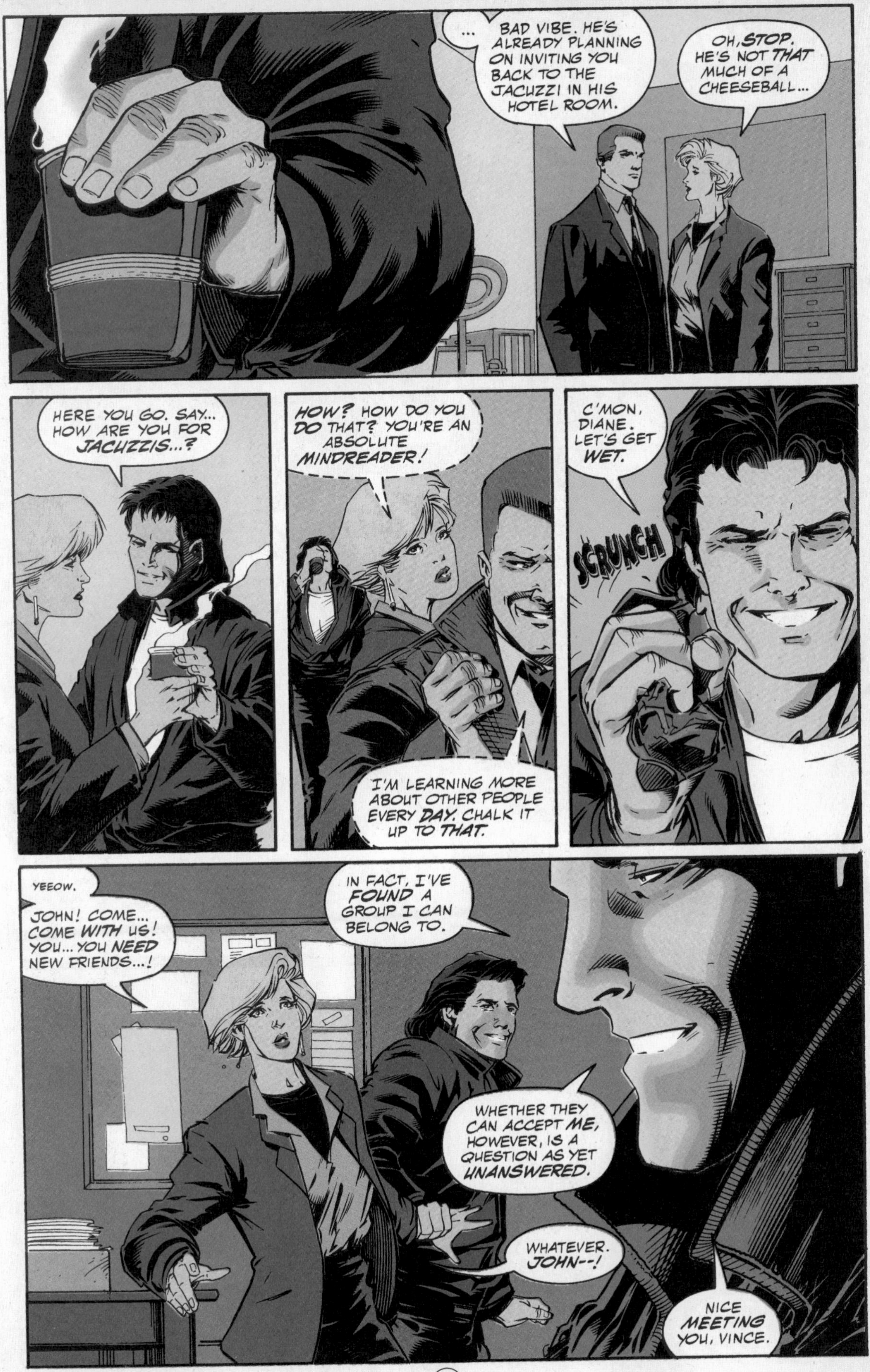
... BAD VIBE. HE'S ALREADY PLANNING ON INVITING YOU BACK TO THE JACUZZI IN HIS HOTEL ROOM.
OH, STOP. HE'S NOT THAT MUCH OF A CHEESEBALL...
HERE YOU GO. SAY... HOW ARE YOU FOR JACUZZIS...?
HOW? HOW DO YOU DO THAT? YOU'RE AN ABSOLUTE MINDREADER!
I'M LEARNING MORE ABOUT OTHER PEOPLE EVERY DAY. CHALK IT UP TO THAT.
C'MON, DIANE. LET'S GET WET.
SCRUNCH
YEEOW.
JOHN! COME... COME WITH US! YOU... YOU NEED NEW FRIENDS...!
IN FACT, I'VE FOUND A GROUP I CAN BELONG TO.
WHETHER THEY CAN ACCEPT ME, HOWEVER, IS A QUESTION AS YET UNANSWERED.
WHATEVER. JOHN--!
NICE MEETING YOU, VINCE.

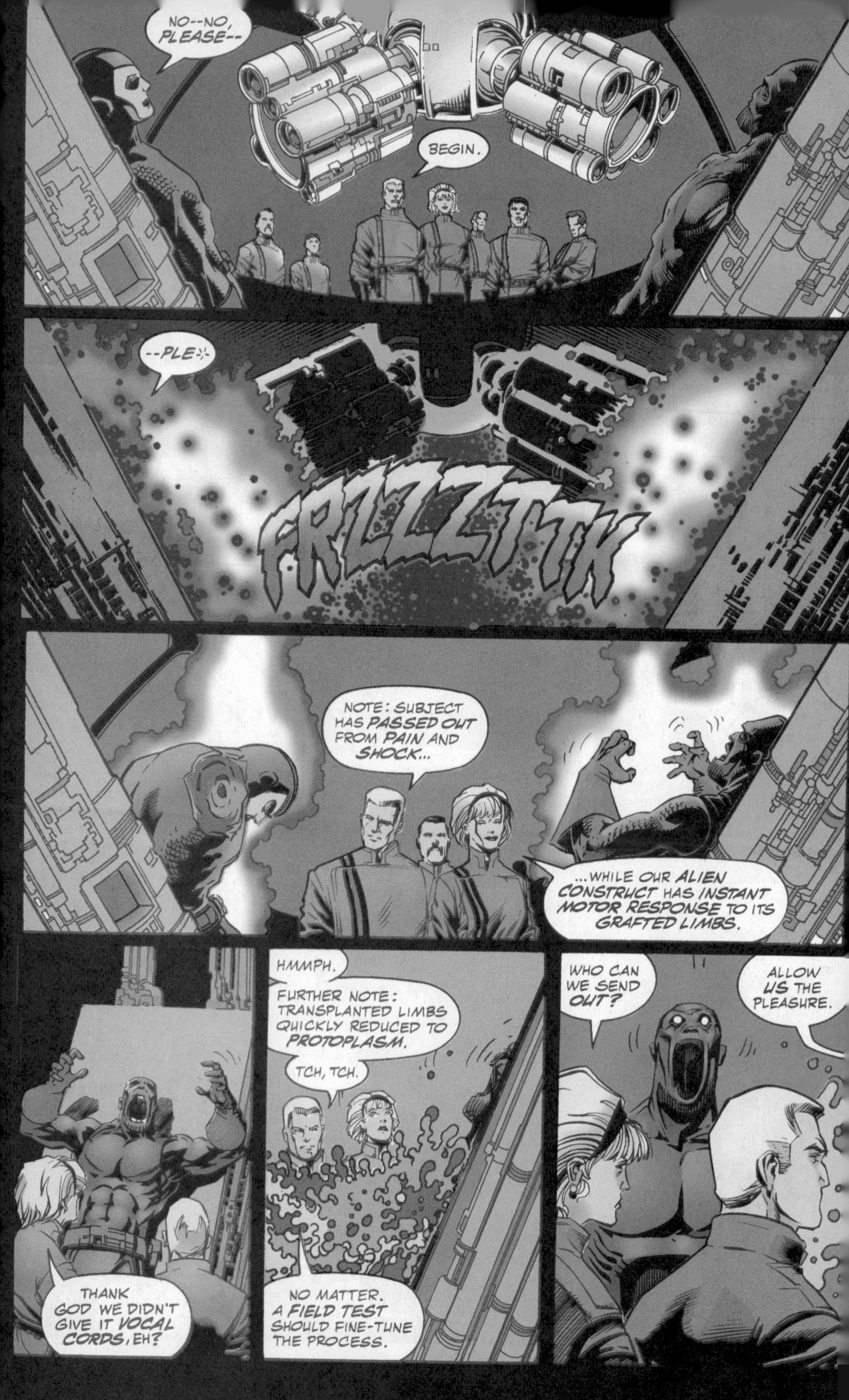
NO--NO, PLEASE--
BEGIN.
--PLE-
FRZZZTTTK
NOTE: SUBJECT HAS PASSED OUT FROM PAIN AND SHOCK...
...WHILE OUR ALIEN CONSTRUCT HAS INSTANT MOTOR RESPONSE TO ITS GRAFTED LIMBS.
THANK GOD WE DIDN'T GIVE IT VOCAL CORDS, EH?
HMMPH.
FURTHER NOTE: TRANSPLANTED LIMBS QUICKLY REDUCED TO PROTOPLASM.
TCH, TCH.
NO MATTER. A FIELD TEST SHOULD FINE-TUNE THE PROCESS.
WHO CAN WE SEND OUT?
ALLOW US THE PLEASURE.

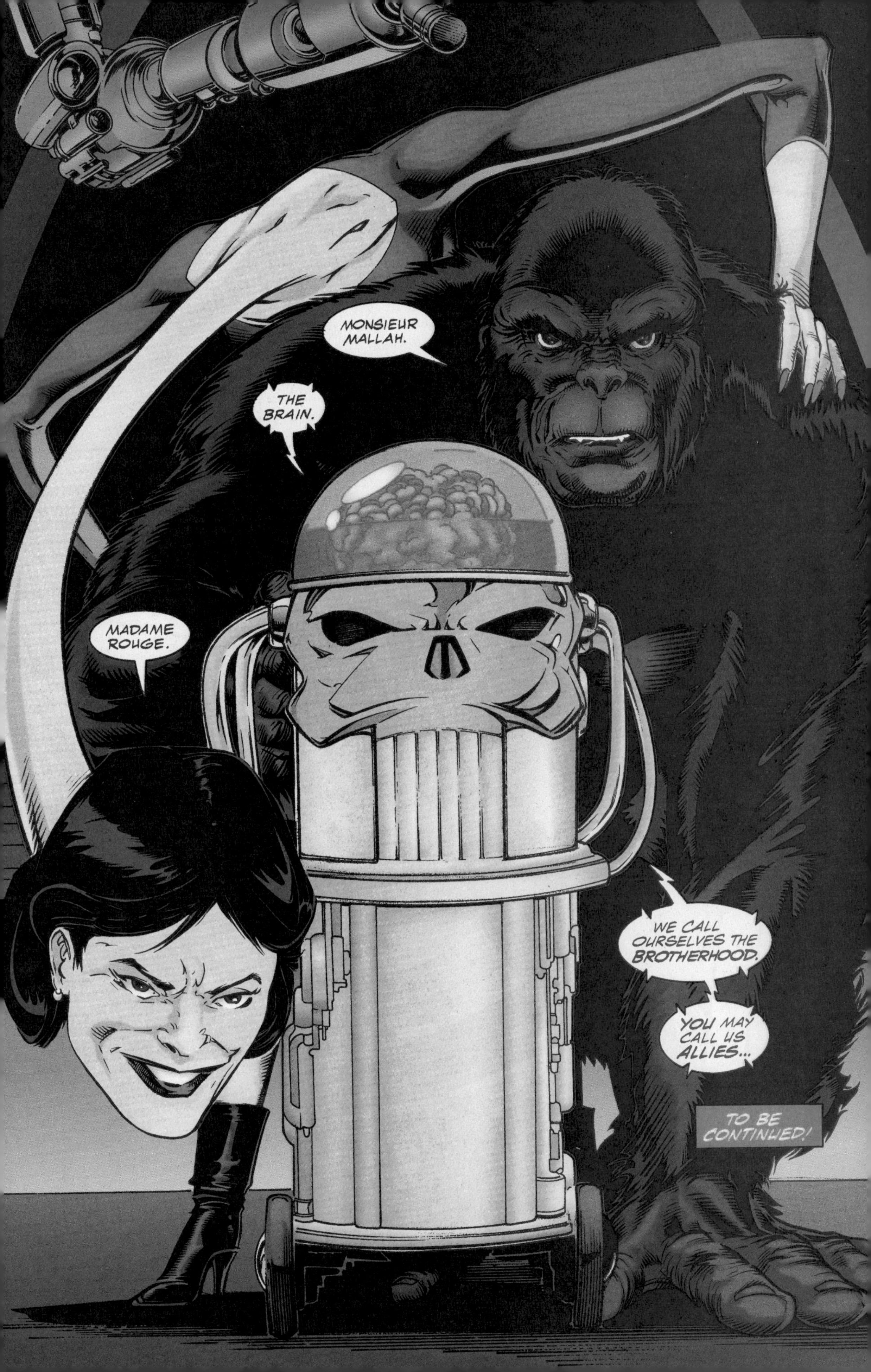
MONSIEUR MALLAH.
THE BRAIN.
MADAME ROUGE.
WE CALL OURSELVES THE BROTHERHOOD.
YOU MAY CALL US ALLIES...
TO BE CONTINUED!

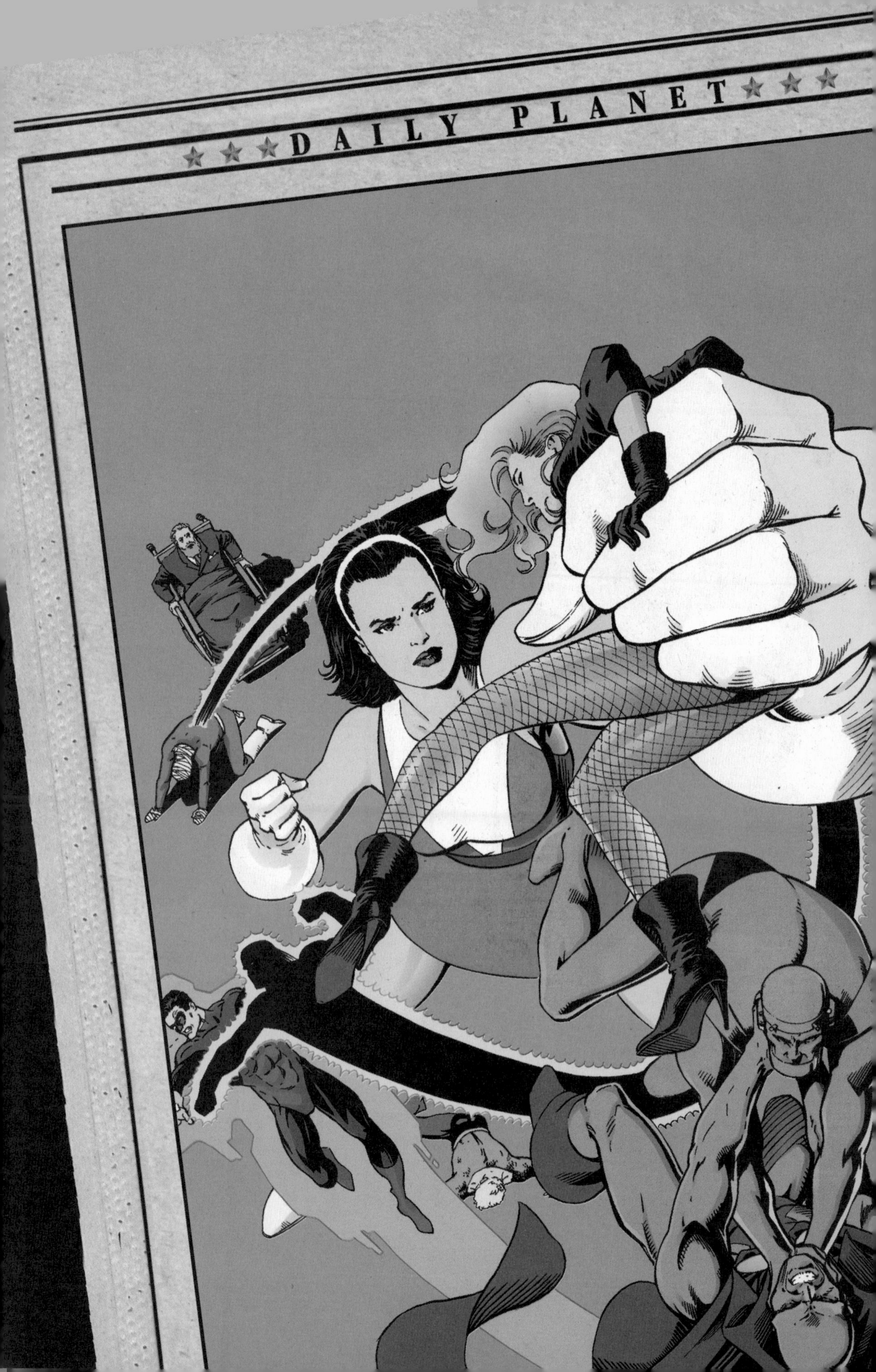
DAILY PLANET

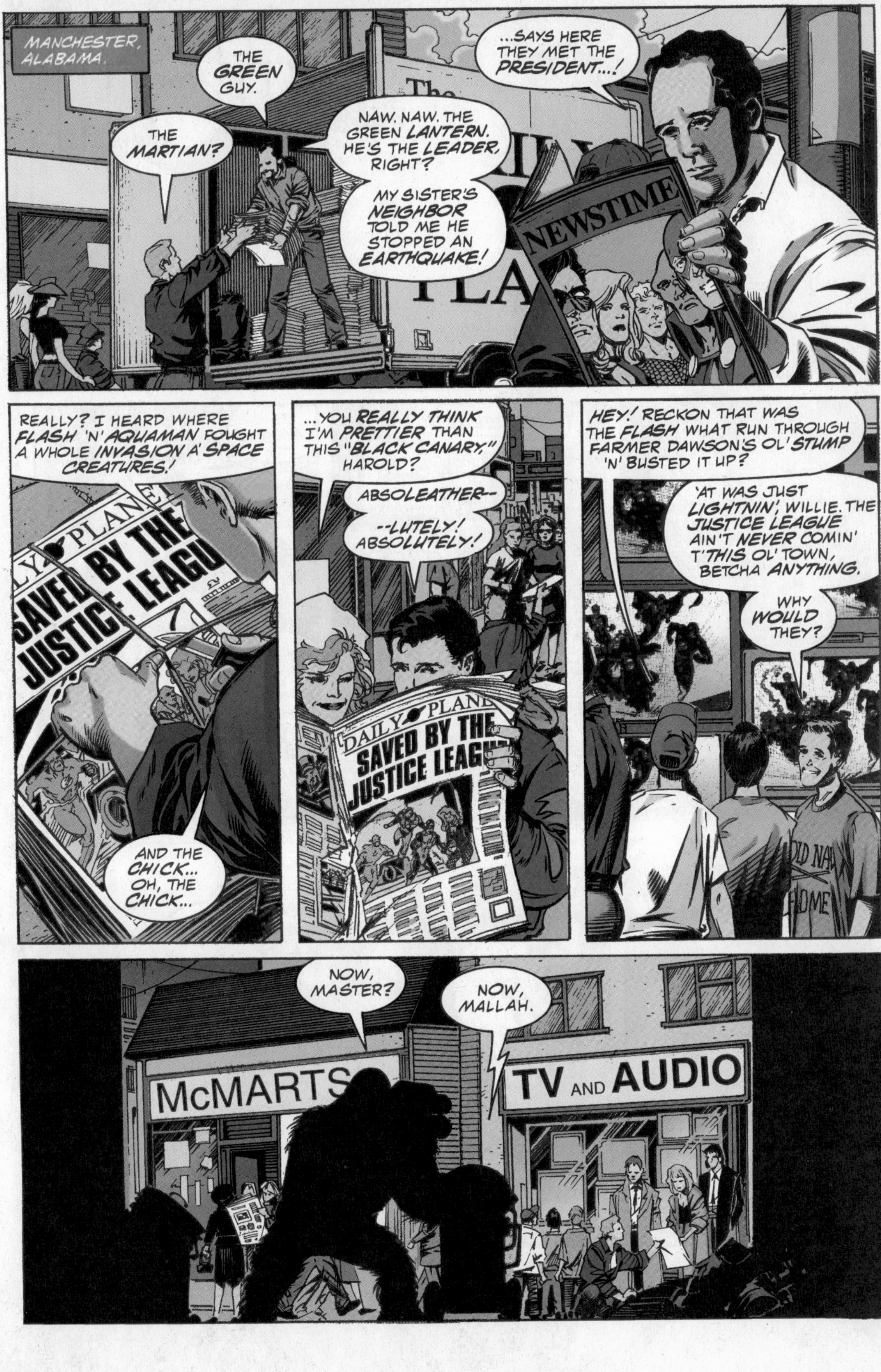
MANCHESTER, ALABAMA.
THE GREEN GUY.
THE MARTIAN?
NAW. NAW. THE GREEN LANTERN. HE'S THE LEADER, RIGHT?
MY SISTER'S NEIGHBOR TOLD ME HE STOPPED AN EARTHQUAKE!
...SAYS HERE THEY MET THE PRESIDENT...!
NEWSTIME
REALLY? I HEARD WHERE FLASH 'N' AQUAMAN FOUGHT A WHOLE INVASION A' SPACE CREATURES!
SAVED BY THE JUSTICE LEAGU
AND THE CHICK... OH, THE CHICK...
...YOU REALLY THINK I'M PRETTIER THAN THIS "BLACK CANARY," HAROLD?
ABSOLEATHER--
--LUTELY! ABSOLUTELY!
DAILY PLANET
SAVED BY THE JUSTICE LEAGU
HEY! RECKON THAT WAS THE FLASH WHAT RUN THROUGH FARMER DAWSON'S OL' STUMP 'N' BUSTED IT UP?
'AT WAS JUST LIGHTNIN', WILLIE. THE JUSTICE LEAGUE AIN'T NEVER COMIN' T'THIS OL' TOWN, BETCHA ANYTHING.
WHY WOULD THEY?
NOW, MASTER?
NOW, MALLAH.
McMARTS
TV AND AUDIO

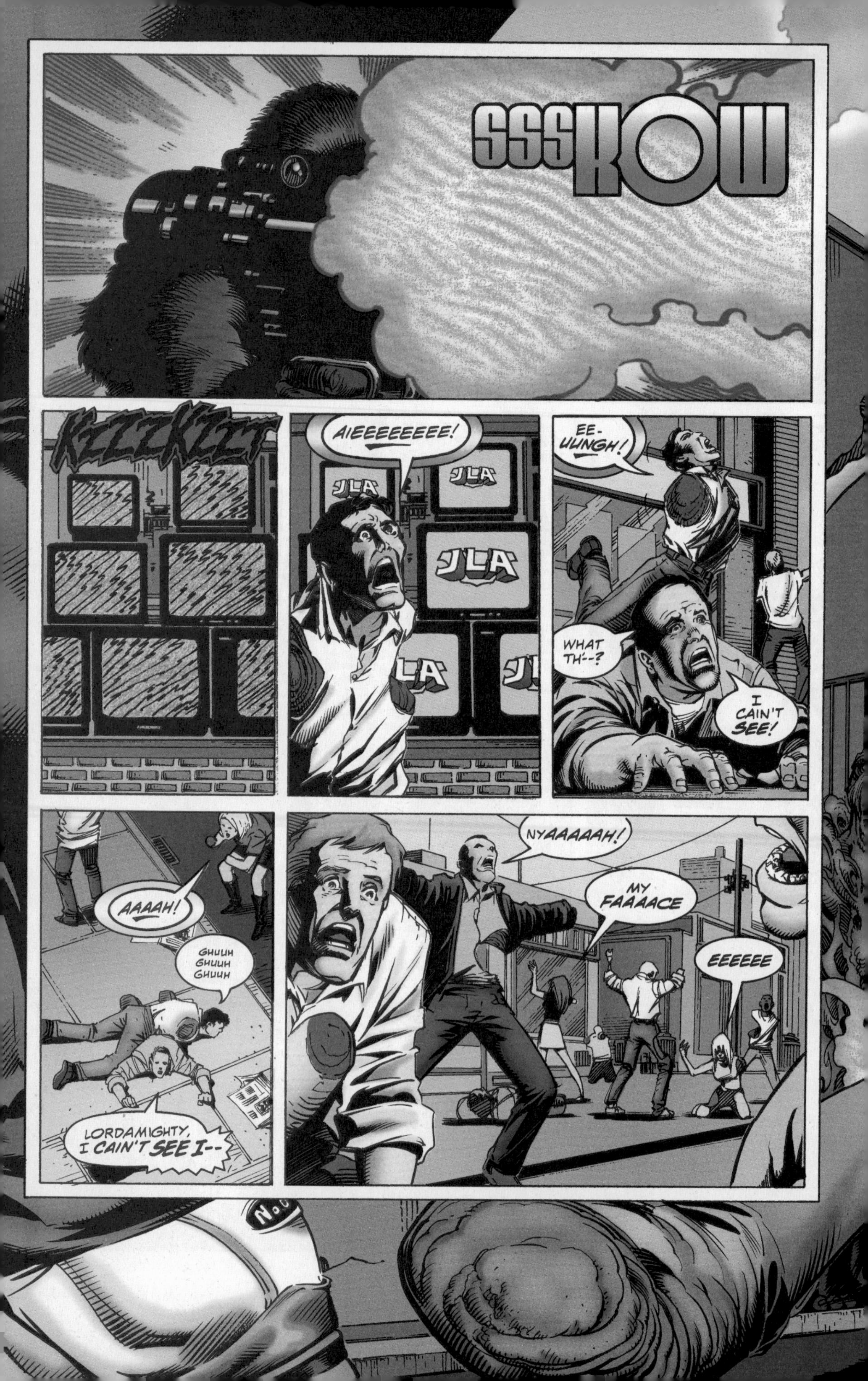
SSSKOW
KZZZKZZZ
AIEEEEEEEE!
JLA
EE-UUNGH!
WHAT TH'--?
I CAIN'T SEE!
AAAAH!
GHUUH GHUUH GHUUH
LORDAMIGHTY, I CAIN'T SEE I--
NYAAAAAH!
MY FAAAACE
EEEEEE

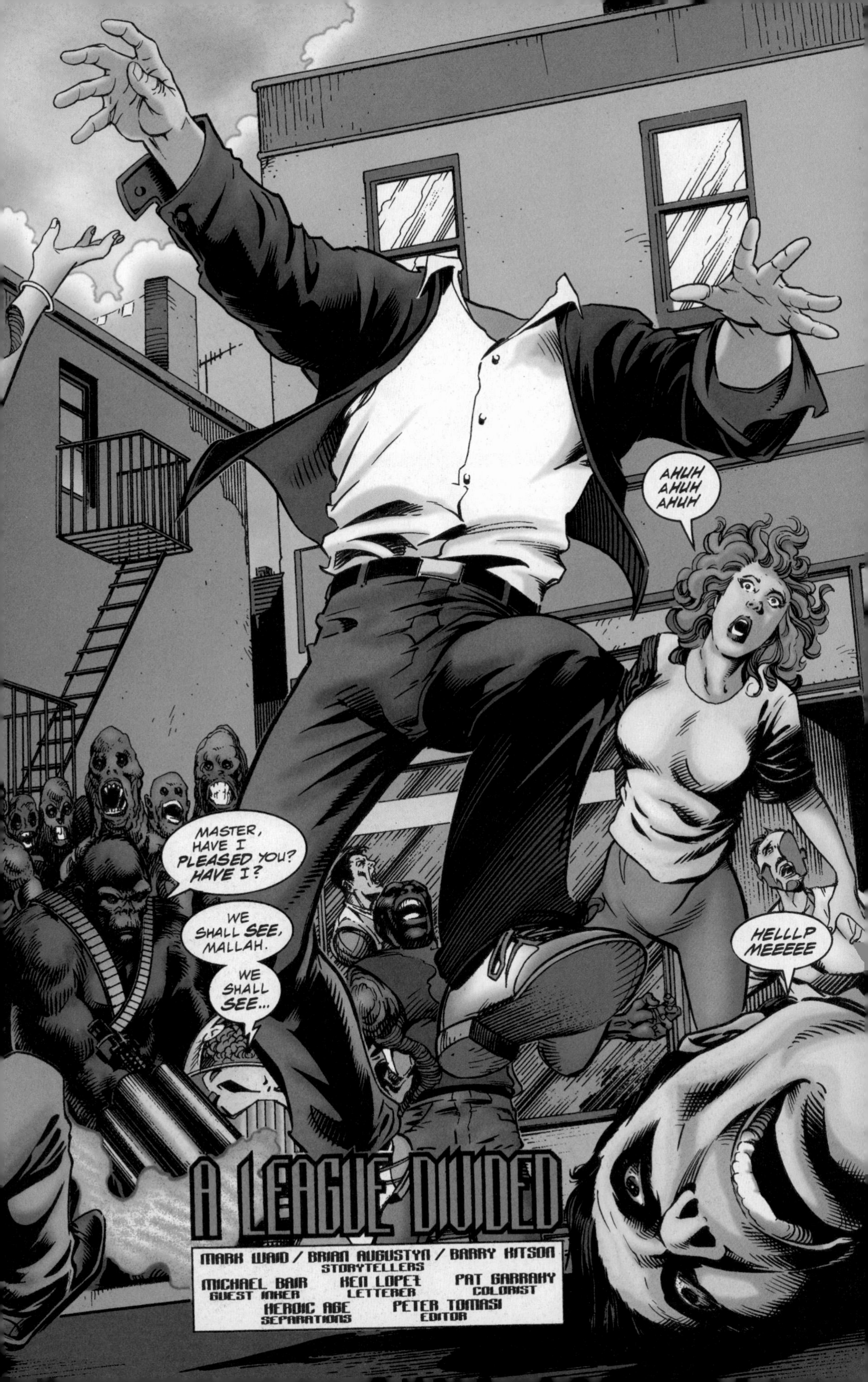
AHUH AHUH AHUH
MASTER, HAVE I PLEASED YOU? HAVE I?
WE SHALL SEE, MALLAH.
WE SHALL SEE...
HELLLP MEEEEE
A LEAGUE DIVIDED
MARK WAID / BRIAN AUGUSTYN / BARRY KITSON
STORYTELLERS
MICHAEL BAIR
GUEST INKER
KEN LOPEZ
LETTERER
PAT GARRAHY
COLORIST
HEROIC AGE
SEPARATIONS
PETER TOMASI
EDITOR

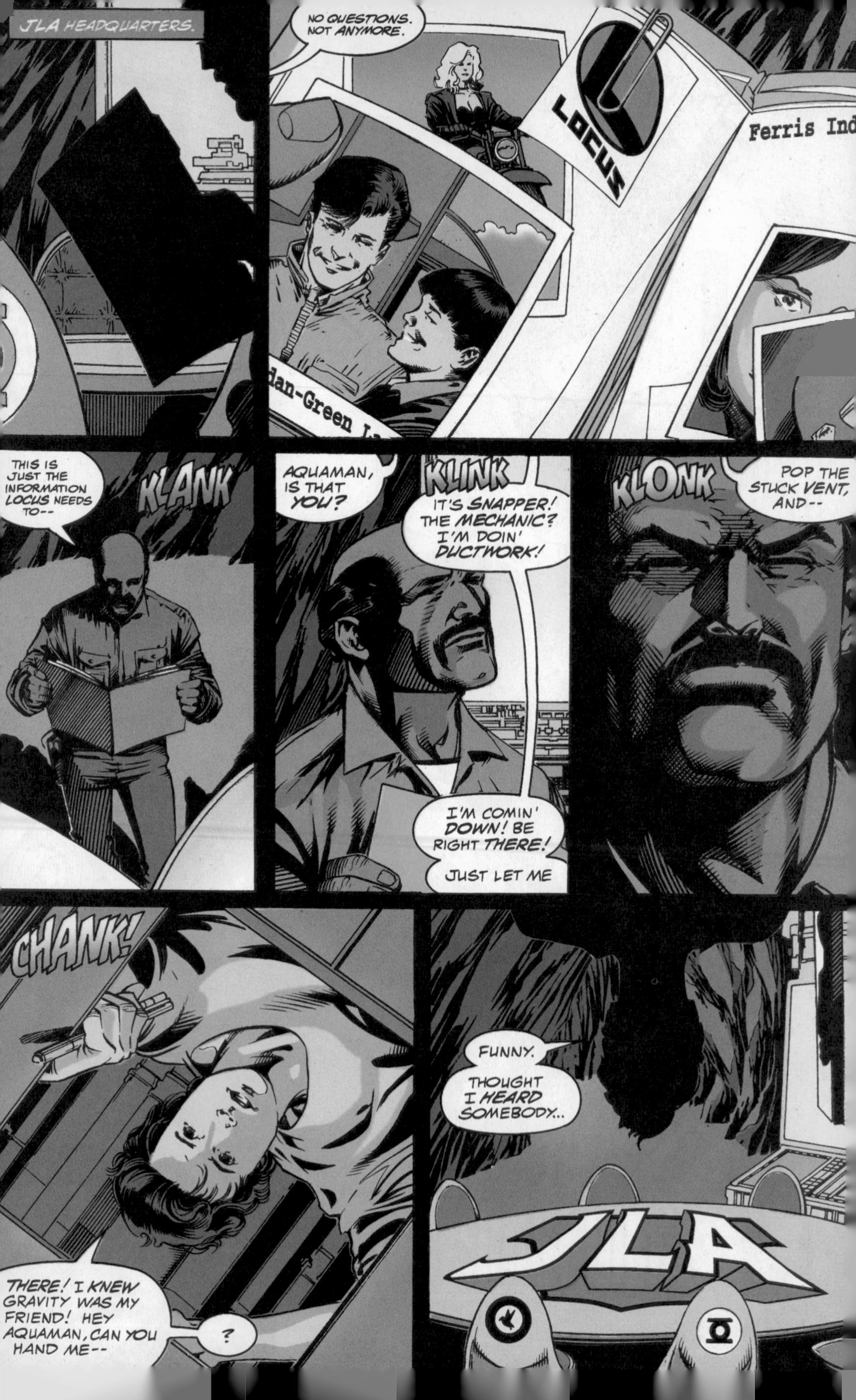
JLA HEADQUARTERS.
NO QUESTIONS. NOT ANYMORE.
LOCUS
Ferris Ind
dan-Green La
THIS IS JUST THE INFORMATION LOCUS NEEDS TO--
KLANK
AQUAMAN, IS THAT YOU?
KLINK
IT'S SNAPPER! THE MECHANIC? I'M DOIN' DUCTWORK!
I'M COMIN' DOWN! BE RIGHT THERE!
JUST LET ME
KLONK
POP THE STUCK VENT, AND--
CHANK!
THERE! I KNEW GRAVITY WAS MY FRIEND! HEY AQUAMAN, CAN YOU HAND ME--
?
FUNNY.
THOUGHT I HEARD SOMEBODY...
JLA

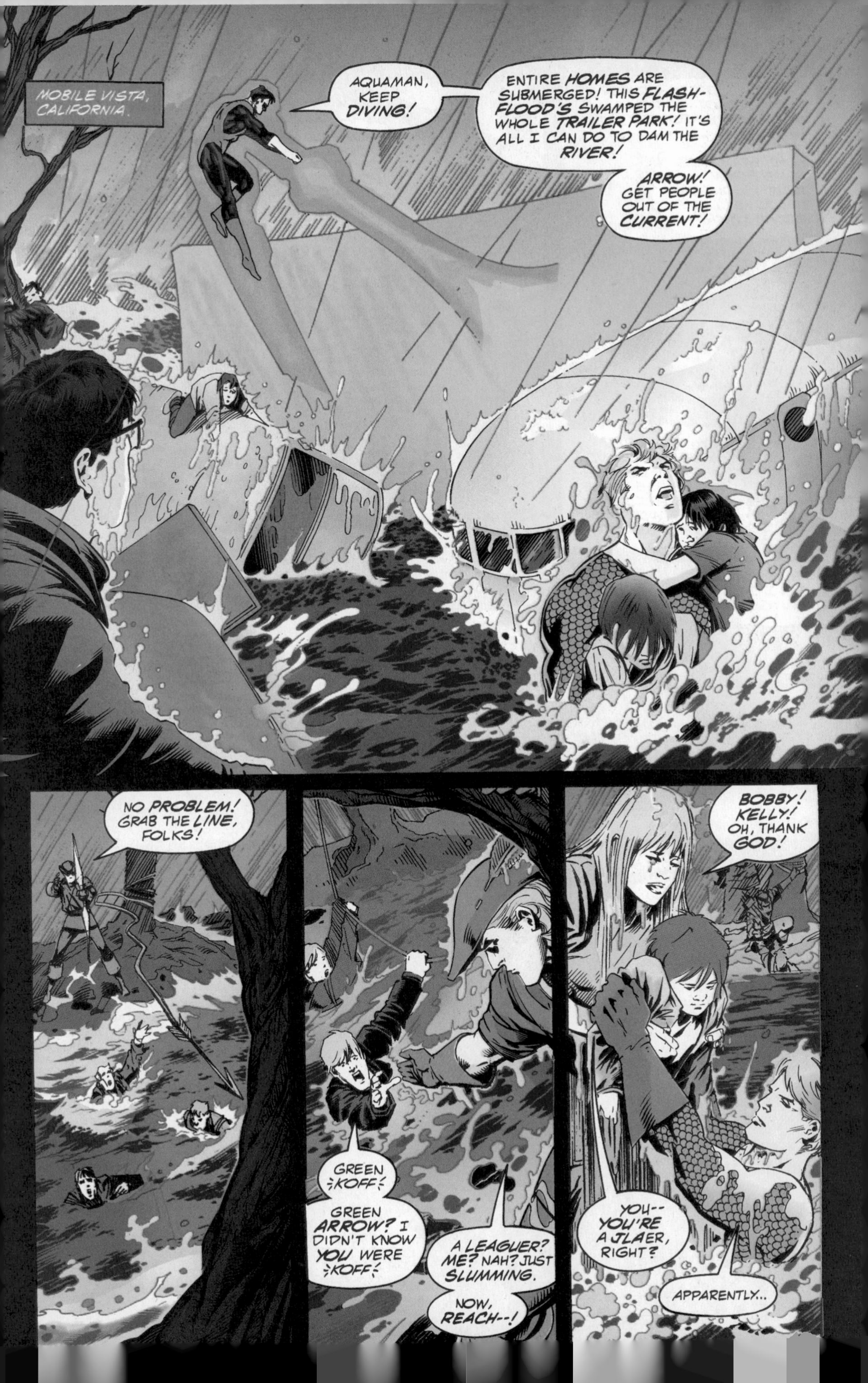
MOBILE VISTA, CALIFORNIA.
AQUAMAN, KEEP DIVING!
ENTIRE HOMES ARE SUBMERGED! THIS FLASH-FLOOD'S SWAMPED THE WHOLE TRAILER PARK! IT'S ALL I CAN DO TO DAM THE RIVER!
ARROW! GET PEOPLE OUT OF THE CURRENT!
NO PROBLEM! GRAB THE LINE, FOLKS!
GREEN KOFF
GREEN ARROW? I DIDN'T KNOW YOU WERE KOFF
A LEAGUER? ME? NAH? JUST SLUMMING.
NOW, REACH--!
BOBBY! KELLY! OH, THANK GOD!
YOU-- YOU'RE A JLAER, RIGHT?
APPARENTLY...

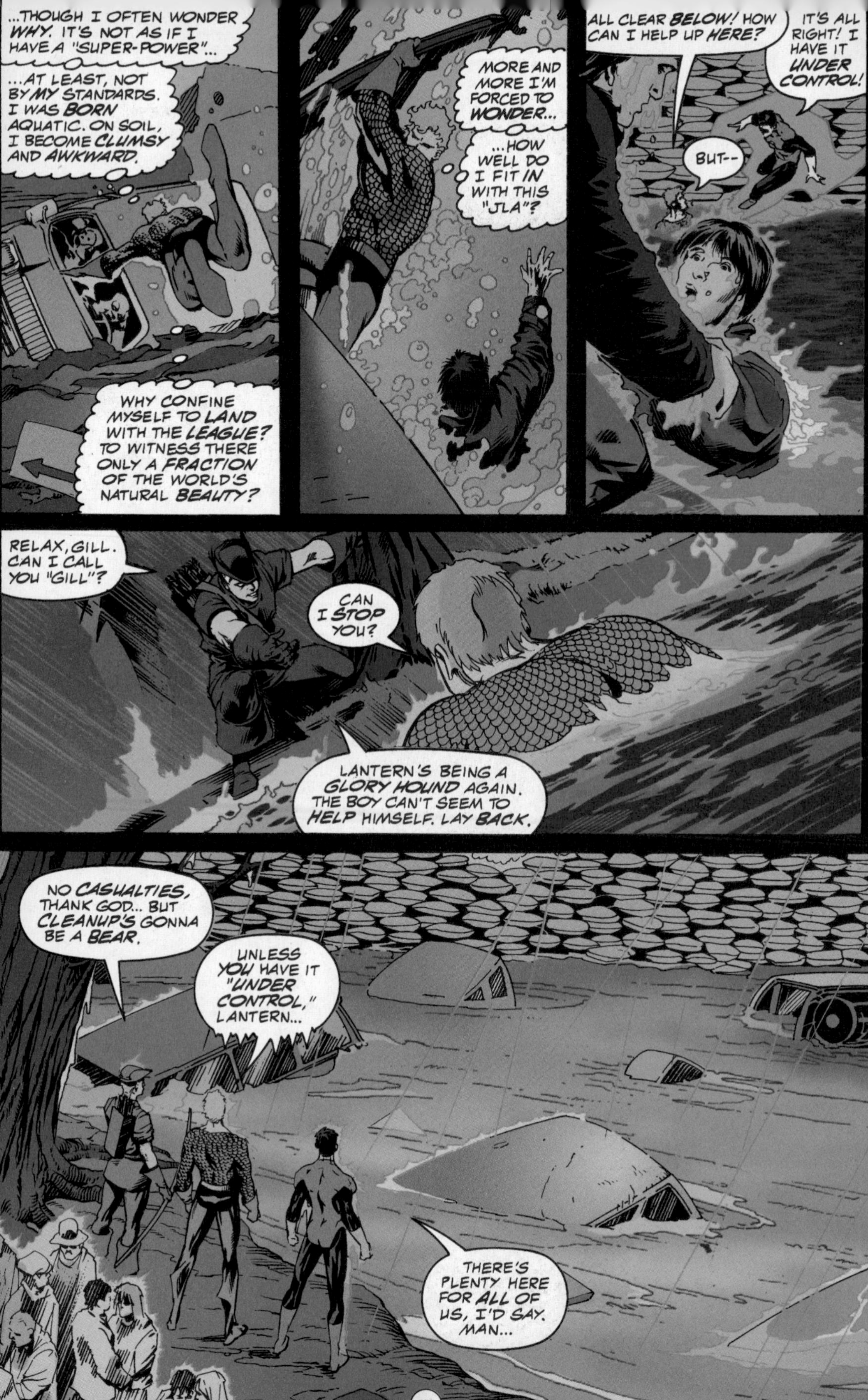
...THOUGH I OFTEN WONDER WHY. IT'S NOT AS IF I HAVE A "SUPER-POWER"...
...AT LEAST, NOT BY MY STANDARDS. I WAS BORN AQUATIC. ON SOIL, I BECOME CLUMSY AND AWKWARD.
WHY CONFINE MYSELF TO LAND WITH THE LEAGUE? TO WITNESS THERE ONLY A FRACTION OF THE WORLD'S NATURAL BEAUTY?
MORE AND MORE I'M FORCED TO WONDER...
...HOW WELL DO I FIT IN WITH THIS "JLA"?
ALL CLEAR BELOW! HOW CAN I HELP UP HERE?
IT'S ALL RIGHT! I HAVE IT UNDER CONTROL!
BUT--
RELAX, GILL. CAN I CALL YOU "GILL"?
CAN I STOP YOU?
LANTERN'S BEING A GLORY HOUND AGAIN. THE BOY CAN'T SEEM TO HELP HIMSELF. LAY BACK.
NO CASUALTIES, THANK GOD... BUT CLEANUP'S GONNA BE A BEAR.
UNLESS YOU HAVE IT "UNDER CONTROL," LANTERN...
THERE'S PLENTY HERE FOR ALL OF US, I'D SAY. MAN...

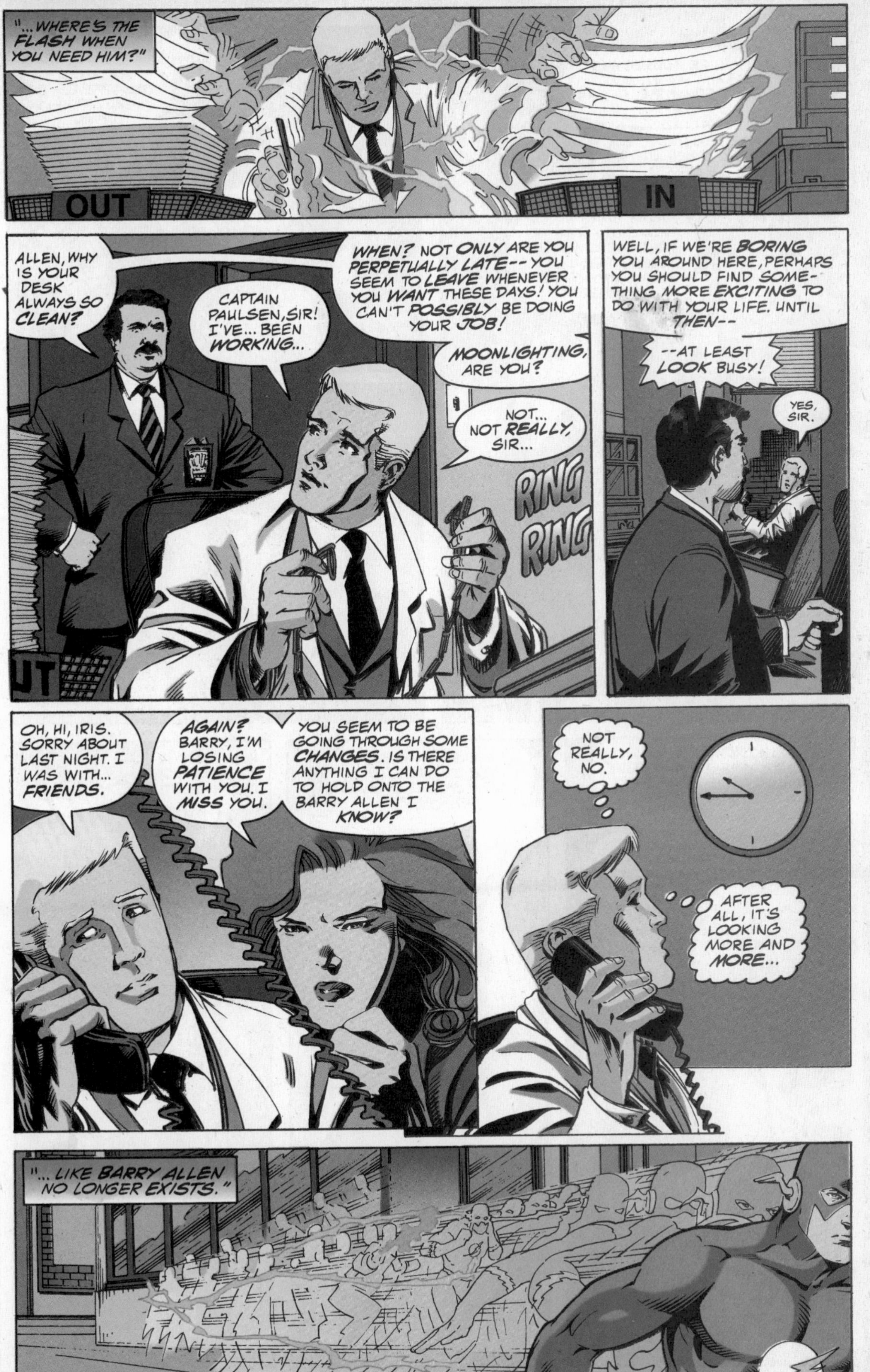
"...WHERE'S THE FLASH WHEN YOU NEED HIM?"
OUT
IN
ALLEN, WHY IS YOUR DESK ALWAYS SO CLEAN?
CAPTAIN PAULSEN, SIR! I'VE... BEEN WORKING...
WHEN? NOT ONLY ARE YOU PERPETUALLY LATE--YOU SEEM TO LEAVE WHENEVER YOU WANT THESE DAYS! YOU CAN'T POSSIBLY BE DOING YOUR JOB!
MOONLIGHTING, ARE YOU?
NOT... NOT REALLY, SIR...
RING
RING
WELL, IF WE'RE BORING YOU AROUND HERE, PERHAPS YOU SHOULD FIND SOMETHING MORE EXCITING TO DO WITH YOUR LIFE. UNTIL THEN--
--AT LEAST LOOK BUSY!
YES, SIR.
OH, HI, IRIS. SORRY ABOUT LAST NIGHT. I WAS WITH... FRIENDS.
AGAIN? BARRY, I'M LOSING PATIENCE WITH YOU. I MISS YOU.
YOU SEEM TO BE GOING THROUGH SOME CHANGES. IS THERE ANYTHING I CAN DO TO HOLD ONTO THE BARRY ALLEN I KNOW?
NOT REALLY, NO.
AFTER ALL, IT'S LOOKING MORE AND MORE...
"...LIKE BARRY ALLEN NO LONGER EXISTS."

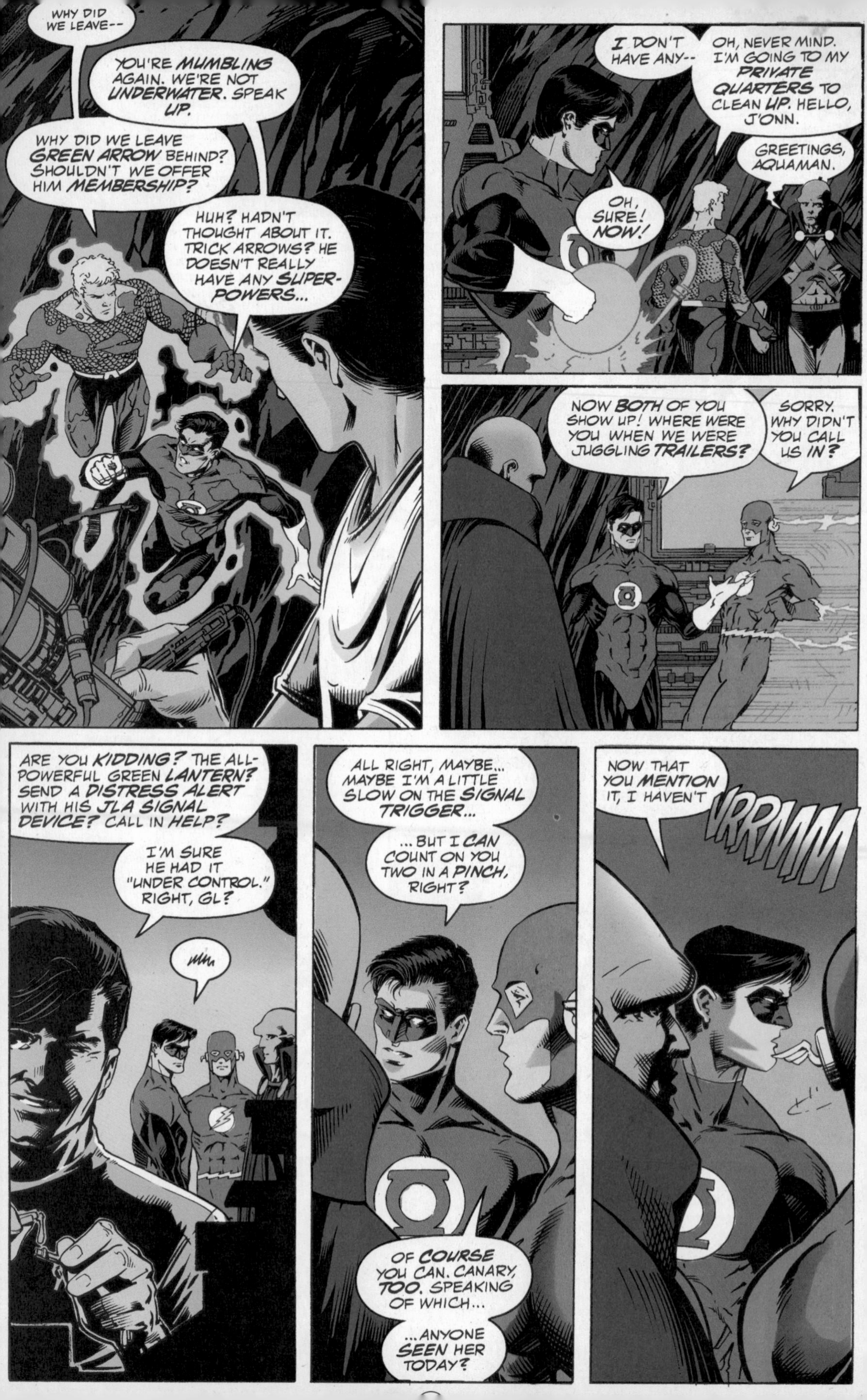
WHY DID WE LEAVE--
YOU'RE MUMBLING AGAIN. WE'RE NOT UNDERWATER. SPEAK UP.
WHY DID WE LEAVE GREEN ARROW BEHIND? SHOULDN'T WE OFFER HIM MEMBERSHIP?
HUH? HADN'T THOUGHT ABOUT IT. TRICK ARROWS? HE DOESN'T REALLY HAVE ANY SUPER-POWERS...
I DON'T HAVE ANY--
OH, NEVER MIND. I'M GOING TO MY PRIVATE QUARTERS TO CLEAN UP. HELLO, J'ONN.
GREETINGS, AQUAMAN.
OH, SURE! NOW!
NOW BOTH OF YOU SHOW UP! WHERE WERE YOU WHEN WE WERE JUGGLING TRAILERS?
SORRY. WHY DIDN'T YOU CALL US IN?
ARE YOU KIDDING? THE ALL-POWERFUL GREEN LANTERN? SEND A DISTRESS ALERT WITH HIS JLA SIGNAL DEVICE? CALL IN HELP?
I'M SURE HE HAD IT "UNDER CONTROL." RIGHT, GL?
MM.
ALL RIGHT, MAYBE... MAYBE I'M A LITTLE SLOW ON THE SIGNAL TRIGGER...
...BUT I CAN COUNT ON YOU TWO IN A PINCH, RIGHT?
OF COURSE YOU CAN. CANARY, TOO. SPEAKING OF WHICH...
...ANYONE SEEN HER TODAY?
NOW THAT YOU MENTION IT, I HAVEN'T
VRRMMM

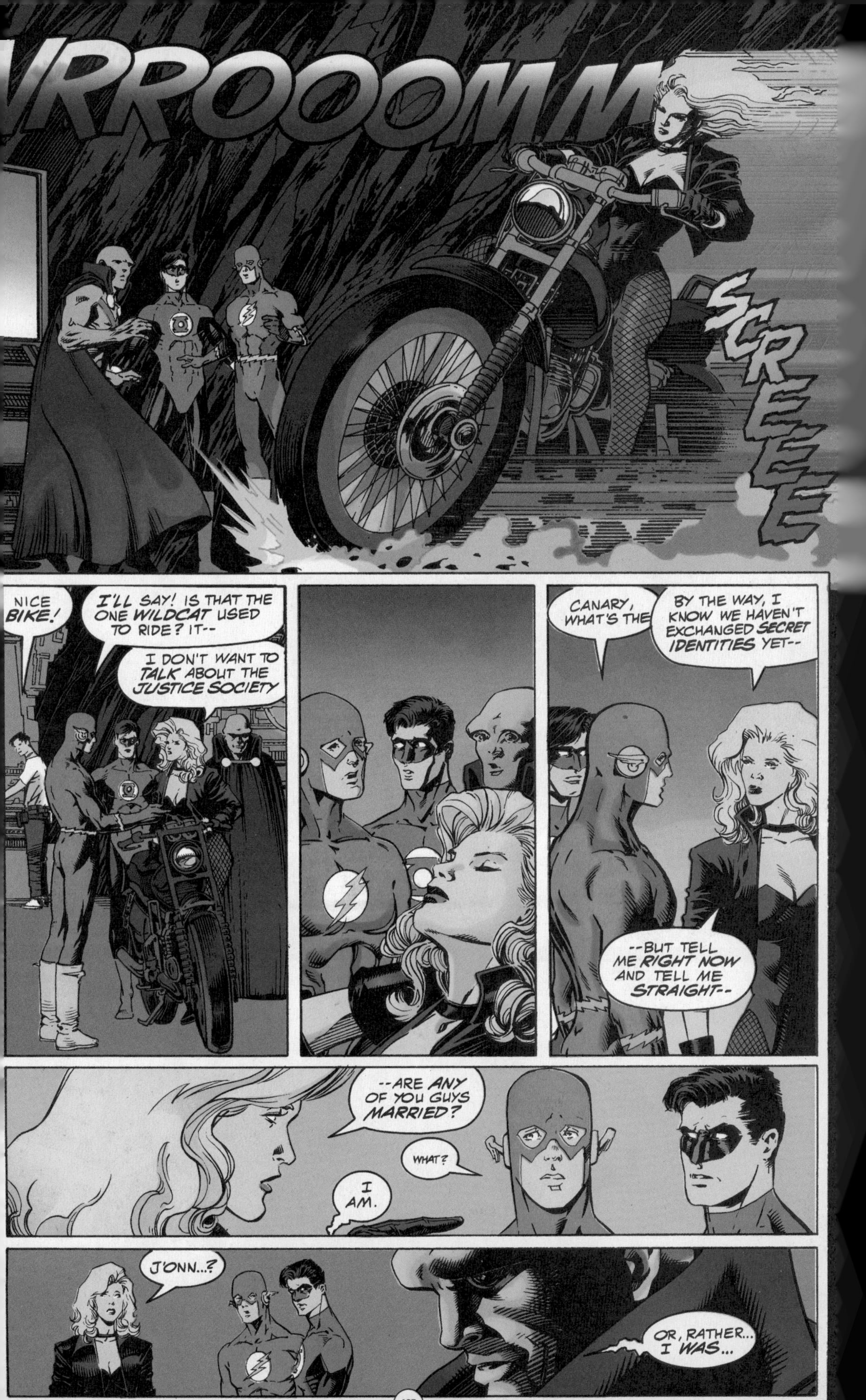
VRROOOMM
SCREEE
NICE BIKE!
I'LL SAY! IS THAT THE ONE WILDCAT USED TO RIDE? IT--
I DON'T WANT TO TALK ABOUT THE JUSTICE SOCIETY
CANARY, WHAT'S THE
BY THE WAY, I KNOW WE HAVEN'T EXCHANGED SECRET IDENTITIES YET--
--BUT TELL ME RIGHT NOW AND TELL ME STRAIGHT--
--ARE ANY OF YOU GUYS MARRIED?
WHAT?
I AM.
J'ONN...?
OR, RATHER... I WAS...

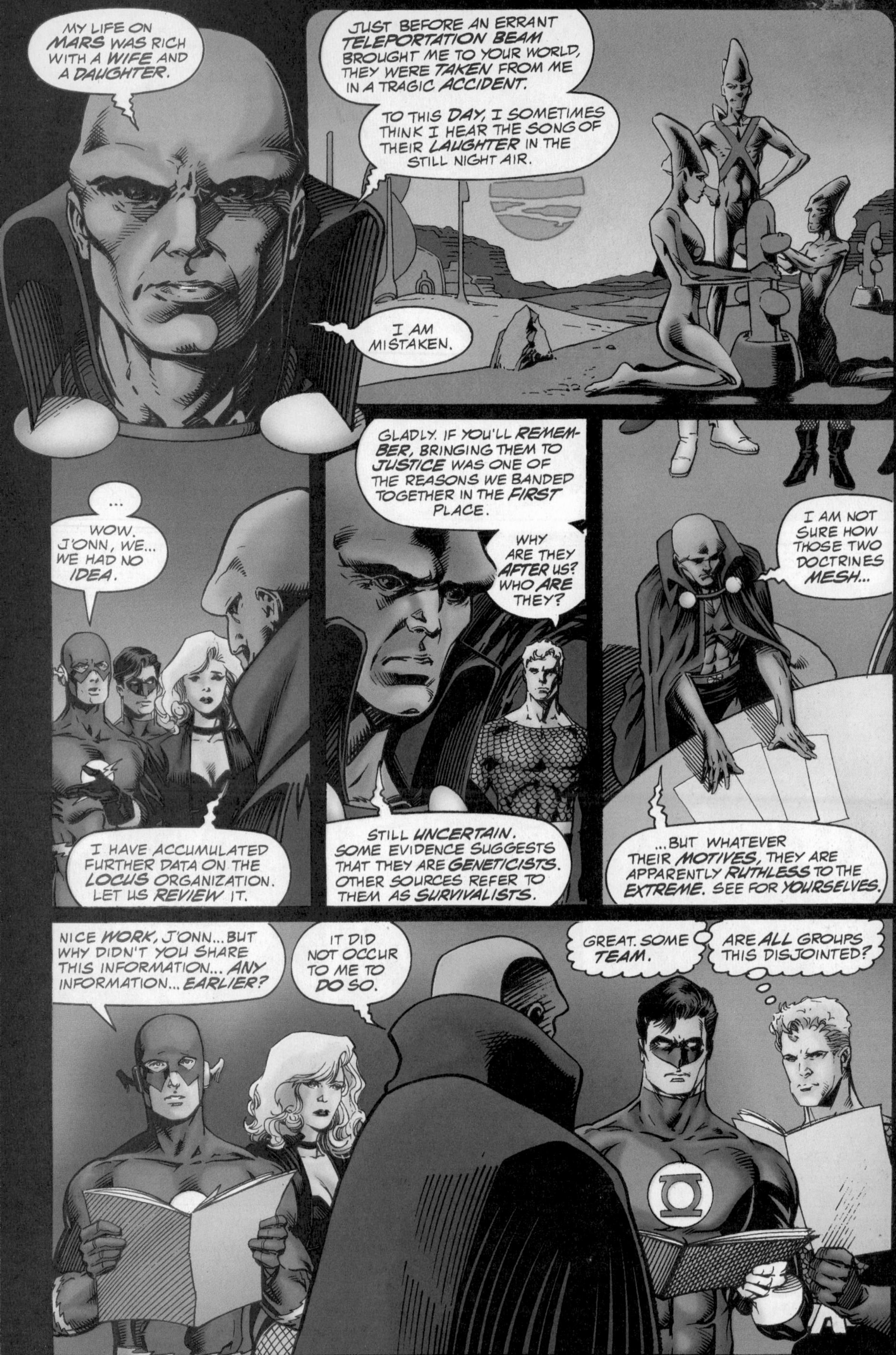

MY LIFE ON MARS WAS RICH WITH A WIFE AND A DAUGHTER.
JUST BEFORE AN ERRANT TELEPORTATION BEAM BROUGHT ME TO YOUR WORLD, THEY WERE TAKEN FROM ME IN A TRAGIC ACCIDENT.
TO THIS DAY, I SOMETIMES THINK I HEAR THE SONG OF THEIR LAUGHTER IN THE STILL NIGHT AIR.
I AM MISTAKEN.
...
WOW. J'ONN, WE... WE HAD NO IDEA.
I HAVE ACCUMULATED FURTHER DATA ON THE LOCUS ORGANIZATION. LET US REVIEW IT.
GLADLY. IF YOU'LL REMEMBER, BRINGING THEM TO JUSTICE WAS ONE OF THE REASONS WE BANDED TOGETHER IN THE FIRST PLACE.
WHY ARE THEY AFTER US? WHO ARE THEY?
STILL UNCERTAIN. SOME EVIDENCE SUGGESTS THAT THEY ARE GENETICISTS. OTHER SOURCES REFER TO THEM AS SURVIVALISTS.
I AM NOT SURE HOW THOSE TWO DOCTRINES MESH...
...BUT WHATEVER THEIR MOTIVES, THEY ARE APPARENTLY RUTHLESS TO THE EXTREME. SEE FOR YOURSELVES.
NICE WORK, J'ONN... BUT WHY DIDN'T YOU SHARE THIS INFORMATION... ANY INFORMATION... EARLIER?
IT DID NOT OCCUR TO ME TO DO SO.
GREAT. SOME TEAM.
ARE ALL GROUPS THIS DISJOINTED?

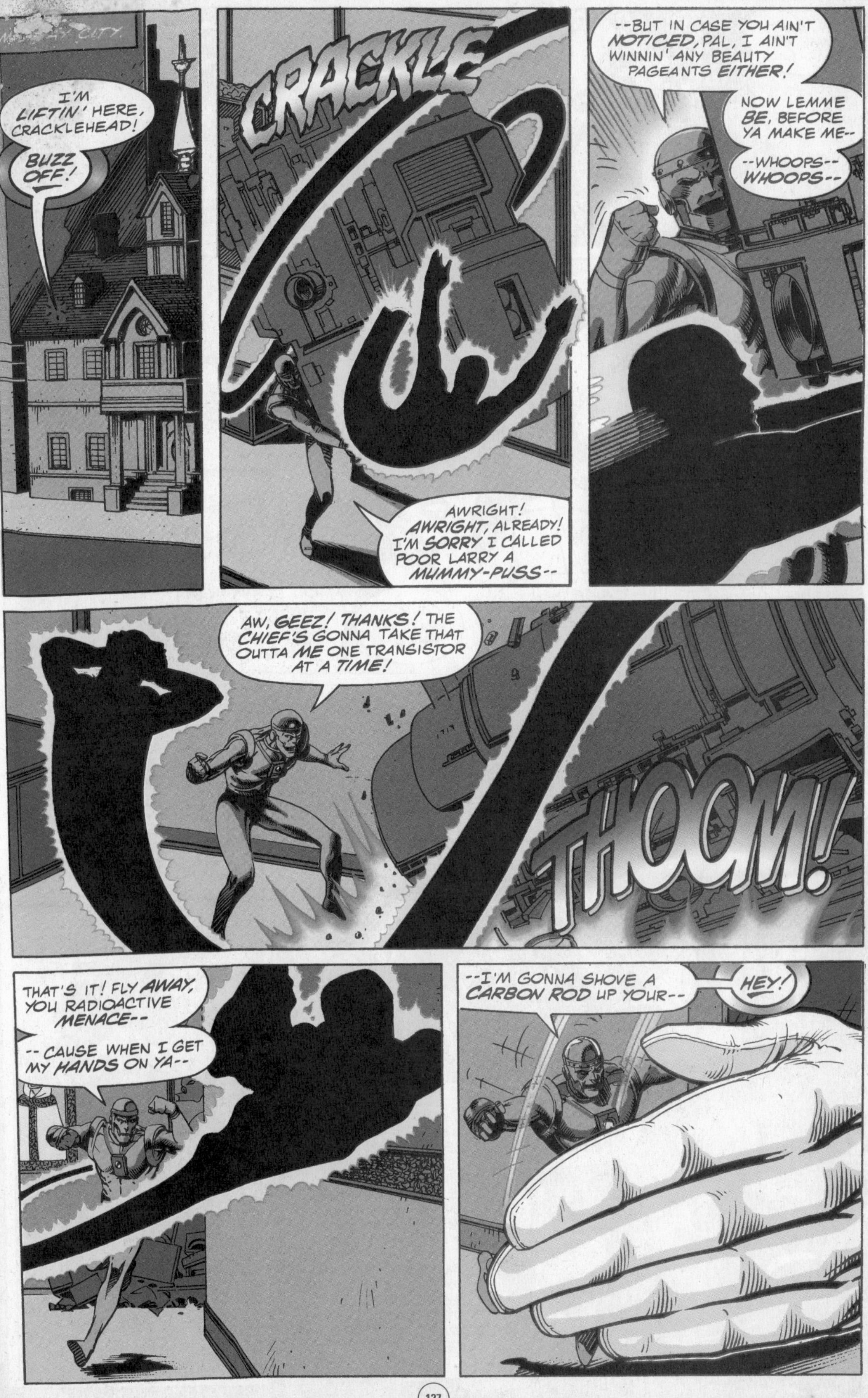
I'M LIFTIN' HERE, CRACKLEHEAD!
BUZZ OFF!
CRACKLE
AWRIGHT! AWRIGHT, ALREADY! I'M SORRY I CALLED POOR LARRY A MUMMY-PUSS--
--BUT IN CASE YOU AIN'T NOTICED, PAL, I AIN'T WINNIN' ANY BEAUTY PAGEANTS EITHER!
NOW LEMME BE, BEFORE YA MAKE ME--
--WHOOPS--
WHOOPS--
AW, GEEZ! THANKS! THE CHIEF'S GONNA TAKE THAT OUTTA ME ONE TRANSISTOR AT A TIME!
THOOM!
THAT'S IT! FLY AWAY, YOU RADIOACTIVE MENACE--
--CAUSE WHEN I GET MY HANDS ON YA--
--I'M GONNA SHOVE A CARBON ROD UP YOUR--
HEY!

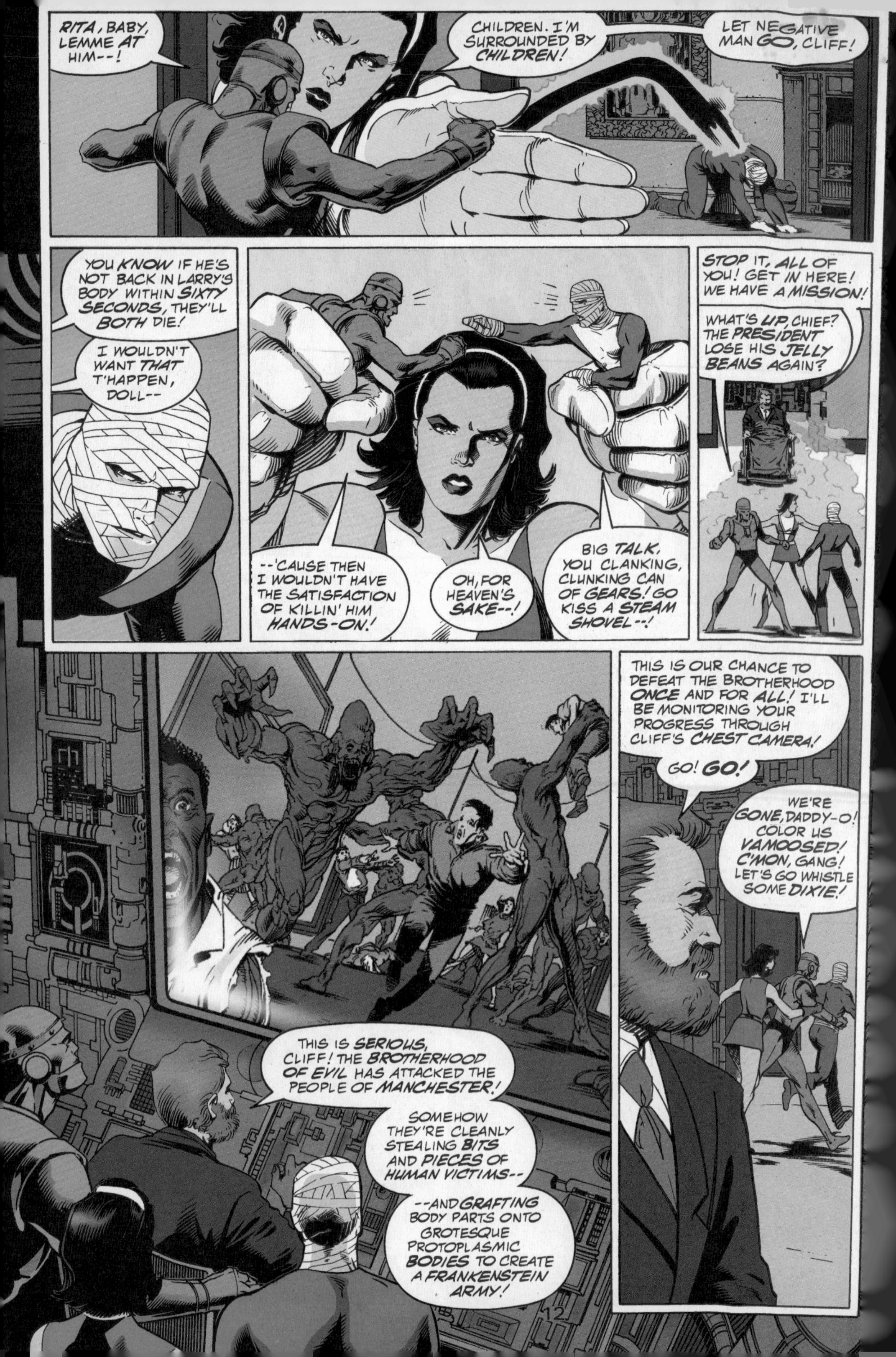

RITA, BABY, LEMME AT HIM--!
CHILDREN. I'M SURROUNDED BY CHILDREN!
LET NEGATIVE MAN GO, CLIFF!
YOU KNOW IF HE'S NOT BACK IN LARRY'S BODY WITHIN SIXTY SECONDS, THEY'LL BOTH DIE!
I WOULDN'T WANT THAT T'HAPPEN, DOLL--
--'CAUSE THEN I WOULDN'T HAVE THE SATISFACTION OF KILLIN' HIM HANDS-ON!
OH, FOR HEAVEN'S SAKE--!
BIG TALK, YOU CLANKING, CLUNKING CAN OF GEARS! GO KISS A STEAM SHOVEL--!
STOP IT, ALL OF YOU! GET IN HERE! WE HAVE A MISSION!
WHAT'S UP, CHIEF? THE PRESIDENT LOSE HIS JELLY BEANS AGAIN?
THIS IS SERIOUS, CLIFF! THE BROTHERHOOD OF EVIL HAS ATTACKED THE PEOPLE OF MANCHESTER!
SOMEHOW THEY'RE CLEANLY STEALING BITS AND PIECES OF HUMAN VICTIMS--
--AND GRAFTING BODY PARTS ONTO GROTESQUE PROTOPLASMIC BODIES TO CREATE A FRANKENSTEIN ARMY!
THIS IS OUR CHANCE TO DEFEAT THE BROTHERHOOD ONCE AND FOR ALL! I'LL BE MONITORING YOUR PROGRESS THROUGH CLIFF'S CHEST CAMERA!
GO! GO!
WE'RE GONE, DADDY-O! COLOR US VAMOOSED! C'MON, GANG! LET'S GO WHISTLE SOME DIXIE!
12

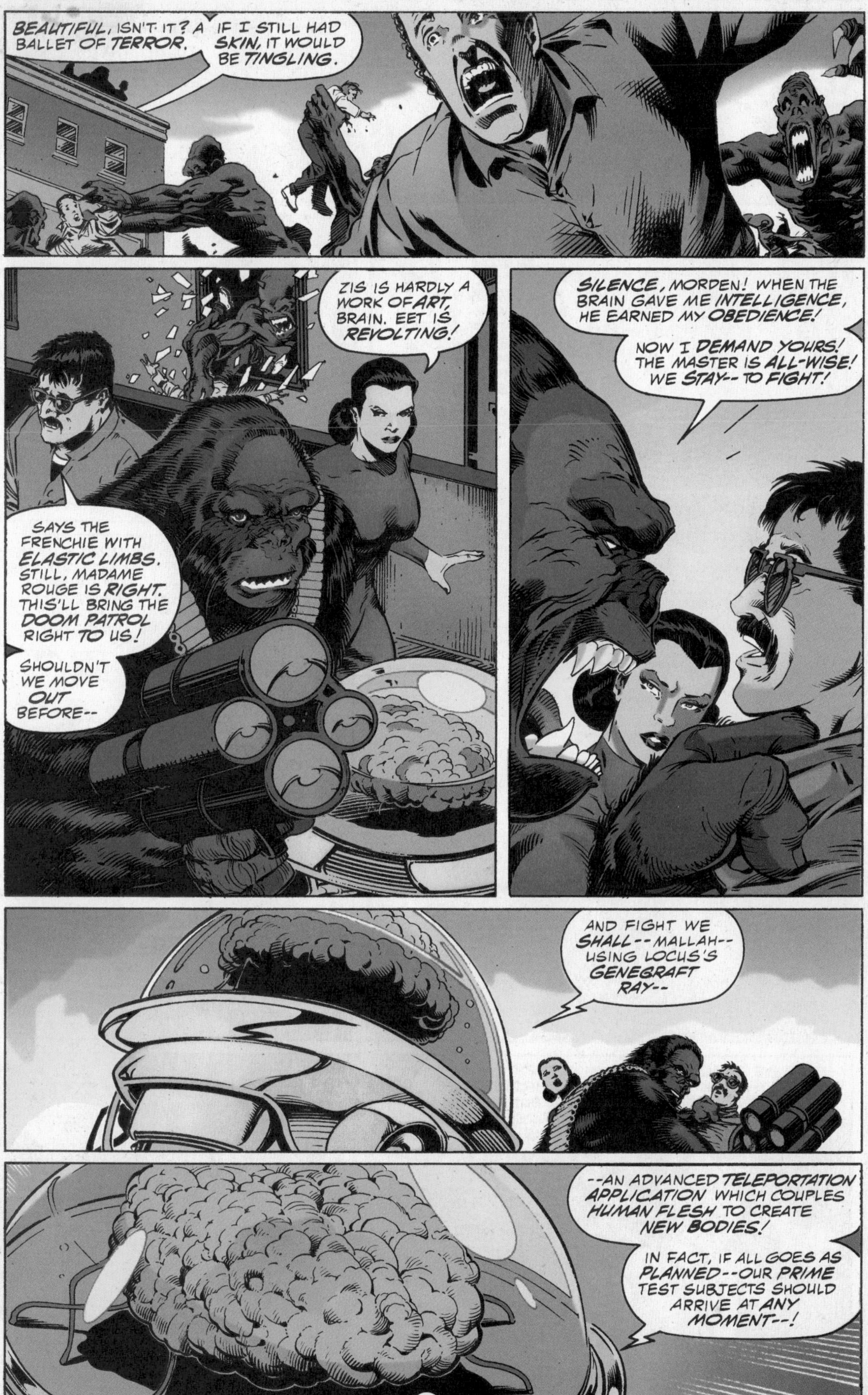

BEAUTIFUL, ISN'T IT? A BALLET OF TERROR.
IF I STILL HAD SKIN, IT WOULD BE TINGLING.
ZIS IS HARDLY A WORK OF ART, BRAIN. EET IS REVOLTING!
SAYS THE FRENCHIE WITH ELASTIC LIMBS. STILL, MADAME ROUGE IS RIGHT. THIS'LL BRING THE DOOM PATROL RIGHT TO US!
SHOULDN'T WE MOVE OUT BEFORE--
SILENCE, MORDEN! WHEN THE BRAIN GAVE ME INTELLIGENCE, HE EARNED MY OBEDIENCE!
NOW I DEMAND YOURS! THE MASTER IS ALL-WISE! WE STAY-- TO FIGHT!
AND FIGHT WE SHALL--MALLAH--USING LOCUS'S GENEGRAFT RAY--
--AN ADVANCED TELEPORTATION APPLICATION WHICH COUPLES HUMAN FLESH TO CREATE NEW BODIES!
IN FACT, IF ALL GOES AS PLANNED--OUR PRIME TEST SUBJECTS SHOULD ARRIVE AT ANY MOMENT--!

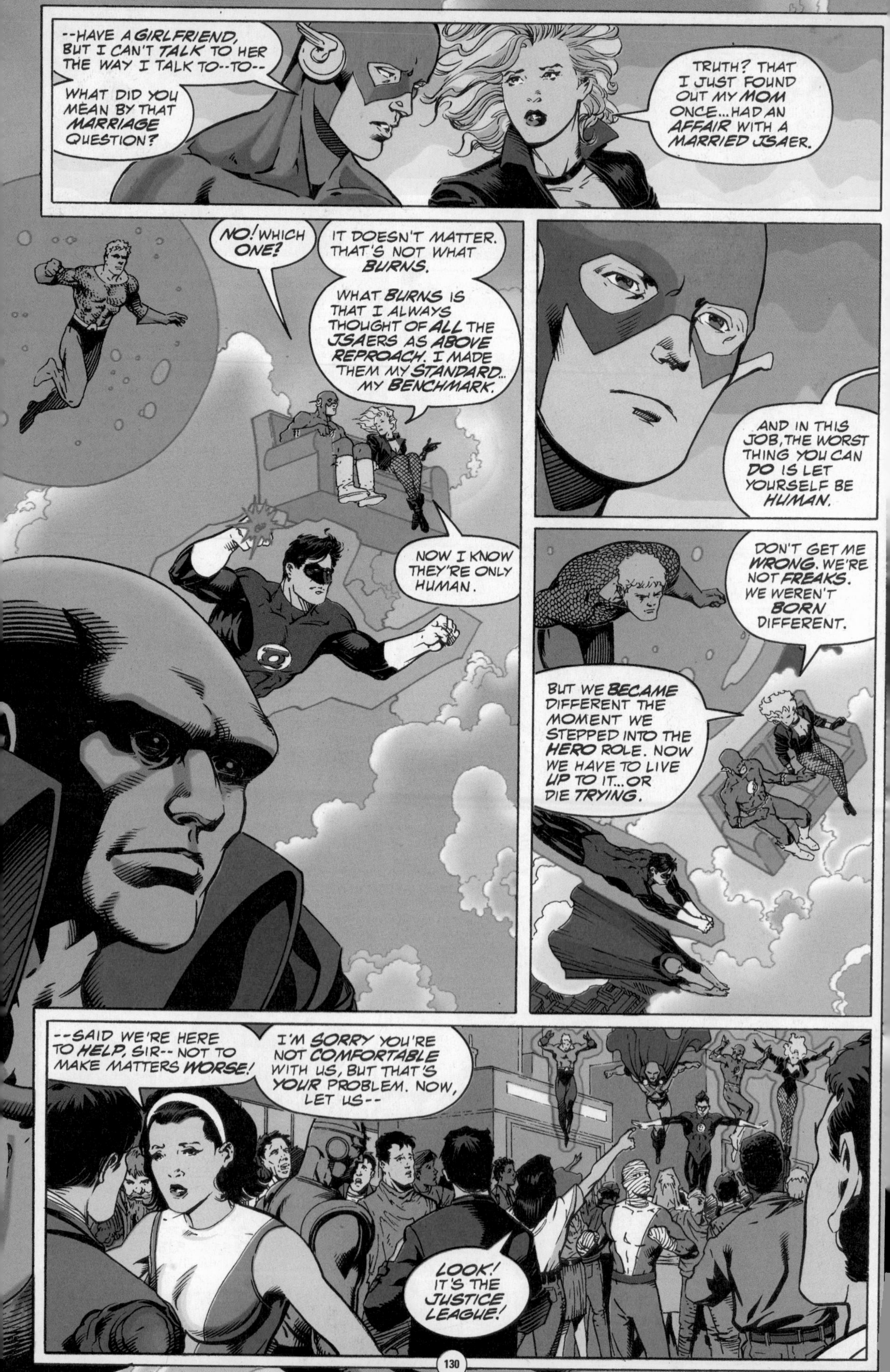

--HAVE A GIRLFRIEND, BUT I CAN'T TALK TO HER THE WAY I TALK TO--TO--
WHAT DID YOU MEAN BY THAT MARRIAGE QUESTION?
TRUTH? THAT I JUST FOUND OUT MY MOM ONCE...HAD AN AFFAIR WITH A MARRIED JSAER.
NO! WHICH ONE?
IT DOESN'T MATTER. THAT'S NOT WHAT BURNS.
WHAT BURNS IS THAT I ALWAYS THOUGHT OF ALL THE JSAERS AS ABOVE REPROACH. I MADE THEM MY STANDARD... MY BENCHMARK.
NOW I KNOW THEY'RE ONLY HUMAN.
AND IN THIS JOB, THE WORST THING YOU CAN DO IS LET YOURSELF BE HUMAN.
DON'T GET ME WRONG. WE'RE NOT FREAKS. WE WEREN'T BORN DIFFERENT.
BUT WE BECAME DIFFERENT THE MOMENT WE STEPPED INTO THE HERO ROLE. NOW WE HAVE TO LIVE UP TO IT...OR DIE TRYING.
--SAID WE'RE HERE TO HELP, SIR-- NOT TO MAKE MATTERS WORSE!
I'M SORRY YOU'RE NOT COMFORTABLE WITH US, BUT THAT'S YOUR PROBLEM. NOW, LET US--
LOOK! IT'S THE JUSTICE LEAGUE!

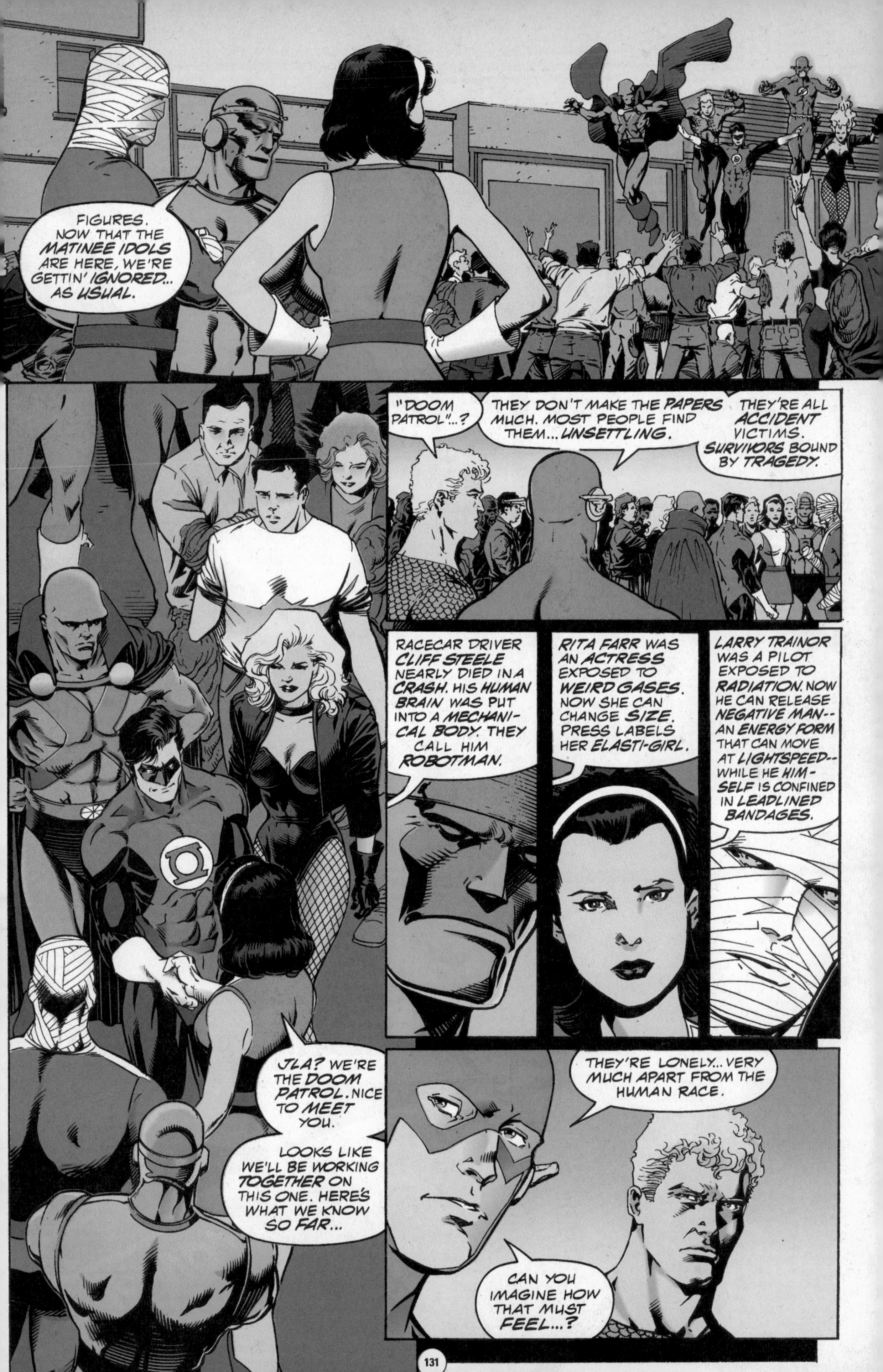
FIGURES. NOW THAT THE MATINEE IDOLS ARE HERE, WE'RE GETTIN' IGNORED... AS USUAL.
"DOOM PATROL"..?
THEY DON'T MAKE THE PAPERS MUCH. MOST PEOPLE FIND THEM... UNSETTLING.
THEY'RE ALL ACCIDENT VICTIMS. SURVIVORS BOUND BY TRAGEDY.
RACECAR DRIVER CLIFF STEELE NEARLY DIED IN A CRASH. HIS HUMAN BRAIN WAS PUT INTO A MECHANICAL BODY. THEY CALL HIM ROBOTMAN.
RITA FARR WAS AN ACTRESS EXPOSED TO WEIRD GASES. NOW SHE CAN CHANGE SIZE. PRESS LABELS HER ELASTI-GIRL.
LARRY TRAINOR WAS A PILOT EXPOSED TO RADIATION. NOW HE CAN RELEASE NEGATIVE MAN-- AN ENERGY FORM THAT CAN MOVE AT LIGHTSPEED-- WHILE HE HIMSELF IS CONFINED IN LEADLINED BANDAGES.
JLA? WE'RE THE DOOM PATROL. NICE TO MEET YOU.
LOOKS LIKE WE'LL BE WORKING TOGETHER ON THIS ONE. HERE'S WHAT WE KNOW SO FAR...
THEY'RE LONELY... VERY MUCH APART FROM THE HUMAN RACE.
CAN YOU IMAGINE HOW THAT MUST FEEL...?

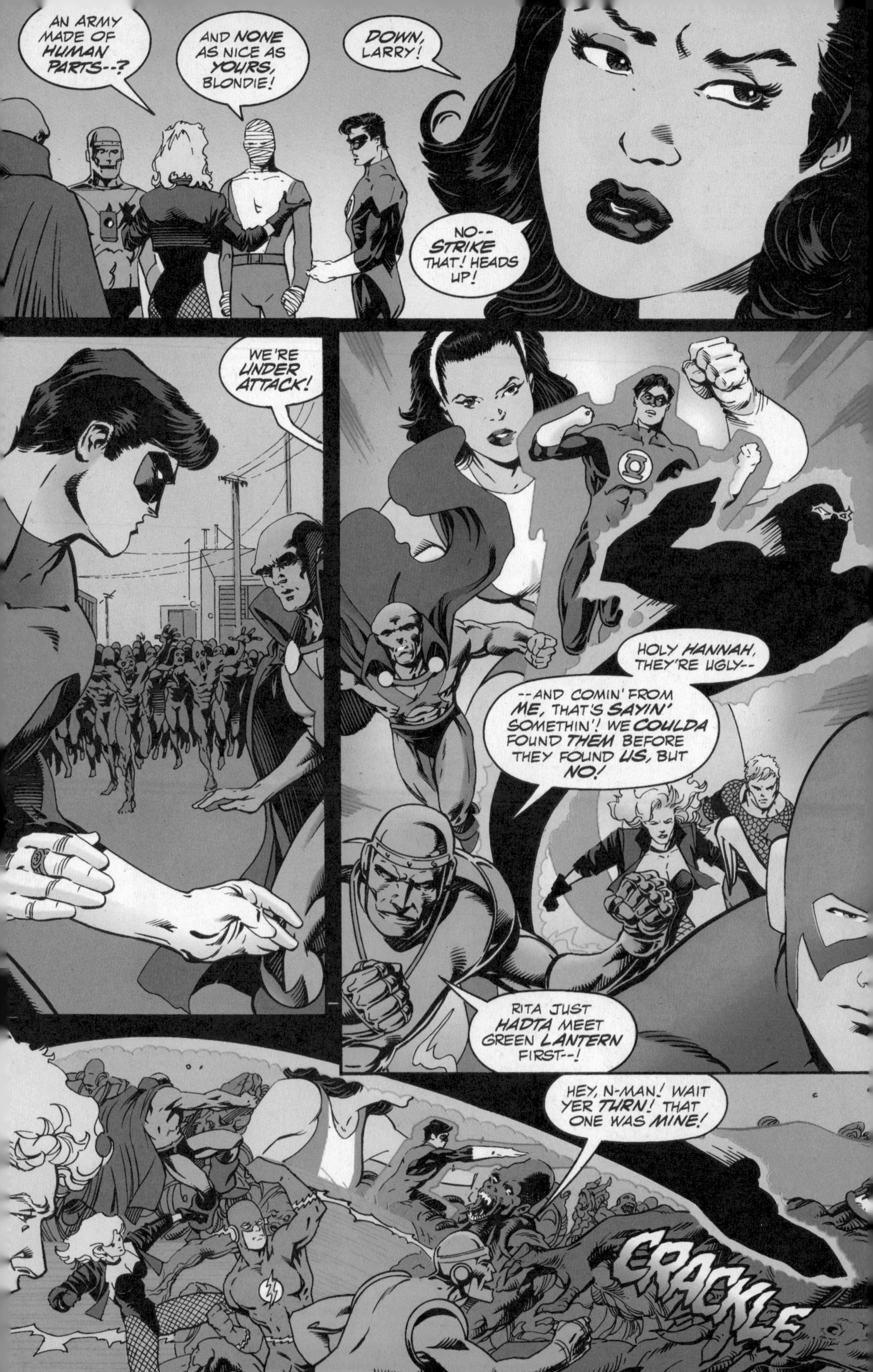
AN ARMY MADE OF HUMAN PARTS--?
AND NONE AS NICE AS YOURS, BLONDIE!
DOWN, LARRY!
NO-- STRIKE THAT! HEADS UP!
WE'RE UNDER ATTACK!
HOLY HANNAH, THEY'RE UGLY--
--AND COMIN' FROM ME, THAT'S SAYIN' SOMETHIN'! WE COULDA FOUND THEM BEFORE THEY FOUND US, BUT NO!
RITA JUST HADTA MEET GREEN LANTERN FIRST--!
HEY, N-MAN! WAIT YER TURN! THAT ONE WAS MINE!
CRACKLE

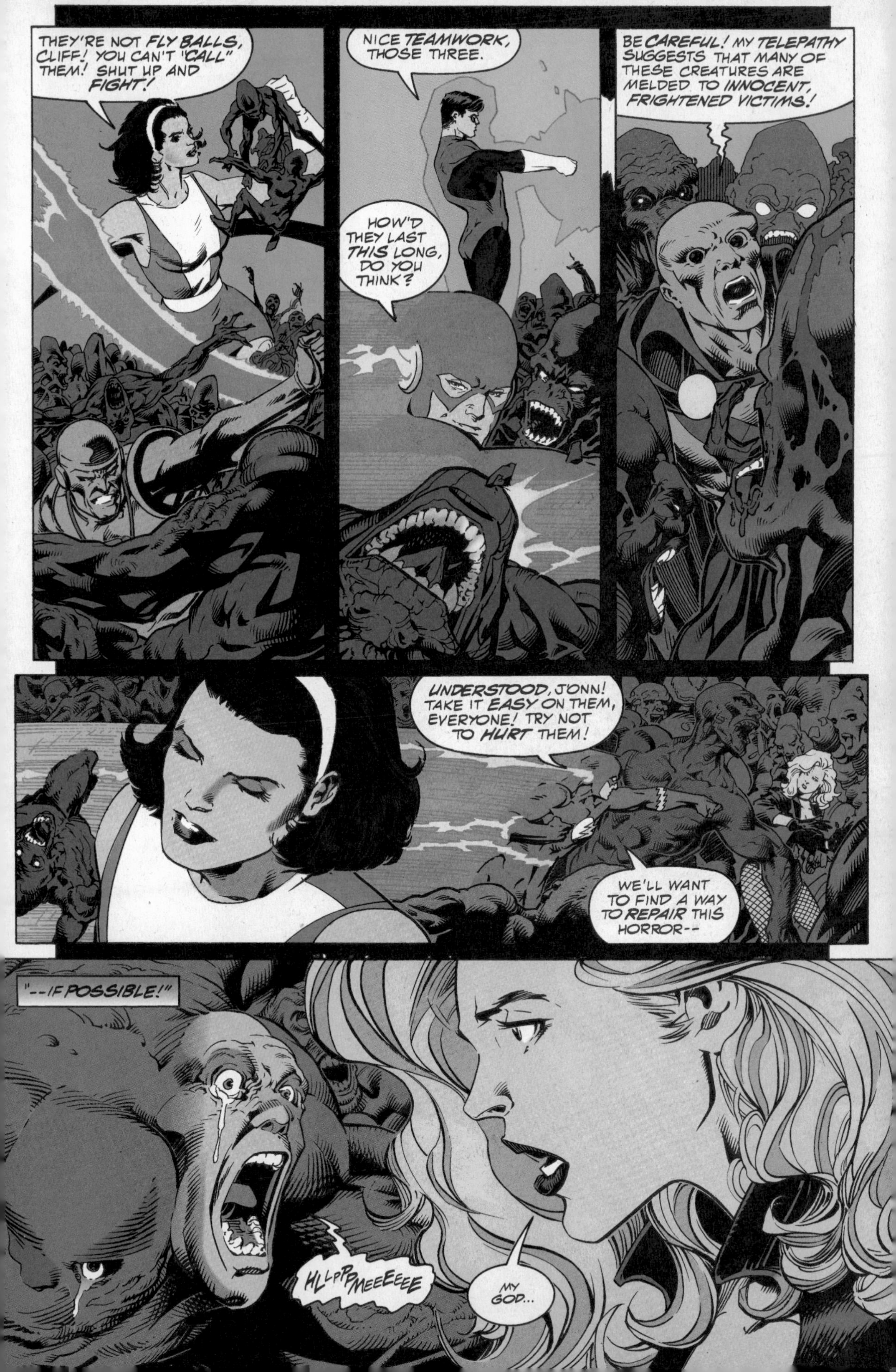
THEY'RE NOT FLY BALLS, CLIFF! YOU CAN'T "CALL" THEM! SHUT UP AND FIGHT!
NICE TEAMWORK, THOSE THREE.
HOW'D THEY LAST THIS LONG, DO YOU THINK?
BE CAREFUL! MY TELEPATHY SUGGESTS THAT MANY OF THESE CREATURES ARE MELDED TO INNOCENT, FRIGHTENED VICTIMS!
UNDERSTOOD, J'ONN! TAKE IT EASY ON THEM, EVERYONE! TRY NOT TO HURT THEM!
WE'LL WANT TO FIND A WAY TO REPAIR THIS HORROR--
"--IF POSSIBLE!"
HLLPPMEEEEEE
MY GOD...

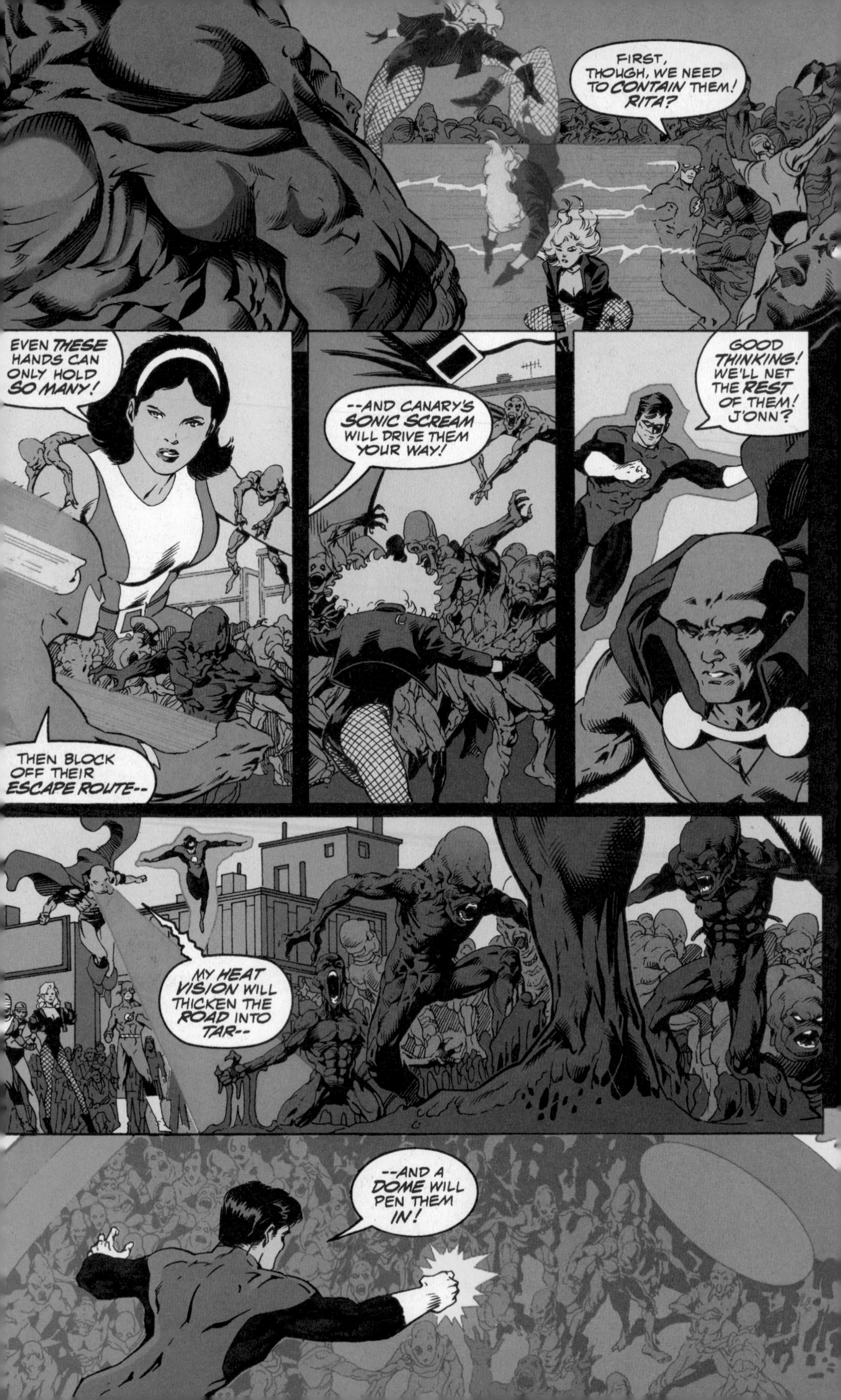
FIRST, THOUGH, WE NEED TO CONTAIN THEM! RITA?
EVEN THESE HANDS CAN ONLY HOLD SO MANY!
THEN BLOCK OFF THEIR ESCAPE ROUTE--
--AND CANARY'S SONIC SCREAM WILL DRIVE THEM YOUR WAY!
GOOD THINKING! WE'LL NET THE REST OF THEM! J'ONN?
MY HEAT VISION WILL THICKEN THE ROAD INTO TAR--
--AND A DOME WILL PEN THEM IN!

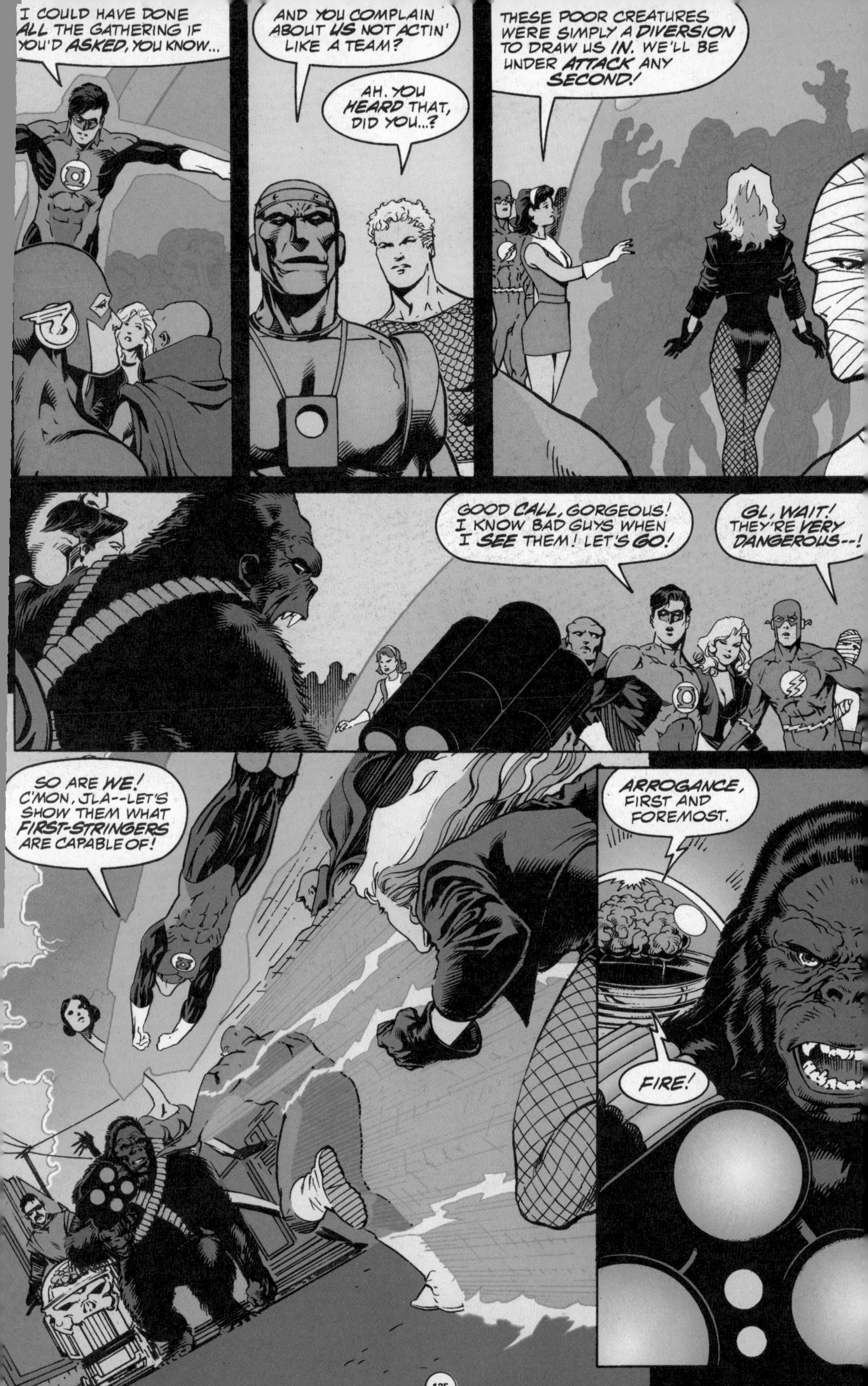
I COULD HAVE DONE ALL THE GATHERING IF YOU'D ASKED, YOU KNOW...
AND YOU COMPLAIN ABOUT US NOT ACTIN' LIKE A TEAM?
AH. YOU HEARD THAT, DID YOU...?
THESE POOR CREATURES WERE SIMPLY A DIVERSION TO DRAW US IN. WE'LL BE UNDER ATTACK ANY SECOND!
GOOD CALL, GORGEOUS! I KNOW BAD GUYS WHEN I SEE THEM! LET'S GO!
GL, WAIT! THEY'RE VERY DANGEROUS--!
SO ARE WE! C'MON, JLA--LET'S SHOW THEM WHAT FIRST-STRINGERS ARE CAPABLE OF!
ARROGANCE, FIRST AND FOREMOST.
FIRE!

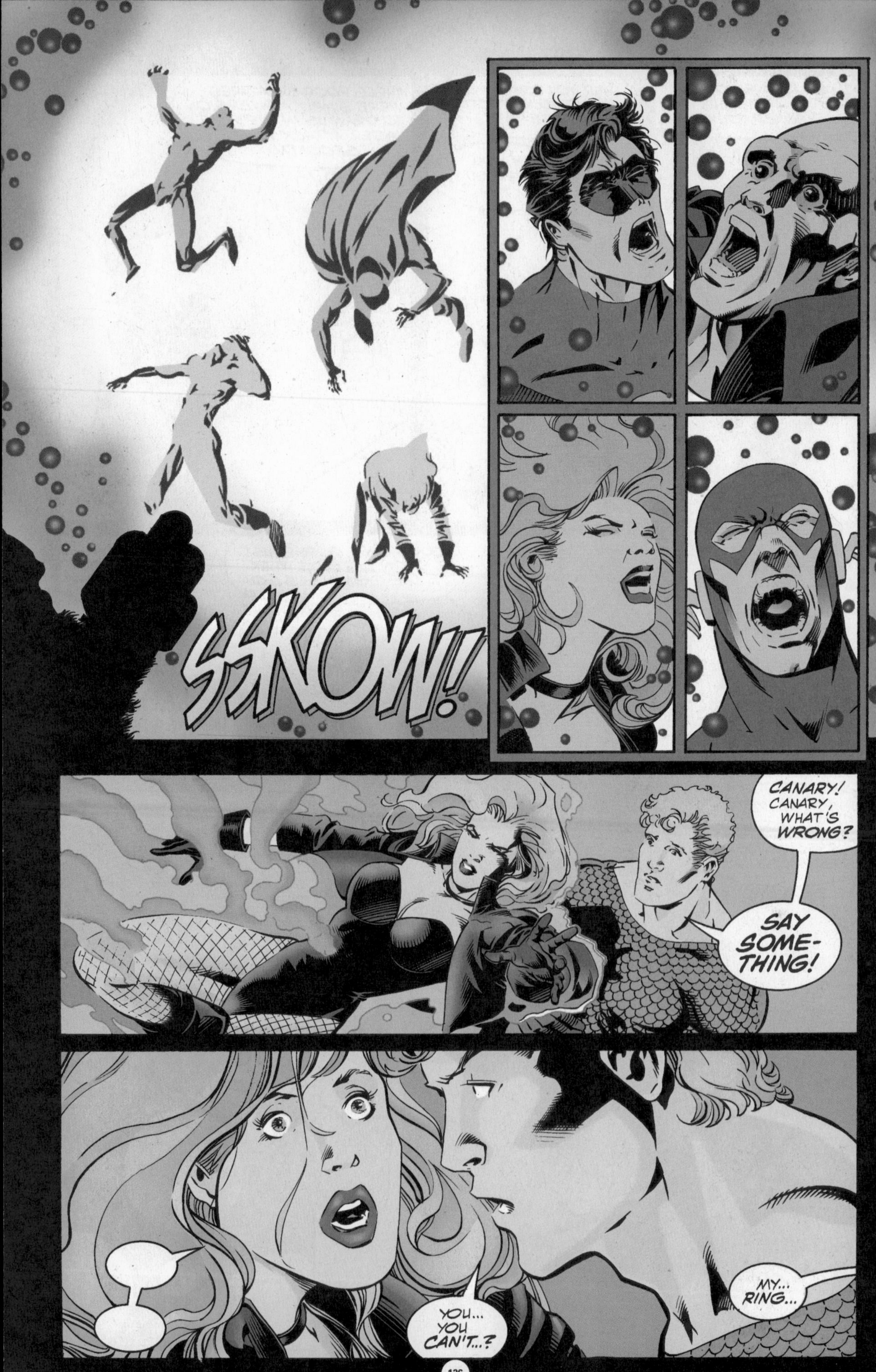
SSKOW!!
CANARY! CANARY, WHAT'S WRONG?
SAY SOME-THING!
YOU... YOU CAN'T...?
MY... RING...

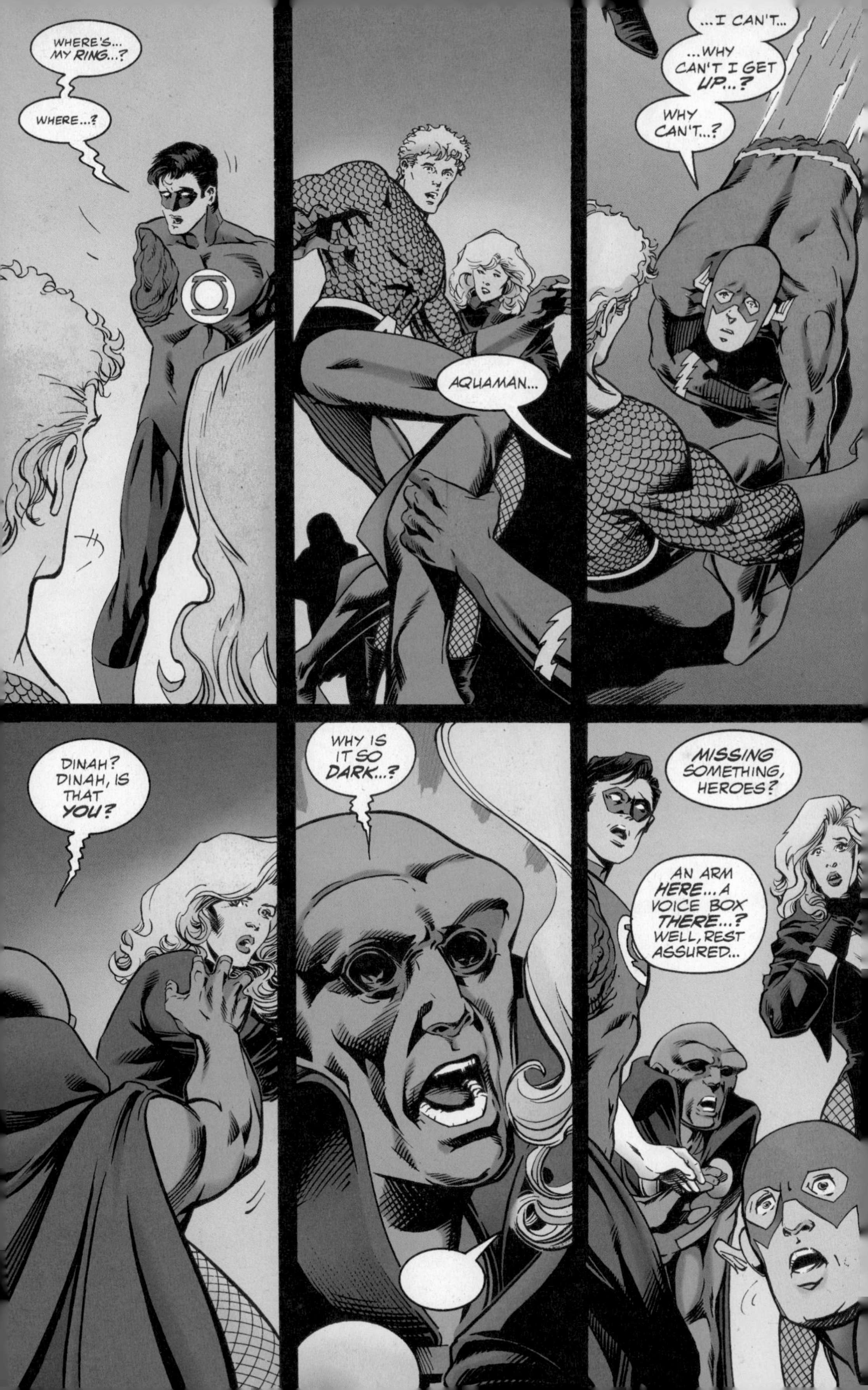
WHERE'S... MY RING...?
WHERE...?
...I CAN'T...
...WHY CAN'T I GET UP...?
WHY CAN'T...?
AQUAMAN...
DINAH? DINAH, IS THAT YOU?
WHY IS IT SO DARK...?
MISSING SOMETHING, HEROES?
AN ARM HERE... A VOICE BOX THERE...? WELL, REST ASSURED...

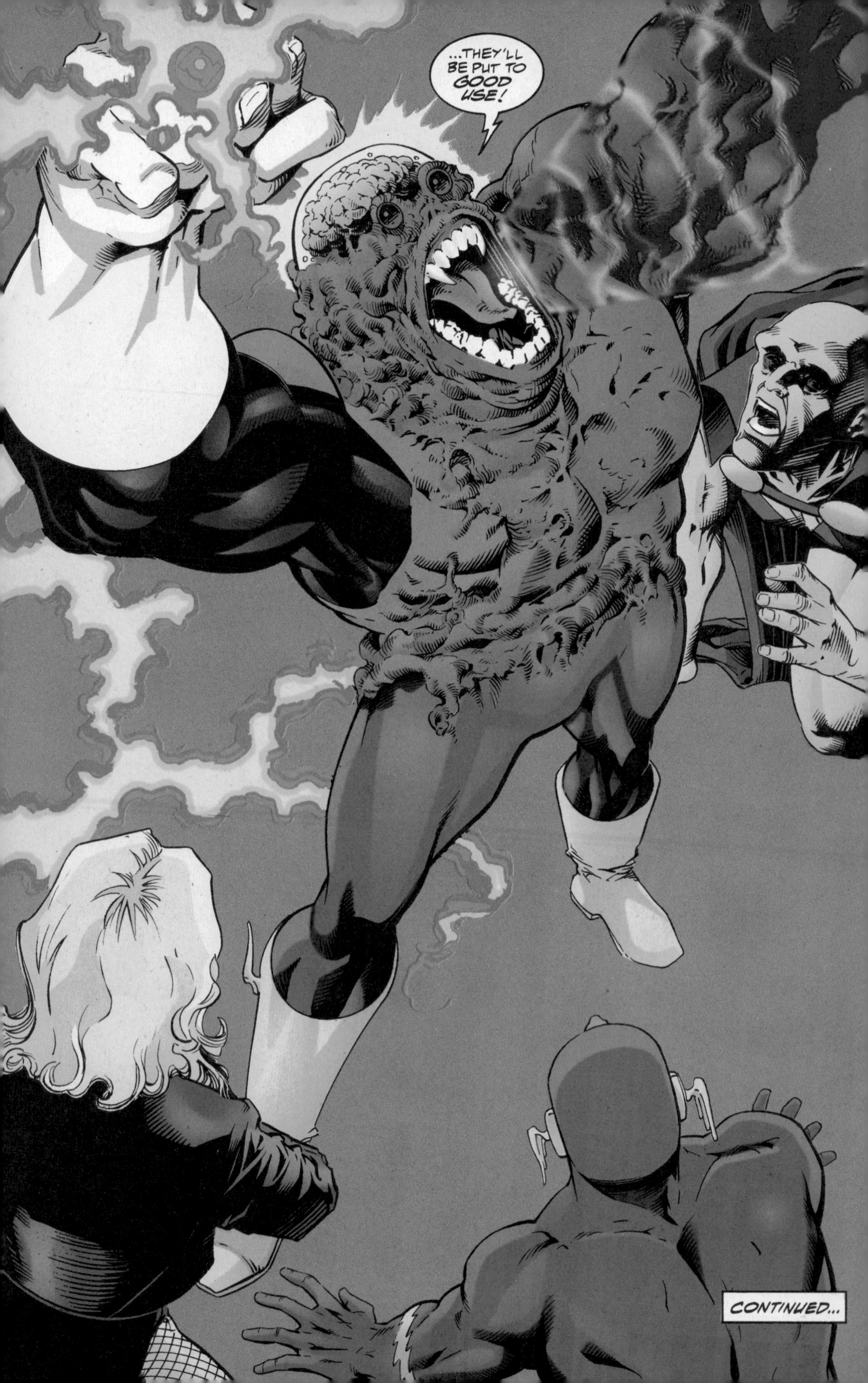
...THEY'LL BE PUT TO GOOD USE!
CONTINUED...

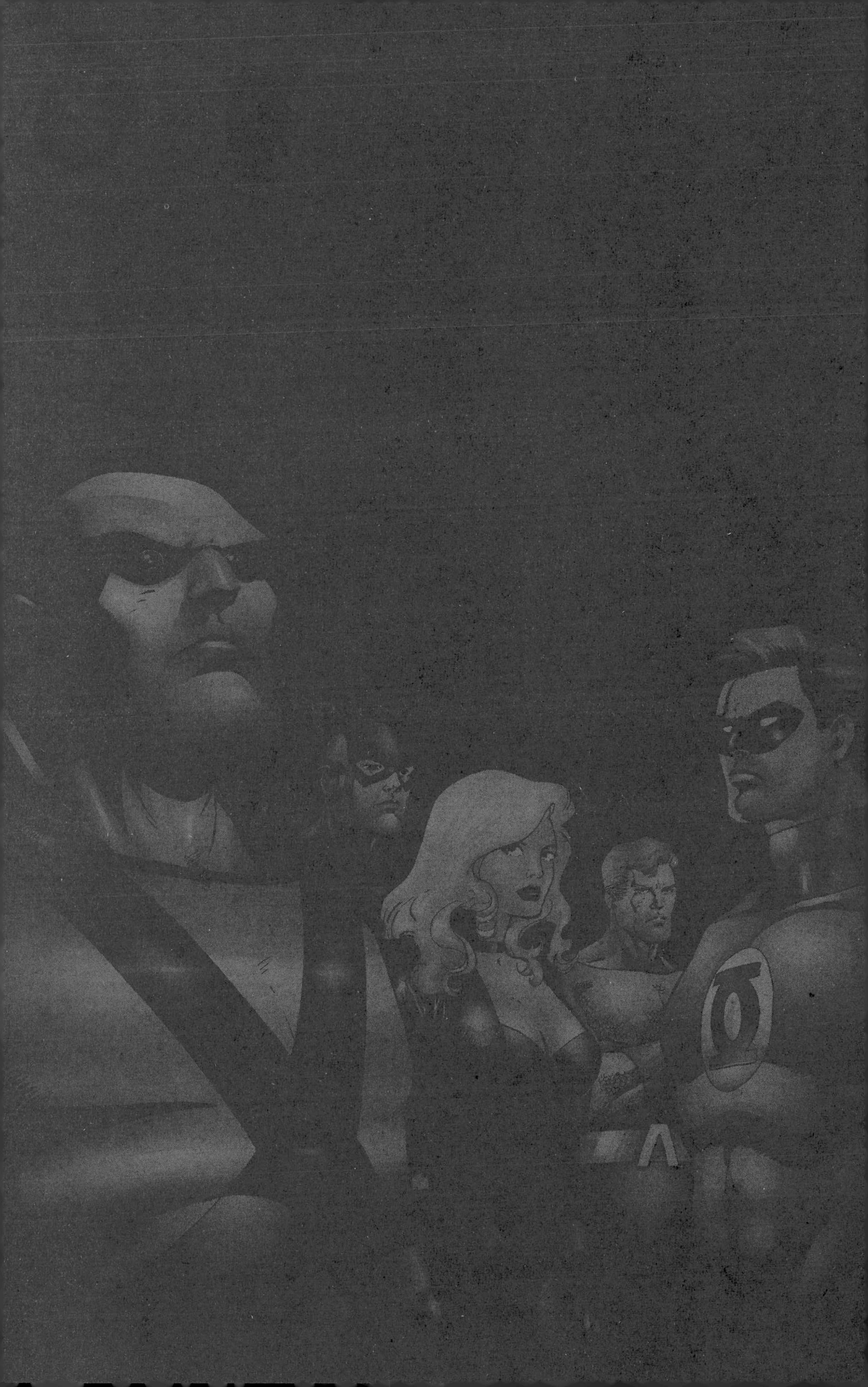

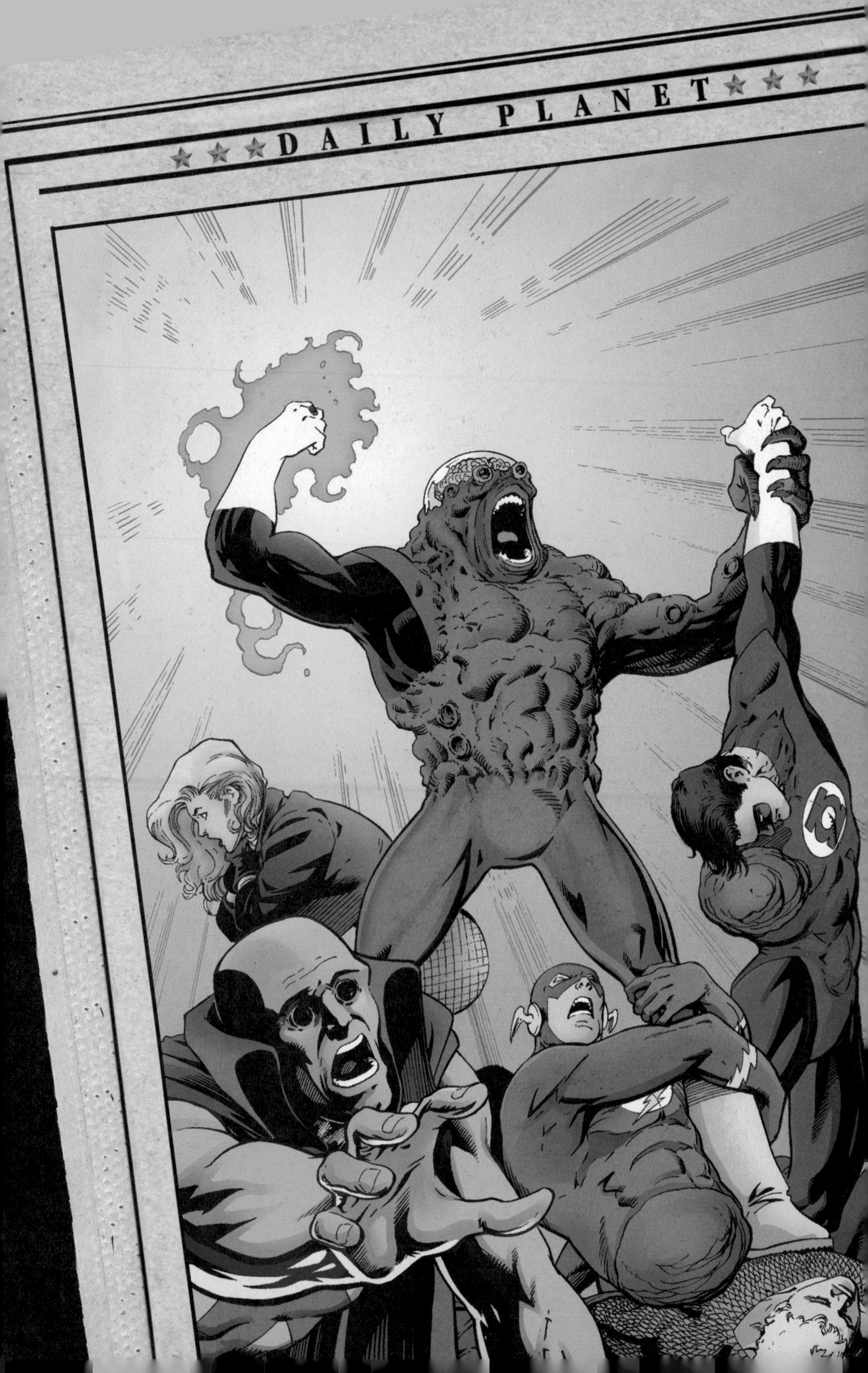
DAILY PLANET

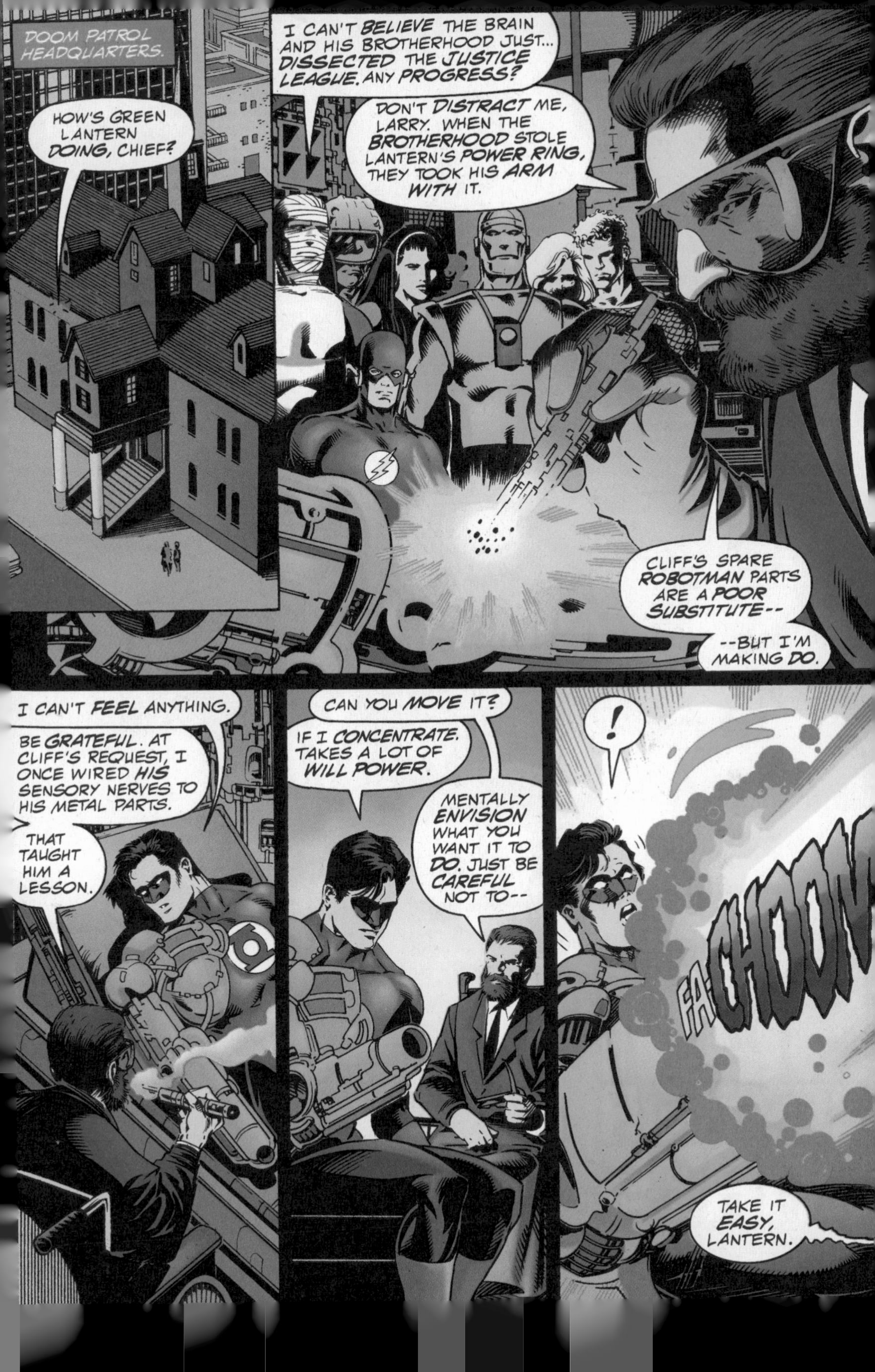
DOOM PATROL HEADQUARTERS.
HOW'S GREEN LANTERN DOING, CHIEF?
I CAN'T BELIEVE THE BRAIN AND HIS BROTHERHOOD JUST... DISSECTED THE JUSTICE LEAGUE. ANY PROGRESS?
DON'T DISTRACT ME, LARRY. WHEN THE BROTHERHOOD STOLE LANTERN'S POWER RING, THEY TOOK HIS ARM WITH IT.
CLIFF'S SPARE ROBOTMAN PARTS ARE A POOR SUBSTITUTE--
--BUT I'M MAKING DO.
I CAN'T FEEL ANYTHING.
BE GRATEFUL. AT CLIFF'S REQUEST, I ONCE WIRED HIS SENSORY NERVES TO HIS METAL PARTS.
THAT TAUGHT HIM A LESSON.
CAN YOU MOVE IT?
IF I CONCENTRATE. TAKES A LOT OF WILL POWER.
MENTALLY ENVISION WHAT YOU WANT IT TO DO. JUST BE CAREFUL NOT TO--
!
FA-CHOON
TAKE IT EASY, LANTERN.

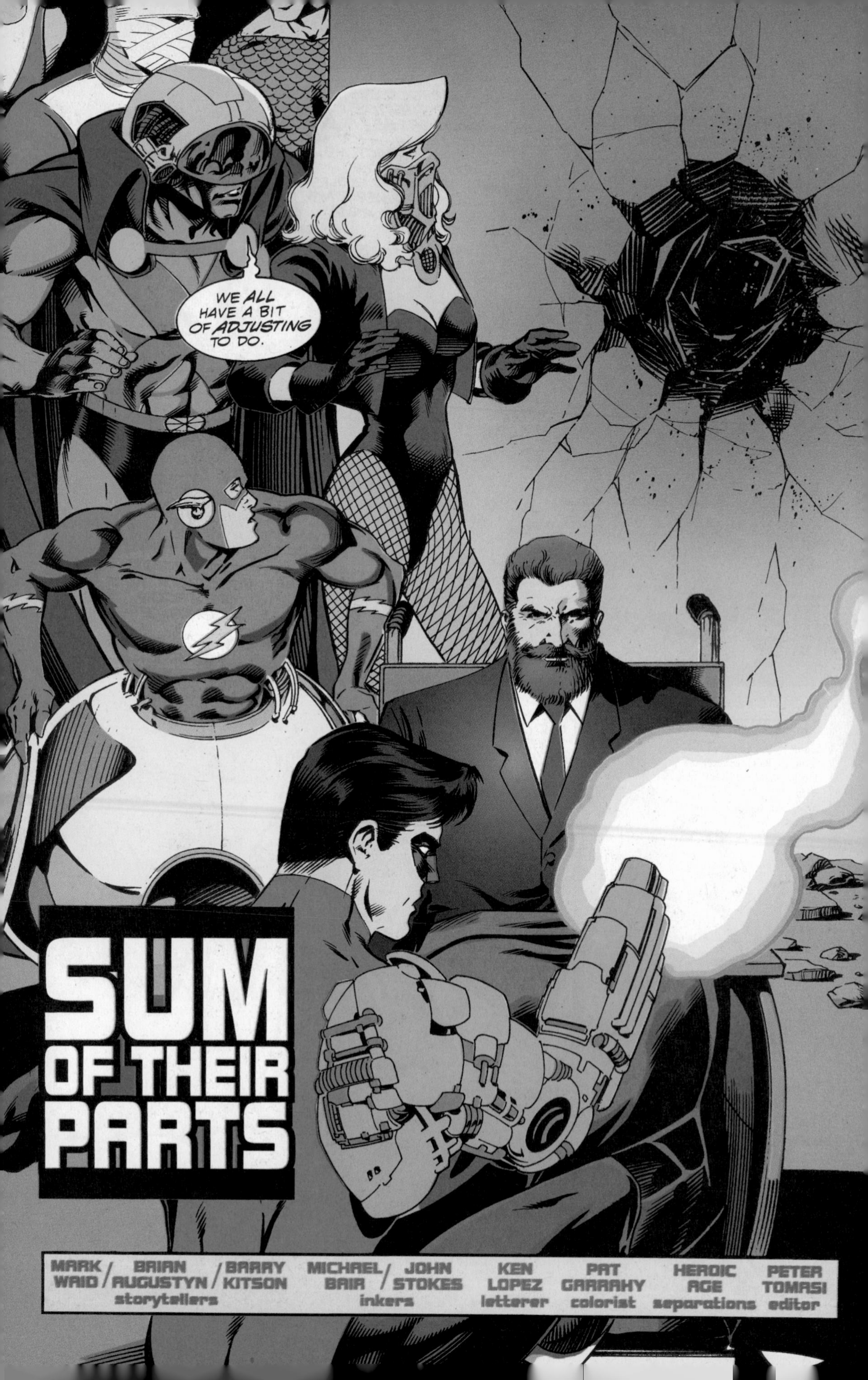
WE ALL HAVE A BIT OF ADJUSTING TO DO.
SUM OF THEIR PARTS
MARK WAID / BRIAN AUGUSTYN / BARRY KITSON storytellers
MICHAEL BAIR / JOHN STOKES inkers
KEN LOPEZ letterer
PAT GARRAHY colorist
HEROIC AGE separations
PETER TOMASI editor

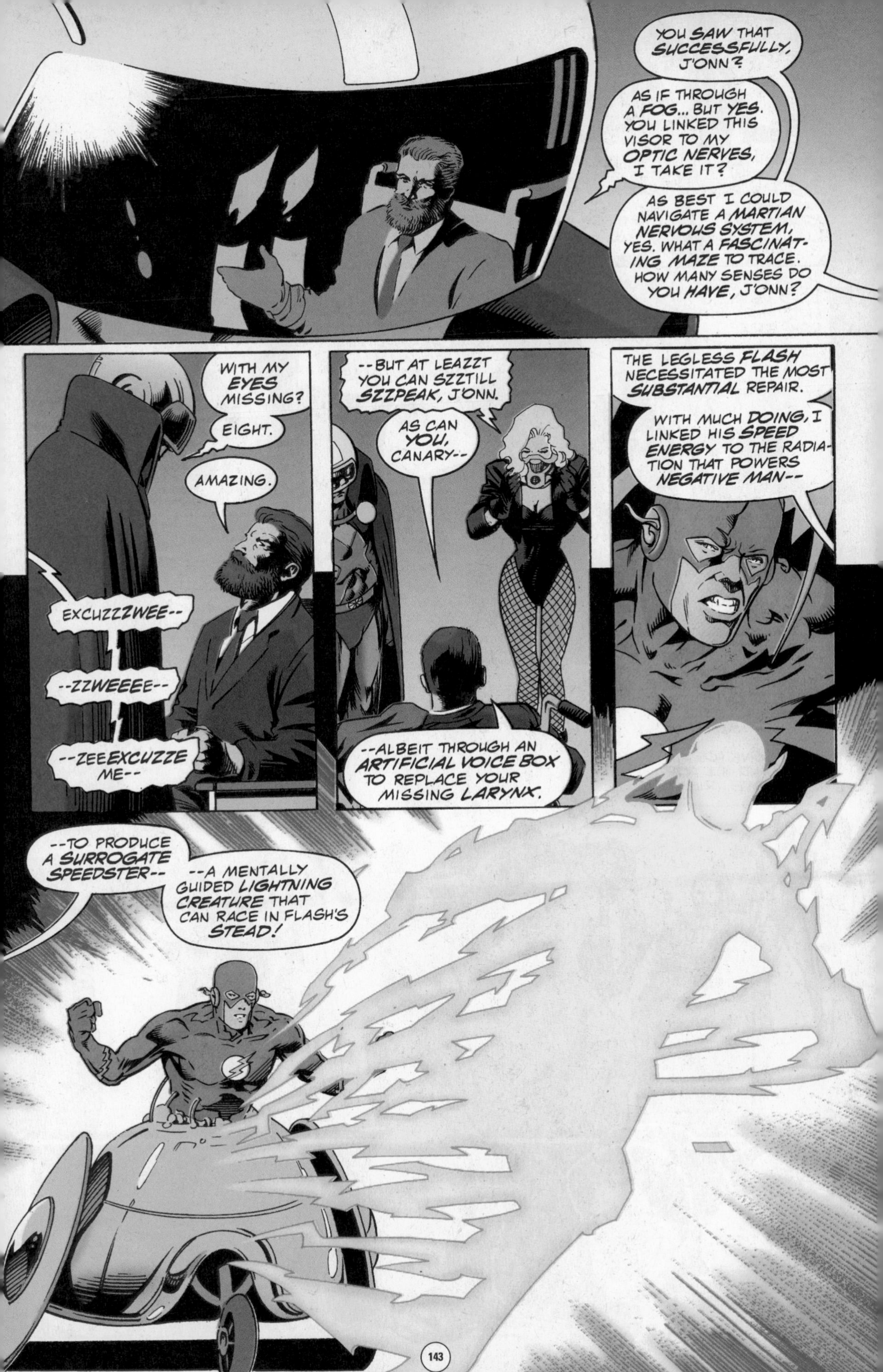

YOU SAW THAT SUCCESSFULLY, J'ONN?
AS IF THROUGH A FOG... BUT YES. YOU LINKED THIS VISOR TO MY OPTIC NERVES, I TAKE IT?
AS BEST I COULD NAVIGATE A MARTIAN NERVOUS SYSTEM, YES. WHAT A FASCINATING MAZE TO TRACE. HOW MANY SENSES DO YOU HAVE, J'ONN?
WITH MY EYES MISSING?
EIGHT.
AMAZING.
EXCUZZZWEE--
--ZZWEEEE--
--ZEEEXCUZZE ME--
--BUT AT LEAZZT YOU CAN SZZTILL SZZPEAK, J'ONN.
AS CAN YOU, CANARY--
--ALBEIT THROUGH AN ARTIFICIAL VOICE BOX TO REPLACE YOUR MISSING LARYNX.
THE LEGLESS FLASH NECESSITATED THE MOST SUBSTANTIAL REPAIR.
WITH MUCH DOING, I LINKED HIS SPEED ENERGY TO THE RADIATION THAT POWERS NEGATIVE MAN--
--TO PRODUCE A SURROGATE SPEEDSTER--
--A MENTALLY GUIDED LIGHTNING CREATURE THAT CAN RACE IN FLASH'S STEAD!

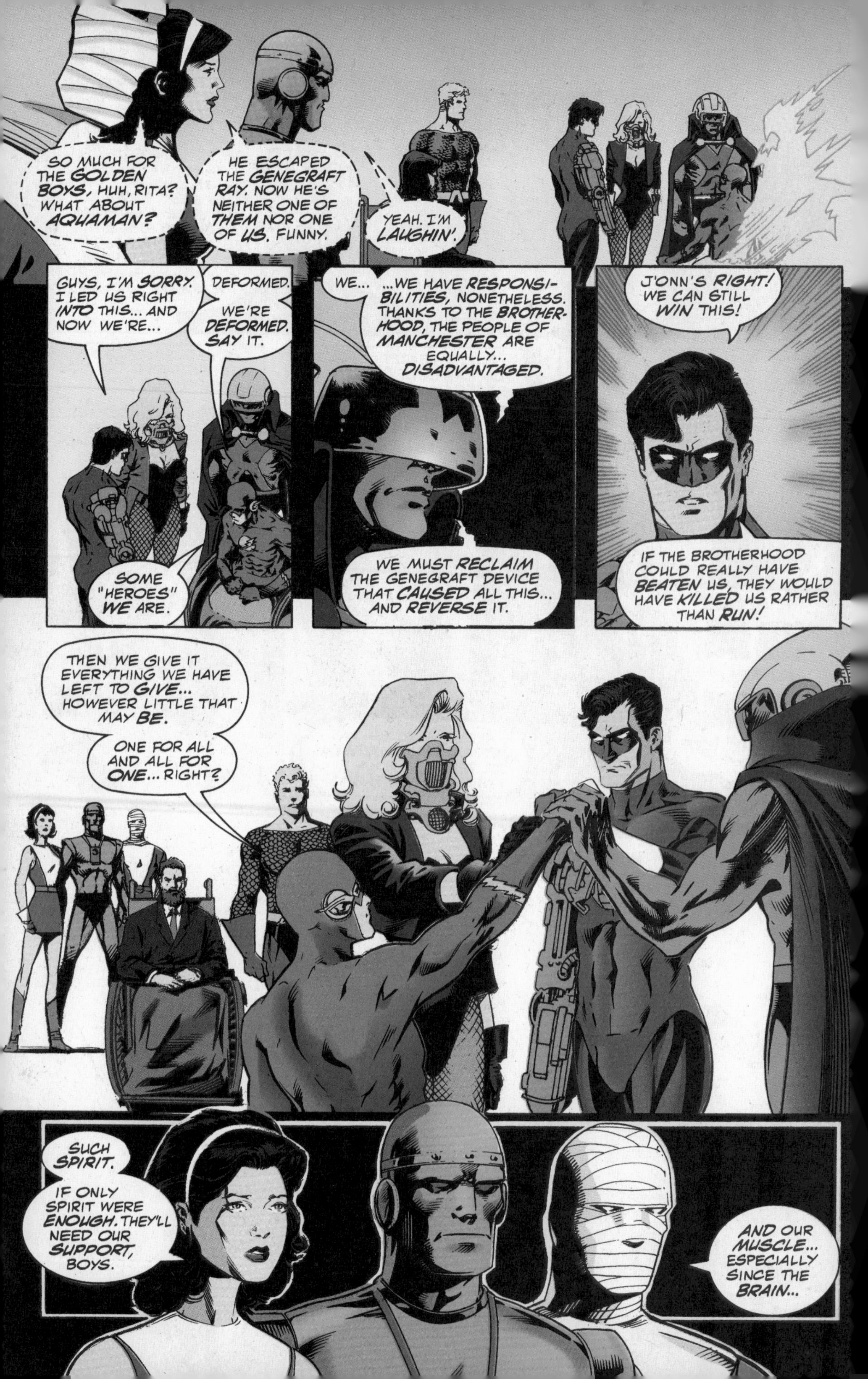
SO MUCH FOR THE GOLDEN BOYS, HUH, RITA? WHAT ABOUT AQUAMAN?
HE ESCAPED THE GENEGRAFT RAY. NOW HE'S NEITHER ONE OF THEM NOR ONE OF US. FUNNY.
YEAH. I'M LAUGHIN'.
GUYS, I'M SORRY. I LED US RIGHT INTO THIS... AND NOW WE'RE...
DEFORMED.
WE'RE DEFORMED. SAY IT.
SOME "HEROES" WE ARE.
WE...
...WE HAVE RESPONSI-BILITIES, NONETHELESS. THANKS TO THE BROTHER-HOOD, THE PEOPLE OF MANCHESTER ARE EQUALLY... DISADVANTAGED.
WE MUST RECLAIM THE GENEGRAFT DEVICE THAT CAUSED ALL THIS... AND REVERSE IT.
J'ONN'S RIGHT! WE CAN STILL WIN THIS!
IF THE BROTHERHOOD COULD REALLY HAVE BEATEN US, THEY WOULD HAVE KILLED US RATHER THAN RUN!
THEN WE GIVE IT EVERYTHING WE HAVE LEFT TO GIVE... HOWEVER LITTLE THAT MAY BE.
ONE FOR ALL AND ALL FOR ONE... RIGHT?
SUCH SPIRIT.
IF ONLY SPIRIT WERE ENOUGH. THEY'LL NEED OUR SUPPORT, BOYS.
AND OUR MUSCLE... ESPECIALLY SINCE THE BRAIN...

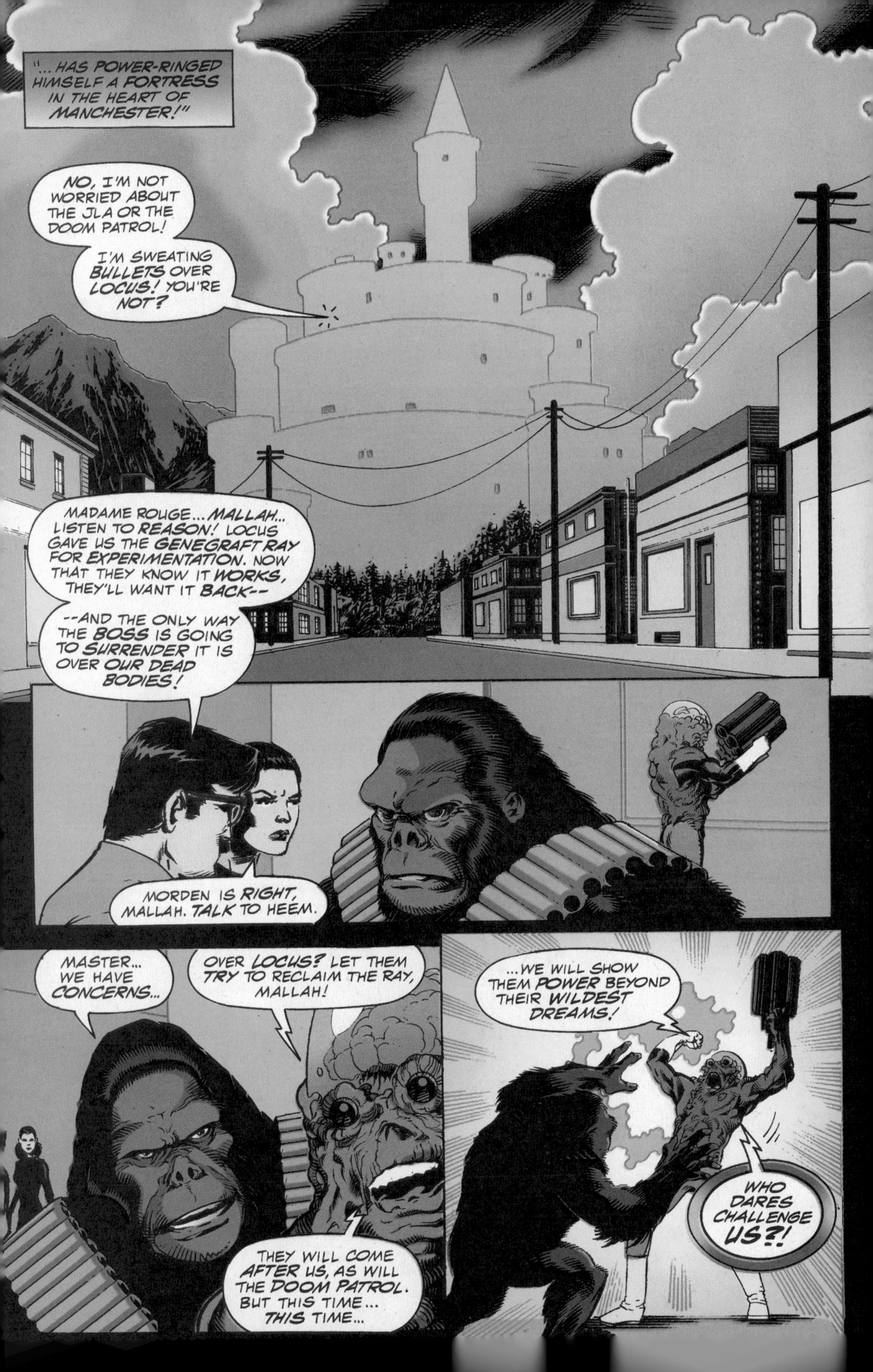
"...HAS POWER-RINGED HIMSELF A FORTRESS IN THE HEART OF MANCHESTER!"
NO, I'M NOT WORRIED ABOUT THE JLA OR THE DOOM PATROL!
I'M SWEATING BULLETS OVER LOCUS! YOU'RE NOT?
MADAME ROUGE... MALLAH... LISTEN TO REASON! LOCUS GAVE US THE GENEGRAFT RAY FOR EXPERIMENTATION. NOW THAT THEY KNOW IT WORKS, THEY'LL WANT IT BACK--
--AND THE ONLY WAY THE BOSS IS GOING TO SURRENDER IT IS OVER OUR DEAD BODIES!
MORDEN IS RIGHT, MALLAH. TALK TO HEEM.
MASTER... WE HAVE CONCERNS...
OVER LOCUS? LET THEM TRY TO RECLAIM THE RAY, MALLAH!
THEY WILL COME AFTER US, AS WILL THE DOOM PATROL. BUT THIS TIME... THIS TIME...
...WE WILL SHOW THEM POWER BEYOND THEIR WILDEST DREAMS!
WHO DARES CHALLENGE US?!

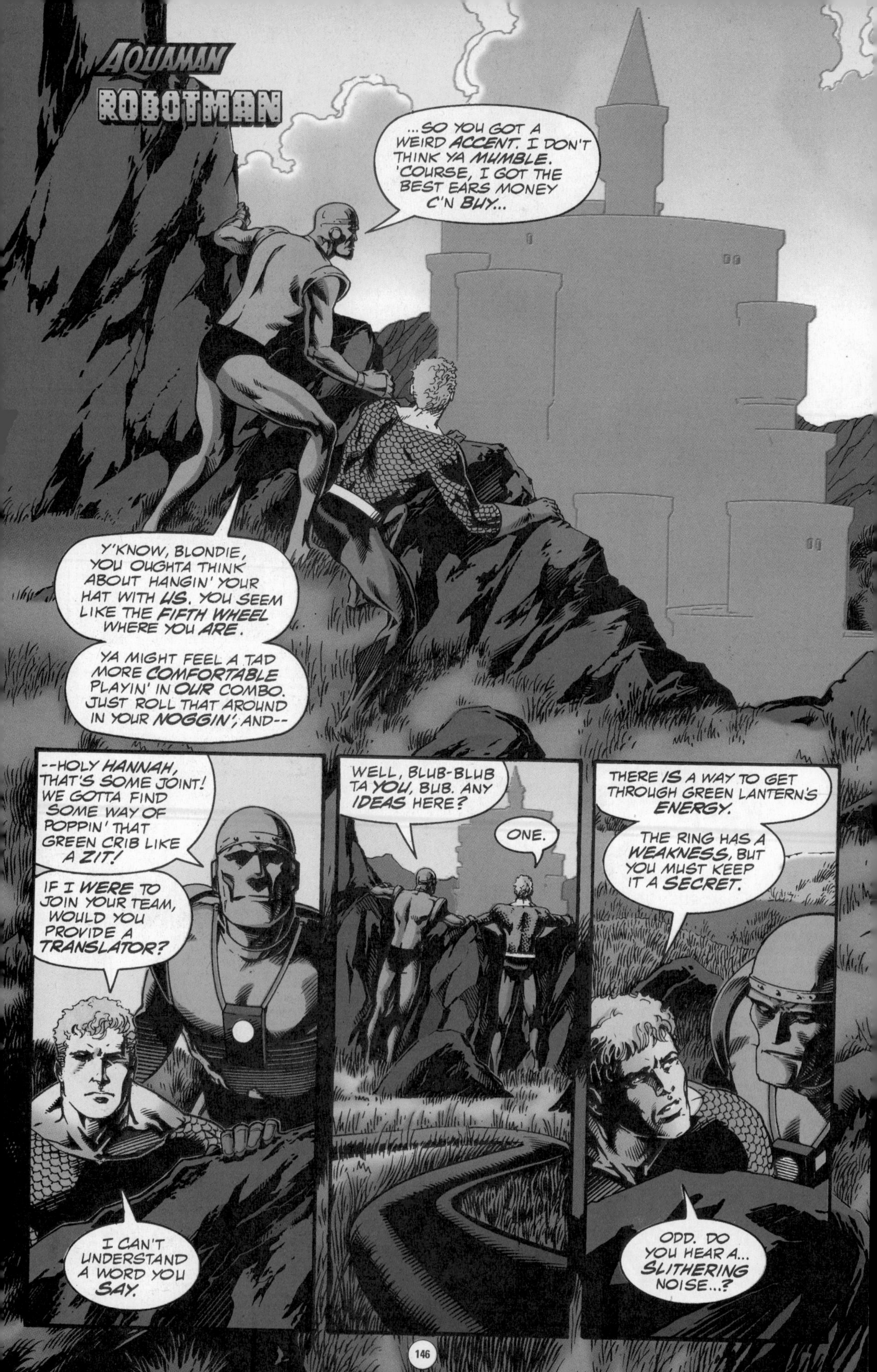
AQUAMAN
ROBOTMAN
...SO YOU GOT A WEIRD ACCENT. I DON'T THINK YA MUMBLE. 'COURSE, I GOT THE BEST EARS MONEY C'N BUY...
Y'KNOW, BLONDIE, YOU OUGHTA THINK ABOUT HANGIN' YOUR HAT WITH US. YOU SEEM LIKE THE FIFTH WHEEL WHERE YOU ARE.
YA MIGHT FEEL A TAD MORE COMFORTABLE PLAYIN' IN OUR COMBO. JUST ROLL THAT AROUND IN YOUR NOGGIN'; AND--
--HOLY HANNAH, THAT'S SOME JOINT! WE GOTTA FIND SOME WAY OF POPPIN' THAT GREEN CRIB LIKE A ZIT!
IF I WERE TO JOIN YOUR TEAM, WOULD YOU PROVIDE A TRANSLATOR?
I CAN'T UNDERSTAND A WORD YOU SAY.
WELL, BLUB-BLUB TA YOU, BUB. ANY IDEAS HERE?
ONE.
THERE IS A WAY TO GET THROUGH GREEN LANTERN'S ENERGY.
THE RING HAS A WEAKNESS, BUT YOU MUST KEEP IT A SECRET.
ODD. DO YOU HEAR A... SLITHERING NOISE...?

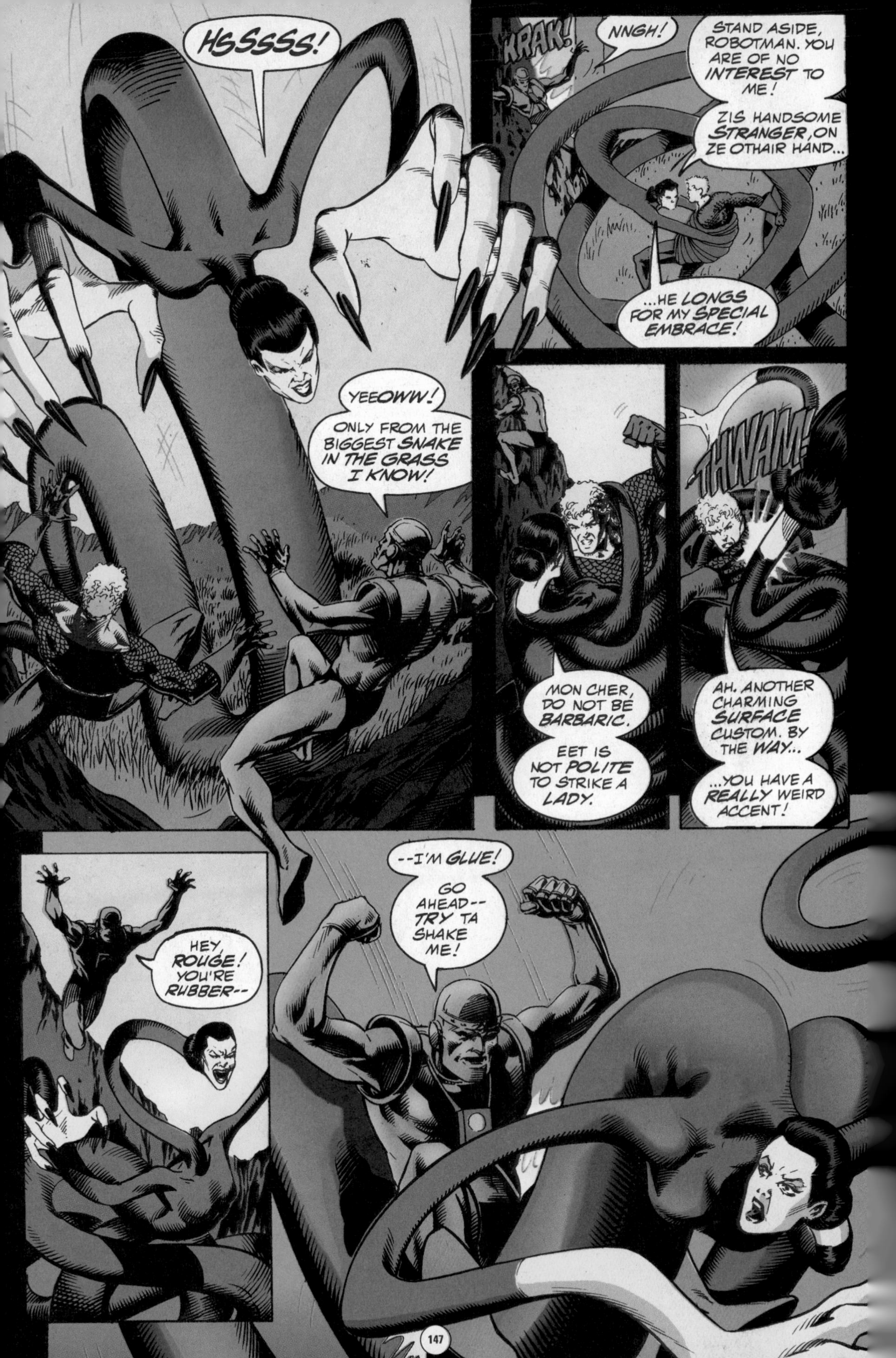
HSSSSS!
YEEOWW!
ONLY FROM THE BIGGEST SNAKE IN THE GRASS I KNOW!
KRAK!
NNGH!
STAND ASIDE, ROBOTMAN. YOU ARE OF NO INTEREST TO ME!
ZIS HANDSOME STRANGER, ON ZE OTHAIR HAND...
...HE LONGS FOR MY SPECIAL EMBRACE!
MON CHER, DO NOT BE BARBARIC.
EET IS NOT POLITE TO STRIKE A LADY.
THWAM!
AH. ANOTHER CHARMING SURFACE CUSTOM. BY THE WAY...
...YOU HAVE A REALLY WEIRD ACCENT!
HEY, ROUGE! YOU'RE RUBBER--
--I'M GLUE!
GO AHEAD-- TRY TA SHAKE ME!

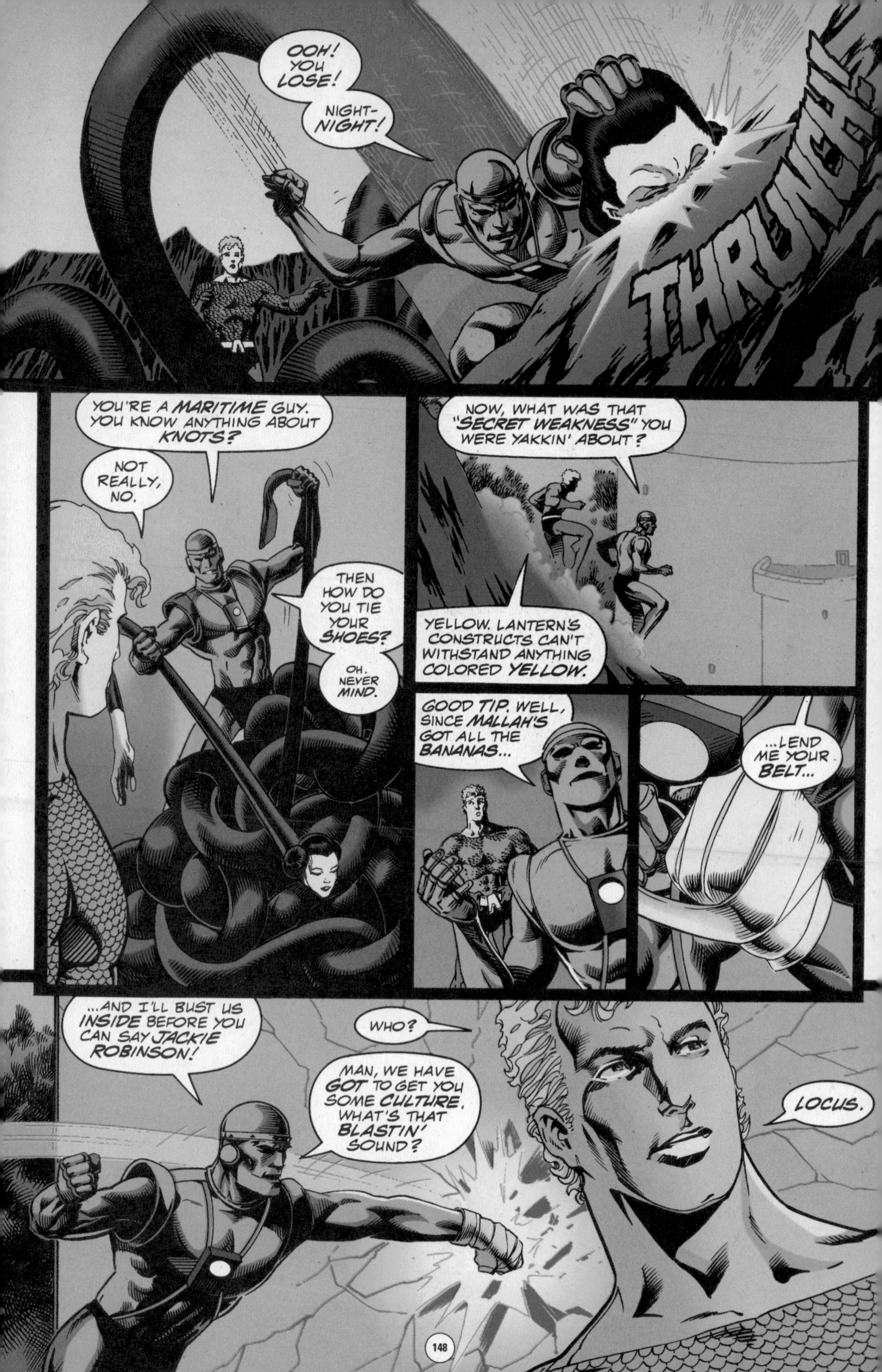
OOH! YOU LOSE!
NIGHT-NIGHT!
THRUNCH!
YOU'RE A MARITIME GUY. YOU KNOW ANYTHING ABOUT KNOTS?
NOT REALLY, NO.
THEN HOW DO YOU TIE YOUR SHOES?
OH. NEVER MIND.
NOW, WHAT WAS THAT "SECRET WEAKNESS" YOU WERE YAKKIN' ABOUT?
YELLOW. LANTERN'S CONSTRUCTS CAN'T WITHSTAND ANYTHING COLORED YELLOW.
GOOD TIP. WELL, SINCE MALLAH'S GOT ALL THE BANANAS...
...LEND ME YOUR BELT...
...AND I'LL BUST US INSIDE BEFORE YOU CAN SAY JACKIE ROBINSON!
WHO?
MAN, WE HAVE GOT TO GET YOU SOME CULTURE. WHAT'S THAT BLASTIN' SOUND?
LOCUS.

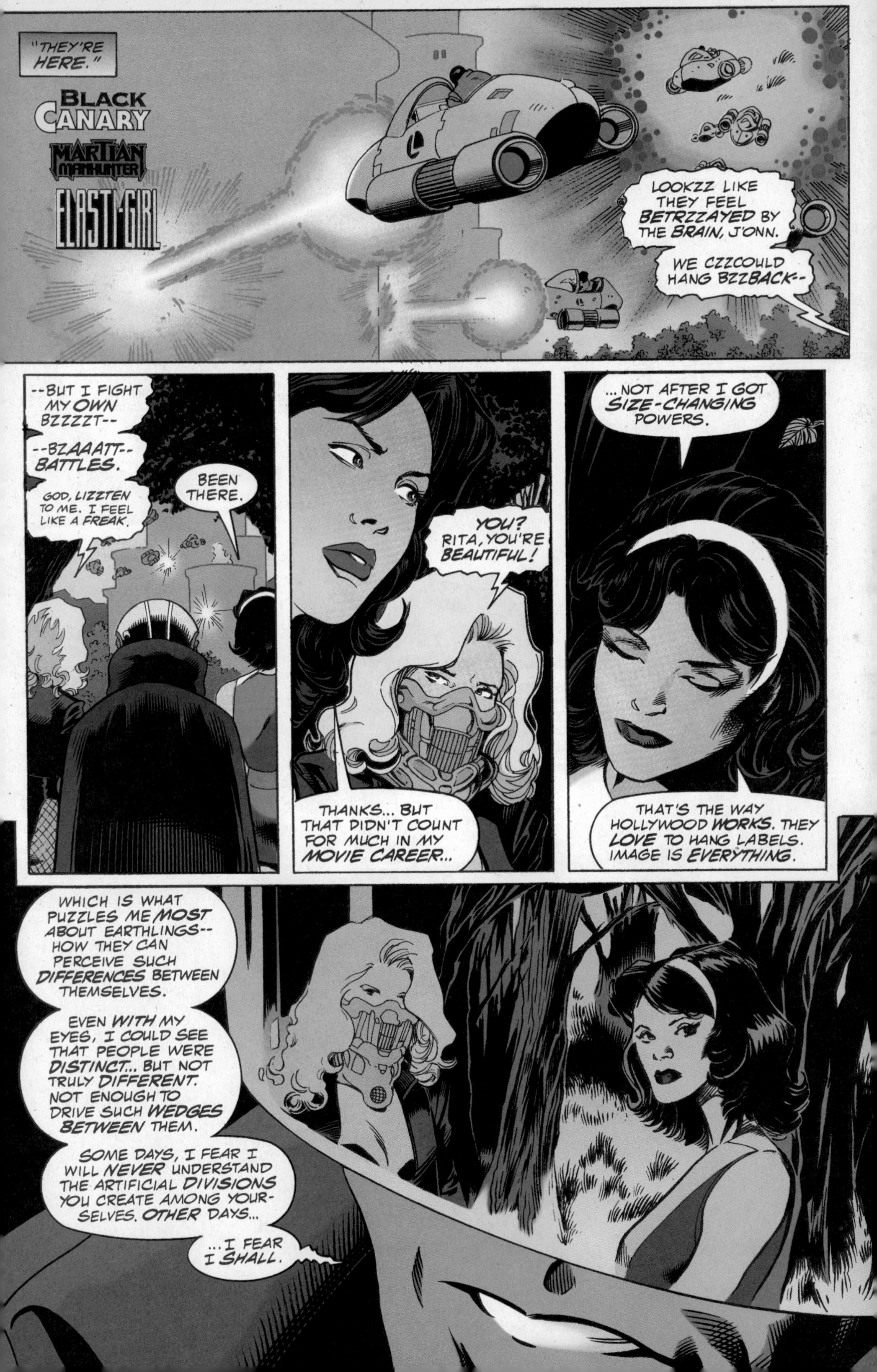
"THEY'RE HERE."
BLACK CANARY
MARTIAN MANHUNTER
ELASTI-GIRL
LOOKZZ LIKE THEY FEEL BETRZZZAYED BY THE BRAIN, J'ONN.
WE CZZCOULD HANG BZZBACK--
--BUT I FIGHT MY OWN BZZZZT--
--BZAAATT-- BATTLES.
GOD, LIZZTEN TO ME. I FEEL LIKE A FREAK.
BEEN THERE.
YOU? RITA, YOU'RE BEAUTIFUL!
THANKS... BUT THAT DIDN'T COUNT FOR MUCH IN MY MOVIE CAREER...
...NOT AFTER I GOT SIZE-CHANGING POWERS.
THAT'S THE WAY HOLLYWOOD WORKS. THEY LOVE TO HANG LABELS. IMAGE IS EVERYTHING.
WHICH IS WHAT PUZZLES ME MOST ABOUT EARTHLINGS-- HOW THEY CAN PERCEIVE SUCH DIFFERENCES BETWEEN THEMSELVES.
EVEN WITH MY EYES, I COULD SEE THAT PEOPLE WERE DISTINCT... BUT NOT TRULY DIFFERENT. NOT ENOUGH TO DRIVE SUCH WEDGES BETWEEN THEM.
SOME DAYS, I FEAR I WILL NEVER UNDERSTAND THE ARTIFICIAL DIVISIONS YOU CREATE AMONG YOURSELVES. OTHER DAYS...
...I FEAR I SHALL.

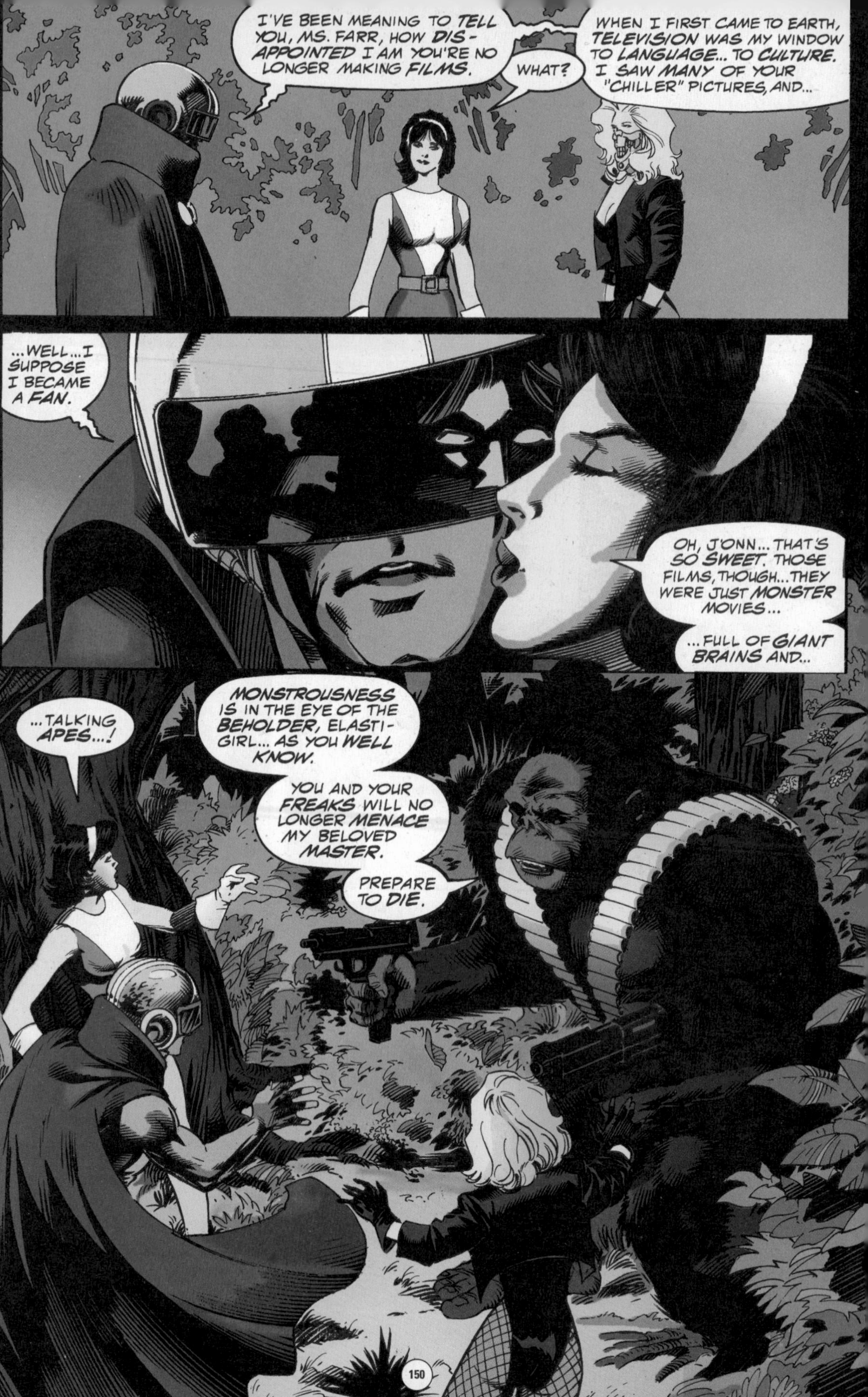
I'VE BEEN MEANING TO TELL YOU, MS. FARR, HOW DIS-APPOINTED I AM YOU'RE NO LONGER MAKING FILMS.
WHAT?
WHEN I FIRST CAME TO EARTH, TELEVISION WAS MY WINDOW TO LANGUAGE... TO CULTURE. I SAW MANY OF YOUR "CHILLER" PICTURES, AND...
...WELL...I SUPPOSE I BECAME A FAN.
OH, J'ONN... THAT'S SO SWEET. THOSE FILMS, THOUGH...THEY WERE JUST MONSTER MOVIES...
...FULL OF GIANT BRAINS AND...
...TALKING APES...!
MONSTROUSNESS IS IN THE EYE OF THE BEHOLDER, ELASTI-GIRL... AS YOU WELL KNOW.
YOU AND YOUR FREAKS WILL NO LONGER MENACE MY BELOVED MASTER.
PREPARE TO DIE.

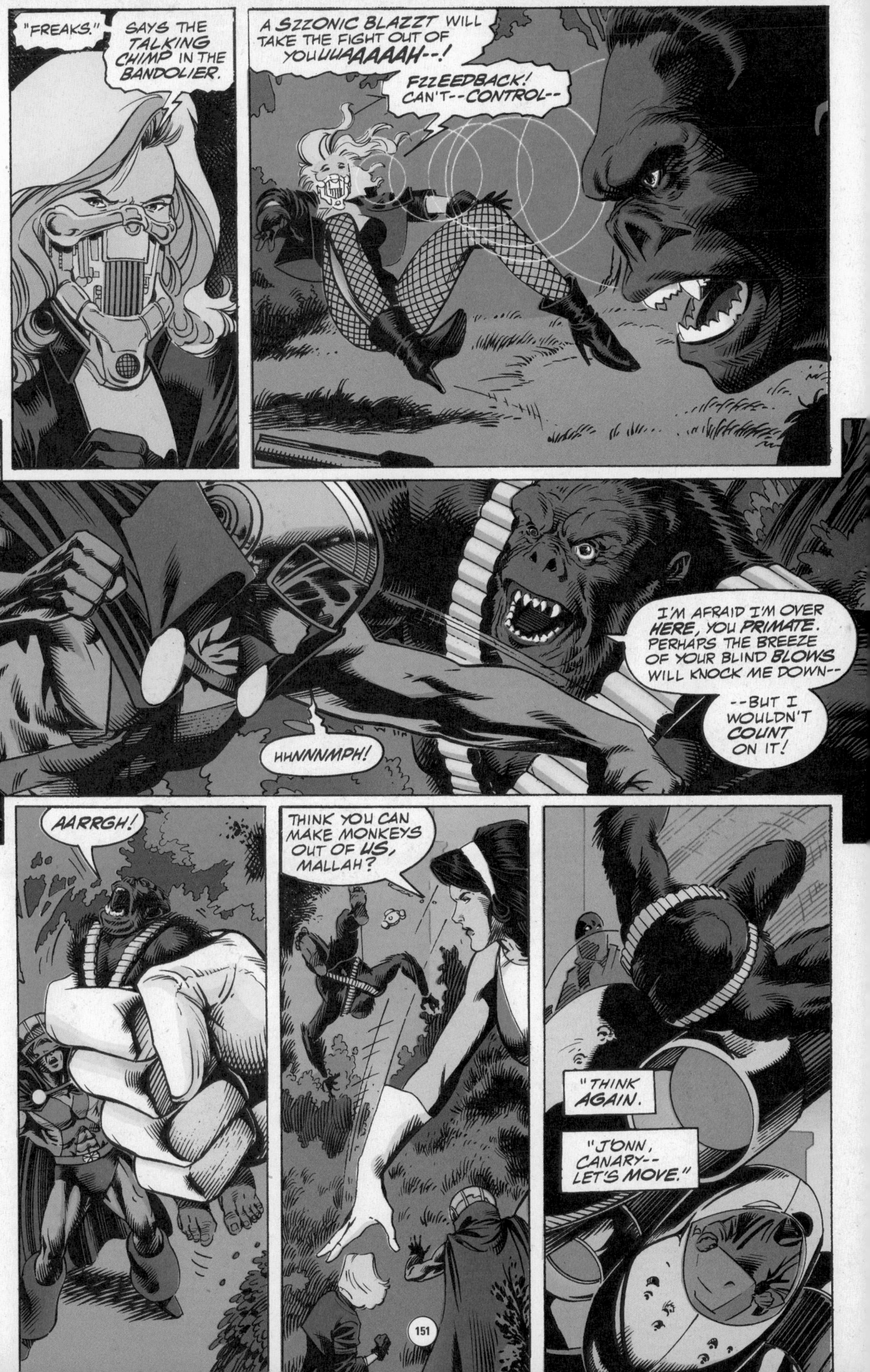
"FREAKS."
SAYS THE TALKING CHIMP IN THE BANDOLIER.
A SZZONIC BLAZZT WILL TAKE THE FIGHT OUT OF YOUUUAAAAAH--!
FZZEEDBACK! CAN'T--CONTROL--
I'M AFRAID I'M OVER HERE, YOU PRIMATE. PERHAPS THE BREEZE OF YOUR BLIND BLOWS WILL KNOCK ME DOWN--
--BUT I WOULDN'T COUNT ON IT!
HHNNNMPH!
AARRGH!
THINK YOU CAN MAKE MONKEYS OUT OF US, MALLAH?
"THINK AGAIN.
"J'ONN, CANARY--LET'S MOVE."

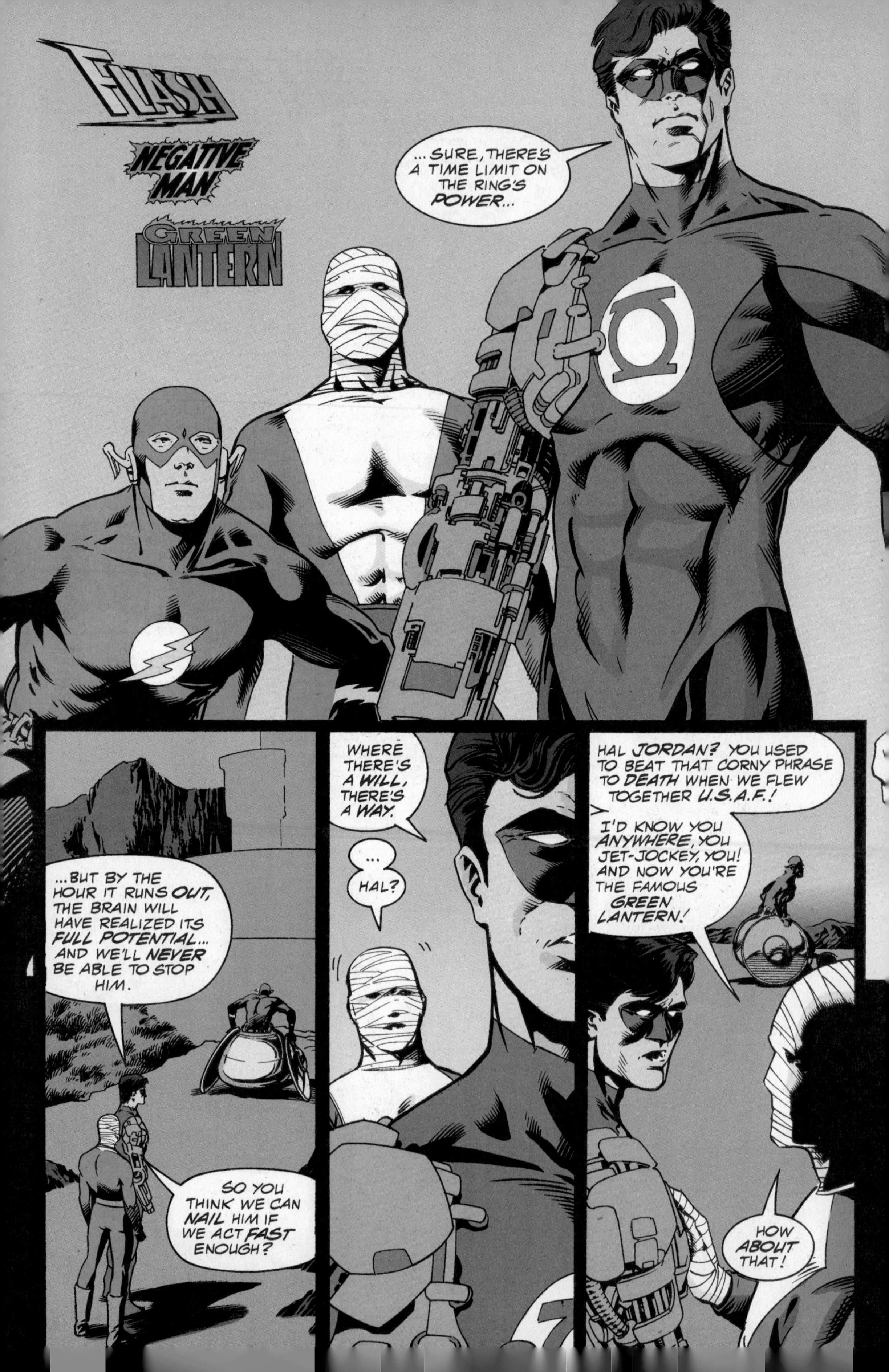
FLASH
NEGATIVE MAN
GREEN LANTERN
... SURE, THERE'S A TIME LIMIT ON THE RING'S POWER...
...BUT BY THE HOUR IT RUNS OUT, THE BRAIN WILL HAVE REALIZED ITS FULL POTENTIAL... AND WE'LL NEVER BE ABLE TO STOP HIM.
SO YOU THINK WE CAN NAIL HIM IF WE ACT FAST ENOUGH?
WHERE THERE'S A WILL, THERE'S A WAY.
... HAL?
HAL JORDAN? YOU USED TO BEAT THAT CORNY PHRASE TO DEATH WHEN WE FLEW TOGETHER U.S.A.F.!
I'D KNOW YOU ANYWHERE, YOU JET-JOCKEY, YOU! AND NOW YOU'RE THE FAMOUS GREEN LANTERN!
HOW ABOUT THAT!

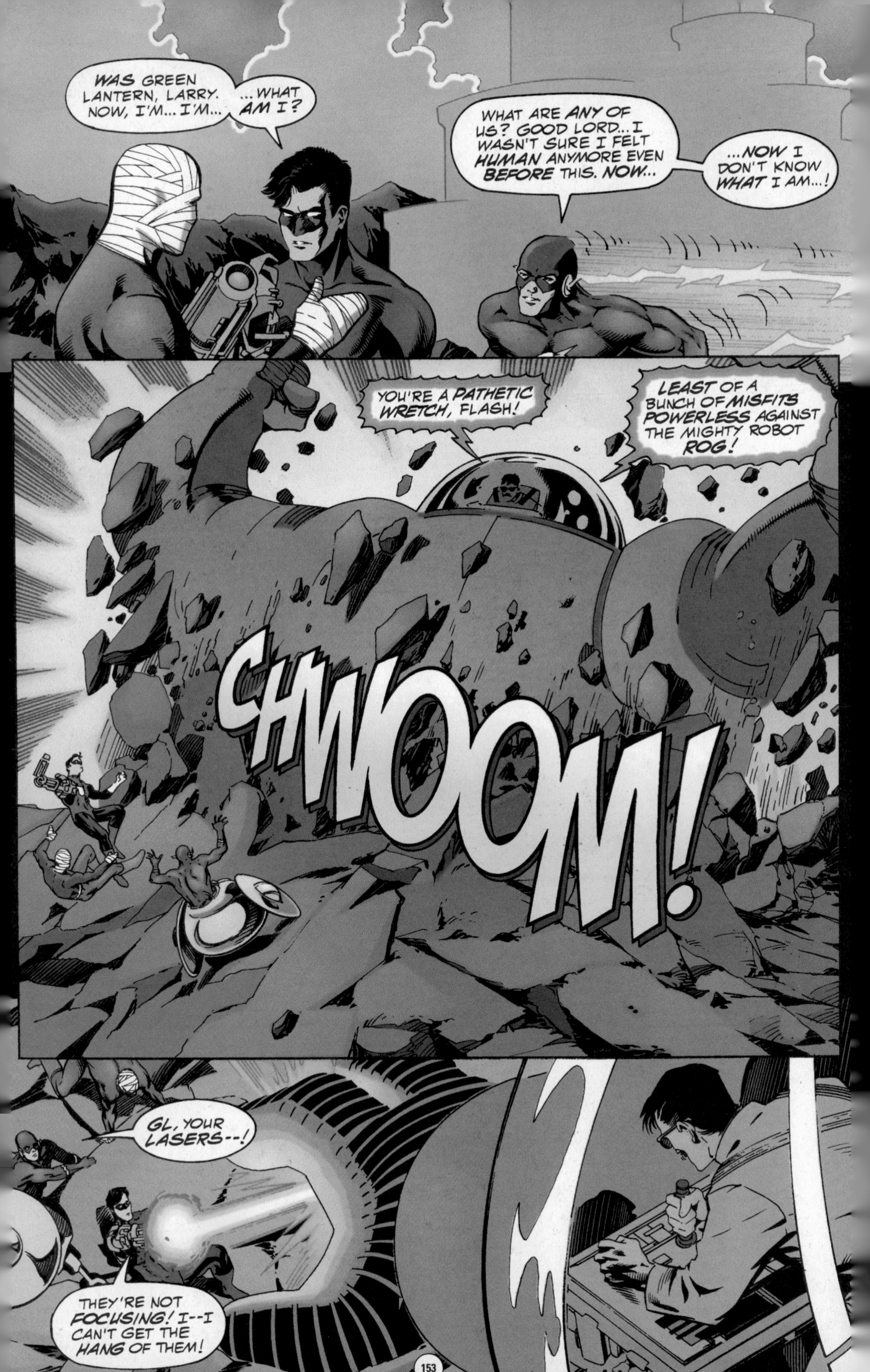
WAS GREEN LANTERN, LARRY. NOW, I'M... I'M...
...WHAT AM I?
WHAT ARE ANY OF US? GOOD LORD... I WASN'T SURE I FELT HUMAN ANYMORE EVEN BEFORE THIS. NOW...
...NOW I DON'T KNOW WHAT I AM...!
YOU'RE A PATHETIC WRETCH, FLASH!
LEAST OF A BUNCH OF MISFITS POWERLESS AGAINST THE MIGHTY ROBOT ROG!
CHWOOM!
GL, YOUR LASERS--!
THEY'RE NOT FOCUSING! I--I CAN'T GET THE HANG OF THEM!

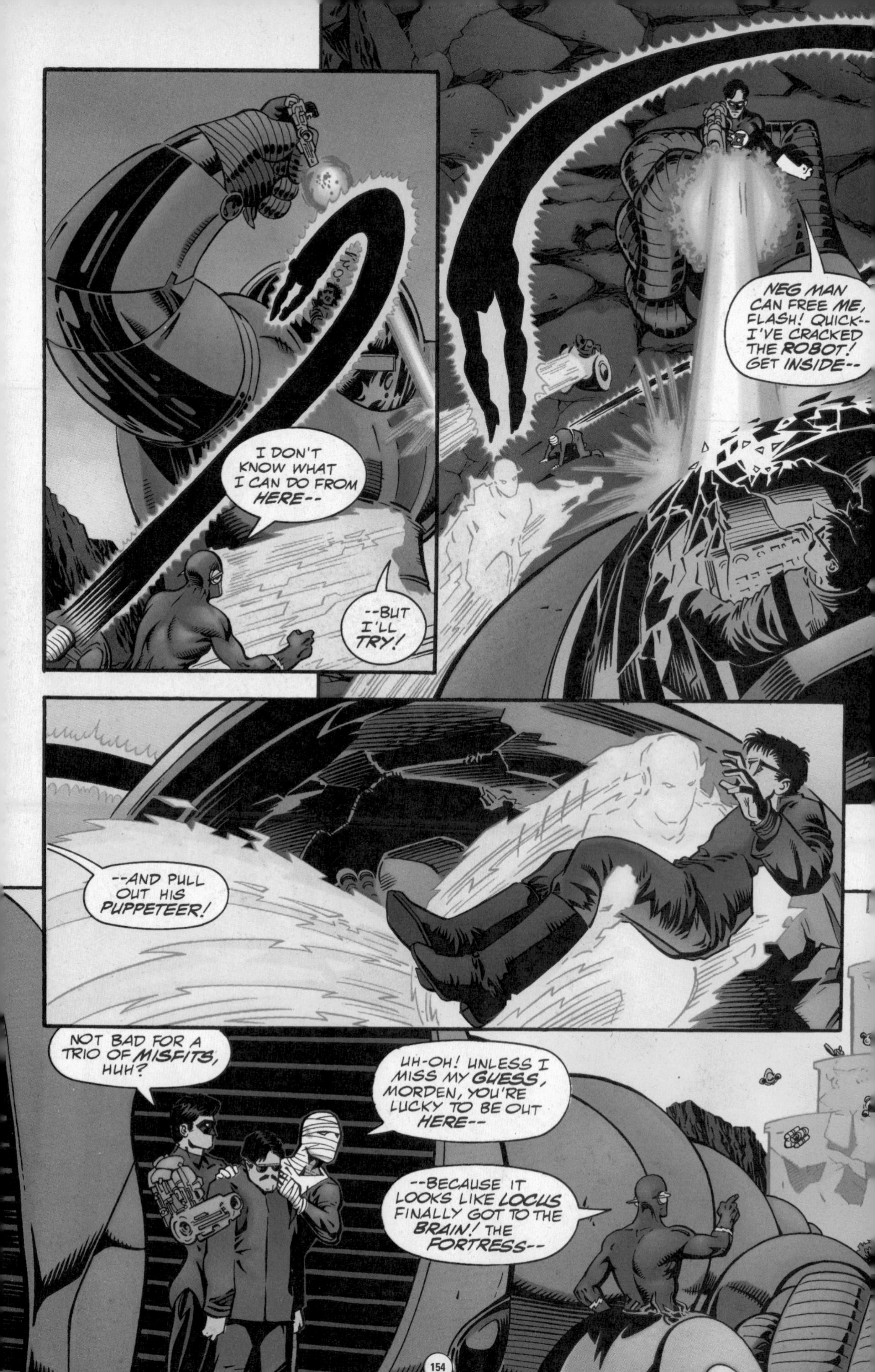

I DON'T KNOW WHAT I CAN DO FROM HERE--
--BUT I'LL TRY!
NEG MAN CAN FREE ME, FLASH! QUICK-- I'VE CRACKED THE ROBOT! GET INSIDE--
--AND PULL OUT HIS PUPPETEER!
NOT BAD FOR A TRIO OF MISFITS, HUH?
UH-OH! UNLESS I MISS MY GUESS, MORDEN, YOU'RE LUCKY TO BE OUT HERE--
--BECAUSE IT LOOKS LIKE LOCUS FINALLY GOT TO THE BRAIN! THE FORTRESS--

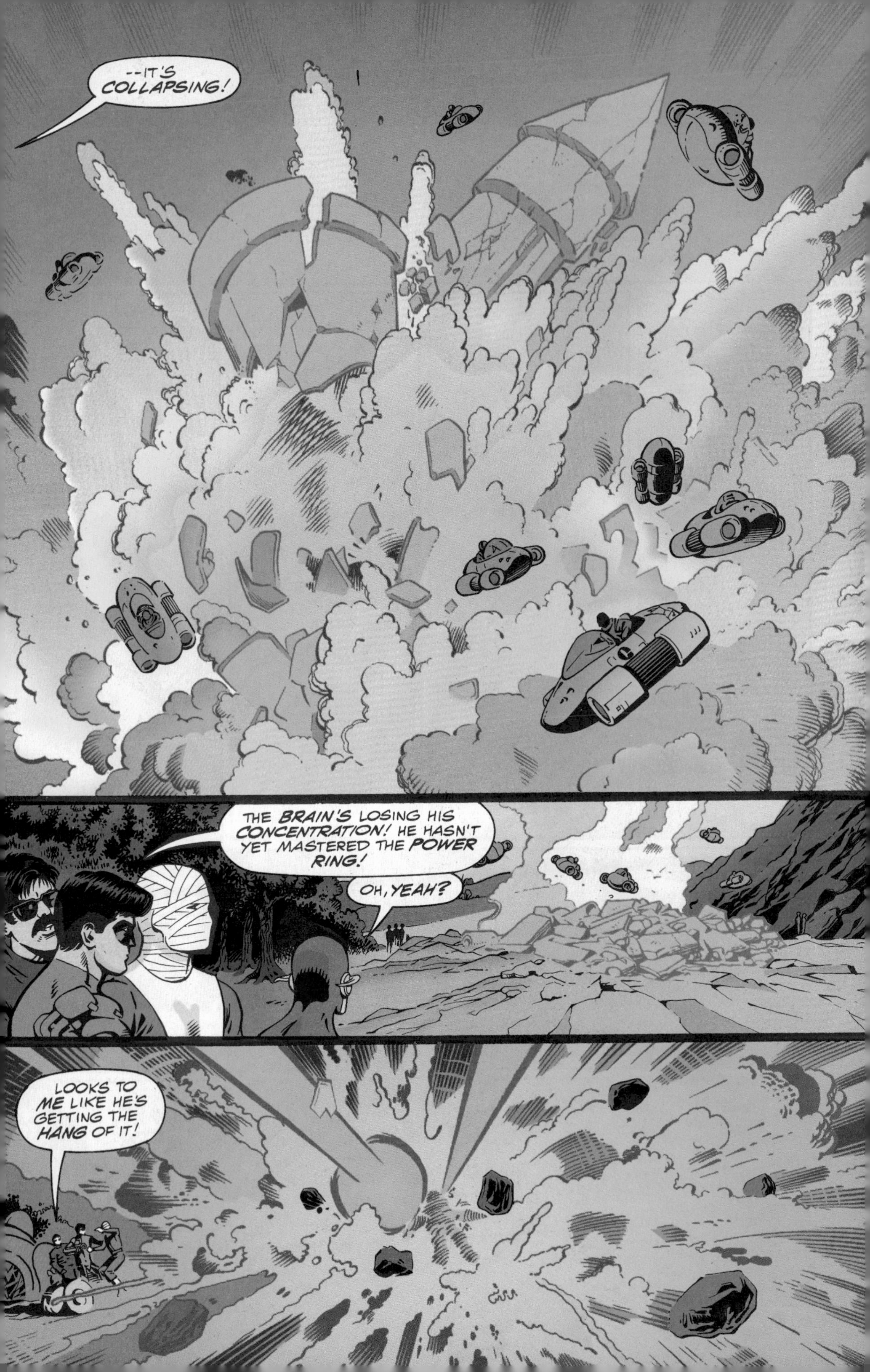
--IT'S COLLAPSING!
THE BRAIN'S LOSING HIS CONCENTRATION! HE HASN'T YET MASTERED THE POWER RING!
OH, YEAH?
LOOKS TO ME LIKE HE'S GETTING THE HANG OF IT!

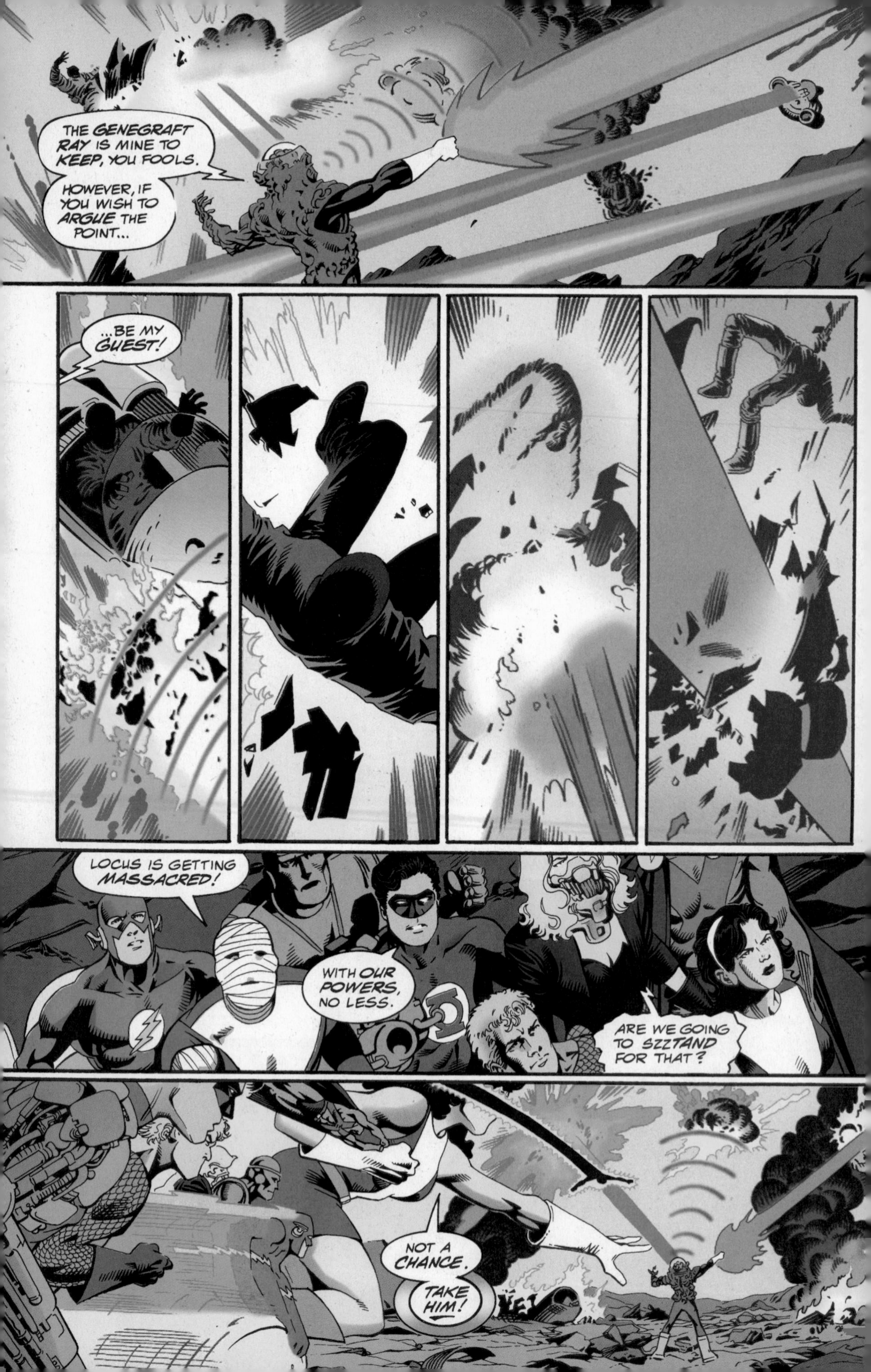
THE GENEGRAFT RAY IS MINE TO KEEP, YOU FOOLS.
HOWEVER, IF YOU WISH TO ARGUE THE POINT...
...BE MY GUEST!
LOCUS IS GETTING MASSACRED!
WITH OUR POWERS, NO LESS.
ARE WE GOING TO SZZTAND FOR THAT?
NOT A CHANCE.
TAKE HIM!

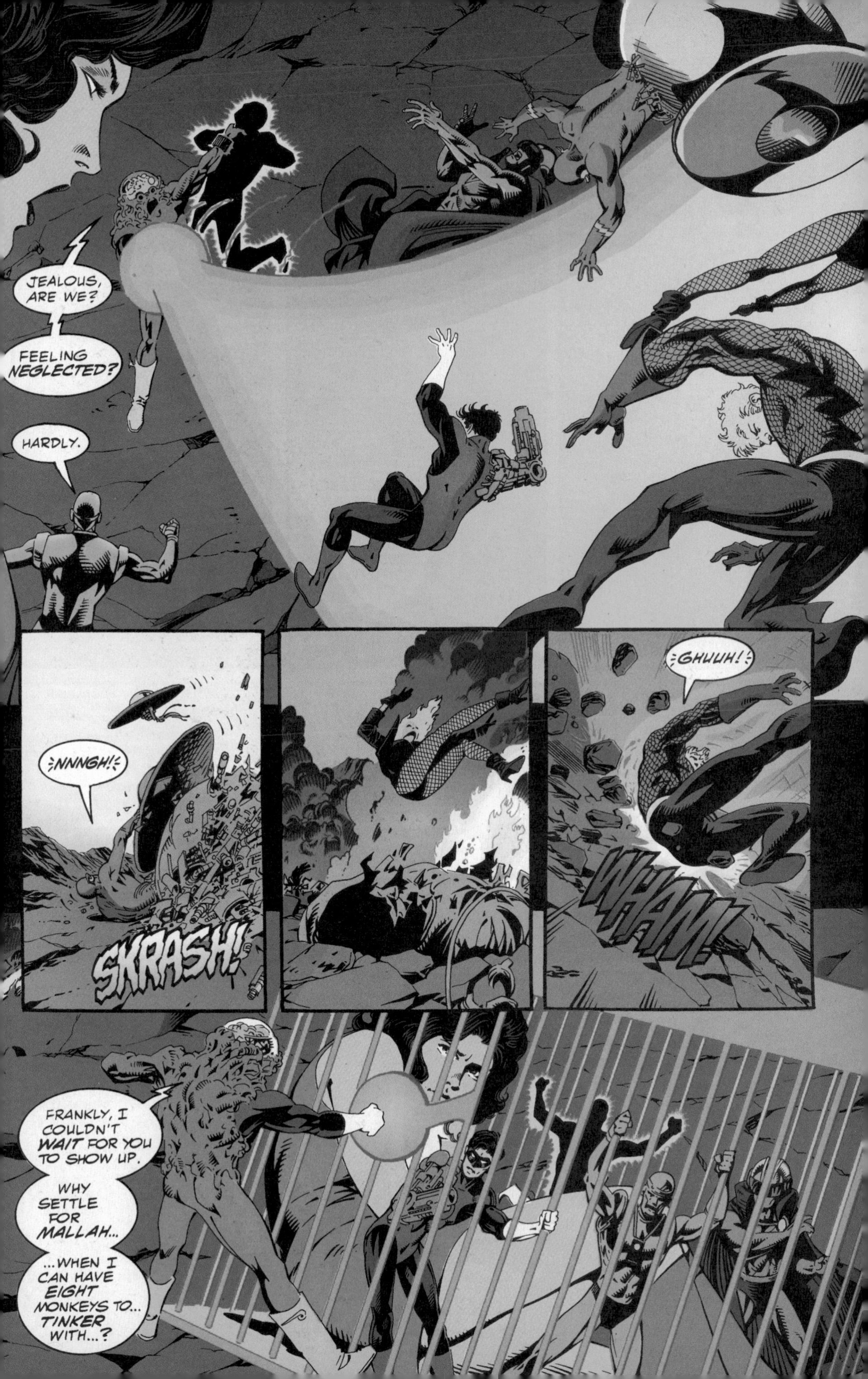
JEALOUS, ARE WE?
FEELING NEGLECTED?
HARDLY.
NNNGH!
SKRASH!
GHUUH!
WHAM!
FRANKLY, I COULDN'T WAIT FOR YOU TO SHOW UP.
WHY SETTLE FOR MALLAH...
...WHEN I CAN HAVE EIGHT MONKEYS TO... TINKER WITH...?

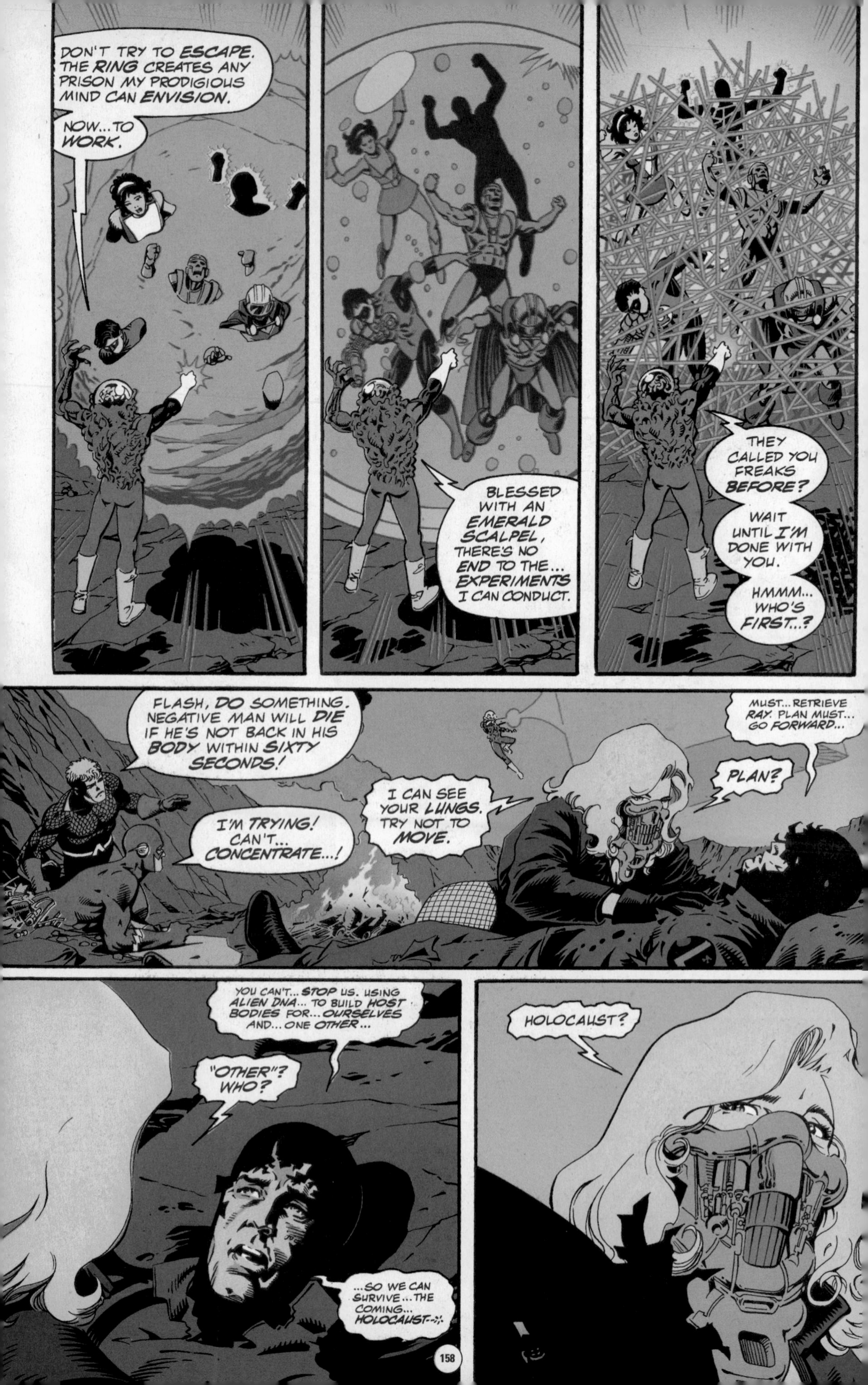

DON'T TRY TO ESCAPE. THE RING CREATES ANY PRISON MY PRODIGIOUS MIND CAN ENVISION.
NOW... TO WORK.
BLESSED WITH AN EMERALD SCALPEL, THERE'S NO END TO THE... EXPERIMENTS I CAN CONDUCT.
THEY CALLED YOU FREAKS BEFORE?
WAIT UNTIL I'M DONE WITH YOU.
HMMM... WHO'S FIRST...?
FLASH, DO SOMETHING. NEGATIVE MAN WILL DIE IF HE'S NOT BACK IN HIS BODY WITHIN SIXTY SECONDS!
I'M TRYING! CAN'T... CONCENTRATE...!
I CAN SEE YOUR LUNGS. TRY NOT TO MOVE.
PLAN?
MUST... RETRIEVE RAY. PLAN MUST... GO FORWARD...
YOU CAN'T... STOP US. USING ALIEN DNA... TO BUILD HOST BODIES FOR... OURSELVES AND... ONE OTHER...
"OTHER"? WHO?
...SO WE CAN SURVIVE... THE COMING... HOLOCAUST--:.
HOLOCAUST?

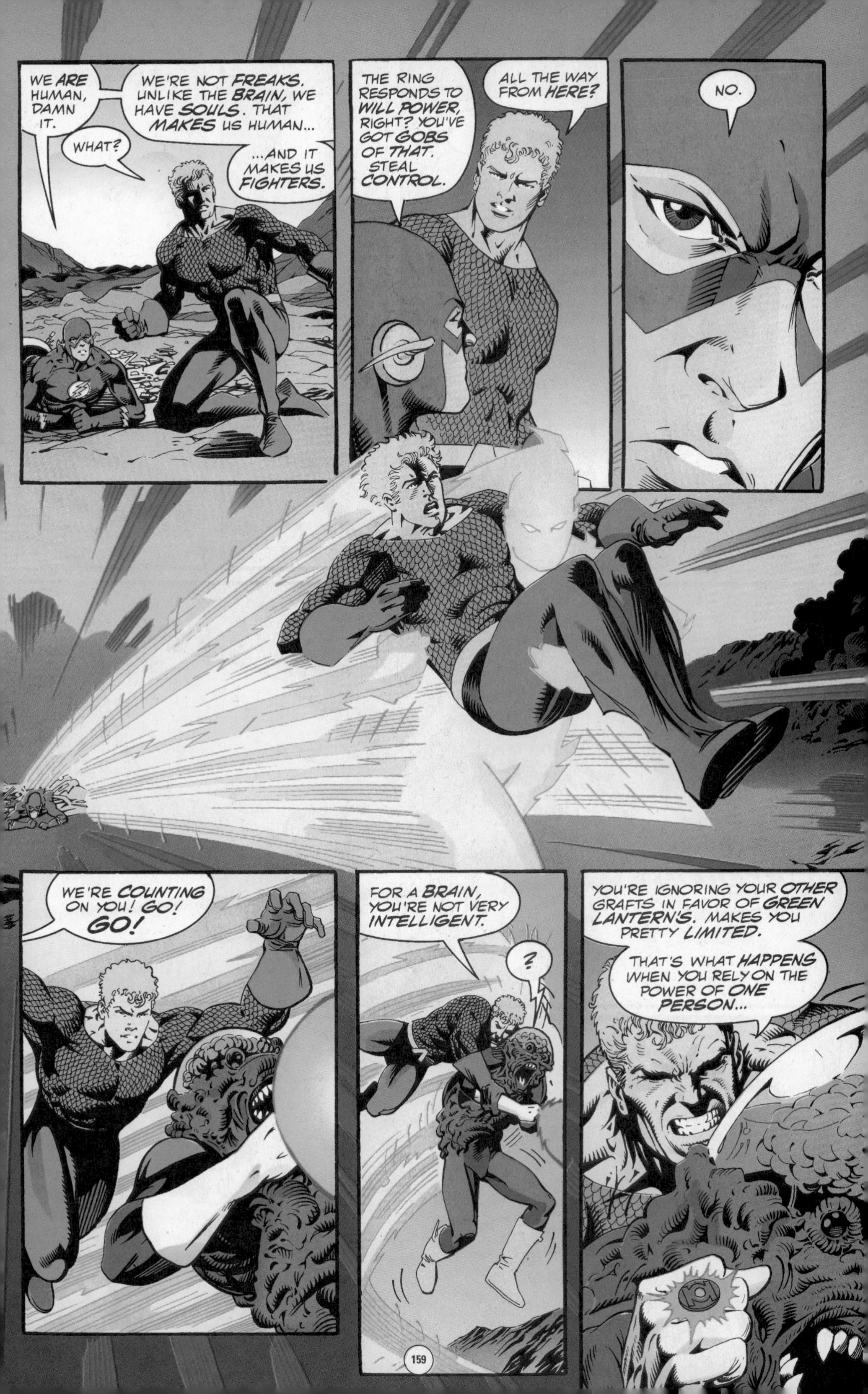

WE ARE HUMAN, DAMN IT.
WE'RE NOT FREAKS. UNLIKE THE BRAIN, WE HAVE SOULS. THAT MAKES US HUMAN...
WHAT?
...AND IT MAKES US FIGHTERS.
THE RING RESPONDS TO WILL POWER, RIGHT? YOU'VE GOT GOBS OF THAT. STEAL CONTROL.
ALL THE WAY FROM HERE?
NO.
WE'RE COUNTING ON YOU! GO! GO!
FOR A BRAIN, YOU'RE NOT VERY INTELLIGENT.
?
YOU'RE IGNORING YOUR OTHER GRAFTS IN FAVOR OF GREEN LANTERN'S. MAKES YOU PRETTY LIMITED.
THAT'S WHAT HAPPENS WHEN YOU RELY ON THE POWER OF ONE PERSON...

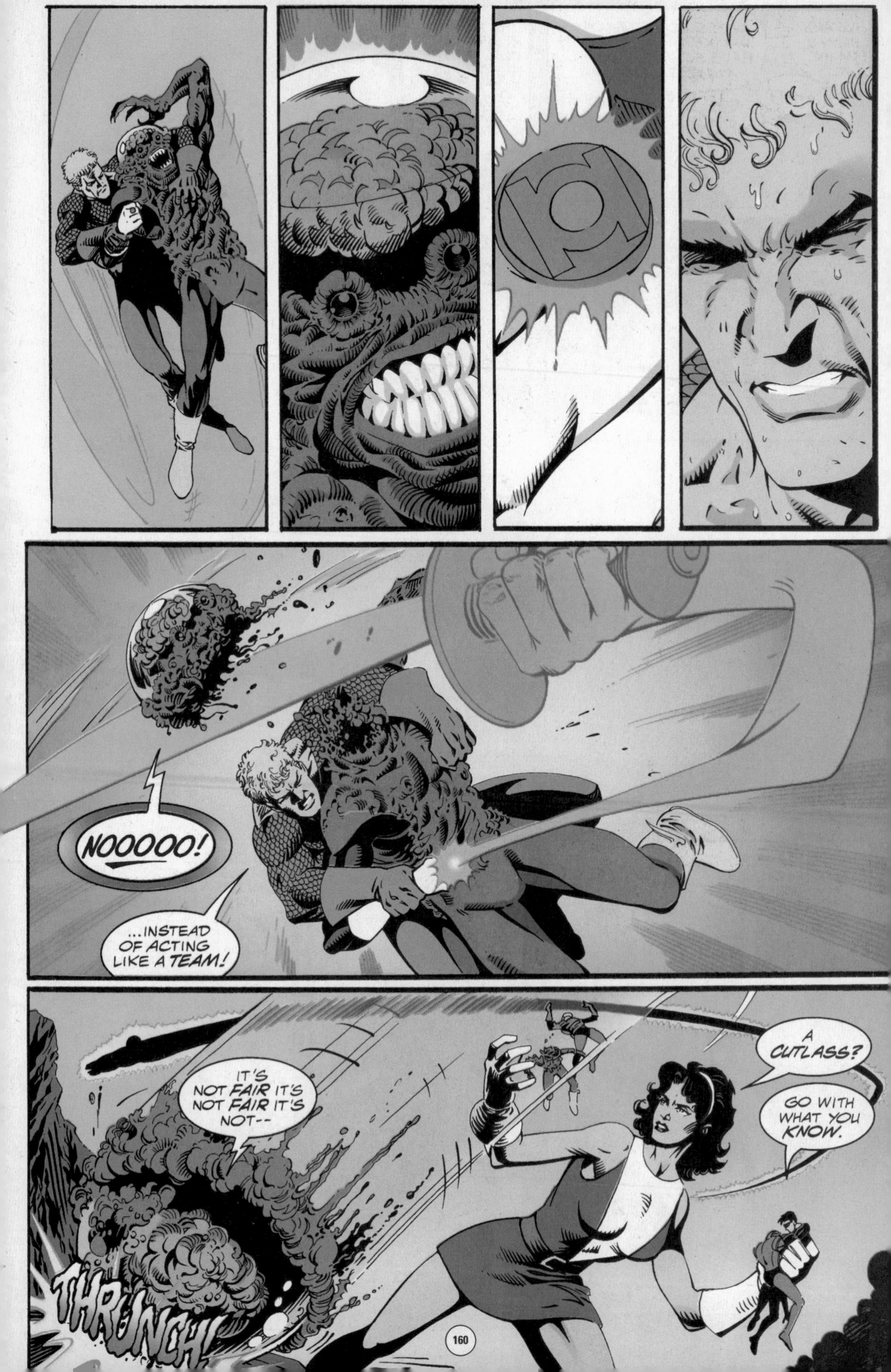
NOOOOO!
...INSTEAD OF ACTING LIKE A TEAM!
IT'S NOT FAIR IT'S NOT FAIR IT'S NOT--
A CUTLASS?
GO WITH WHAT YOU KNOW.
THRUNCH!

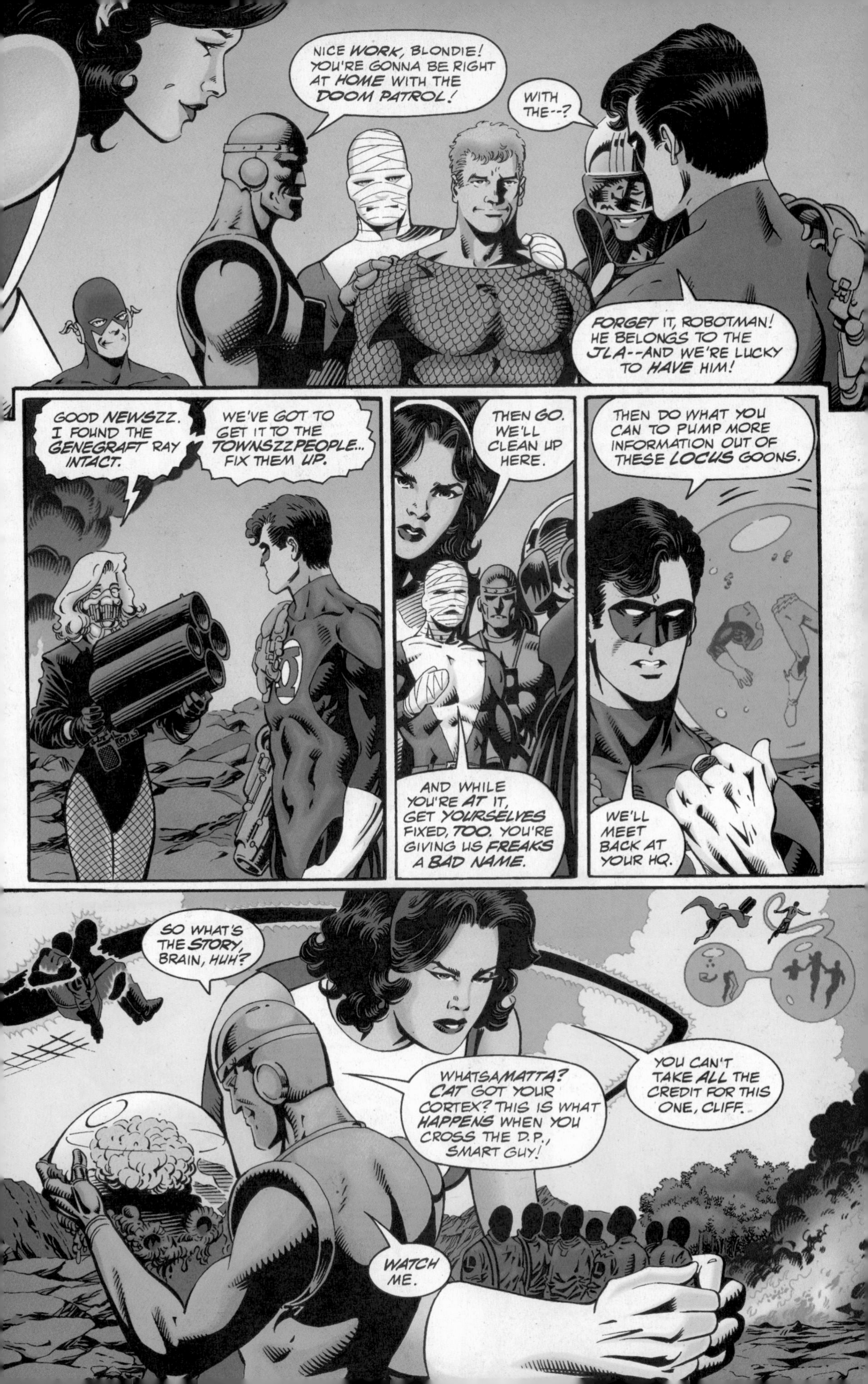
NICE WORK, BLONDIE! YOU'RE GONNA BE RIGHT AT HOME WITH THE DOOM PATROL!
WITH THE--?
FORGET IT, ROBOTMAN! HE BELONGS TO THE JLA--AND WE'RE LUCKY TO HAVE HIM!
GOOD NEWSZZ. I FOUND THE GENEGRAFT RAY INTACT.
WE'VE GOT TO GET IT TO THE TOWNSZZPEOPLE... FIX THEM UP.
THEN GO. WE'LL CLEAN UP HERE.
AND WHILE YOU'RE AT IT, GET YOURSELVES FIXED, TOO. YOU'RE GIVING US FREAKS A BAD NAME.
THEN DO WHAT YOU CAN TO PUMP MORE INFORMATION OUT OF THESE LOCUS GOONS.
WE'LL MEET BACK AT YOUR HQ.
SO WHAT'S THE STORY, BRAIN, HUH?
WHATSAMATTA? CAT GOT YOUR CORTEX? THIS IS WHAT HAPPENS WHEN YOU CROSS THE D.P., SMART GUY!
YOU CAN'T TAKE ALL THE CREDIT FOR THIS ONE, CLIFF.
WATCH ME.

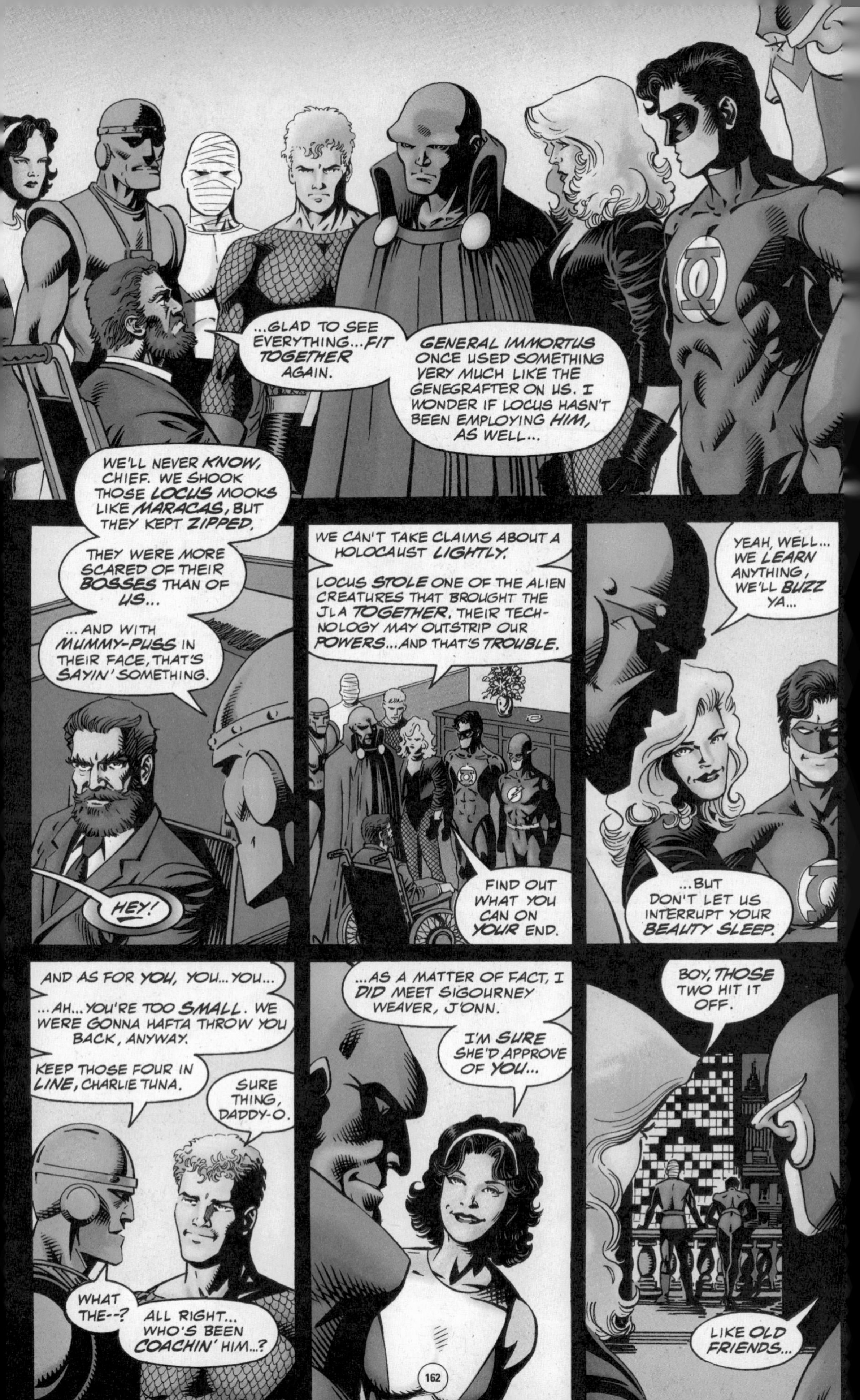
...GLAD TO SEE EVERYTHING... FIT TOGETHER AGAIN.
GENERAL IMMORTUS ONCE USED SOMETHING VERY MUCH LIKE THE GENEGRAFTER ON US. I WONDER IF LOCUS HASN'T BEEN EMPLOYING HIM, AS WELL...
WE'LL NEVER KNOW, CHIEF. WE SHOOK THOSE LOCUS MOOKS LIKE MARACAS, BUT THEY KEPT ZIPPED.
THEY WERE MORE SCARED OF THEIR BOSSES THAN OF US...
...AND WITH MUMMY-PUSS IN THEIR FACE, THAT'S SAYIN' SOMETHING.
HEY!
WE CAN'T TAKE CLAIMS ABOUT A HOLOCAUST LIGHTLY.
LOCUS STOLE ONE OF THE ALIEN CREATURES THAT BROUGHT THE JLA TOGETHER. THEIR TECHNOLOGY MAY OUTSTRIP OUR POWERS... AND THAT'S TROUBLE.
FIND OUT WHAT YOU CAN ON YOUR END.
YEAH, WELL... WE LEARN ANYTHING, WE'LL BUZZ YA...
...BUT DON'T LET US INTERRUPT YOUR BEAUTY SLEEP.
AND AS FOR YOU, YOU... YOU...
...AH... YOU'RE TOO SMALL. WE WERE GONNA HAFTA THROW YOU BACK, ANYWAY.
KEEP THOSE FOUR IN LINE, CHARLIE TUNA.
SURE THING, DADDY-O.
WHAT THE--?
ALL RIGHT... WHO'S BEEN COACHIN' HIM...?
...AS A MATTER OF FACT, I DID MEET SIGOURNEY WEAVER, J'ONN.
I'M SURE SHE'D APPROVE OF YOU...
BOY, THOSE TWO HIT IT OFF.
LIKE OLD FRIENDS...

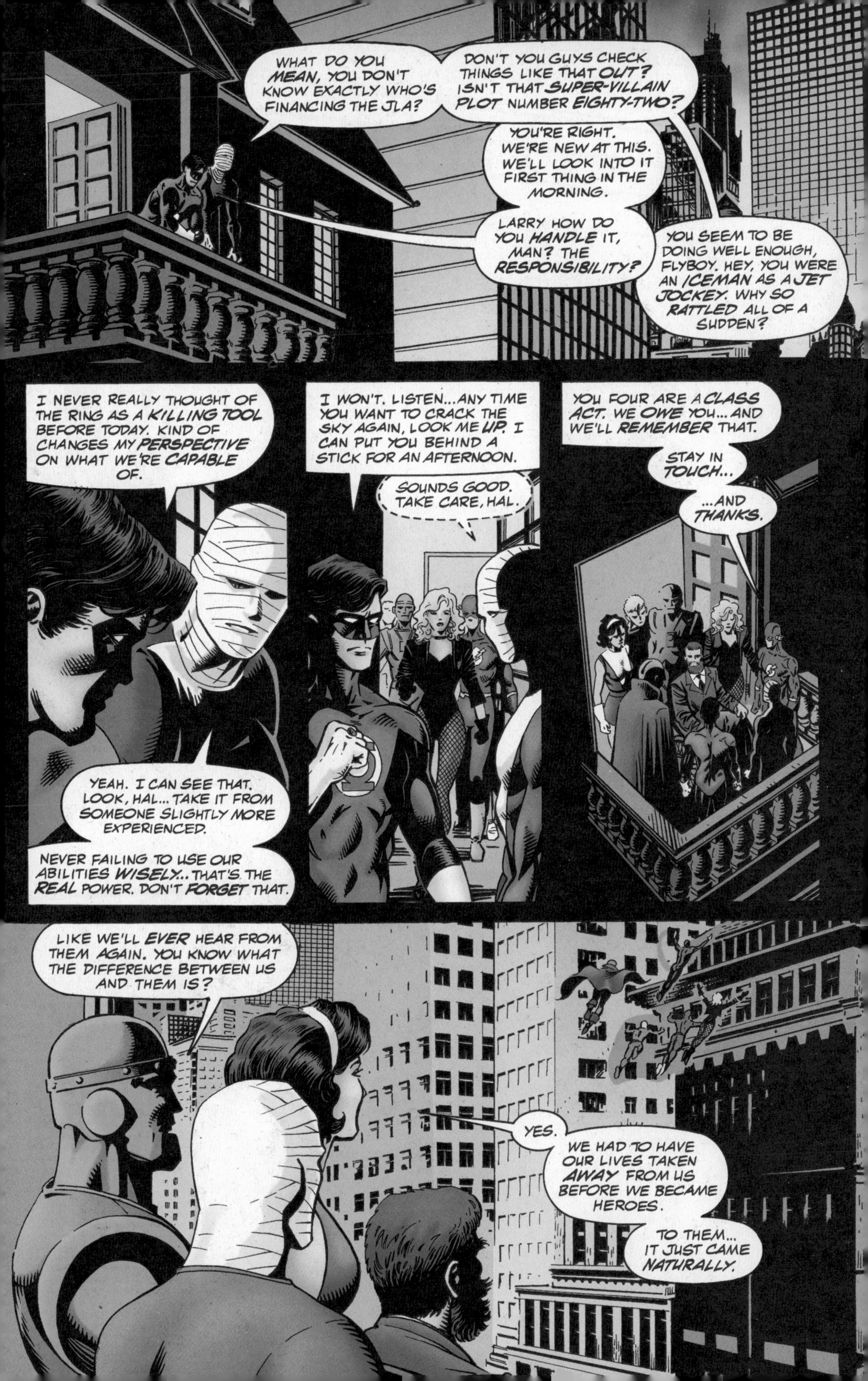
WHAT DO YOU MEAN, YOU DON'T KNOW EXACTLY WHO'S FINANCING THE JLA?
DON'T YOU GUYS CHECK THINGS LIKE THAT OUT? ISN'T THAT SUPER-VILLAIN PLOT NUMBER EIGHTY-TWO?
YOU'RE RIGHT. WE'RE NEW AT THIS. WE'LL LOOK INTO IT FIRST THING IN THE MORNING.
LARRY HOW DO YOU HANDLE IT, MAN? THE RESPONSIBILITY?
YOU SEEM TO BE DOING WELL ENOUGH, FLYBOY. HEY, YOU WERE AN ICEMAN AS A JET JOCKEY. WHY SO RATTLED ALL OF A SUDDEN?
I NEVER REALLY THOUGHT OF THE RING AS A KILLING TOOL BEFORE TODAY. KIND OF CHANGES MY PERSPECTIVE ON WHAT WE'RE CAPABLE OF.
YEAH. I CAN SEE THAT. LOOK, HAL... TAKE IT FROM SOMEONE SLIGHTLY MORE EXPERIENCED.
NEVER FAILING TO USE OUR ABILITIES WISELY... THAT'S THE REAL POWER. DON'T FORGET THAT.
I WON'T. LISTEN... ANY TIME YOU WANT TO CRACK THE SKY AGAIN, LOOK ME UP. I CAN PUT YOU BEHIND A STICK FOR AN AFTERNOON.
SOUNDS GOOD. TAKE CARE, HAL.
YOU FOUR ARE A CLASS ACT. WE OWE YOU... AND WE'LL REMEMBER THAT.
STAY IN TOUCH...
...AND THANKS.
LIKE WE'LL EVER HEAR FROM THEM AGAIN. YOU KNOW WHAT THE DIFFERENCE BETWEEN US AND THEM IS?
YES.
WE HAD TO HAVE OUR LIVES TAKEN AWAY FROM US BEFORE WE BECAME HEROES.
TO THEM... IT JUST CAME NATURALLY.

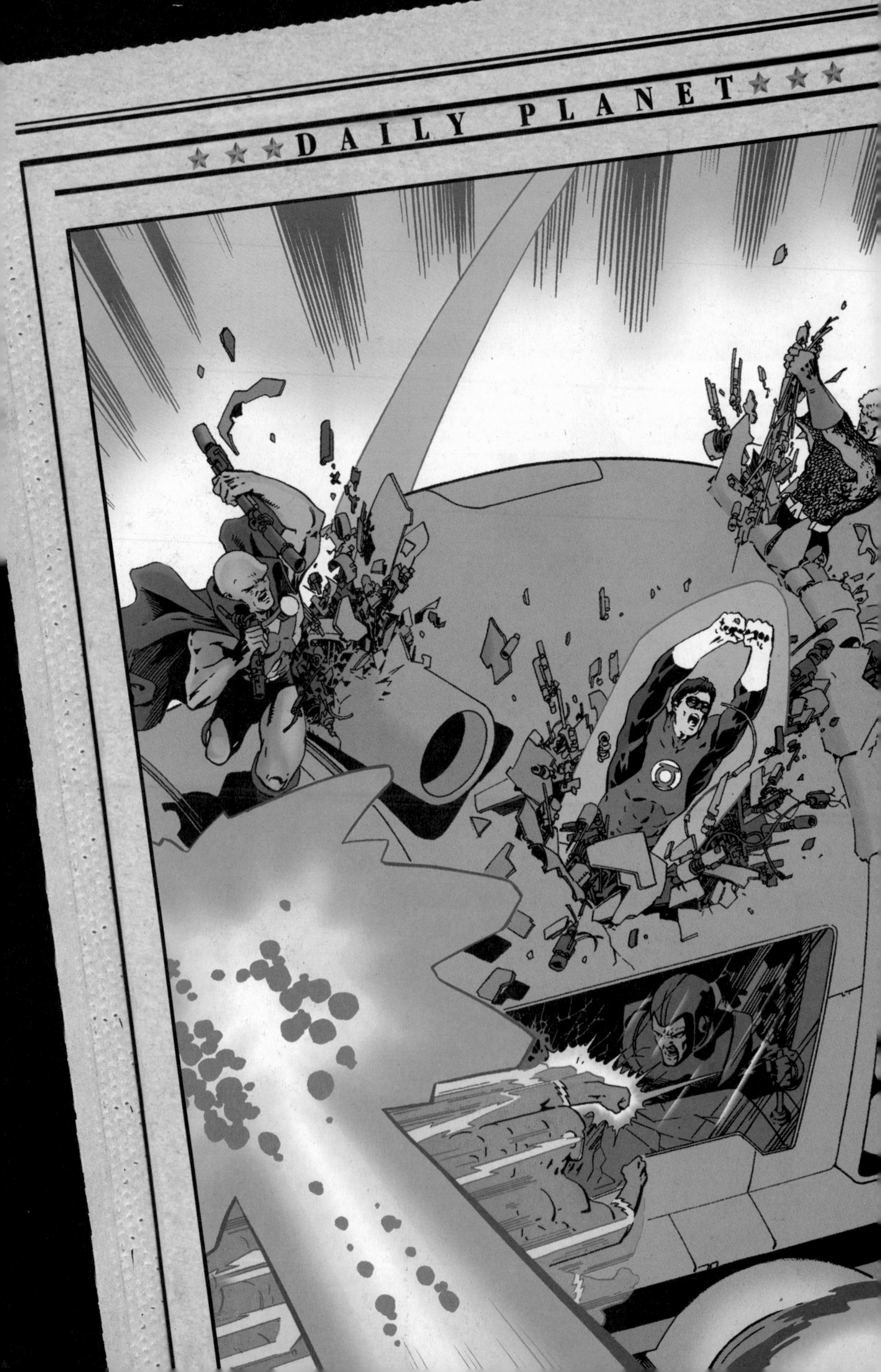
DAILY PLANET

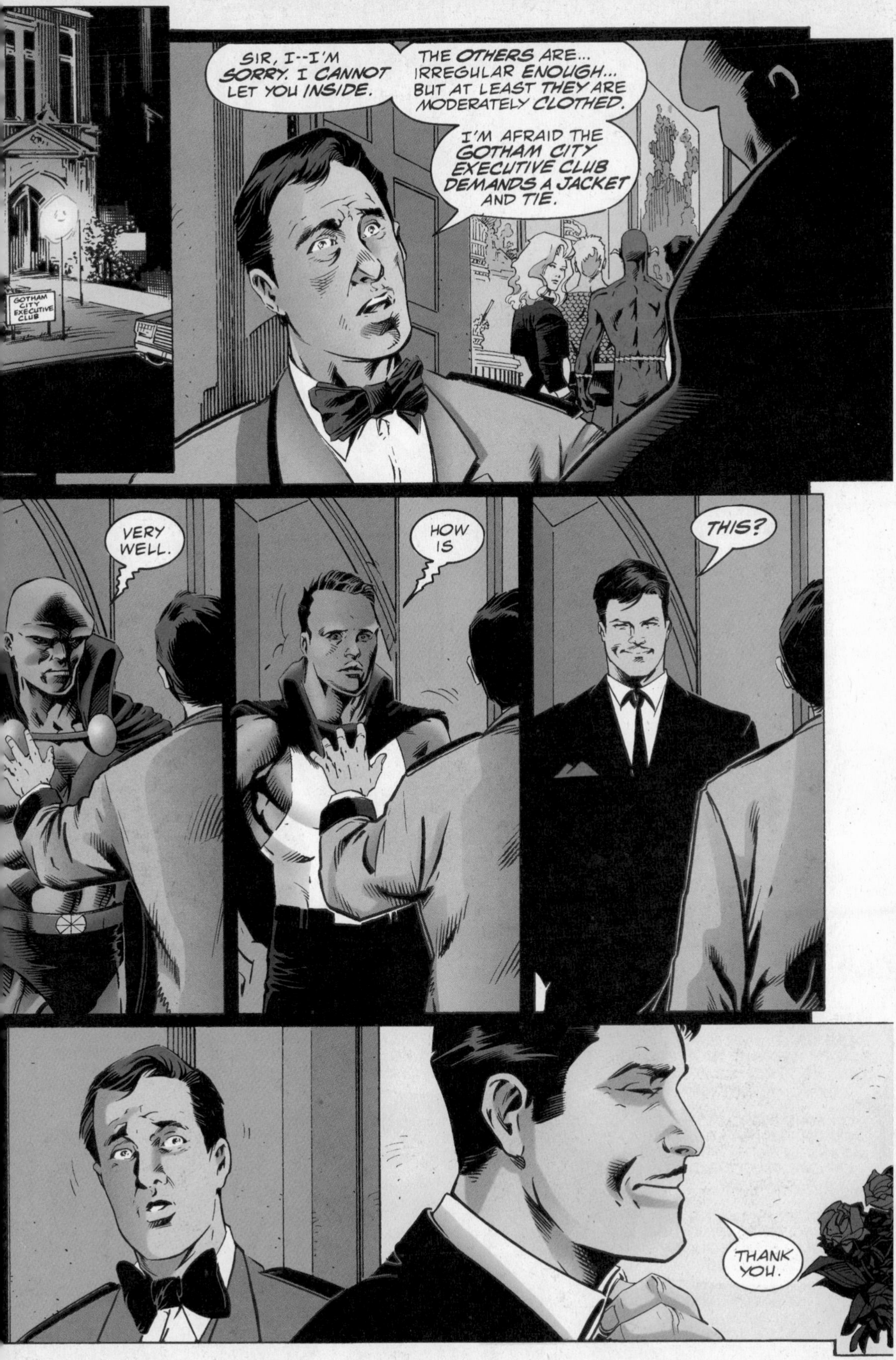
GOTHAM CITY EXECUTIVE CLUB
SIR, I--I'M SORRY. I CANNOT LET YOU INSIDE.
THE OTHERS ARE... IRREGULAR ENOUGH... BUT AT LEAST THEY ARE MODERATELY CLOTHED.
I'M AFRAID THE GOTHAM CITY EXECUTIVE CLUB DEMANDS A JACKET AND TIE.
VERY WELL.
HOW IS
THIS?
THANK YOU.

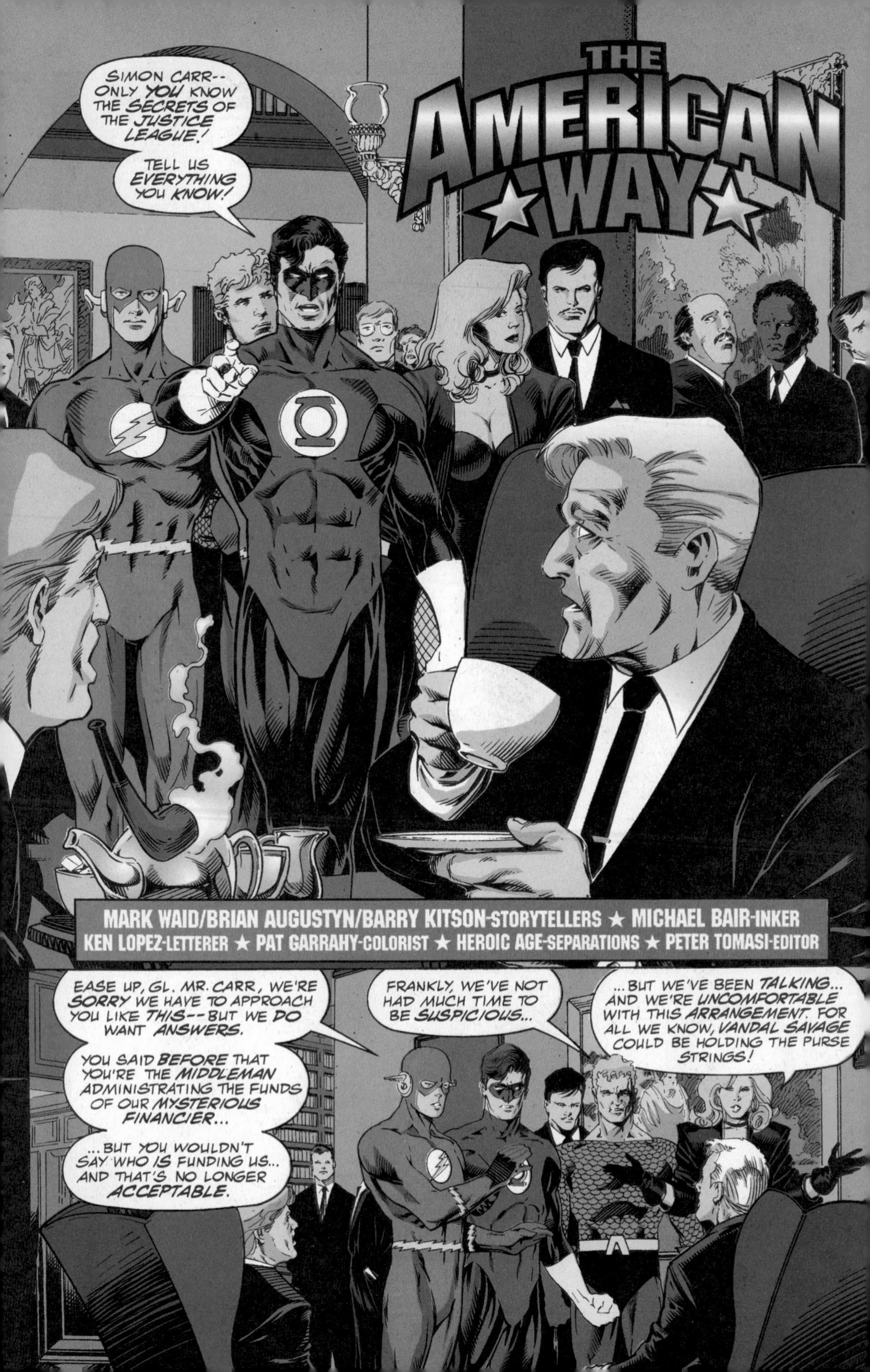
THE AMERICAN WAY
SIMON CARR-- ONLY YOU KNOW THE SECRETS OF THE JUSTICE LEAGUE!
TELL US EVERYTHING YOU KNOW!
MARK WAID/BRIAN AUGUSTYN/BARRY KITSON-STORYTELLERS ★ MICHAEL BAIR-INKER
KEN LOPEZ-LETTERER ★ PAT GARRAHY-COLORIST ★ HEROIC AGE-SEPARATIONS ★ PETER TOMASI-EDITOR
EASE UP, GL. MR. CARR, WE'RE SORRY WE HAVE TO APPROACH YOU LIKE THIS--BUT WE DO WANT ANSWERS.
YOU SAID BEFORE THAT YOU'RE THE MIDDLEMAN ADMINISTRATING THE FUNDS OF OUR MYSTERIOUS FINANCIER...
...BUT YOU WOULDN'T SAY WHO IS FUNDING US... AND THAT'S NO LONGER ACCEPTABLE.
FRANKLY, WE'VE NOT HAD MUCH TIME TO BE SUSPICIOUS...
...BUT WE'VE BEEN TALKING... AND WE'RE UNCOMFORTABLE WITH THIS ARRANGEMENT. FOR ALL WE KNOW, VANDAL SAVAGE COULD BE HOLDING THE PURSE STRINGS!

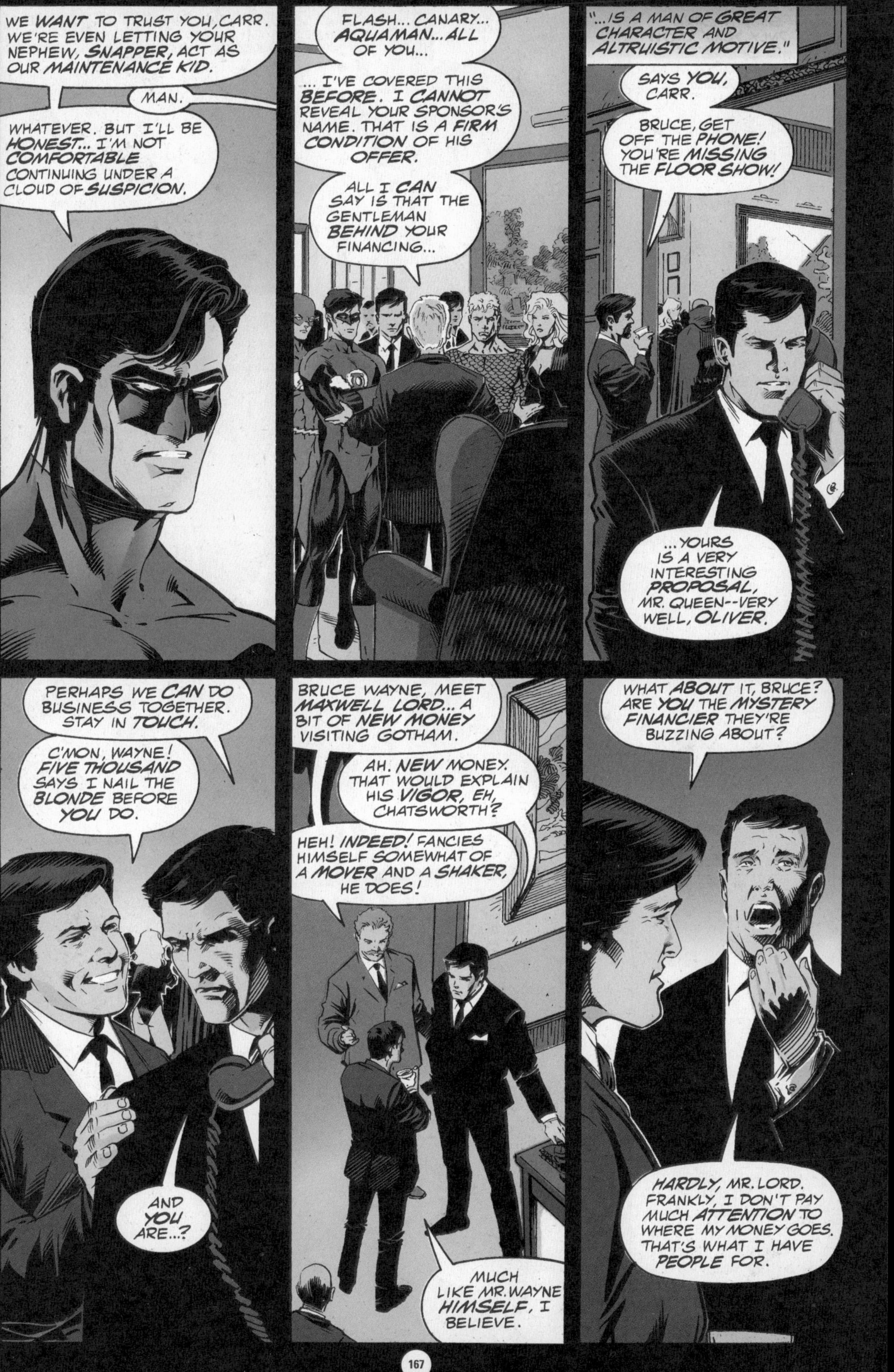

WE WANT TO TRUST YOU, CARR. WE'RE EVEN LETTING YOUR NEPHEW, SNAPPER, ACT AS OUR MAINTENANCE KID.
MAN.
WHATEVER. BUT I'LL BE HONEST... I'M NOT COMFORTABLE CONTINUING UNDER A CLOUD OF SUSPICION.
FLASH... CANARY... AQUAMAN... ALL OF YOU...
... I'VE COVERED THIS BEFORE. I CANNOT REVEAL YOUR SPONSOR'S NAME. THAT IS A FIRM CONDITION OF HIS OFFER.
ALL I CAN SAY IS THAT THE GENTLEMAN BEHIND YOUR FINANCING...
"...IS A MAN OF GREAT CHARACTER AND ALTRUISTIC MOTIVE."
SAYS YOU, CARR.
BRUCE, GET OFF THE PHONE! YOU'RE MISSING THE FLOOR SHOW!
...YOURS IS A VERY INTERESTING PROPOSAL, MR. QUEEN--VERY WELL, OLIVER.
PERHAPS WE CAN DO BUSINESS TOGETHER. STAY IN TOUCH.
C'MON, WAYNE! FIVE THOUSAND SAYS I NAIL THE BLONDE BEFORE YOU DO.
AND YOU ARE...?
BRUCE WAYNE, MEET MAXWELL LORD... A BIT OF NEW MONEY VISITING GOTHAM.
AH. NEW MONEY. THAT WOULD EXPLAIN HIS VIGOR, EH, CHATSWORTH?
HEH! INDEED! FANCIES HIMSELF SOMEWHAT OF A MOVER AND A SHAKER, HE DOES!
MUCH LIKE MR. WAYNE HIMSELF, I BELIEVE.
WHAT ABOUT IT, BRUCE? ARE YOU THE MYSTERY FINANCIER THEY'RE BUZZING ABOUT?
HARDLY, MR. LORD. FRANKLY, I DON'T PAY MUCH ATTENTION TO WHERE MY MONEY GOES. THAT'S WHAT I HAVE PEOPLE FOR.

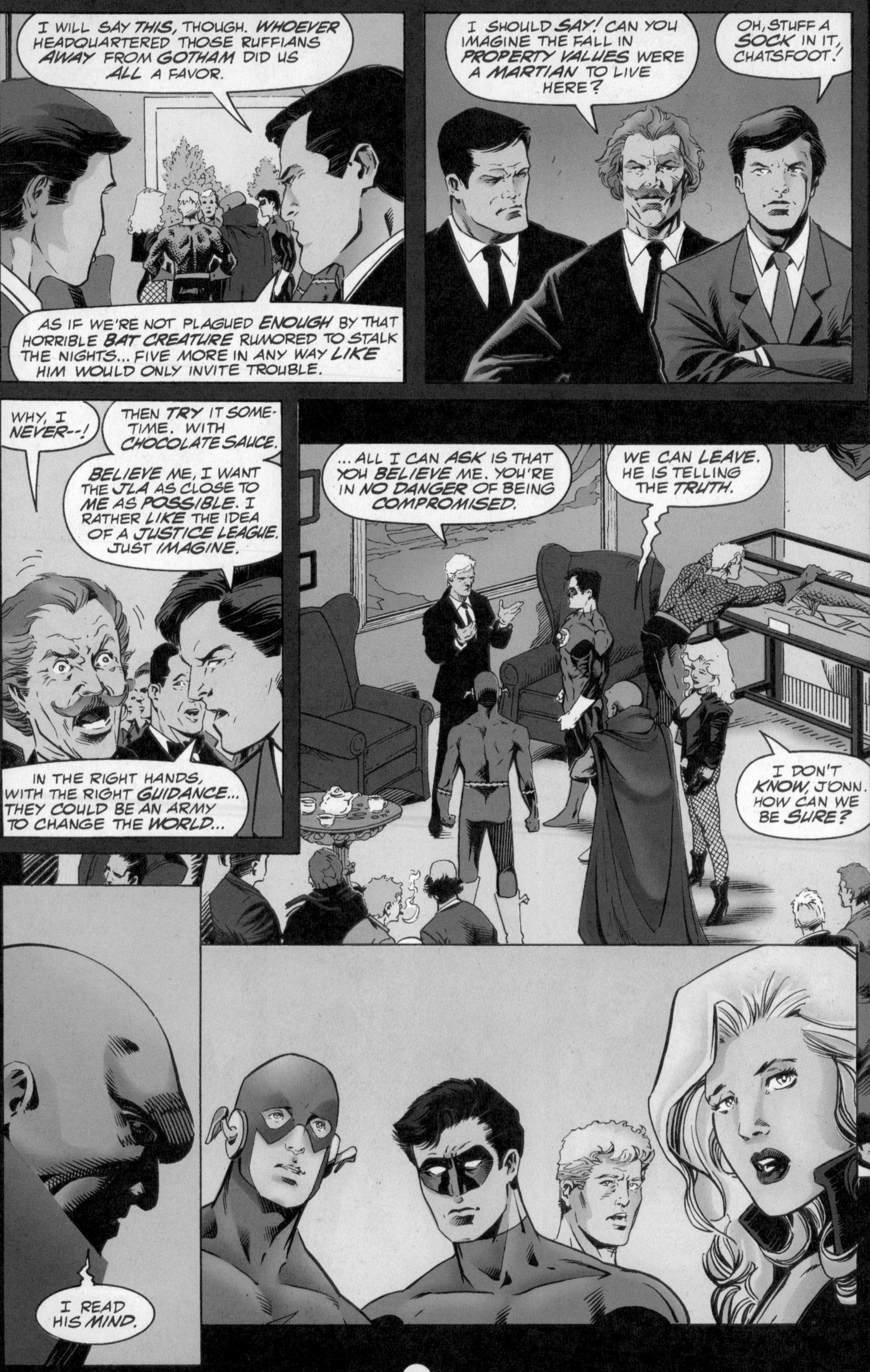

I WILL SAY THIS, THOUGH. WHOEVER HEADQUARTERED THOSE RUFFIANS AWAY FROM GOTHAM DID US ALL A FAVOR.
AS IF WE'RE NOT PLAGUED ENOUGH BY THAT HORRIBLE BAT CREATURE RUMORED TO STALK THE NIGHTS... FIVE MORE IN ANY WAY LIKE HIM WOULD ONLY INVITE TROUBLE.
I SHOULD SAY! CAN YOU IMAGINE THE FALL IN PROPERTY VALUES WERE A MARTIAN TO LIVE HERE?
OH, STUFF A SOCK IN IT, CHATSFOOT!
WHY, I NEVER--!
THEN TRY IT SOMETIME. WITH CHOCOLATE SAUCE.
BELIEVE ME, I WANT THE JLA AS CLOSE TO ME AS POSSIBLE. I RATHER LIKE THE IDEA OF A JUSTICE LEAGUE. JUST IMAGINE.
IN THE RIGHT HANDS, WITH THE RIGHT GUIDANCE... THEY COULD BE AN ARMY TO CHANGE THE WORLD...
...ALL I CAN ASK IS THAT YOU BELIEVE ME. YOU'RE IN NO DANGER OF BEING COMPROMISED.
WE CAN LEAVE. HE IS TELLING THE TRUTH.
I DON'T KNOW, J'ONN. HOW CAN WE BE SURE?
I READ HIS MIND.

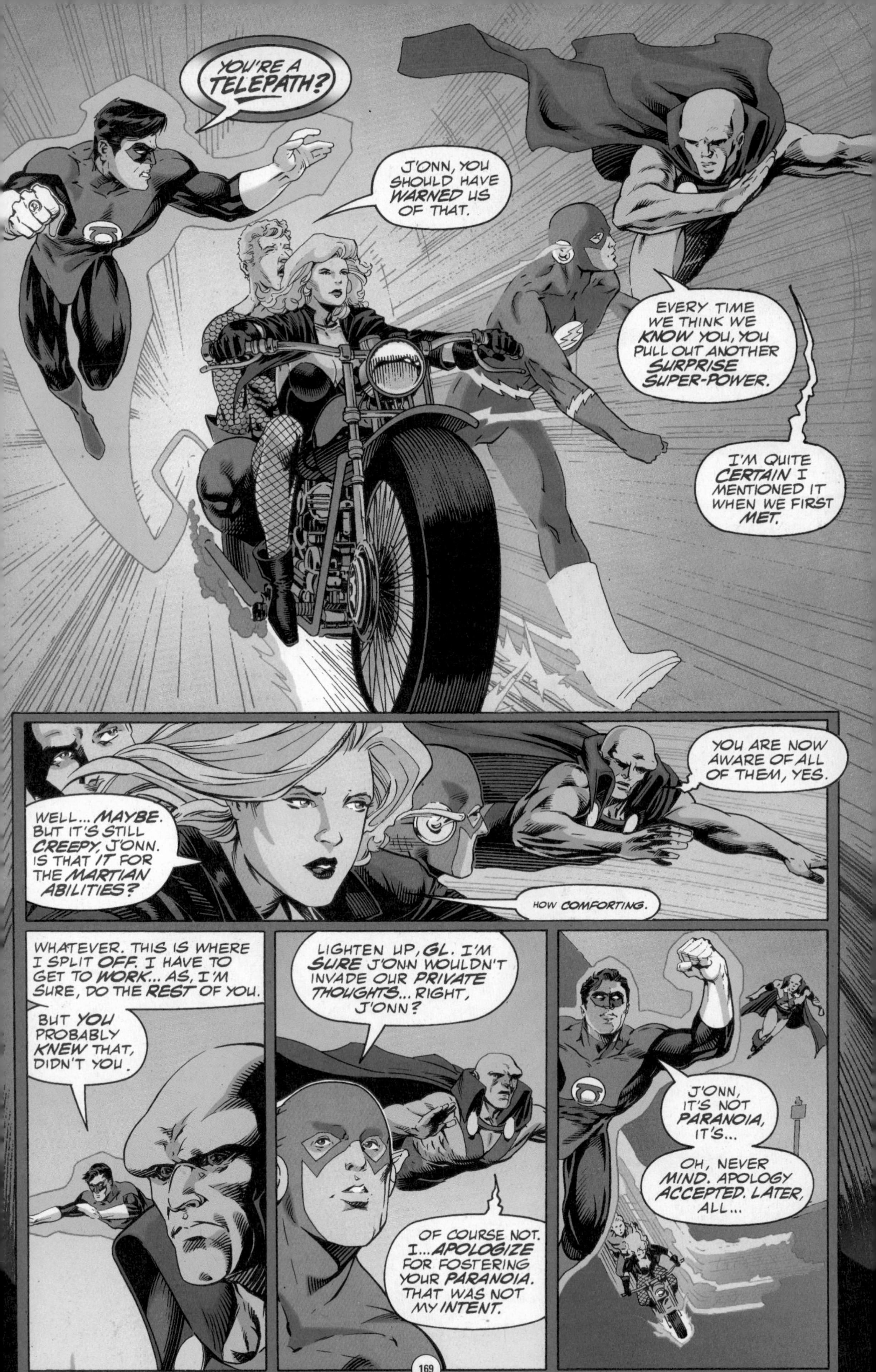

YOU'RE A TELEPATH?
J'ONN, YOU SHOULD HAVE WARNED US OF THAT.
EVERY TIME WE THINK WE KNOW YOU, YOU PULL OUT ANOTHER SURPRISE SUPER-POWER.
I'M QUITE CERTAIN I MENTIONED IT WHEN WE FIRST MET.
WELL... MAYBE. BUT IT'S STILL CREEPY, J'ONN. IS THAT IT FOR THE MARTIAN ABILITIES?
YOU ARE NOW AWARE OF ALL OF THEM, YES.
HOW COMFORTING.
WHATEVER. THIS IS WHERE I SPLIT OFF. I HAVE TO GET TO WORK... AS, I'M SURE, DO THE REST OF YOU.
BUT YOU PROBABLY KNEW THAT, DIDN'T YOU.
LIGHTEN UP, GL. I'M SURE J'ONN WOULDN'T INVADE OUR PRIVATE THOUGHTS... RIGHT, J'ONN?
OF COURSE NOT. I... APOLOGIZE FOR FOSTERING YOUR PARANOIA. THAT WAS NOT MY INTENT.
J'ONN, IT'S NOT PARANOIA, IT'S...
OH, NEVER MIND. APOLOGY ACCEPTED. LATER, ALL...

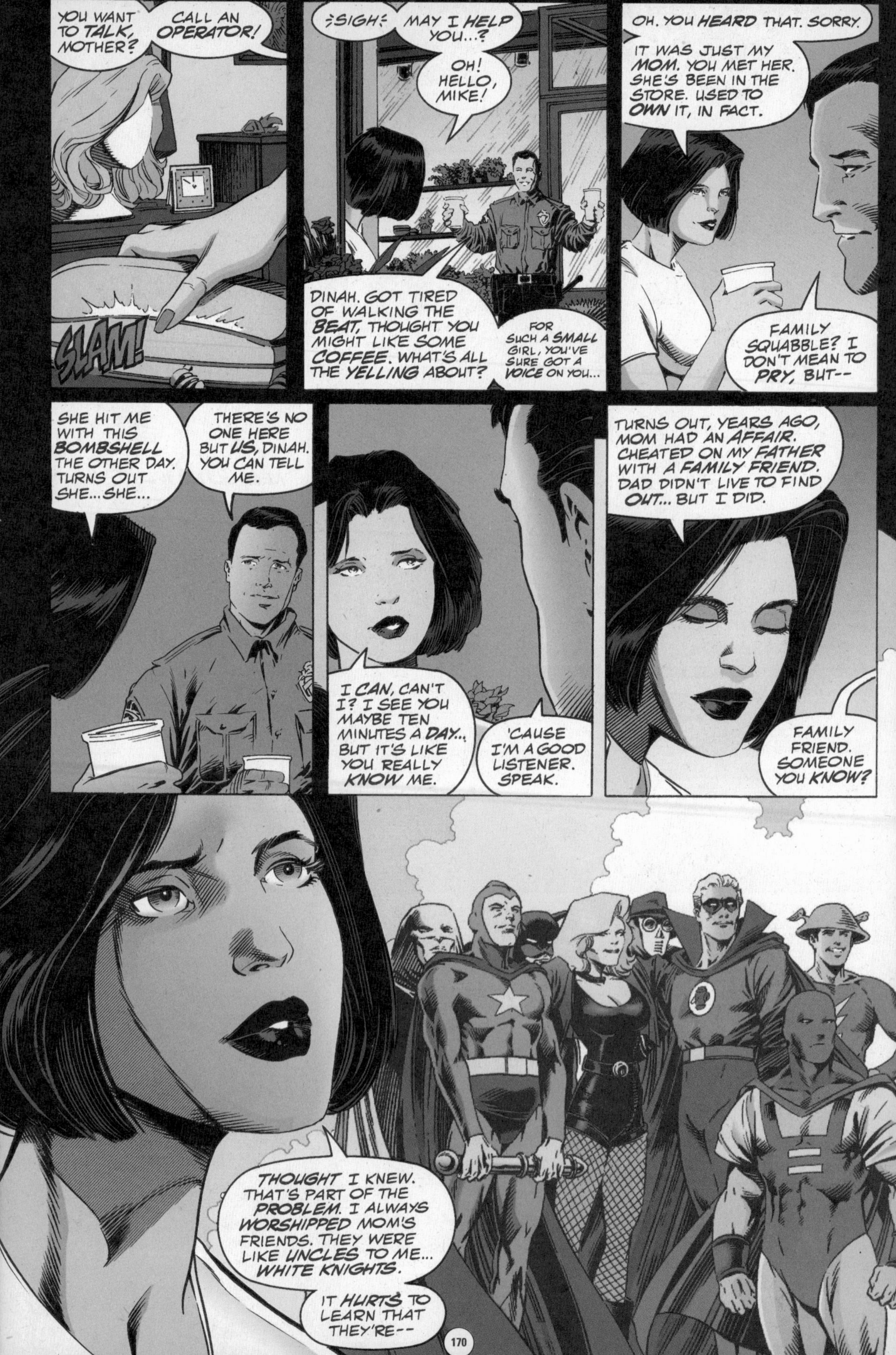
YOU WANT TO TALK, MOTHER?
CALL AN OPERATOR!
SLAM!
SIGH
MAY I HELP YOU...?
OH! HELLO, MIKE!
DINAH. GOT TIRED OF WALKING THE BEAT, THOUGHT YOU MIGHT LIKE SOME COFFEE. WHAT'S ALL THE YELLING ABOUT?
FOR SUCH A SMALL GIRL, YOU'VE SURE GOT A VOICE ON YOU...
OH. YOU HEARD THAT. SORRY.
IT WAS JUST MY MOM. YOU MET HER. SHE'S BEEN IN THE STORE. USED TO OWN IT, IN FACT.
FAMILY SQUABBLE? I DON'T MEAN TO PRY, BUT--
SHE HIT ME WITH THIS BOMBSHELL THE OTHER DAY. TURNS OUT SHE... SHE...
THERE'S NO ONE HERE BUT US, DINAH. YOU CAN TELL ME.
I CAN, CAN'T I? I SEE YOU MAYBE TEN MINUTES A DAY... BUT IT'S LIKE YOU REALLY KNOW ME.
'CAUSE I'M A GOOD LISTENER. SPEAK.
TURNS OUT, YEARS AGO, MOM HAD AN AFFAIR. CHEATED ON MY FATHER WITH A FAMILY FRIEND. DAD DIDN'T LIVE TO FIND OUT... BUT I DID.
FAMILY FRIEND. SOMEONE YOU KNOW?
THOUGHT I KNEW. THAT'S PART OF THE PROBLEM. I ALWAYS WORSHIPPED MOM'S FRIENDS. THEY WERE LIKE UNCLES TO ME... WHITE KNIGHTS.
IT HURTS TO LEARN THAT THEY'RE--

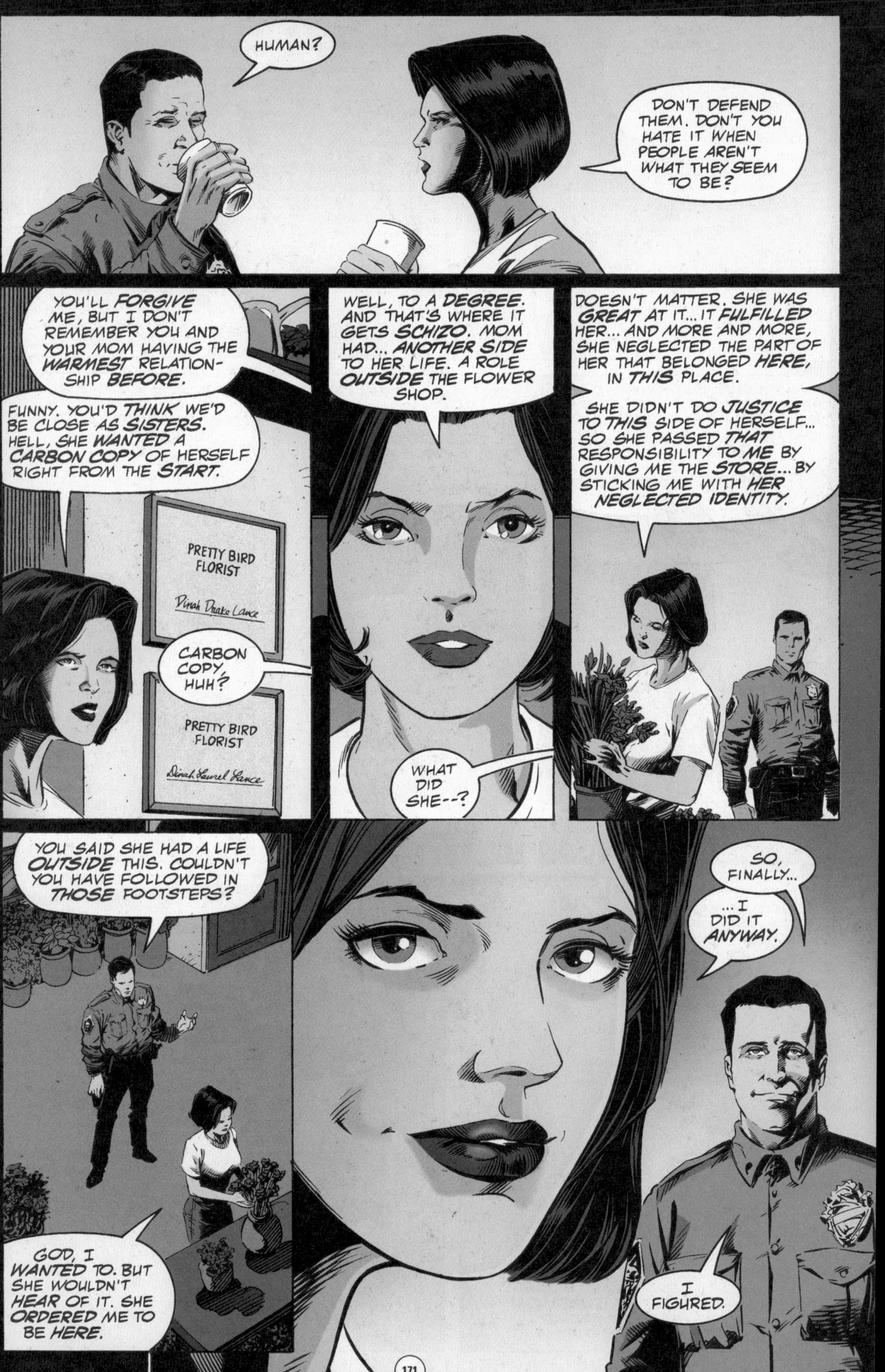
HUMAN?
DON'T DEFEND THEM. DON'T YOU HATE IT WHEN PEOPLE AREN'T WHAT THEY SEEM TO BE?
YOU'LL FORGIVE ME, BUT I DON'T REMEMBER YOU AND YOUR MOM HAVING THE WARMEST RELATIONSHIP BEFORE.
FUNNY. YOU'D THINK WE'D BE CLOSE AS SISTERS. HELL, SHE WANTED A CARBON COPY OF HERSELF RIGHT FROM THE START.
PRETTY BIRD FLORIST
Dinah Drake Lance
CARBON COPY, HUH?
PRETTY BIRD FLORIST
Dinah Laurel Lance
WELL, TO A DEGREE. AND THAT'S WHERE IT GETS SCHIZO. MOM HAD... ANOTHER SIDE TO HER LIFE. A ROLE OUTSIDE THE FLOWER SHOP.
WHAT DID SHE--?
DOESN'T MATTER. SHE WAS GREAT AT IT... IT FULFILLED HER... AND MORE AND MORE, SHE NEGLECTED THE PART OF HER THAT BELONGED HERE, IN THIS PLACE.
SHE DIDN'T DO JUSTICE TO THIS SIDE OF HERSELF... SO SHE PASSED THAT RESPONSIBILITY TO ME BY GIVING ME THE STORE... BY STICKING ME WITH HER NEGLECTED IDENTITY.
YOU SAID SHE HAD A LIFE OUTSIDE THIS. COULDN'T YOU HAVE FOLLOWED IN THOSE FOOTSTEPS?
GOD, I WANTED TO. BUT SHE WOULDN'T HEAR OF IT. SHE ORDERED ME TO BE HERE.
SO, FINALLY...
...I DID IT ANYWAY.
I FIGURED.

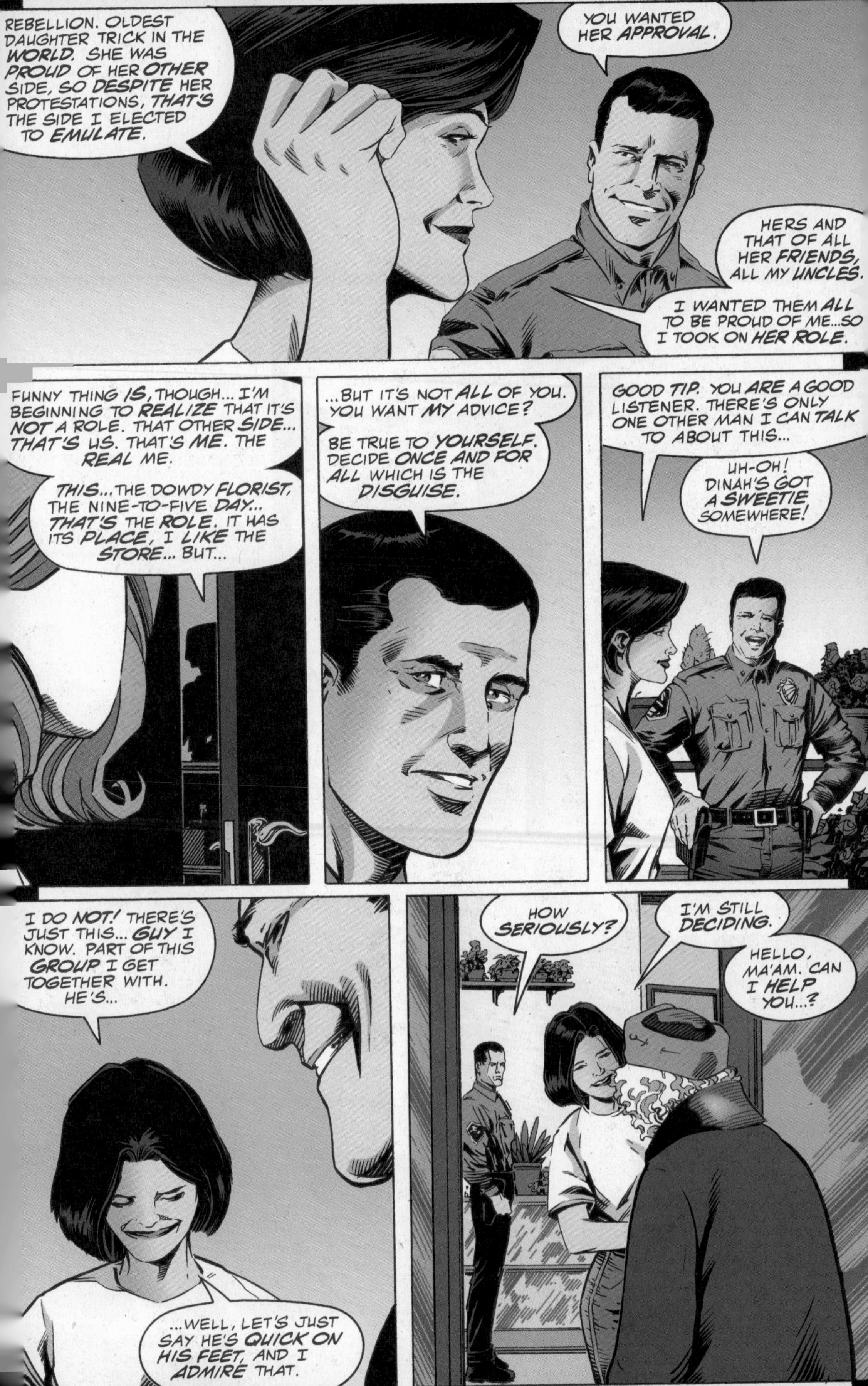
REBELLION. OLDEST DAUGHTER TRICK IN THE WORLD. SHE WAS PROUD OF HER OTHER SIDE, SO DESPITE HER PROTESTATIONS, THAT'S THE SIDE I ELECTED TO EMULATE.
YOU WANTED HER APPROVAL.
HERS AND THAT OF ALL HER FRIENDS, ALL MY UNCLES.
I WANTED THEM ALL TO BE PROUD OF ME...SO I TOOK ON HER ROLE.
FUNNY THING IS, THOUGH... I'M BEGINNING TO REALIZE THAT IT'S NOT A ROLE. THAT OTHER SIDE... THAT'S US. THAT'S ME. THE REAL ME.
THIS... THE DOWDY FLORIST, THE NINE-TO-FIVE DAY... THAT'S THE ROLE. IT HAS ITS PLACE, I LIKE THE STORE... BUT...
...BUT IT'S NOT ALL OF YOU. YOU WANT MY ADVICE?
BE TRUE TO YOURSELF. DECIDE ONCE AND FOR ALL WHICH IS THE DISGUISE.
GOOD TIP. YOU ARE A GOOD LISTENER. THERE'S ONLY ONE OTHER MAN I CAN TALK TO ABOUT THIS...
UH-OH! DINAH'S GOT A SWEETIE SOMEWHERE!
I DO NOT! THERE'S JUST THIS... GUY I KNOW. PART OF THIS GROUP I GET TOGETHER WITH. HE'S...
...WELL, LET'S JUST SAY HE'S QUICK ON HIS FEET, AND I ADMIRE THAT.
HOW SERIOUSLY?
I'M STILL DECIDING.
HELLO, MA'AM. CAN I HELP YOU...?

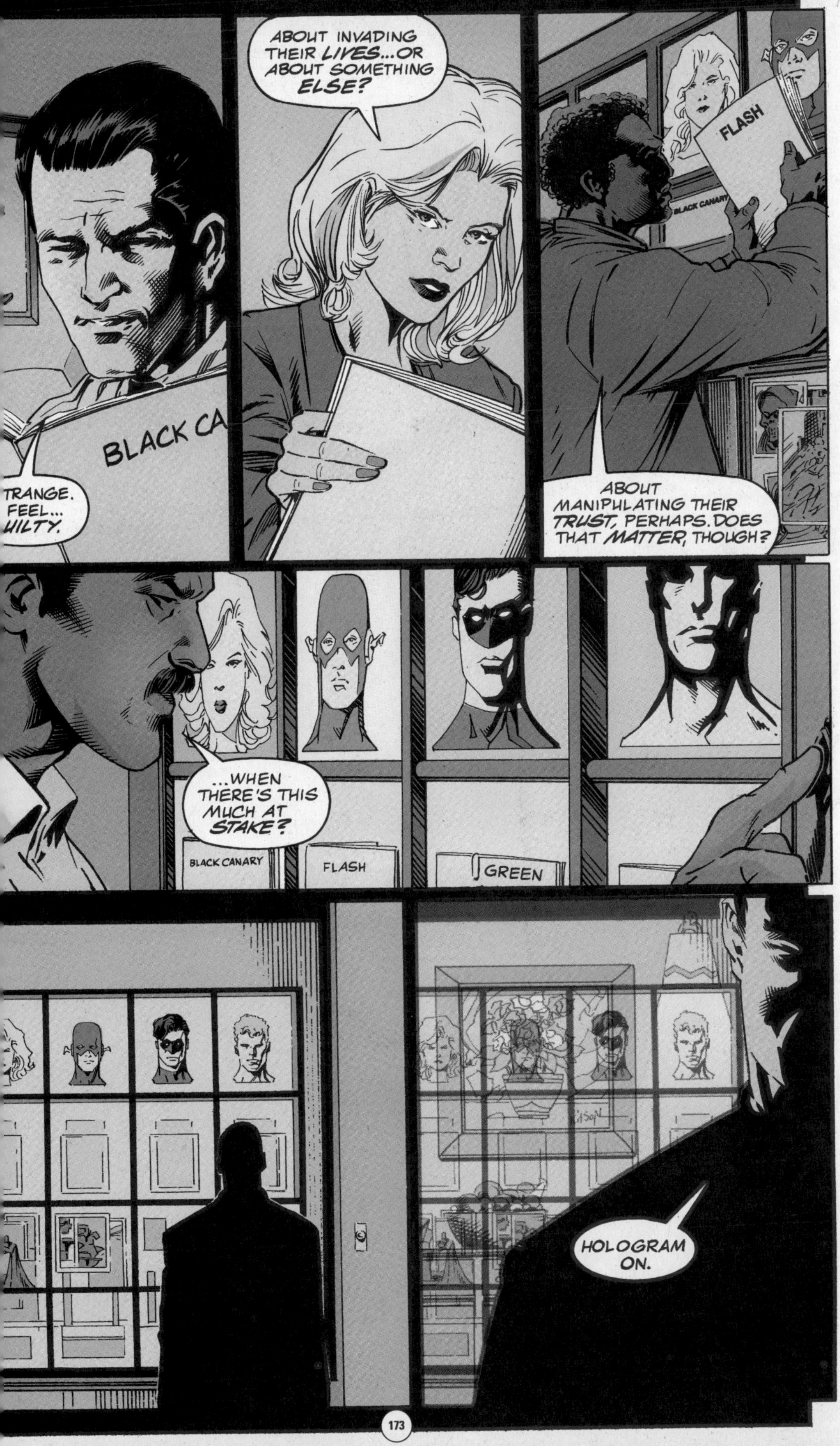
TRANGE.
FEEL...
UILTY.
ABOUT INVADING THEIR LIVES...OR ABOUT SOMETHING ELSE?
BLACK CA
FLASH
BLACK CANARY
ABOUT MANIPULATING THEIR TRUST, PERHAPS. DOES THAT MATTER, THOUGH?
...WHEN THERE'S THIS MUCH AT STAKE?
BLACK CANARY
FLASH
GREEN
HOLOGRAM ON.

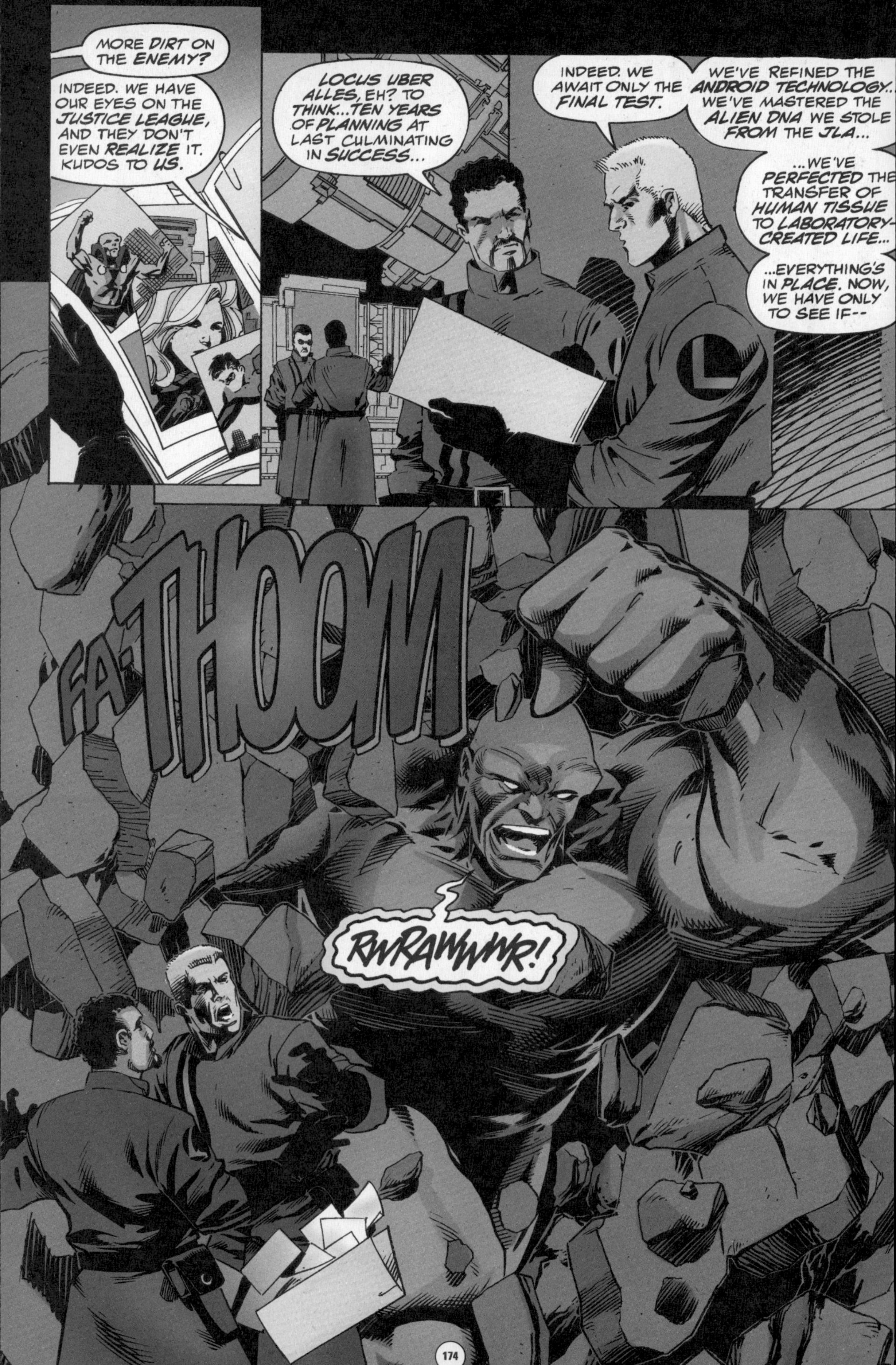
MORE DIRT ON THE ENEMY?
INDEED. WE HAVE OUR EYES ON THE JUSTICE LEAGUE, AND THEY DON'T EVEN REALIZE IT. KUDOS TO US.
LOCUS UBER ALLES, EH? TO THINK...TEN YEARS OF PLANNING AT LAST CULMINATING IN SUCCESS...
INDEED. WE AWAIT ONLY THE FINAL TEST.
WE'VE REFINED THE ANDROID TECHNOLOGY... WE'VE MASTERED THE ALIEN DNA WE STOLE FROM THE JLA...
...WE'VE PERFECTED THE TRANSFER OF HUMAN TISSUE TO LABORATORY-CREATED LIFE...
...EVERYTHING'S IN PLACE. NOW, WE HAVE ONLY TO SEE IF--
FA-THOOM
RWRAWWWR!

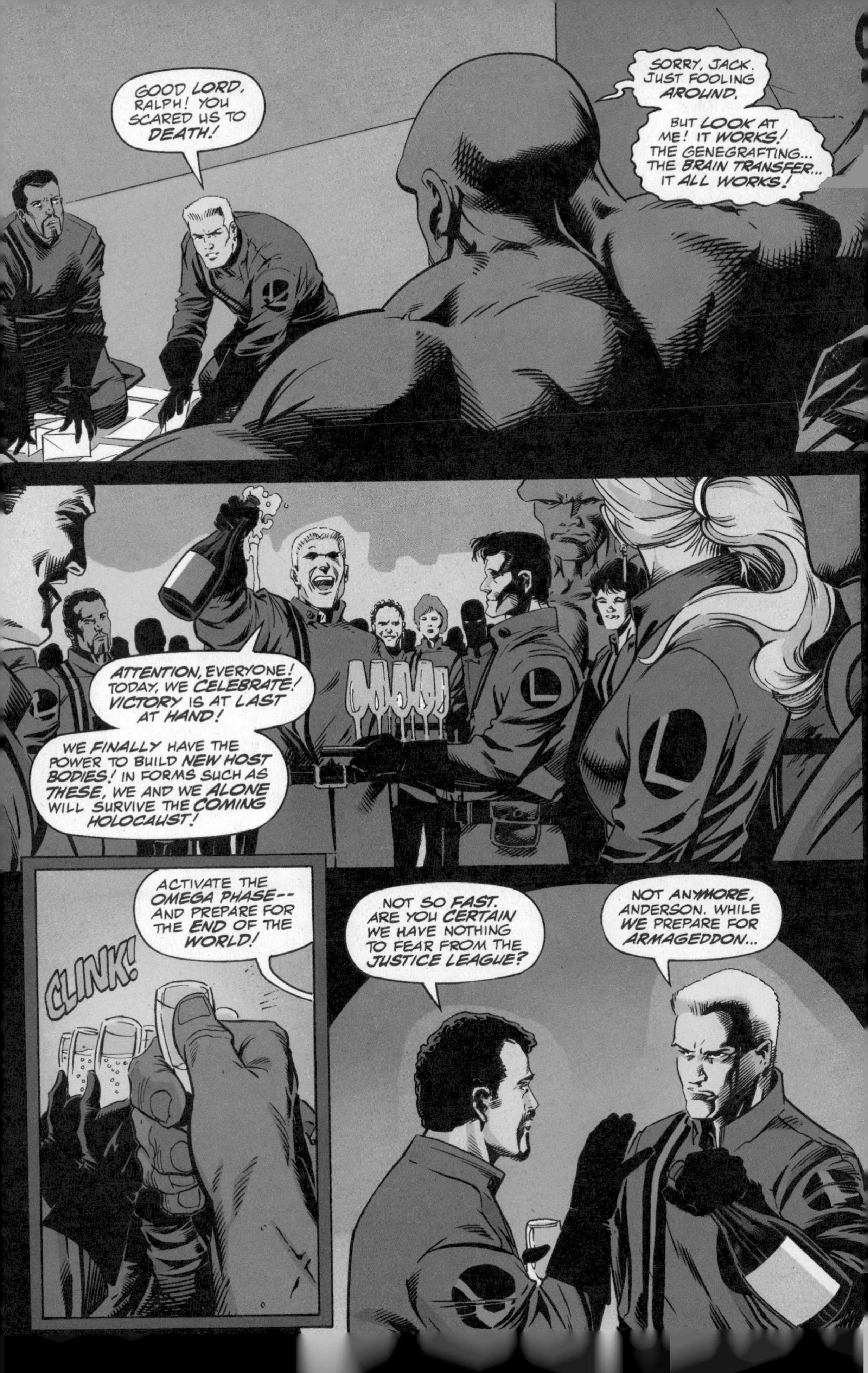
GOOD LORD, RALPH! YOU SCARED US TO DEATH!
SORRY, JACK. JUST FOOLING AROUND.
BUT LOOK AT ME! IT WORKS! THE GENEGRAFTING... THE BRAIN TRANSFER... IT ALL WORKS!
ATTENTION, EVERYONE! TODAY, WE CELEBRATE! VICTORY IS AT LAST AT HAND!
WE FINALLY HAVE THE POWER TO BUILD NEW HOST BODIES! IN FORMS SUCH AS THESE, WE AND WE ALONE WILL SURVIVE THE COMING HOLOCAUST!
ACTIVATE THE OMEGA PHASE-- AND PREPARE FOR THE END OF THE WORLD!
CLINK!
NOT SO FAST. ARE YOU CERTAIN WE HAVE NOTHING TO FEAR FROM THE JUSTICE LEAGUE?
NOT ANYMORE, ANDERSON. WHILE WE PREPARE FOR ARMAGEDDON...

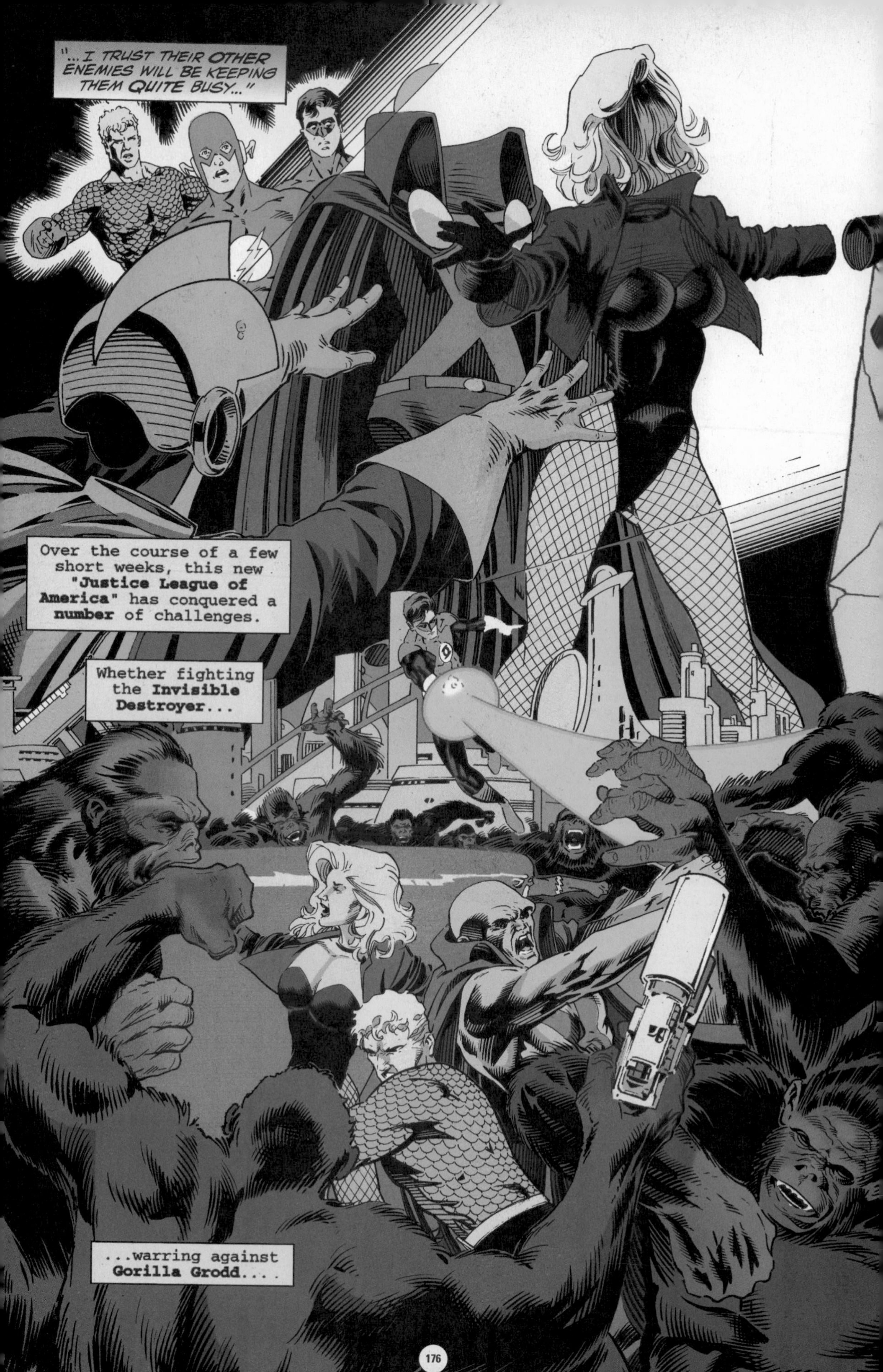
"...I TRUST THEIR OTHER ENEMIES WILL BE KEEPING THEM QUITE BUSY..."
Over the course of a few short weeks, this new "Justice League of America" has conquered a number of challenges.
Whether fighting the Invisible Destroyer...
...warring against Gorilla Grodd....

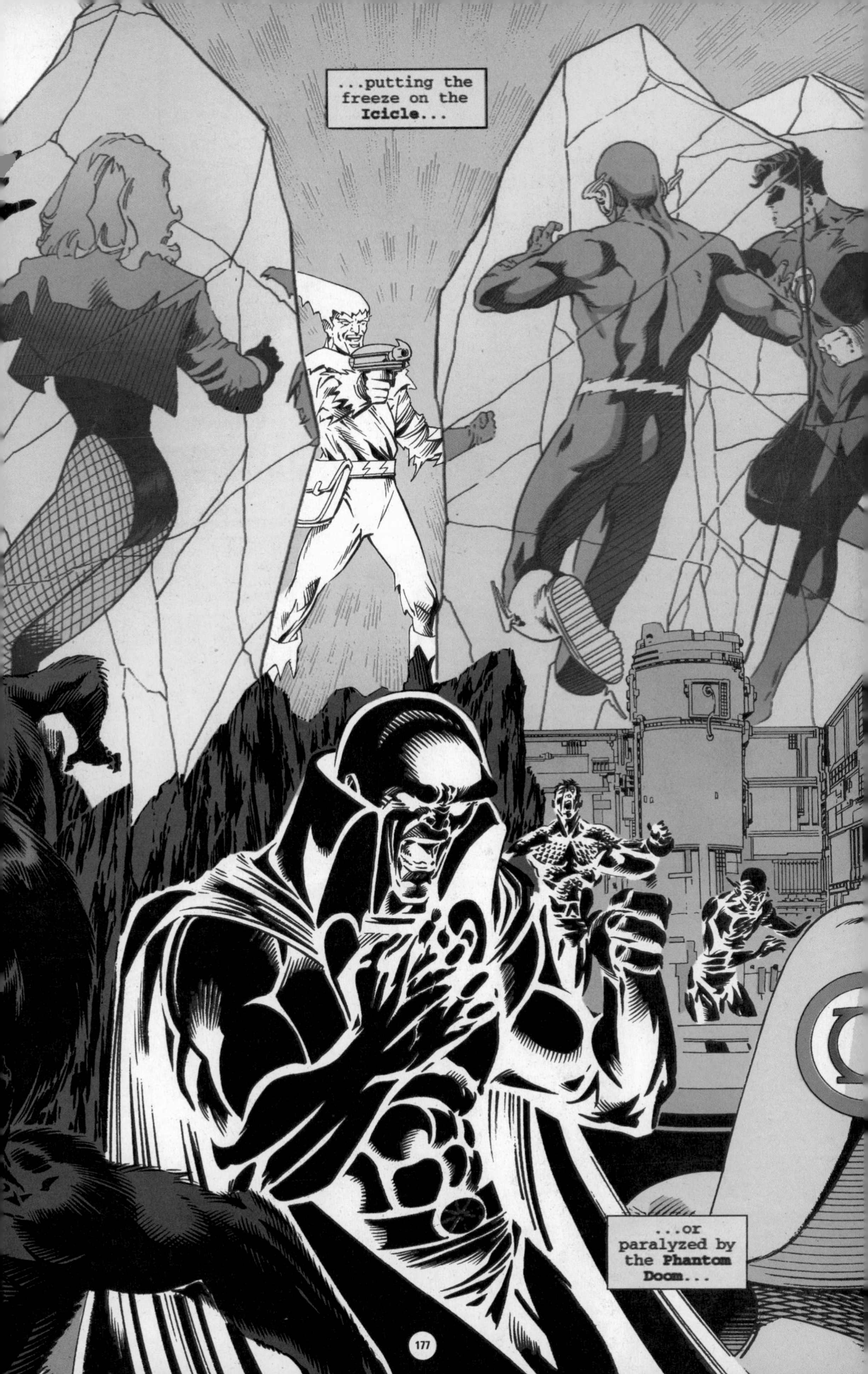
...putting the freeze on the Icicle...
...or paralyzed by the Phantom Doom...

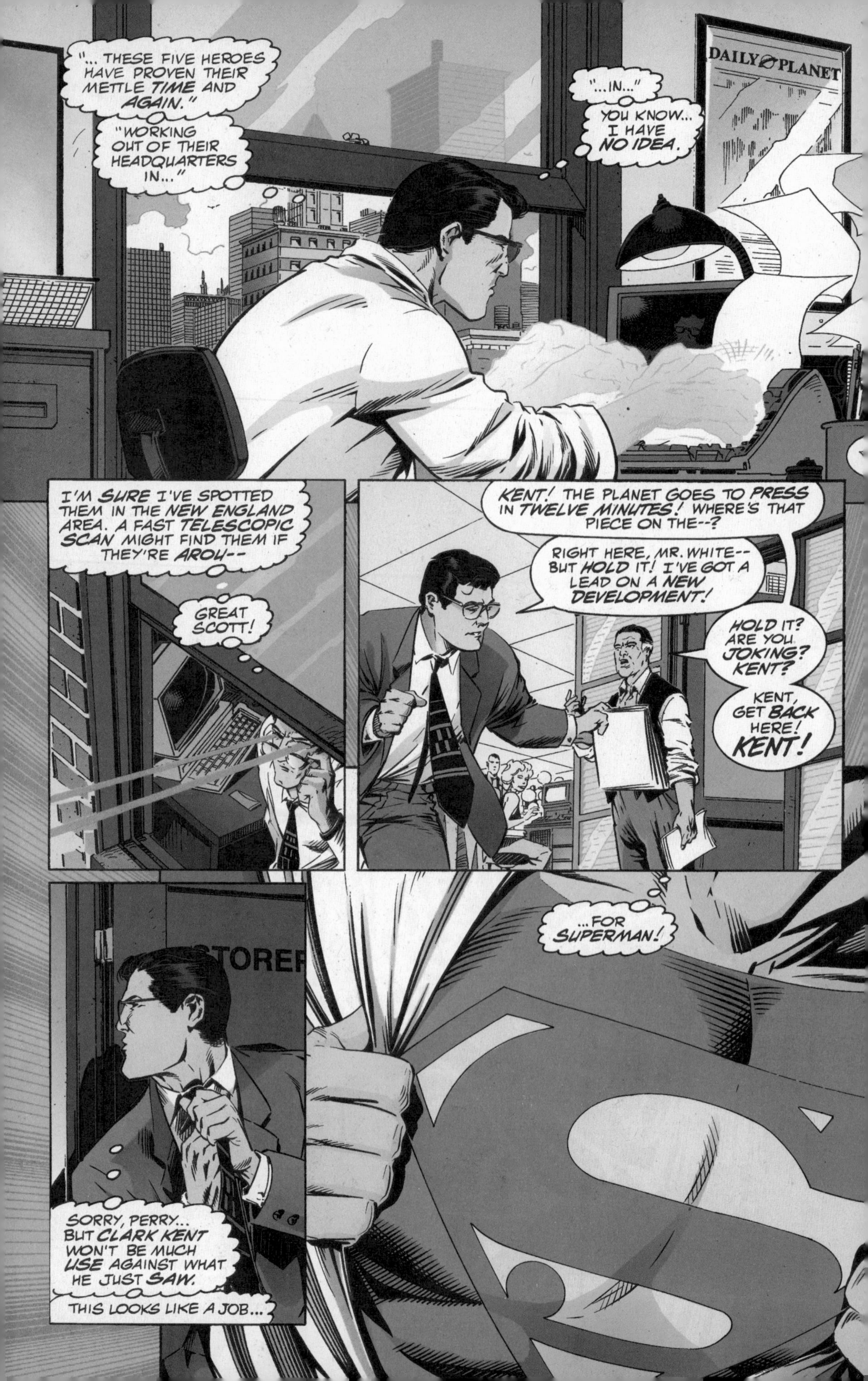
"... THESE FIVE HEROES HAVE PROVEN THEIR METTLE TIME AND AGAIN."
"WORKING OUT OF THEIR HEADQUARTERS IN..."
"...IN..."
YOU KNOW... I HAVE NO IDEA.
DAILY PLANET
I'M SURE I'VE SPOTTED THEM IN THE NEW ENGLAND AREA. A FAST TELESCOPIC SCAN MIGHT FIND THEM IF THEY'RE AROU--
GREAT SCOTT!
KENT! THE PLANET GOES TO PRESS IN TWELVE MINUTES! WHERE'S THAT PIECE ON THE--?
RIGHT HERE, MR. WHITE-- BUT HOLD IT! I'VE GOT A LEAD ON A NEW DEVELOPMENT!
HOLD IT? ARE YOU JOKING? KENT?
KENT, GET BACK HERE! KENT!
STORER
SORRY, PERRY... BUT CLARK KENT WON'T BE MUCH USE AGAINST WHAT HE JUST SAW.
THIS LOOKS LIKE A JOB...
...FOR SUPERMAN!

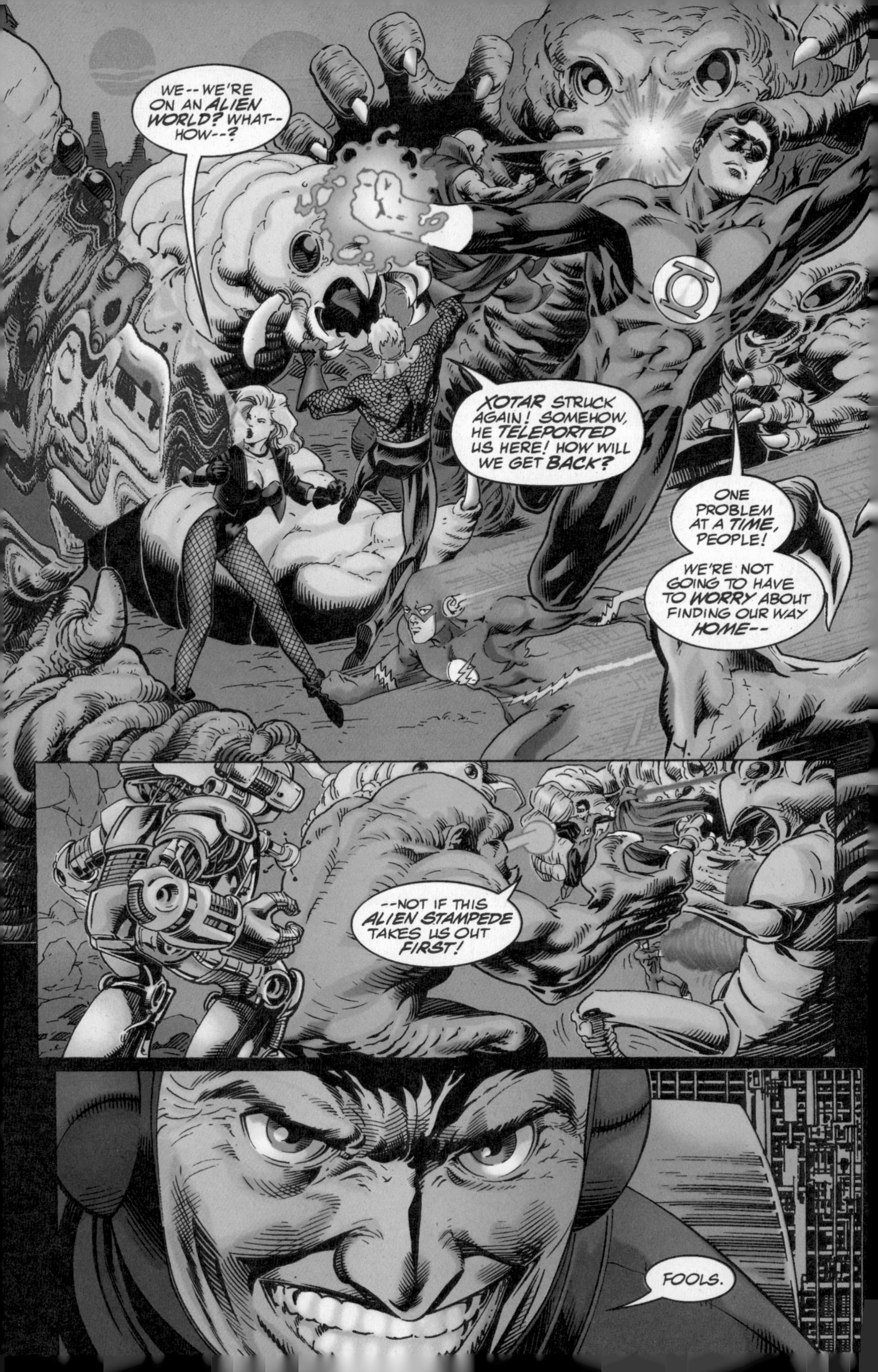
WE--WE'RE ON AN ALIEN WORLD? WHAT-- HOW--?
XOTAR STRUCK AGAIN! SOMEHOW, HE TELEPORTED US HERE! HOW WILL WE GET BACK?
ONE PROBLEM AT A TIME, PEOPLE!
WE'RE NOT GOING TO HAVE TO WORRY ABOUT FINDING OUR WAY HOME--
--NOT IF THIS ALIEN STAMPEDE TAKES US OUT FIRST!
FOOLS.

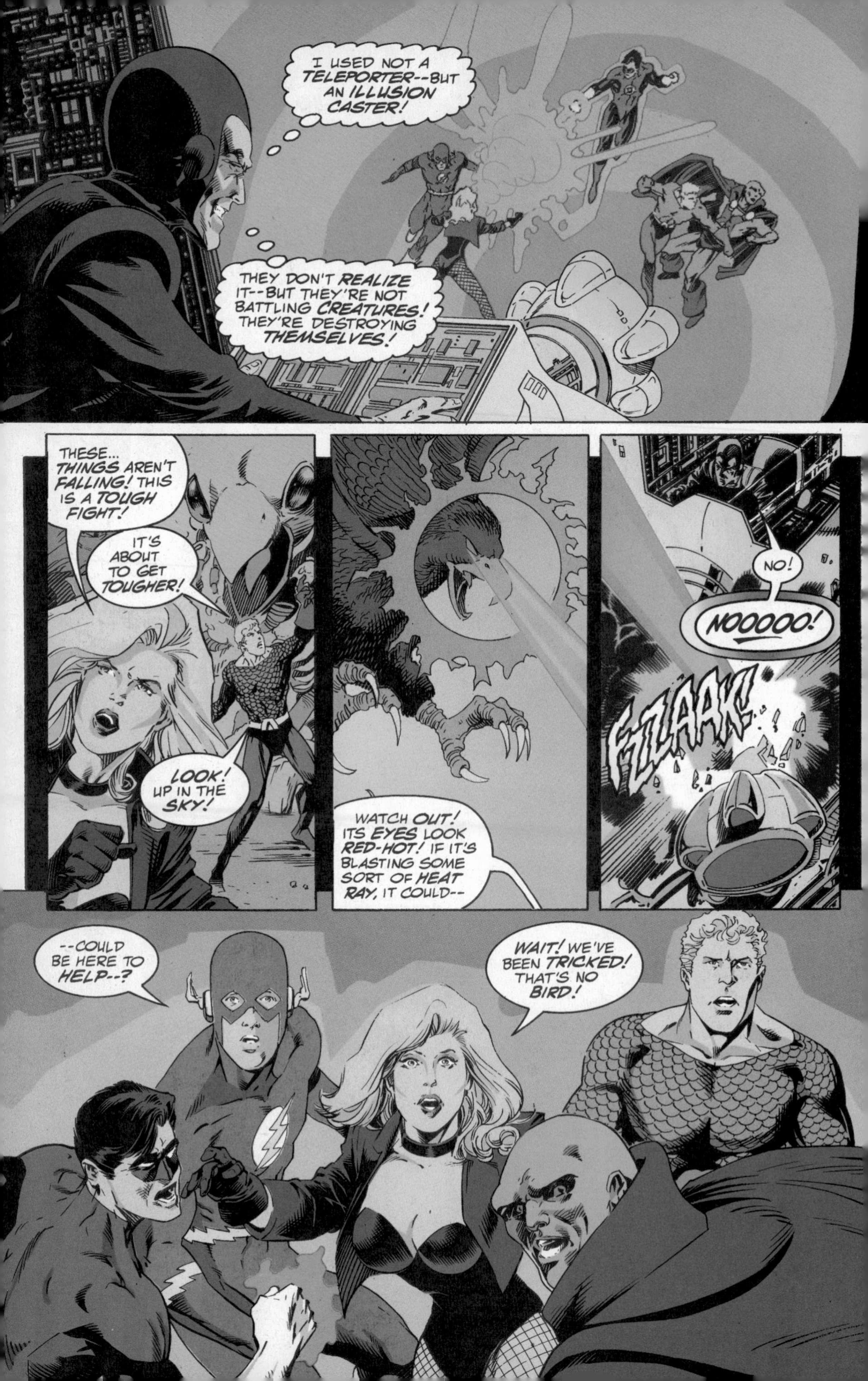
I USED NOT A TELEPORTER--BUT AN ILLUSION CASTER!
THEY DON'T REALIZE IT--BUT THEY'RE NOT BATTLING CREATURES! THEY'RE DESTROYING THEMSELVES!
THESE... THINGS AREN'T FALLING! THIS IS A TOUGH FIGHT!
IT'S ABOUT TO GET TOUGHER!
LOOK! UP IN THE SKY!
WATCH OUT! ITS EYES LOOK RED-HOT! IF IT'S BLASTING SOME SORT OF HEAT RAY, IT COULD--
NO!
NOOOOO!
FZZAAK!
--COULD BE HERE TO HELP--?
WAIT! WE'VE BEEN TRICKED! THAT'S NO BIRD!

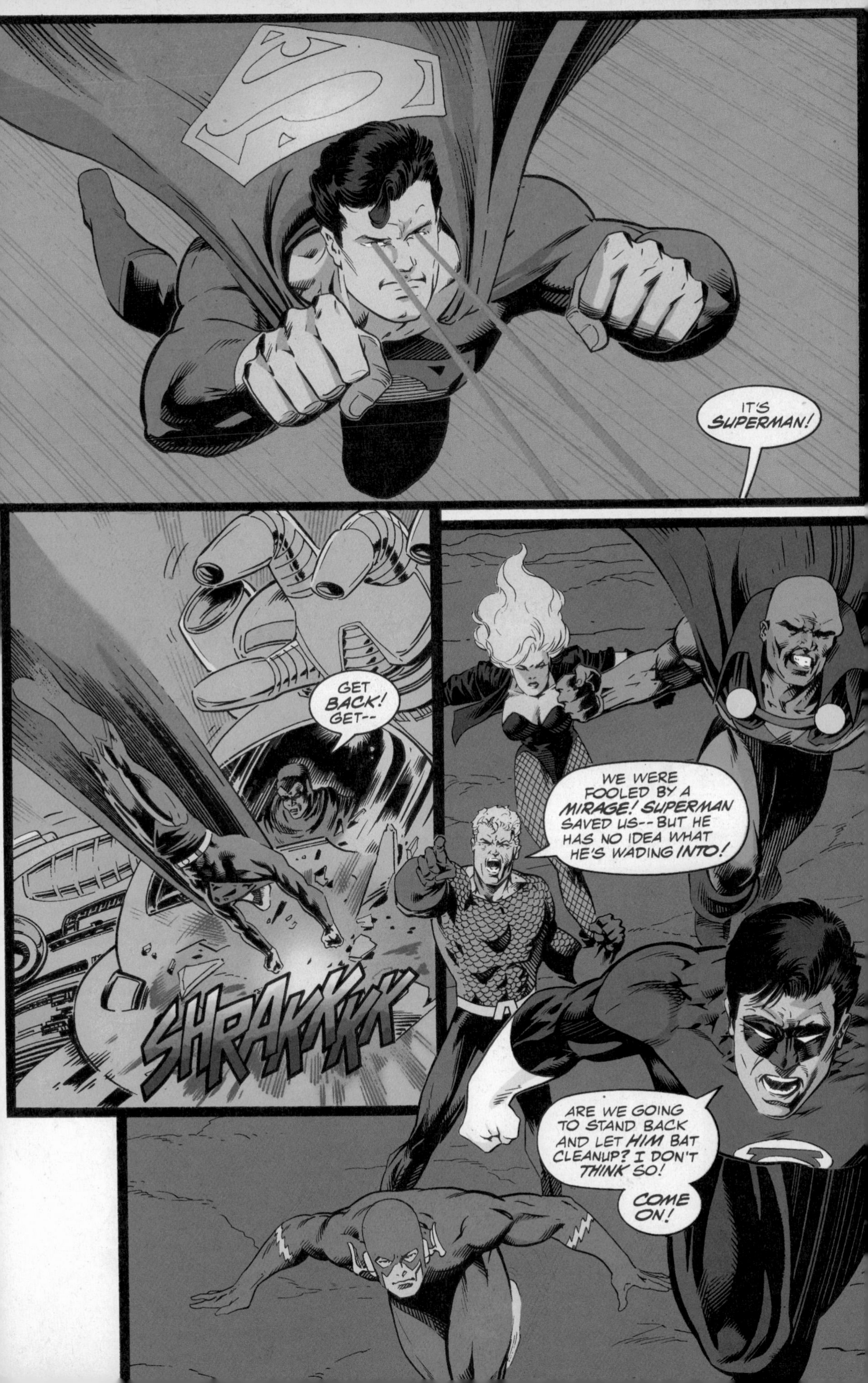
IT'S SUPERMAN!
GET BACK! GET--
SHRAKKKK
WE WERE FOOLED BY A MIRAGE! SUPERMAN SAVED US-- BUT HE HAS NO IDEA WHAT HE'S WADING INTO!
ARE WE GOING TO STAND BACK AND LET HIM BAT CLEANUP? I DON'T THINK SO!
COME ON!

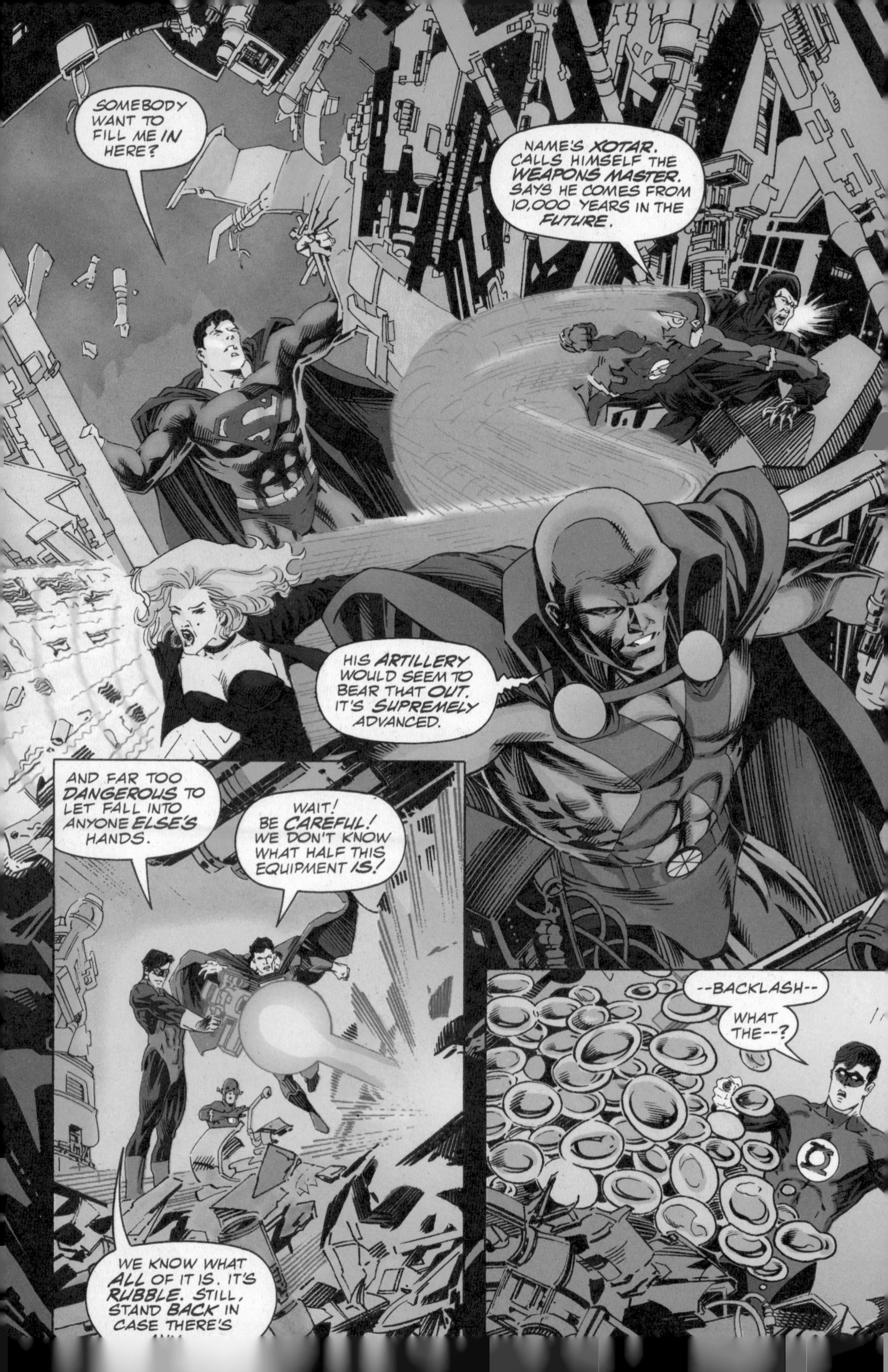
SOMEBODY WANT TO FILL ME IN HERE?
NAME'S XOTAR. CALLS HIMSELF THE WEAPONS MASTER. SAYS HE COMES FROM 10,000 YEARS IN THE FUTURE.
HIS ARTILLERY WOULD SEEM TO BEAR THAT OUT. IT'S SUPREMELY ADVANCED.
AND FAR TOO DANGEROUS TO LET FALL INTO ANYONE ELSE'S HANDS.
WAIT! BE CAREFUL! WE DON'T KNOW WHAT HALF THIS EQUIPMENT IS!
WE KNOW WHAT ALL OF IT IS. IT'S RUBBLE. STILL, STAND BACK IN CASE THERE'S
--BACKLASH--
WHAT THE--?

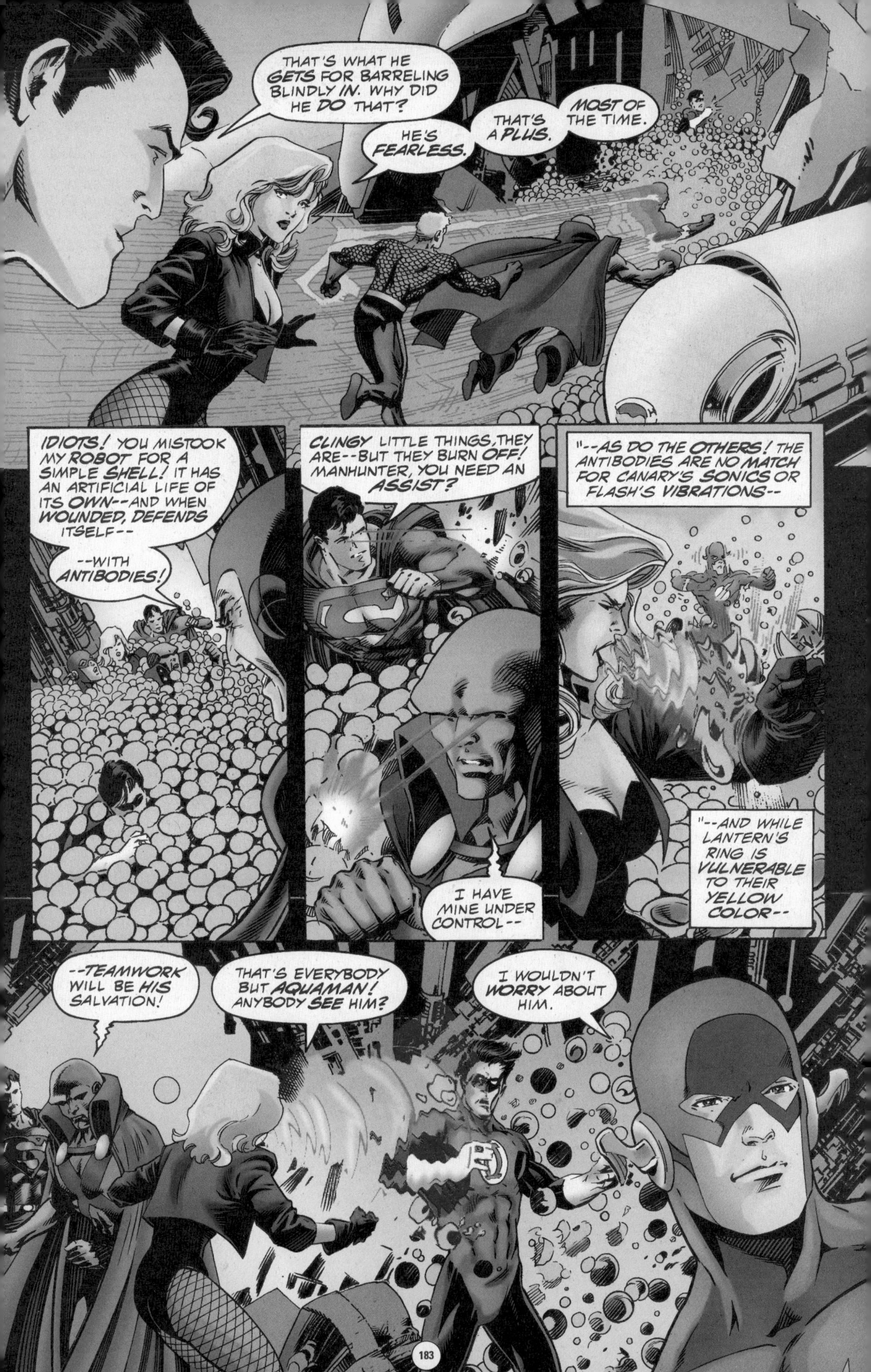
THAT'S WHAT HE GETS FOR BARRELING BLINDLY IN. WHY DID HE DO THAT?
HE'S FEARLESS.
THAT'S A PLUS.
MOST OF THE TIME.
IDIOTS! YOU MISTOOK MY ROBOT FOR A SIMPLE SHELL! IT HAS AN ARTIFICIAL LIFE OF ITS OWN--AND WHEN WOUNDED, DEFENDS ITSELF--
--WITH ANTIBODIES!
CLINGY LITTLE THINGS, THEY ARE--BUT THEY BURN OFF! MANHUNTER, YOU NEED AN ASSIST?
I HAVE MINE UNDER CONTROL--
"--AS DO THE OTHERS! THE ANTIBODIES ARE NO MATCH FOR CANARY'S SONICS OR FLASH'S VIBRATIONS--
"--AND WHILE LANTERN'S RING IS VULNERABLE TO THEIR YELLOW COLOR--
--TEAMWORK WILL BE HIS SALVATION!
THAT'S EVERYBODY BUT AQUAMAN! ANYBODY SEE HIM?
I WOULDN'T WORRY ABOUT HIM.

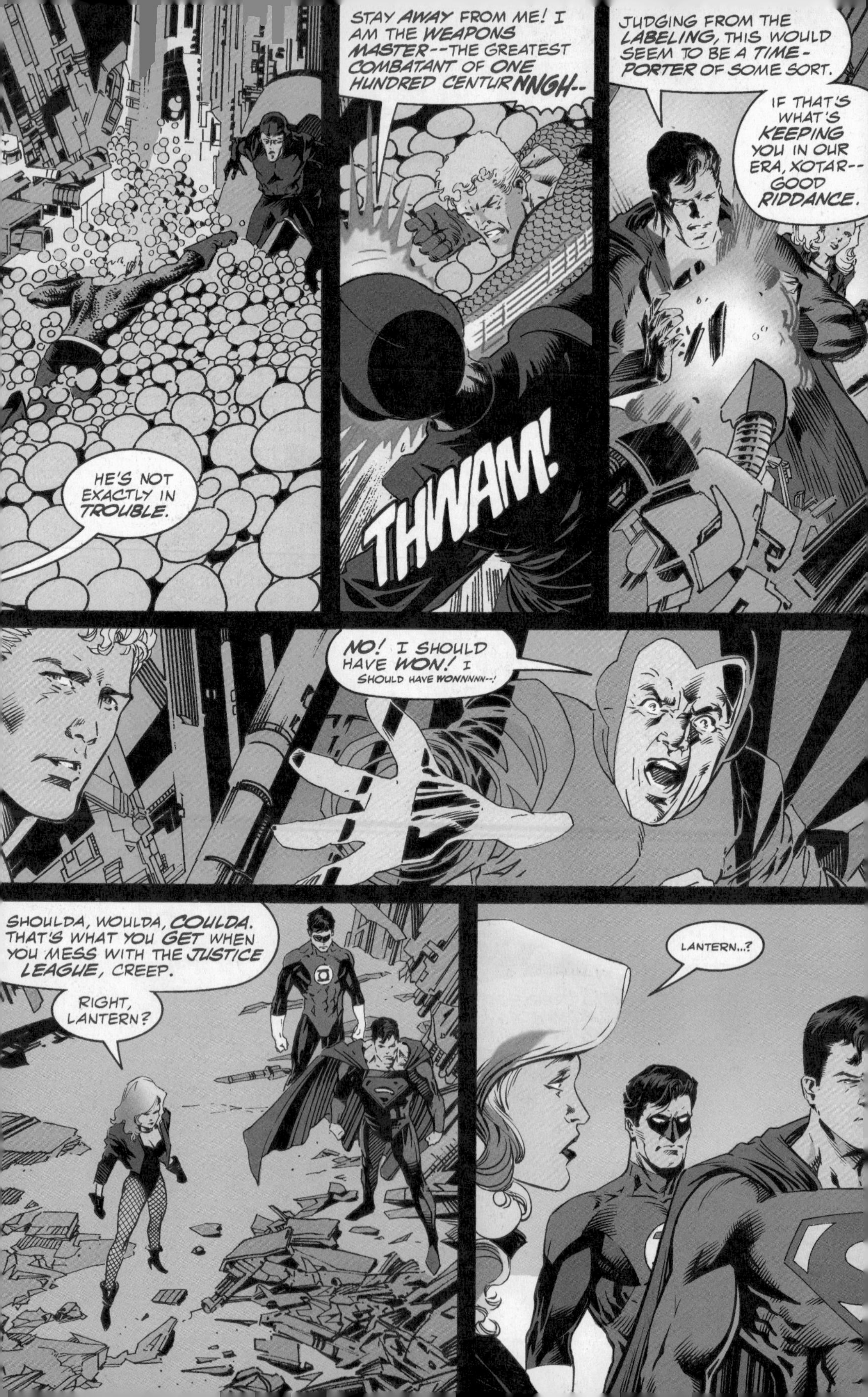

HE'S NOT EXACTLY IN TROUBLE.
STAY AWAY FROM ME! I AM THE WEAPONS MASTER--THE GREATEST COMBATANT OF ONE HUNDRED CENTURNNGH--
THWAM!
JUDGING FROM THE LABELING, THIS WOULD SEEM TO BE A TIME-PORTER OF SOME SORT.
IF THAT'S WHAT'S KEEPING YOU IN OUR ERA, XOTAR--GOOD RIDDANCE.
NO! I SHOULD HAVE WON! I SHOULD HAVE WONNNNN--!
SHOULDA, WOULDA, COULDA. THAT'S WHAT YOU GET WHEN YOU MESS WITH THE JUSTICE LEAGUE, CREEP.
RIGHT, LANTERN?
LANTERN...?

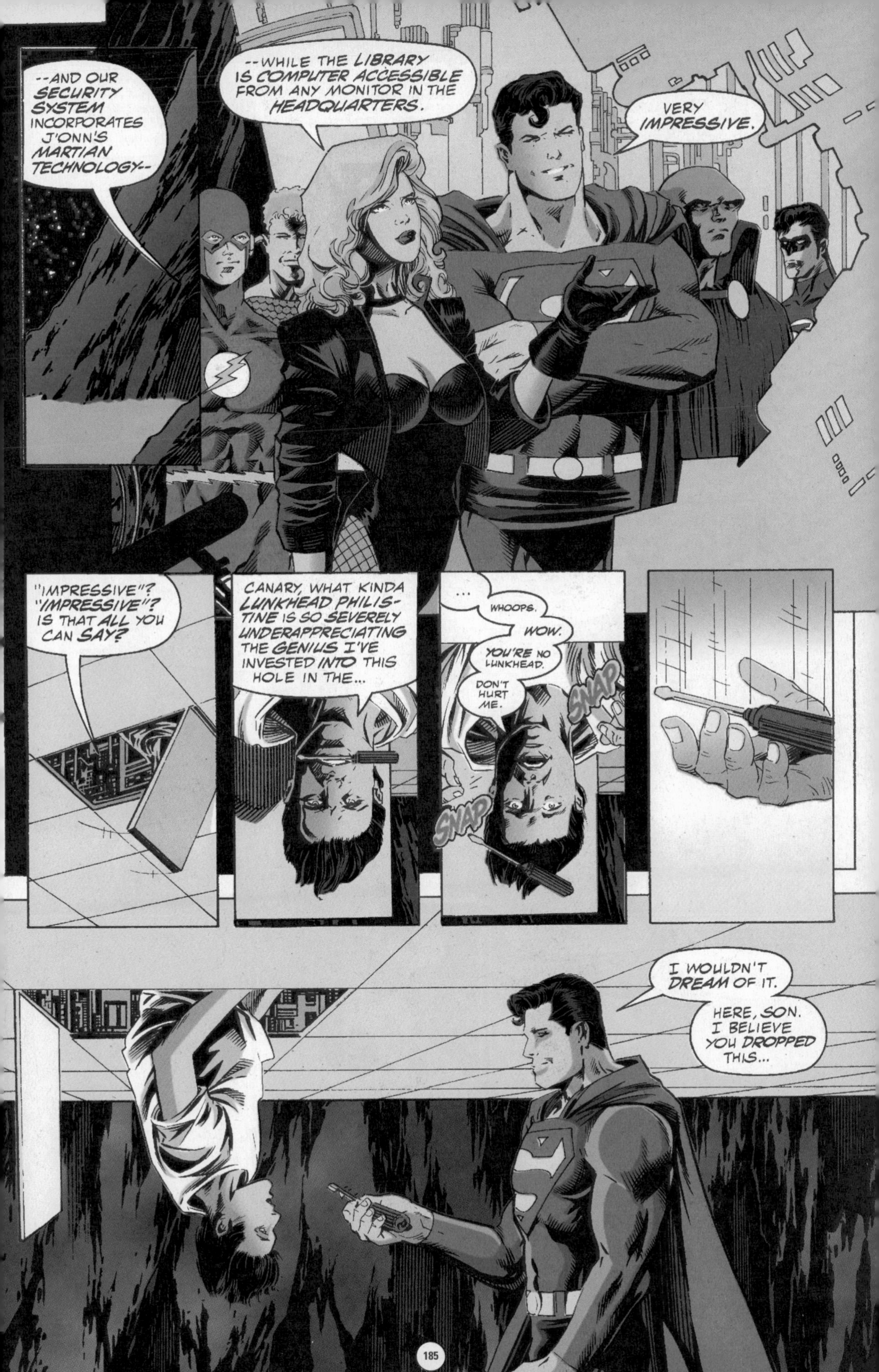
--AND OUR SECURITY SYSTEM INCORPORATES J'ONN'S MARTIAN TECHNOLOGY--
--WHILE THE LIBRARY IS COMPUTER ACCESSIBLE FROM ANY MONITOR IN THE HEADQUARTERS.
VERY IMPRESSIVE.
"IMPRESSIVE"? "IMPRESSIVE"? IS THAT ALL YOU CAN SAY?
CANARY, WHAT KINDA LUNKHEAD PHILIS-TINE IS SO SEVERELY UNDERAPPRECIATING THE GENIUS I'VE INVESTED INTO THIS HOLE IN THE...
...
WHOOPS.
WOW.
YOU'RE NO LUNKHEAD.
DON'T HURT ME.
SNAP
SNAP
I WOULDN'T DREAM OF IT.
HERE, SON. I BELIEVE YOU DROPPED THIS...

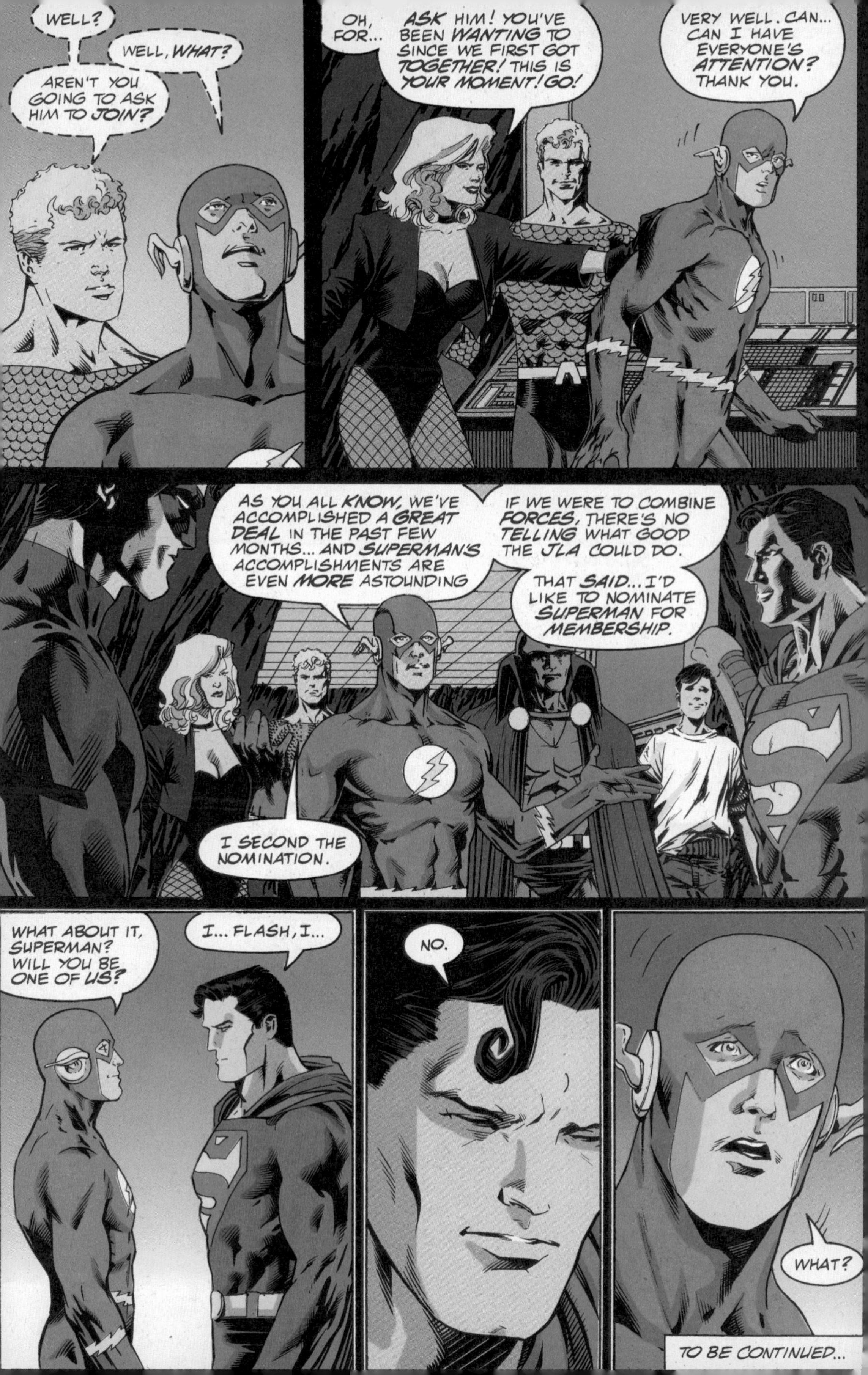
WELL?
WELL, WHAT?
AREN'T YOU GOING TO ASK HIM TO JOIN?
OH, FOR...
ASK HIM! YOU'VE BEEN WANTING TO SINCE WE FIRST GOT TOGETHER! THIS IS YOUR MOMENT! GO!
VERY WELL. CAN... CAN I HAVE EVERYONE'S ATTENTION? THANK YOU.
AS YOU ALL KNOW, WE'VE ACCOMPLISHED A GREAT DEAL IN THE PAST FEW MONTHS... AND SUPERMAN'S ACCOMPLISHMENTS ARE EVEN MORE ASTOUNDING
IF WE WERE TO COMBINE FORCES, THERE'S NO TELLING WHAT GOOD THE JLA COULD DO.
THAT SAID... I'D LIKE TO NOMINATE SUPERMAN FOR MEMBERSHIP.
I SECOND THE NOMINATION.
WHAT ABOUT IT, SUPERMAN? WILL YOU BE ONE OF US?
I... FLASH, I...
NO.
WHAT?
TO BE CONTINUED...

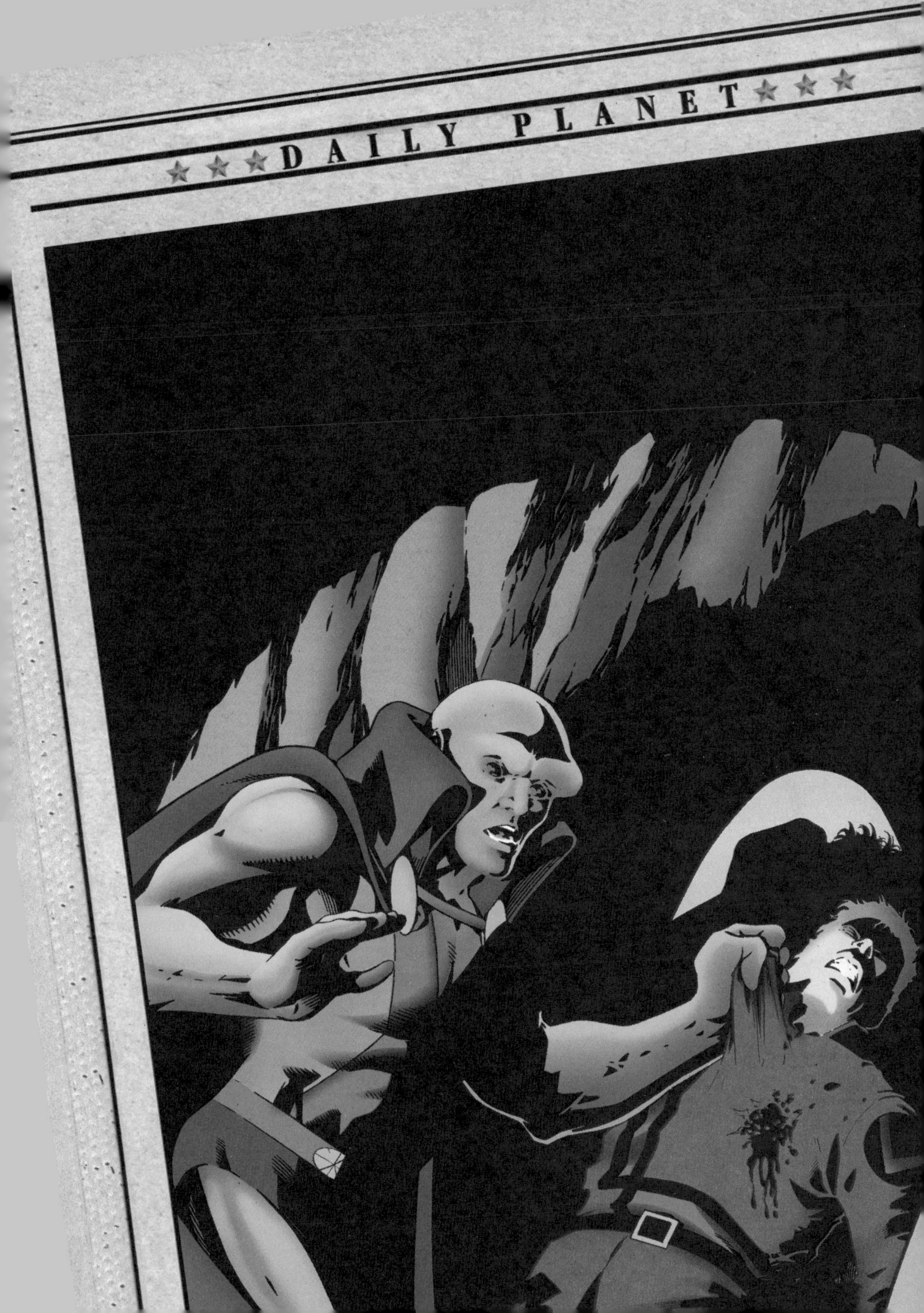

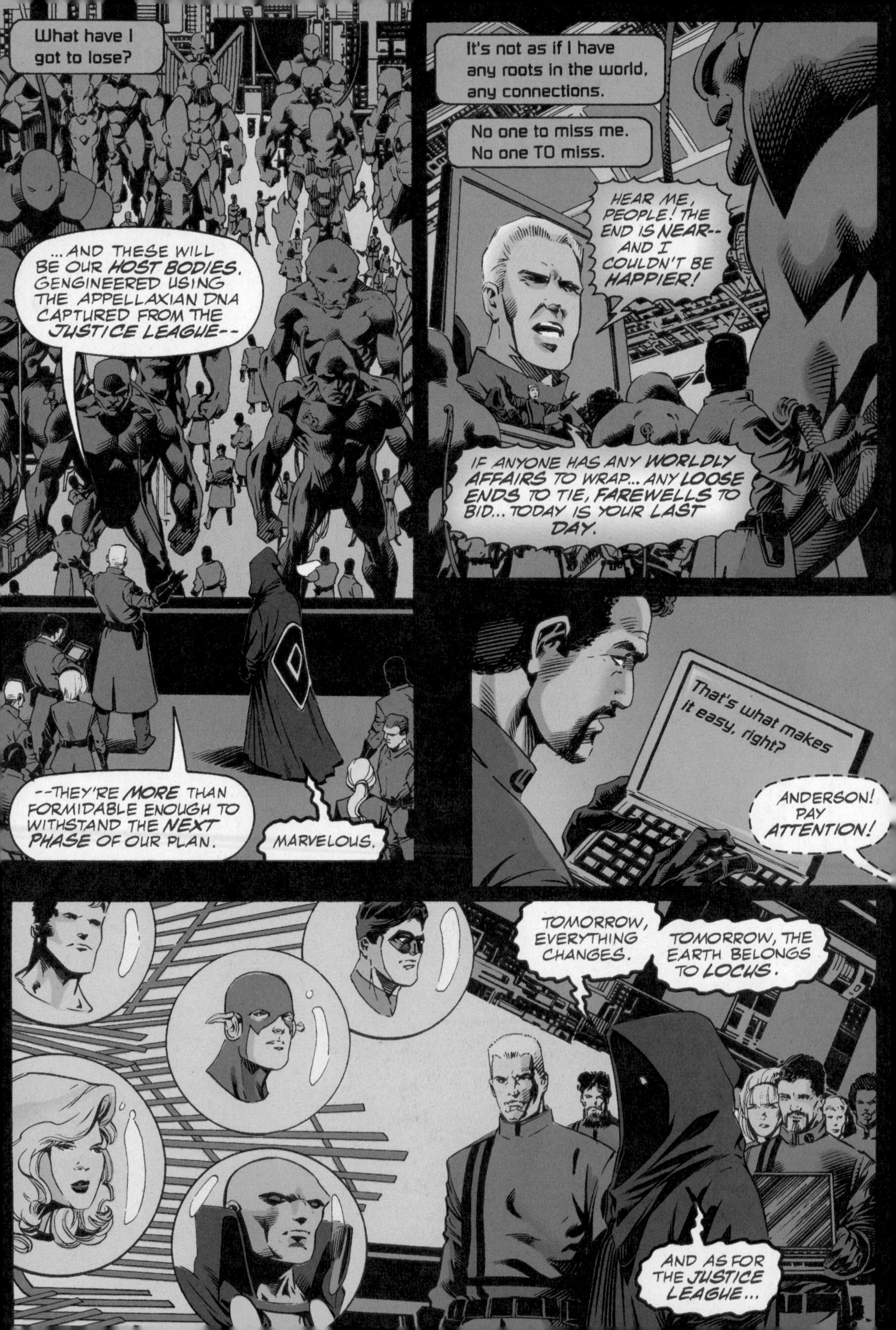
What have I got to lose?
It's not as if I have any roots in the world, any connections.
No one to miss me. No one TO miss.
HEAR ME, PEOPLE! THE END IS NEAR-- AND I COULDN'T BE HAPPIER!
IF ANYONE HAS ANY WORLDLY AFFAIRS TO WRAP... ANY LOOSE ENDS TO TIE, FAREWELLS TO BID... TODAY IS YOUR LAST DAY.
...AND THESE WILL BE OUR HOST BODIES. GENGINEERED USING THE APPELLAXIAN DNA CAPTURED FROM THE JUSTICE LEAGUE--
--THEY'RE MORE THAN FORMIDABLE ENOUGH TO WITHSTAND THE NEXT PHASE OF OUR PLAN.
MARVELOUS.
That's what makes it easy, right?
ANDERSON! PAY ATTENTION!
TOMORROW, EVERYTHING CHANGES.
TOMORROW, THE EARTH BELONGS TO LOCUS.
AND AS FOR THE JUSTICE LEAGUE...

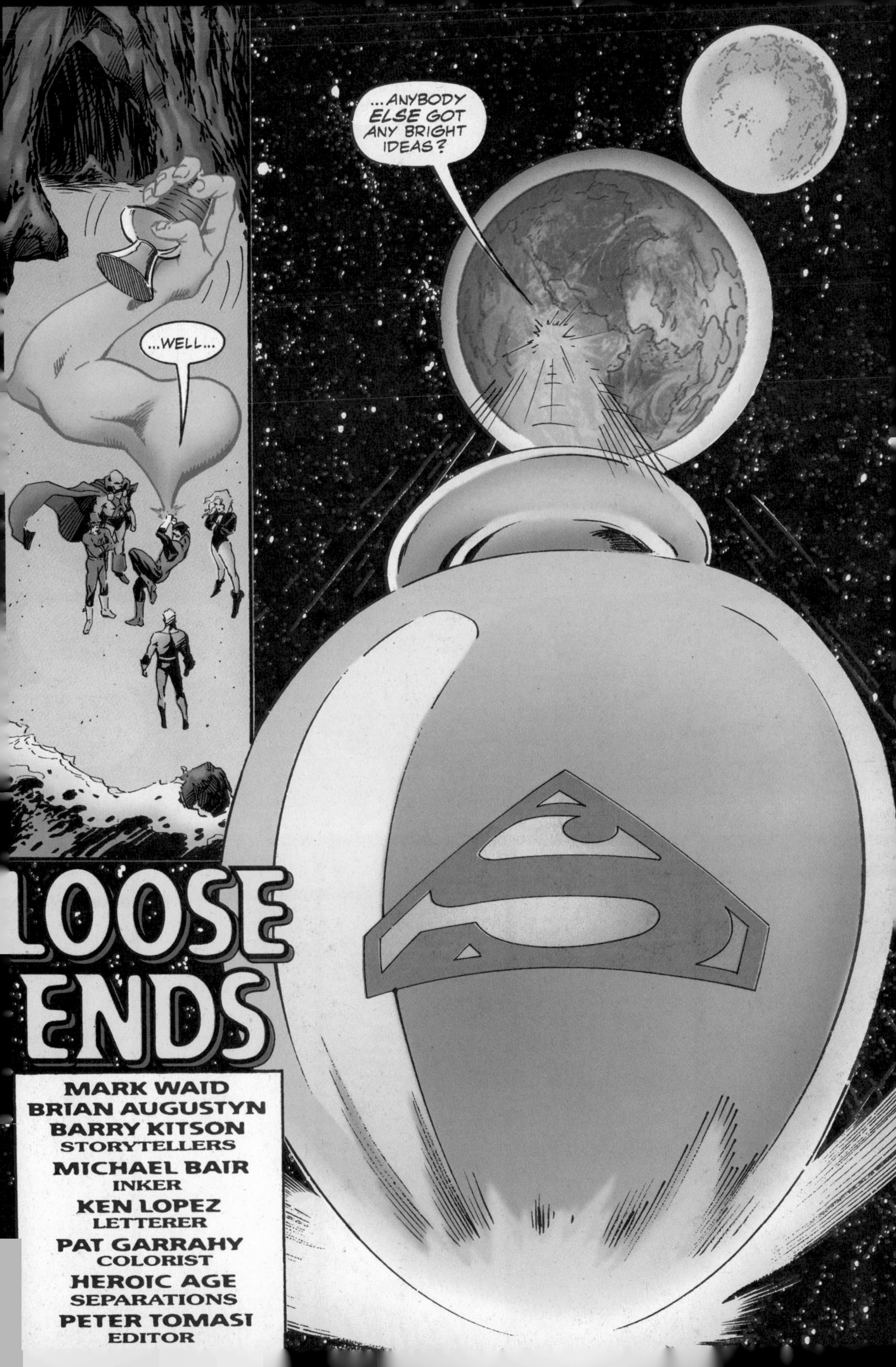
...WELL...
...ANYBODY ELSE GOT ANY BRIGHT IDEAS?
LOOSE ENDS
MARK WAID
BRIAN AUGUSTYN
BARRY KITSON
STORYTELLERS
MICHAEL BAIR
INKER
KEN LOPEZ
LETTERER
PAT GARRAHY
COLORIST
HEROIC AGE
SEPARATIONS
PETER TOMASI
EDITOR

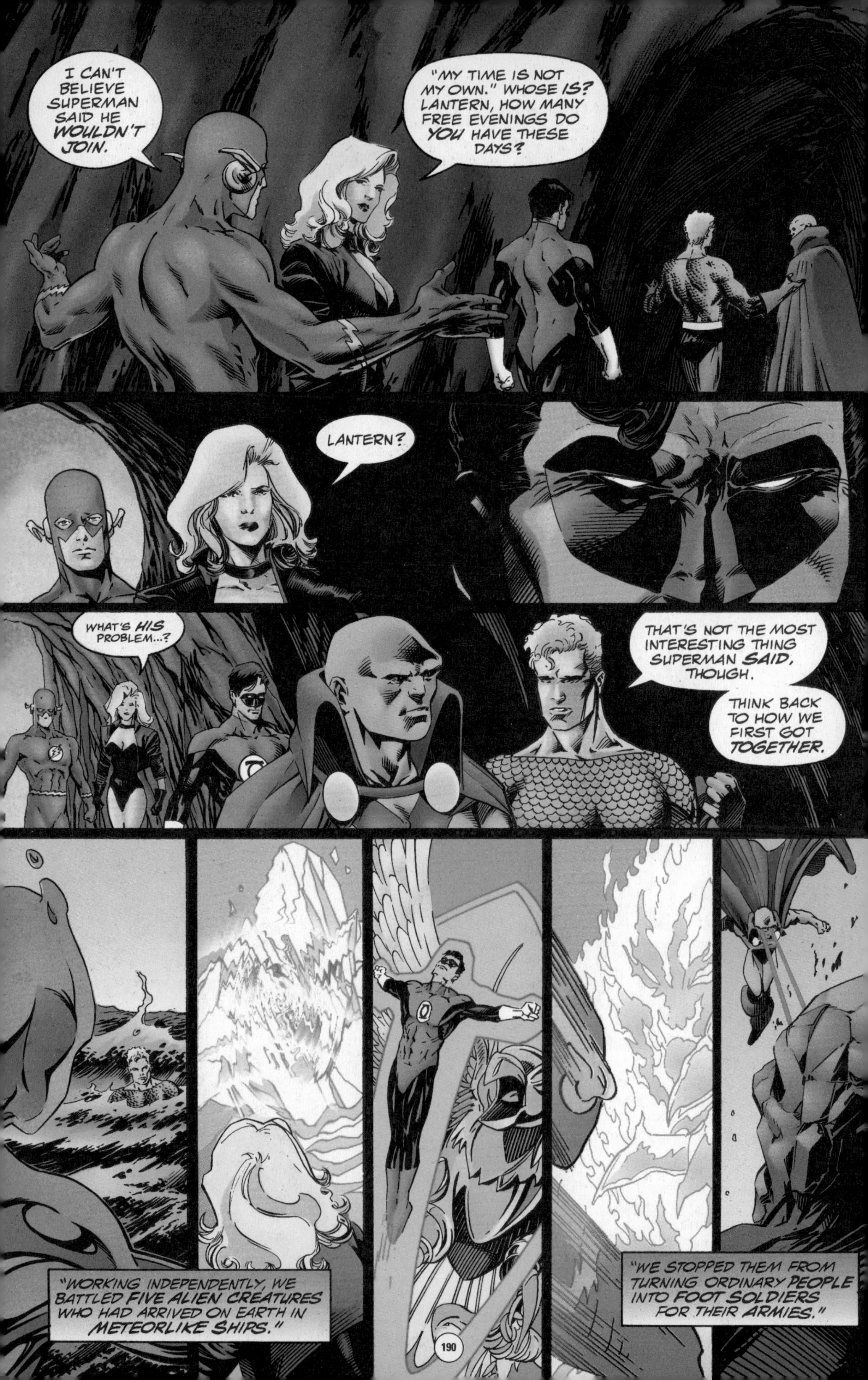
I CAN'T BELIEVE SUPERMAN SAID HE WOULDN'T JOIN.
"MY TIME IS NOT MY OWN." WHOSE IS? LANTERN, HOW MANY FREE EVENINGS DO YOU HAVE THESE DAYS?
LANTERN?
WHAT'S HIS PROBLEM...?
THAT'S NOT THE MOST INTERESTING THING SUPERMAN SAID, THOUGH.
THINK BACK TO HOW WE FIRST GOT TOGETHER.
"WORKING INDEPENDENTLY, WE BATTLED FIVE ALIEN CREATURES WHO HAD ARRIVED ON EARTH IN METEORLIKE SHIPS."
"WE STOPPED THEM FROM TURNING ORDINARY PEOPLE INTO FOOT SOLDIERS FOR THEIR ARMIES."

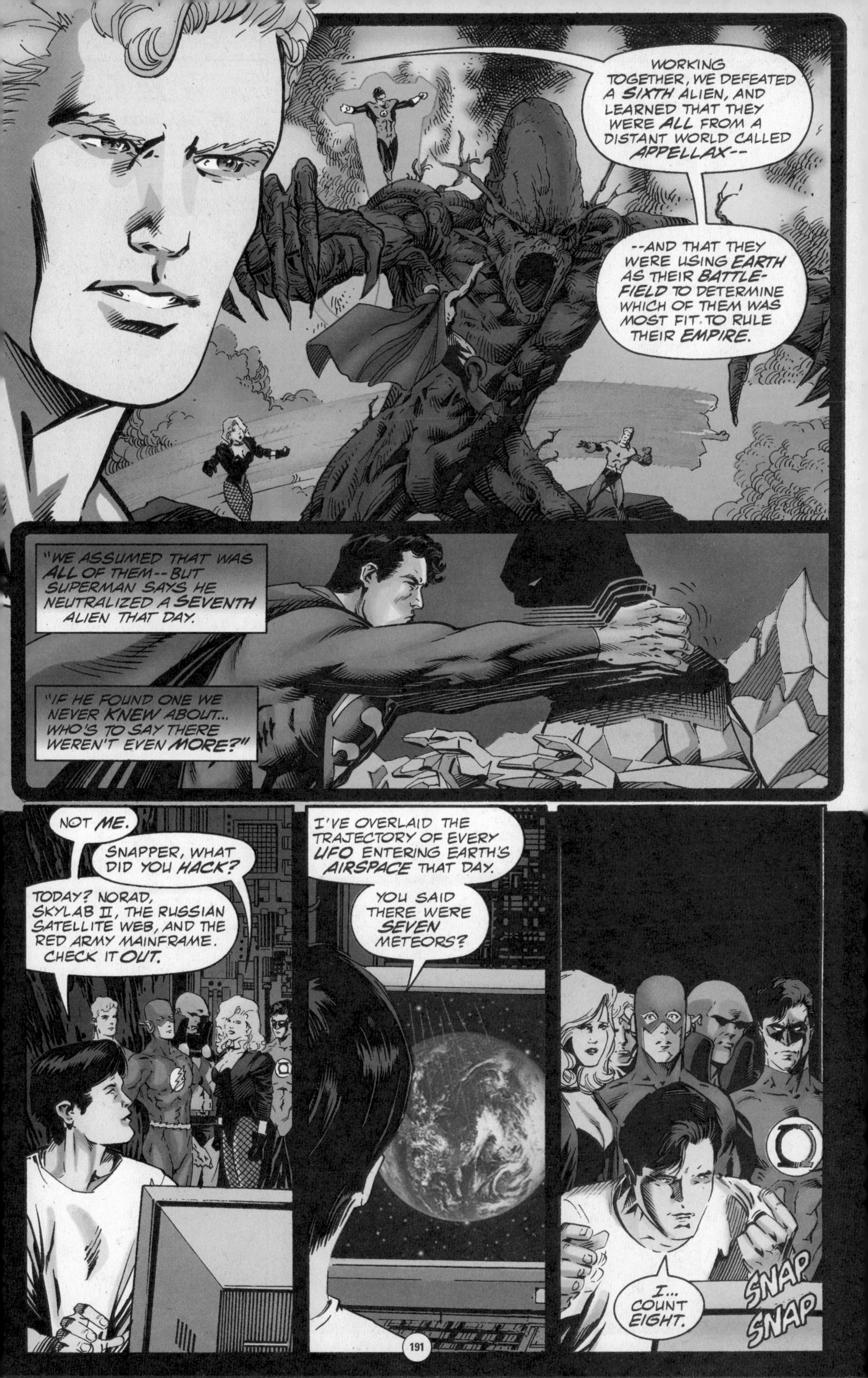
WORKING TOGETHER, WE DEFEATED A SIXTH ALIEN, AND LEARNED THAT THEY WERE ALL FROM A DISTANT WORLD CALLED APPELLAX--
--AND THAT THEY WERE USING EARTH AS THEIR BATTLE-FIELD TO DETERMINE WHICH OF THEM WAS MOST FIT TO RULE THEIR EMPIRE.
"WE ASSUMED THAT WAS ALL OF THEM--BUT SUPERMAN SAYS HE NEUTRALIZED A SEVENTH ALIEN THAT DAY.
"IF HE FOUND ONE WE NEVER KNEW ABOUT... WHO'S TO SAY THERE WEREN'T EVEN MORE?"
NOT ME.
SNAPPER, WHAT DID YOU HACK?
TODAY? NORAD, SKYLAB II, THE RUSSIAN SATELLITE WEB, AND THE RED ARMY MAINFRAME. CHECK IT OUT.
I'VE OVERLAID THE TRAJECTORY OF EVERY UFO ENTERING EARTH'S AIRSPACE THAT DAY.
YOU SAID THERE WERE SEVEN METEORS?
I... COUNT EIGHT.
SNAP
SNAP

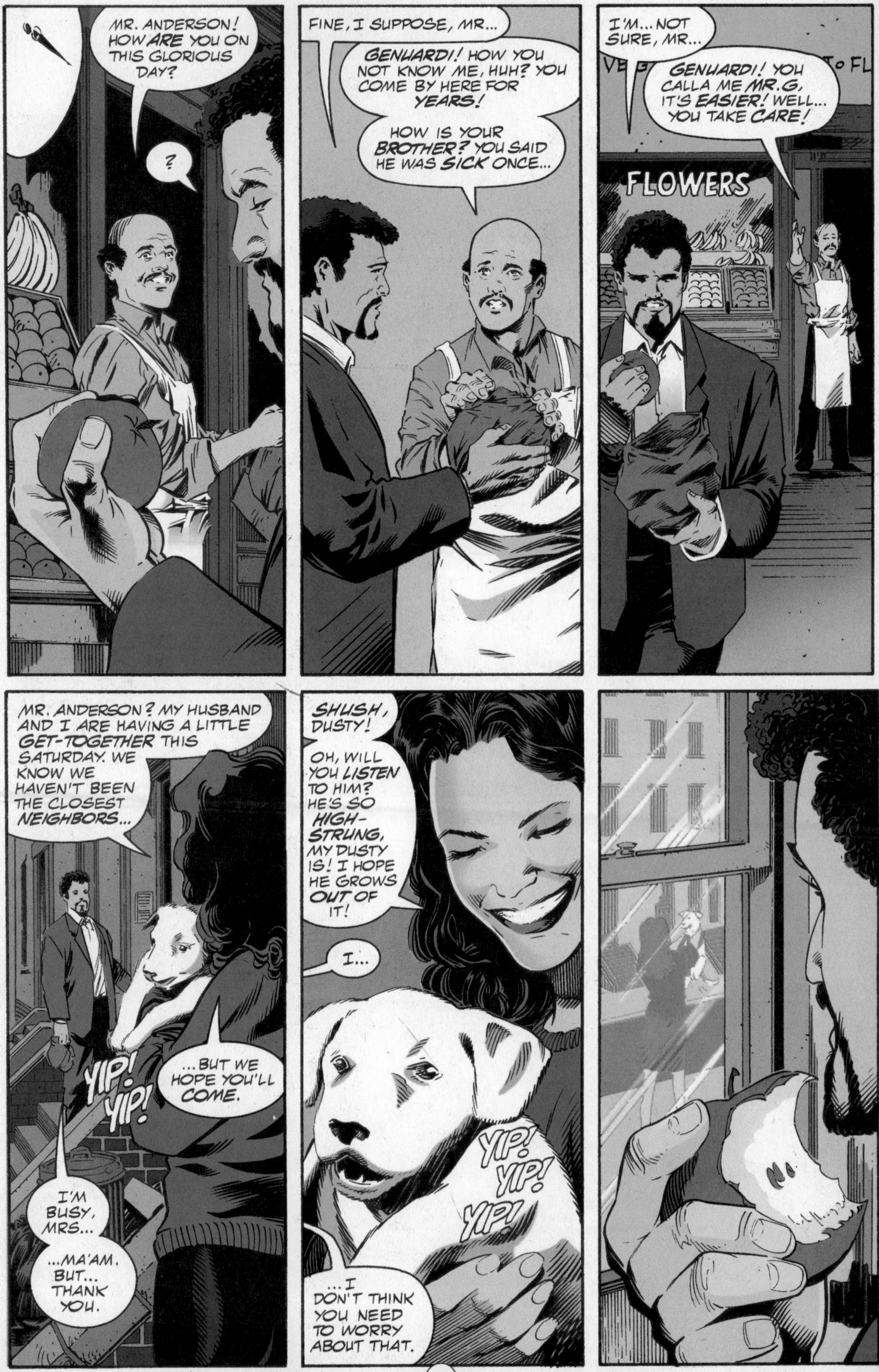
MR. ANDERSON! HOW ARE YOU ON THIS GLORIOUS DAY?
?
FINE, I SUPPOSE, MR...
GENUARDI! HOW YOU NOT KNOW ME, HUH? YOU COME BY HERE FOR YEARS!
HOW IS YOUR BROTHER? YOU SAID HE WAS SICK ONCE...
I'M... NOT SURE, MR...
GENUARDI! YOU CALLA ME MR. G, IT'S EASIER! WELL... YOU TAKE CARE!
FLOWERS
MR. ANDERSON? MY HUSBAND AND I ARE HAVING A LITTLE GET-TOGETHER THIS SATURDAY. WE KNOW WE HAVEN'T BEEN THE CLOSEST NEIGHBORS...
YIP! YIP!
...BUT WE HOPE YOU'LL COME.
I'M BUSY, MRS...
...MA'AM. BUT... THANK YOU.
SHUSH, DUSTY!
OH, WILL YOU LISTEN TO HIM? HE'S SO HIGH-STRUNG, MY DUSTY IS! I HOPE HE GROWS OUT OF IT!
I...
YIP! YIP! YIP!
...I DON'T THINK YOU NEED TO WORRY ABOUT THAT.

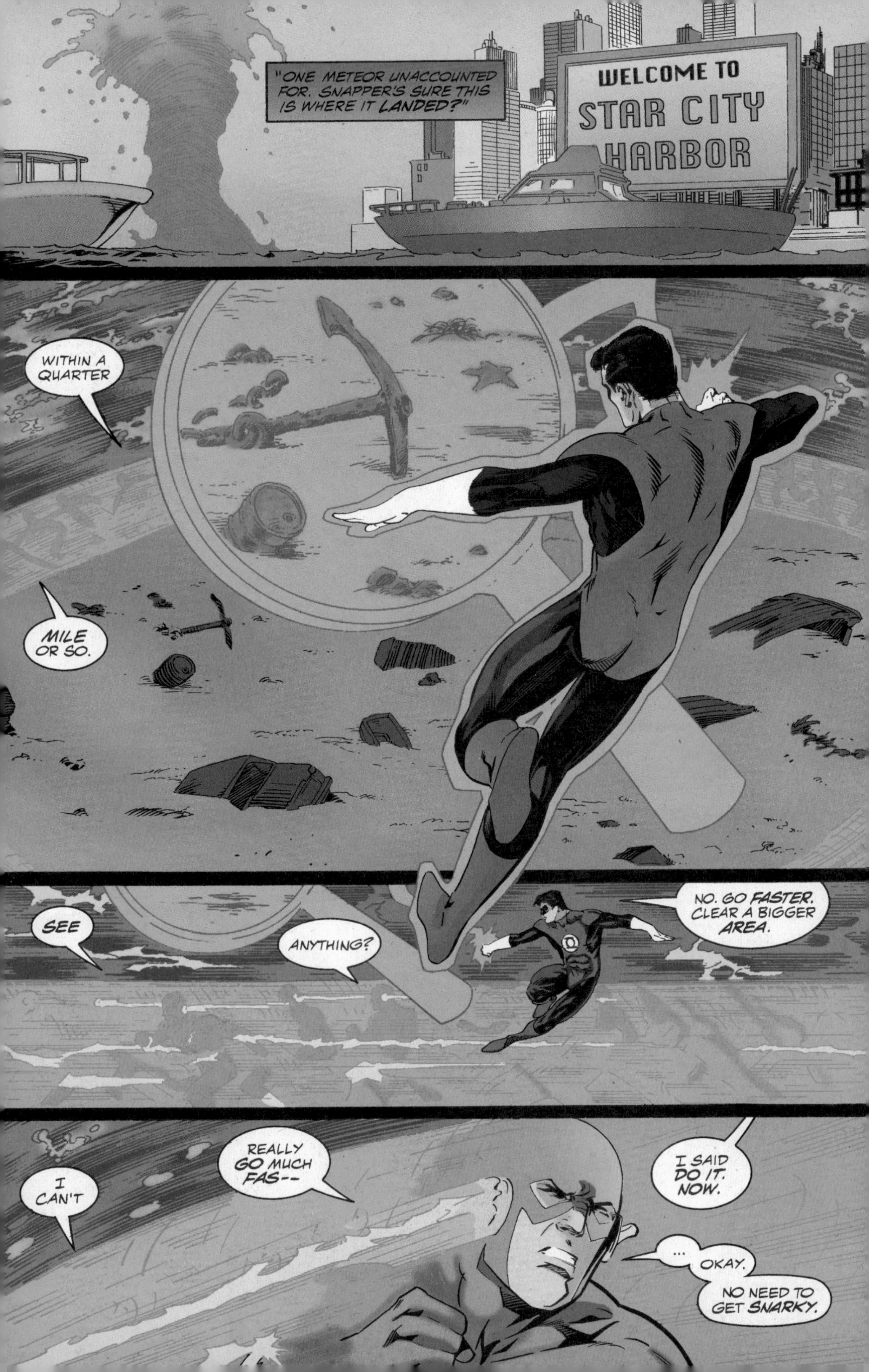
"ONE METEOR UNACCOUNTED FOR. SNAPPER'S SURE THIS IS WHERE IT LANDED?"
WELCOME TO STAR CITY HARBOR
WITHIN A QUARTER
MILE OR SO.
SEE
ANYTHING?
NO. GO FASTER. CLEAR A BIGGER AREA.
I CAN'T
REALLY GO MUCH FAS--
I SAID DO IT. NOW.
... OKAY.
NO NEED TO GET SNARKY.

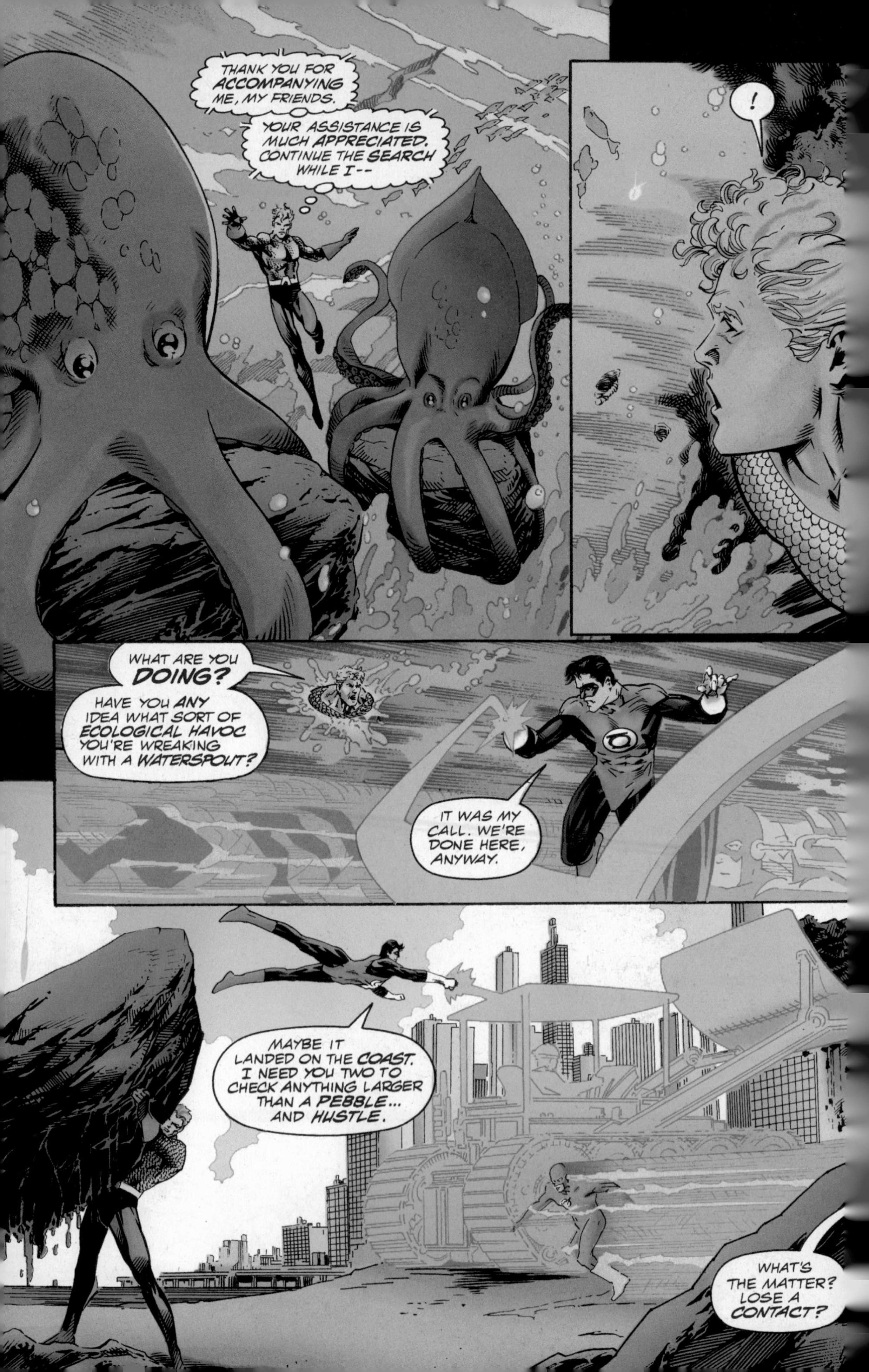
THANK YOU FOR ACCOMPANYING ME, MY FRIENDS.
YOUR ASSISTANCE IS MUCH APPRECIATED. CONTINUE THE SEARCH WHILE I--
!
WHAT ARE YOU DOING?
HAVE YOU ANY IDEA WHAT SORT OF ECOLOGICAL HAVOC YOU'RE WREAKING WITH A WATERSPOUT?
IT WAS MY CALL. WE'RE DONE HERE, ANYWAY.
MAYBE IT LANDED ON THE COAST. I NEED YOU TWO TO CHECK ANYTHING LARGER THAN A PEBBLE... AND HUSTLE.
WHAT'S THE MATTER? LOSE A CONTACT?

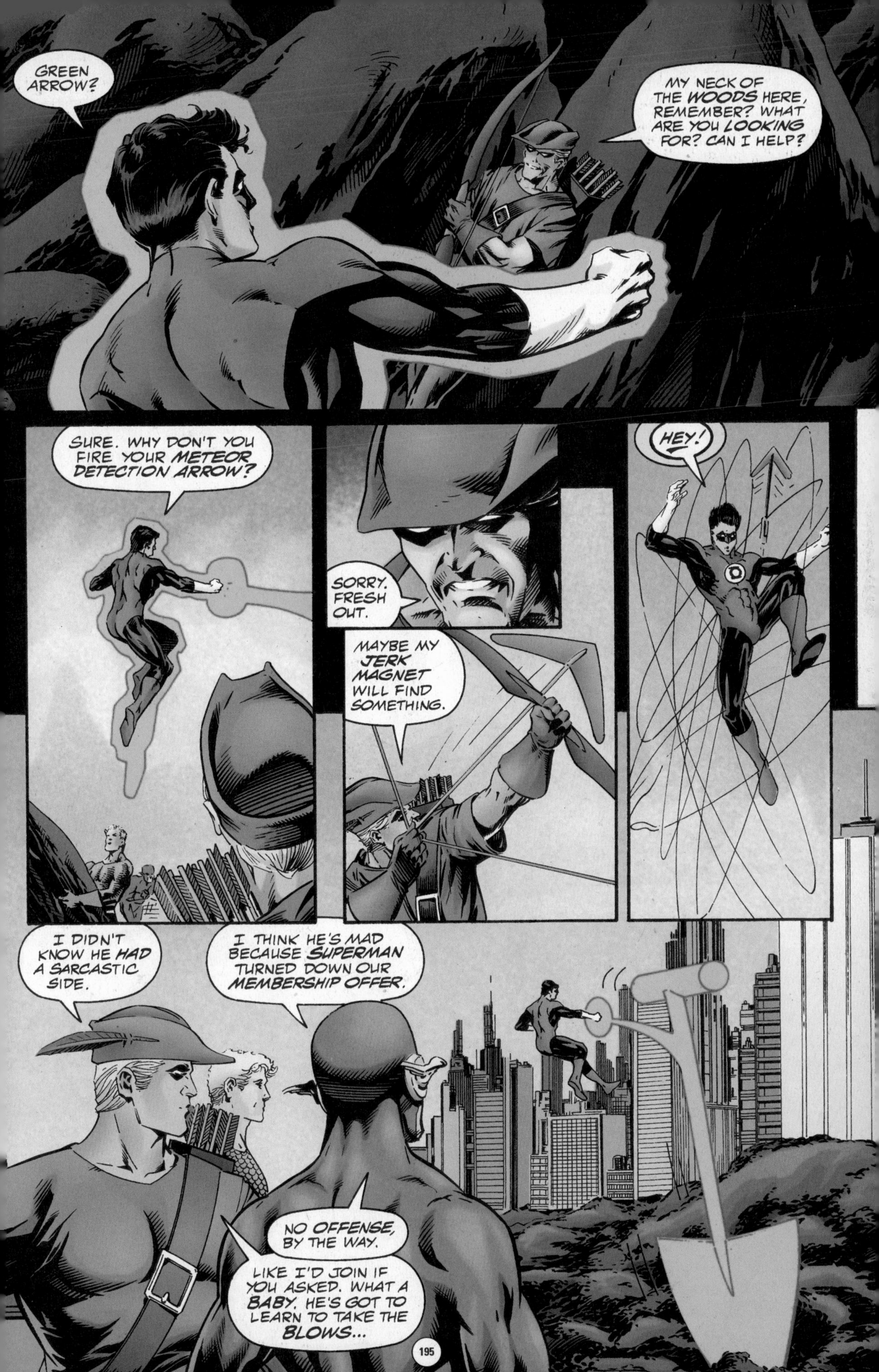
GREEN ARROW?
MY NECK OF THE WOODS HERE, REMEMBER? WHAT ARE YOU LOOKING FOR? CAN I HELP?
SURE. WHY DON'T YOU FIRE YOUR METEOR DETECTION ARROW?
SORRY. FRESH OUT.
MAYBE MY JERK MAGNET WILL FIND SOMETHING.
HEY!
I DIDN'T KNOW HE HAD A SARCASTIC SIDE.
I THINK HE'S MAD BECAUSE SUPERMAN TURNED DOWN OUR MEMBERSHIP OFFER.
NO OFFENSE, BY THE WAY.
LIKE I'D JOIN IF YOU ASKED. WHAT A BABY. HE'S GOT TO LEARN TO TAKE THE BLOWS...

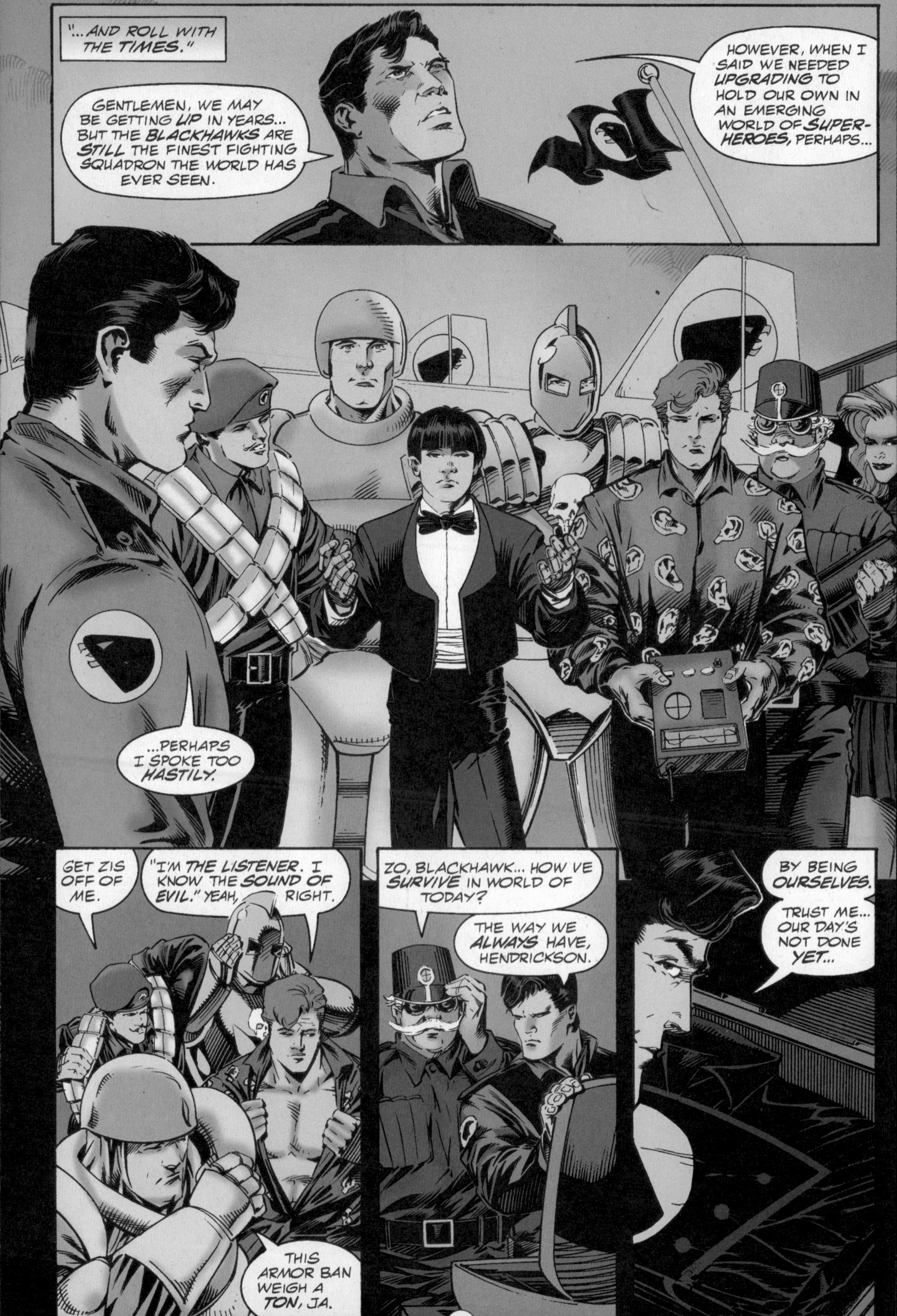

"...AND ROLL WITH THE TIMES."
GENTLEMEN, WE MAY BE GETTING UP IN YEARS... BUT THE BLACKHAWKS ARE STILL THE FINEST FIGHTING SQUADRON THE WORLD HAS EVER SEEN.
HOWEVER, WHEN I SAID WE NEEDED UPGRADING TO HOLD OUR OWN IN AN EMERGING WORLD OF SUPER-HEROES, PERHAPS...
...PERHAPS I SPOKE TOO HASTILY.
GET ZIS OFF OF ME.
"I'M THE LISTENER. I KNOW THE SOUND OF EVIL." YEAH, RIGHT.
THIS ARMOR BAN WEIGH A TON, JA.
ZO, BLACKHAWK... HOW VE SURVIVE IN WORLD OF TODAY?
THE WAY WE ALWAYS HAVE, HENDRICKSON.
BY BEING OURSELVES.
TRUST ME... OUR DAY'S NOT DONE YET...

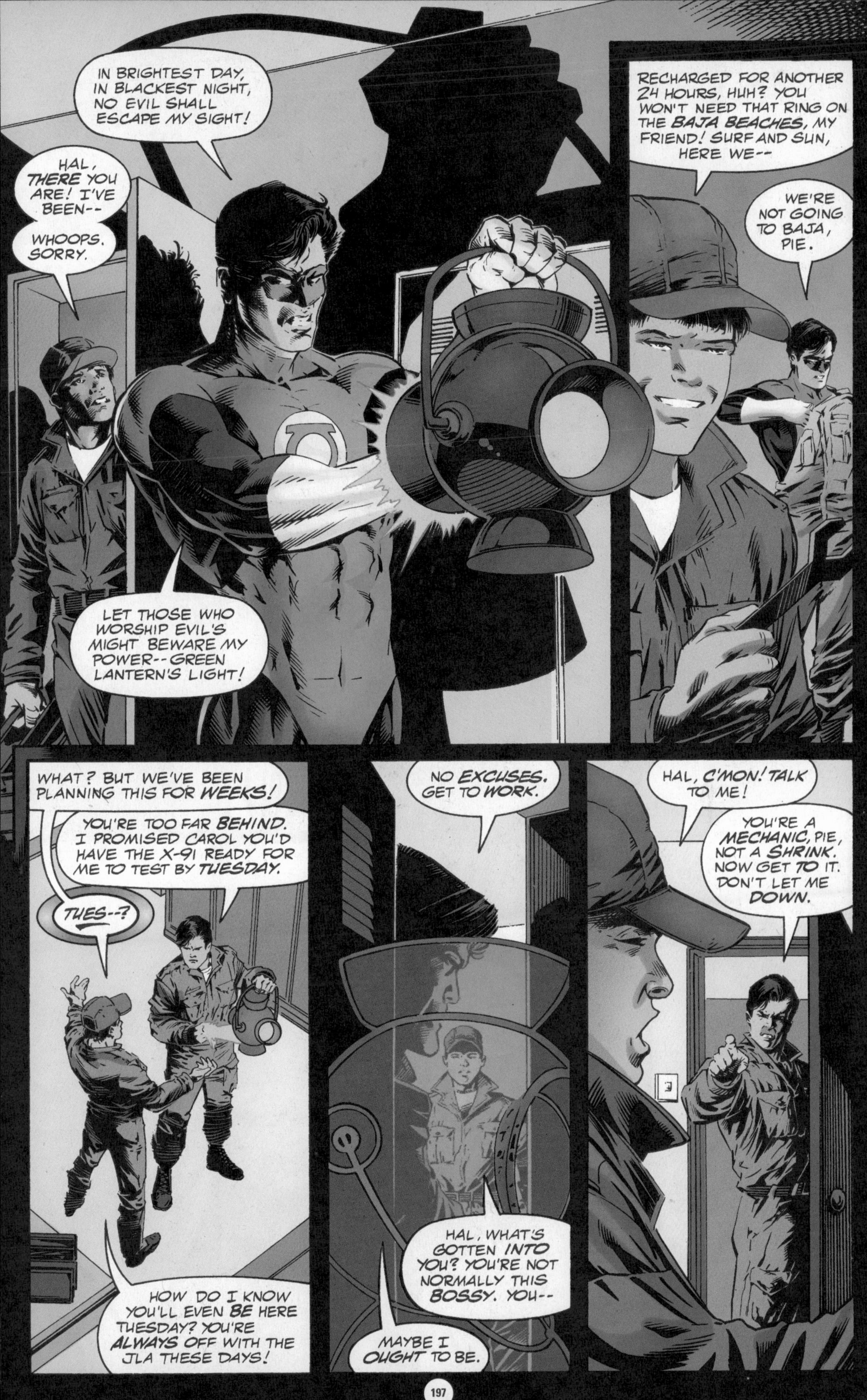
IN BRIGHTEST DAY, IN BLACKEST NIGHT, NO EVIL SHALL ESCAPE MY SIGHT!
HAL, THERE YOU ARE! I'VE BEEN--
WHOOPS. SORRY.
LET THOSE WHO WORSHIP EVIL'S MIGHT BEWARE MY POWER--GREEN LANTERN'S LIGHT!
RECHARGED FOR ANOTHER 24 HOURS, HUH? YOU WON'T NEED THAT RING ON THE BAJA BEACHES, MY FRIEND! SURF AND SUN, HERE WE--
WE'RE NOT GOING TO BAJA, PIE.
WHAT? BUT WE'VE BEEN PLANNING THIS FOR WEEKS!
YOU'RE TOO FAR BEHIND. I PROMISED CAROL YOU'D HAVE THE X-91 READY FOR ME TO TEST BY TUESDAY.
TUES--?
HOW DO I KNOW YOU'LL EVEN BE HERE TUESDAY? YOU'RE ALWAYS OFF WITH THE JLA THESE DAYS!
NO EXCUSES. GET TO WORK.
HAL, WHAT'S GOTTEN INTO YOU? YOU'RE NOT NORMALLY THIS BOSSY. YOU--
MAYBE I OUGHT TO BE.
HAL, C'MON! TALK TO ME!
YOU'RE A MECHANIC, PIE, NOT A SHRINK. NOW GET TO IT. DON'T LET ME DOWN.

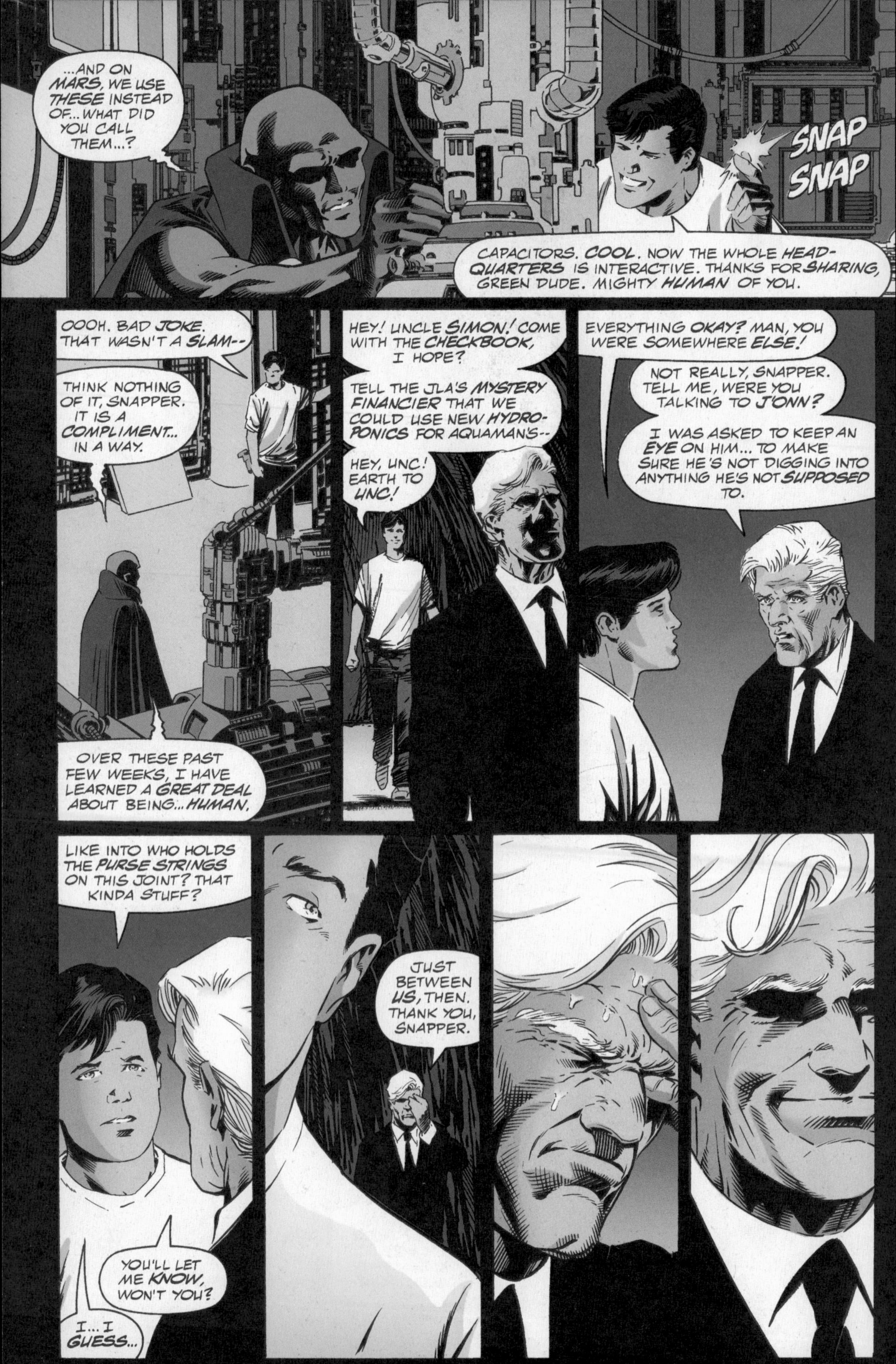
...AND ON MARS, WE USE THESE INSTEAD OF... WHAT DID YOU CALL THEM...?
SNAP SNAP
CAPACITORS. COOL. NOW THE WHOLE HEADQUARTERS IS INTERACTIVE. THANKS FOR SHARING, GREEN DUDE. MIGHTY HUMAN OF YOU.
OOOH. BAD JOKE. THAT WASN'T A SLAM--
THINK NOTHING OF IT, SNAPPER. IT IS A COMPLIMENT... IN A WAY.
OVER THESE PAST FEW WEEKS, I HAVE LEARNED A GREAT DEAL ABOUT BEING... HUMAN.
HEY! UNCLE SIMON! COME WITH THE CHECKBOOK, I HOPE?
TELL THE JLA'S MYSTERY FINANCIER THAT WE COULD USE NEW HYDROPONICS FOR AQUAMAN'S--
HEY, UNC! EARTH TO UNC!
EVERYTHING OKAY? MAN, YOU WERE SOMEWHERE ELSE!
NOT REALLY, SNAPPER. TELL ME, WERE YOU TALKING TO J'ONN?
I WAS ASKED TO KEEP AN EYE ON HIM... TO MAKE SURE HE'S NOT DIGGING INTO ANYTHING HE'S NOT SUPPOSED TO.
LIKE INTO WHO HOLDS THE PURSE STRINGS ON THIS JOINT? THAT KINDA STUFF?
YOU'LL LET ME KNOW, WON'T YOU?
I... I GUESS...
JUST BETWEEN US, THEN. THANK YOU, SNAPPER.

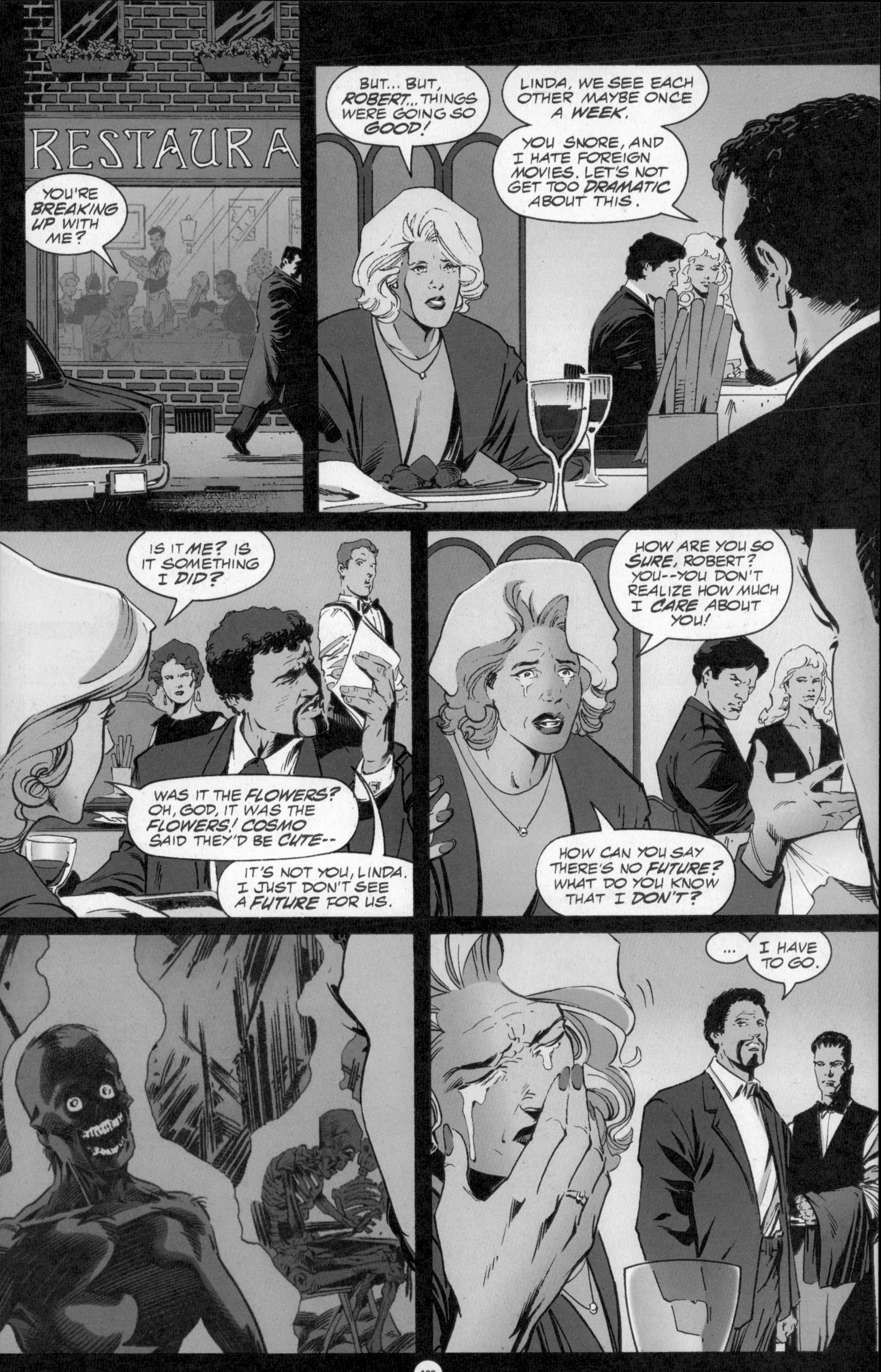
RESTAURA
YOU'RE BREAKING UP WITH ME?
BUT... BUT, ROBERT... THINGS WERE GOING SO GOOD!
LINDA, WE SEE EACH OTHER MAYBE ONCE A WEEK.
YOU SNORE, AND I HATE FOREIGN MOVIES. LET'S NOT GET TOO DRAMATIC ABOUT THIS.
IS IT ME? IS IT SOMETHING I DID?
WAS IT THE FLOWERS? OH, GOD, IT WAS THE FLOWERS! COSMO SAID THEY'D BE CUTE--
IT'S NOT YOU, LINDA. I JUST DON'T SEE A FUTURE FOR US.
HOW ARE YOU SO SURE, ROBERT? YOU--YOU DON'T REALIZE HOW MUCH I CARE ABOUT YOU!
HOW CAN YOU SAY THERE'S NO FUTURE? WHAT DO YOU KNOW THAT I DON'T?
... I HAVE TO GO.

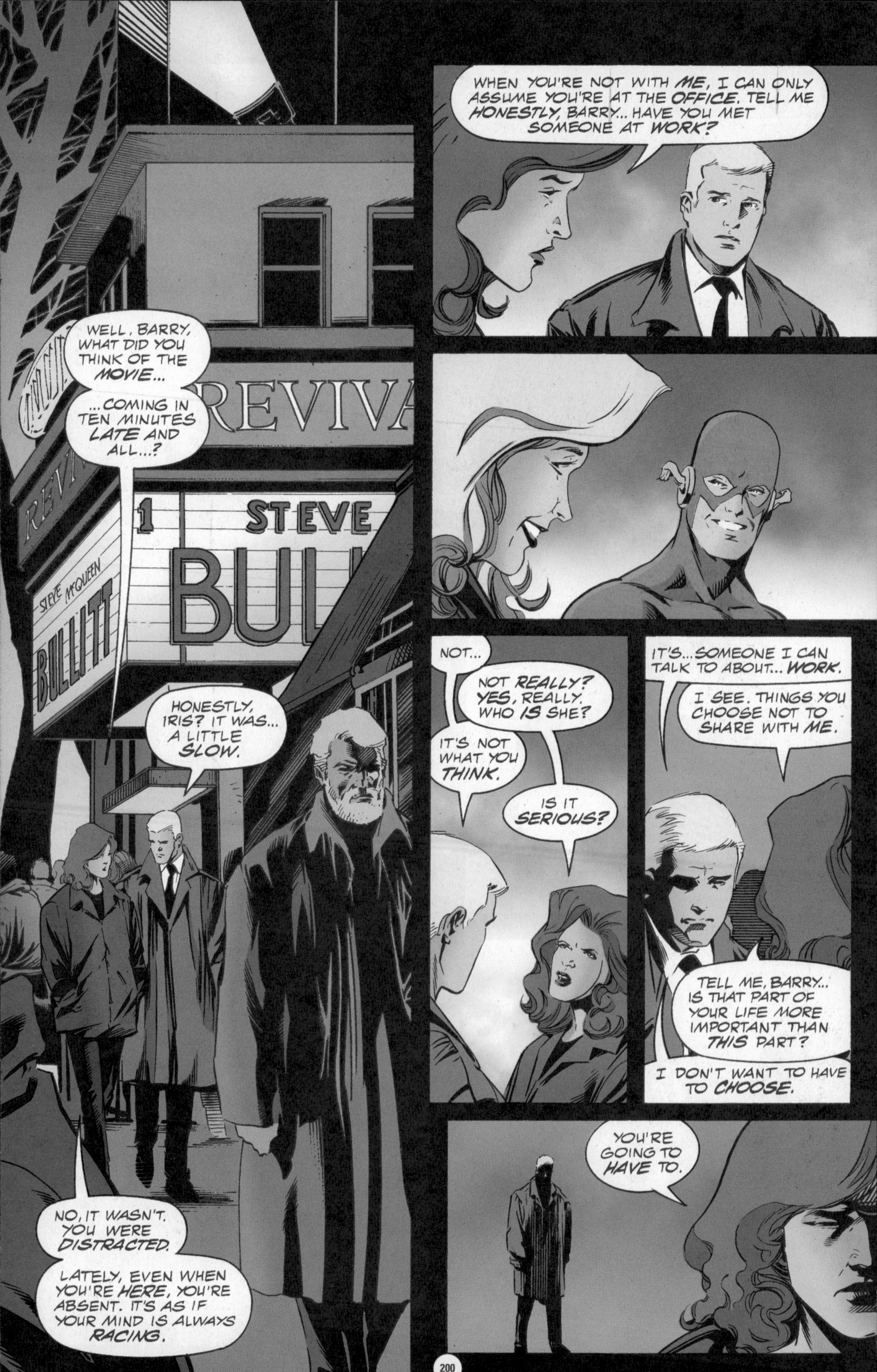
REVIVAL
STEVE
BULL
STEVE McQUEEN
BULLITT
WELL, BARRY, WHAT DID YOU THINK OF THE MOVIE...
...COMING IN TEN MINUTES LATE AND ALL...?
HONESTLY, IRIS? IT WAS... A LITTLE SLOW.
NO, IT WASN'T. YOU WERE DISTRACTED.
LATELY, EVEN WHEN YOU'RE HERE, YOU'RE ABSENT. IT'S AS IF YOUR MIND IS ALWAYS RACING.
WHEN YOU'RE NOT WITH ME, I CAN ONLY ASSUME YOU'RE AT THE OFFICE. TELL ME HONESTLY, BARRY... HAVE YOU MET SOMEONE AT WORK?
NOT...
NOT REALLY? YES, REALLY. WHO IS SHE?
IT'S NOT WHAT YOU THINK.
IS IT SERIOUS?
IT'S... SOMEONE I CAN TALK TO ABOUT... WORK.
I SEE. THINGS YOU CHOOSE NOT TO SHARE WITH ME.
TELL ME, BARRY... IS THAT PART OF YOUR LIFE MORE IMPORTANT THAN THIS PART?
I DON'T WANT TO HAVE TO CHOOSE.
YOU'RE GOING TO HAVE TO.

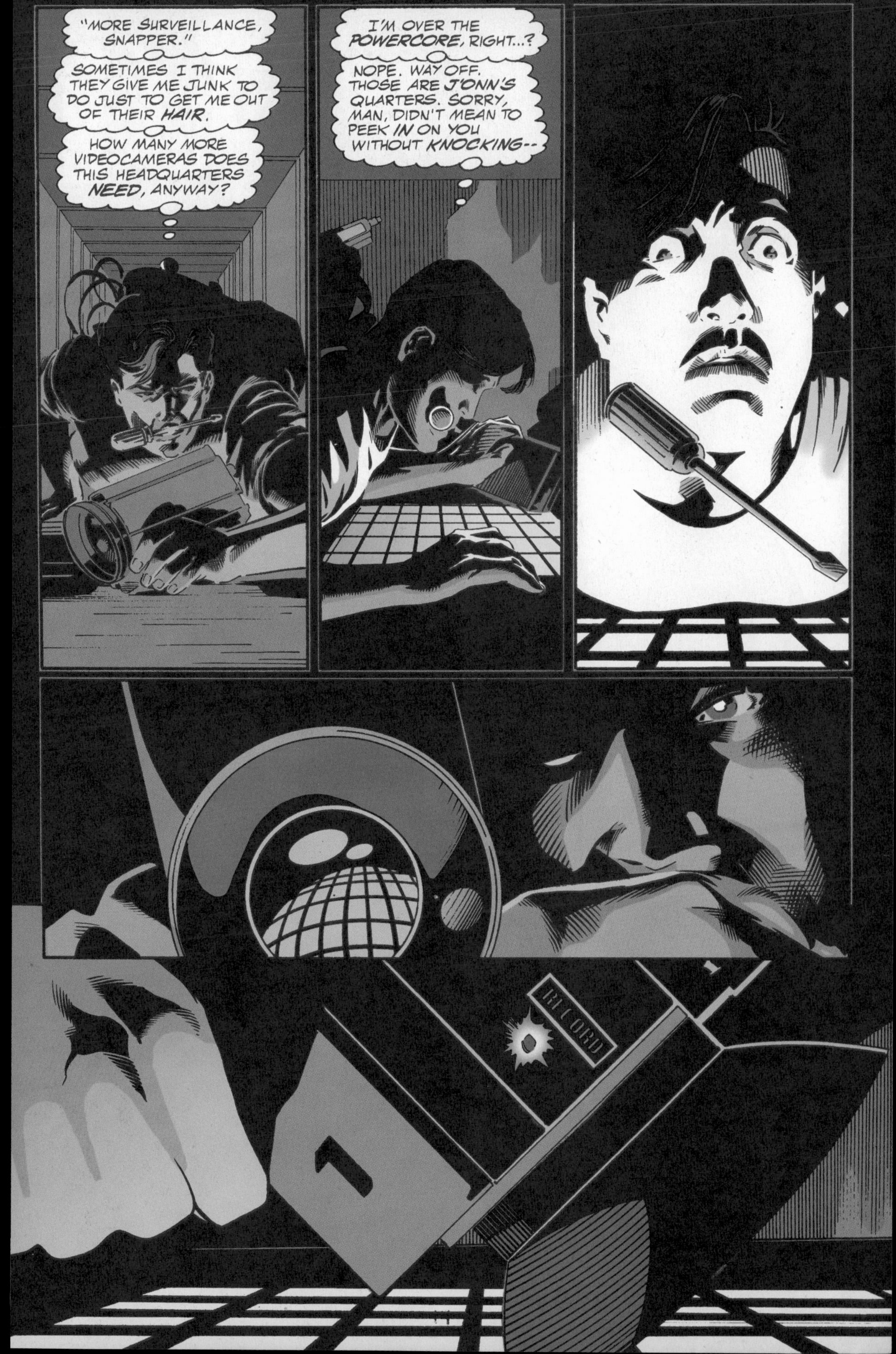
"MORE SURVEILLANCE, SNAPPER."
SOMETIMES I THINK THEY GIVE ME JUNK TO DO JUST TO GET ME OUT OF THEIR HAIR.
HOW MANY MORE VIDEOCAMERAS DOES THIS HEADQUARTERS NEED, ANYWAY?
I'M OVER THE POWERCORE, RIGHT...?
NOPE. WAY OFF. THOSE ARE J'ONN'S QUARTERS. SORRY, MAN, DIDN'T MEAN TO PEEK IN ON YOU WITHOUT KNOCKING--
RECORD

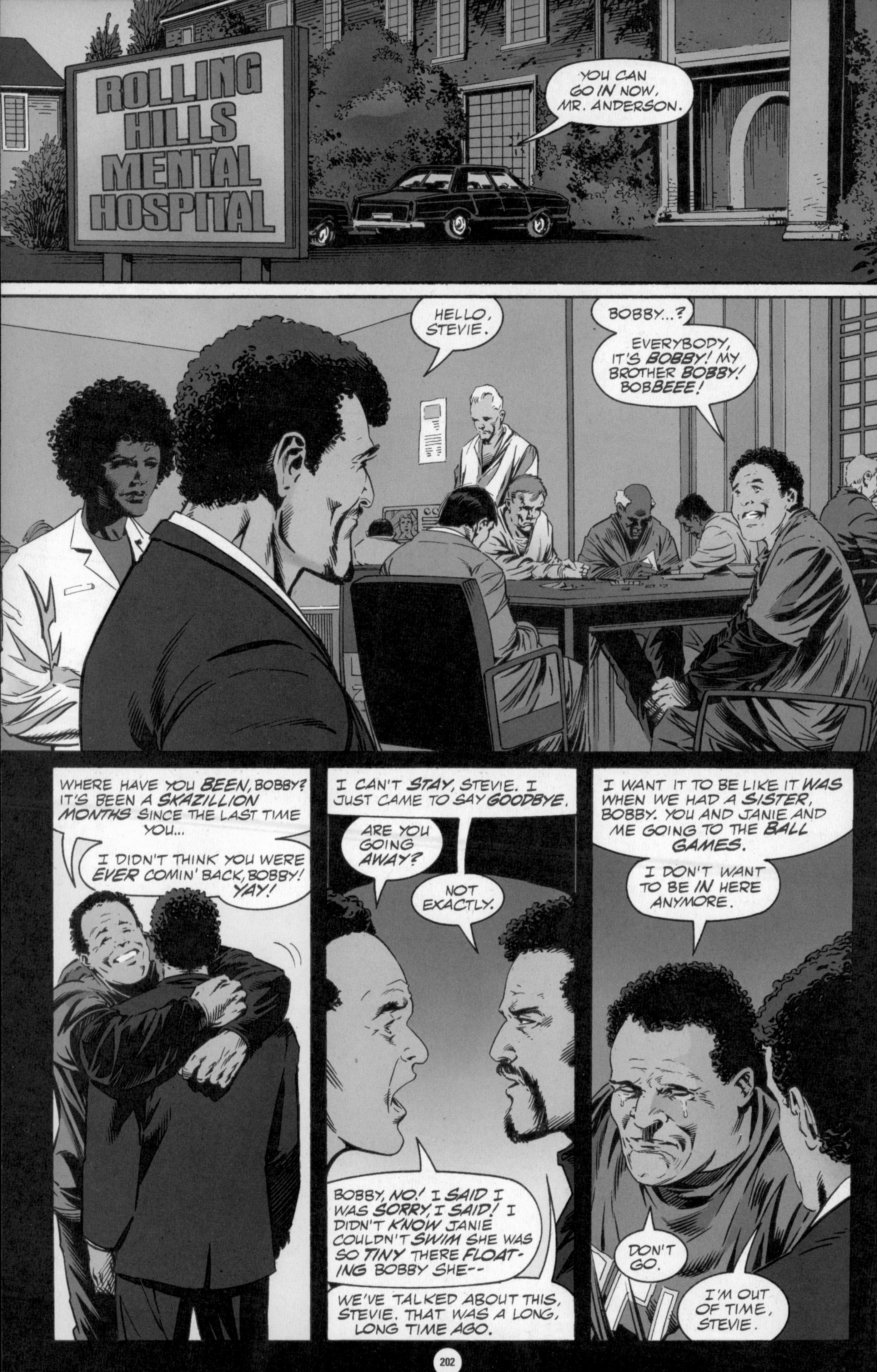
ROLLING HILLS MENTAL HOSPITAL
YOU CAN GO IN NOW, MR. ANDERSON.
HELLO, STEVIE.
BOBBY...?
EVERYBODY, IT'S BOBBY! MY BROTHER BOBBY! BOBBEEE!
WHERE HAVE YOU BEEN, BOBBY? IT'S BEEN A SKAZILLION MONTHS SINCE THE LAST TIME YOU...
I DIDN'T THINK YOU WERE EVER COMIN' BACK, BOBBY! YAY!
I CAN'T STAY, STEVIE. I JUST CAME TO SAY GOODBYE.
ARE YOU GOING AWAY?
NOT EXACTLY.
BOBBY, NO! I SAID I WAS SORRY, I SAID! I DIDN'T KNOW JANIE COULDN'T SWIM SHE WAS SO TINY THERE FLOATING BOBBY SHE--
WE'VE TALKED ABOUT THIS, STEVIE. THAT WAS A LONG, LONG TIME AGO.
I WANT IT TO BE LIKE IT WAS WHEN WE HAD A SISTER, BOBBY. YOU AND JANIE AND ME GOING TO THE BALL GAMES.
I DON'T WANT TO BE IN HERE ANYMORE.
DON'T GO.
I'M OUT OF TIME, STEVIE.

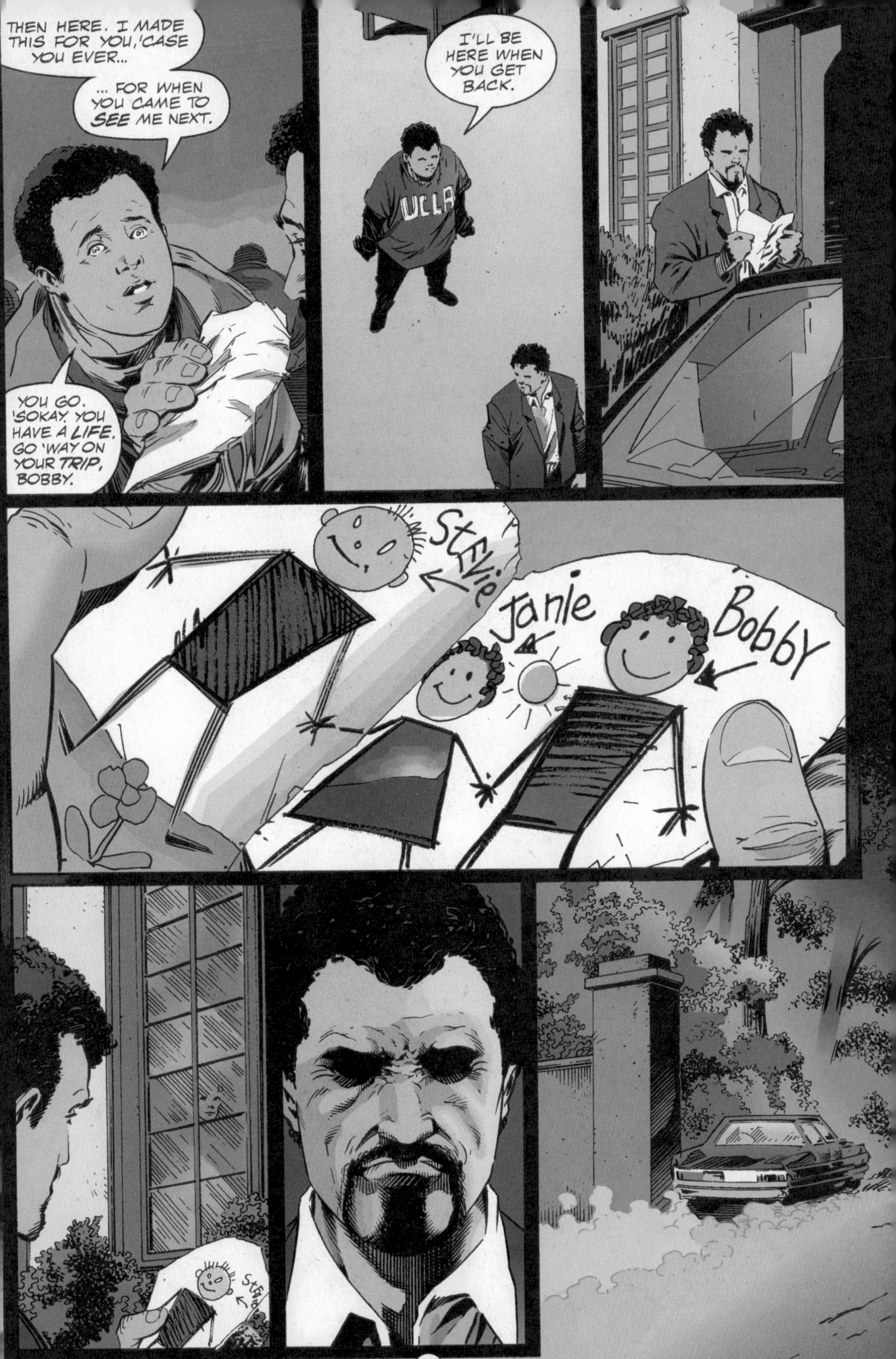
THEN HERE. I MADE THIS FOR YOU, 'CASE YOU EVER...
... FOR WHEN YOU CAME TO SEE ME NEXT.
YOU GO. 'SOKAY. YOU HAVE A LIFE. GO 'WAY ON YOUR TRIP, BOBBY.
I'LL BE HERE WHEN YOU GET BACK.
UCLA
StEvie
Janie
Bobby
StEvie

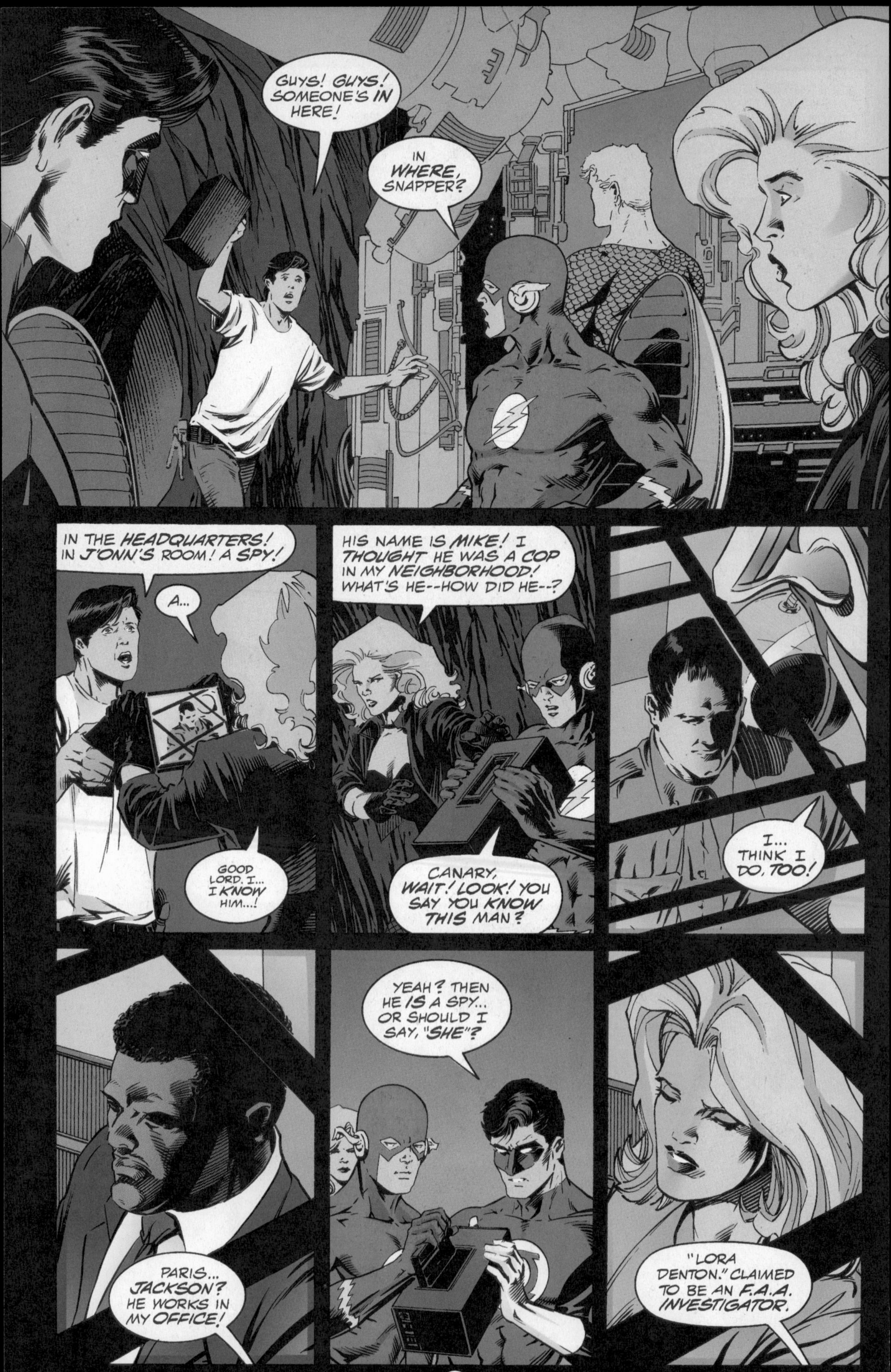
GUYS! GUYS! SOMEONE'S IN HERE!
IN WHERE, SNAPPER?
IN THE HEADQUARTERS! IN J'ONN'S ROOM! A SPY!
A...
GOOD LORD, I... I KNOW HIM...!
HIS NAME IS MIKE! I THOUGHT HE WAS A COP IN MY NEIGHBORHOOD! WHAT'S HE--HOW DID HE--?
CANARY, WAIT! LOOK! YOU SAY YOU KNOW THIS MAN?
I... THINK I DO, TOO!
PARIS... JACKSON? HE WORKS IN MY OFFICE!
YEAH? THEN HE IS A SPY... OR SHOULD I SAY, "SHE"?
"LORA DENTON." CLAIMED TO BE AN F.A.A. INVESTIGATOR.

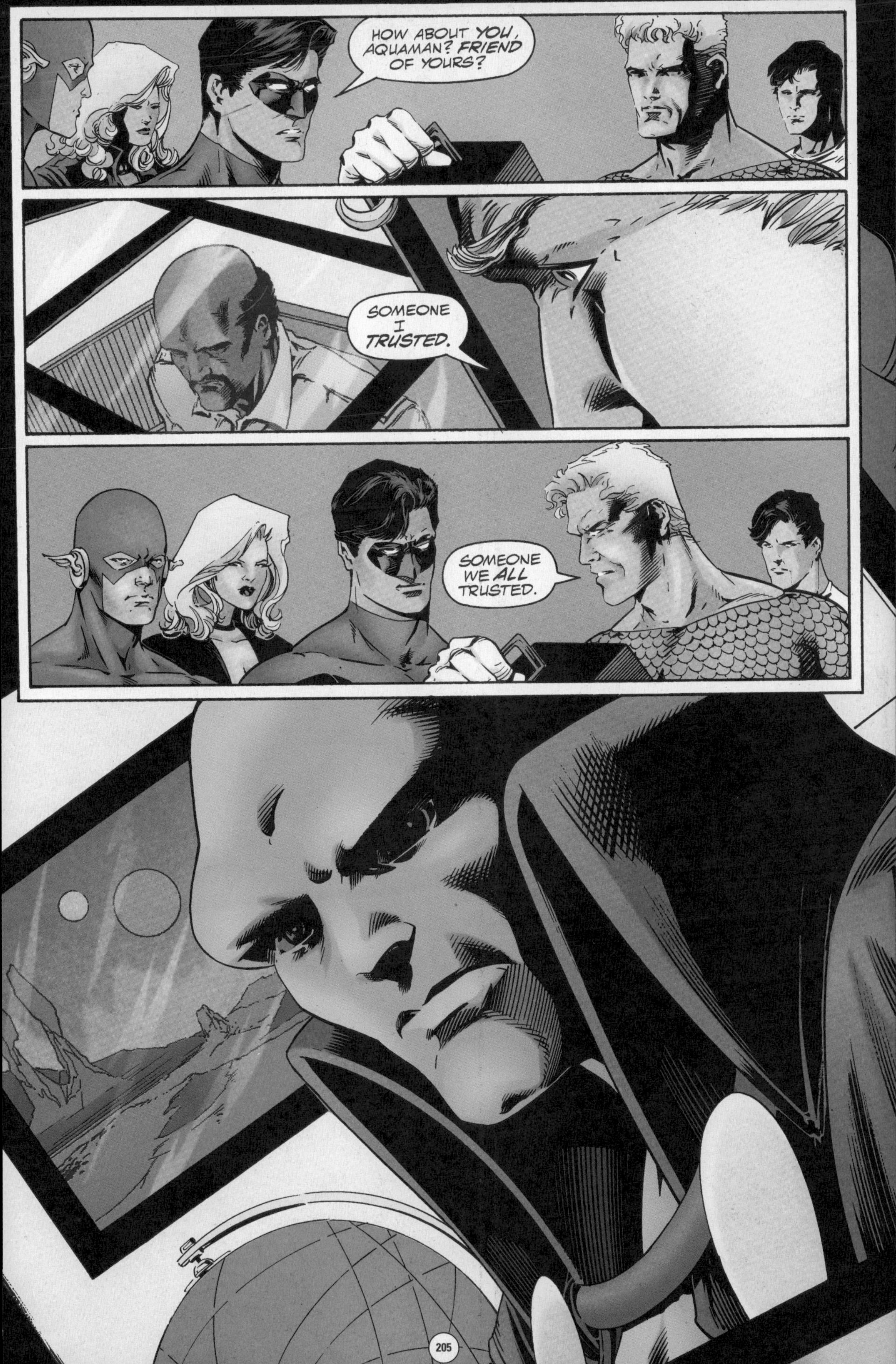
HOW ABOUT YOU, AQUAMAN? FRIEND OF YOURS?
SOMEONE I TRUSTED.
SOMEONE WE ALL TRUSTED.

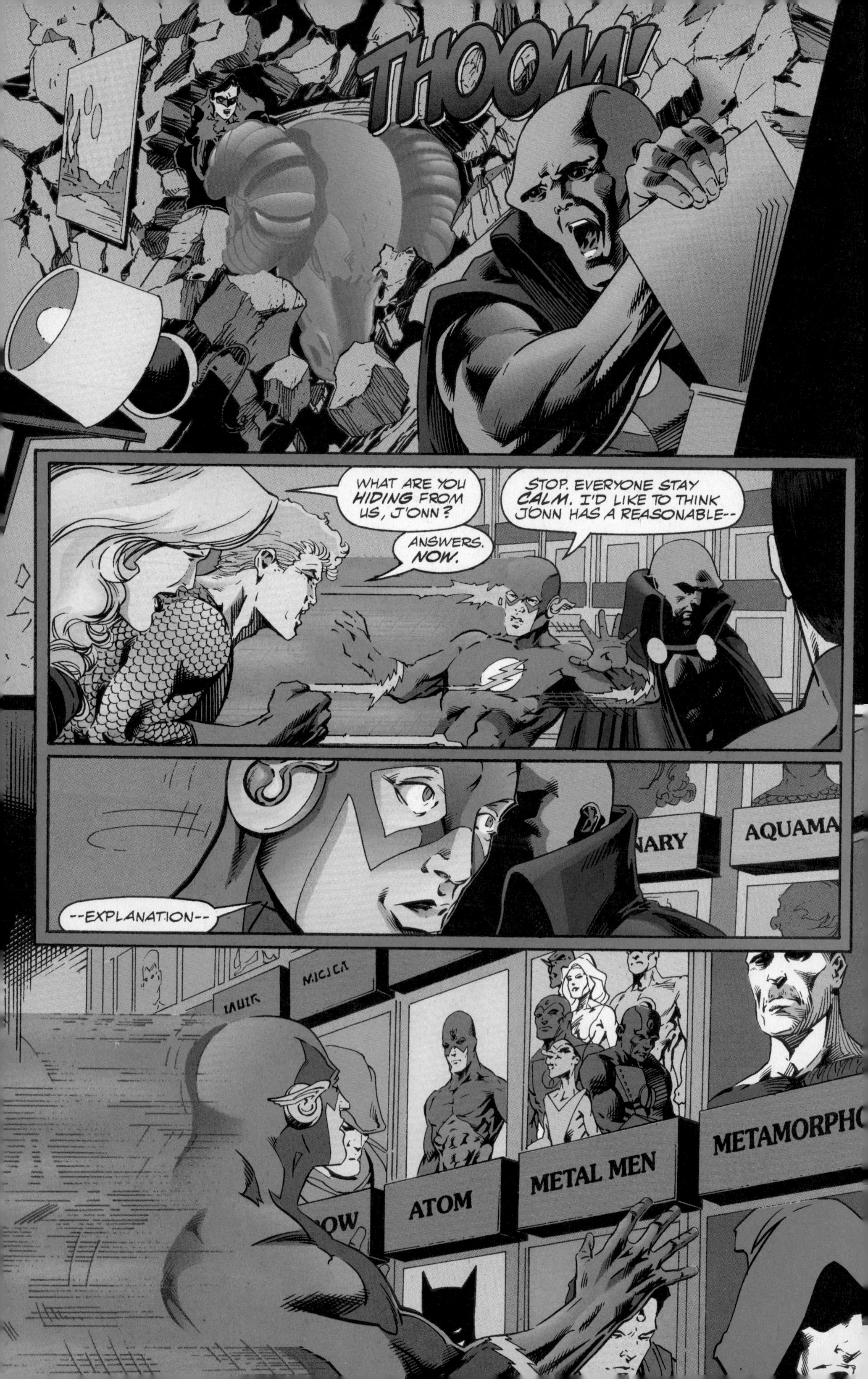
THOOM!
WHAT ARE YOU HIDING FROM US, J'ONN?
ANSWERS. NOW.
STOP. EVERYONE STAY CALM. I'D LIKE TO THINK J'ONN HAS A REASONABLE--
--EXPLANATION--
AQUAMA
ATOM
METAL MEN
METAMORPHO

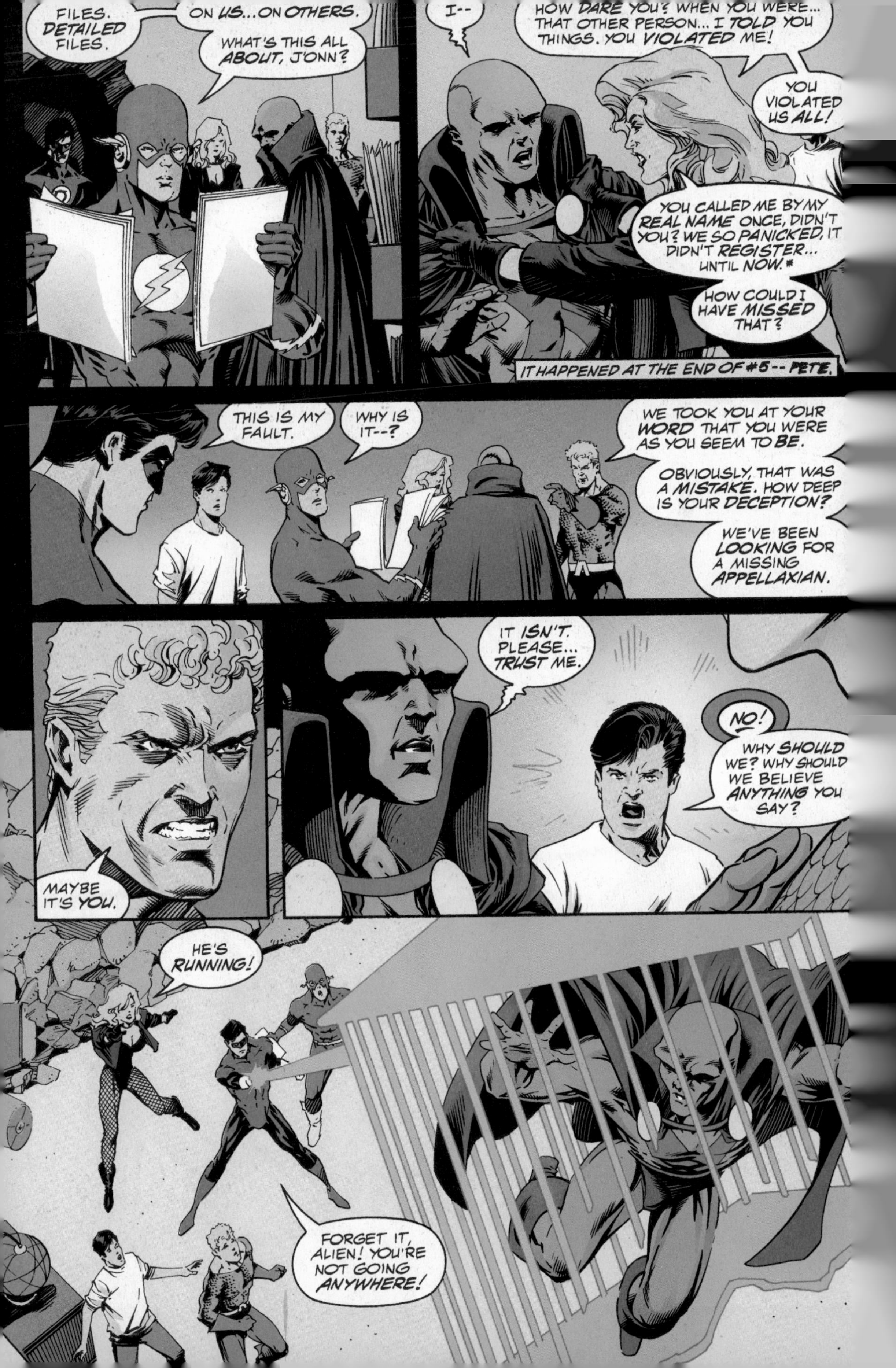
FILES. DETAILED FILES.
ON US...ON OTHERS.
WHAT'S THIS ALL ABOUT, J'ONN?
I--
HOW DARE YOU? WHEN YOU WERE... THAT OTHER PERSON... I TOLD YOU THINGS. YOU VIOLATED ME!
YOU VIOLATED US ALL!
YOU CALLED ME BY MY REAL NAME ONCE, DIDN'T YOU? WE SO PANICKED, IT DIDN'T REGISTER... UNTIL NOW.*
HOW COULD I HAVE MISSED THAT?
*IT HAPPENED AT THE END OF #5 -- PETE.
THIS IS MY FAULT.
WHY IS IT--?
WE TOOK YOU AT YOUR WORD THAT YOU WERE AS YOU SEEM TO BE.
OBVIOUSLY, THAT WAS A MISTAKE. HOW DEEP IS YOUR DECEPTION?
WE'VE BEEN LOOKING FOR A MISSING APPELLAXIAN.
MAYBE IT'S YOU.
IT ISN'T. PLEASE... TRUST ME.
NO!
WHY SHOULD WE? WHY SHOULD WE BELIEVE ANYTHING YOU SAY?
HE'S RUNNING!
FORGET IT, ALIEN! YOU'RE NOT GOING ANYWHERE!

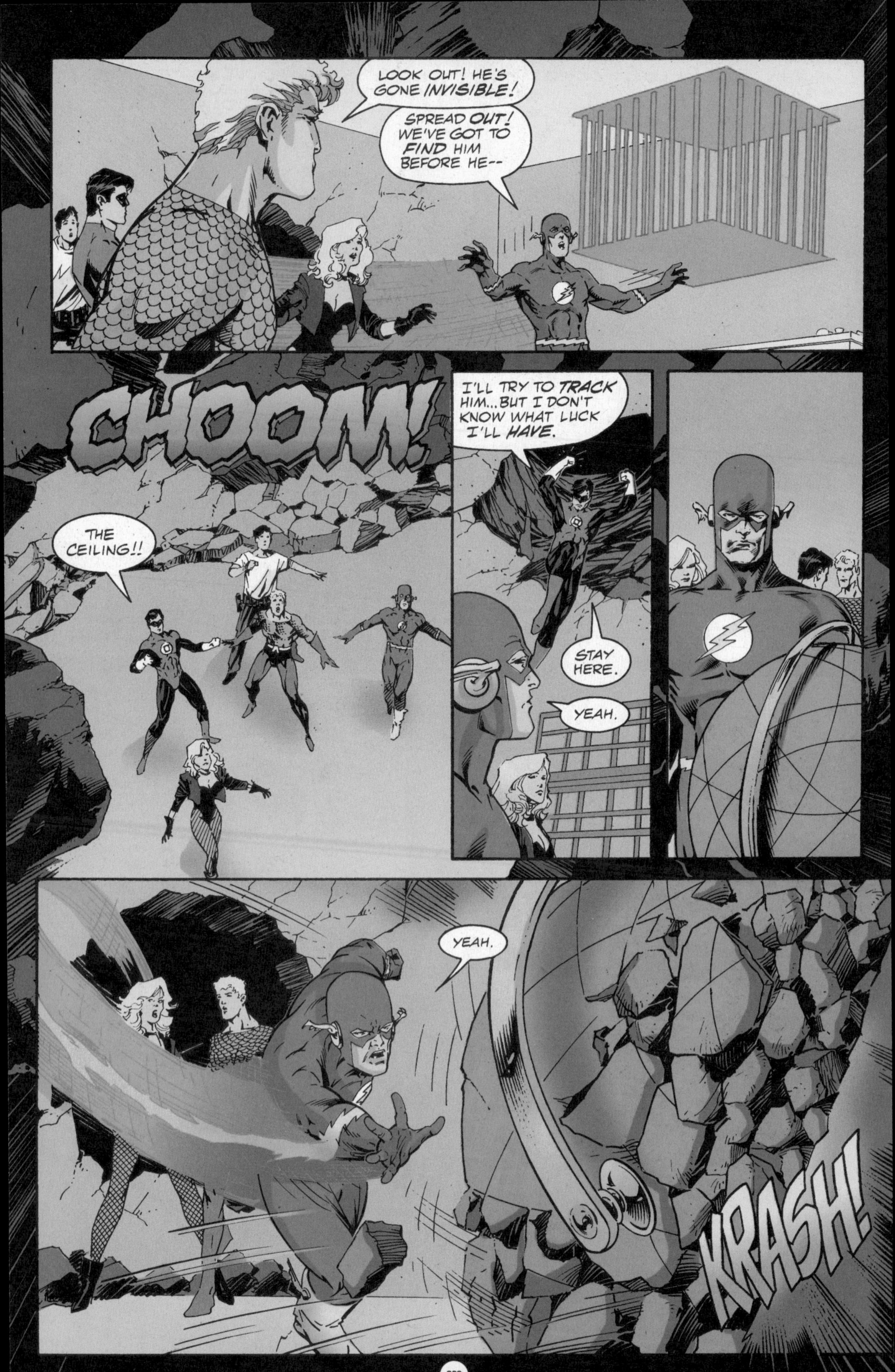
LOOK OUT! HE'S GONE INVISIBLE!
SPREAD OUT! WE'VE GOT TO FIND HIM BEFORE HE--
CHOOM!
THE CEILING!!
I'LL TRY TO TRACK HIM... BUT I DON'T KNOW WHAT LUCK I'LL HAVE.
STAY HERE.
YEAH.
YEAH.
KRASH!

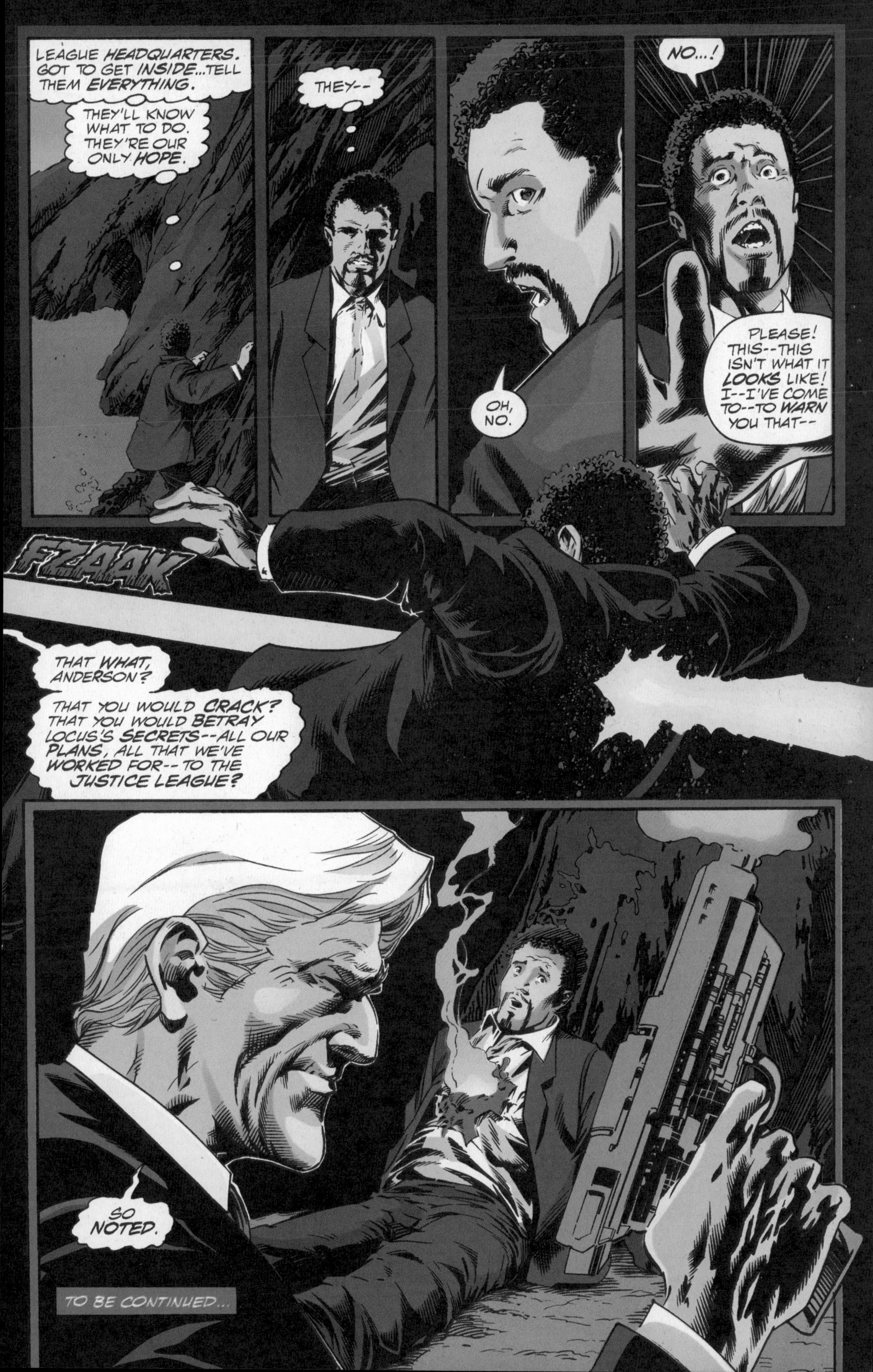
LEAGUE HEADQUARTERS. GOT TO GET INSIDE...TELL THEM EVERYTHING.
THEY'LL KNOW WHAT TO DO. THEY'RE OUR ONLY HOPE.
THEY--
OH, NO.
NO...!
PLEASE! THIS--THIS ISN'T WHAT IT LOOKS LIKE! I--I'VE COME TO--TO WARN YOU THAT--
FZAAK
THAT WHAT, ANDERSON?
THAT YOU WOULD CRACK? THAT YOU WOULD BETRAY LOCUS'S SECRETS--ALL OUR PLANS, ALL THAT WE'VE WORKED FOR--TO THE JUSTICE LEAGUE?
SO NOTED.
TO BE CONTINUED...

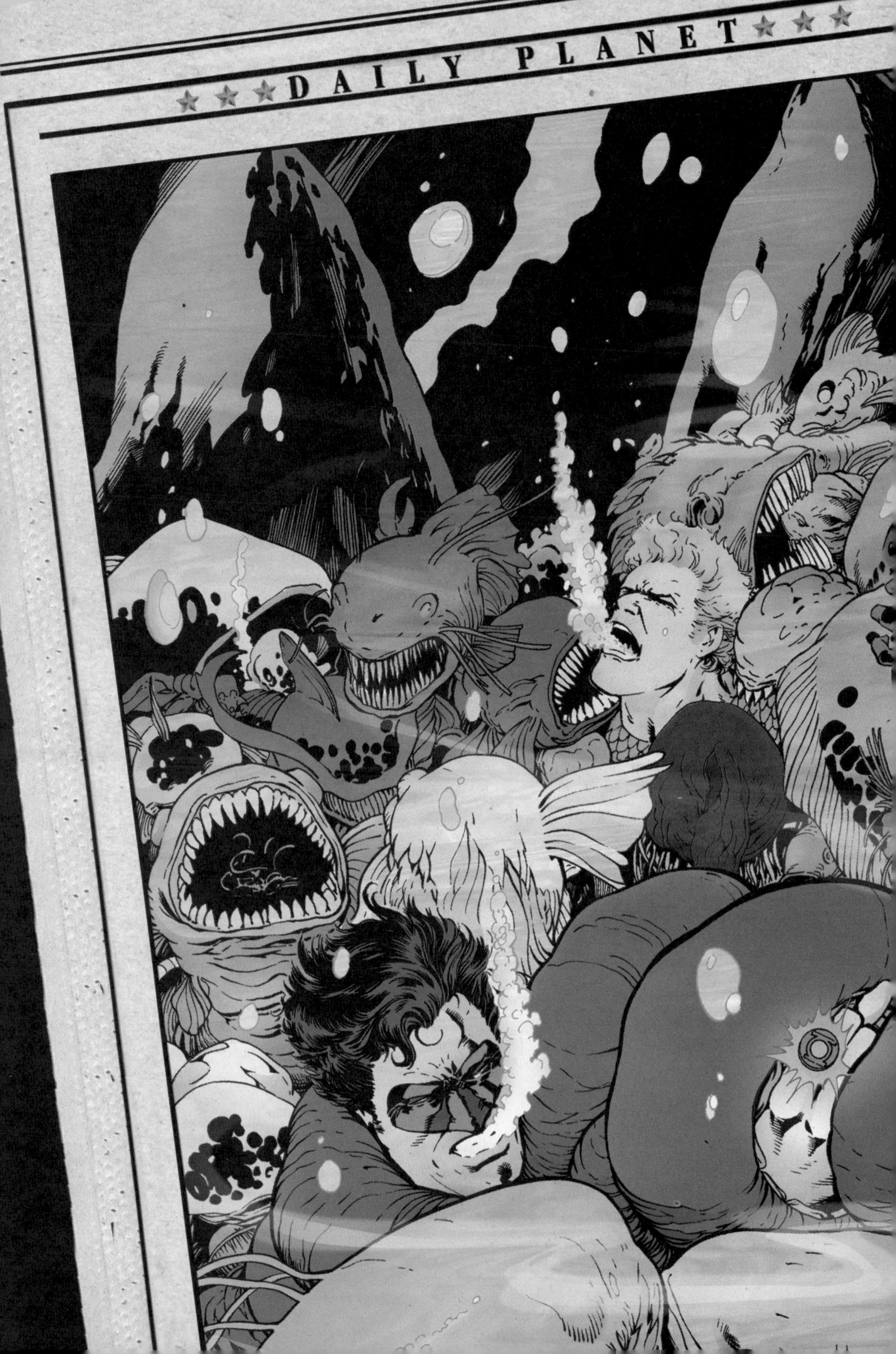
DAILY PLANET

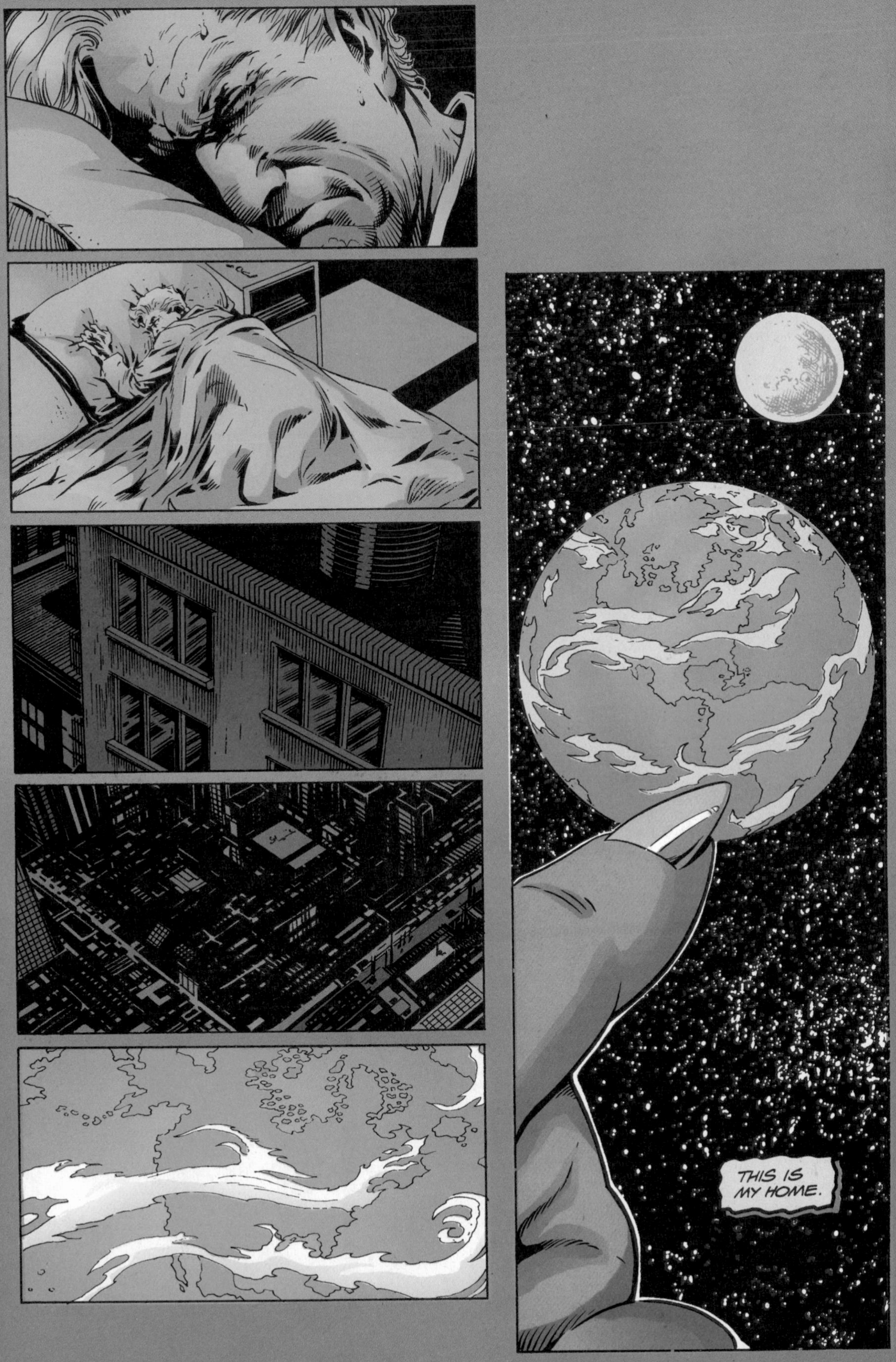
THIS IS MY HOME.

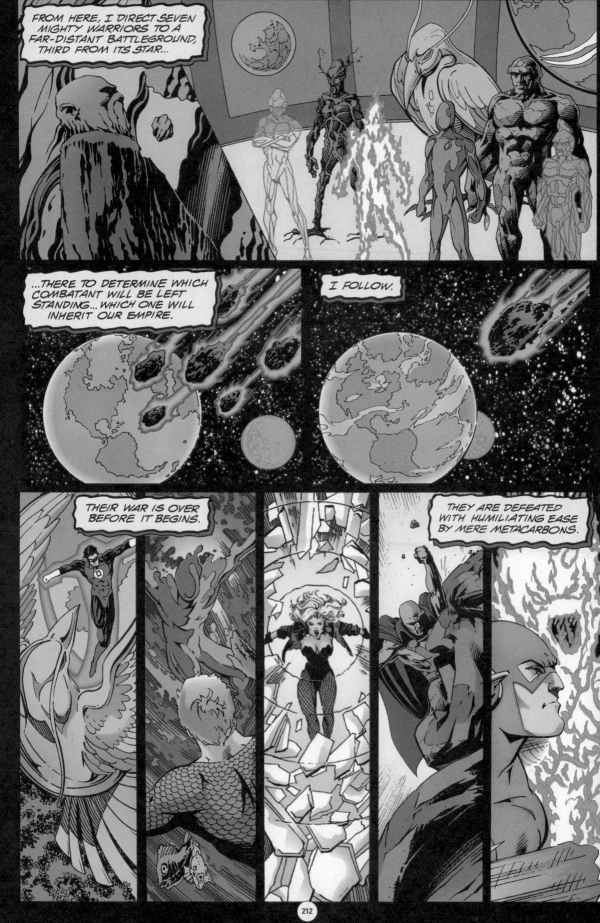

FROM HERE, I DIRECT SEVEN MIGHTY WARRIORS TO A FAR-DISTANT BATTLEGROUND, THIRD FROM ITS STAR...

...THERE TO DETERMINE WHICH COMBATANT WILL BE LEFT STANDING...WHICH ONE WILL INHERIT OUR EMPIRE.

I FOLLOW.

THEIR WAR IS OVER BEFORE IT BEGINS.

THEY ARE DEFEATED WITH HUMILIATING EASE BY MERE METACARBONS.

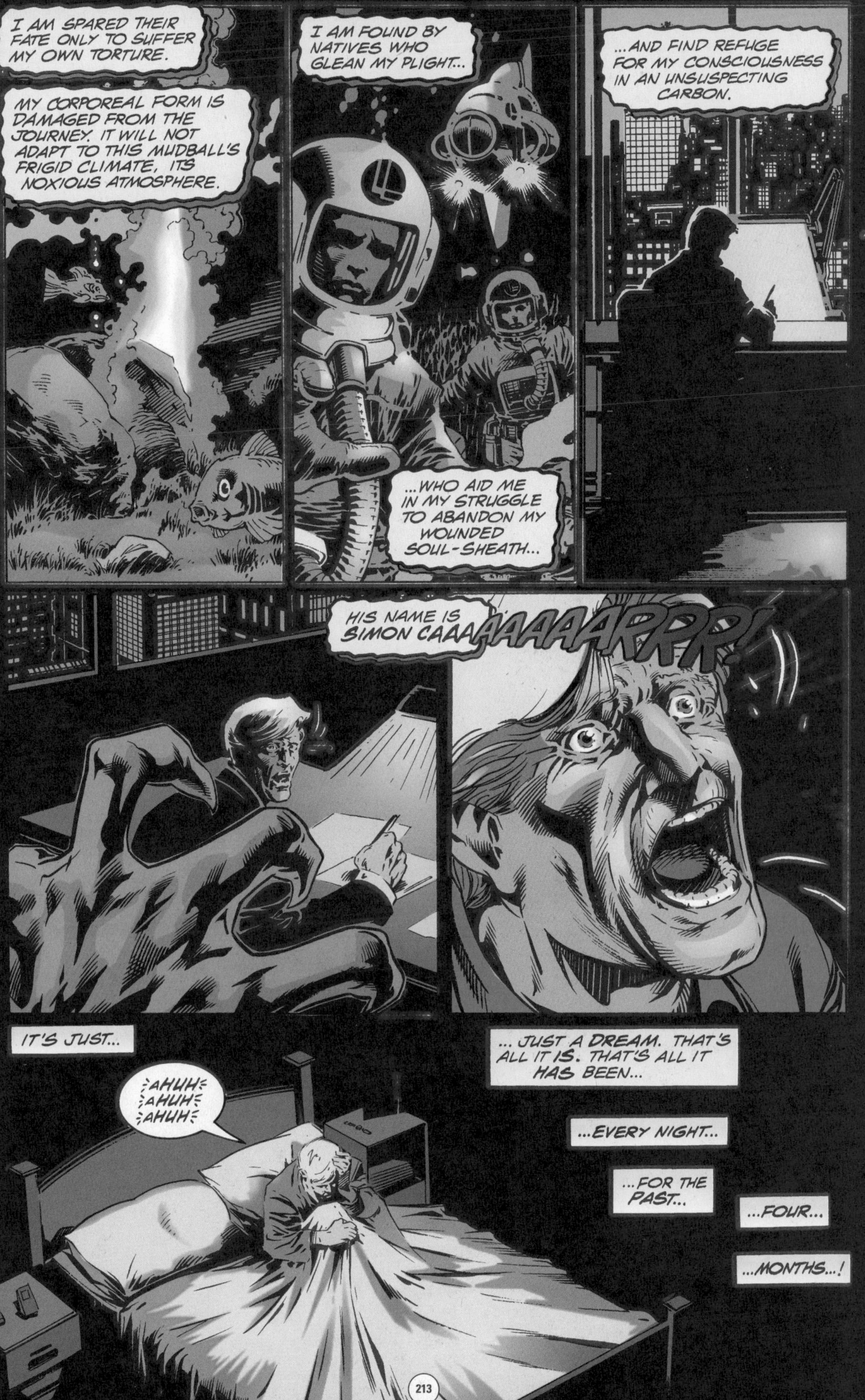
I AM SPARED THEIR FATE ONLY TO SUFFER MY OWN TORTURE.
MY CORPOREAL FORM IS DAMAGED FROM THE JOURNEY. IT WILL NOT ADAPT TO THIS MUDBALL'S FRIGID CLIMATE, ITS NOXIOUS ATMOSPHERE.
I AM FOUND BY NATIVES WHO GLEAN MY PLIGHT...
...WHO AID ME IN MY STRUGGLE TO ABANDON MY WOUNDED SOUL-SHEATH...
...AND FIND REFUGE FOR MY CONSCIOUSNESS IN AN UNSUSPECTING CARBON.
HIS NAME IS SIMON CAAA
AAAAARRPP!
IT'S JUST...
AHUH AHUH AHUH
... JUST A DREAM. THAT'S ALL IT IS. THAT'S ALL IT HAS BEEN...
...EVERY NIGHT...
...FOR THE PAST...
...FOUR...
...MONTHS...!

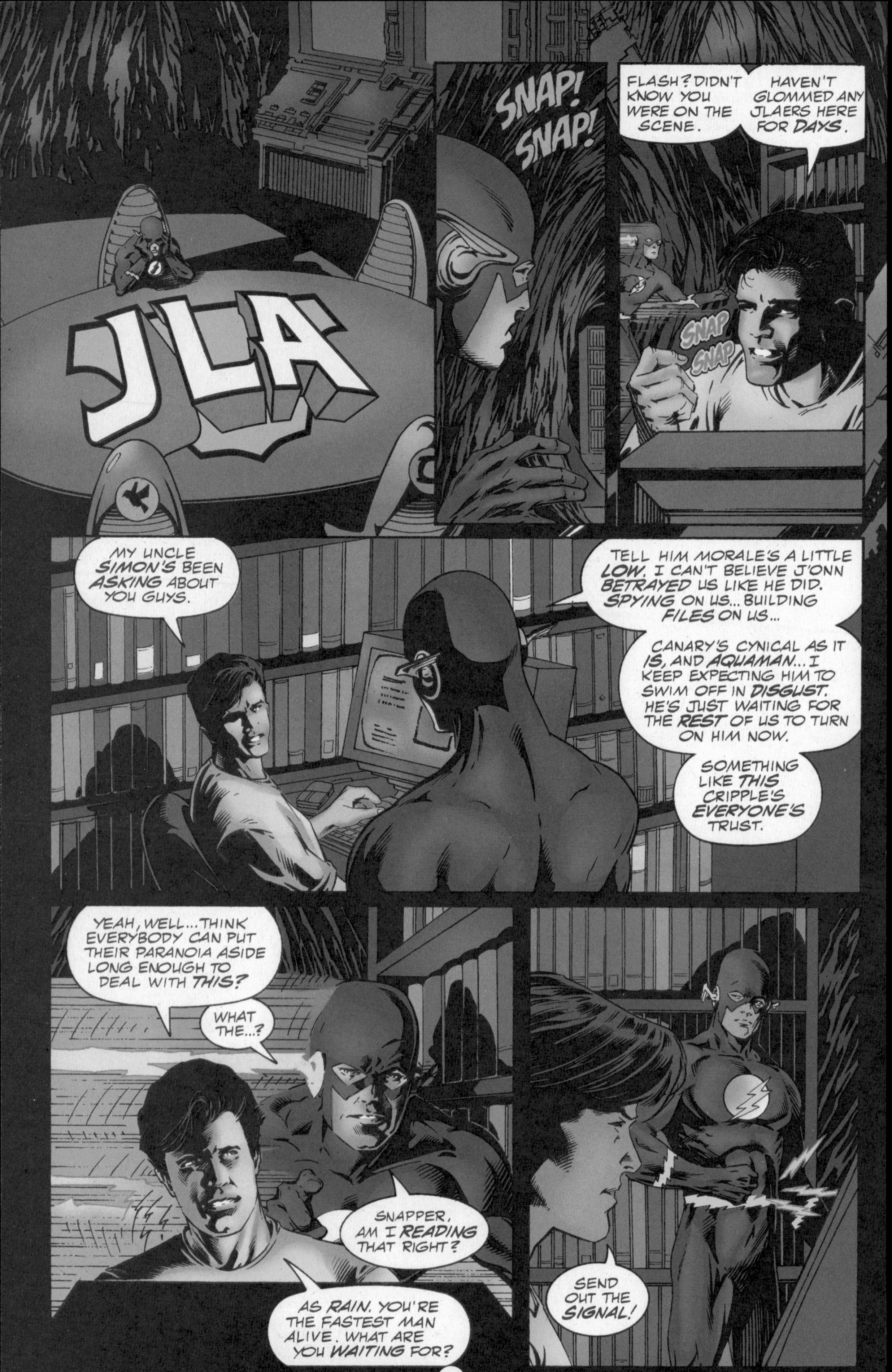
JLA
SNAP! SNAP!
FLASH? DIDN'T KNOW YOU WERE ON THE SCENE.
HAVEN'T GLOMMED ANY JLAERS HERE FOR DAYS.
SNAP SNAP
MY UNCLE SIMON'S BEEN ASKING ABOUT YOU GUYS.
TELL HIM MORALE'S A LITTLE LOW. I CAN'T BELIEVE J'ONN BETRAYED US LIKE HE DID. SPYING ON US... BUILDING FILES ON US...
CANARY'S CYNICAL AS IT IS, AND AQUAMAN... I KEEP EXPECTING HIM TO SWIM OFF IN DISGUST. HE'S JUST WAITING FOR THE REST OF US TO TURN ON HIM NOW.
SOMETHING LIKE THIS CRIPPLE'S EVERYONE'S TRUST.
YEAH, WELL... THINK EVERYBODY CAN PUT THEIR PARANOIA ASIDE LONG ENOUGH TO DEAL WITH THIS?
WHAT THE...?
SNAPPER, AM I READING THAT RIGHT?
AS RAIN. YOU'RE THE FASTEST MAN ALIVE. WHAT ARE YOU WAITING FOR?
SEND OUT THE SIGNAL!

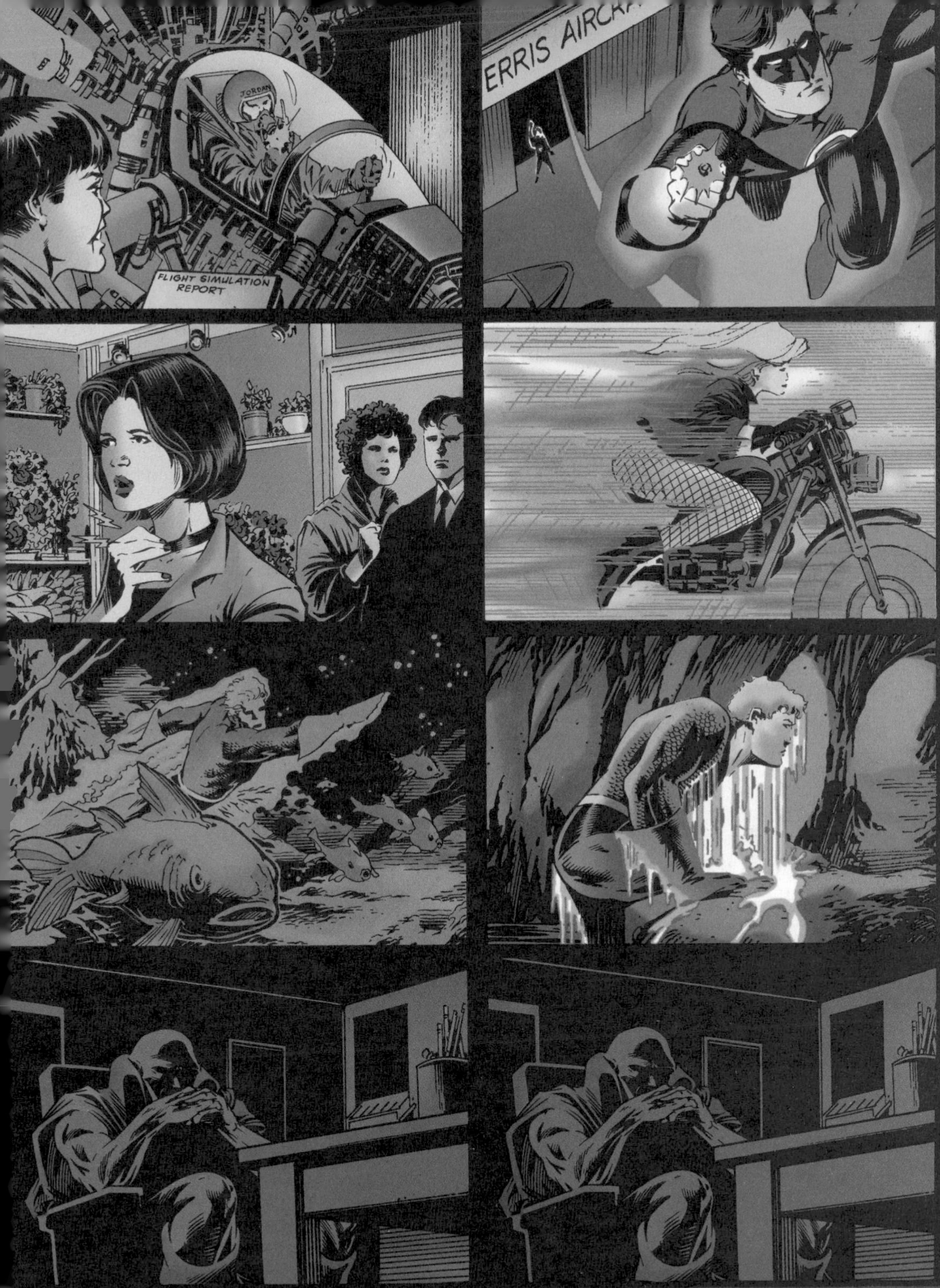

JORDAN
FLIGHT SIMULATION REPORT
ERRIS AIRCRA

CHANGE THE WORLD

MARK WAID / BRIAN AUGUSTYN / BARRY KITSON
storytellers

MICHAEL BAIR
inker

KEN LOPEZ
letterer

PAT GARRAHY
colorist

HEROIC AGE
separations

PETER TOMASI
editor

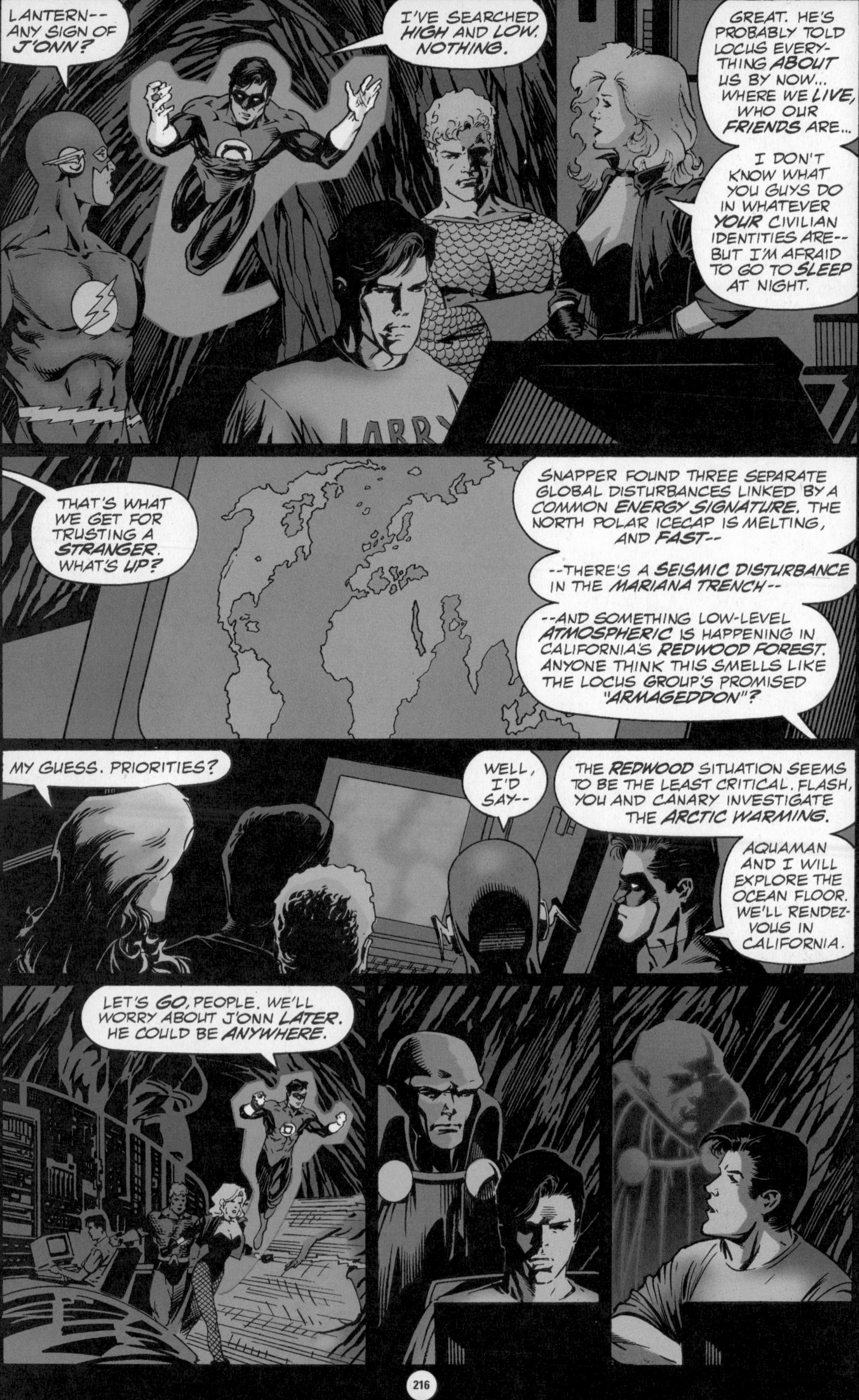
LANTERN-- ANY SIGN OF J'ONN?
I'VE SEARCHED HIGH AND LOW. NOTHING.
GREAT. HE'S PROBABLY TOLD LOCUS EVERYTHING ABOUT US BY NOW... WHERE WE LIVE, WHO OUR FRIENDS ARE...
I DON'T KNOW WHAT YOU GUYS DO IN WHATEVER YOUR CIVILIAN IDENTITIES ARE-- BUT I'M AFRAID TO GO TO SLEEP AT NIGHT.
THAT'S WHAT WE GET FOR TRUSTING A STRANGER. WHAT'S UP?
SNAPPER FOUND THREE SEPARATE GLOBAL DISTURBANCES LINKED BY A COMMON ENERGY SIGNATURE. THE NORTH POLAR ICECAP IS MELTING, AND FAST--
--THERE'S A SEISMIC DISTURBANCE IN THE MARIANA TRENCH--
--AND SOMETHING LOW-LEVEL ATMOSPHERIC IS HAPPENING IN CALIFORNIA'S REDWOOD FOREST. ANYONE THINK THIS SMELLS LIKE THE LOCUS GROUP'S PROMISED "ARMAGEDDON"?
MY GUESS. PRIORITIES?
WELL, I'D SAY--
THE REDWOOD SITUATION SEEMS TO BE THE LEAST CRITICAL. FLASH, YOU AND CANARY INVESTIGATE THE ARCTIC WARMING.
AQUAMAN AND I WILL EXPLORE THE OCEAN FLOOR. WE'LL RENDEZVOUS IN CALIFORNIA.
LET'S GO, PEOPLE. WE'LL WORRY ABOUT J'ONN LATER. HE COULD BE ANYWHERE.
LARRY

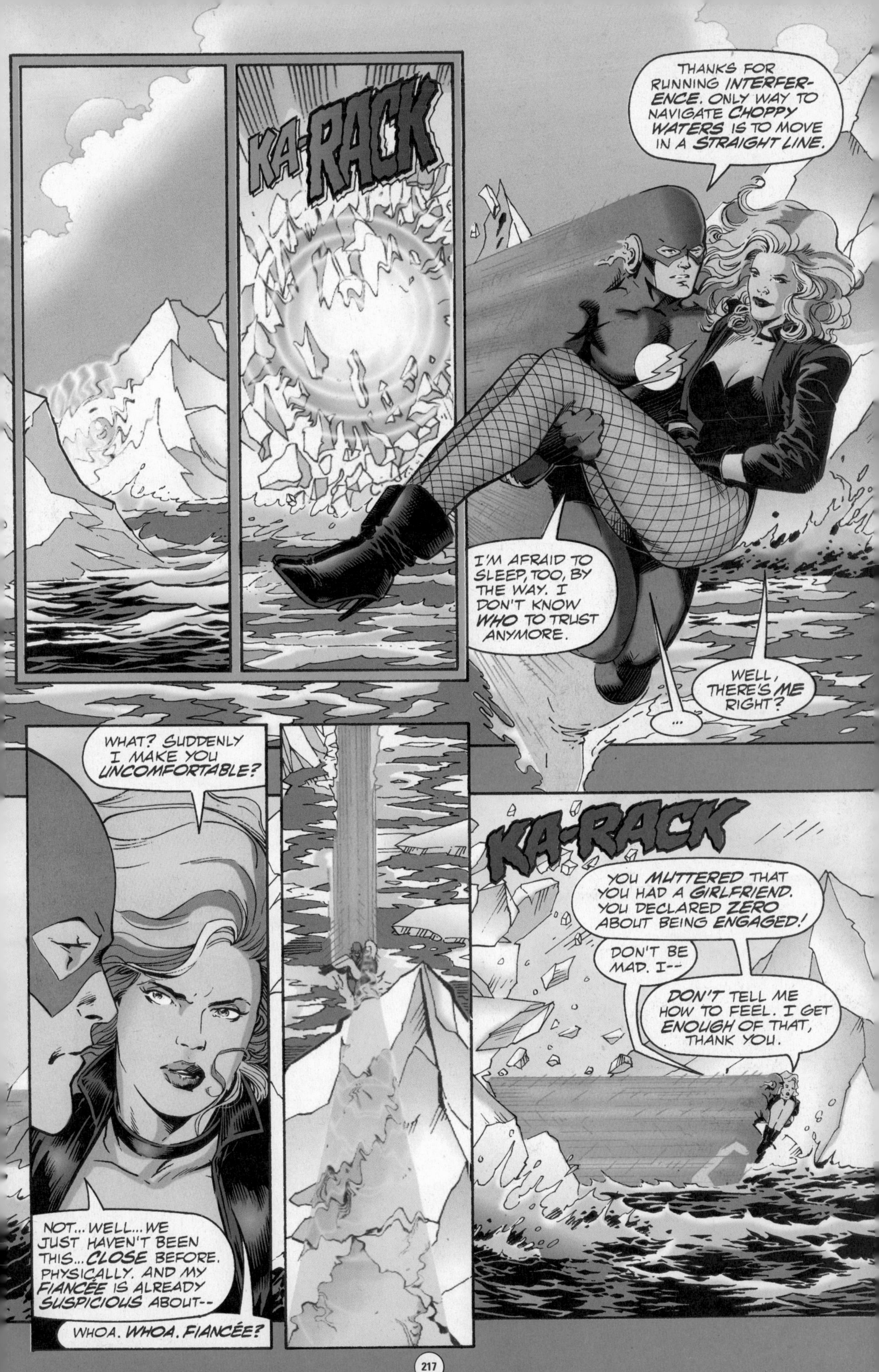
KA-RACK
THANKS FOR RUNNING INTERFERENCE. ONLY WAY TO NAVIGATE CHOPPY WATERS IS TO MOVE IN A STRAIGHT LINE.
I'M AFRAID TO SLEEP, TOO, BY THE WAY. I DON'T KNOW WHO TO TRUST ANYMORE.
WELL, THERE'S ME RIGHT?
...
WHAT? SUDDENLY I MAKE YOU UNCOMFORTABLE?
NOT... WELL... WE JUST HAVEN'T BEEN THIS... CLOSE BEFORE. PHYSICALLY. AND MY FIANCÉE IS ALREADY SUSPICIOUS ABOUT--
WHOA. WHOA. FIANCÉE?
KA-RACK
YOU MUTTERED THAT YOU HAD A GIRLFRIEND. YOU DECLARED ZERO ABOUT BEING ENGAGED!
DON'T BE MAD. I--
DON'T TELL ME HOW TO FEEL. I GET ENOUGH OF THAT, THANK YOU.

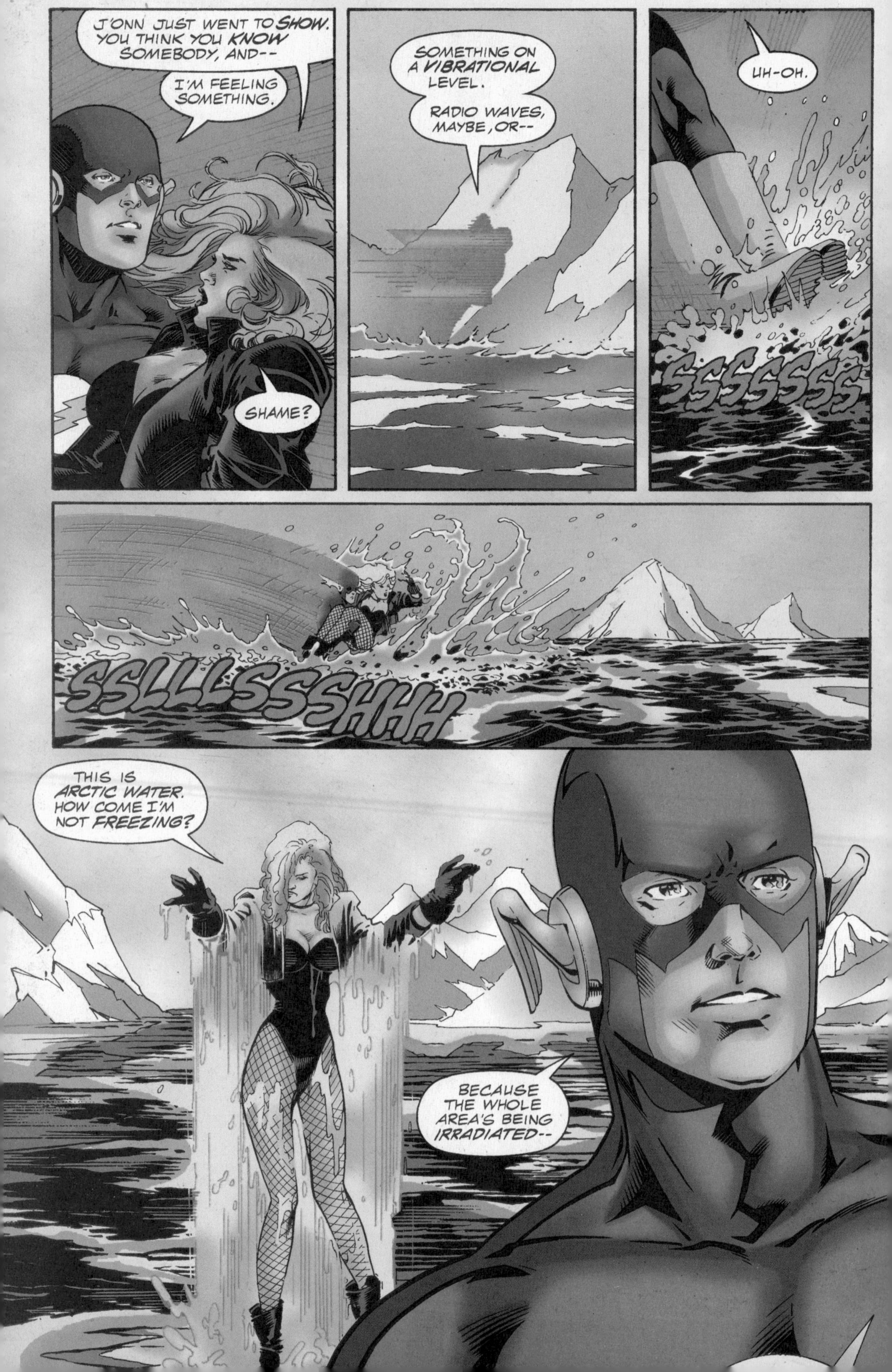

J'ONN JUST WENT TO SHOW. YOU THINK YOU KNOW SOMEBODY, AND--
I'M FEELING SOMETHING.
SHAME?
SOMETHING ON A VIBRATIONAL LEVEL.
RADIO WAVES, MAYBE, OR--
UH-OH.
SSSSSSSS
SSLLLSSSHHH
THIS IS ARCTIC WATER. HOW COME I'M NOT FREEZING?
BECAUSE THE WHOLE AREA'S BEING IRRADIATED--

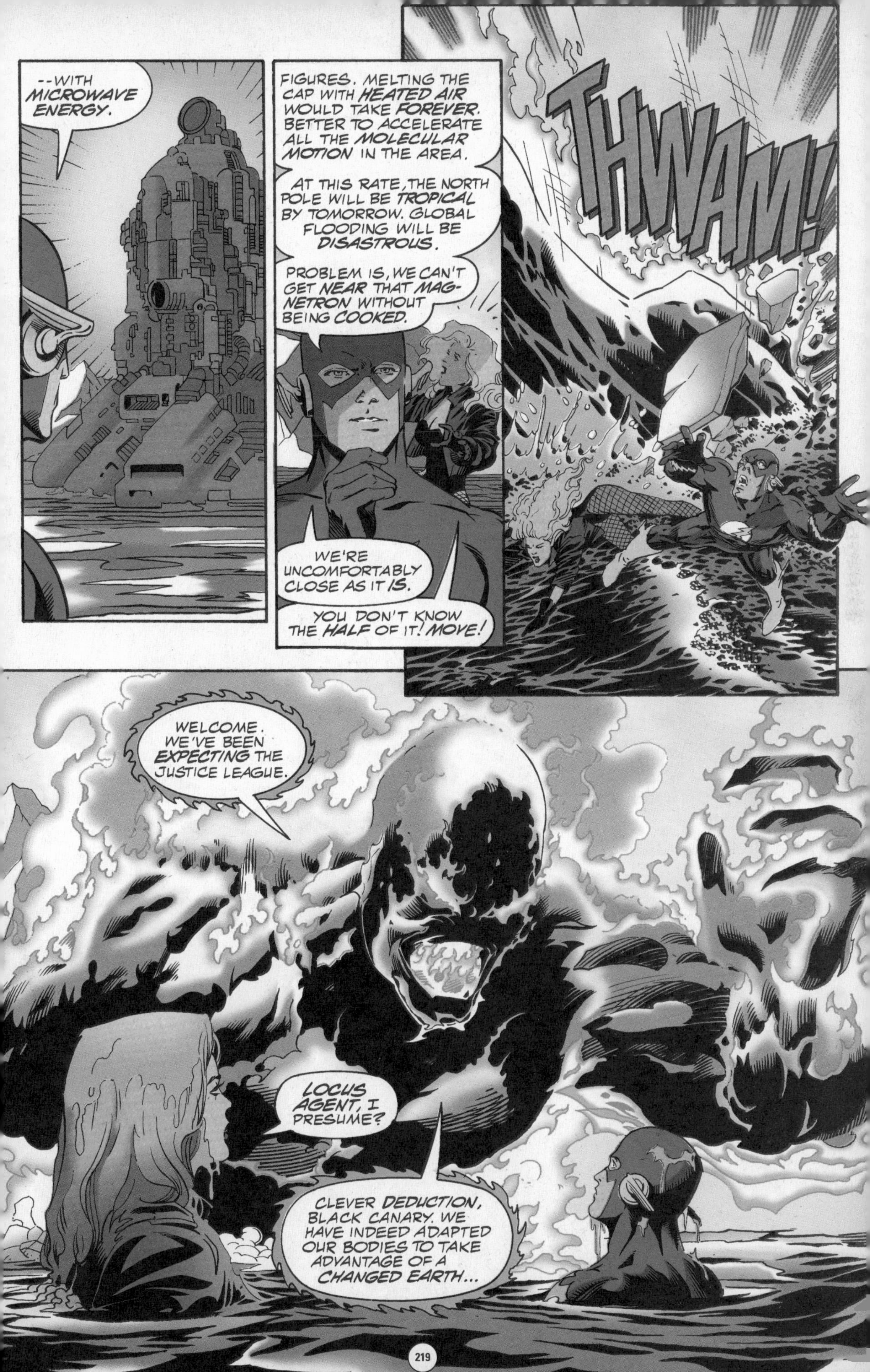
--WITH MICROWAVE ENERGY.
FIGURES. MELTING THE CAP WITH HEATED AIR WOULD TAKE FOREVER. BETTER TO ACCELERATE ALL THE MOLECULAR MOTION IN THE AREA.
AT THIS RATE, THE NORTH POLE WILL BE TROPICAL BY TOMORROW. GLOBAL FLOODING WILL BE DISASTROUS.
PROBLEM IS, WE CAN'T GET NEAR THAT MAG-NETRON WITHOUT BEING COOKED.
WE'RE UNCOMFORTABLY CLOSE AS IT IS.
YOU DON'T KNOW THE HALF OF IT! MOVE!
THWAM!
WELCOME. WE'VE BEEN EXPECTING THE JUSTICE LEAGUE.
LOCUS AGENT, I PRESUME?
CLEVER DEDUCTION, BLACK CANARY. WE HAVE INDEED ADAPTED OUR BODIES TO TAKE ADVANTAGE OF A CHANGED EARTH...

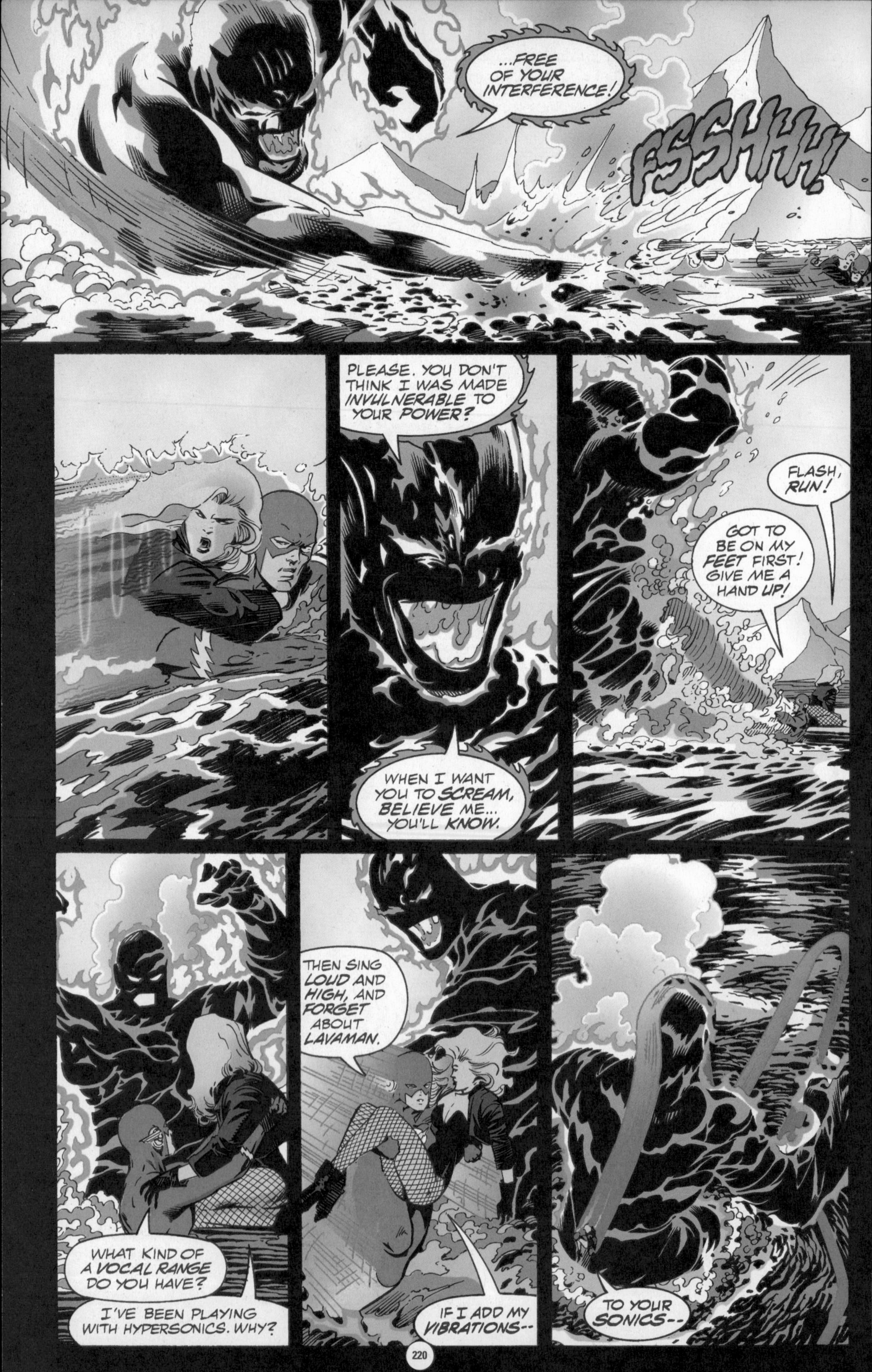
...FREE OF YOUR INTERFERENCE!
FSSHHH!
PLEASE. YOU DON'T THINK I WAS MADE INVULNERABLE TO YOUR POWER?
WHEN I WANT YOU TO SCREAM, BELIEVE ME... YOU'LL KNOW.
FLASH, RUN!
GOT TO BE ON MY FEET FIRST! GIVE ME A HAND UP!
WHAT KIND OF A VOCAL RANGE DO YOU HAVE?
I'VE BEEN PLAYING WITH HYPERSONICS. WHY?
THEN SING LOUD AND HIGH, AND FORGET ABOUT LAVAMAN.
IF I ADD MY VIBRATIONS--
TO YOUR SONICS--

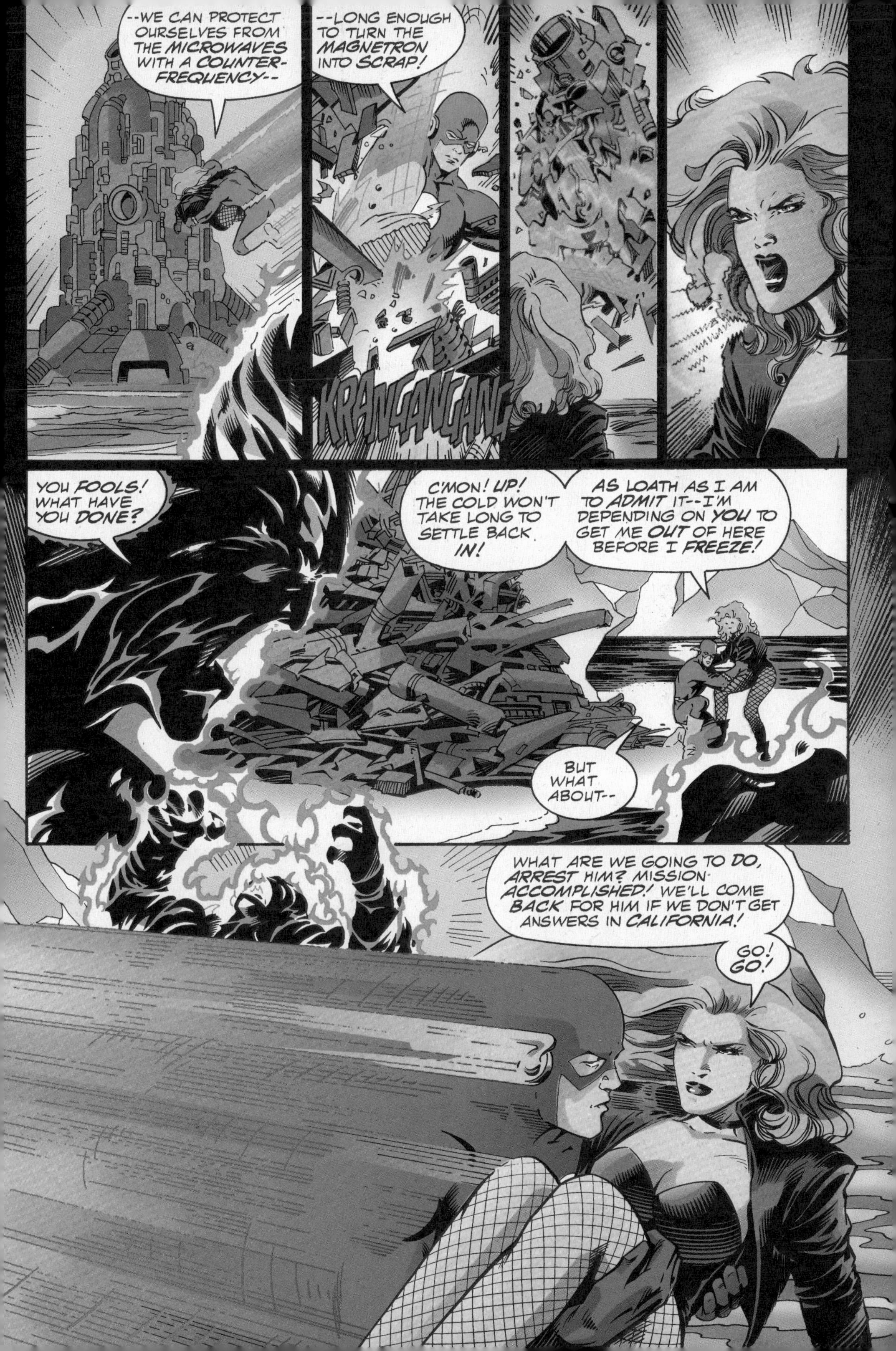
--WE CAN PROTECT OURSELVES FROM THE MICROWAVES WITH A COUNTER-FREQUENCY--
--LONG ENOUGH TO TURN THE MAGNETRON INTO SCRAP!
KRANGANGANG
YOU FOOLS! WHAT HAVE YOU DONE?
C'MON! UP! THE COLD WON'T TAKE LONG TO SETTLE BACK IN!
AS LOATH AS I AM TO ADMIT IT--I'M DEPENDING ON YOU TO GET ME OUT OF HERE BEFORE I FREEZE!
BUT WHAT ABOUT--
WHAT ARE WE GOING TO DO, ARREST HIM? MISSION ACCOMPLISHED! WE'LL COME BACK FOR HIM IF WE DON'T GET ANSWERS IN CALIFORNIA!
GO! GO!

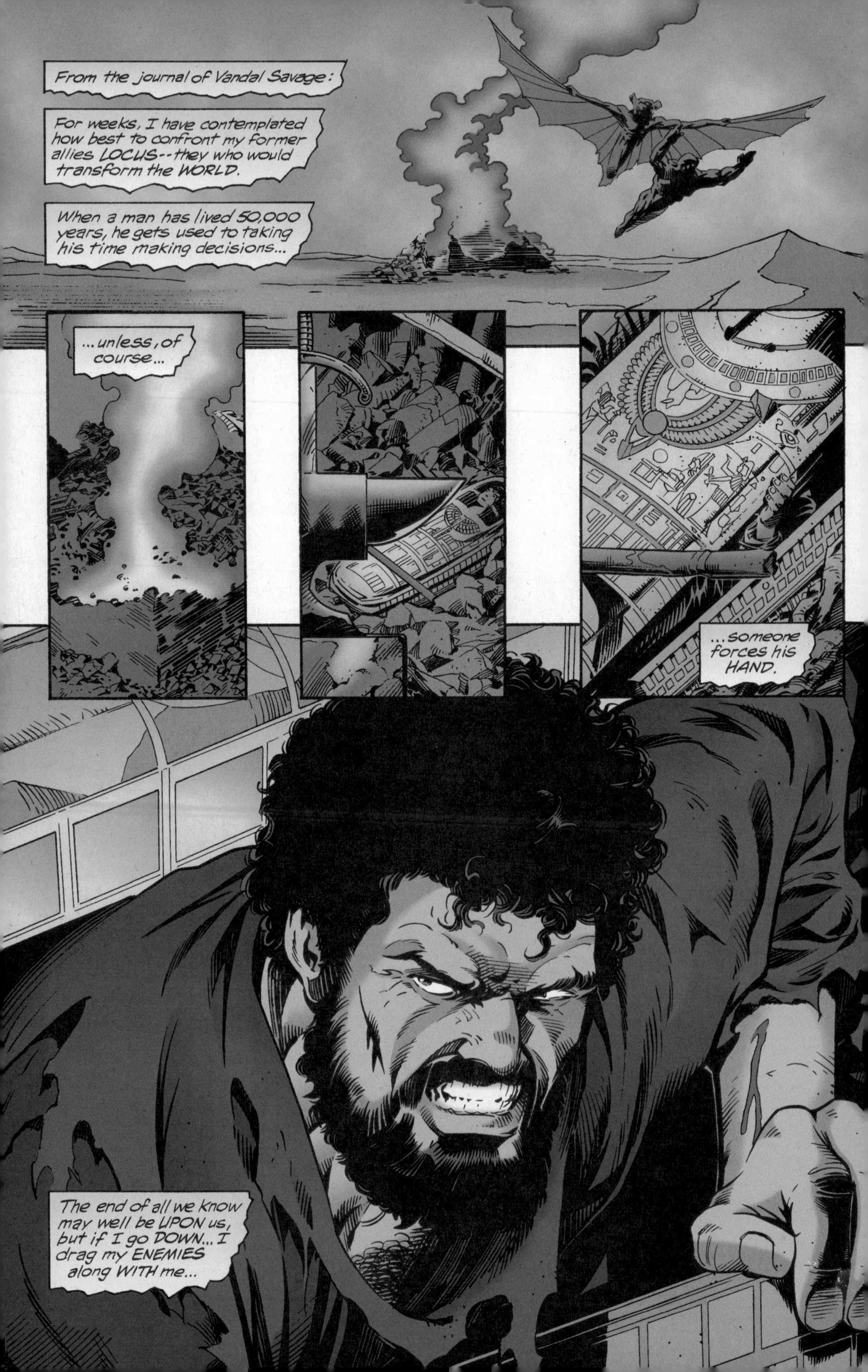
From the journal of Vandal Savage:
For weeks, I have contemplated how best to confront my former allies LOCUS--they who would transform the WORLD.
When a man has lived 50,000 years, he gets used to taking his time making decisions...
...unless, of course...
...someone forces his HAND.
The end of all we know may well be UPON us, but if I go DOWN... I drag my ENEMIES along WITH me...

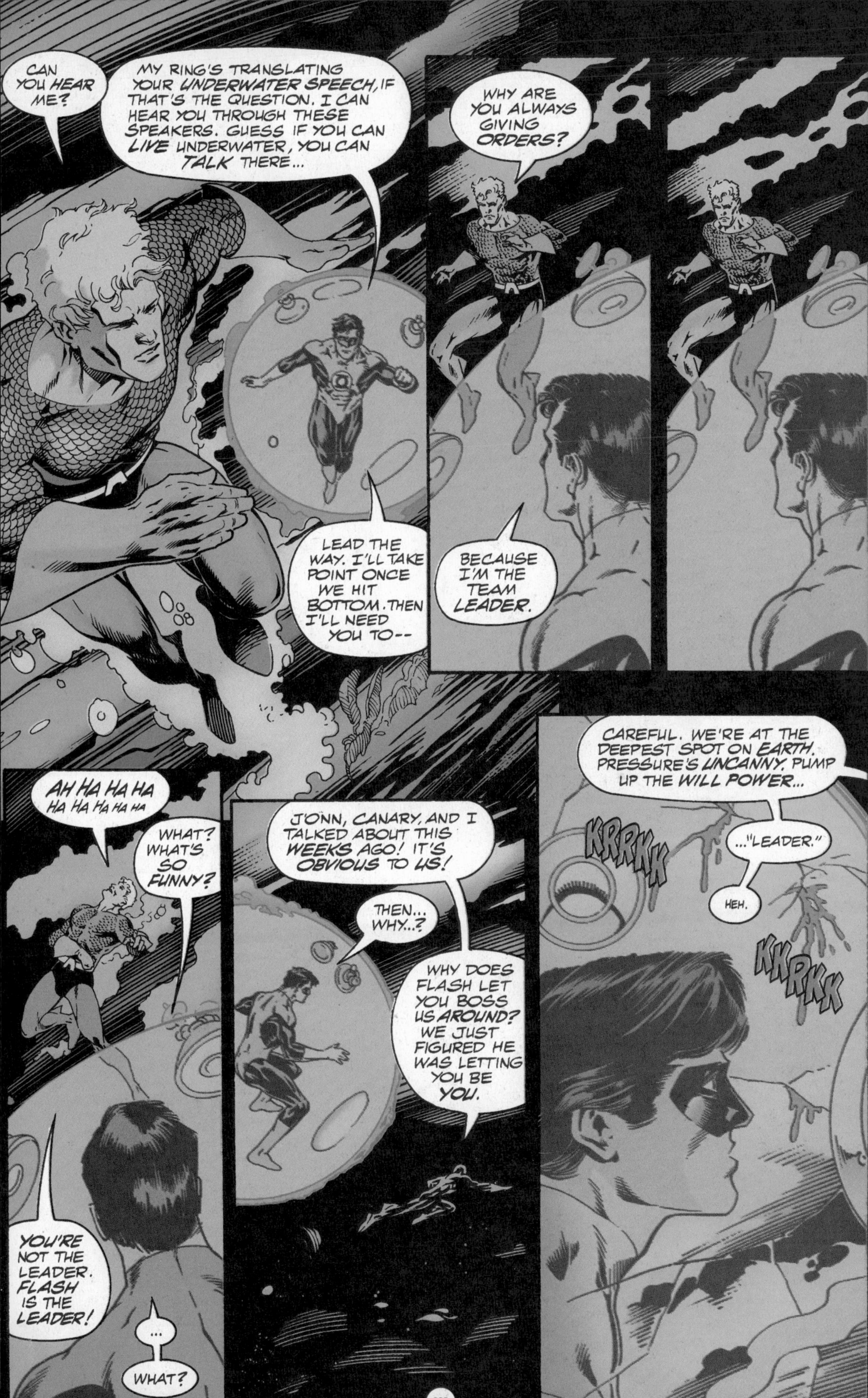
CAN YOU HEAR ME?
MY RING'S TRANSLATING YOUR UNDERWATER SPEECH, IF THAT'S THE QUESTION. I CAN HEAR YOU THROUGH THESE SPEAKERS. GUESS IF YOU CAN LIVE UNDERWATER, YOU CAN TALK THERE...
LEAD THE WAY. I'LL TAKE POINT ONCE WE HIT BOTTOM. THEN I'LL NEED YOU TO--
WHY ARE YOU ALWAYS GIVING ORDERS?
BECAUSE I'M THE TEAM LEADER.
AH HA HA HA HA HA HA HA HA HA
WHAT? WHAT'S SO FUNNY?
YOU'RE NOT THE LEADER. FLASH IS THE LEADER!
...
WHAT?
J'ONN, CANARY, AND I TALKED ABOUT THIS WEEKS AGO! IT'S OBVIOUS TO US!
THEN... WHY..?
WHY DOES FLASH LET YOU BOSS US AROUND? WE JUST FIGURED HE WAS LETTING YOU BE YOU.
CAREFUL. WE'RE AT THE DEEPEST SPOT ON EARTH. PRESSURE'S UNCANNY. PUMP UP THE WILL POWER...
KRRKKK
..."LEADER."
HEH.
KKRKKK

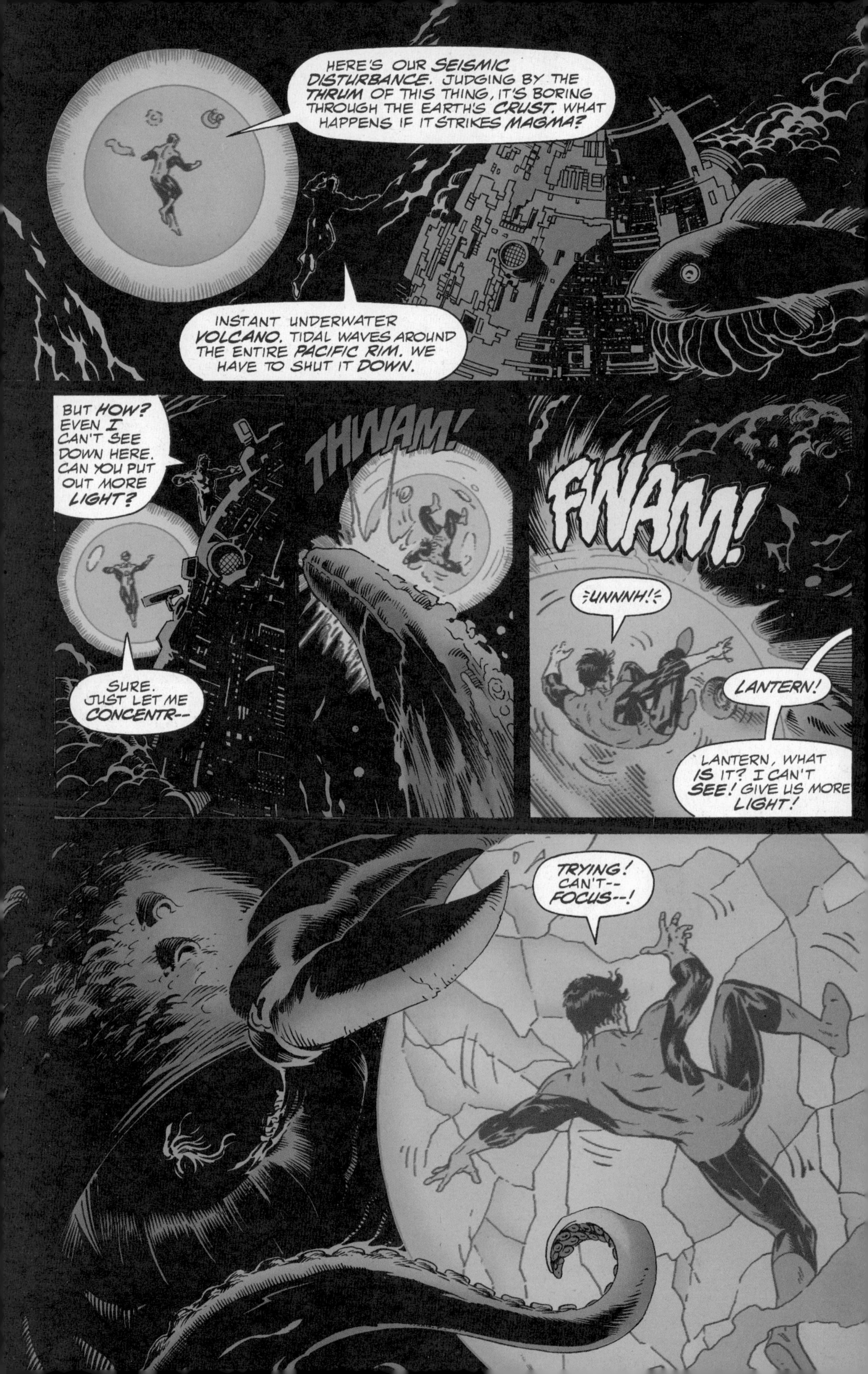
HERE'S OUR SEISMIC DISTURBANCE. JUDGING BY THE THRUM OF THIS THING, IT'S BORING THROUGH THE EARTH'S CRUST. WHAT HAPPENS IF IT STRIKES MAGMA?
INSTANT UNDERWATER VOLCANO. TIDAL WAVES AROUND THE ENTIRE PACIFIC RIM. WE HAVE TO SHUT IT DOWN.
BUT HOW? EVEN I CAN'T SEE DOWN HERE. CAN YOU PUT OUT MORE LIGHT?
SURE. JUST LET ME CONCENTR--
THWAM!
FWAM!
UNNNH!
LANTERN!
LANTERN, WHAT IS IT? I CAN'T SEE! GIVE US MORE LIGHT!
TRYING! CAN'T-- FOCUS--!

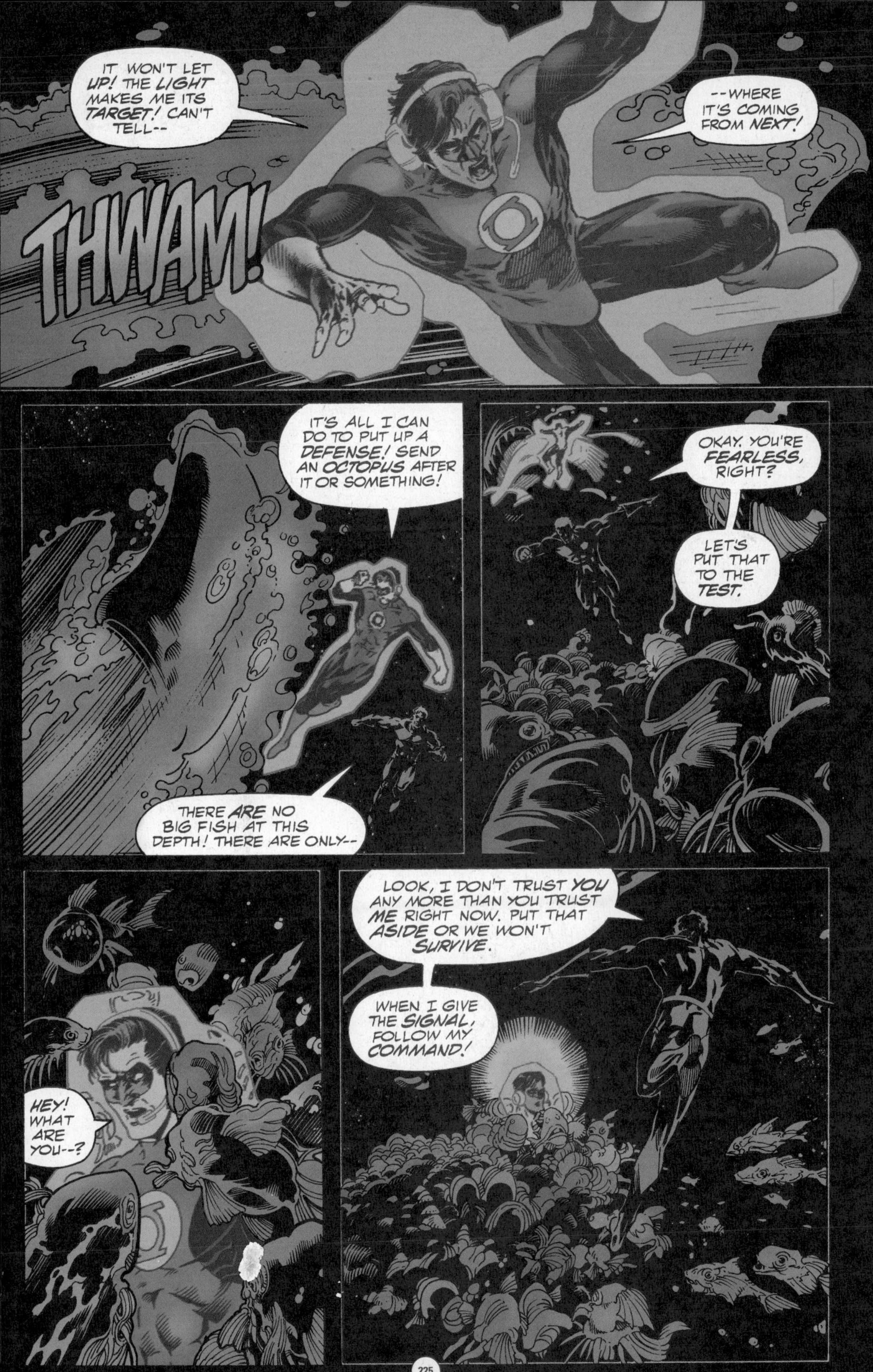
IT WON'T LET UP! THE LIGHT MAKES ME ITS TARGET! CAN'T TELL--
--WHERE IT'S COMING FROM NEXT!
THWAM!
IT'S ALL I CAN DO TO PUT UP A DEFENSE! SEND AN OCTOPUS AFTER IT OR SOMETHING!
THERE ARE NO BIG FISH AT THIS DEPTH! THERE ARE ONLY--
OKAY. YOU'RE FEARLESS, RIGHT?
LET'S PUT THAT TO THE TEST.
HEY! WHAT ARE YOU--?
LOOK, I DON'T TRUST YOU ANY MORE THAN YOU TRUST ME RIGHT NOW. PUT THAT ASIDE OR WE WON'T SURVIVE.
WHEN I GIVE THE SIGNAL, FOLLOW MY COMMAND!

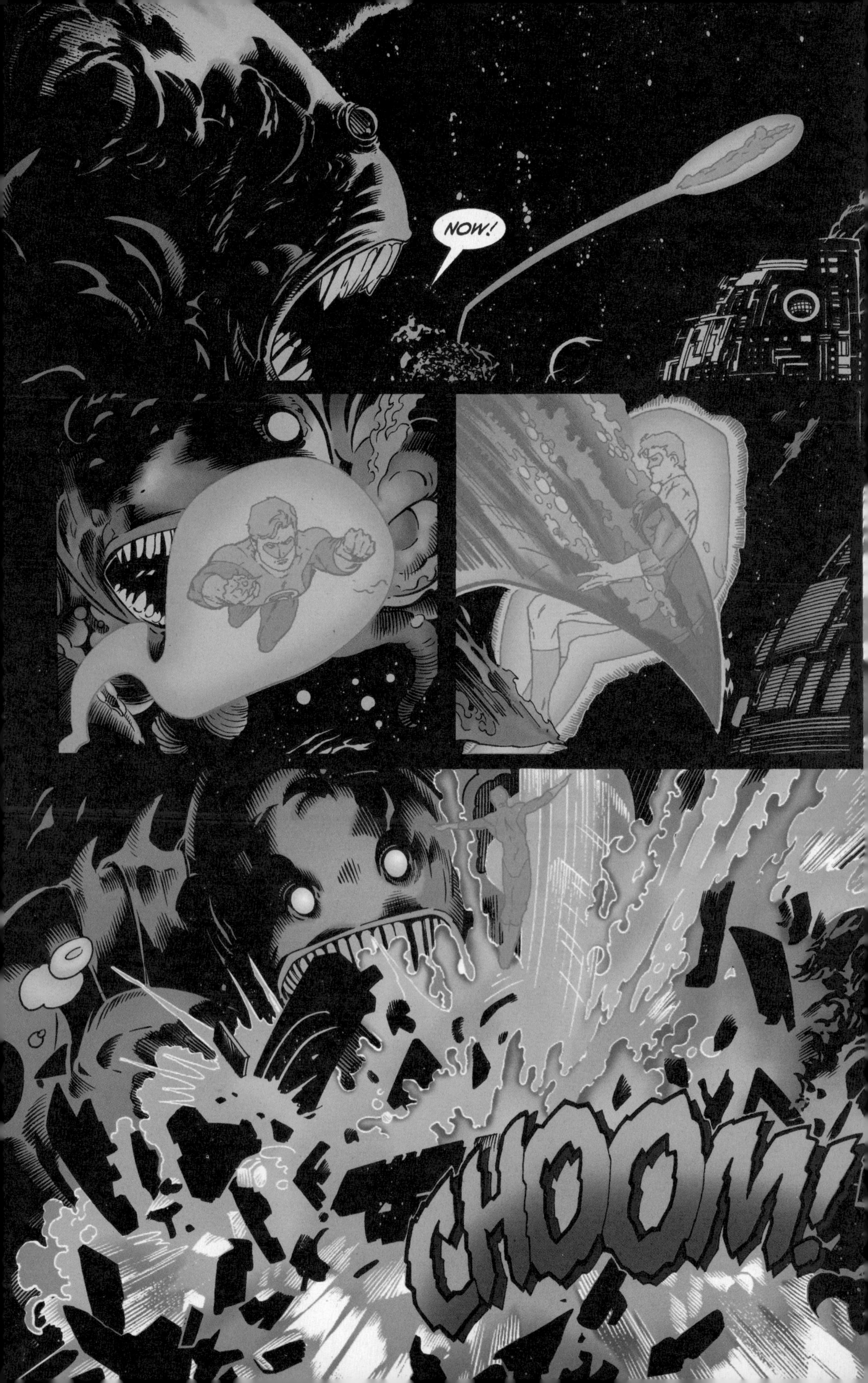
NOW!
CHOOM!

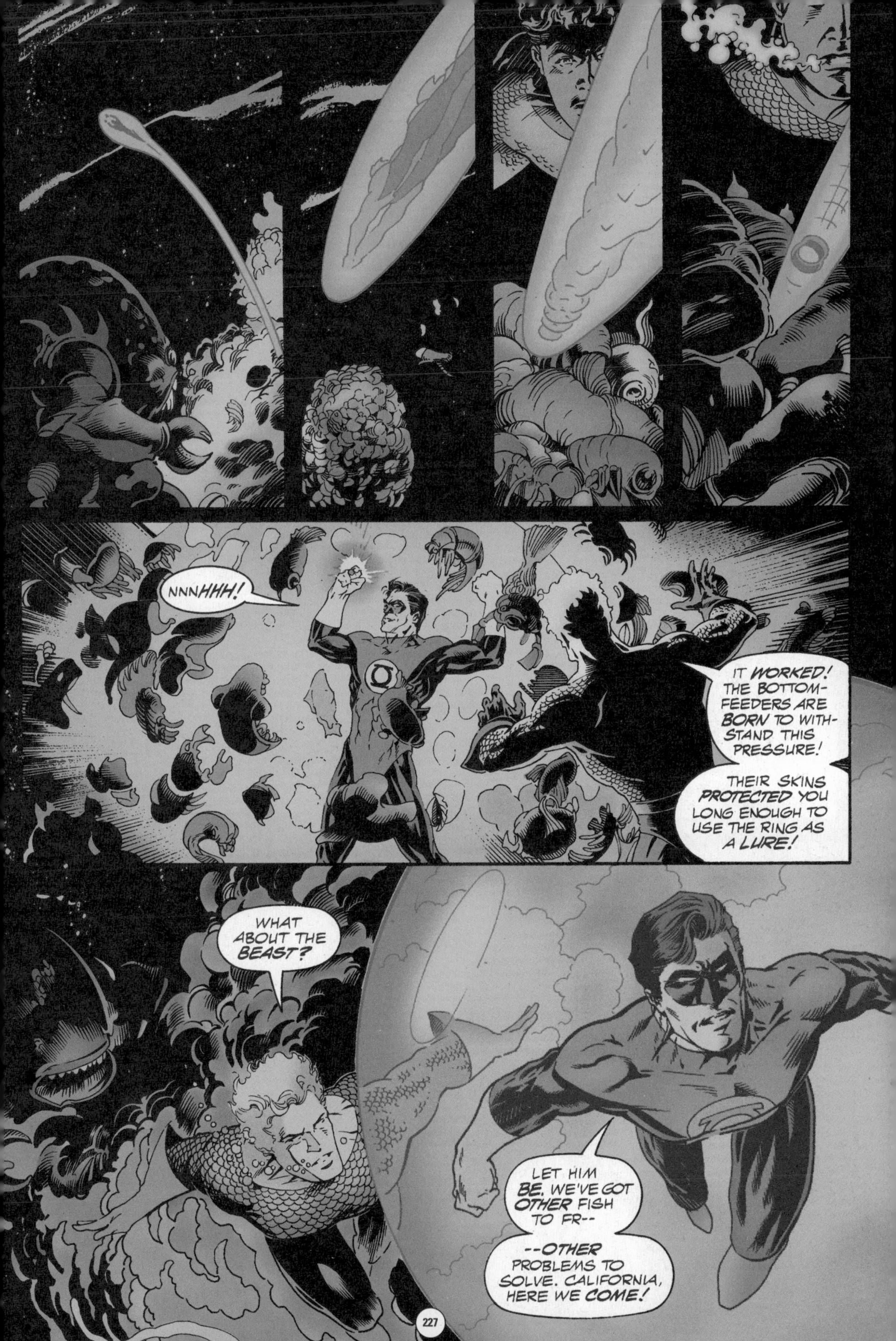
NNNHHH!
IT WORKED! THE BOTTOM-FEEDERS ARE BORN TO WITH-STAND THIS PRESSURE!
THEIR SKINS PROTECTED YOU LONG ENOUGH TO USE THE RING AS A LURE!
WHAT ABOUT THE BEAST?
LET HIM BE. WE'VE GOT OTHER FISH TO FR--
--OTHER PROBLEMS TO SOLVE. CALIFORNIA, HERE WE COME!

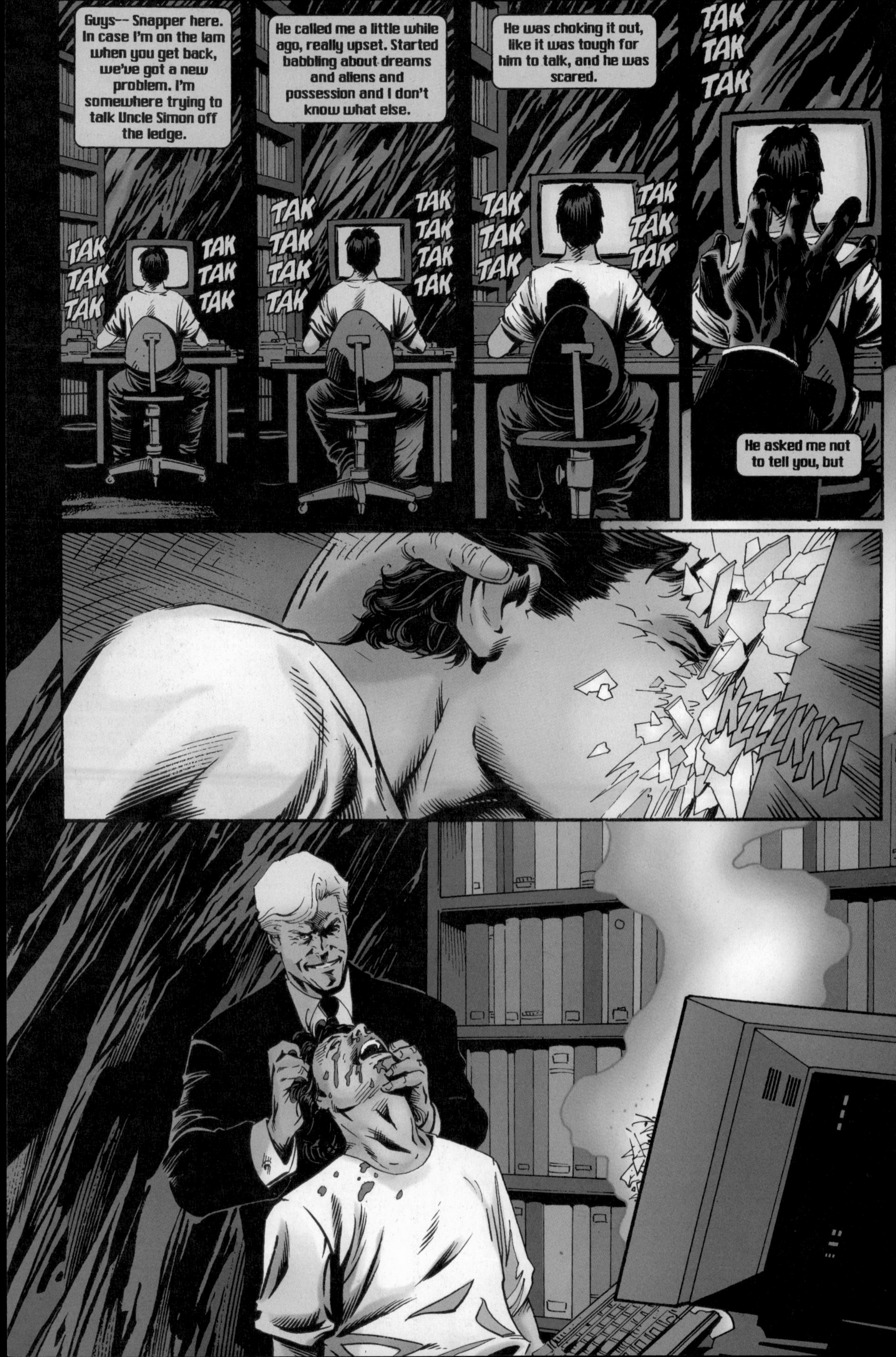
Guys-- Snapper here. In case I'm on the lam when you get back, we've got a new problem. I'm somewhere trying to talk Uncle Simon off the ledge.
TAK TAK TAK
TAK TAK TAK
He called me a little while ago, really upset. Started babbling about dreams and aliens and possession and I don't know what else.
TAK TAK TAK TAK
TAK TAK TAK TAK
He was choking it out, like it was tough for him to talk, and he was scared.
TAK TAK TAK
TAK TAK TAK
TAK TAK TAK
He asked me not to tell you, but
KZZZKKT

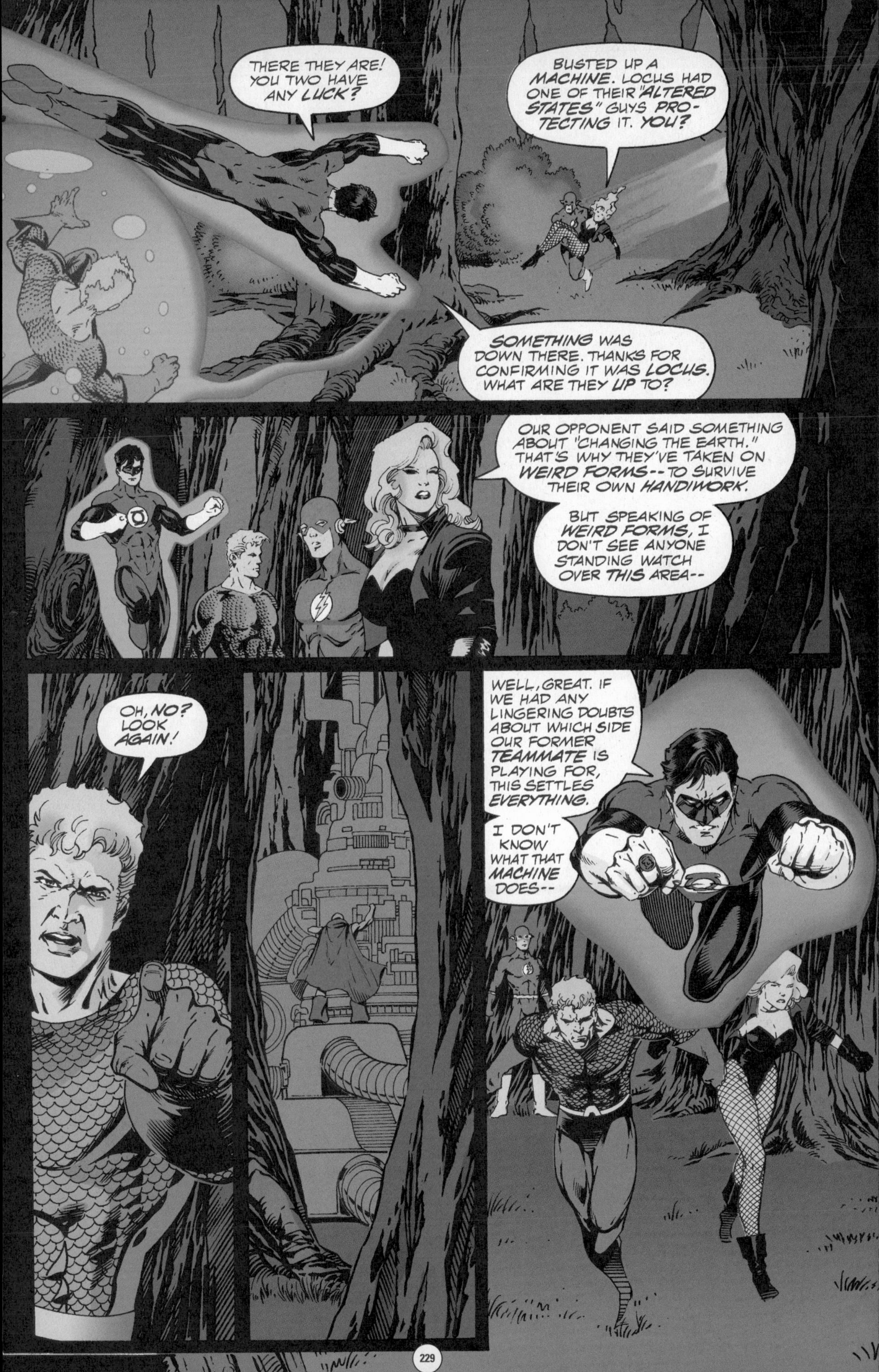
THERE THEY ARE! YOU TWO HAVE ANY LUCK?
BUSTED UP A MACHINE. LOCUS HAD ONE OF THEIR "ALTERED STATES" GUYS PROTECTING IT. YOU?
SOMETHING WAS DOWN THERE. THANKS FOR CONFIRMING IT WAS LOCUS. WHAT ARE THEY UP TO?
OUR OPPONENT SAID SOMETHING ABOUT "CHANGING THE EARTH." THAT'S WHY THEY'VE TAKEN ON WEIRD FORMS--TO SURVIVE THEIR OWN HANDIWORK.
BUT SPEAKING OF WEIRD FORMS, I DON'T SEE ANYONE STANDING WATCH OVER THIS AREA--
OH, NO? LOOK AGAIN!
WELL, GREAT. IF WE HAD ANY LINGERING DOUBTS ABOUT WHICH SIDE OUR FORMER TEAMMATE IS PLAYING FOR, THIS SETTLES EVERYTHING.
I DON'T KNOW WHAT THAT MACHINE DOES--

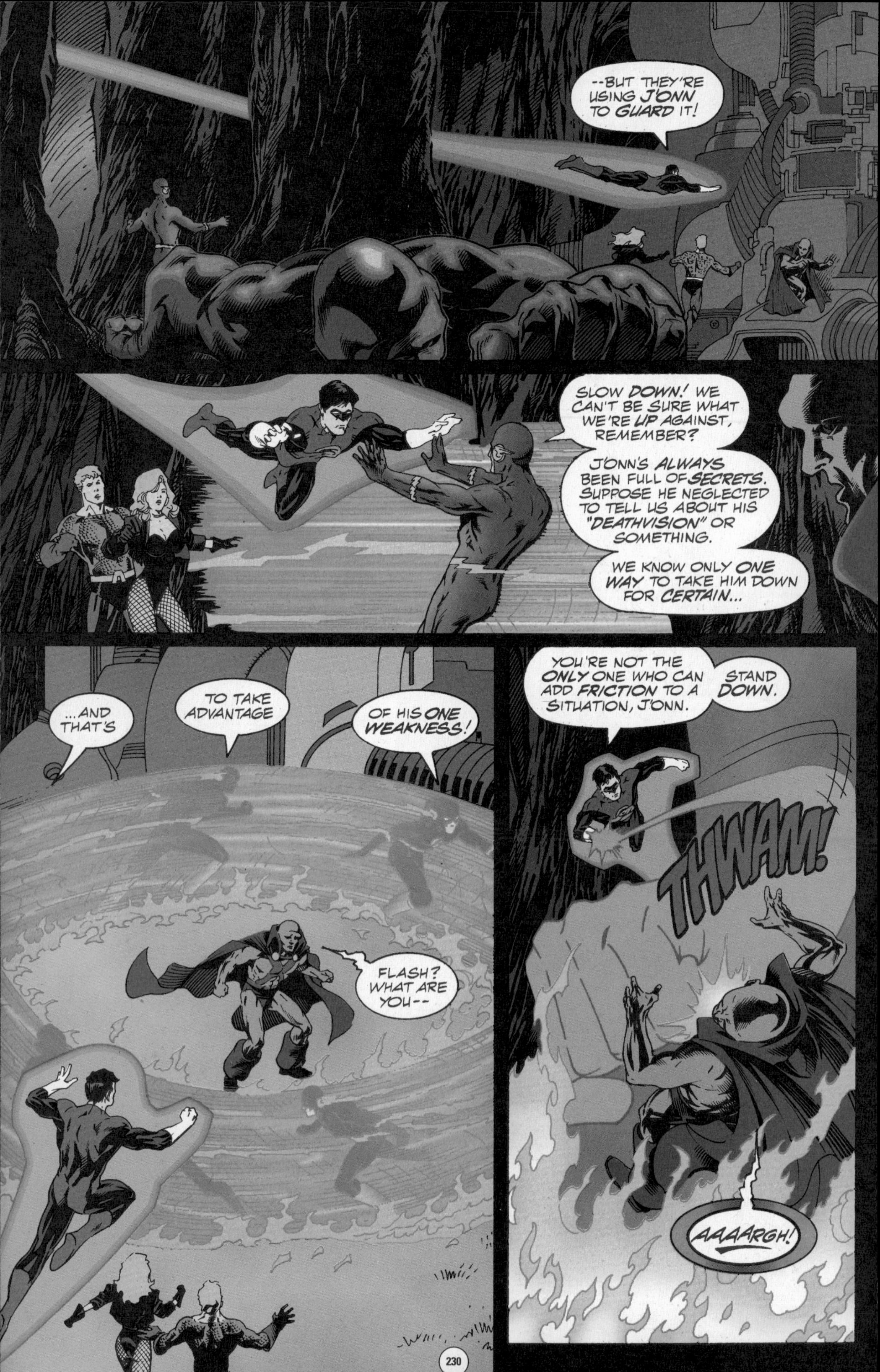
--BUT THEY'RE USING J'ONN TO GUARD IT!
SLOW DOWN! WE CAN'T BE SURE WHAT WE'RE UP AGAINST, REMEMBER?
J'ONN'S ALWAYS BEEN FULL OF SECRETS. SUPPOSE HE NEGLECTED TO TELL US ABOUT HIS "DEATHVISION" OR SOMETHING.
WE KNOW ONLY ONE WAY TO TAKE HIM DOWN FOR CERTAIN...
...AND THAT'S
TO TAKE ADVANTAGE
OF HIS ONE WEAKNESS!
FLASH? WHAT ARE YOU--
YOU'RE NOT THE ONLY ONE WHO CAN ADD FRICTION TO A SITUATION, J'ONN.
STAND DOWN.
THWAM!
AAAARGH!

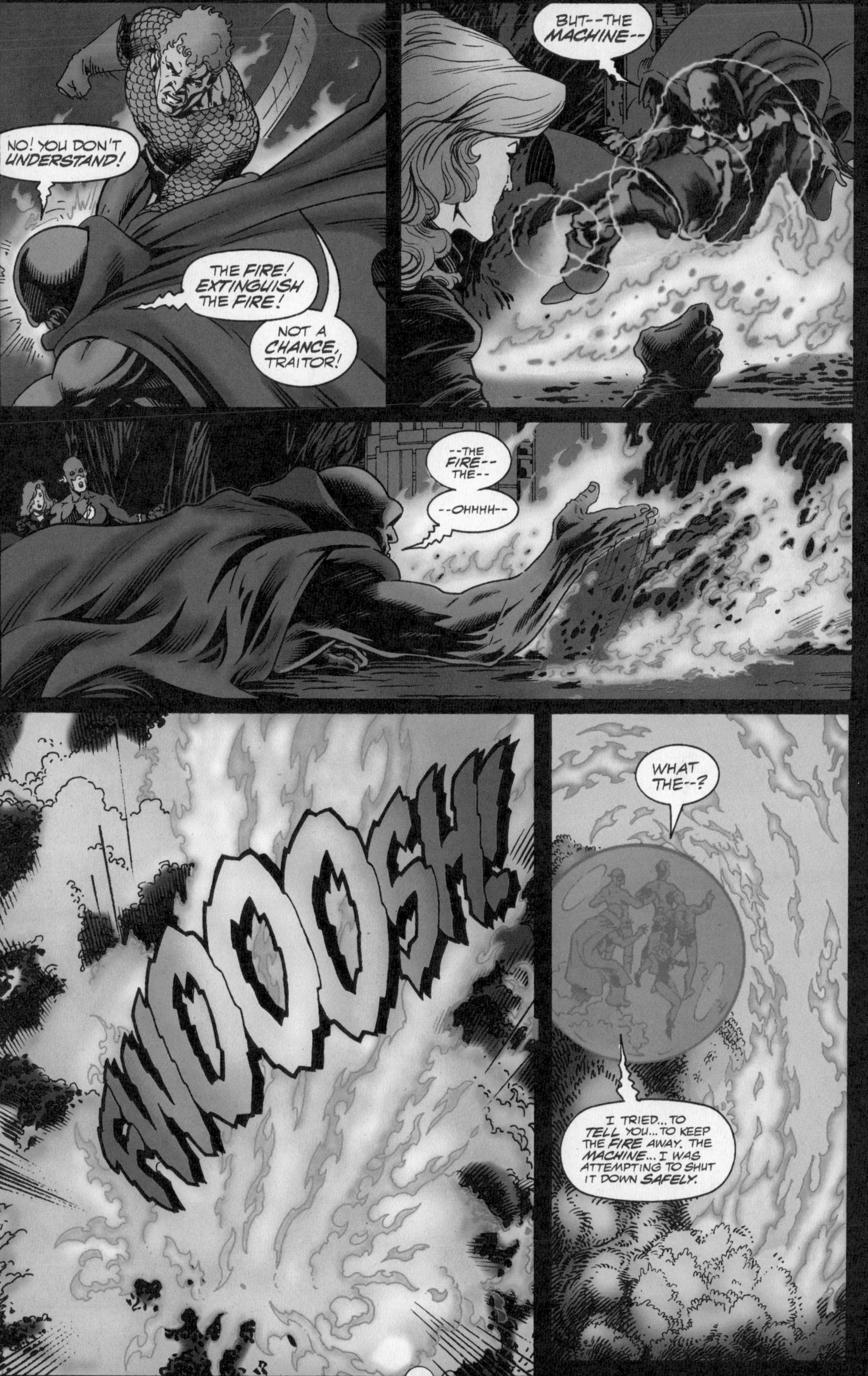
NO! YOU DON'T UNDERSTAND!
THE FIRE! EXTINGUISH THE FIRE!
NOT A CHANCE, TRAITOR!
BUT--THE MACHINE--
--THE FIRE-- THE--
--OHHHH--
WHOOOSH!
WHAT THE--?
I TRIED...TO TELL YOU...TO KEEP THE FIRE AWAY. THE MACHINE...I WAS ATTEMPTING TO SHUT IT DOWN SAFELY.

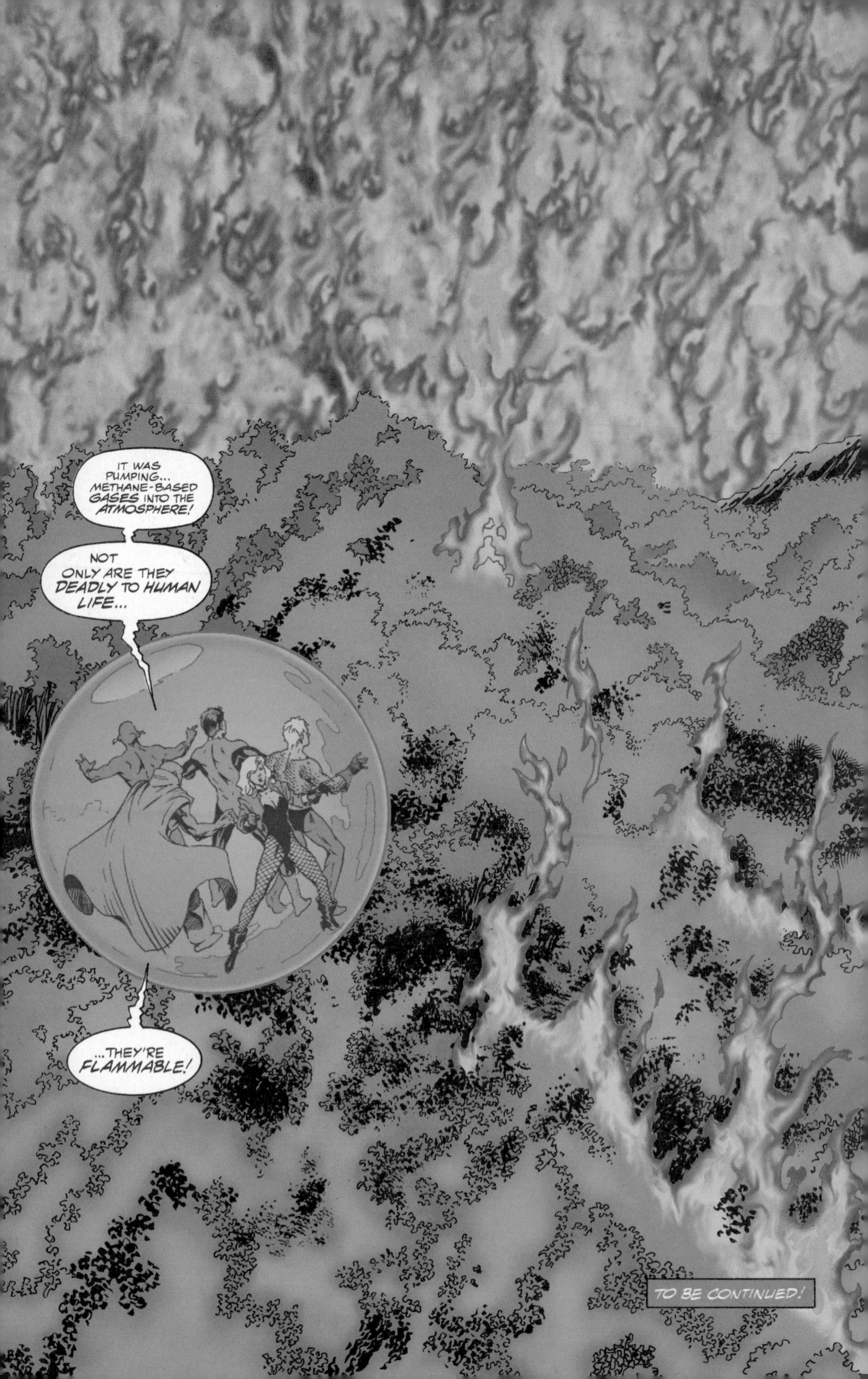
IT WAS PUMPING... METHANE-BASED GASES INTO THE ATMOSPHERE!
NOT ONLY ARE THEY DEADLY TO HUMAN LIFE...
...THEY'RE FLAMMABLE!
TO BE CONTINUED!

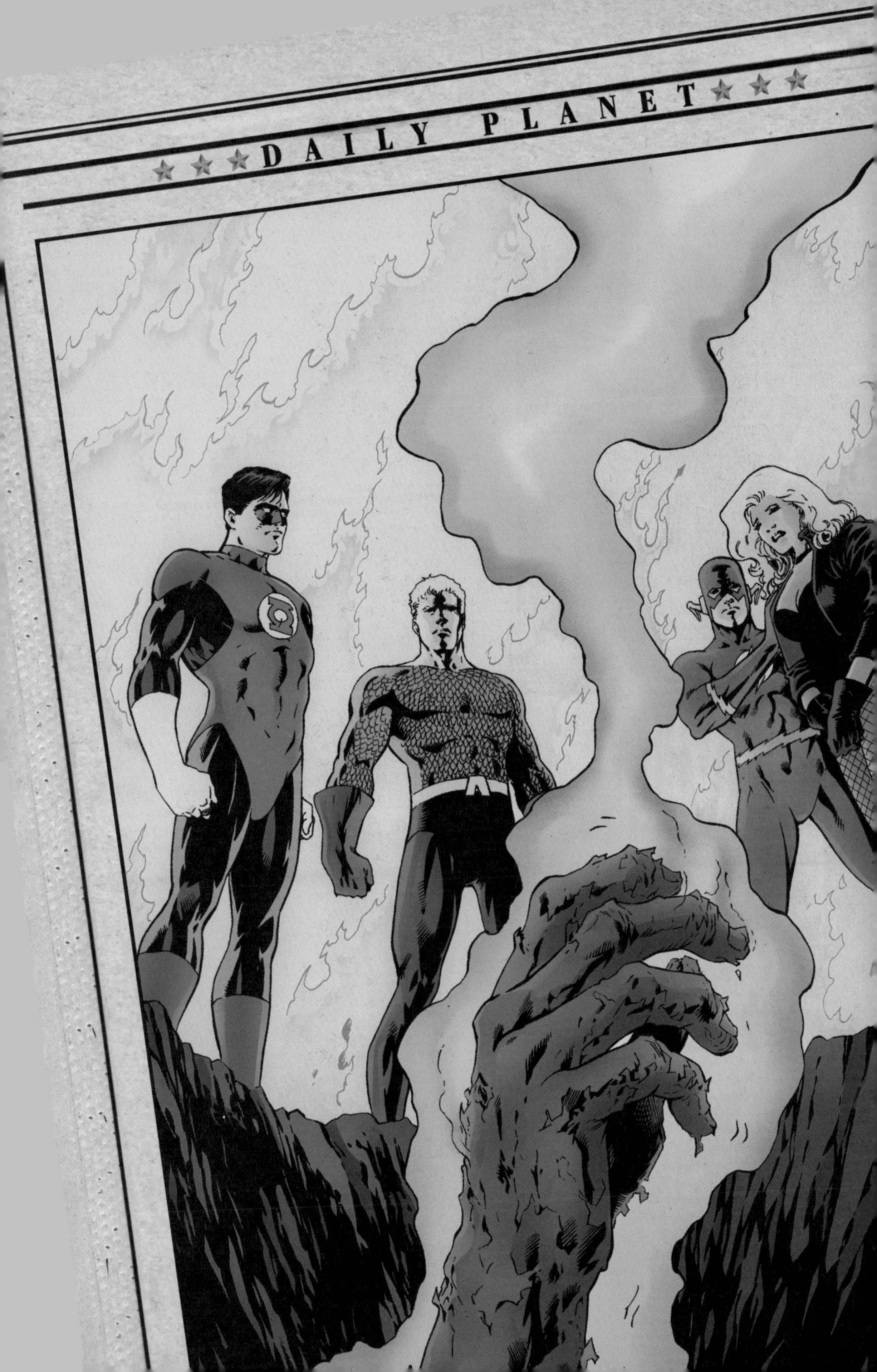
DAILY PLANET

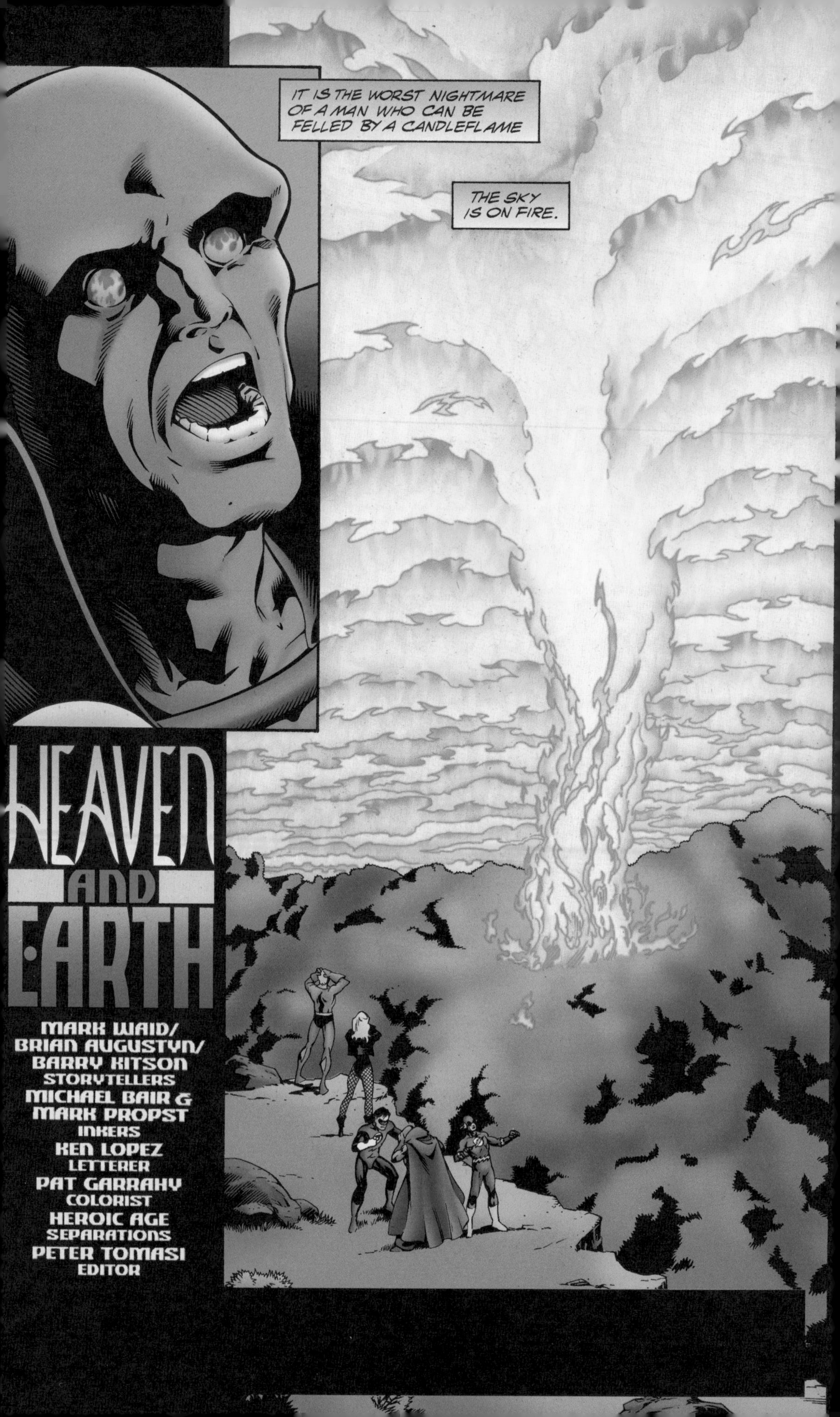
IT IS THE WORST NIGHTMARE OF A MAN WHO CAN BE FELLED BY A CANDLEFLAME
THE SKY IS ON FIRE.
HEAVEN AND EARTH
MARK WAID/ BRIAN AUGUSTYN/ BARRY KITSON STORYTELLERS
MICHAEL BAIR & MARK PROPST INKERS
KEN LOPEZ LETTERER
PAT GARRAHY COLORIST
HEROIC AGE SEPARATIONS
PETER TOMASI EDITOR

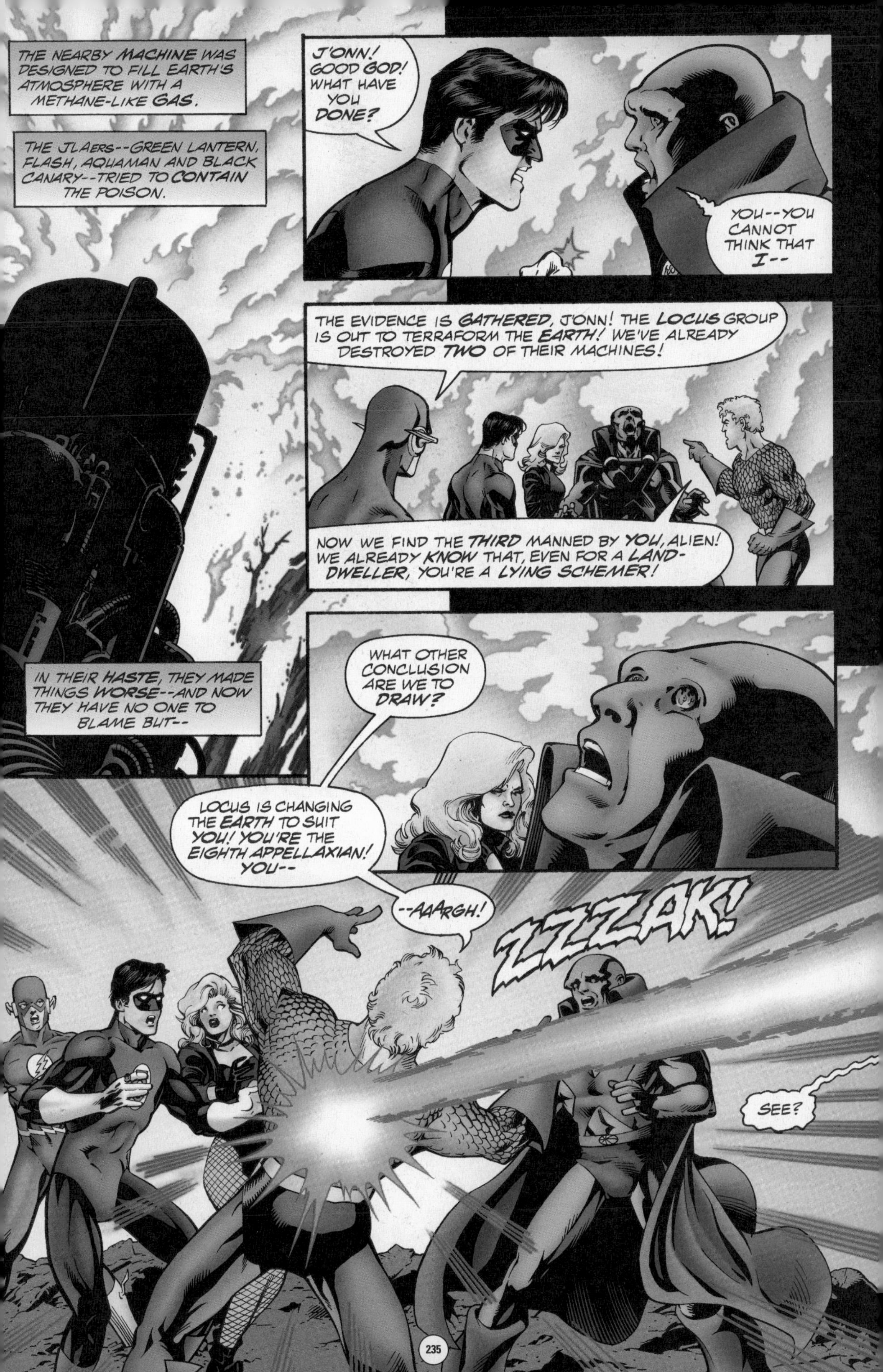
THE NEARBY MACHINE WAS DESIGNED TO FILL EARTH'S ATMOSPHERE WITH A METHANE-LIKE GAS.
THE JLAers--GREEN LANTERN, FLASH, AQUAMAN AND BLACK CANARY--TRIED TO CONTAIN THE POISON.
J'ONN! GOOD GOD! WHAT HAVE YOU DONE?
YOU--YOU CANNOT THINK THAT I--
THE EVIDENCE IS GATHERED, J'ONN! THE LOCUS GROUP IS OUT TO TERRAFORM THE EARTH! WE'VE ALREADY DESTROYED TWO OF THEIR MACHINES!
NOW WE FIND THE THIRD MANNED BY YOU, ALIEN! WE ALREADY KNOW THAT, EVEN FOR A LAND-DWELLER, YOU'RE A LYING SCHEMER!
IN THEIR HASTE, THEY MADE THINGS WORSE--AND NOW THEY HAVE NO ONE TO BLAME BUT--
WHAT OTHER CONCLUSION ARE WE TO DRAW?
LOCUS IS CHANGING THE EARTH TO SUIT YOU! YOU'RE THE EIGHTH APPELLAXIAN! YOU--
--AAARGH!
ZZZAK!
SEE?

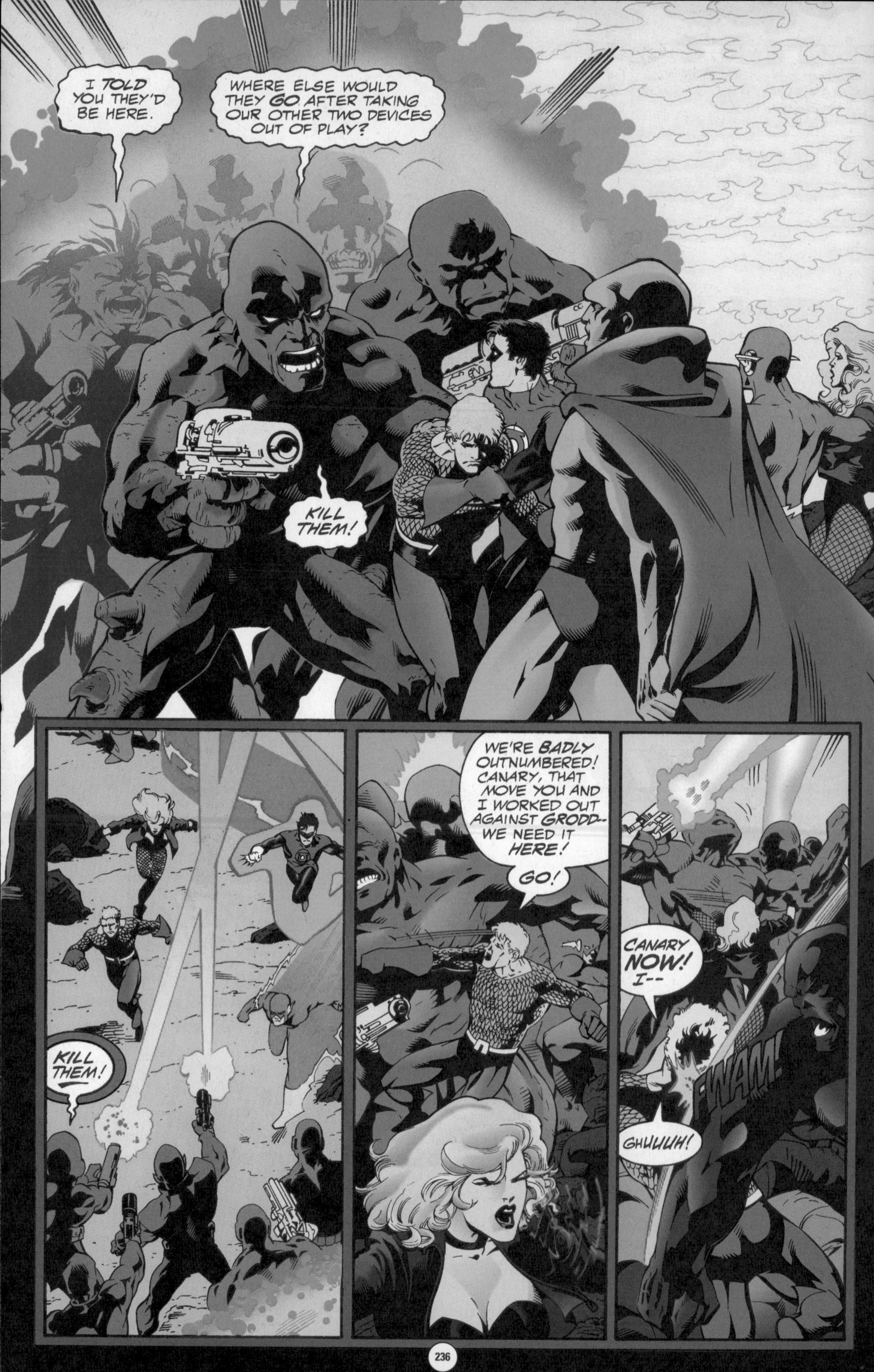
I TOLD YOU THEY'D BE HERE.
WHERE ELSE WOULD THEY GO AFTER TAKING OUR OTHER TWO DEVICES OUT OF PLAY?
KILL THEM!
KILL THEM!
WE'RE BADLY OUTNUMBERED! CANARY, THAT MOVE YOU AND I WORKED OUT AGAINST GRODD-- WE NEED IT HERE!
GO!
CANARY NOW! I--
FWAM!
GHUUUH!

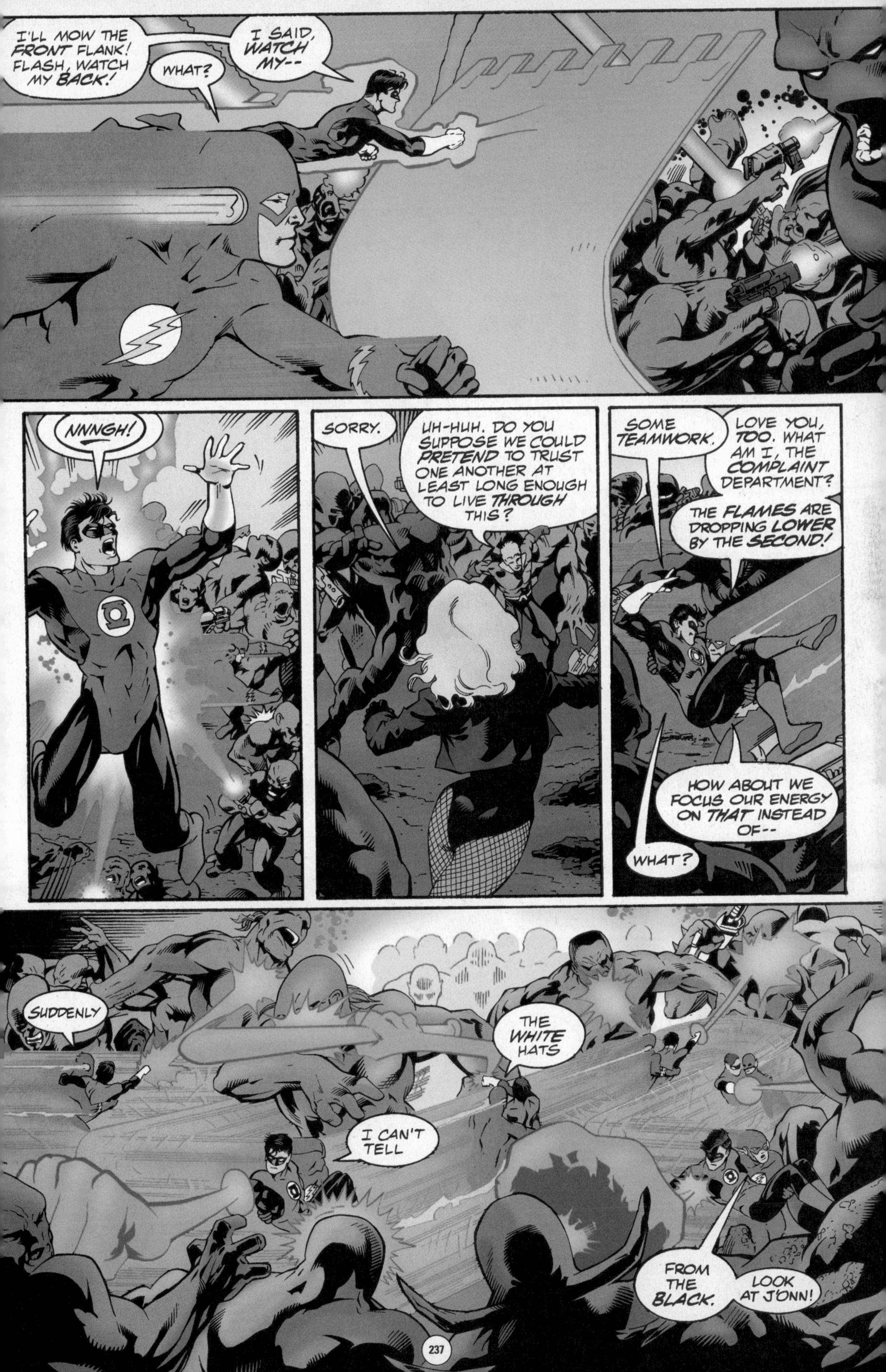
I'LL MOW THE FRONT FLANK! FLASH, WATCH MY BACK!
WHAT?
I SAID, WATCH MY--
NNNGH!
SORRY.
UH-HUH. DO YOU SUPPOSE WE COULD PRETEND TO TRUST ONE ANOTHER AT LEAST LONG ENOUGH TO LIVE THROUGH THIS?
SOME TEAMWORK.
LOVE YOU, TOO. WHAT AM I, THE COMPLAINT DEPARTMENT?
THE FLAMES ARE DROPPING LOWER BY THE SECOND!
HOW ABOUT WE FOCUS OUR ENERGY ON THAT INSTEAD OF--
WHAT?
SUDDENLY
THE WHITE HATS
I CAN'T TELL
FROM THE BLACK.
LOOK AT J'ONN!

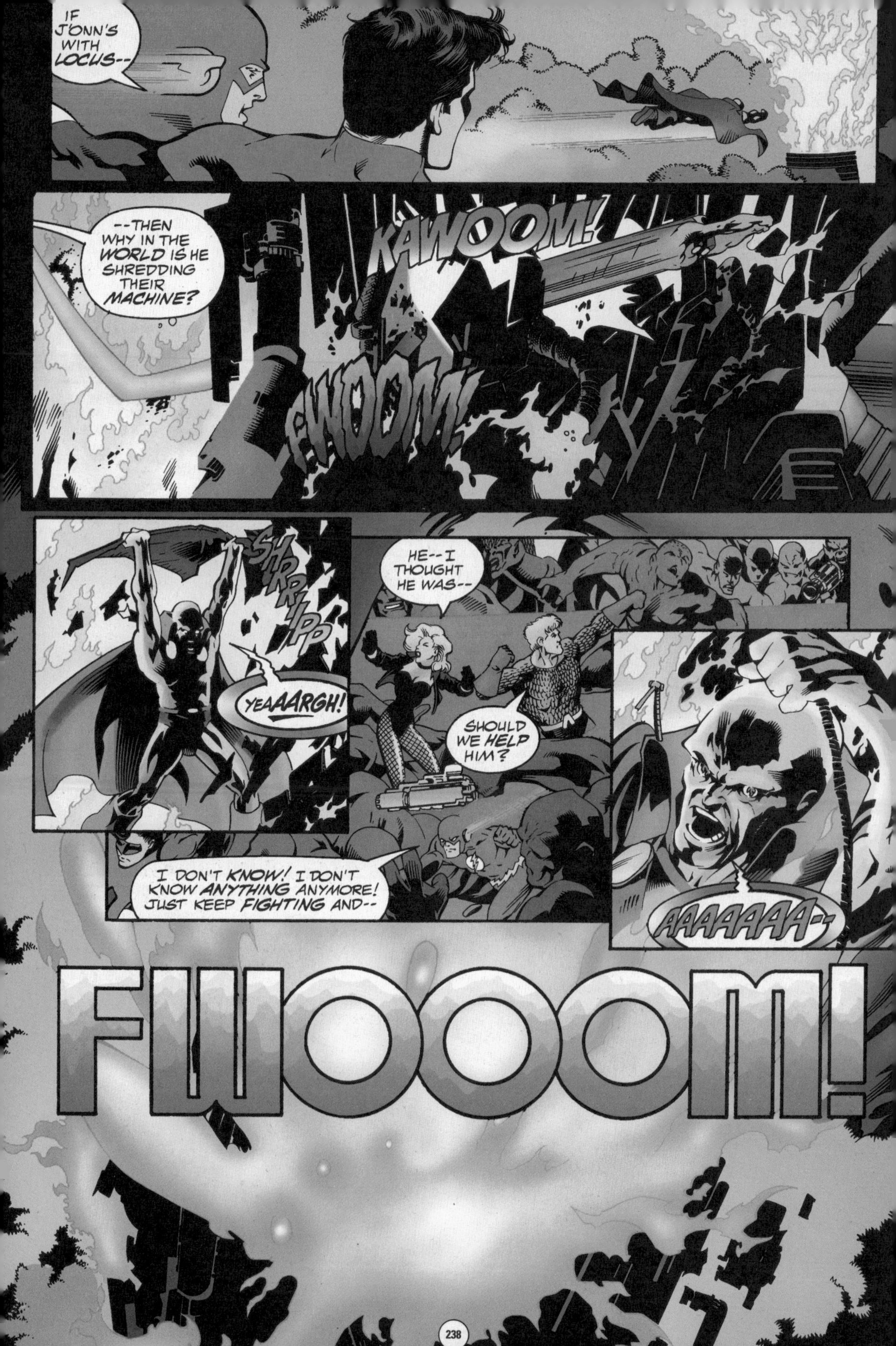
IF J'ONN'S WITH LOCUS--
--THEN WHY IN THE WORLD IS HE SHREDDING THEIR MACHINE?
KAWOOM!
FWOOM!
SHRRIPP
YEAAARGH!
HE--I THOUGHT HE WAS--
SHOULD WE HELP HIM?
I DON'T KNOW! I DON'T KNOW ANYTHING ANYMORE! JUST KEEP FIGHTING AND--
AAAAAAA--
FWOOOM!

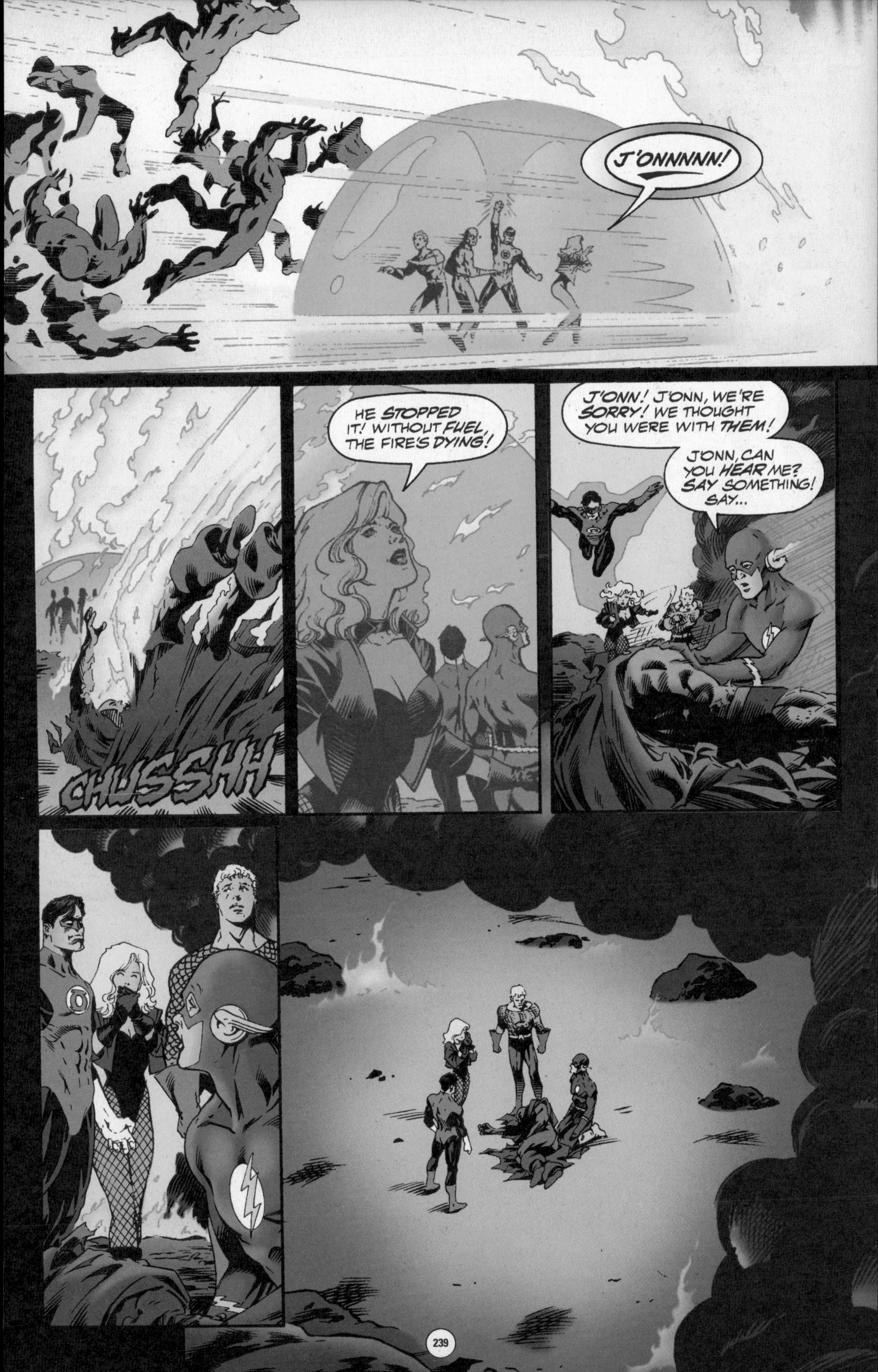
J'ONNNNN!
CHUSSHH
HE STOPPED IT! WITHOUT FUEL, THE FIRE'S DYING!
J'ONN! J'ONN, WE'RE SORRY! WE THOUGHT YOU WERE WITH THEM!
J'ONN, CAN YOU HEAR ME? SAY SOMETHING! SAY...

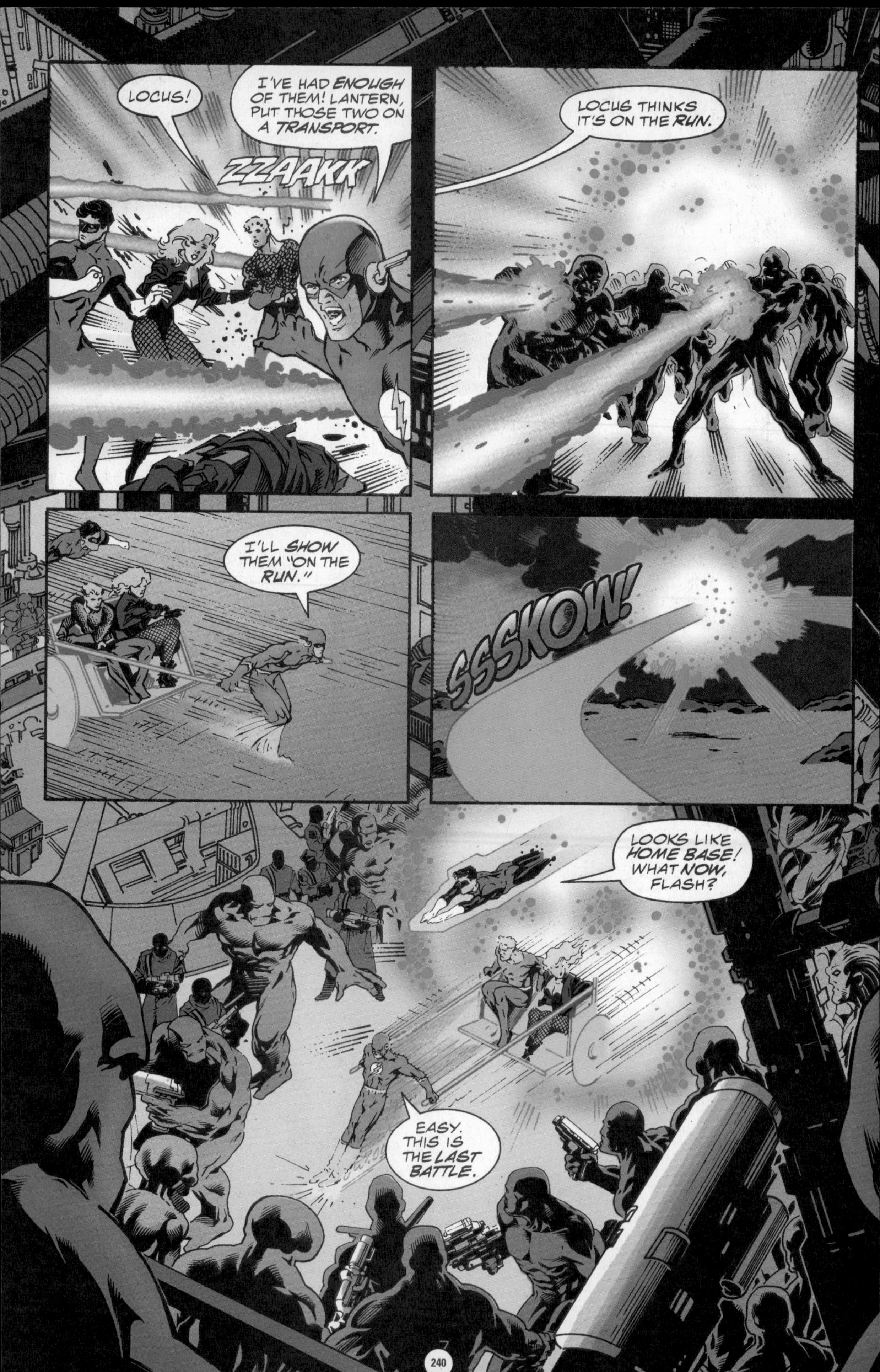
LOCUS!
I'VE HAD ENOUGH OF THEM! LANTERN, PUT THOSE TWO ON A TRANSPORT.
ZZAAKK
LOCUS THINKS IT'S ON THE RUN.
I'LL SHOW THEM "ON THE RUN."
SSSKOW!
LOOKS LIKE HOME BASE! WHAT NOW, FLASH?
EASY. THIS IS THE LAST BATTLE.

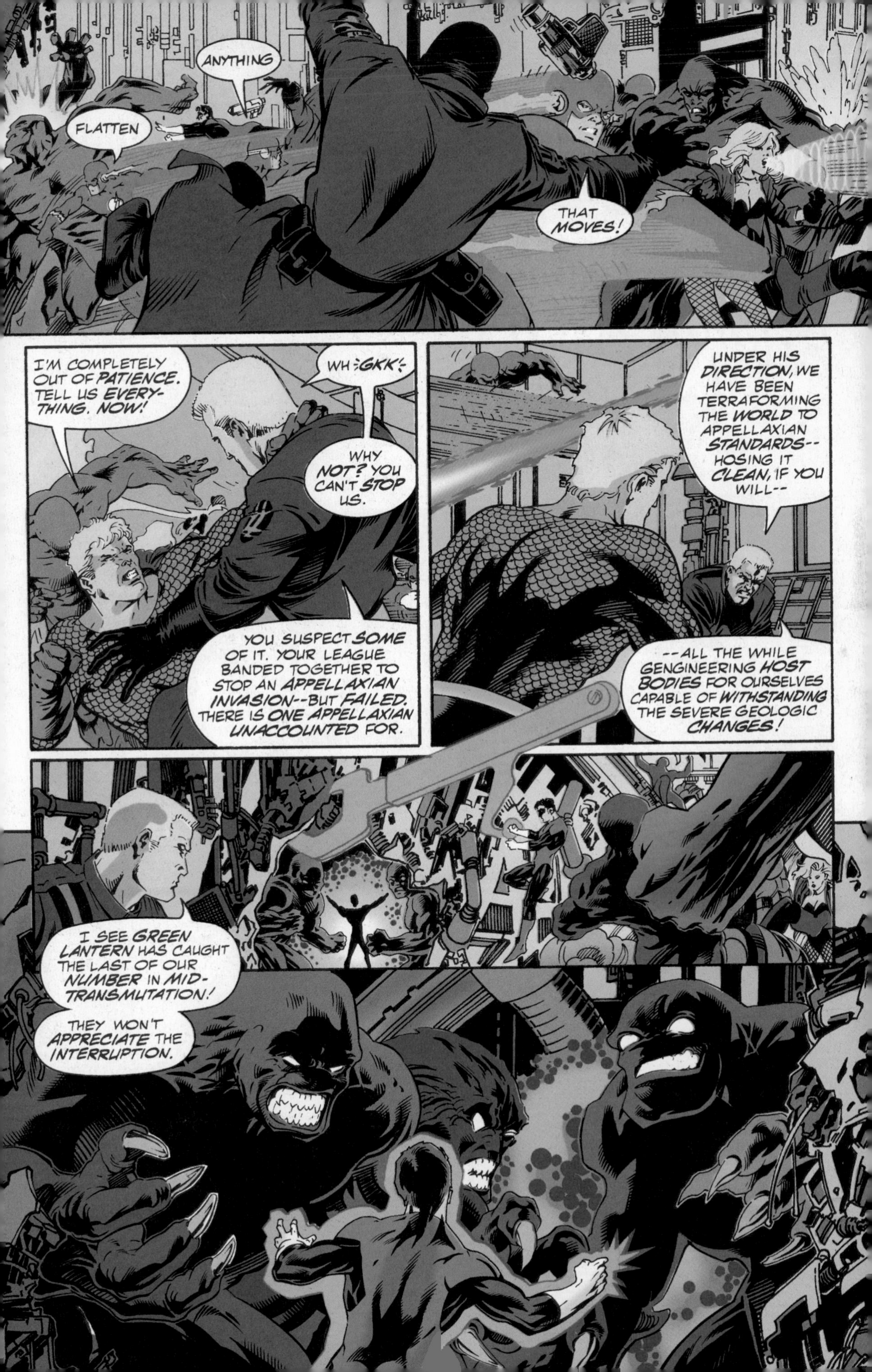
ANYTHING
FLATTEN
THAT MOVES!
I'M COMPLETELY OUT OF PATIENCE. TELL US EVERYTHING. NOW!
WH -GKK-
WHY NOT? YOU CAN'T STOP US.
YOU SUSPECT SOME OF IT. YOUR LEAGUE BANDED TOGETHER TO STOP AN APPELLAXIAN INVASION--BUT FAILED. THERE IS ONE APPELLAXIAN UNACCOUNTED FOR.
UNDER HIS DIRECTION, WE HAVE BEEN TERRAFORMING THE WORLD TO APPELLAXIAN STANDARDS--HOSING IT CLEAN, IF YOU WILL--
--ALL THE WHILE GENGINEERING HOST BODIES FOR OURSELVES CAPABLE OF WITHSTANDING THE SEVERE GEOLOGIC CHANGES!
I SEE GREEN LANTERN HAS CAUGHT THE LAST OF OUR NUMBER IN MID-TRANSMUTATION!
THEY WON'T APPRECIATE THE INTERRUPTION.

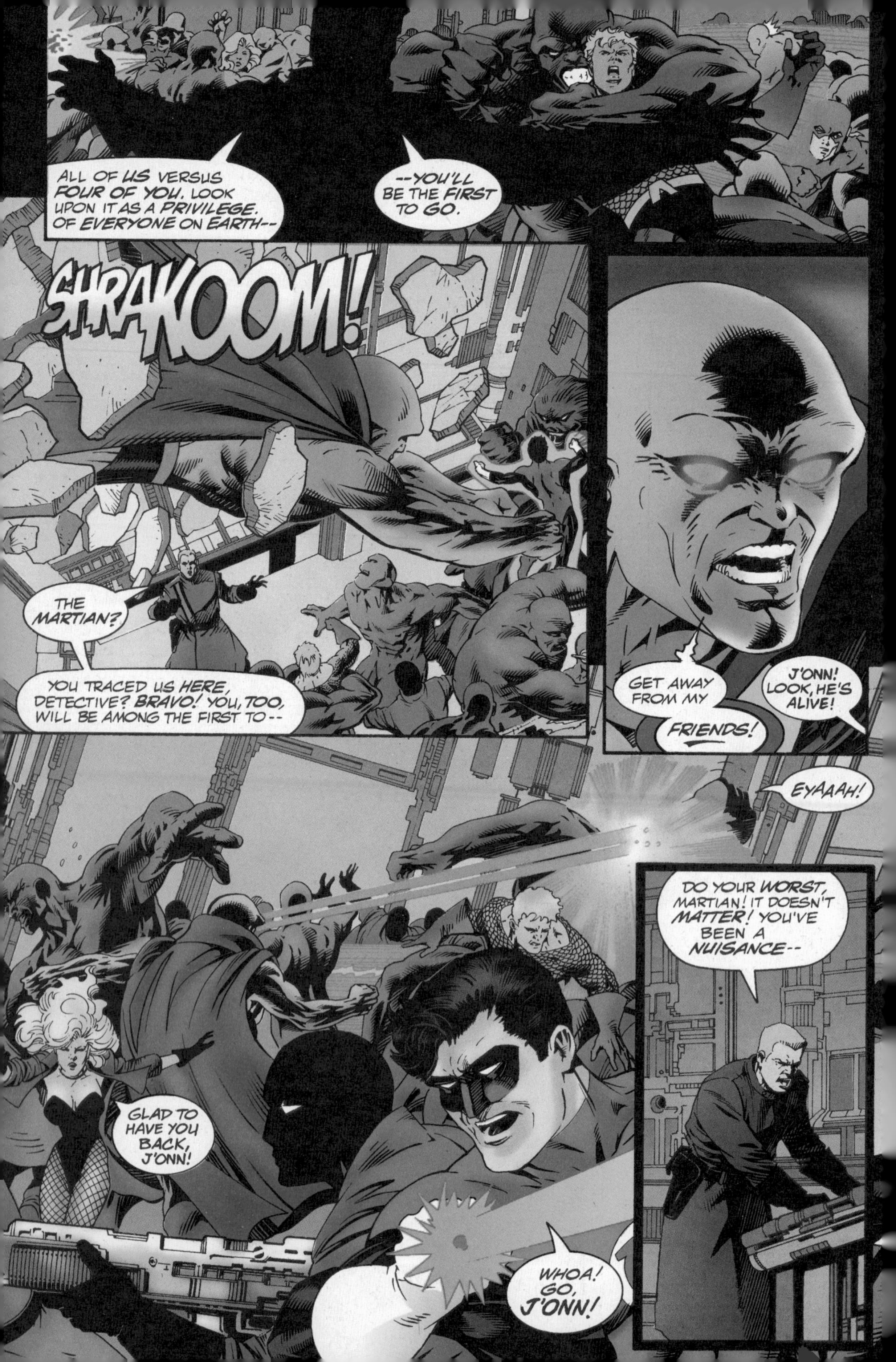
ALL OF US VERSUS FOUR OF YOU. LOOK UPON IT AS A PRIVILEGE. OF EVERYONE ON EARTH--
--YOU'LL BE THE FIRST TO GO.
SHRAKOOM!
THE MARTIAN?
YOU TRACED US HERE, DETECTIVE? BRAVO! YOU, TOO, WILL BE AMONG THE FIRST TO--
GET AWAY FROM MY FRIENDS!
J'ONN! LOOK, HE'S ALIVE!
EYAAAH!
DO YOUR WORST, MARTIAN! IT DOESN'T MATTER! YOU'VE BEEN A NUISANCE--
GLAD TO HAVE YOU BACK, J'ONN!
WHOA! GO, J'ONN!

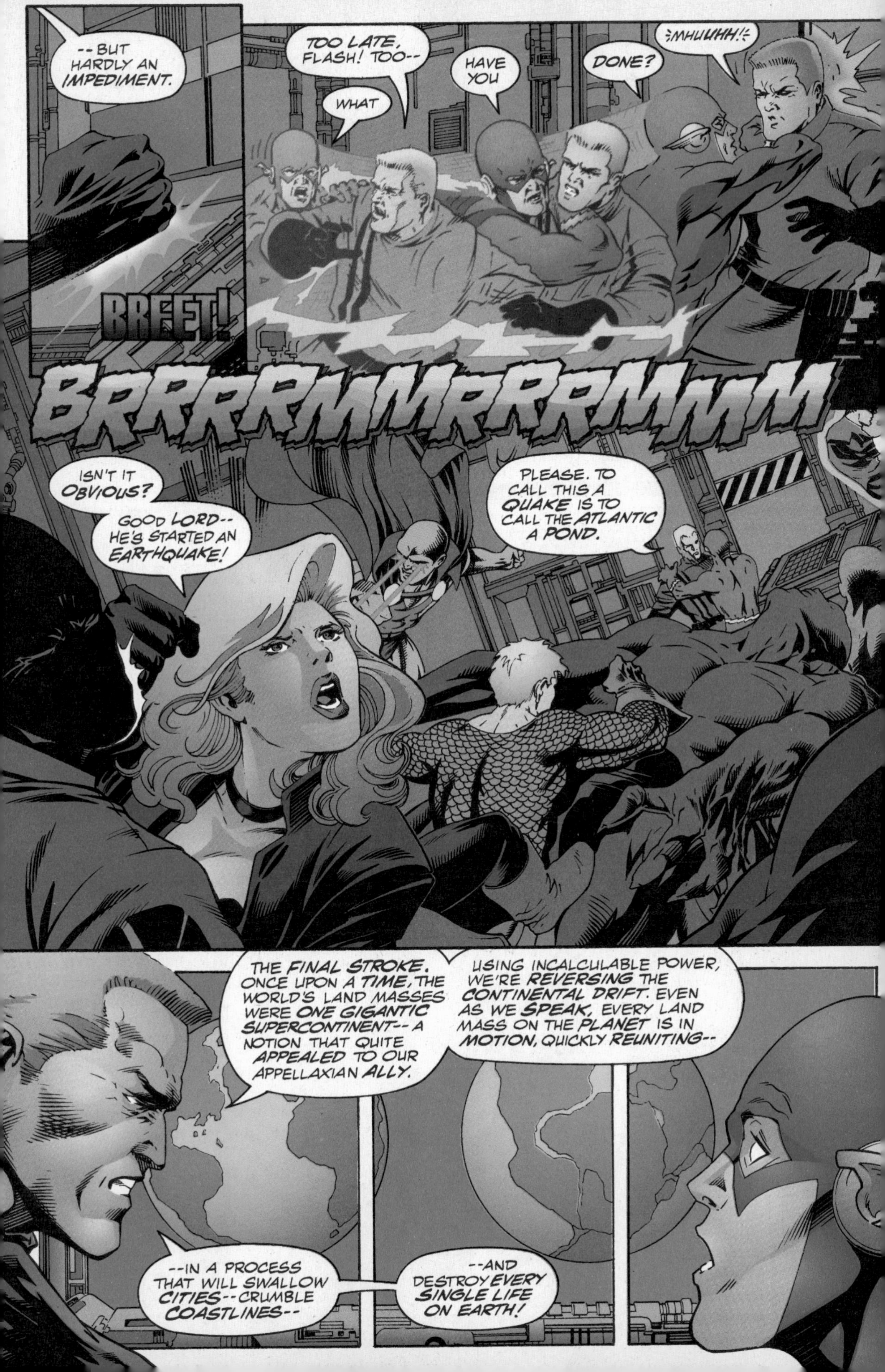
--BUT HARDLY AN IMPEDIMENT.
BREET!
TOO LATE, FLASH! TOO--
WHAT
HAVE YOU
DONE?
MHUUHH!
BRRRRMMMRRRRMMMM
ISN'T IT OBVIOUS?
GOOD LORD-- HE'S STARTED AN EARTHQUAKE!
PLEASE. TO CALL THIS A QUAKE IS TO CALL THE ATLANTIC A POND.
THE FINAL STROKE. ONCE UPON A TIME, THE WORLD'S LAND MASSES WERE ONE GIGANTIC SUPERCONTINENT-- A NOTION THAT QUITE APPEALED TO OUR APPELLAXIAN ALLY.
USING INCALCULABLE POWER, WE'RE REVERSING THE CONTINENTAL DRIFT. EVEN AS WE SPEAK, EVERY LAND MASS ON THE PLANET IS IN MOTION, QUICKLY REUNITING--
--IN A PROCESS THAT WILL SWALLOW CITIES--CRUMBLE COASTLINES--
--AND DESTROY EVERY SINGLE LIFE ON EARTH!

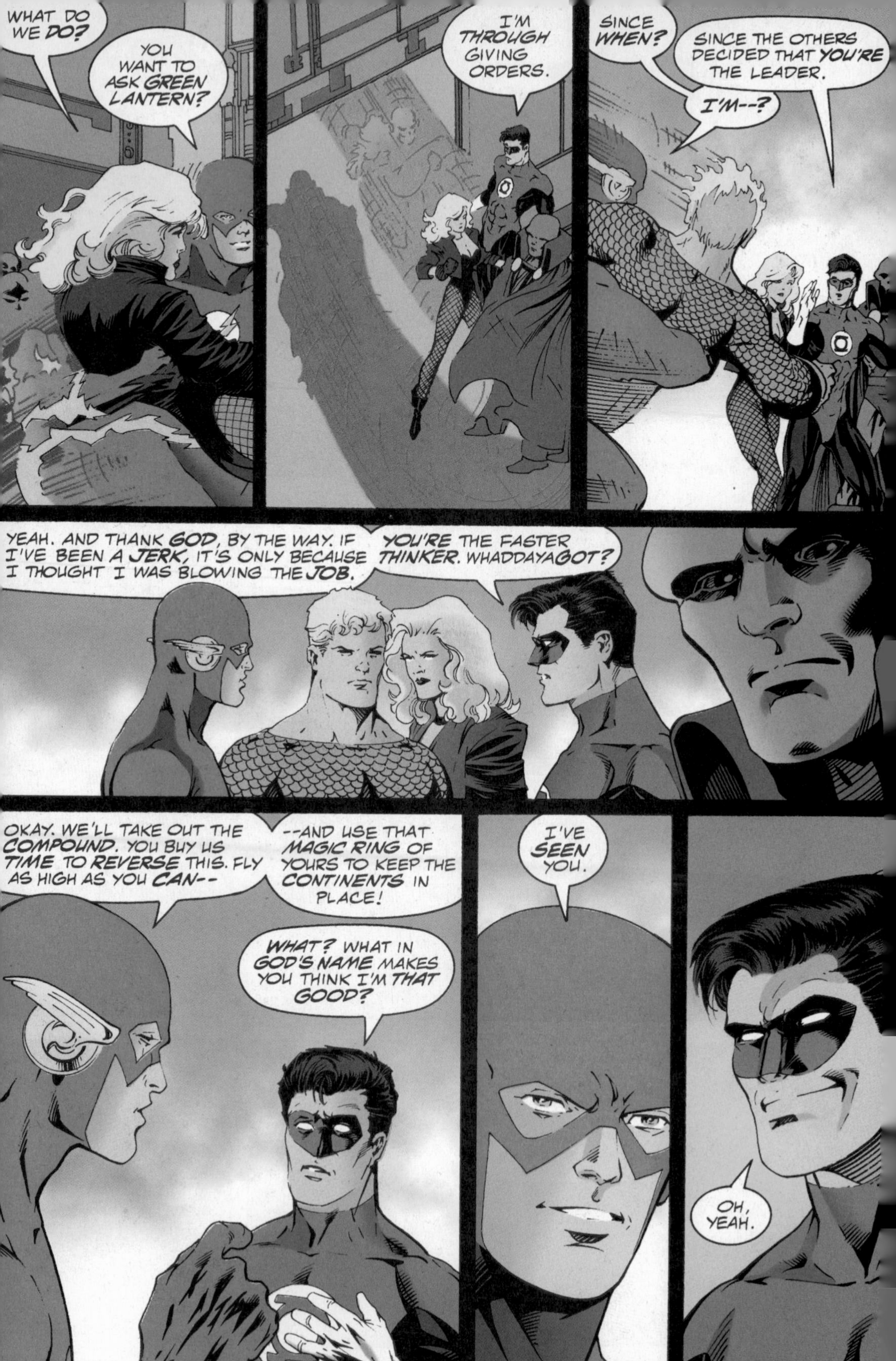
WHAT DO WE DO?
YOU WANT TO ASK GREEN LANTERN?
I'M THROUGH GIVING ORDERS.
SINCE WHEN?
SINCE THE OTHERS DECIDED THAT YOU'RE THE LEADER.
I'M--?
YEAH. AND THANK GOD, BY THE WAY. IF I'VE BEEN A JERK, IT'S ONLY BECAUSE I THOUGHT I WAS BLOWING THE JOB.
YOU'RE THE FASTER THINKER. WHADDAYA GOT?
OKAY. WE'LL TAKE OUT THE COMPOUND. YOU BUY US TIME TO REVERSE THIS. FLY AS HIGH AS YOU CAN--
--AND USE THAT MAGIC RING OF YOURS TO KEEP THE CONTINENTS IN PLACE!
WHAT? WHAT IN GOD'S NAME MAKES YOU THINK I'M THAT GOOD?
I'VE SEEN YOU.
OH, YEAH.

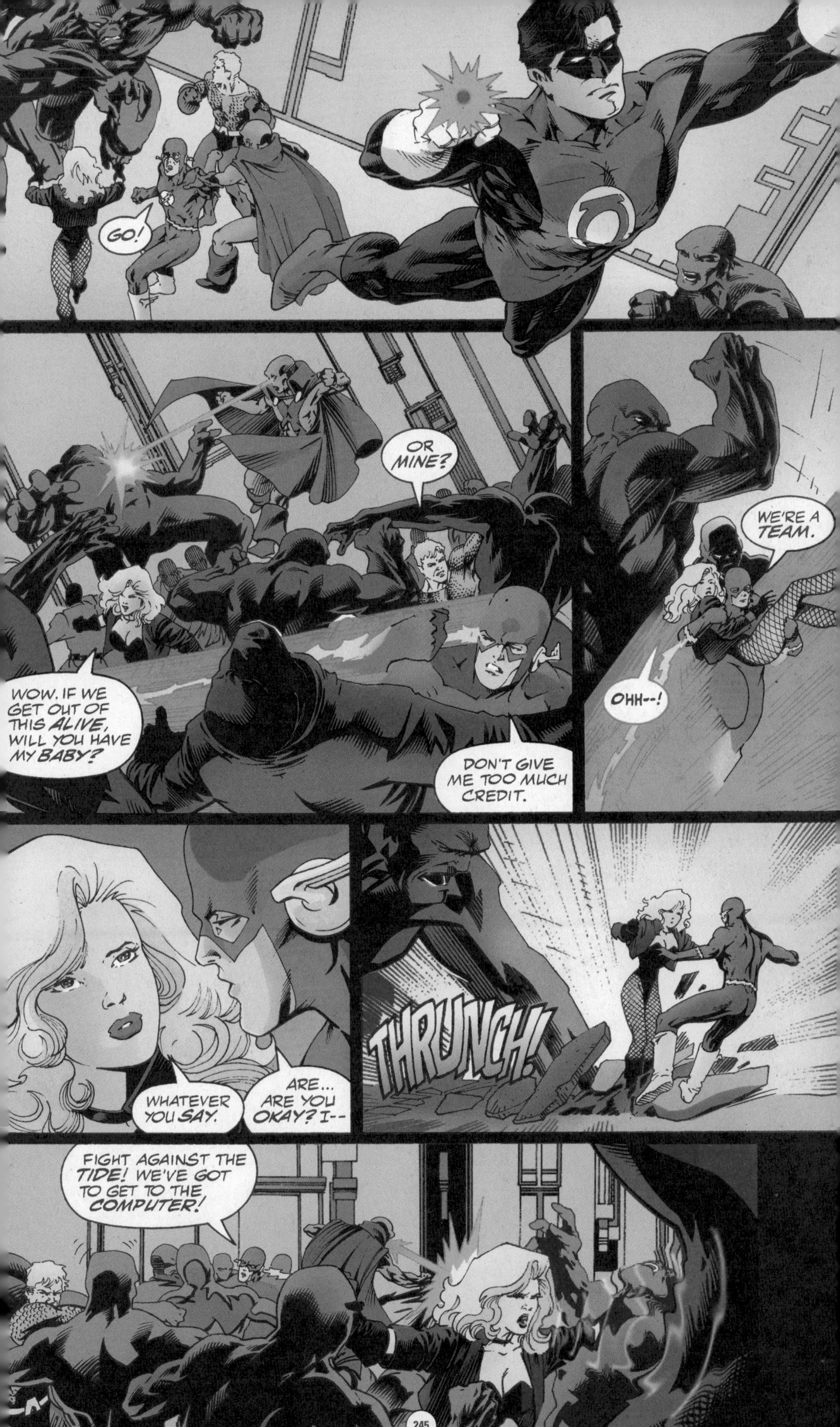
GO!
OR MINE?
WE'RE A TEAM.
WOW. IF WE GET OUT OF THIS ALIVE, WILL YOU HAVE MY BABY?
OHH--!
DON'T GIVE ME TOO MUCH CREDIT.
WHATEVER YOU SAY.
ARE... ARE YOU OKAY? I--
THRUNCH!
FIGHT AGAINST THE TIDE! WE'VE GOT TO GET TO THE COMPUTER!

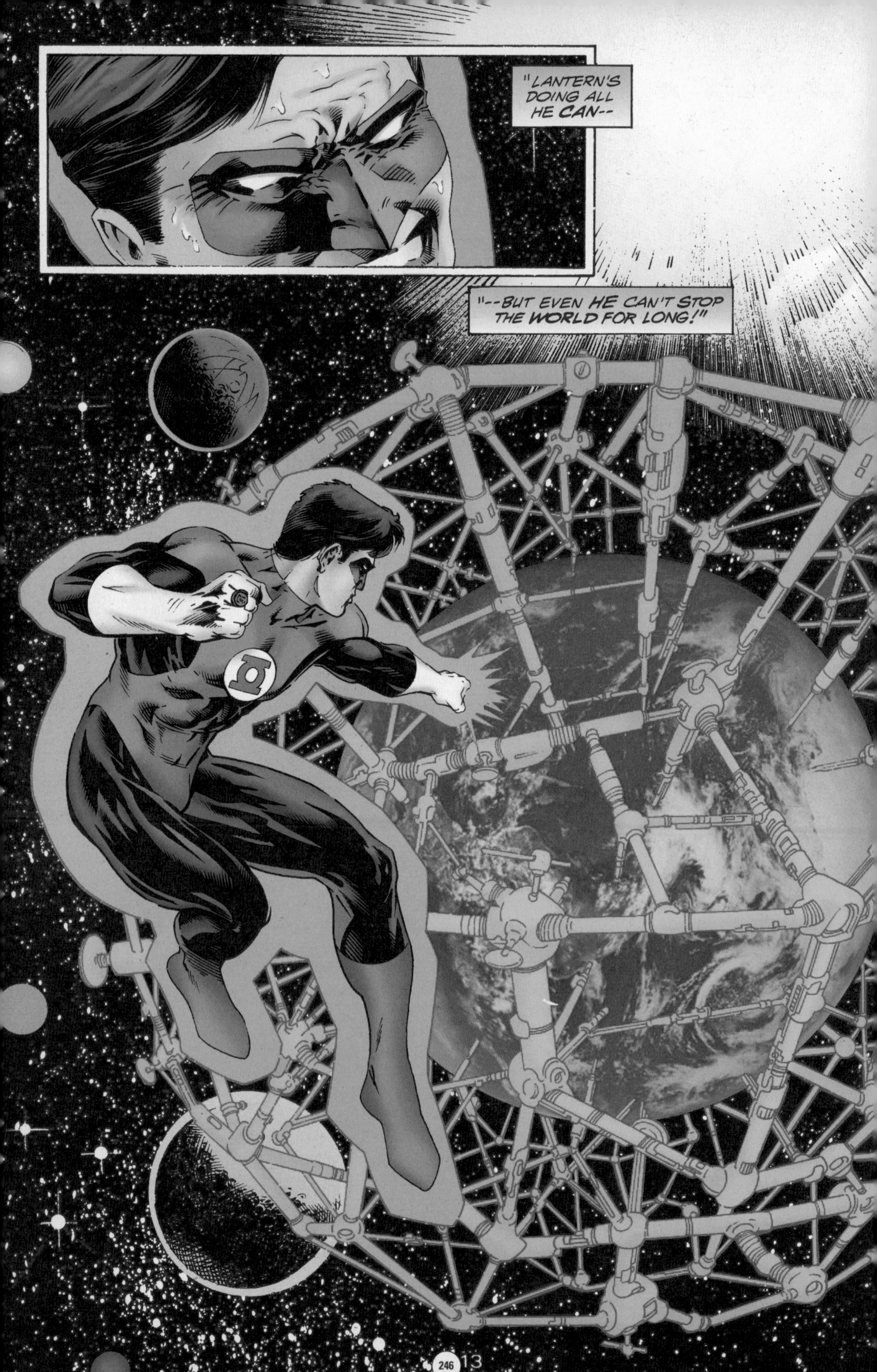
"LANTERN'S DOING ALL HE CAN--
"--BUT EVEN HE CAN'T STOP THE WORLD FOR LONG!"

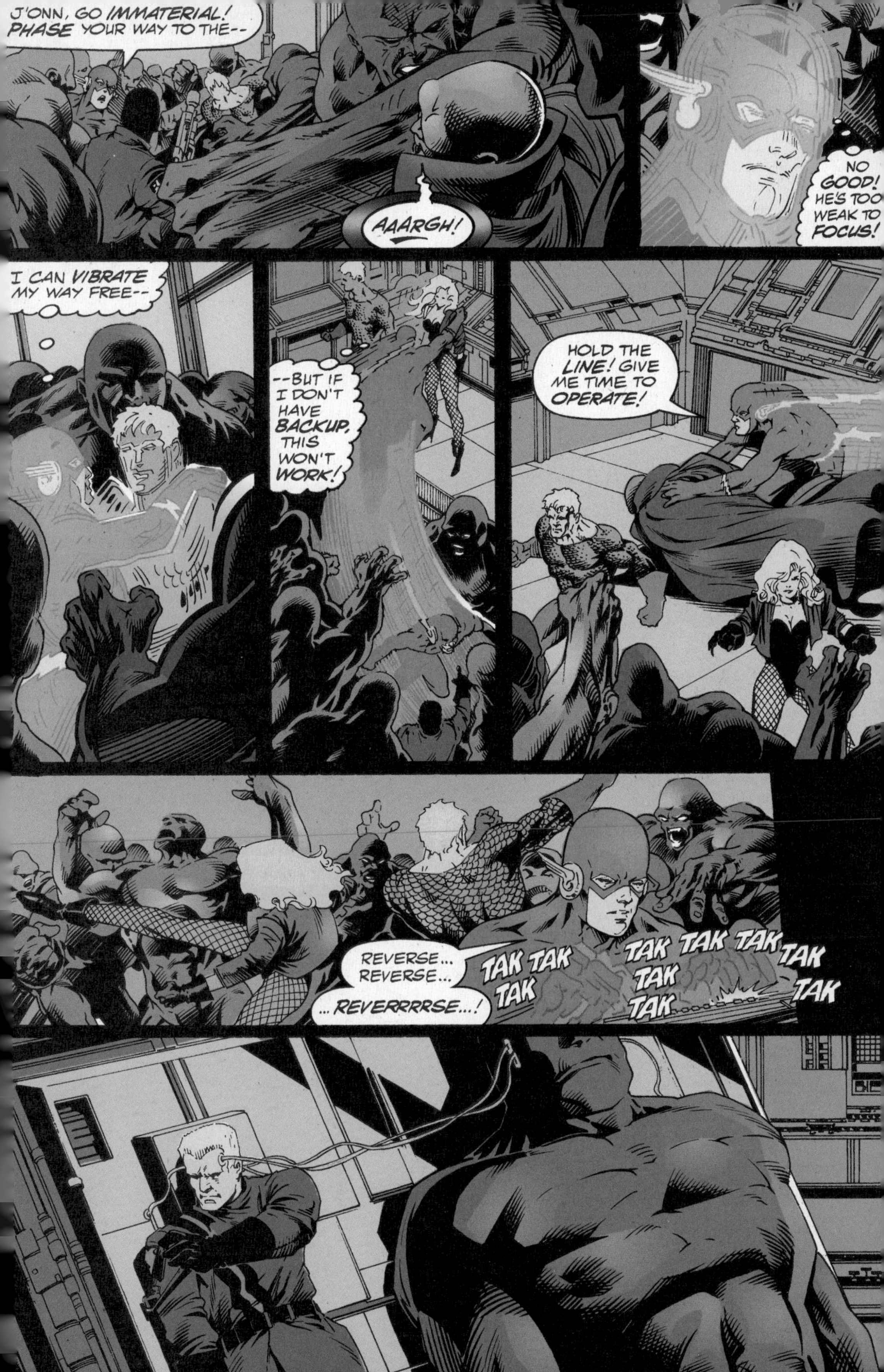
J'ONN, GO IMMATERIAL! PHASE YOUR WAY TO THE--
AAARGH!
NO GOOD! HE'S TOO WEAK TO FOCUS!
I CAN VIBRATE MY WAY FREE--
--BUT IF I DON'T HAVE BACKUP, THIS WON'T WORK!
HOLD THE LINE! GIVE ME TIME TO OPERATE!
REVERSE... REVERSE...
...REVERRRRSE...!
TAK TAK TAK
TAK TAK TAK
TAK TAK TAK
TAK TAK

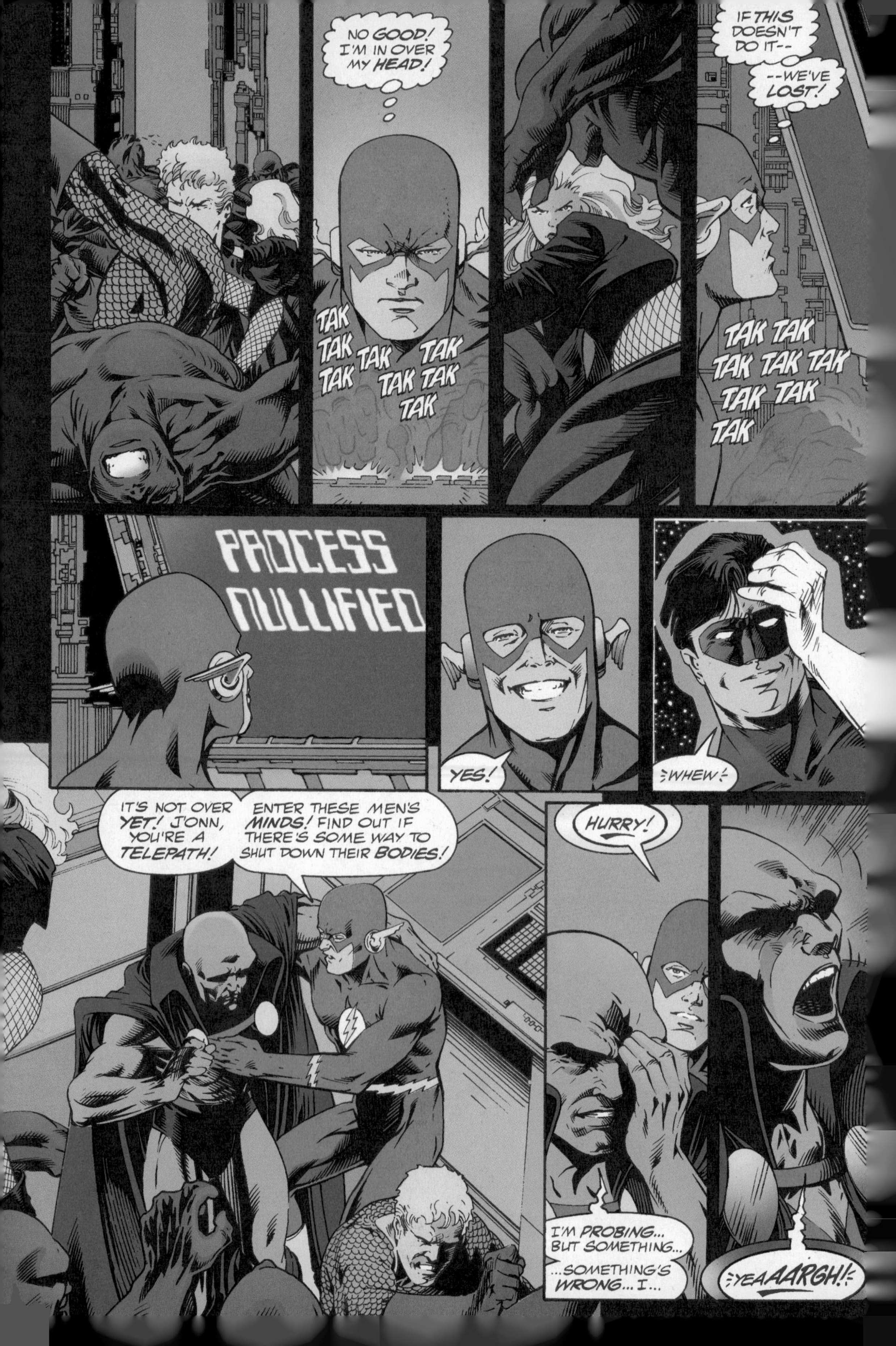
NO GOOD! I'M IN OVER MY HEAD!
TAK TAK TAK TAK TAK TAK TAK TAK
IF THIS DOESN'T DO IT--
--WE'VE LOST!
TAK TAK TAK TAK TAK TAK TAK TAK
PROCESS NULLIFIED
YES!
WHEW
IT'S NOT OVER YET! J'ONN, YOU'RE A TELEPATH!
ENTER THESE MEN'S MINDS! FIND OUT IF THERE'S SOME WAY TO SHUT DOWN THEIR BODIES!
HURRY!
I'M PROBING... BUT SOMETHING...
...SOMETHING'S WRONG... I...
YEAAARGH!

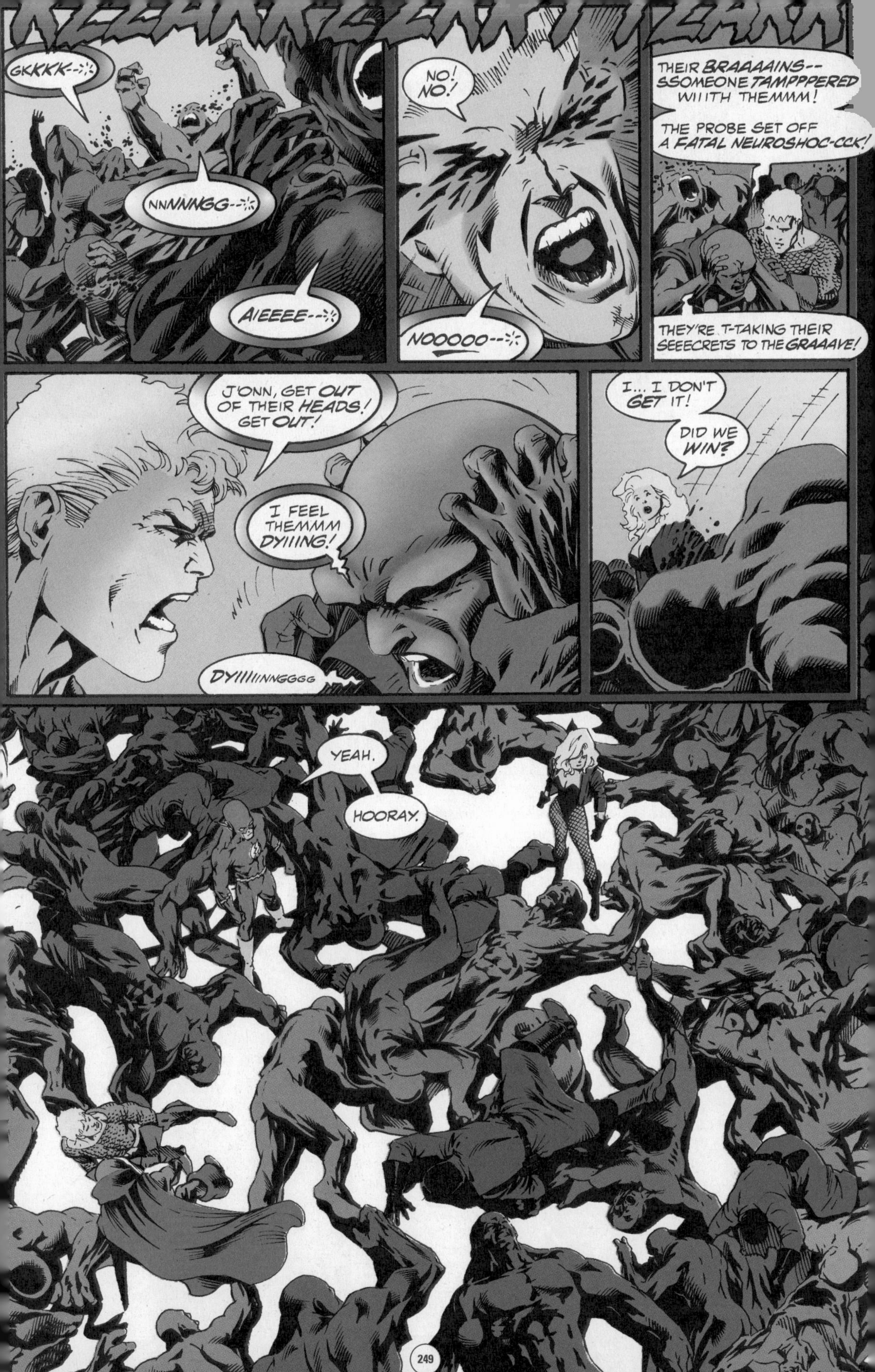
GKKKK--
NNNNNGG--
AIEEEE--
NO! NO!
NOOOOO--
THEIR BRAAAAINS-- SSOMEONE TAMPPPERED WIIITH THEMMM!
THE PROBE SET OFF A FATAL NEUROSHOC-CCK!
THEY'RE T-TAKING THEIR SEEECRETS TO THE GRAAAVE!
J'ONN, GET OUT OF THEIR HEADS! GET OUT!
I FEEL THEMMM DYIIING!
DYIIIINNGGGG
I... I DON'T GET IT!
DID WE WIN?
YEAH.
HOORAY.

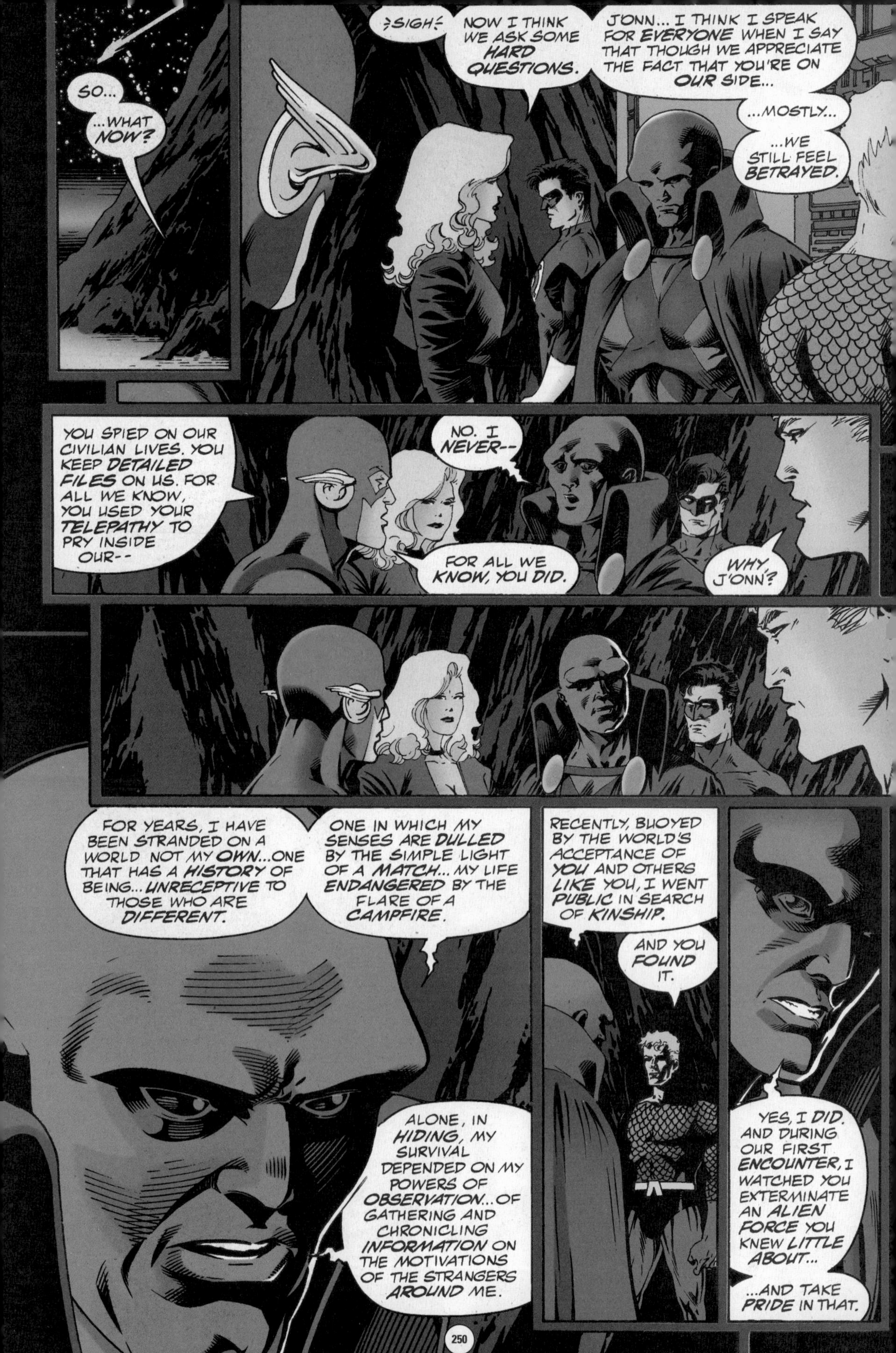

SO... ...WHAT NOW?
SIGH
NOW I THINK WE ASK SOME HARD QUESTIONS.
J'ONN... I THINK I SPEAK FOR EVERYONE WHEN I SAY THAT THOUGH WE APPRECIATE THE FACT THAT YOU'RE ON OUR SIDE...
...MOSTLY...
...WE STILL FEEL BETRAYED.
YOU SPIED ON OUR CIVILIAN LIVES. YOU KEEP DETAILED FILES ON US. FOR ALL WE KNOW, YOU USED YOUR TELEPATHY TO PRY INSIDE OUR--
NO. I NEVER--
FOR ALL WE KNOW, YOU DID.
WHY, J'ONN?
FOR YEARS, I HAVE BEEN STRANDED ON A WORLD NOT MY OWN...ONE THAT HAS A HISTORY OF BEING... UNRECEPTIVE TO THOSE WHO ARE DIFFERENT.
ONE IN WHICH MY SENSES ARE DULLED BY THE SIMPLE LIGHT OF A MATCH... MY LIFE ENDANGERED BY THE FLARE OF A CAMPFIRE.
ALONE, IN HIDING, MY SURVIVAL DEPENDED ON MY POWERS OF OBSERVATION...OF GATHERING AND CHRONICLING INFORMATION ON THE MOTIVATIONS OF THE STRANGERS AROUND ME.
RECENTLY, BUOYED BY THE WORLD'S ACCEPTANCE OF YOU AND OTHERS LIKE YOU, I WENT PUBLIC IN SEARCH OF KINSHIP.
AND YOU FOUND IT.
YES, I DID. AND DURING OUR FIRST ENCOUNTER, I WATCHED YOU EXTERMINATE AN ALIEN FORCE YOU KNEW LITTLE ABOUT...
...AND TAKE PRIDE IN THAT.

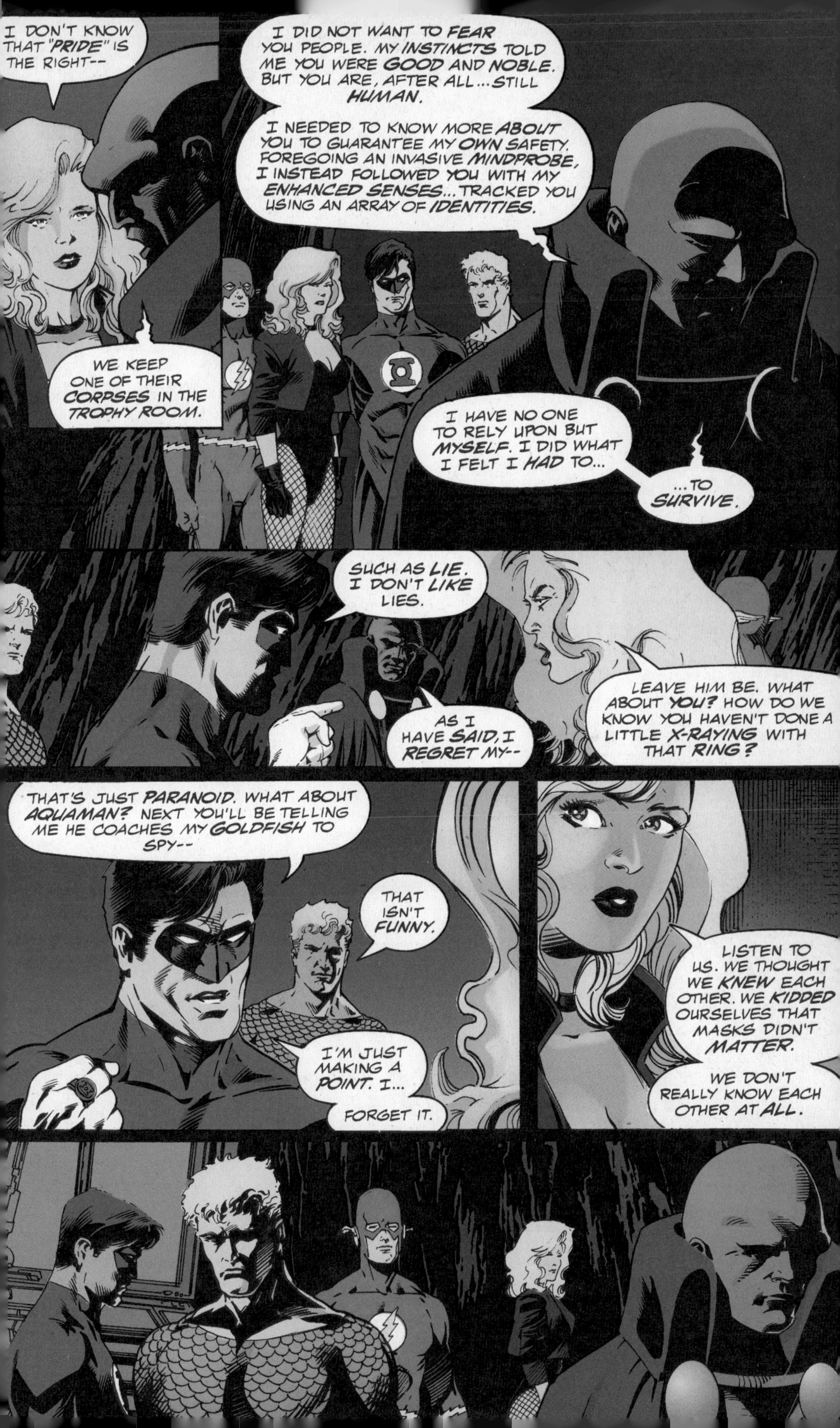

I DON'T KNOW THAT "PRIDE" IS THE RIGHT--
WE KEEP ONE OF THEIR CORPSES IN THE TROPHY ROOM.
I DID NOT WANT TO FEAR YOU PEOPLE. MY INSTINCTS TOLD ME YOU WERE GOOD AND NOBLE. BUT YOU ARE, AFTER ALL... STILL HUMAN.
I NEEDED TO KNOW MORE ABOUT YOU TO GUARANTEE MY OWN SAFETY. FOREGOING AN INVASIVE MINDPROBE, I INSTEAD FOLLOWED YOU WITH MY ENHANCED SENSES... TRACKED YOU USING AN ARRAY OF IDENTITIES.
I HAVE NO ONE TO RELY UPON BUT MYSELF. I DID WHAT I FELT I HAD TO...
...TO SURVIVE.
SUCH AS LIE. I DON'T LIKE LIES.
AS I HAVE SAID, I REGRET MY--
LEAVE HIM BE. WHAT ABOUT YOU? HOW DO WE KNOW YOU HAVEN'T DONE A LITTLE X-RAYING WITH THAT RING?
THAT'S JUST PARANOID. WHAT ABOUT AQUAMAN? NEXT YOU'LL BE TELLING ME HE COACHES MY GOLDFISH TO SPY--
THAT ISN'T FUNNY.
I'M JUST MAKING A POINT. I...
FORGET IT.
LISTEN TO US. WE THOUGHT WE KNEW EACH OTHER. WE KIDDED OURSELVES THAT MASKS DIDN'T MATTER.
WE DON'T REALLY KNOW EACH OTHER AT ALL.

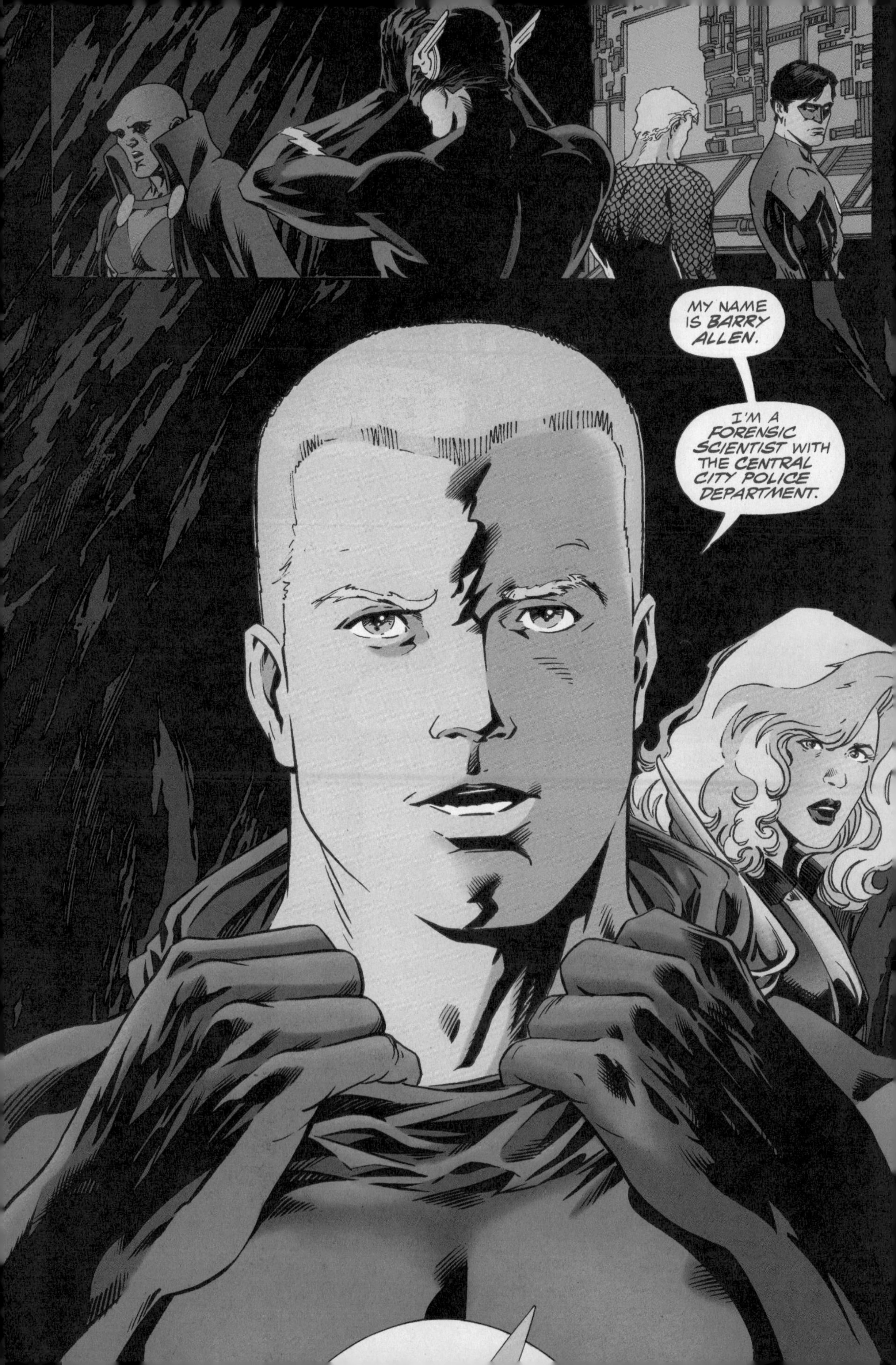
MY NAME IS BARRY ALLEN.
I'M A FORENSIC SCIENTIST WITH THE CENTRAL CITY POLICE DEPARTMENT.

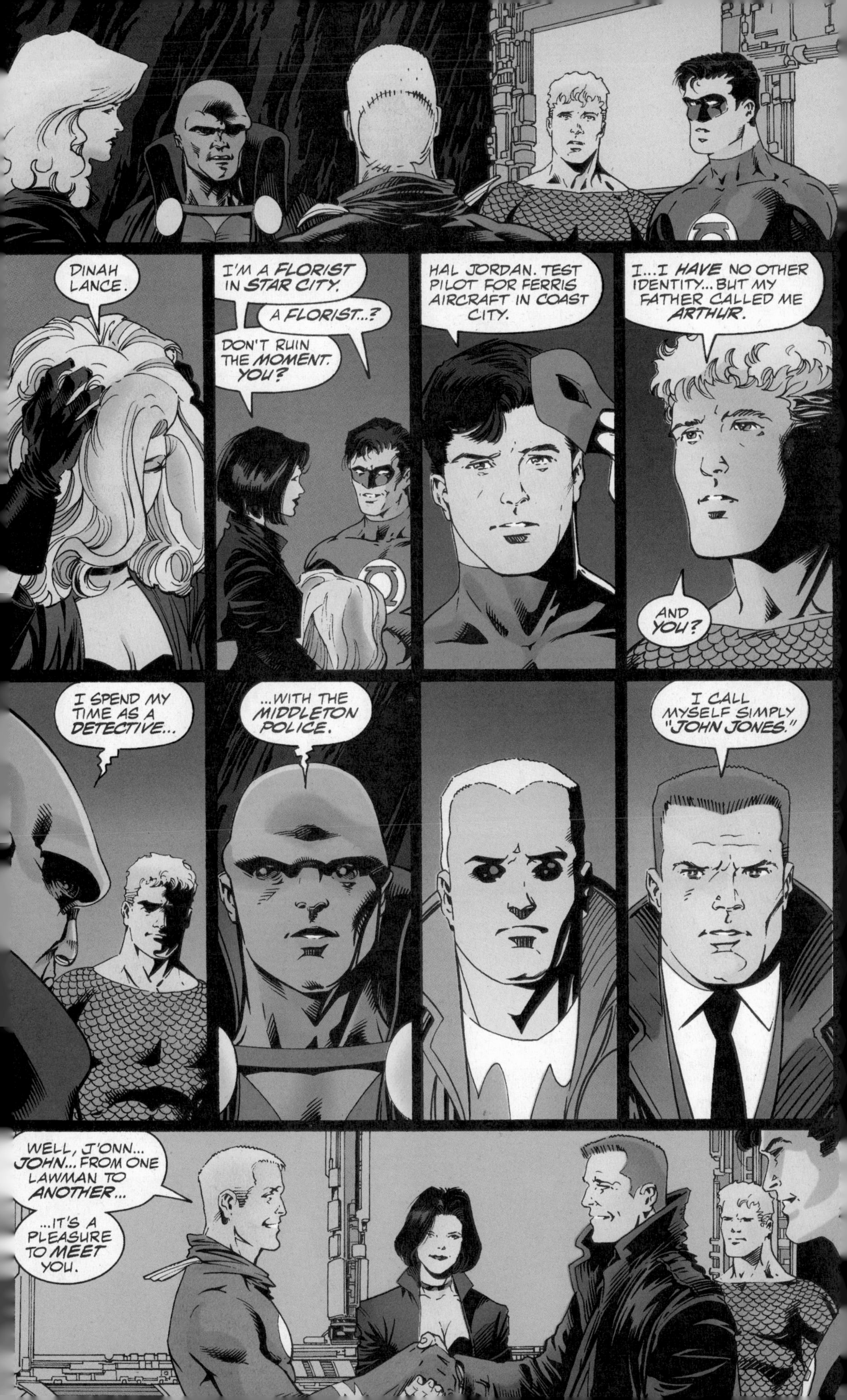
DINAH LANCE.
I'M A FLORIST IN STAR CITY.
A FLORIST...?
DON'T RUIN THE MOMENT. YOU?
HAL JORDAN. TEST PILOT FOR FERRIS AIRCRAFT IN COAST CITY.
I...I HAVE NO OTHER IDENTITY... BUT MY FATHER CALLED ME ARTHUR.
AND YOU?
I SPEND MY TIME AS A DETECTIVE...
...WITH THE MIDDLETON POLICE.
I CALL MYSELF SIMPLY "JOHN JONES."
WELL, J'ONN... JOHN... FROM ONE LAWMAN TO ANOTHER...
...IT'S A PLEASURE TO MEET YOU.

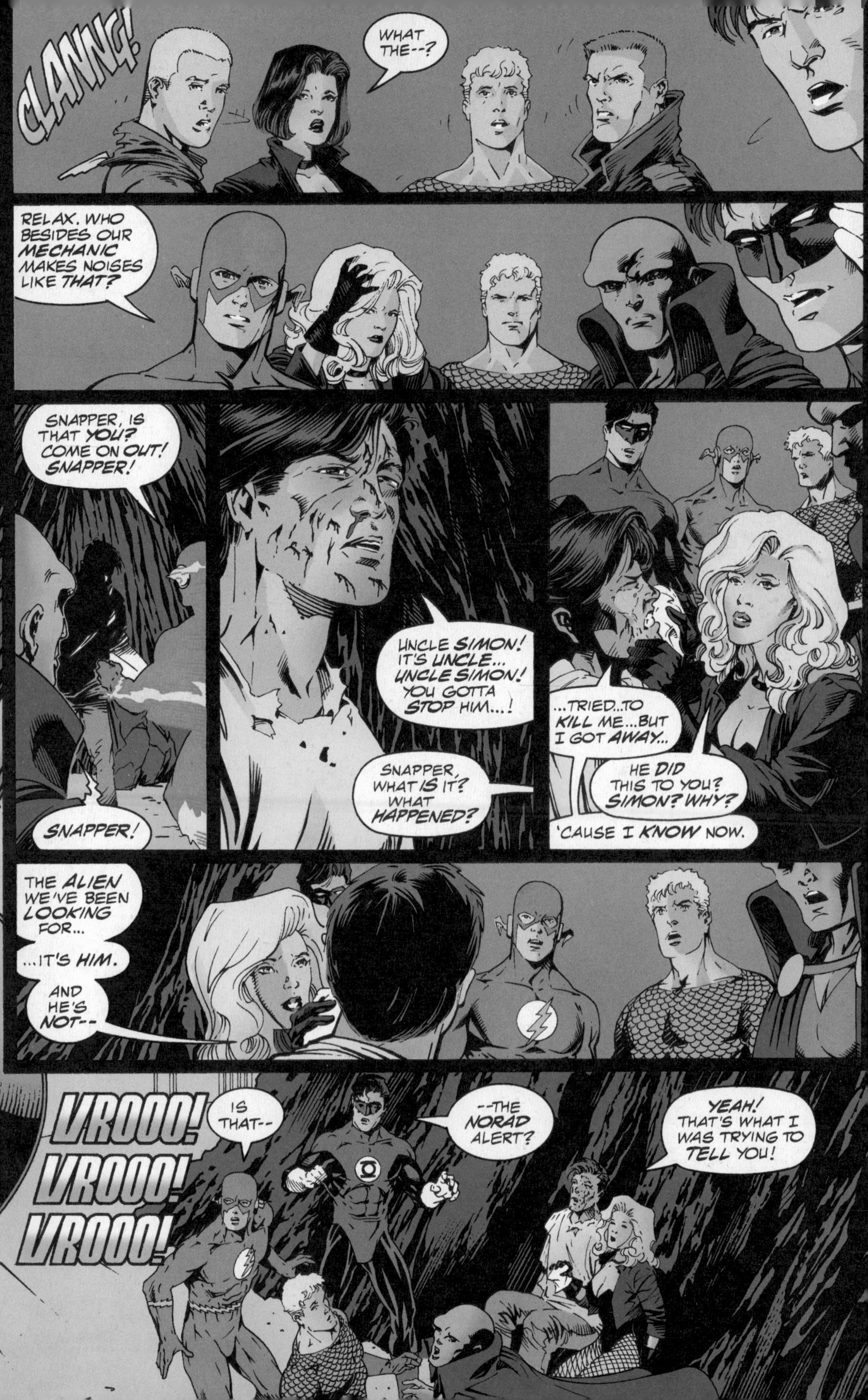
CLANNG!
WHAT THE--?
RELAX. WHO BESIDES OUR MECHANIC MAKES NOISES LIKE THAT?
SNAPPER, IS THAT YOU? COME ON OUT! SNAPPER!
SNAPPER!
UNCLE SIMON! IT'S UNCLE... UNCLE SIMON! YOU GOTTA STOP HIM...!
SNAPPER, WHAT IS IT? WHAT HAPPENED?
...TRIED...TO KILL ME...BUT I GOT AWAY...
HE DID THIS TO YOU? SIMON? WHY?
'CAUSE I KNOW NOW.
THE ALIEN WE'VE BEEN LOOKING FOR...
...IT'S HIM.
AND HE'S NOT--
VROOO! VROOO! VROOO!
IS THAT--
--THE NORAD ALERT?
YEAH! THAT'S WHAT I WAS TRYING TO TELL YOU!

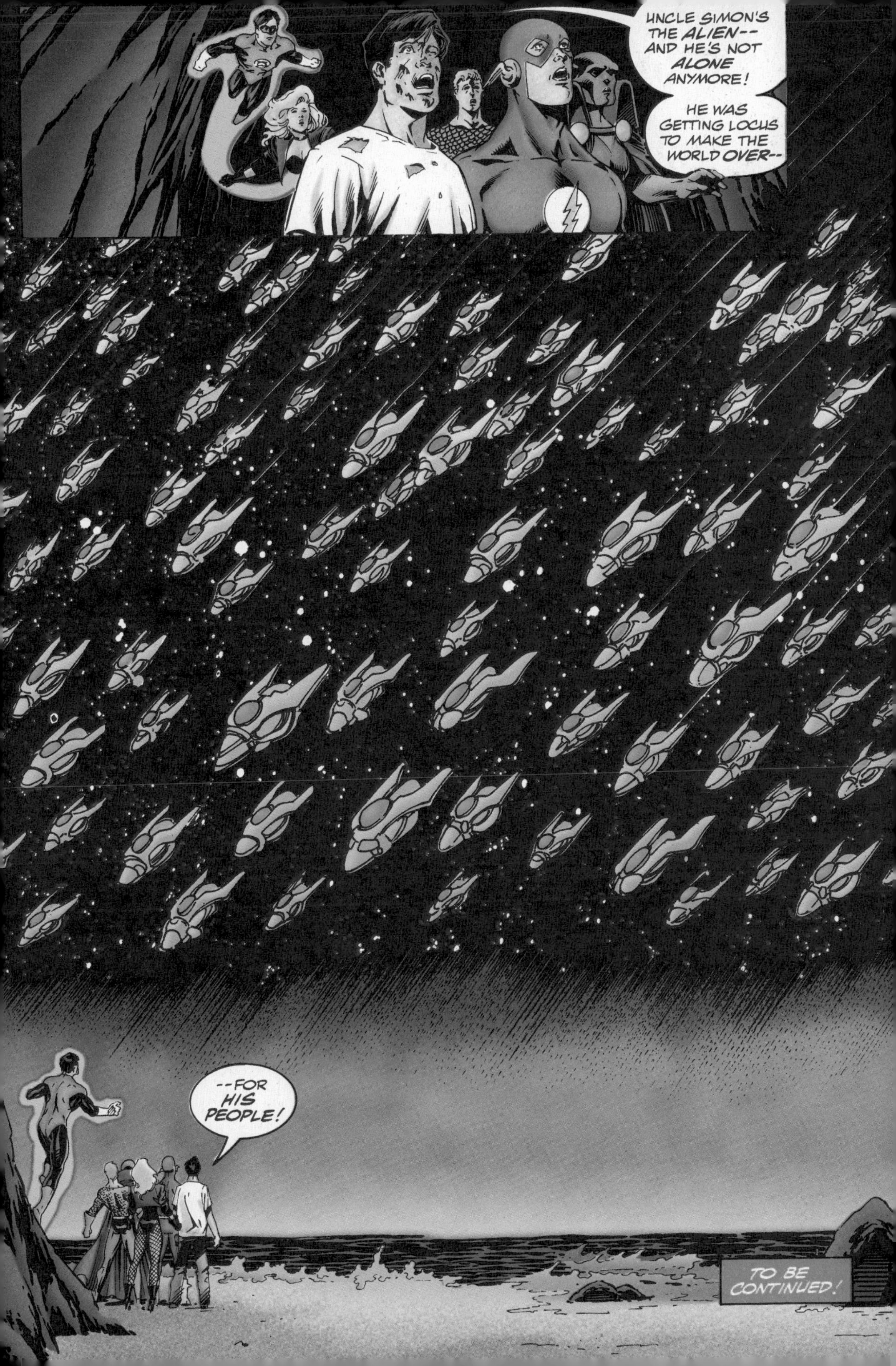
UNCLE SIMON'S THE ALIEN-- AND HE'S NOT ALONE ANYMORE!
HE WAS GETTING LOCUS TO MAKE THE WORLD OVER--
--FOR HIS PEOPLE!
TO BE CONTINUED!

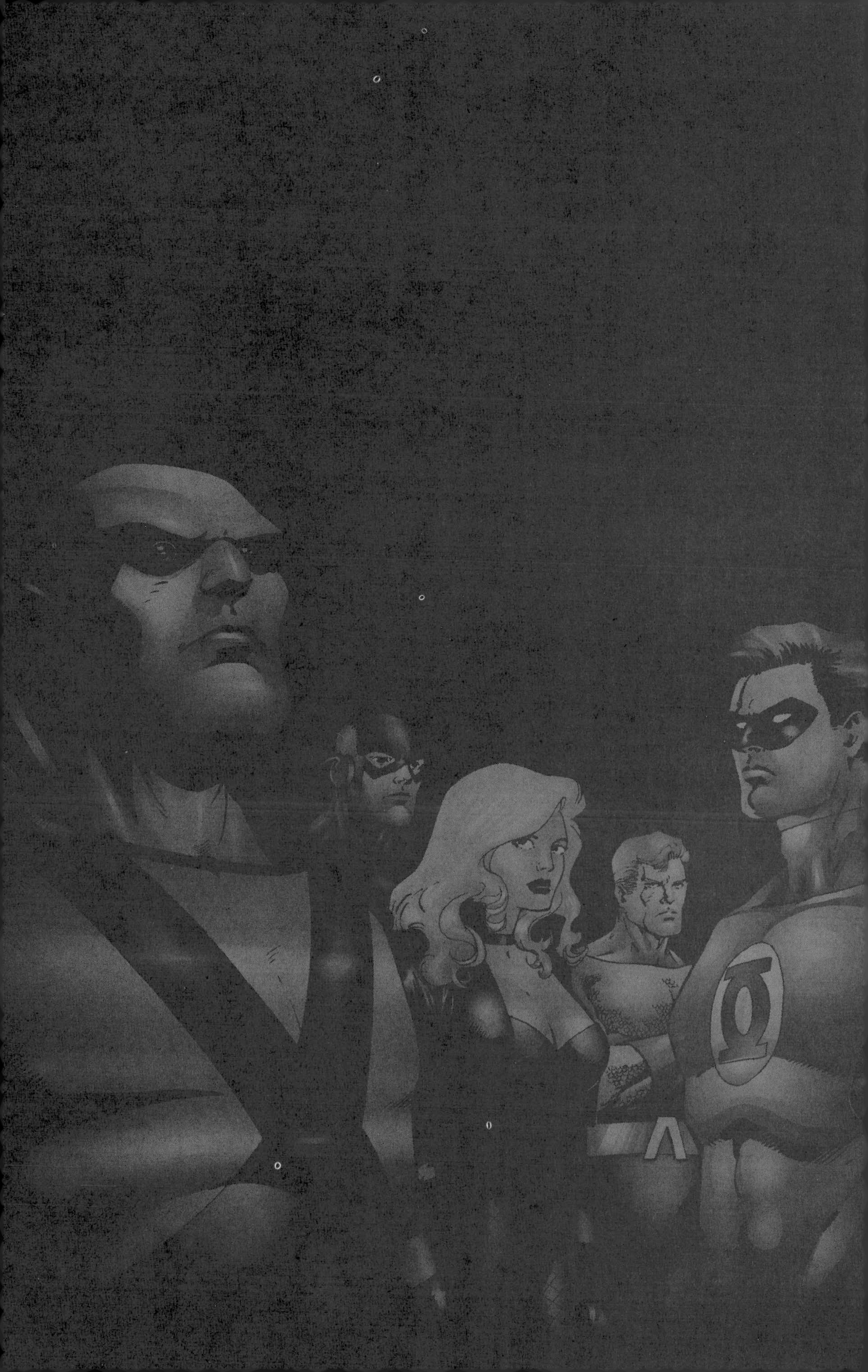

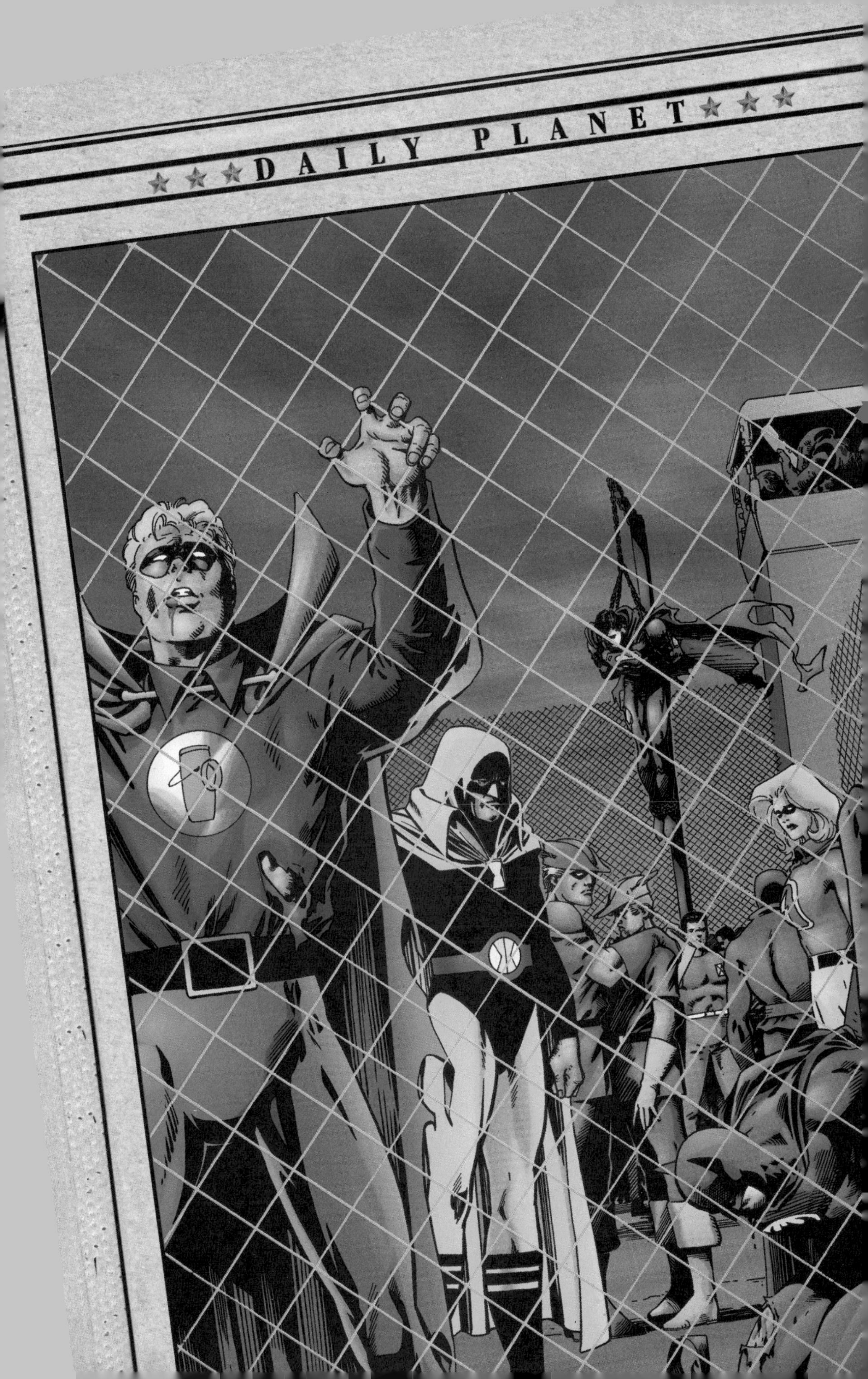
DAILY PLANET

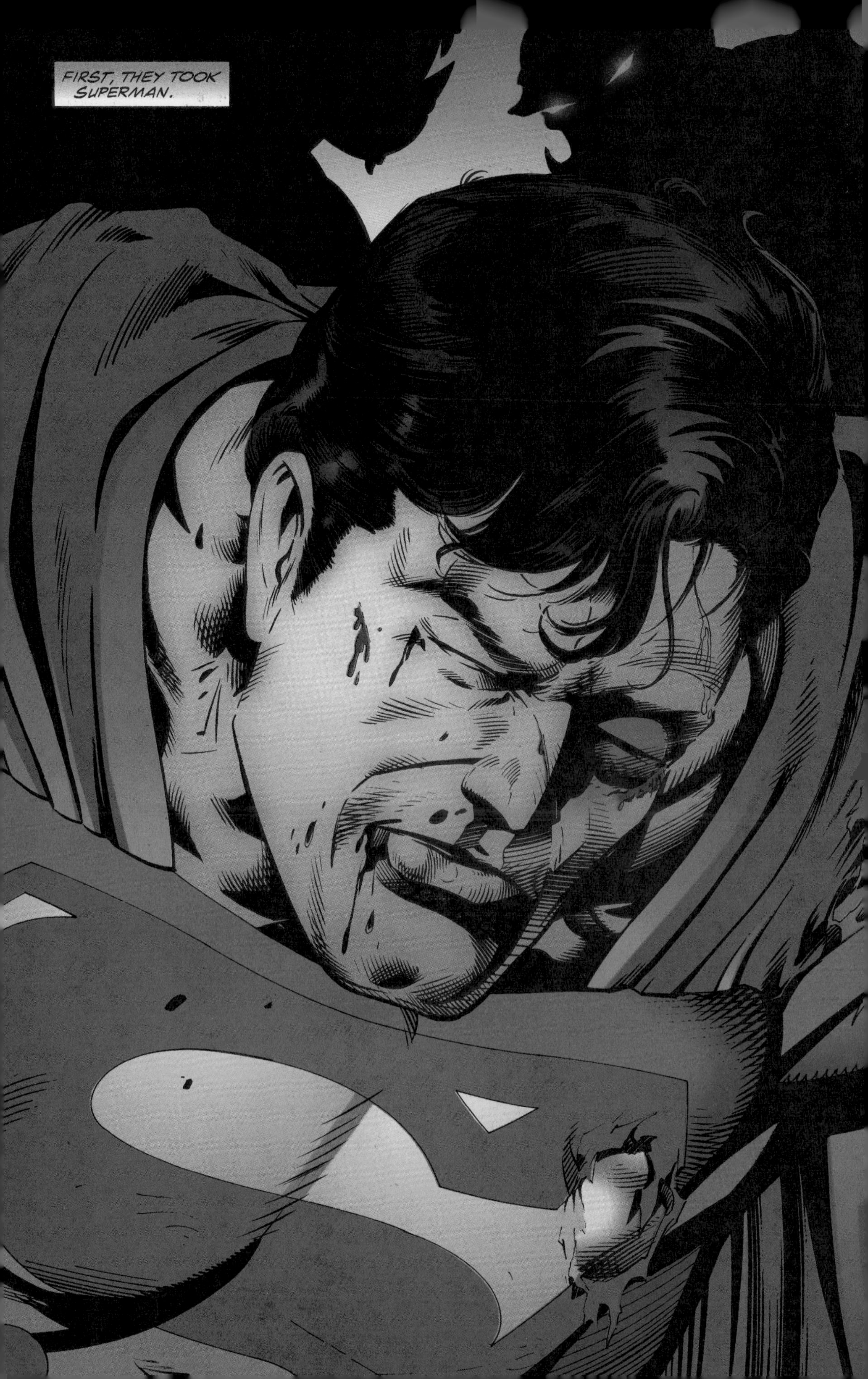
FIRST, THEY TOOK SUPERMAN.

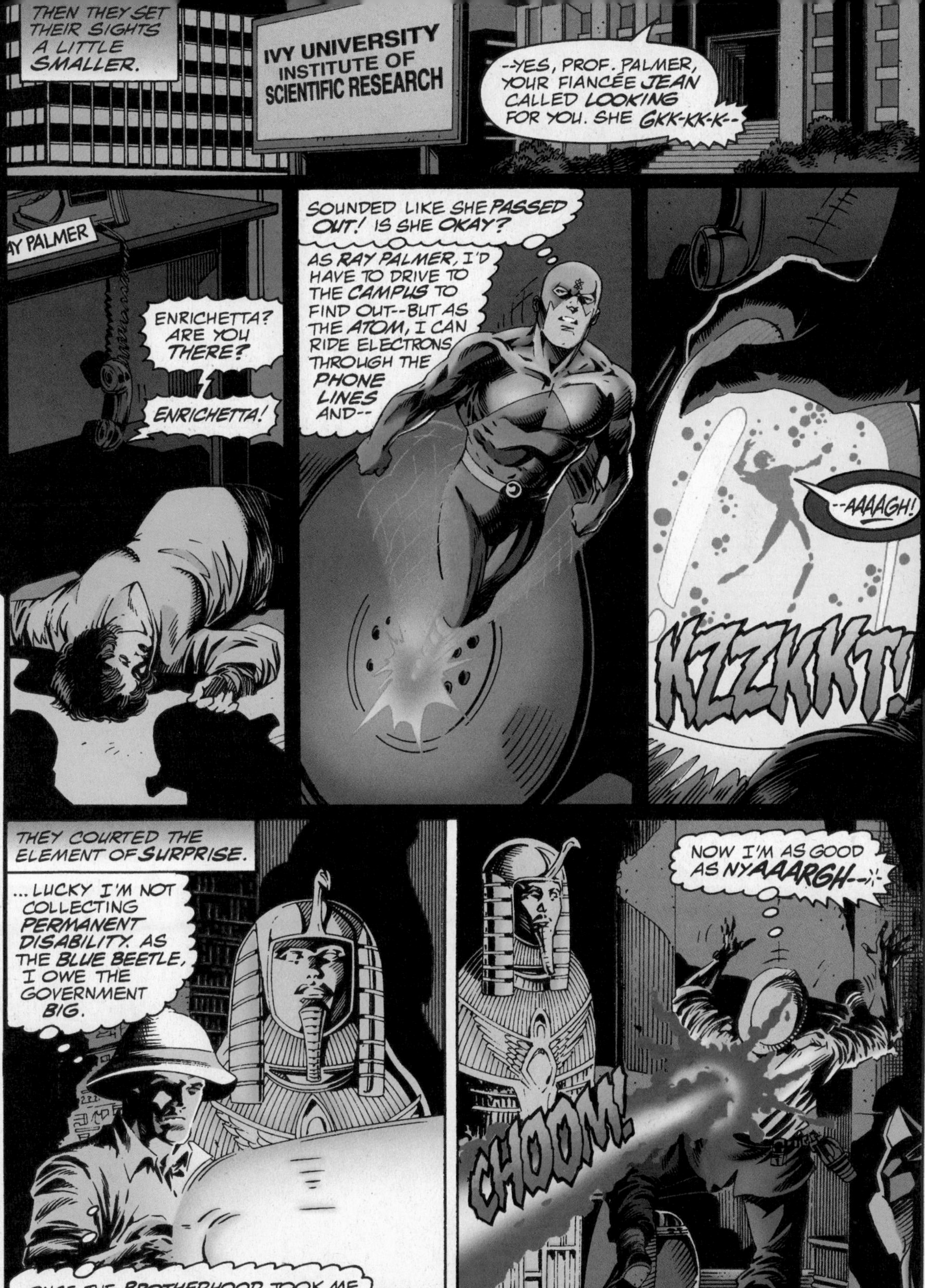
THEN THEY SET THEIR SIGHTS A LITTLE SMALLER.
IVY UNIVERSITY INSTITUTE OF SCIENTIFIC RESEARCH
--YES, PROF. PALMER, YOUR FIANCÉE JEAN CALLED LOOKING FOR YOU. SHE GKK-KK-K--
AY PALMER
ENRICHETTA? ARE YOU THERE?
ENRICHETTA!
SOUNDED LIKE SHE PASSED OUT! IS SHE OKAY?
AS RAY PALMER, I'D HAVE TO DRIVE TO THE CAMPUS TO FIND OUT--BUT AS THE ATOM, I CAN RIDE ELECTRONS THROUGH THE PHONE LINES AND--
--AAAAGH!
KZZKKT!
THEY COURTED THE ELEMENT OF SURPRISE.
...LUCKY I'M NOT COLLECTING PERMANENT DISABILITY. AS THE BLUE BEETLE, I OWE THE GOVERNMENT BIG.
ONCE THE BROTHERHOOD TOOK ME APART, THE NATIONAL GUARD USED THE GENEGRAFT RAY TO PUT ME BACK TOGETHER AGAIN.
NOW I'M AS GOOD AS NYAAARGH--
CHOOM!

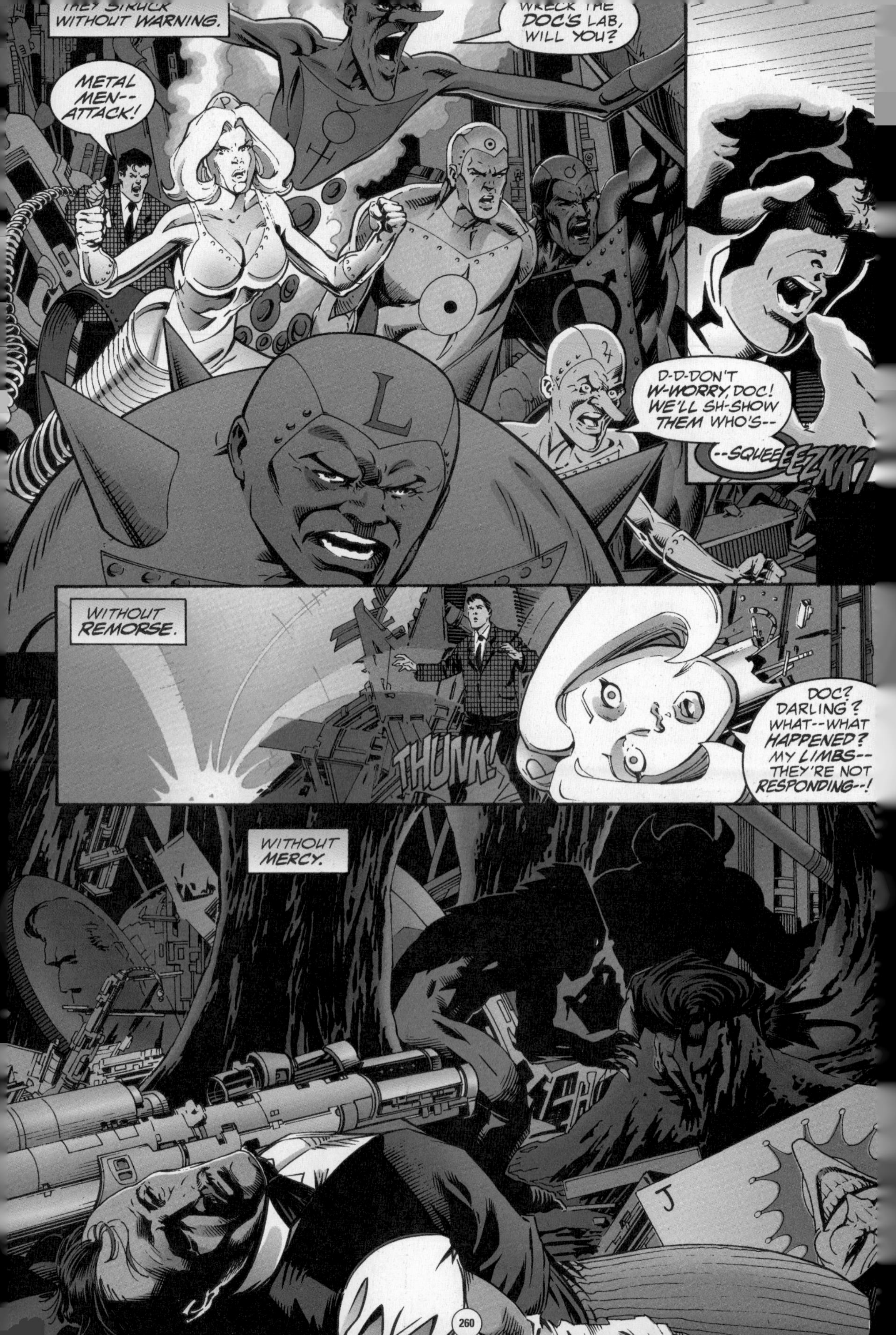
THEY STRUCK WITHOUT WARNING.
WRECK THE DOC'S LAB, WILL YOU?
METAL MEN--ATTACK!
D-D-DON'T W-WORRY, DOC! WE'LL SH-SHOW THEM WHO'S--
--SQUEEEEEZKKT
WITHOUT REMORSE.
THUNK!
DOC? DARLING? WHAT--WHAT HAPPENED? MY LIMBS--THEY'RE NOT RESPONDING--!
WITHOUT MERCY.

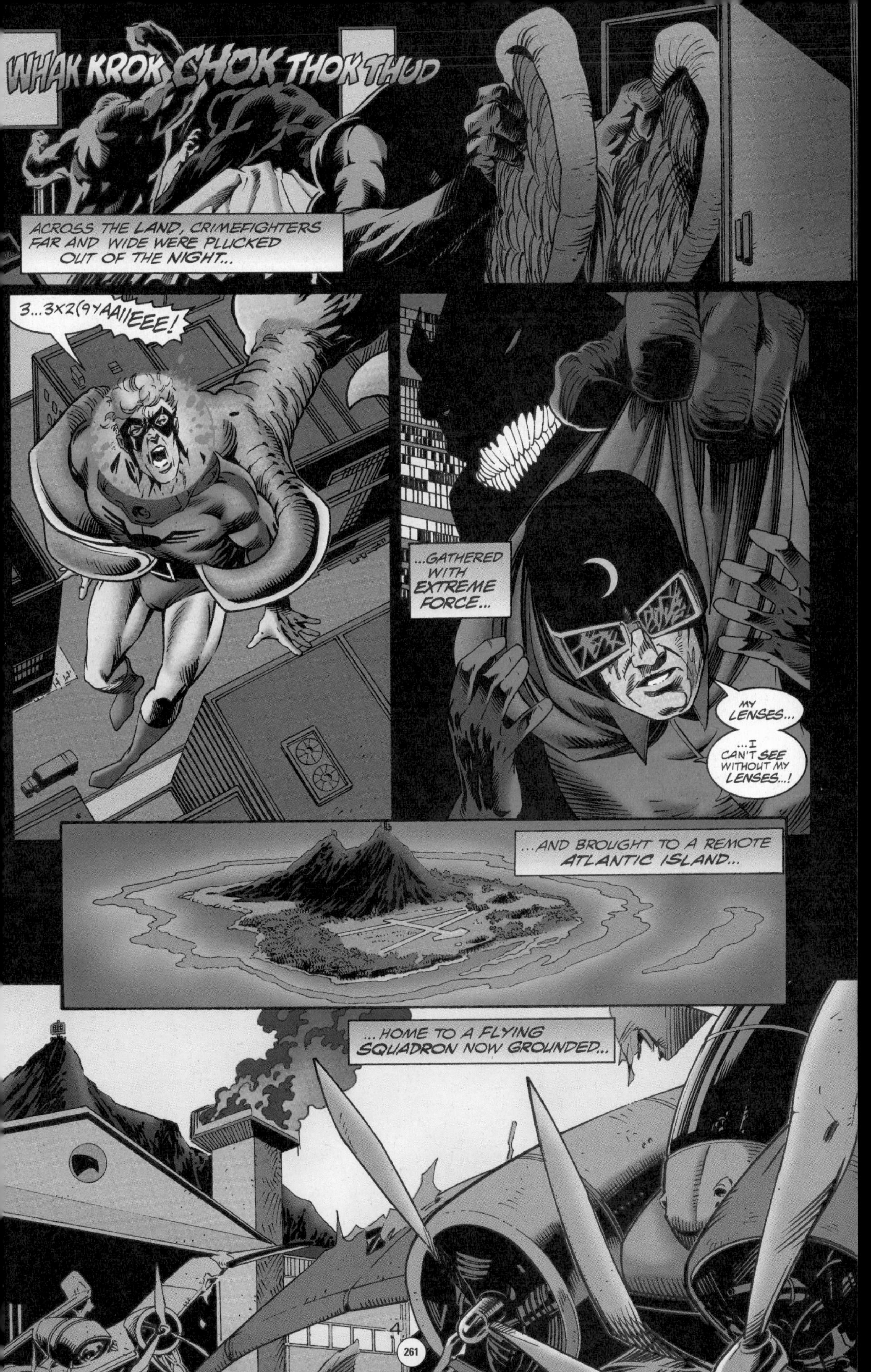
WHAK KROK CHOK THOK THUD
ACROSS THE LAND, CRIMEFIGHTERS FAR AND WIDE WERE PLUCKED OUT OF THE NIGHT...
3...3X2(9YAAIIEEE!
...GATHERED WITH EXTREME FORCE...
MY LENSES...
...I CAN'T SEE WITHOUT MY LENSES...!
...AND BROUGHT TO A REMOTE ATLANTIC ISLAND...
...HOME TO A FLYING SQUADRON NOW GROUNDED...

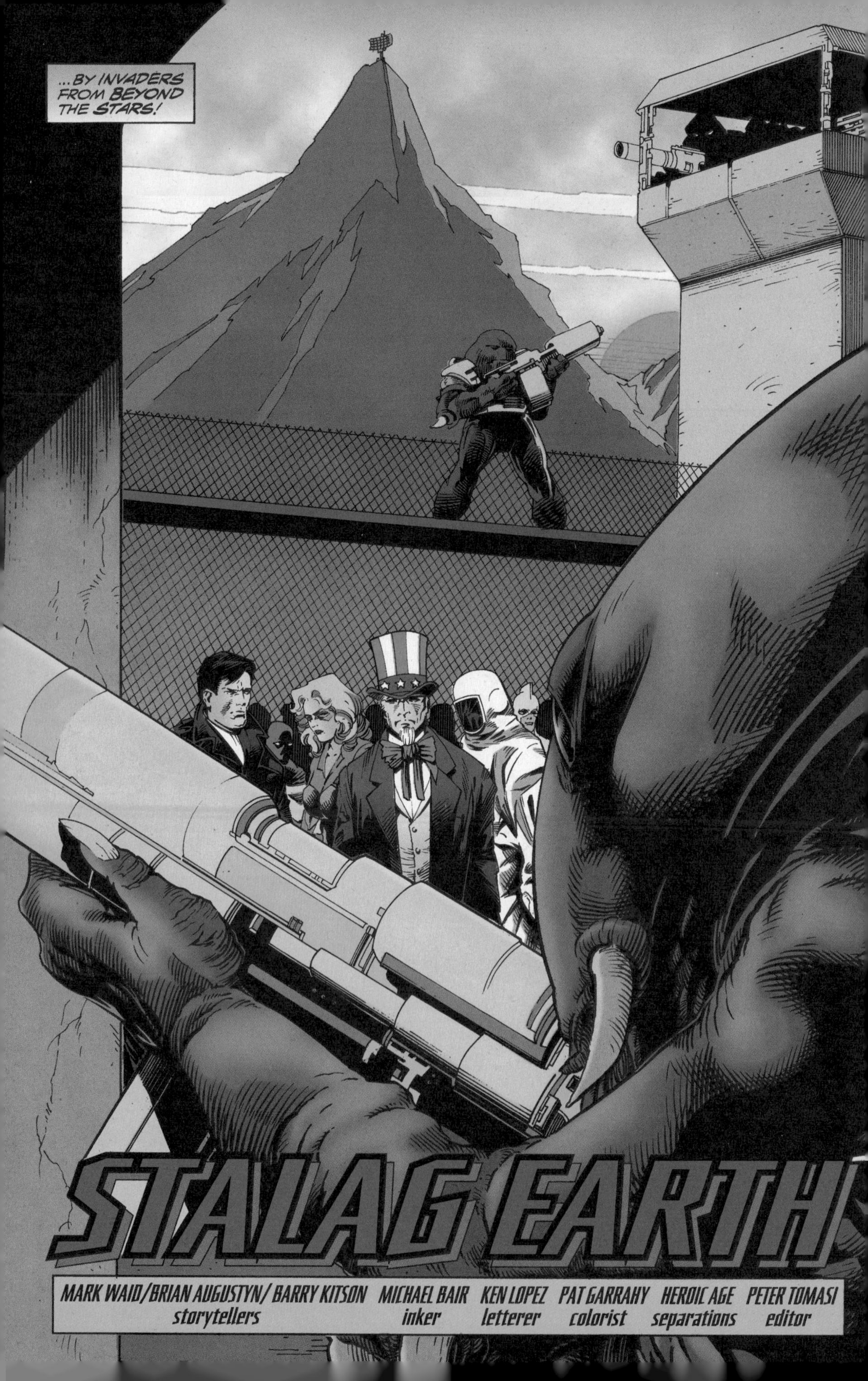
...BY INVADERS FROM BEYOND THE STARS!
STALAG EARTH
MARK WAID/BRIAN AUGUSTYN/ BARRY KITSON storytellers
MICHAEL BAIR inker
KEN LOPEZ letterer
PAT GARRAHY colorist
HEROIC AGE separations
PETER TOMASI editor

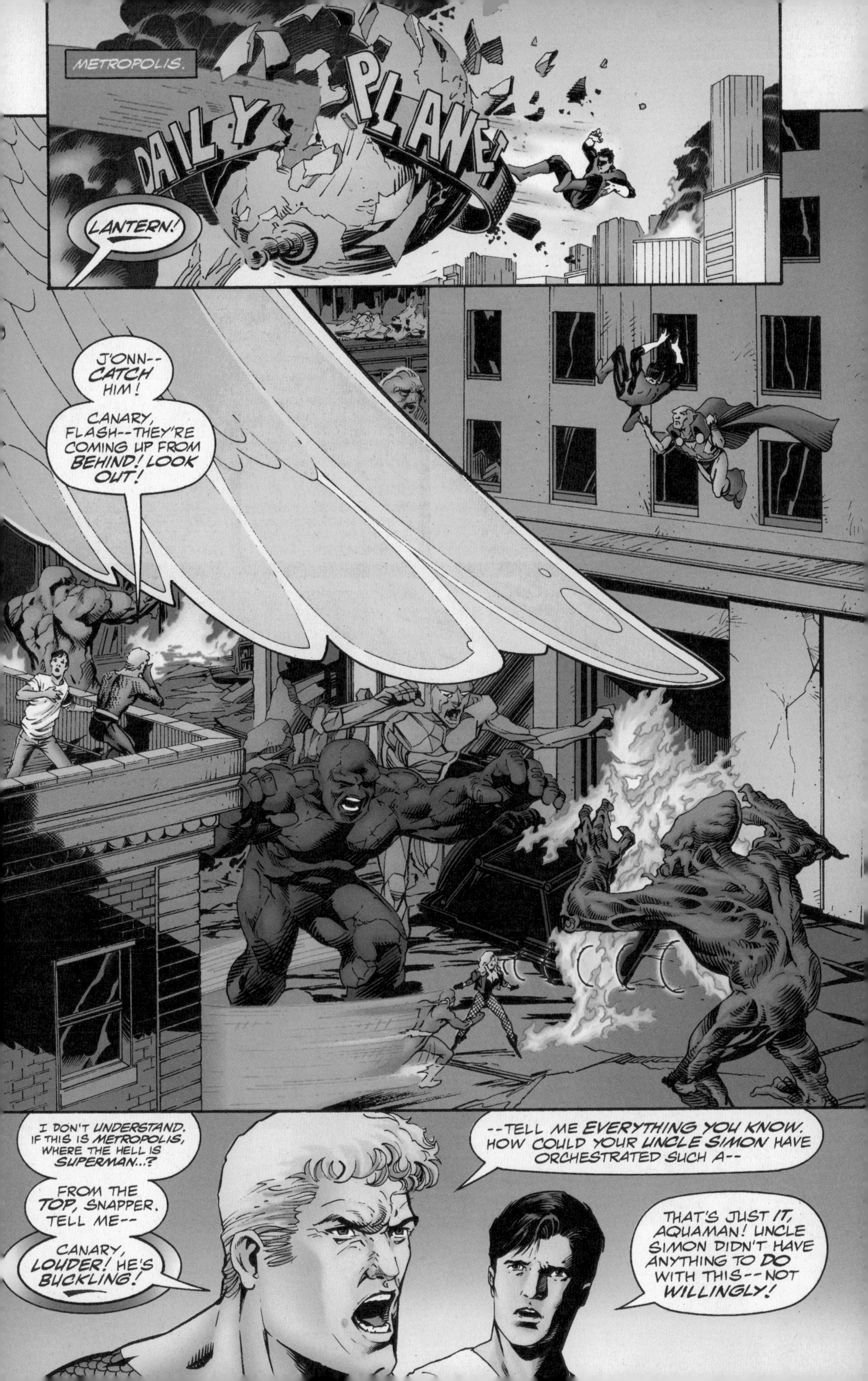
METROPOLIS.
DAILY PLANET
LANTERN!
J'ONN--CATCH HIM!
CANARY, FLASH--THEY'RE COMING UP FROM BEHIND! LOOK OUT!
I DON'T UNDERSTAND. IF THIS IS METROPOLIS, WHERE THE HELL IS SUPERMAN...?
FROM THE TOP, SNAPPER. TELL ME--
CANARY, LOUDER! HE'S BUCKLING!
--TELL ME EVERYTHING YOU KNOW. HOW COULD YOUR UNCLE SIMON HAVE ORCHESTRATED SUCH A--
THAT'S JUST IT, AQUAMAN! UNCLE SIMON DIDN'T HAVE ANYTHING TO DO WITH THIS--NOT WILLINGLY!

"A FEW MONTHS AGO, SEVEN *ALIENS* SHOWED UP, RIGHT? THAT'S WHAT BROUGHT THE JUSTICE LEAGUE TOGETHER IN THE *FIRST PLACE!*"

"THEY CAME HERE IN A BUNCH OF DIFFERENT *HOST BODIES* TO FIGHT A *DUEL* -- FIGURING THE *WINNER* WOULD BECOME KING OF THEIR PLANET, *APPELLAX!* INSTEAD, YOU GUYS SHUT THE SEVEN *DOWN* --"

"-- BUT YOU MISSED AN *EIGHTH*, 'CAUSE HIS HOST BODY MAL-FUNCTIONED -- AND THAT'S WHAT *SAVED* HIM! HE WAS RESCUED BY *LOCUS* --"

"-- AND AFTER HE SAW HOW EASILY *YOU* FIVE TRASHED THE OTHER APPELLAX-IANS, HE GRABBED A NEW HOST BODY. HE LEARNED HOW UNCLE SIMON WAS *CONNECTED* WITH THE LEAGUE -- THAT SIMON WAS WORKING FOR YOUR FINANCIAL *BACKER* --"

"-- SO HE -- HE TOOK SIMON. USED HIM AS A *SPY-EYE.* SIMON DIDN'T *KNOW* HE WAS SHARING HIS BODY WITH AN *ALIEN MIND.* HE THOUGHT HE WAS HAVING *BLACKOUTS.*"

"THE ALIEN LAY LOW EVERY TIME J'ONN WAS NEARBY, 'CAUSE HE DIDN'T WANT TO GET RATTED OUT BY J'ONN'S *TELEP-ATHY* -- BUT THE REST OF THE TIME, HE WAS SENDING WORD *HOME!*"

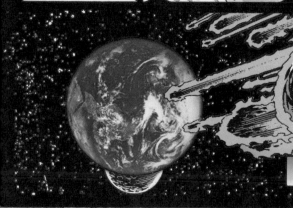

"GUESS HE GOT AFRAID I'D CAUGHT ON, SO HE BASHED ME UP PRETTY *GOOD* -- BUT I GOT *AWAY* AFTER HE *BRAGGED* ABOUT WHAT HE'D BEEN UP TO!"

"HE'D TOLD THE APPELLAXIANS HOW *POWERFUL* EARTH'S HEROES WERE, THAT THEY MIGHT SOMEDAY BE A THREAT TO APPELLAX --"

"-- SO THEY SENT AN ENTIRE INVASION *FORCE* TO WIPE OUR PLANET *OUT!*"

HOW *MANY?* ORIGINALLY WE FOUGHT JUST *SEVEN* ...

TRY SEVEN ... *THOUSAND.*

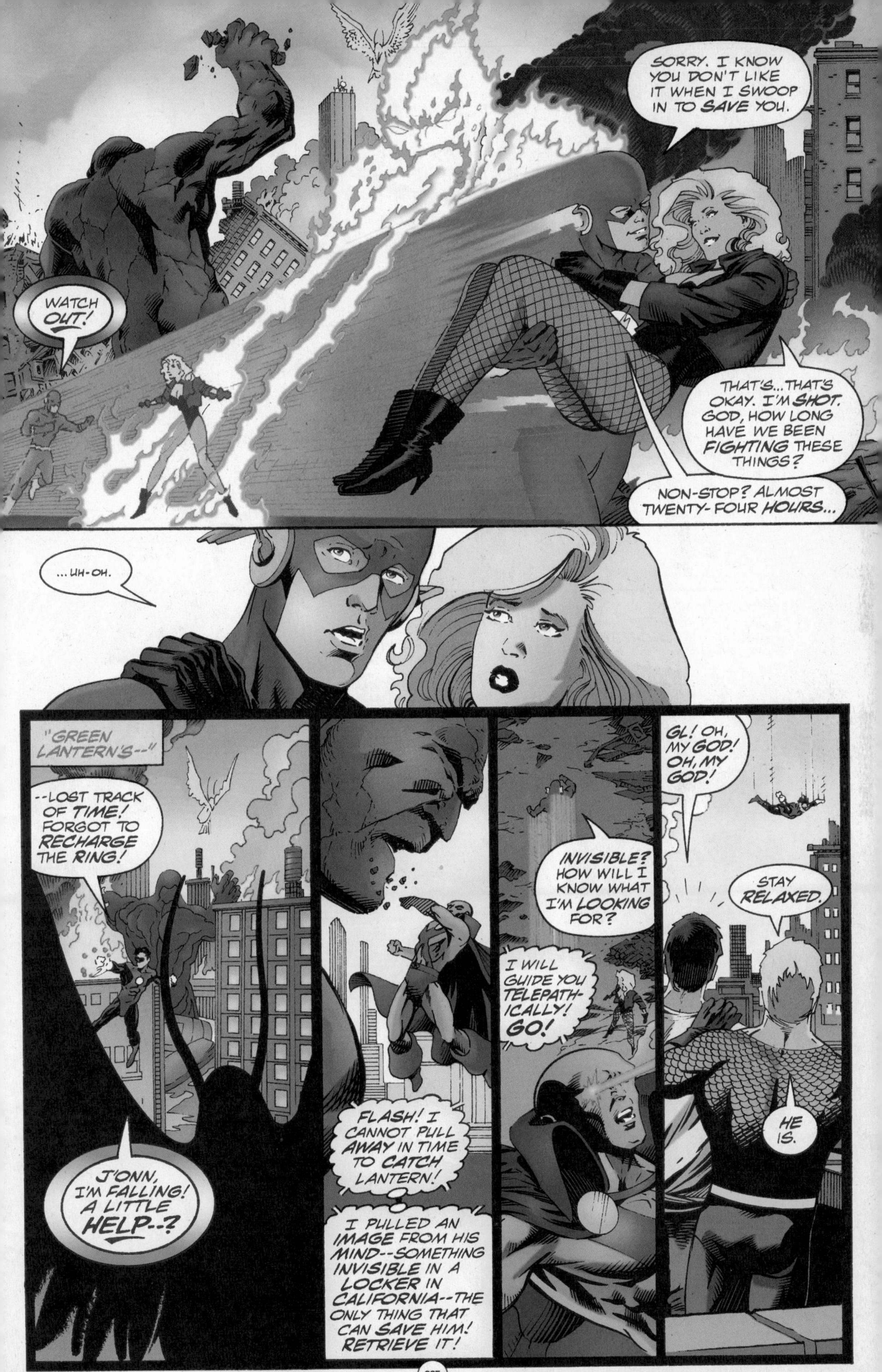
SORRY. I KNOW YOU DON'T LIKE IT WHEN I SWOOP IN TO SAVE YOU.
WATCH OUT!
THAT'S...THAT'S OKAY. I'M SHOT. GOD, HOW LONG HAVE WE BEEN FIGHTING THESE THINGS?
NON-STOP? ALMOST TWENTY-FOUR HOURS...
...UH-OH.
"GREEN LANTERN'S--"
--LOST TRACK OF TIME! FORGOT TO RECHARGE THE RING!
J'ONN, I'M FALLING! A LITTLE HELP--?
FLASH! I CANNOT PULL AWAY IN TIME TO CATCH LANTERN!
I PULLED AN IMAGE FROM HIS MIND--SOMETHING INVISIBLE IN A LOCKER IN CALIFORNIA--THE ONLY THING THAT CAN SAVE HIM! RETRIEVE IT!
INVISIBLE? HOW WILL I KNOW WHAT I'M LOOKING FOR?
I WILL GUIDE YOU TELEPATHICALLY! GO!
GL! OH, MY GOD! OH, MY GOD!
STAY RELAXED.
HE IS.

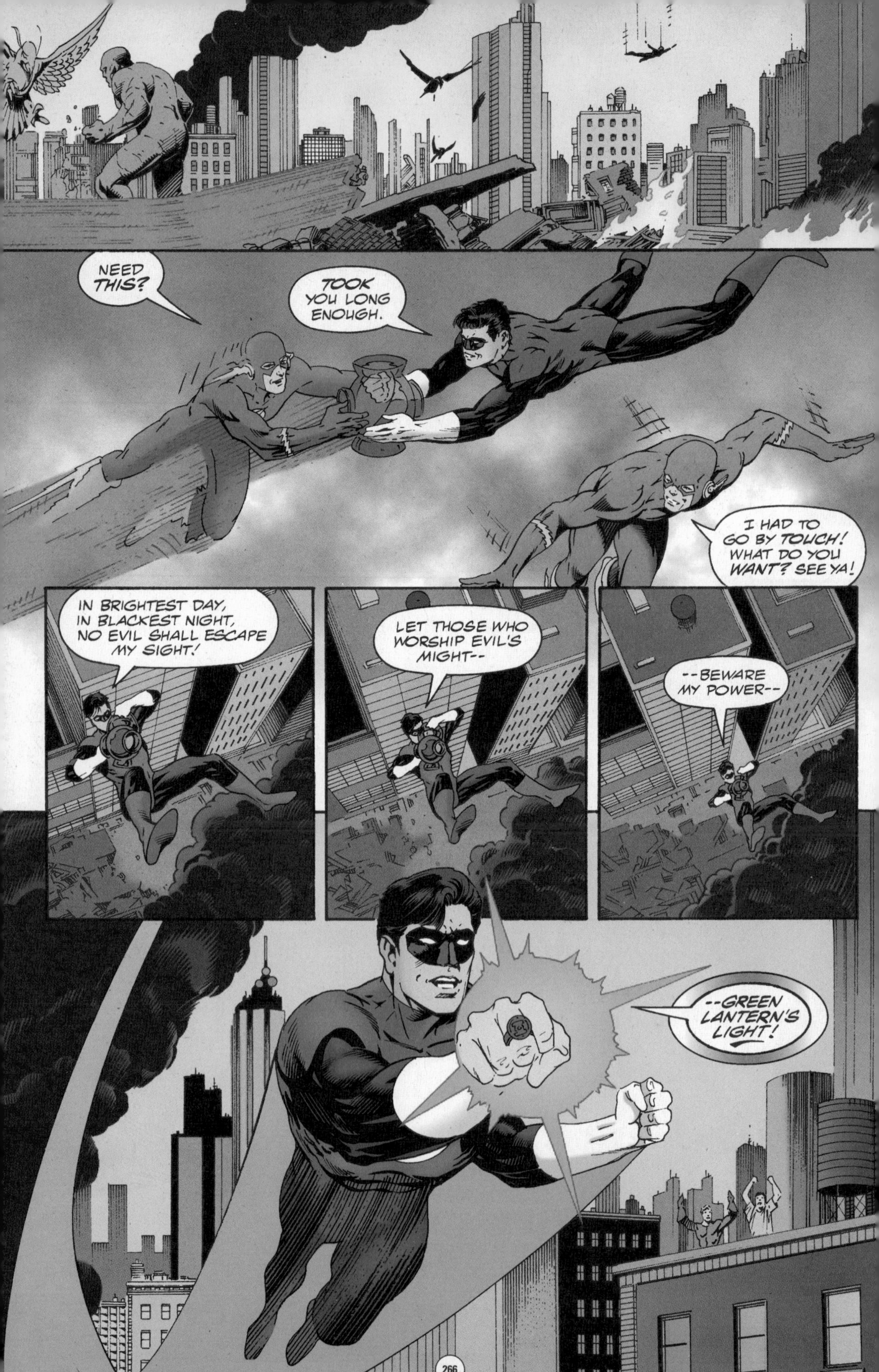
NEED THIS?
TOOK YOU LONG ENOUGH.
I HAD TO GO BY TOUCH! WHAT DO YOU WANT? SEE YA!
IN BRIGHTEST DAY, IN BLACKEST NIGHT, NO EVIL SHALL ESCAPE MY SIGHT!
LET THOSE WHO WORSHIP EVIL'S MIGHT--
--BEWARE MY POWER--
--GREEN LANTERN'S LIGHT!

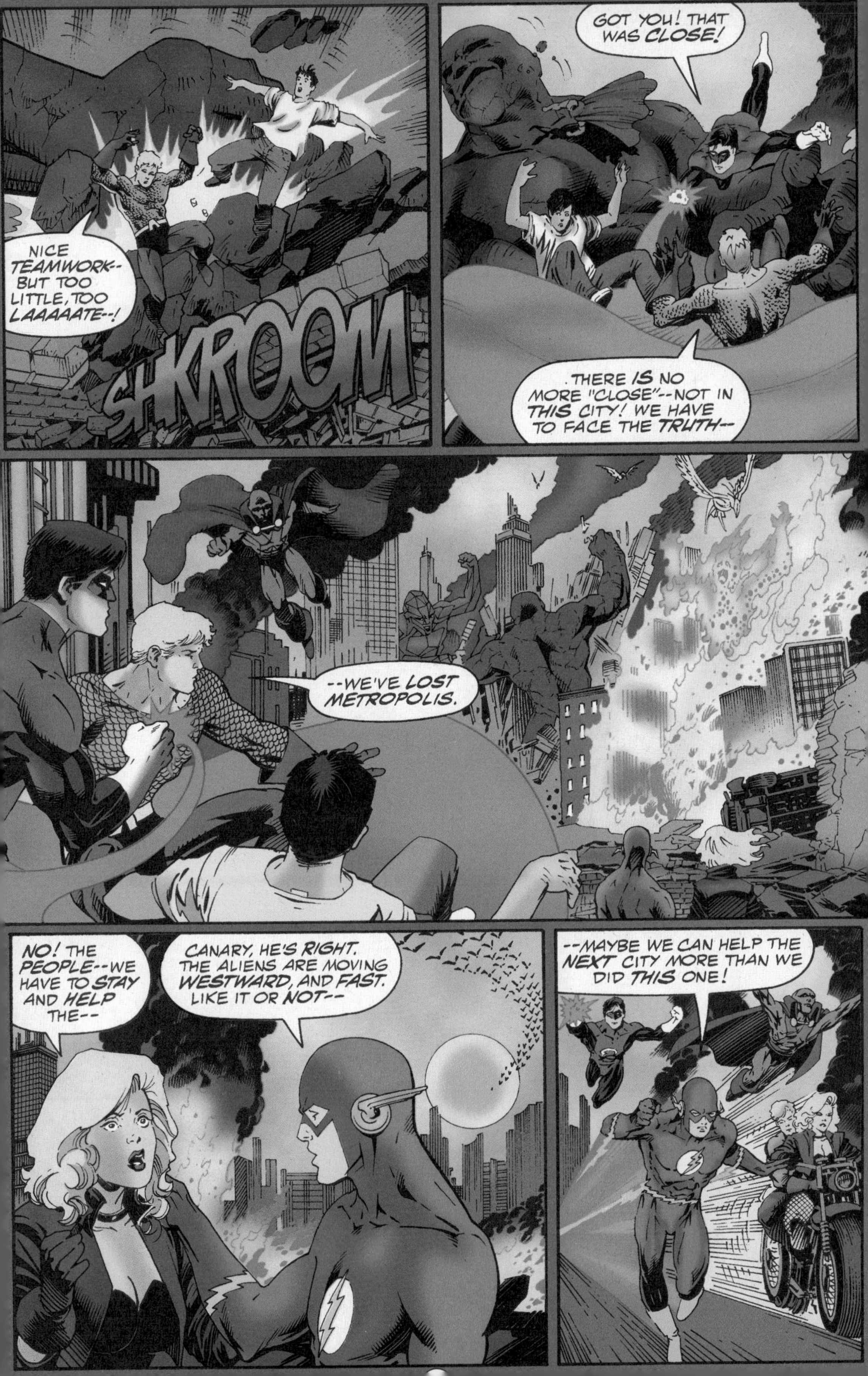
NICE TEAMWORK--BUT TOO LITTLE, TOO LAAAAATE--!
SHKROOM
GOT YOU! THAT WAS CLOSE!
THERE IS NO MORE "CLOSE"--NOT IN THIS CITY! WE HAVE TO FACE THE TRUTH--
--WE'VE LOST METROPOLIS.
NO! THE PEOPLE--WE HAVE TO STAY AND HELP THE--
CANARY, HE'S RIGHT. THE ALIENS ARE MOVING WESTWARD, AND FAST. LIKE IT OR NOT--
--MAYBE WE CAN HELP THE NEXT CITY MORE THAN WE DID THIS ONE!

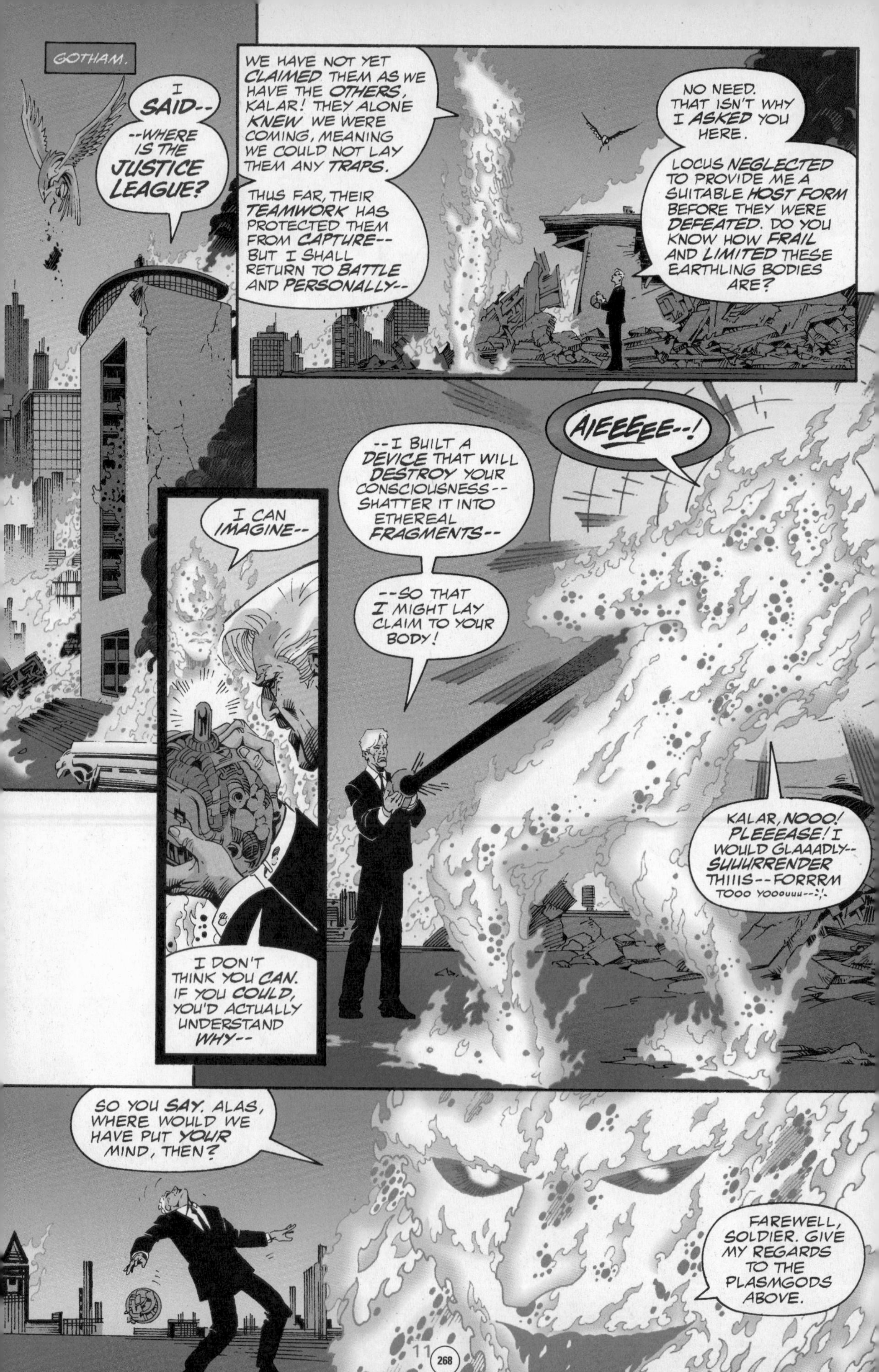

GOTHAM.
I SAID-- --WHERE IS THE JUSTICE LEAGUE?
WE HAVE NOT YET CLAIMED THEM AS WE HAVE THE OTHERS, KALAR! THEY ALONE KNEW WE WERE COMING, MEANING WE COULD NOT LAY THEM ANY TRAPS.
THUS FAR, THEIR TEAMWORK HAS PROTECTED THEM FROM CAPTURE-- BUT I SHALL RETURN TO BATTLE AND PERSONALLY--
NO NEED. THAT ISN'T WHY I ASKED YOU HERE.
LOCUS NEGLECTED TO PROVIDE ME A SUITABLE HOST FORM BEFORE THEY WERE DEFEATED. DO YOU KNOW HOW FRAIL AND LIMITED THESE EARTHLING BODIES ARE?
I CAN IMAGINE--
I DON'T THINK YOU CAN. IF YOU COULD, YOU'D ACTUALLY UNDERSTAND WHY--
--I BUILT A DEVICE THAT WILL DESTROY YOUR CONSCIOUSNESS--SHATTER IT INTO ETHEREAL FRAGMENTS--
--SO THAT I MIGHT LAY CLAIM TO YOUR BODY!
AIEEEEE--!
KALAR, NOOO! PLEEEASE! I WOULD GLAAADLY--SUUURRENDER THIIIS--FORRRM TOOO YOOouuu--
SO YOU SAY. ALAS, WHERE WOULD WE HAVE PUT YOUR MIND, THEN?
FAREWELL, SOLDIER. GIVE MY REGARDS TO THE PLASMGODS ABOVE.
11

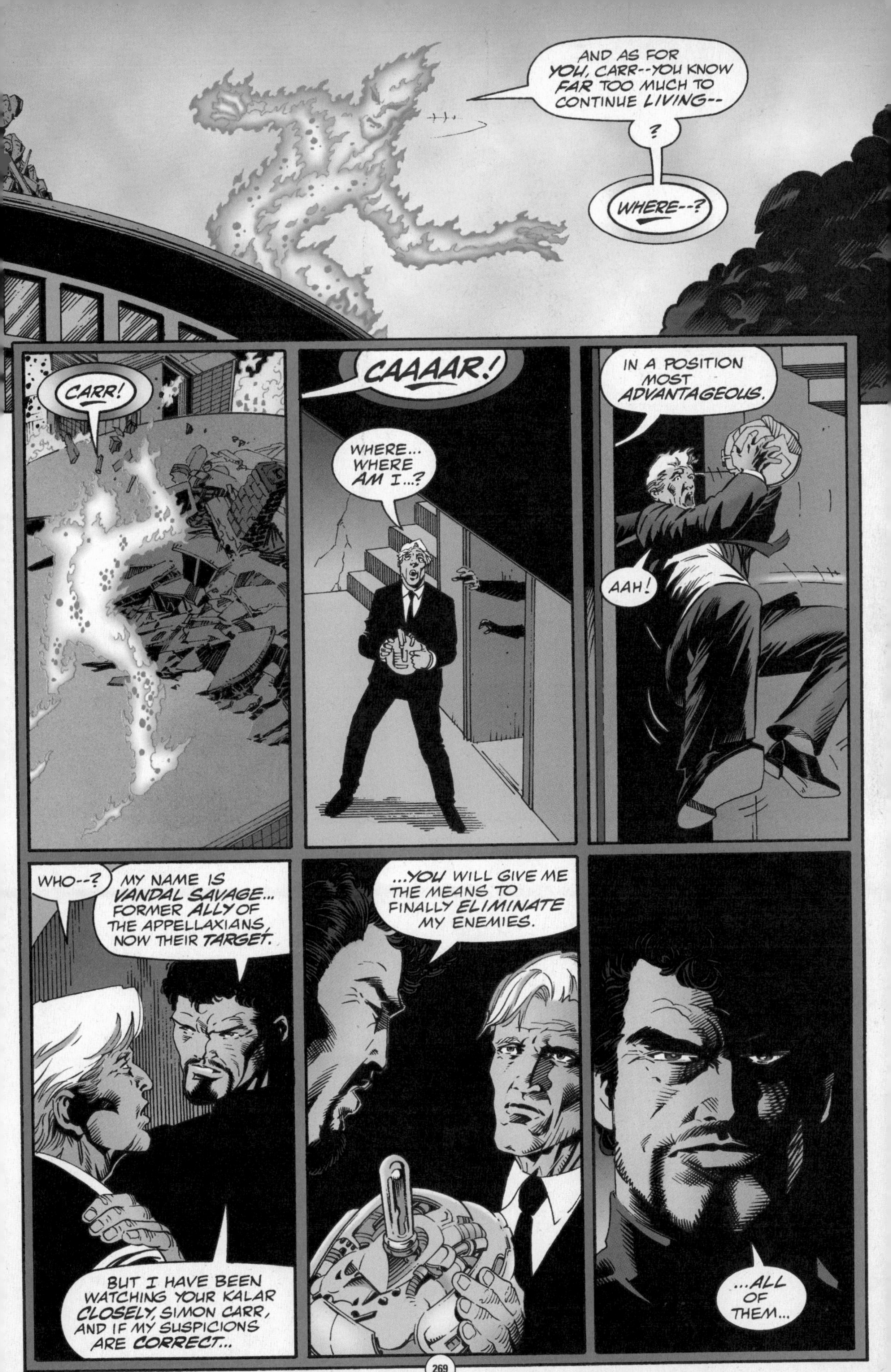

AND AS FOR YOU, CARR--YOU KNOW FAR TOO MUCH TO CONTINUE LIVING--
?
WHERE--?
CARR!
CAAAAR!
WHERE... WHERE AM I...?
IN A POSITION MOST ADVANTAGEOUS.
AAH!
WHO--?
MY NAME IS VANDAL SAVAGE... FORMER ALLY OF THE APPELLAXIANS, NOW THEIR TARGET.
BUT I HAVE BEEN WATCHING YOUR KALAR CLOSELY, SIMON CARR, AND IF MY SUSPICIONS ARE CORRECT...
...YOU WILL GIVE ME THE MEANS TO FINALLY ELIMINATE MY ENEMIES.
...ALL OF THEM...

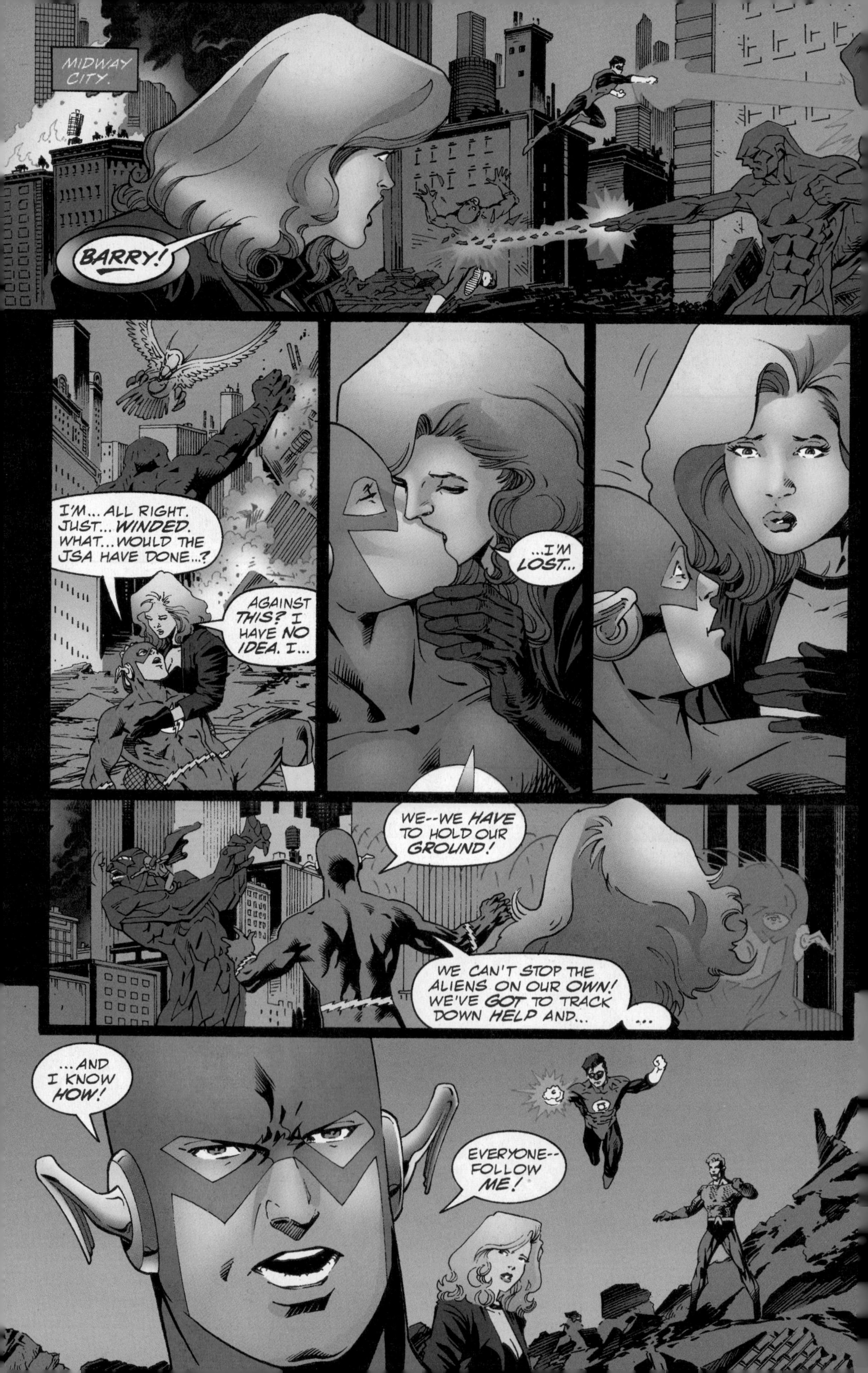
MIDWAY CITY.
BARRY!
I'M... ALL RIGHT. JUST... WINDED. WHAT... WOULD THE JSA HAVE DONE...?
AGAINST THIS? I HAVE NO IDEA. I...
...I'M LOST...
WE--WE HAVE TO HOLD OUR GROUND!
WE CAN'T STOP THE ALIENS ON OUR OWN! WE'VE GOT TO TRACK DOWN HELP AND...
...
...AND I KNOW HOW!
EVERYONE-- FOLLOW ME!

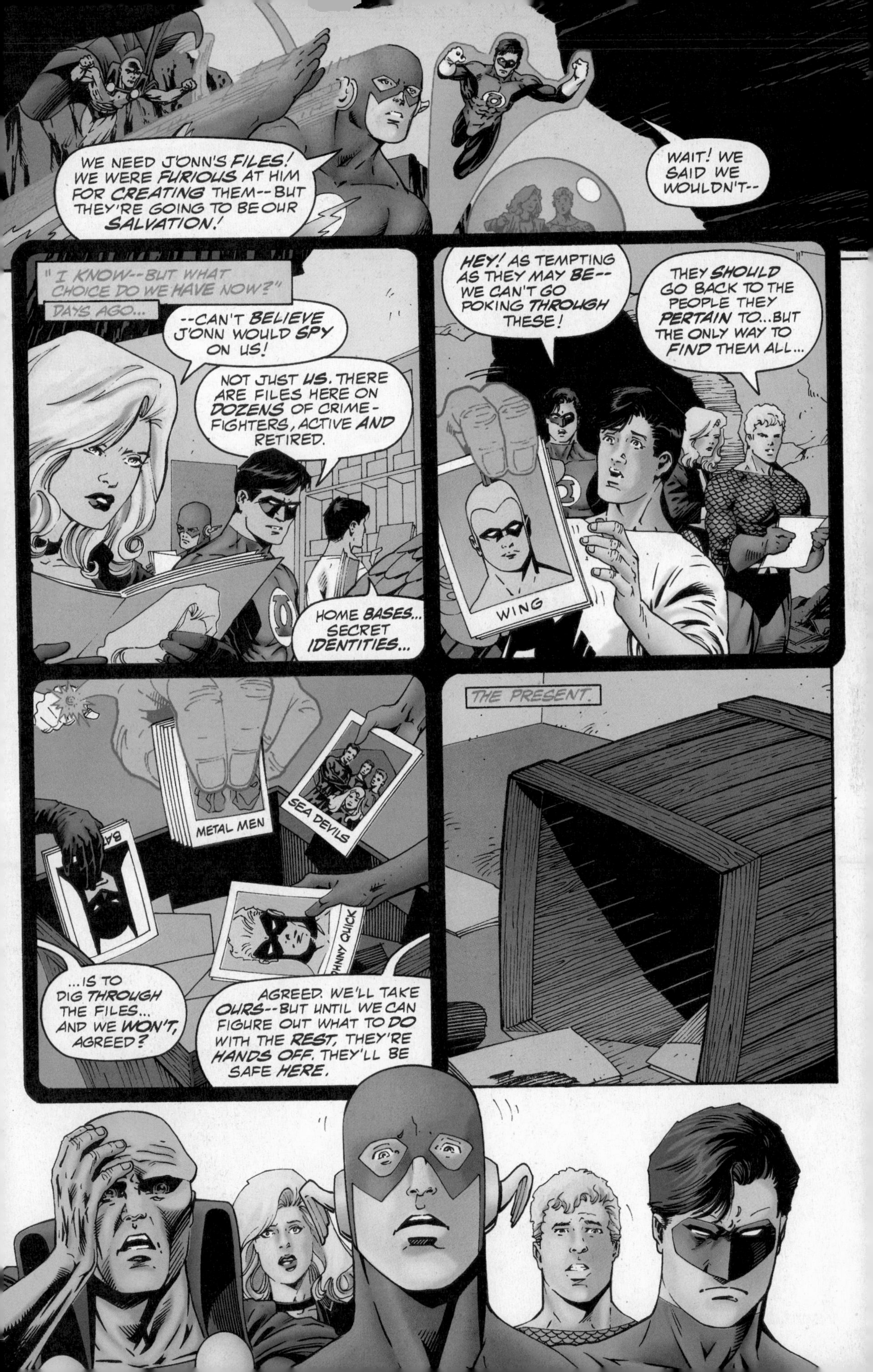

WE NEED J'ONN'S FILES! WE WERE FURIOUS AT HIM FOR CREATING THEM--BUT THEY'RE GOING TO BE OUR SALVATION!
WAIT! WE SAID WE WOULDN'T--
"I KNOW--BUT WHAT CHOICE DO WE HAVE NOW?"
DAYS AGO...
--CAN'T BELIEVE J'ONN WOULD SPY ON US!
NOT JUST US. THERE ARE FILES HERE ON DOZENS OF CRIME-FIGHTERS, ACTIVE AND RETIRED.
HOME BASES... SECRET IDENTITIES...
HEY! AS TEMPTING AS THEY MAY BE--WE CAN'T GO POKING THROUGH THESE!
THEY SHOULD GO BACK TO THE PEOPLE THEY PERTAIN TO...BUT THE ONLY WAY TO FIND THEM ALL...
WING
METAL MEN
SEA DEVILS
JOHNNY QUICK
...IS TO DIG THROUGH THE FILES... AND WE WON'T, AGREED?
AGREED. WE'LL TAKE OURS--BUT UNTIL WE CAN FIGURE OUT WHAT TO DO WITH THE REST, THEY'RE HANDS OFF. THEY'LL BE SAFE HERE.
THE PRESENT.

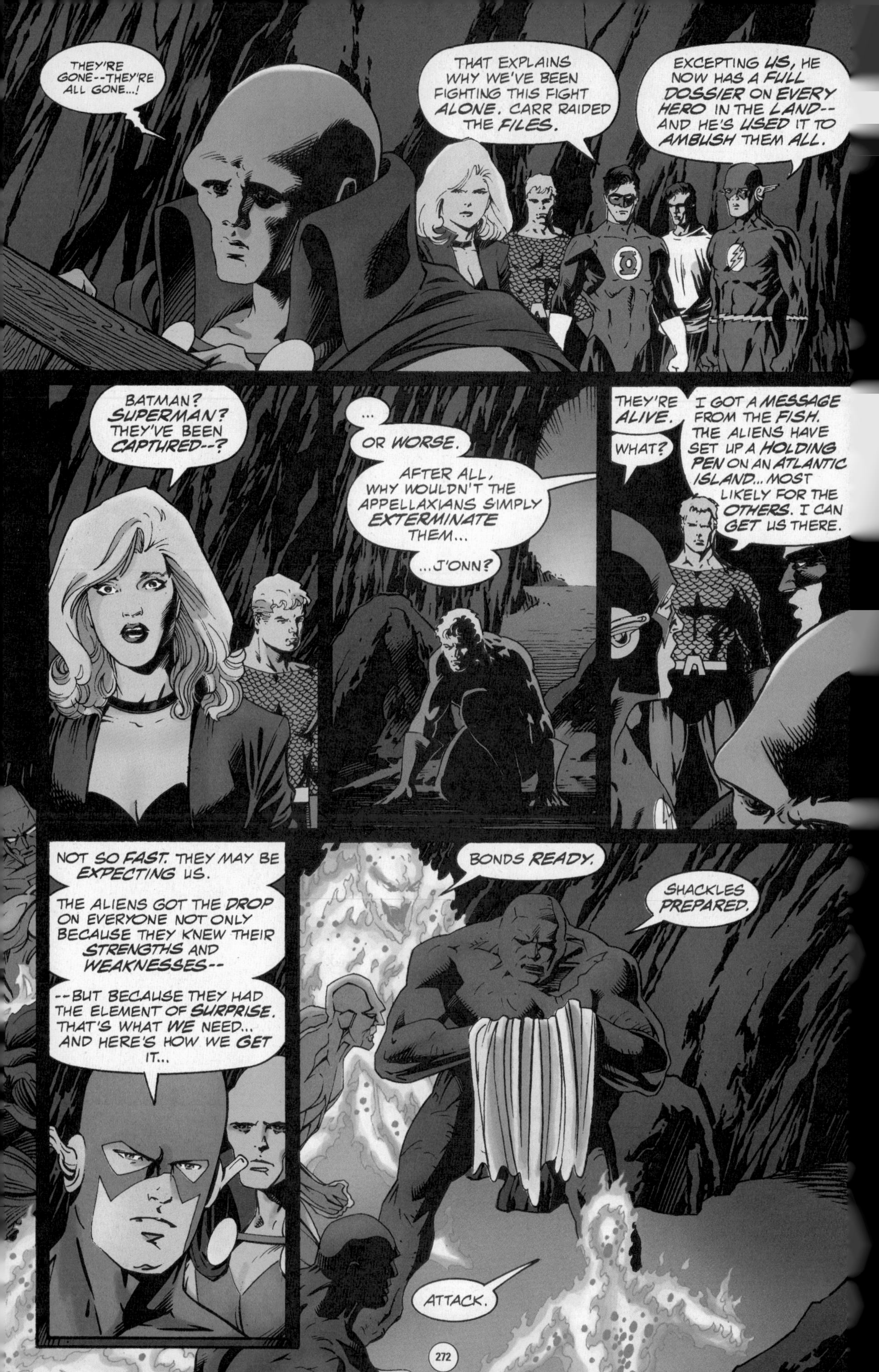
THEY'RE GONE--THEY'RE ALL GONE...!
THAT EXPLAINS WHY WE'VE BEEN FIGHTING THIS FIGHT ALONE. CARR RAIDED THE FILES.
EXCEPTING US, HE NOW HAS A FULL DOSSIER ON EVERY HERO IN THE LAND--AND HE'S USED IT TO AMBUSH THEM ALL.
BATMAN? SUPERMAN? THEY'VE BEEN CAPTURED--?
...
OR WORSE.
AFTER ALL, WHY WOULDN'T THE APPELLAXIANS SIMPLY EXTERMINATE THEM...
...J'ONN?
THEY'RE ALIVE.
WHAT?
I GOT A MESSAGE FROM THE FISH. THE ALIENS HAVE SET UP A HOLDING PEN ON AN ATLANTIC ISLAND... MOST LIKELY FOR THE OTHERS. I CAN GET US THERE.
NOT SO FAST. THEY MAY BE EXPECTING US.
THE ALIENS GOT THE DROP ON EVERYONE NOT ONLY BECAUSE THEY KNEW THEIR STRENGTHS AND WEAKNESSES--
--BUT BECAUSE THEY HAD THE ELEMENT OF SURPRISE. THAT'S WHAT WE NEED... AND HERE'S HOW WE GET IT...
BONDS READY.
SHACKLES PREPARED.
ATTACK.

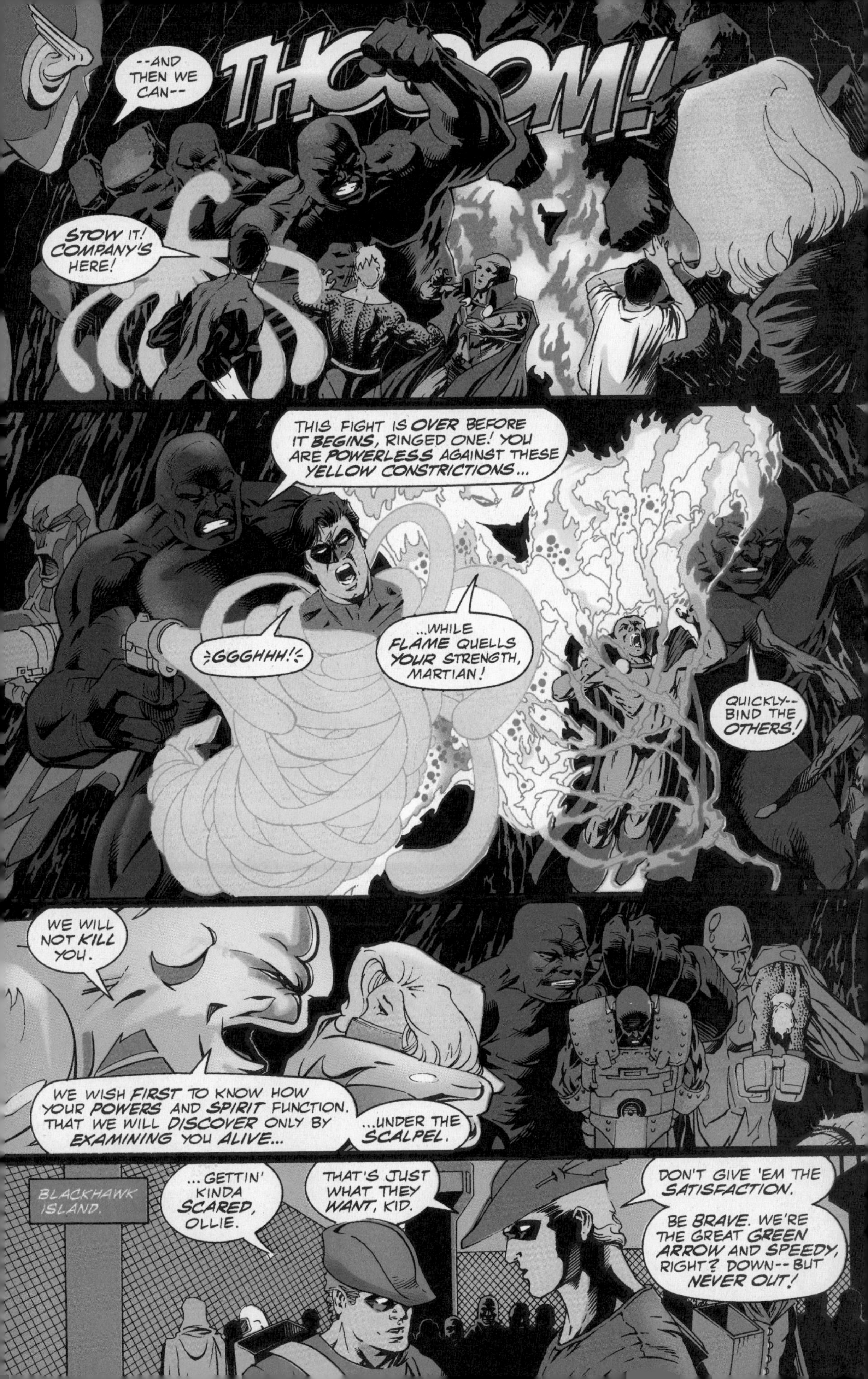
--AND THEN WE CAN--
THOOOM!
STOW IT! COMPANY'S HERE!
THIS FIGHT IS OVER BEFORE IT BEGINS, RINGED ONE! YOU ARE POWERLESS AGAINST THESE YELLOW CONSTRICTIONS...
GGGHHH!
...WHILE FLAME QUELLS YOUR STRENGTH, MARTIAN!
QUICKLY-- BIND THE OTHERS!
WE WILL NOT KILL YOU.
WE WISH FIRST TO KNOW HOW YOUR POWERS AND SPIRIT FUNCTION. THAT WE WILL DISCOVER ONLY BY EXAMINING YOU ALIVE...
...UNDER THE SCALPEL.
BLACKHAWK ISLAND.
...GETTIN' KINDA SCARED, OLLIE.
THAT'S JUST WHAT THEY WANT, KID.
DON'T GIVE 'EM THE SATISFACTION.
BE BRAVE. WE'RE THE GREAT GREEN ARROW AND SPEEDY, RIGHT? DOWN-- BUT NEVER OUT!

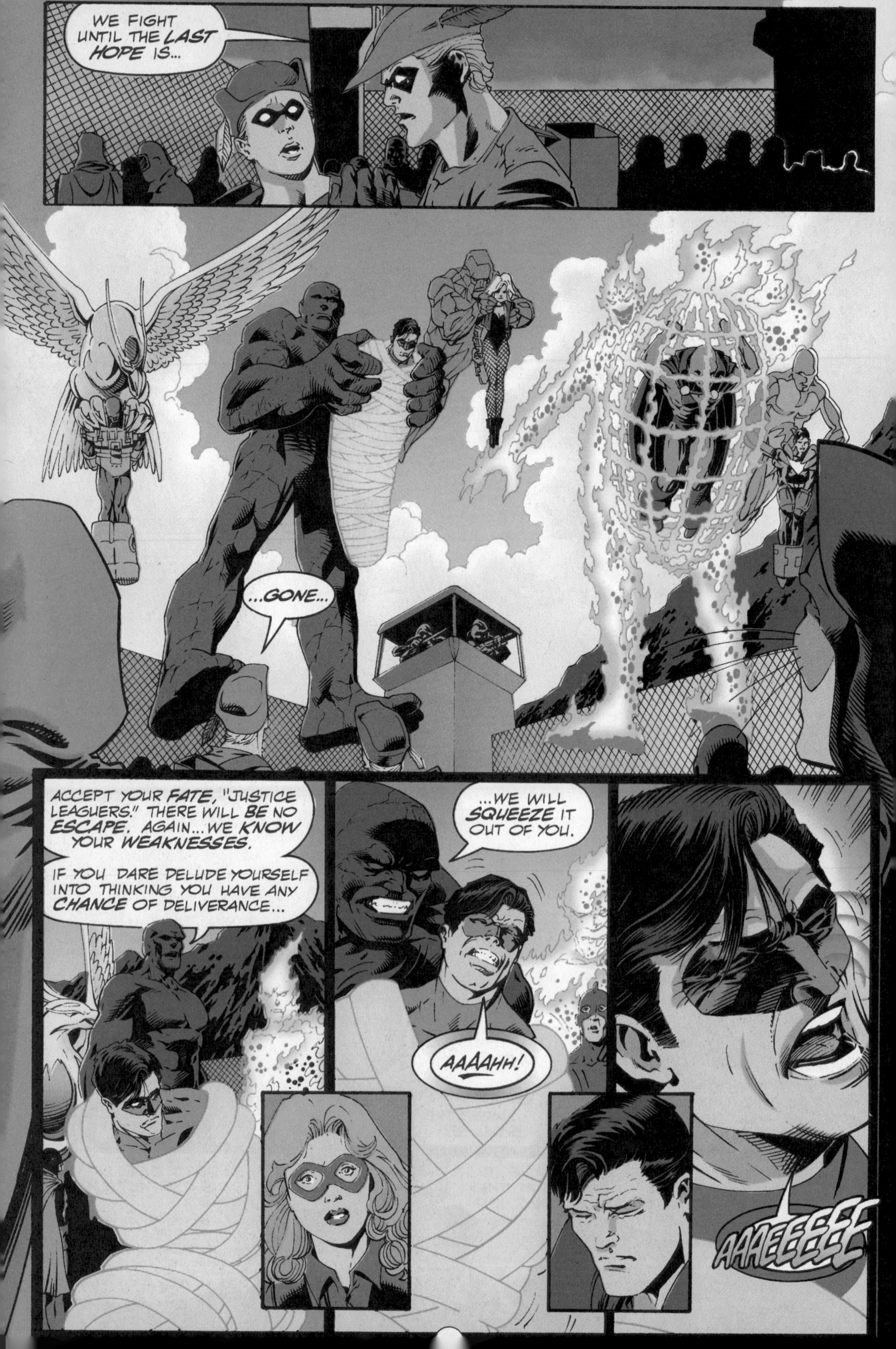
WE FIGHT UNTIL THE LAST HOPE IS...
...GONE...
ACCEPT YOUR FATE, "JUSTICE LEAGUERS." THERE WILL BE NO ESCAPE. AGAIN...WE KNOW YOUR WEAKNESSES.
IF YOU DARE DELUDE YOURSELF INTO THINKING YOU HAVE ANY CHANCE OF DELIVERANCE...
...WE WILL SQUEEZE IT OUT OF YOU.
AAAAHH!
AAAEEEEEE

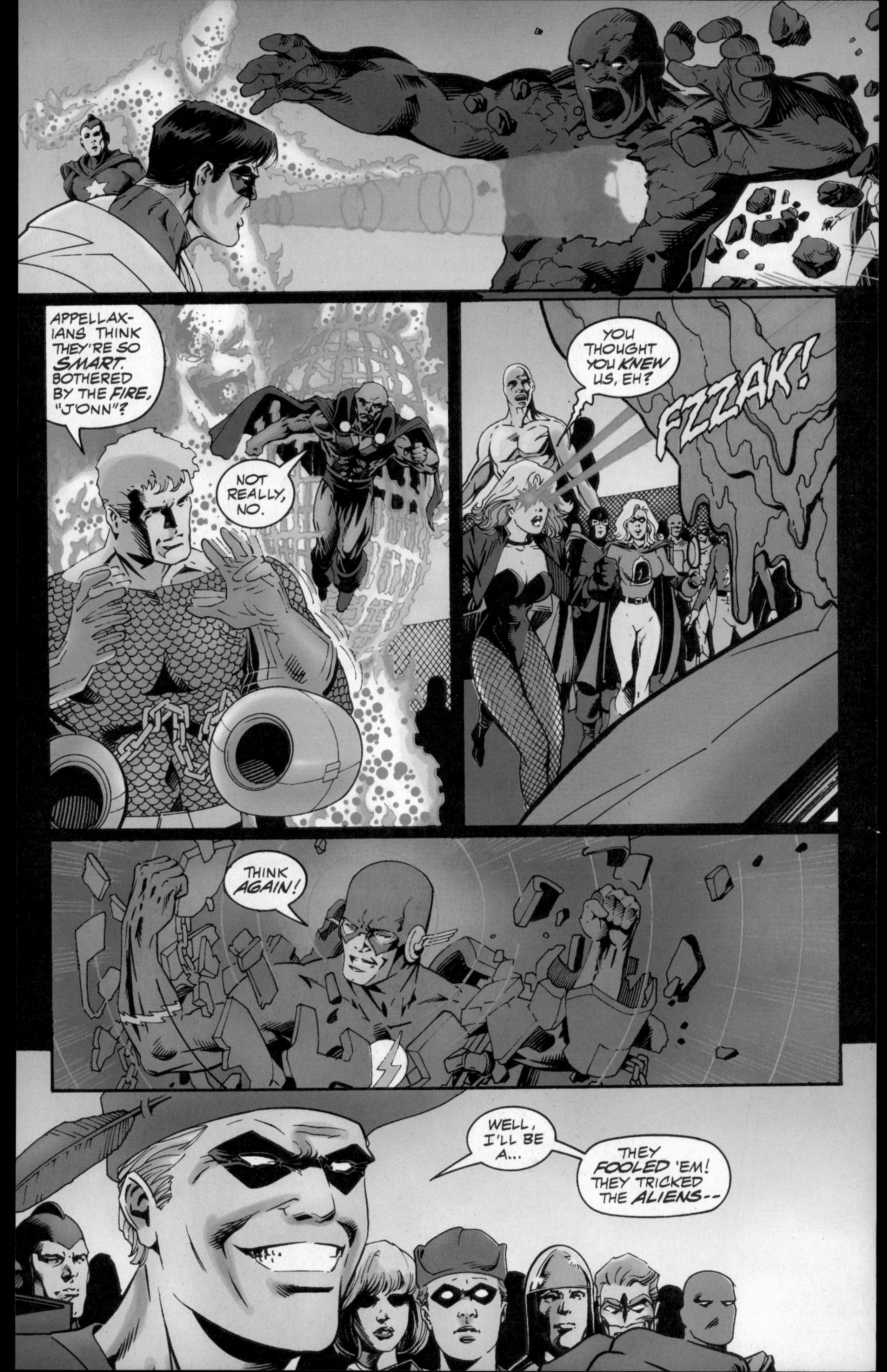
APPELLAX-IANS THINK THEY'RE SO SMART. BOTHERED BY THE FIRE, "J'ONN"?
NOT REALLY, NO.
YOU THOUGHT YOU KNEW US, EH?
FZZAK!
THINK AGAIN!
WELL, I'LL BE A...
THEY FOOLED 'EM! THEY TRICKED THE ALIENS--

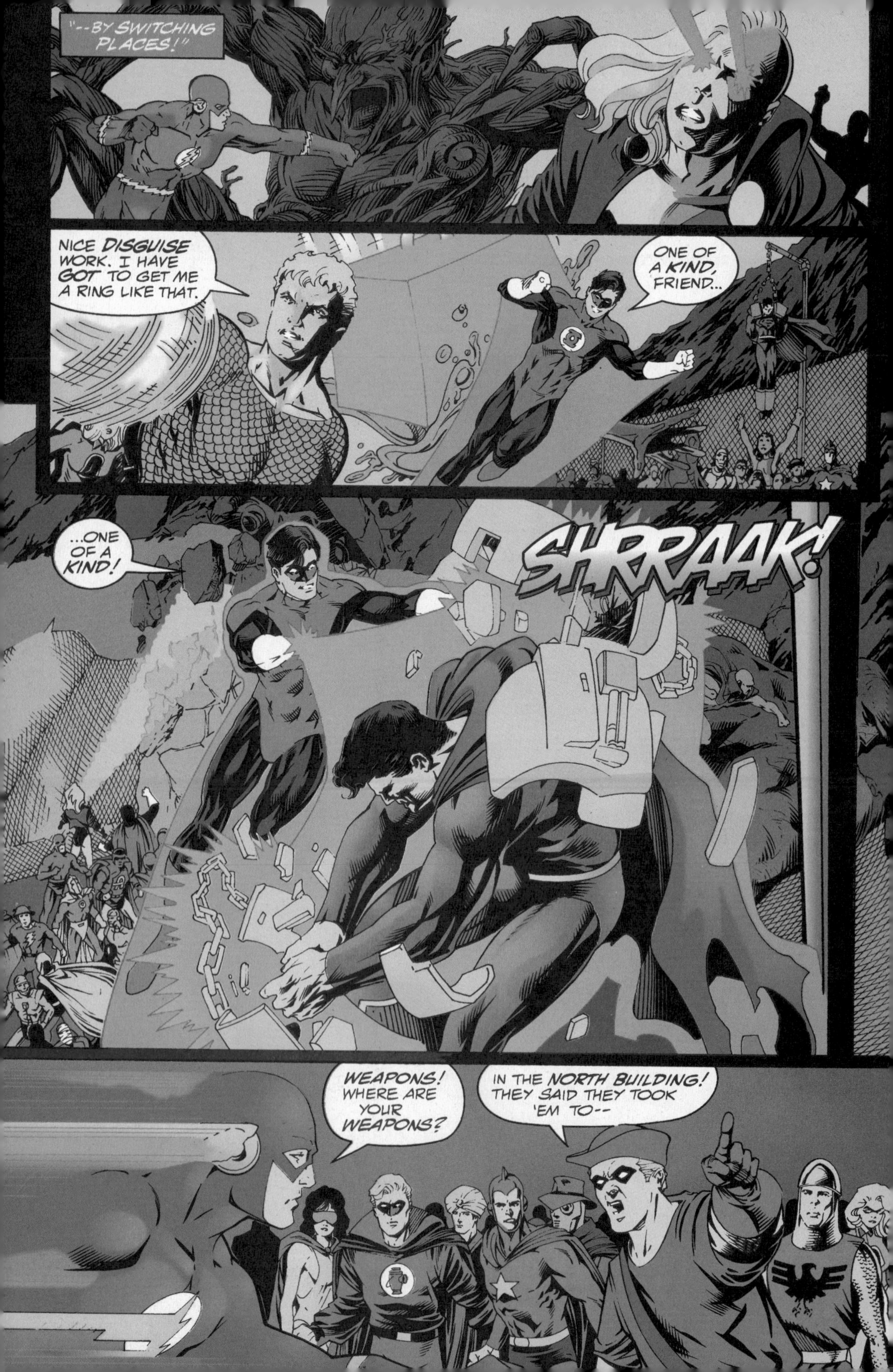
"--BY SWITCHING PLACES!"
NICE DISGUISE WORK. I HAVE GOT TO GET ME A RING LIKE THAT.
ONE OF A KIND, FRIEND...
...ONE OF A KIND!
SHRRAAK!
WEAPONS! WHERE ARE YOUR WEAPONS?
IN THE NORTH BUILDING! THEY SAID THEY TOOK 'EM TO--

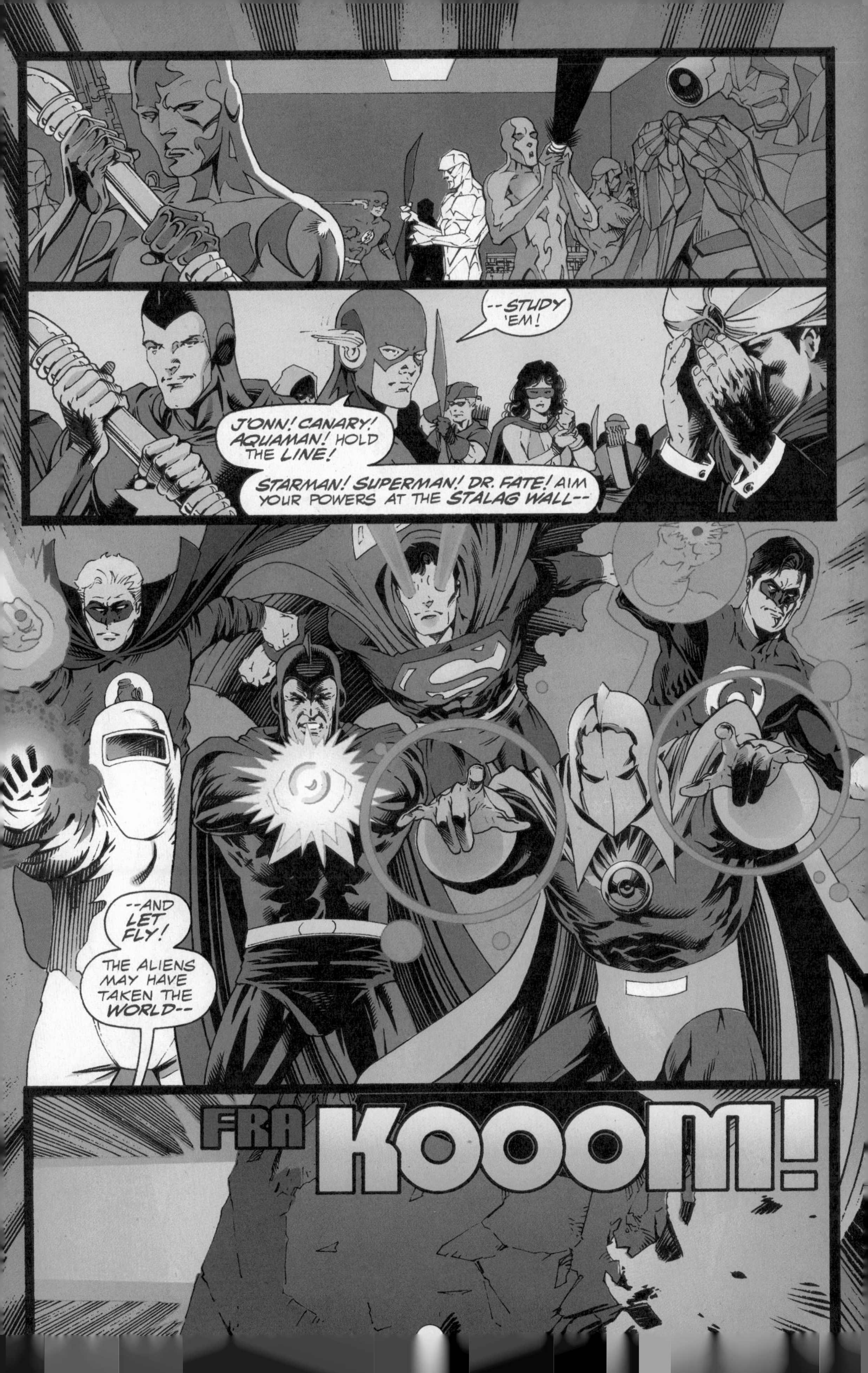
--STUDY 'EM!
J'ONN! CANARY! AQUAMAN! HOLD THE LINE!
STARMAN! SUPERMAN! DR. FATE! AIM YOUR POWERS AT THE STALAG WALL--
--AND LET FLY!
THE ALIENS MAY HAVE TAKEN THE WORLD--
FRA KOOOM!

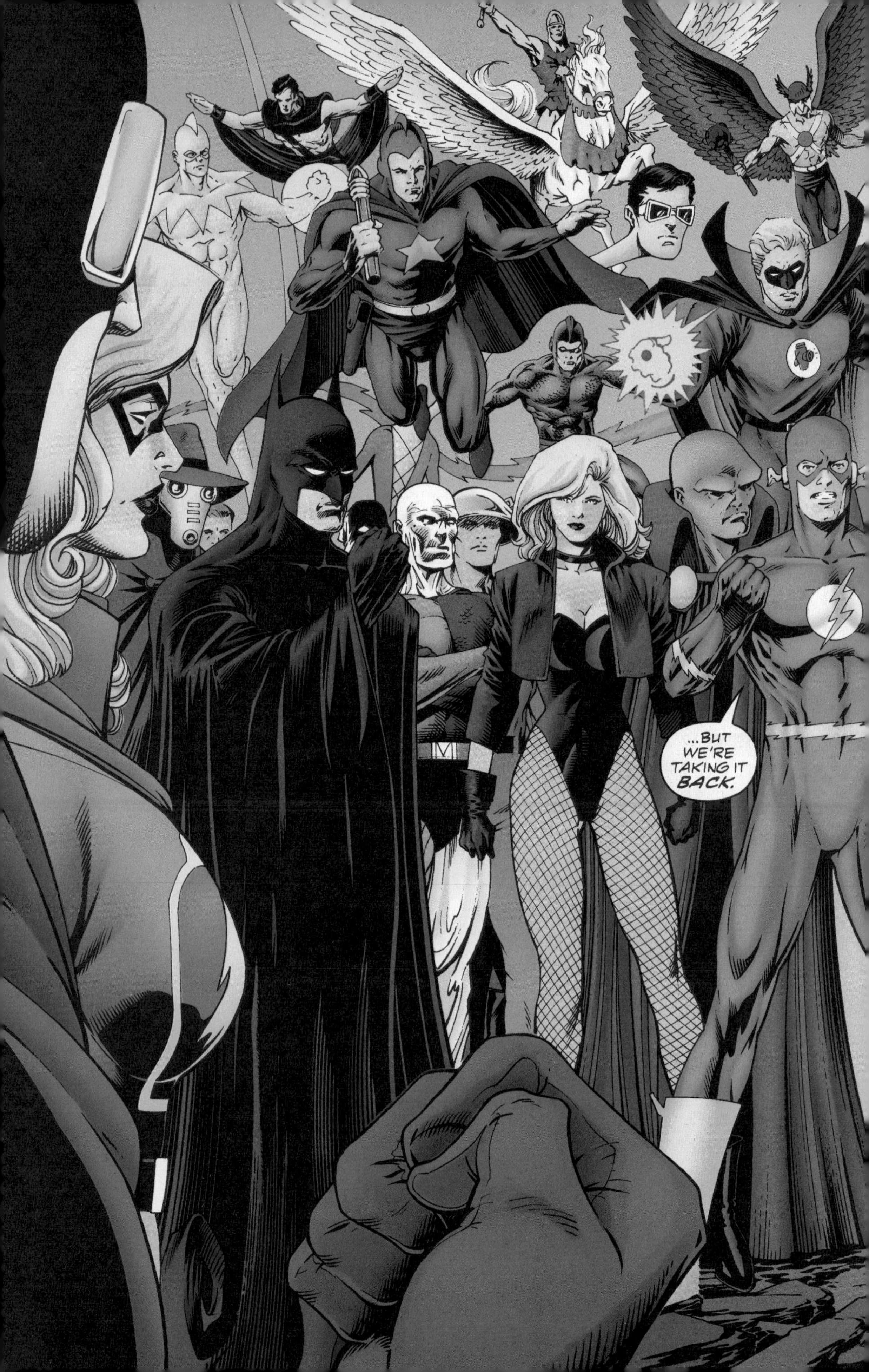
...BUT WE'RE TAKING IT BACK.

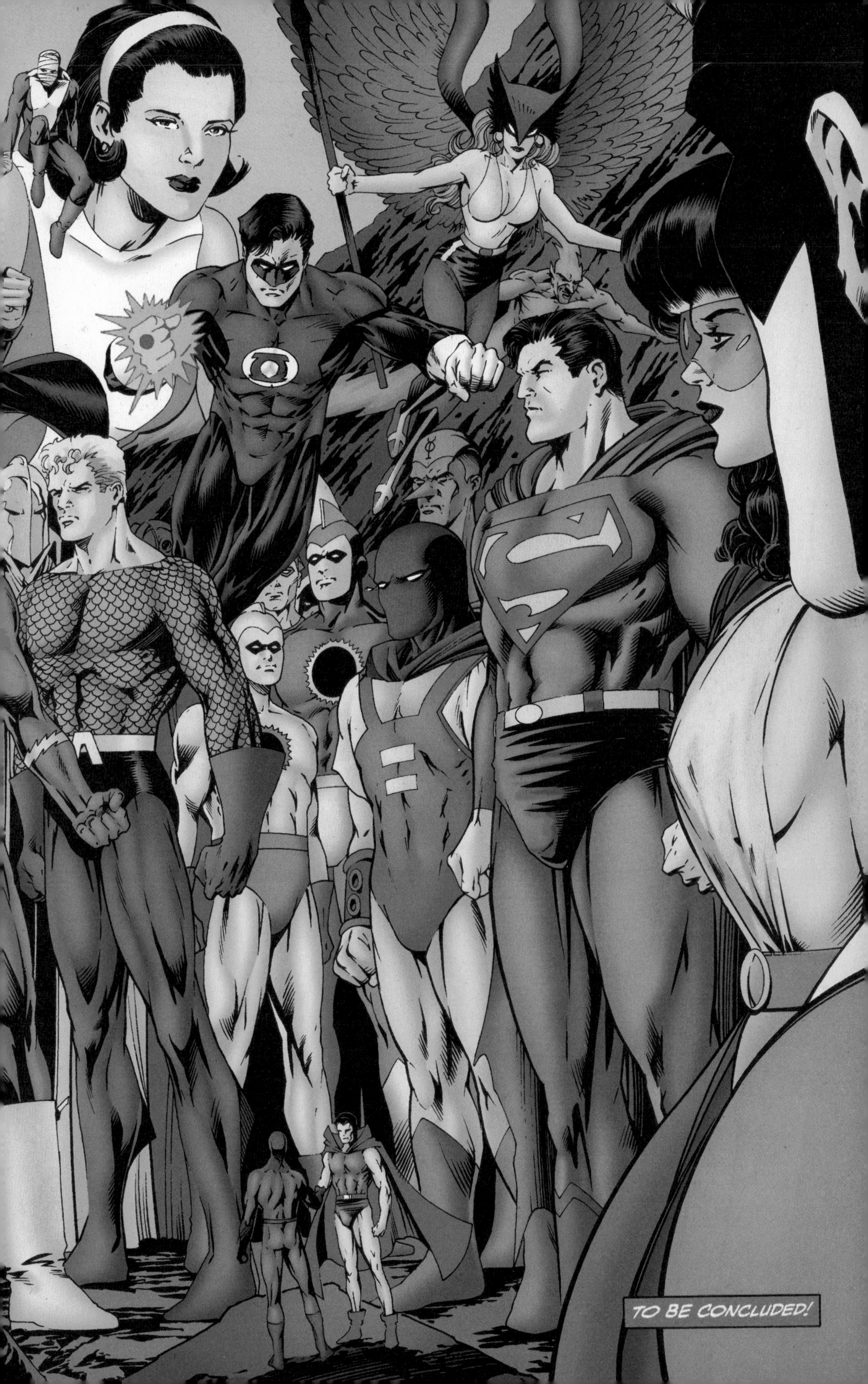
TO BE CONCLUDED!

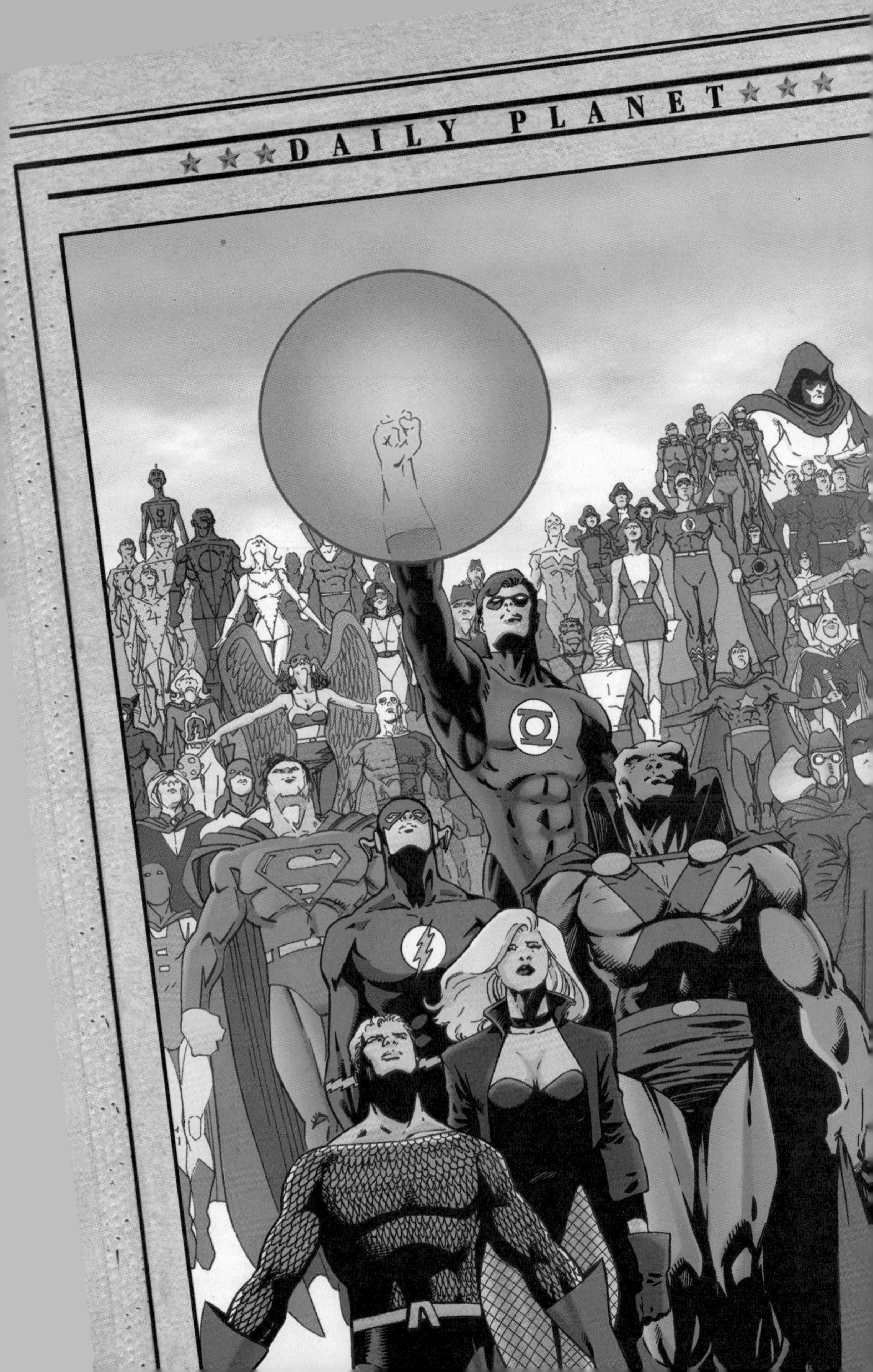
DAILY PLANET

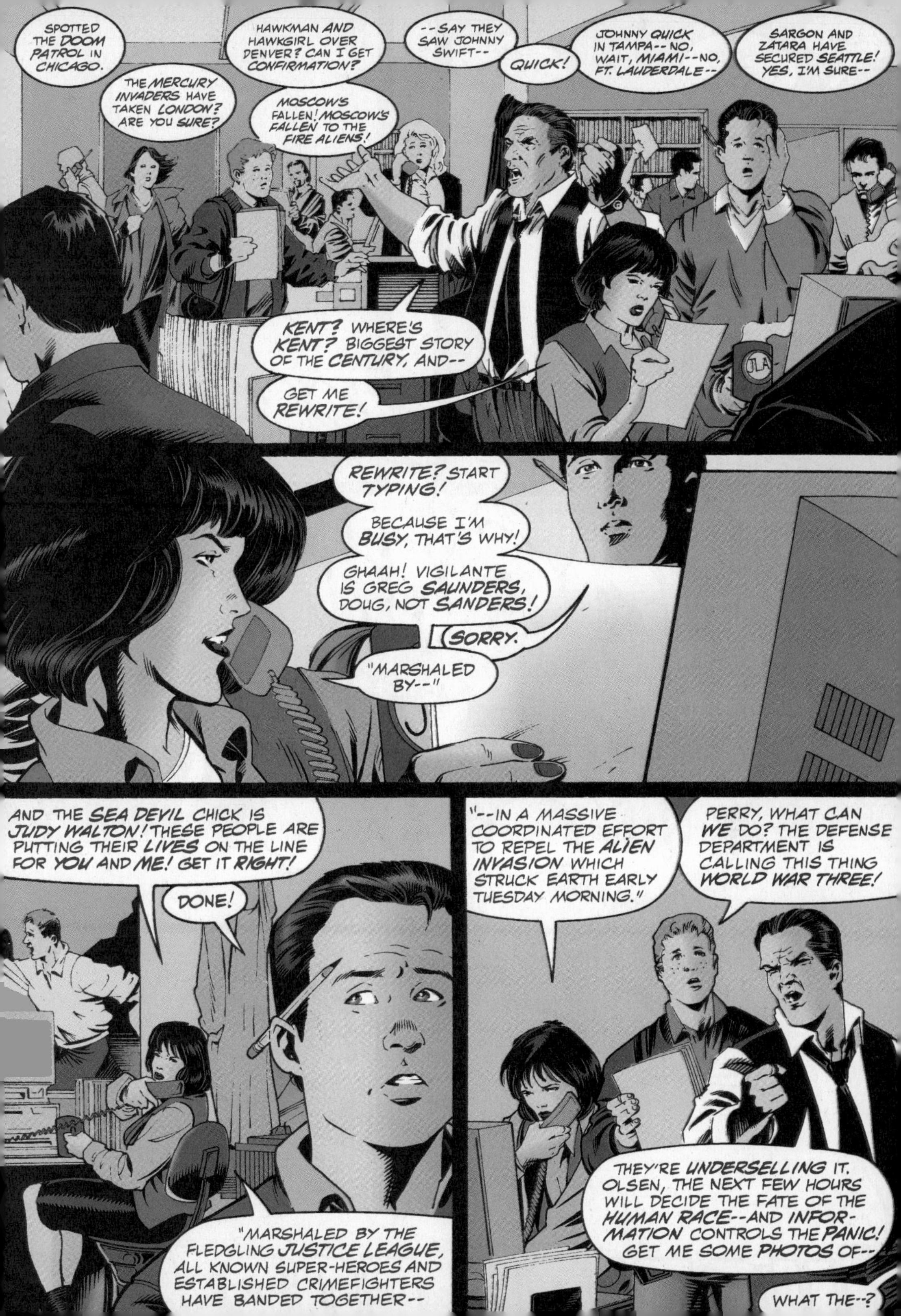

SPOTTED THE DOOM PATROL IN CHICAGO.
HAWKMAN AND HAWKGIRL OVER DENVER? CAN I GET CONFIRMATION?
--SAY THEY SAW JOHNNY SWIFT--
QUICK!
JOHNNY QUICK IN TAMPA--NO, WAIT, MIAMI--NO, FT. LAUDERDALE--
SARGON AND ZATARA HAVE SECURED SEATTLE! YES, I'M SURE--
THE MERCURY INVADERS HAVE TAKEN LONDON? ARE YOU SURE?
MOSCOW'S FALLEN! MOSCOW'S FALLEN TO THE FIRE ALIENS!
KENT? WHERE'S KENT? BIGGEST STORY OF THE CENTURY, AND--
GET ME REWRITE!
REWRITE? START TYPING!
BECAUSE I'M BUSY, THAT'S WHY!
GHAAH! VIGILANTE IS GREG SAUNDERS, DOUG, NOT SANDERS!
SORRY.
"MARSHALED BY--"
AND THE SEA DEVIL CHICK IS JUDY WALTON! THESE PEOPLE ARE PUTTING THEIR LIVES ON THE LINE FOR YOU AND ME! GET IT RIGHT!
DONE!
"MARSHALED BY THE FLEDGLING JUSTICE LEAGUE, ALL KNOWN SUPER-HEROES AND ESTABLISHED CRIMEFIGHTERS HAVE BANDED TOGETHER--
"--IN A MASSIVE COORDINATED EFFORT TO REPEL THE ALIEN INVASION WHICH STRUCK EARTH EARLY TUESDAY MORNING."
PERRY, WHAT CAN WE DO? THE DEFENSE DEPARTMENT IS CALLING THIS THING WORLD WAR THREE!
THEY'RE UNDERSELLING IT. OLSEN, THE NEXT FEW HOURS WILL DECIDE THE FATE OF THE HUMAN RACE--AND INFORMATION CONTROLS THE PANIC! GET ME SOME PHOTOS OF--
WHAT THE--?

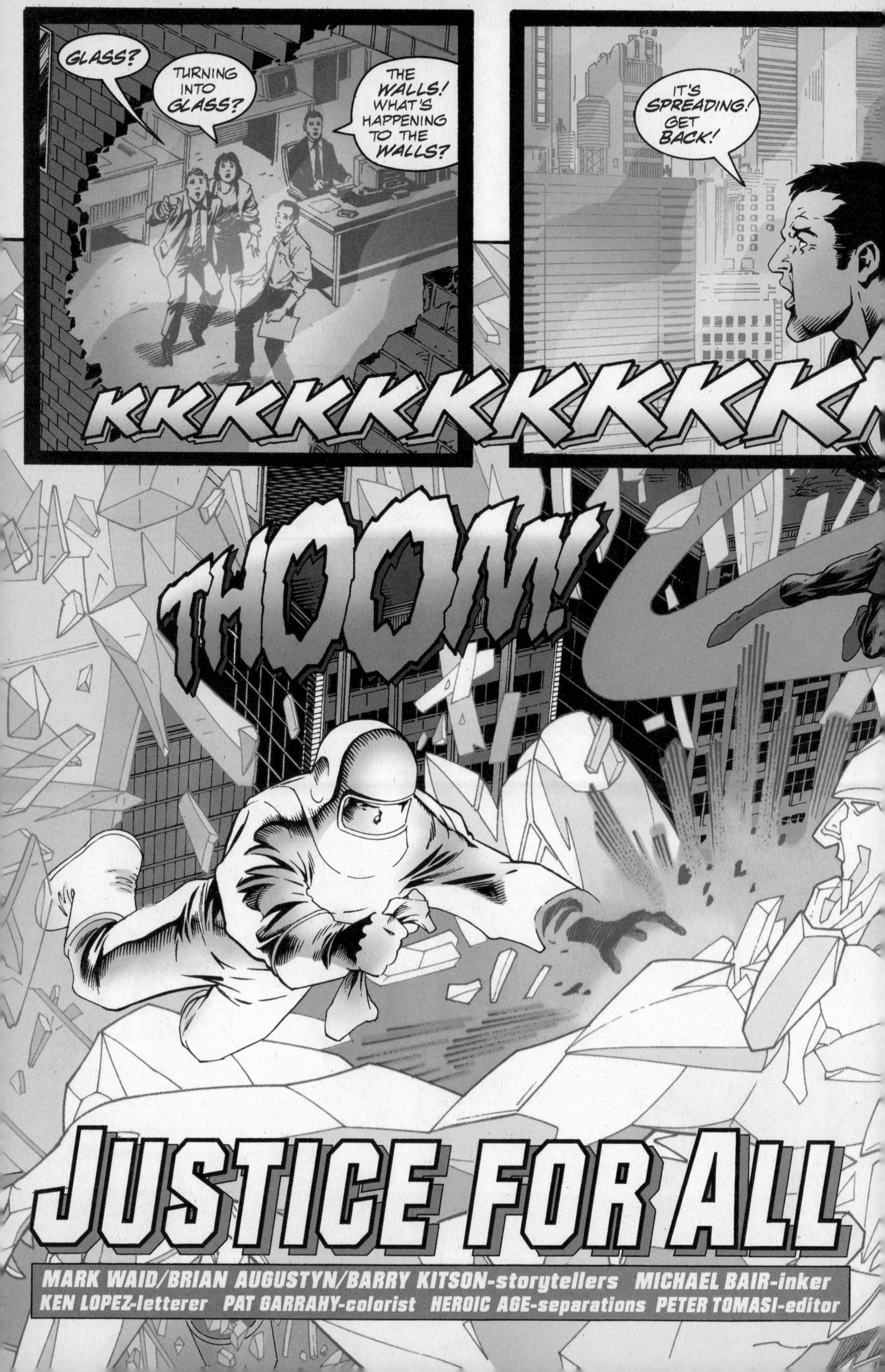
GLASS?
TURNING INTO GLASS?
THE WALLS! WHAT'S HAPPENING TO THE WALLS?
IT'S SPREADING! GET BACK!
KKKKKKKKKKKK
THOOM!
JUSTICE FOR ALL
MARK WAID/BRIAN AUGUSTYN/BARRY KITSON-storytellers MICHAEL BAIR-inker
KEN LOPEZ-letterer PAT GARRAHY-colorist HEROIC AGE-separations PETER TOMASI-editor

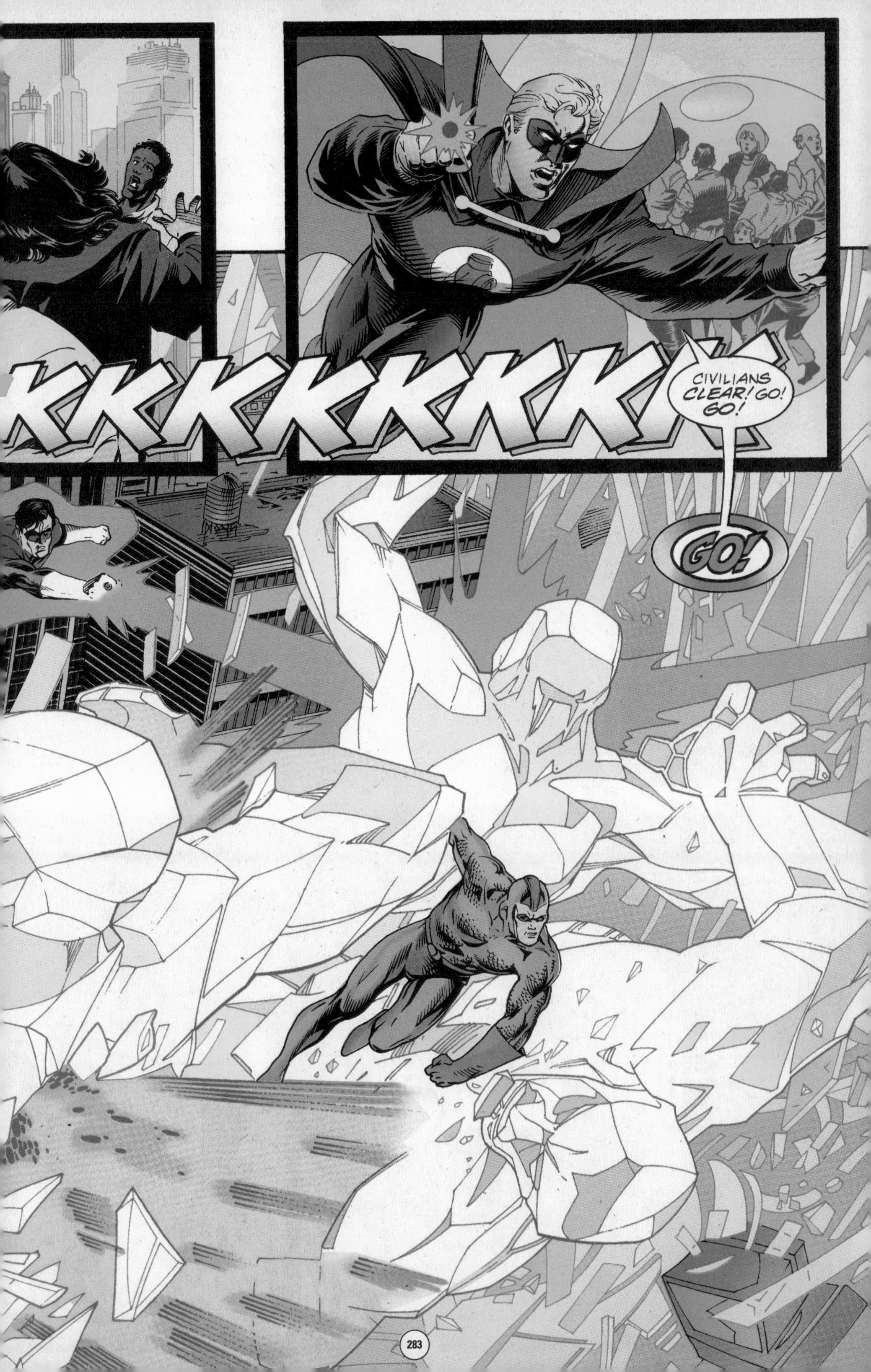
KKKKKKKKK
CIVILIANS CLEAR! GO! GO!
GO!

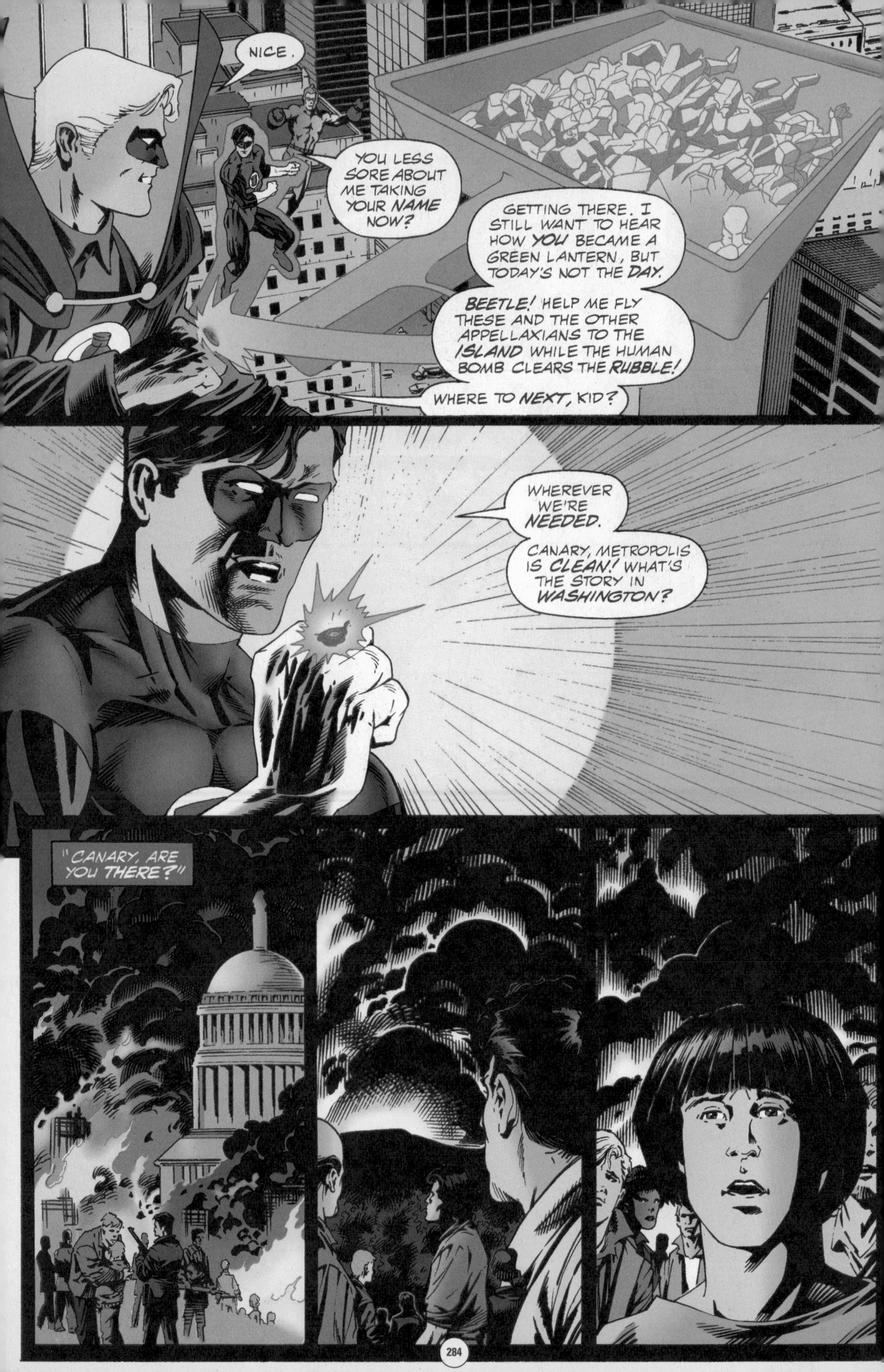
NICE.
YOU LESS SORE ABOUT ME TAKING YOUR NAME NOW?
GETTING THERE. I STILL WANT TO HEAR HOW YOU BECAME A GREEN LANTERN, BUT TODAY'S NOT THE DAY.
BEETLE! HELP ME FLY THESE AND THE OTHER APPELLAXIANS TO THE ISLAND WHILE THE HUMAN BOMB CLEARS THE RUBBLE!
WHERE TO NEXT, KID?
WHEREVER WE'RE NEEDED.
CANARY, METROPOLIS IS CLEAN! WHAT'S THE STORY IN WASHINGTON?
"CANARY, ARE YOU THERE?"

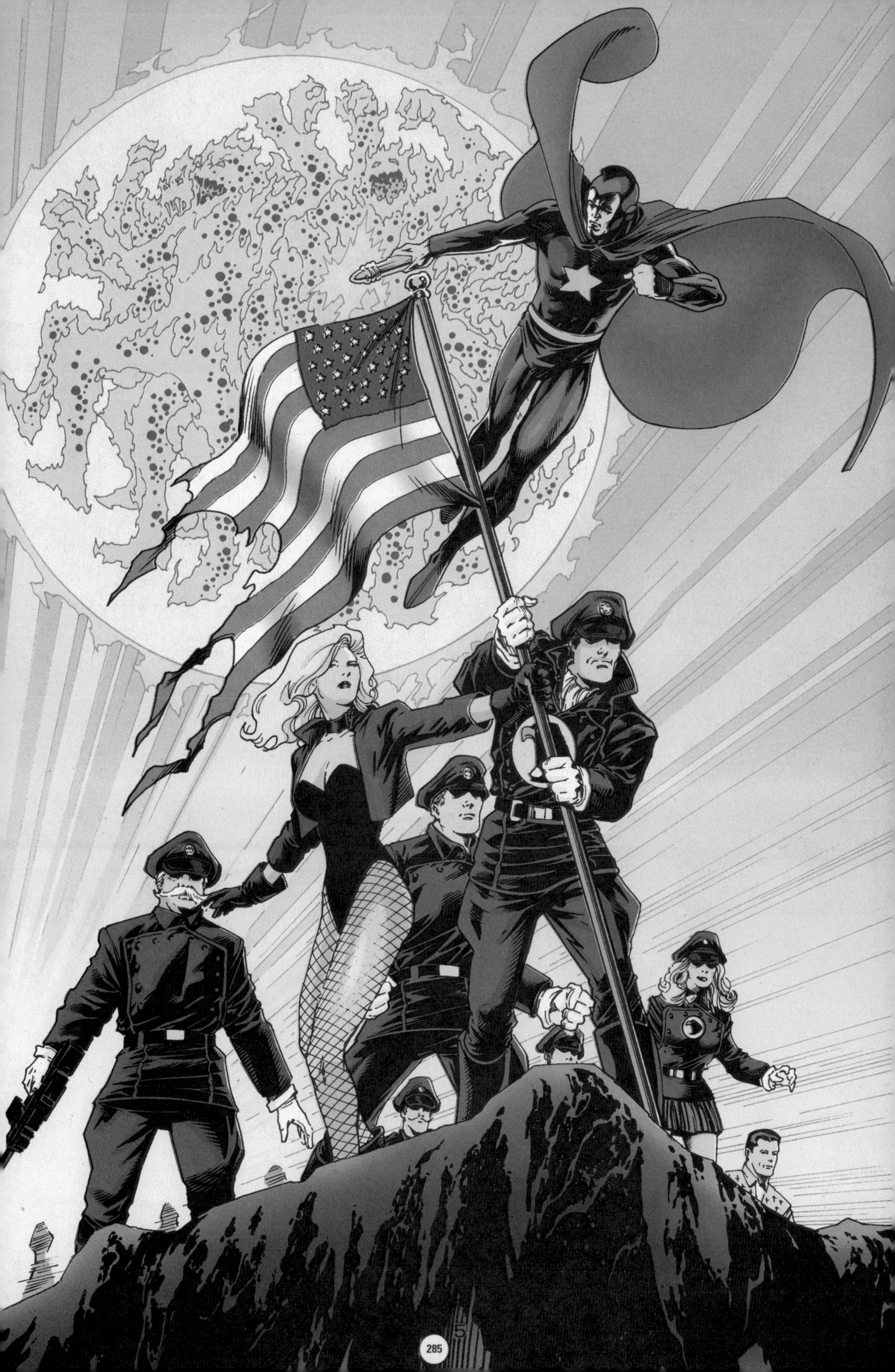

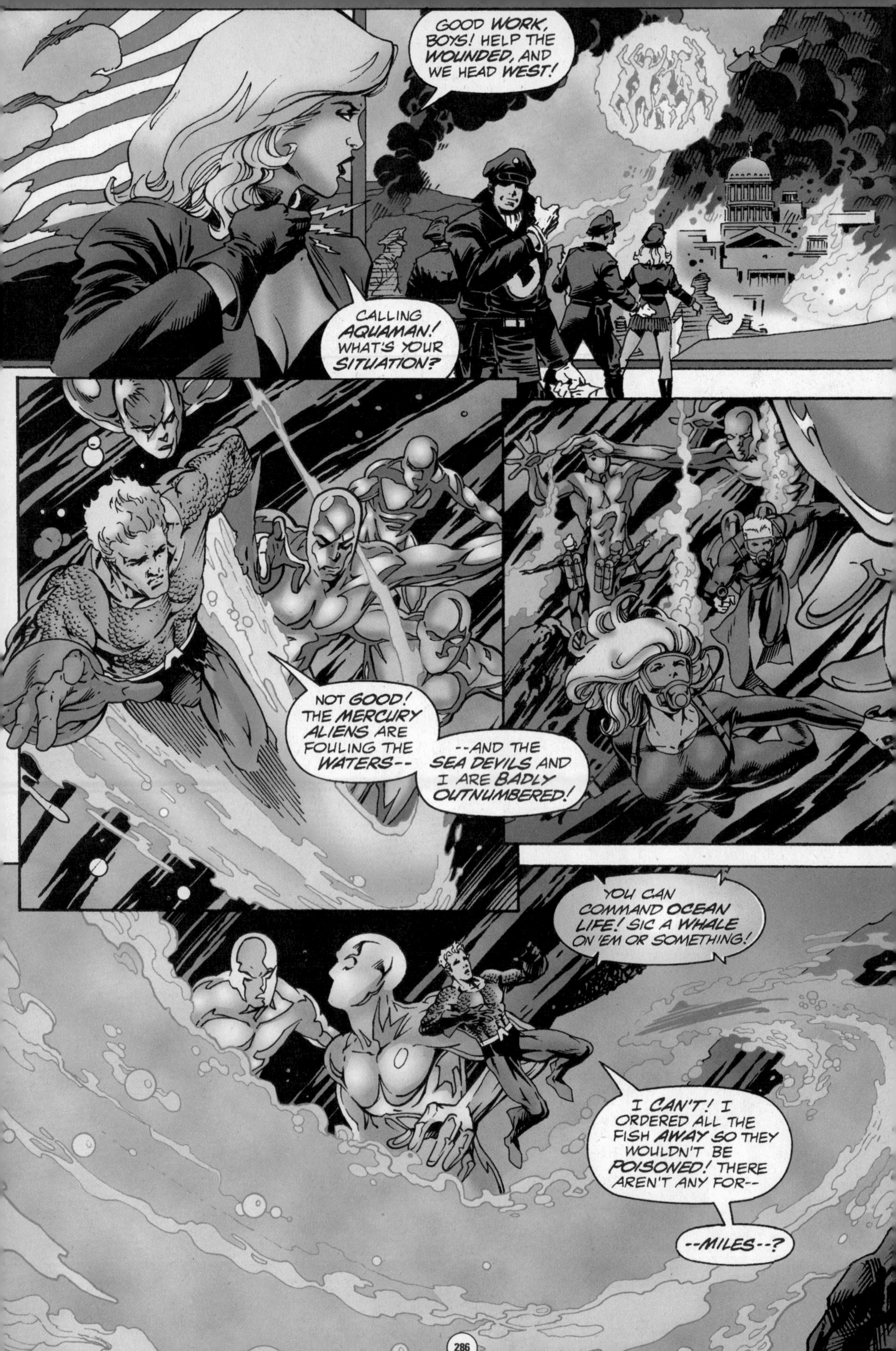
GOOD WORK, BOYS! HELP THE WOUNDED, AND WE HEAD WEST!
CALLING AQUAMAN! WHAT'S YOUR SITUATION?
NOT GOOD! THE MERCURY ALIENS ARE FOULING THE WATERS--
--AND THE SEA DEVILS AND I ARE BADLY OUTNUMBERED!
YOU CAN COMMAND OCEAN LIFE! SIC A WHALE ON 'EM OR SOMETHING!
I CAN'T! I ORDERED ALL THE FISH AWAY SO THEY WOULDN'T BE POISONED! THERE AREN'T ANY FOR--
--MILES--?

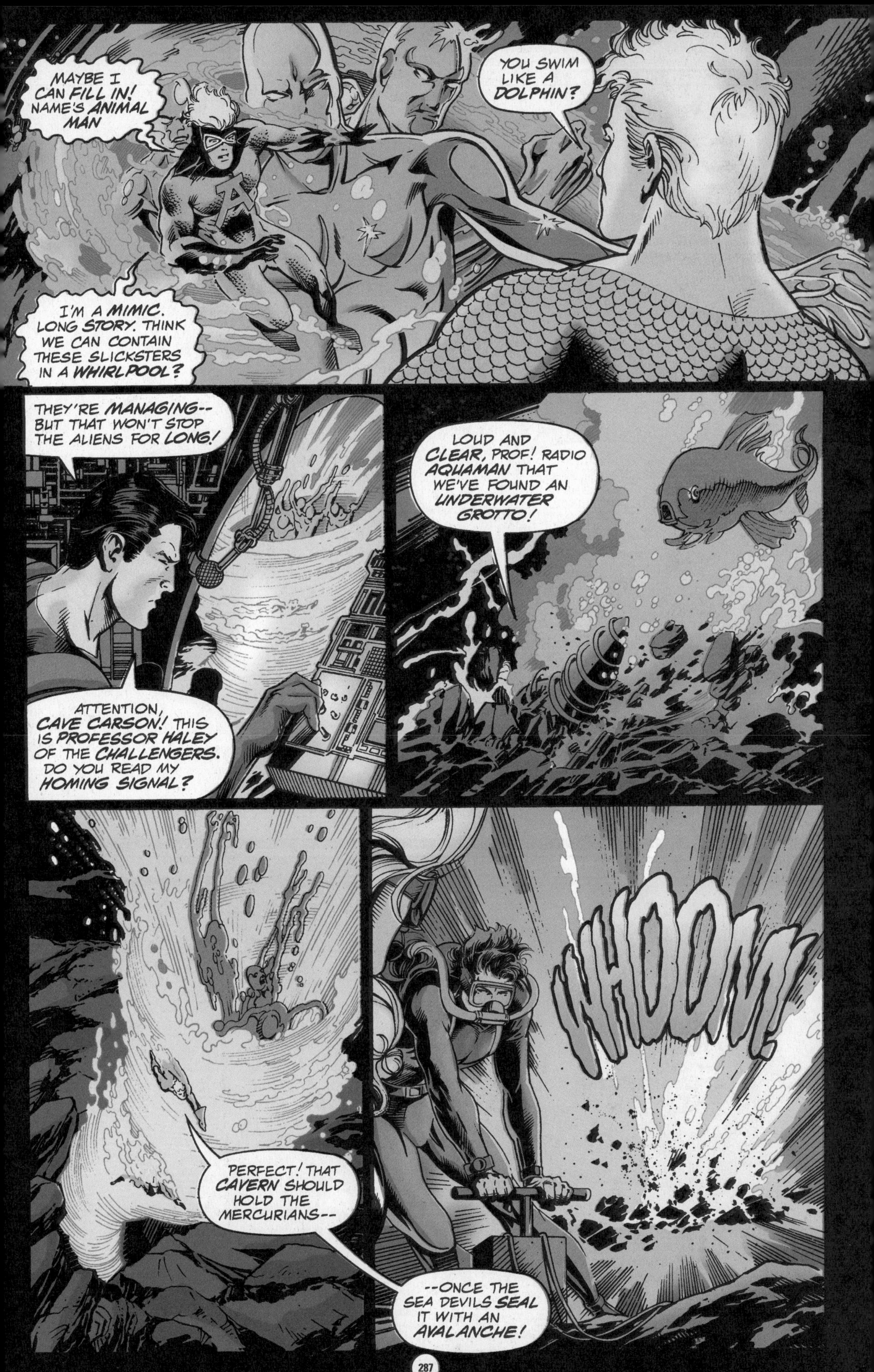
MAYBE I CAN FILL IN! NAME'S ANIMAL MAN
YOU SWIM LIKE A DOLPHIN?
I'M A MIMIC. LONG STORY. THINK WE CAN CONTAIN THESE SLICKSTERS IN A WHIRLPOOL?
THEY'RE MANAGING--BUT THAT WON'T STOP THE ALIENS FOR LONG!
ATTENTION, CAVE CARSON! THIS IS PROFESSOR HALEY OF THE CHALLENGERS. DO YOU READ MY HOMING SIGNAL?
LOUD AND CLEAR, PROF! RADIO AQUAMAN THAT WE'VE FOUND AN UNDERWATER GROTTO!
PERFECT! THAT CAVERN SHOULD HOLD THE MERCURIANS--
--ONCE THE SEA DEVILS SEAL IT WITH AN AVALANCHE!
WHOOM!

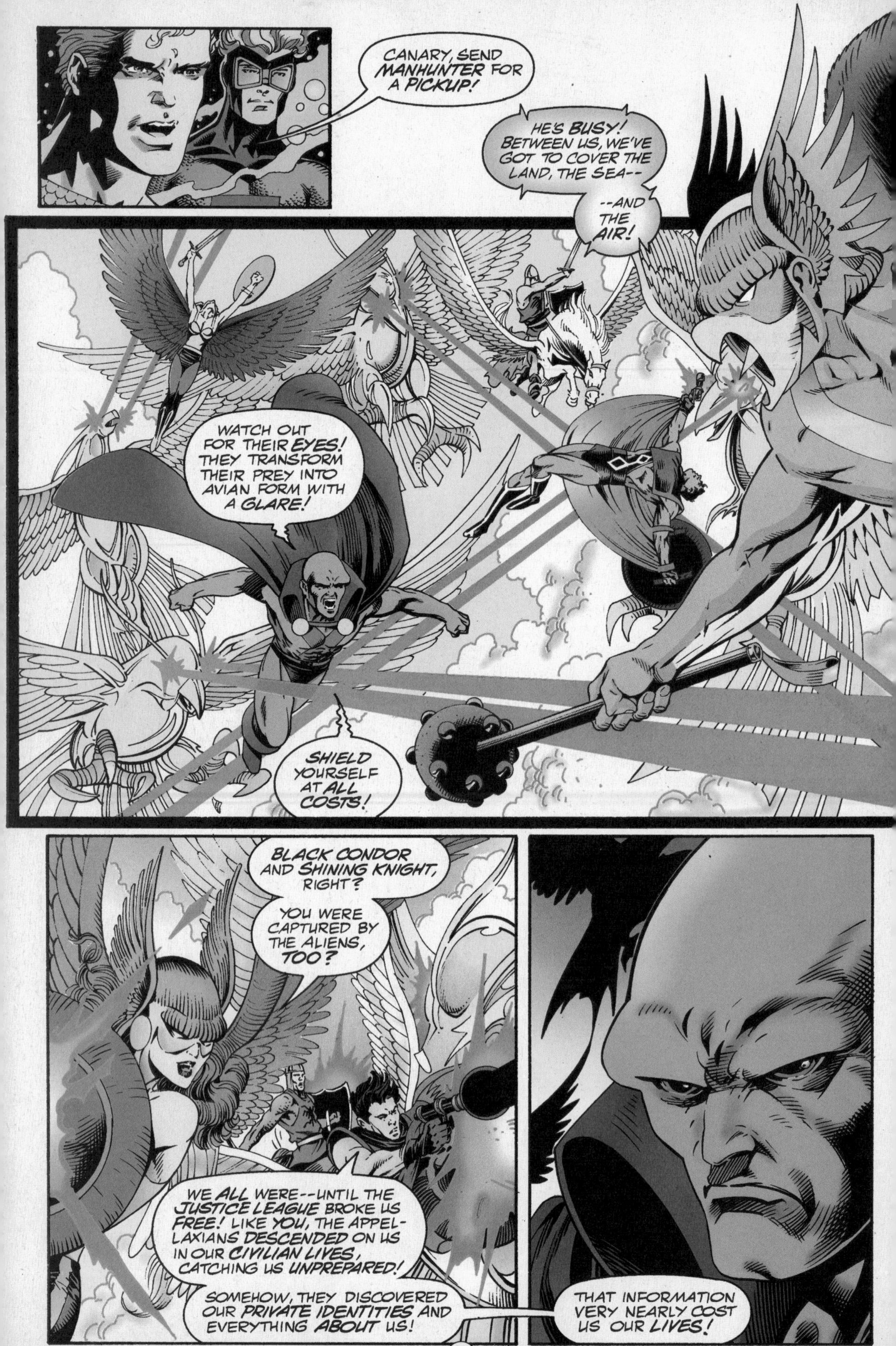
CANARY, SEND MANHUNTER FOR A PICKUP!
HE'S BUSY! BETWEEN US, WE'VE GOT TO COVER THE LAND, THE SEA--
--AND THE AIR!
WATCH OUT FOR THEIR EYES! THEY TRANSFORM THEIR PREY INTO AVIAN FORM WITH A GLARE!
SHIELD YOURSELF AT ALL COSTS!
BLACK CONDOR AND SHINING KNIGHT, RIGHT?
YOU WERE CAPTURED BY THE ALIENS, TOO?
WE ALL WERE--UNTIL THE JUSTICE LEAGUE BROKE US FREE! LIKE YOU, THE APPEL-LAXIANS DESCENDED ON US IN OUR CIVILIAN LIVES, CATCHING US UNPREPARED!
SOMEHOW, THEY DISCOVERED OUR PRIVATE IDENTITIES AND EVERYTHING ABOUT US!
THAT INFORMATION VERY NEARLY COST US OUR LIVES!

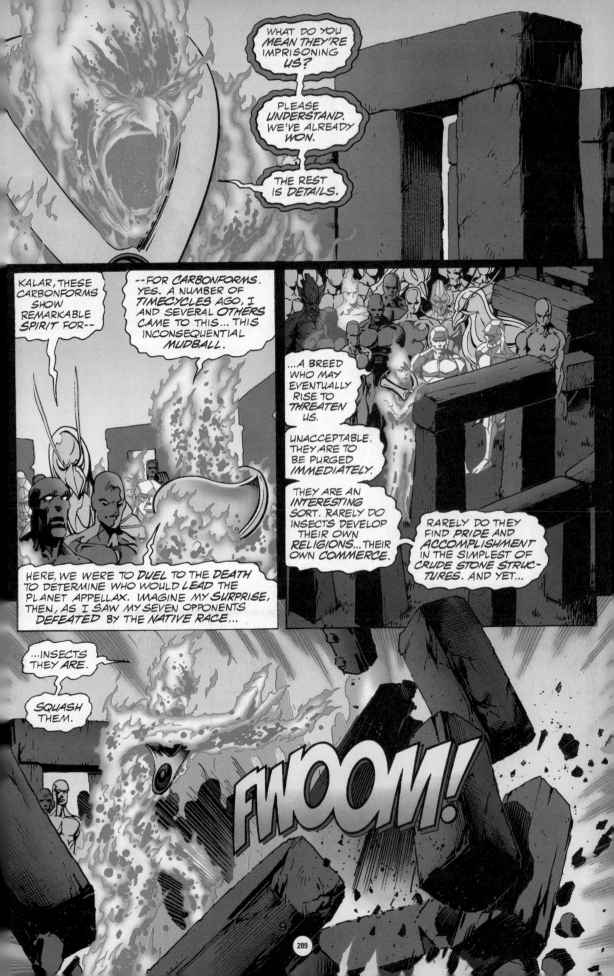

WHAT DO YOU *MEAN* THEY'RE *IMPRISONING* US?

PLEASE *UNDERSTAND*. WE'VE ALREADY *WON*.

THE REST IS *DETAILS*.

KALAR, THESE CARBONFORMS SHOW REMARKABLE *SPIRIT* FOR--

--FOR *CARBONFORMS*. YES. A NUMBER OF *TIMECYCLES* AGO, I AND SEVERAL *OTHERS* CAME TO THIS... THIS *INCONSEQUENTIAL MUDBALL*.

HERE, WE WERE TO *DUEL* TO THE *DEATH* TO DETERMINE WHO WOULD *LEAD* THE PLANET APPELLAX. IMAGINE MY *SURPRISE*, THEN, AS I SAW MY SEVEN OPPONENTS *DEFEATED* BY THE *NATIVE RACE*...

...A BREED WHO MAY EVENTUALLY RISE TO *THREATEN* US.

UNACCEPTABLE. THEY ARE TO BE *PURGED IMMEDIATELY*.

THEY ARE AN *INTERESTING* SORT. RARELY DO INSECTS DEVELOP THEIR OWN *RELIGIONS*... THEIR OWN *COMMERCE*.

RARELY DO THEY FIND *PRIDE* AND *ACCOMPLISHMENT* IN THE SIMPLEST OF *CRUDE STONE STRUC-TURES*. AND YET...

...*INSECTS* THEY ARE.

SQUASH THEM.

FWOOM!

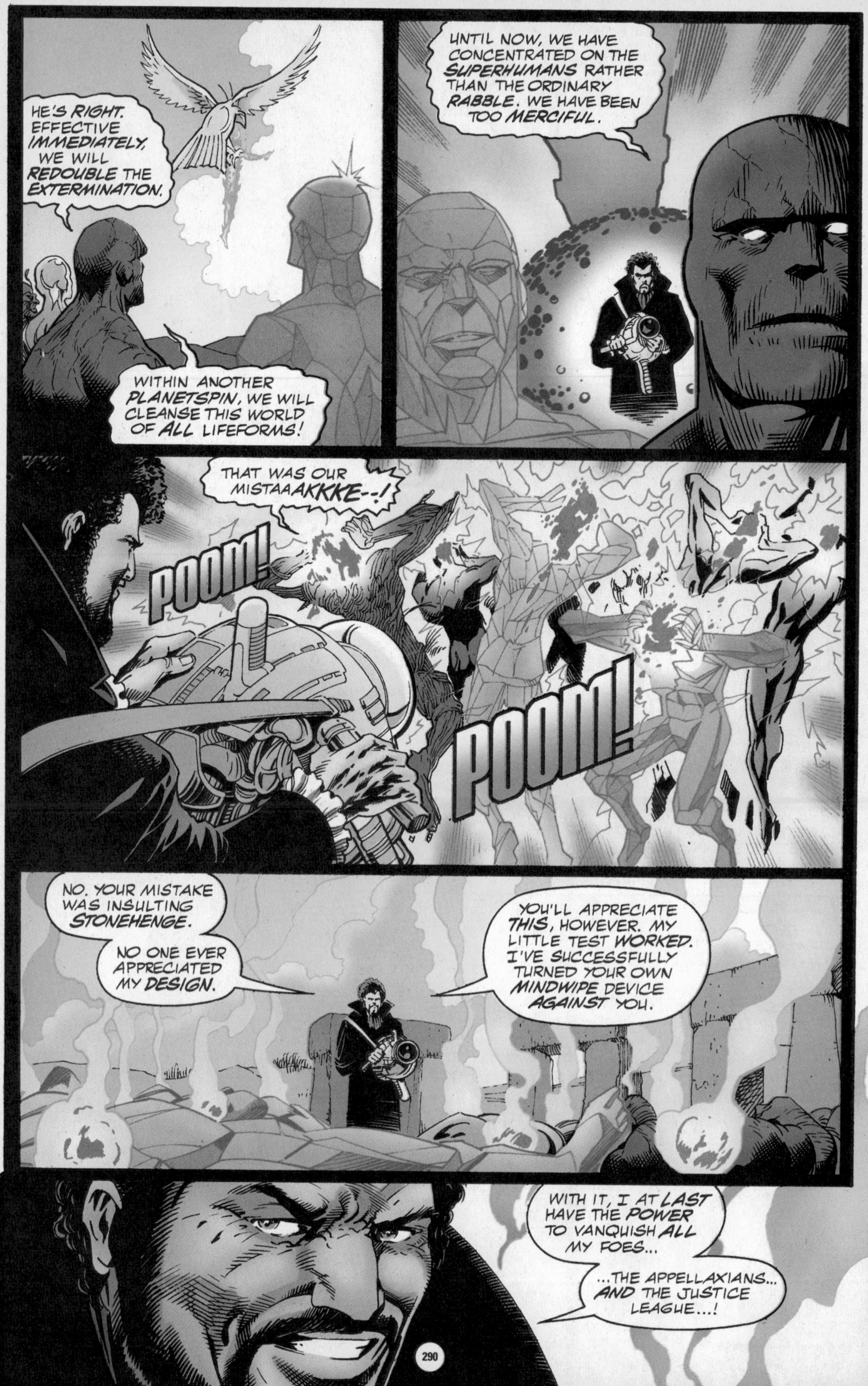
HE'S RIGHT. EFFECTIVE IMMEDIATELY, WE WILL REDOUBLE THE EXTERMINATION.
WITHIN ANOTHER PLANETSPIN, WE WILL CLEANSE THIS WORLD OF ALL LIFEFORMS!
UNTIL NOW, WE HAVE CONCENTRATED ON THE SUPERHUMANS RATHER THAN THE ORDINARY RABBLE. WE HAVE BEEN TOO MERCIFUL.
THAT WAS OUR MISTAAAKKKE--!
POOM!
POOM!
NO. YOUR MISTAKE WAS INSULTING STONEHENGE.
NO ONE EVER APPRECIATED MY DESIGN.
YOU'LL APPRECIATE THIS, HOWEVER. MY LITTLE TEST WORKED. I'VE SUCCESSFULLY TURNED YOUR OWN MINDWIPE DEVICE AGAINST YOU.
WITH IT, I AT LAST HAVE THE POWER TO VANQUISH ALL MY FOES...
...THE APPELLAXIANS... AND THE JUSTICE LEAGUE...!

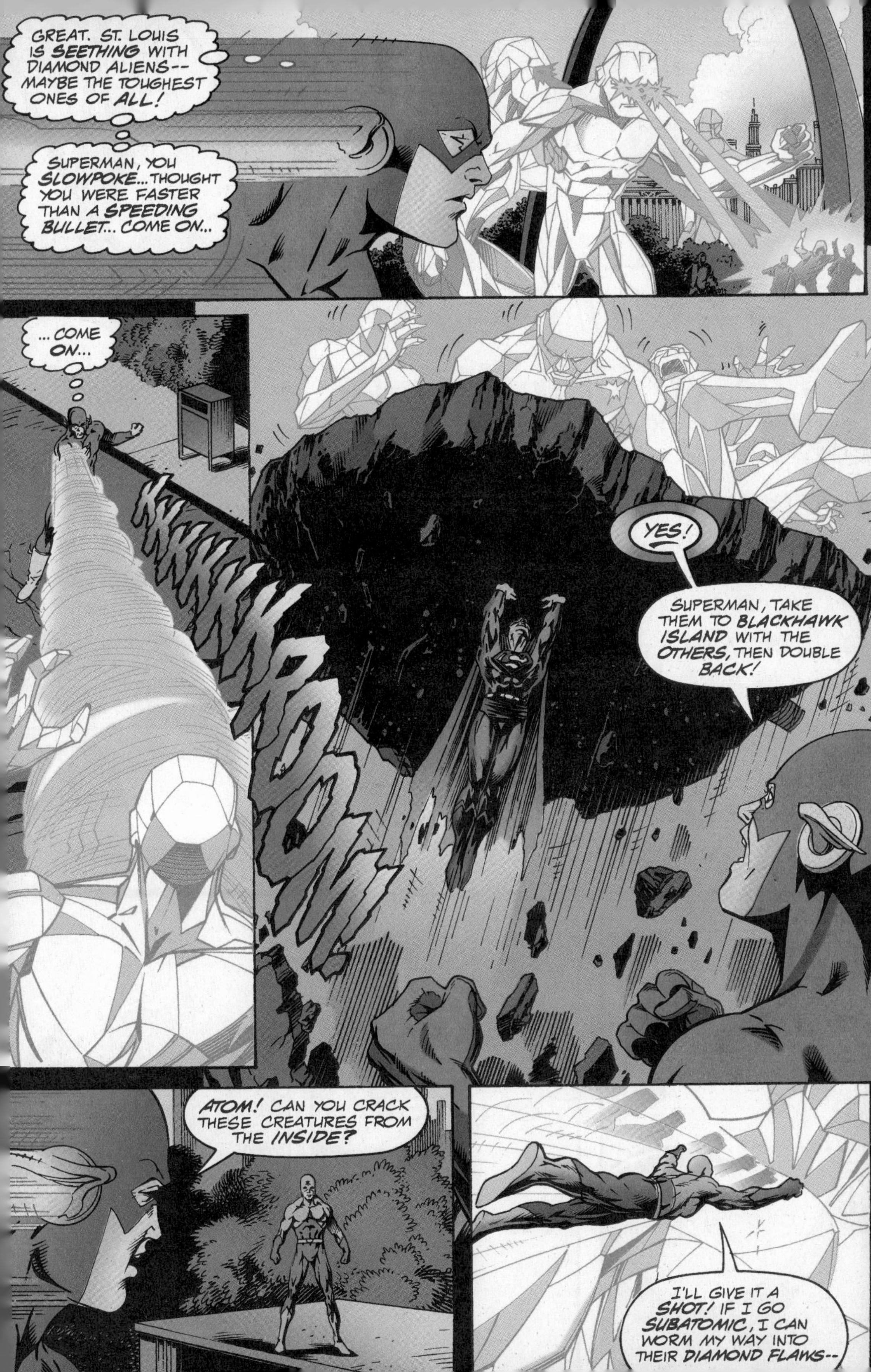
GREAT. ST. LOUIS IS SEETHING WITH DIAMOND ALIENS--MAYBE THE TOUGHEST ONES OF ALL!
SUPERMAN, YOU SLOWPOKE... THOUGHT YOU WERE FASTER THAN A SPEEDING BULLET... COME ON...
...COME ON...
KKKKKKKROOOM!
YES!
SUPERMAN, TAKE THEM TO BLACKHAWK ISLAND WITH THE OTHERS, THEN DOUBLE BACK!
ATOM! CAN YOU CRACK THESE CREATURES FROM THE INSIDE?
I'LL GIVE IT A SHOT! IF I GO SUBATOMIC, I CAN WORM MY WAY INTO THEIR DIAMOND FLAWS--

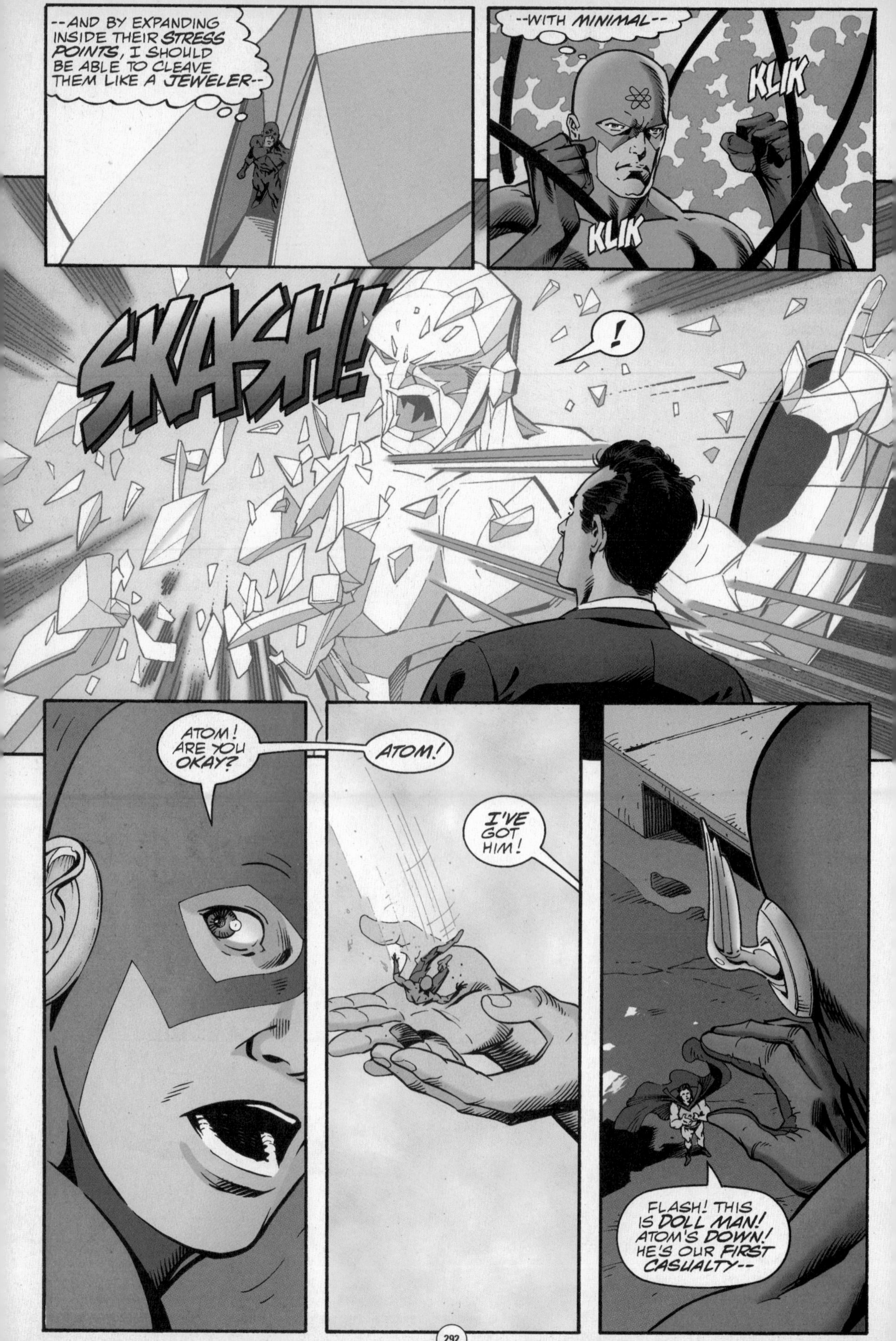
--AND BY EXPANDING INSIDE THEIR STRESS POINTS, I SHOULD BE ABLE TO CLEAVE THEM LIKE A JEWELER--
--WITH MINIMAL--
KLIK
KLIK
SKASH!
!
ATOM! ARE YOU OKAY?
ATOM!
I'VE GOT HIM!
FLASH! THIS IS DOLL MAN! ATOM'S DOWN! HE'S OUR FIRST CASUALTY--

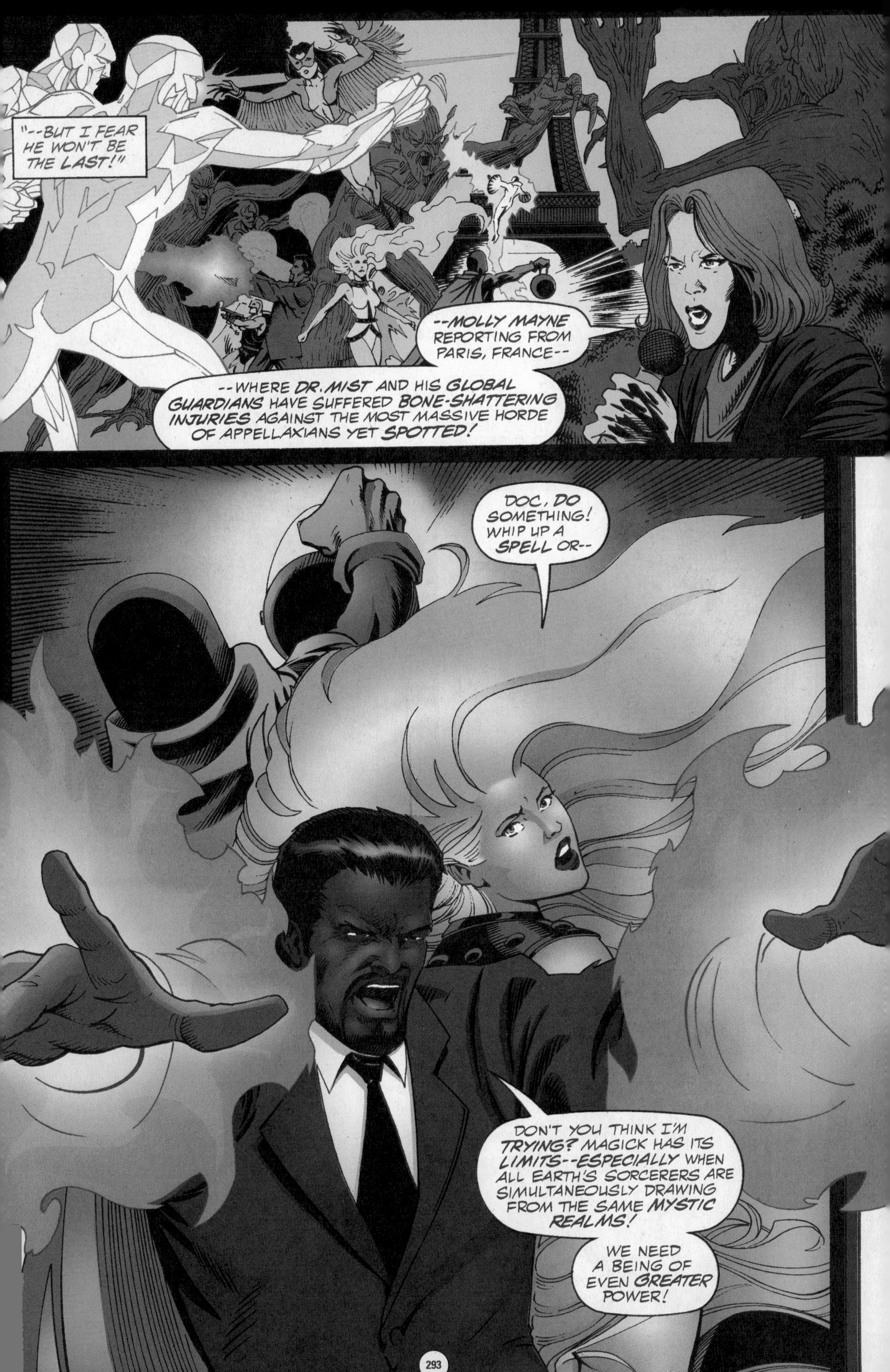
"--BUT I FEAR HE WON'T BE THE LAST!"
--MOLLY MAYNE REPORTING FROM PARIS, FRANCE--
--WHERE DR. MIST AND HIS GLOBAL GUARDIANS HAVE SUFFERED BONE-SHATTERING INJURIES AGAINST THE MOST MASSIVE HORDE OF APPELLAXIANS YET SPOTTED!
DOC, DO SOMETHING! WHIP UP A SPELL OR--
DON'T YOU THINK I'M TRYING? MAGICK HAS ITS LIMITS--ESPECIALLY WHEN ALL EARTH'S SORCERERS ARE SIMULTANEOUSLY DRAWING FROM THE SAME MYSTIC REALMS!
WE NEED A BEING OF EVEN GREATER POWER!

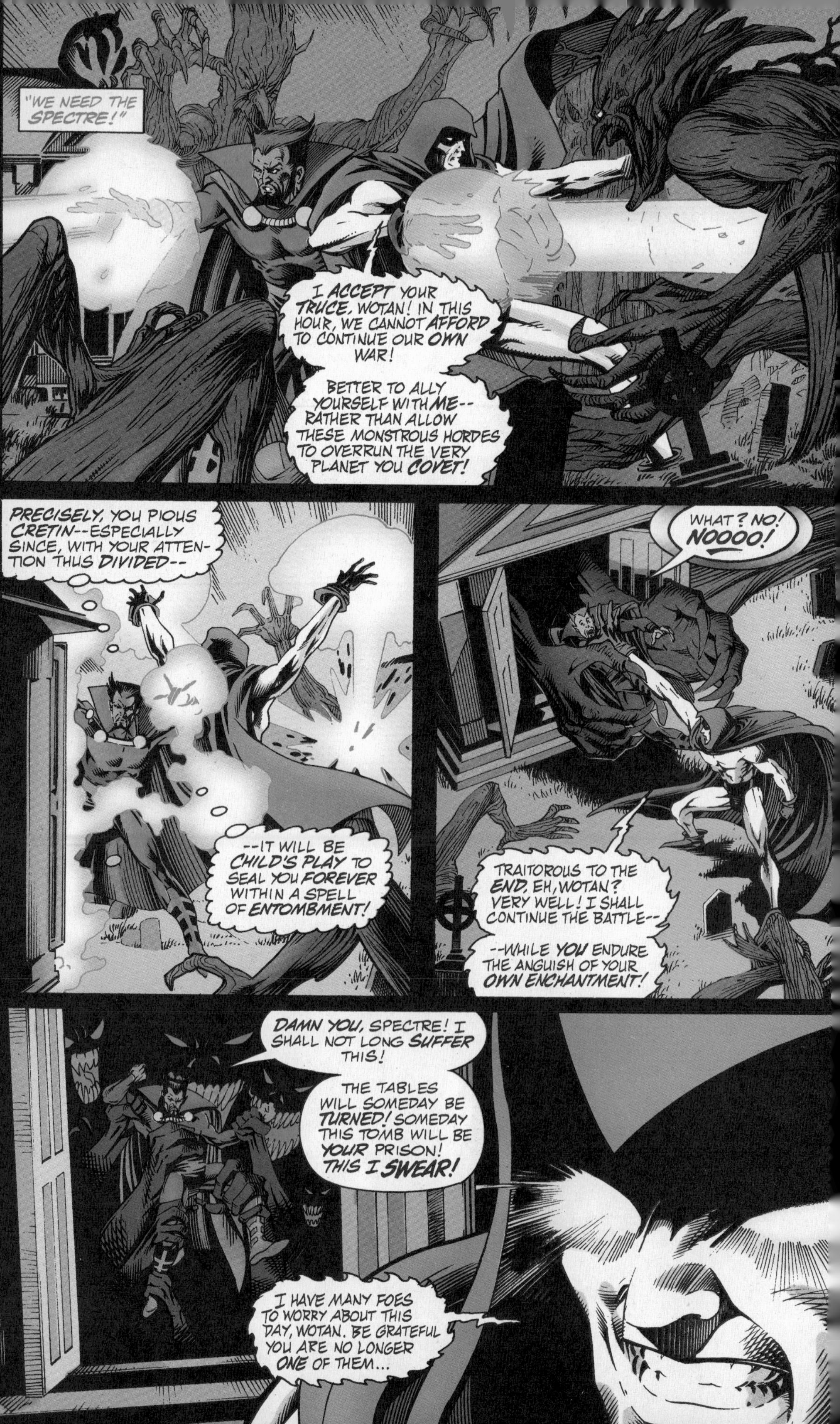
"WE NEED THE SPECTRE!"
I ACCEPT YOUR TRUCE, WOTAN! IN THIS HOUR, WE CANNOT AFFORD TO CONTINUE OUR OWN WAR!
BETTER TO ALLY YOURSELF WITH ME-- RATHER THAN ALLOW THESE MONSTROUS HORDES TO OVERRUN THE VERY PLANET YOU COVET!
PRECISELY, YOU PIOUS CRETIN--ESPECIALLY SINCE, WITH YOUR ATTENTION THUS DIVIDED--
--IT WILL BE CHILD'S PLAY TO SEAL YOU FOREVER WITHIN A SPELL OF ENTOMBMENT!
WHAT? NO! NOOOO!
TRAITOROUS TO THE END, EH, WOTAN? VERY WELL! I SHALL CONTINUE THE BATTLE--
--WHILE YOU ENDURE THE ANGUISH OF YOUR OWN ENCHANTMENT!
DAMN YOU, SPECTRE! I SHALL NOT LONG SUFFER THIS!
THE TABLES WILL SOMEDAY BE TURNED! SOMEDAY THIS TOMB WILL BE YOUR PRISON! THIS I SWEAR!
I HAVE MANY FOES TO WORRY ABOUT THIS DAY, WOTAN. BE GRATEFUL YOU ARE NO LONGER ONE OF THEM...

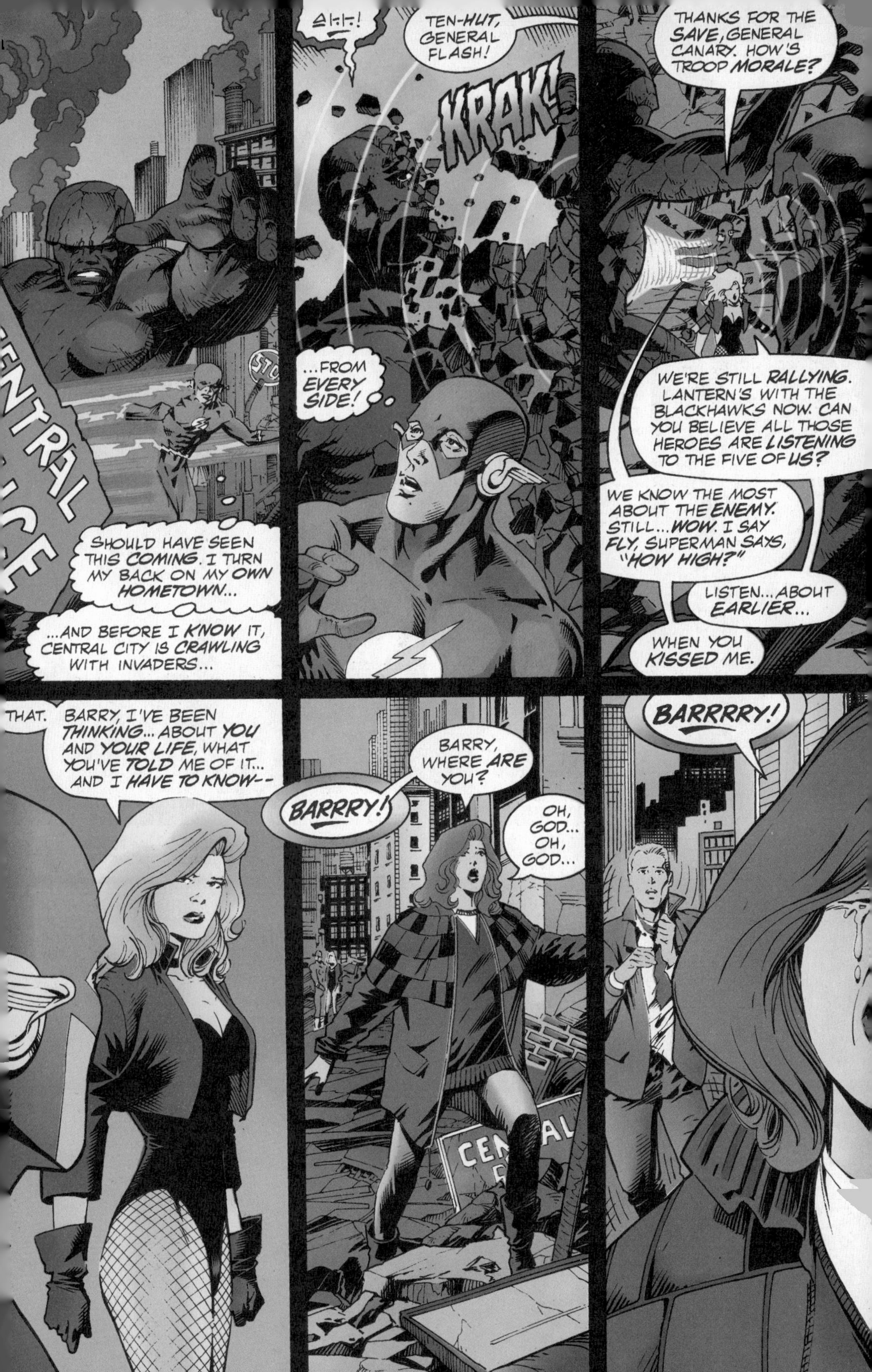
SHOULD HAVE SEEN THIS COMING. I TURN MY BACK ON MY OWN HOMETOWN...
...AND BEFORE I KNOW IT, CENTRAL CITY IS CRAWLING WITH INVADERS...
TEN-HUT, GENERAL FLASH!
KRAK!
...FROM EVERY SIDE!
THANKS FOR THE SAVE, GENERAL CANARY. HOW'S TROOP MORALE?
WE'RE STILL RALLYING. LANTERN'S WITH THE BLACKHAWKS NOW. CAN YOU BELIEVE ALL THOSE HEROES ARE LISTENING TO THE FIVE OF US?
WE KNOW THE MOST ABOUT THE ENEMY. STILL...WOW. I SAY FLY, SUPERMAN SAYS, "HOW HIGH?"
LISTEN...ABOUT EARLIER...
WHEN YOU KISSED ME.
THAT.
BARRY, I'VE BEEN THINKING... ABOUT YOU AND YOUR LIFE, WHAT YOU'VE TOLD ME OF IT... AND I HAVE TO KNOW--
BARRRY!
BARRY, WHERE ARE YOU?
OH, GOD... OH, GOD...
BARRRRY!

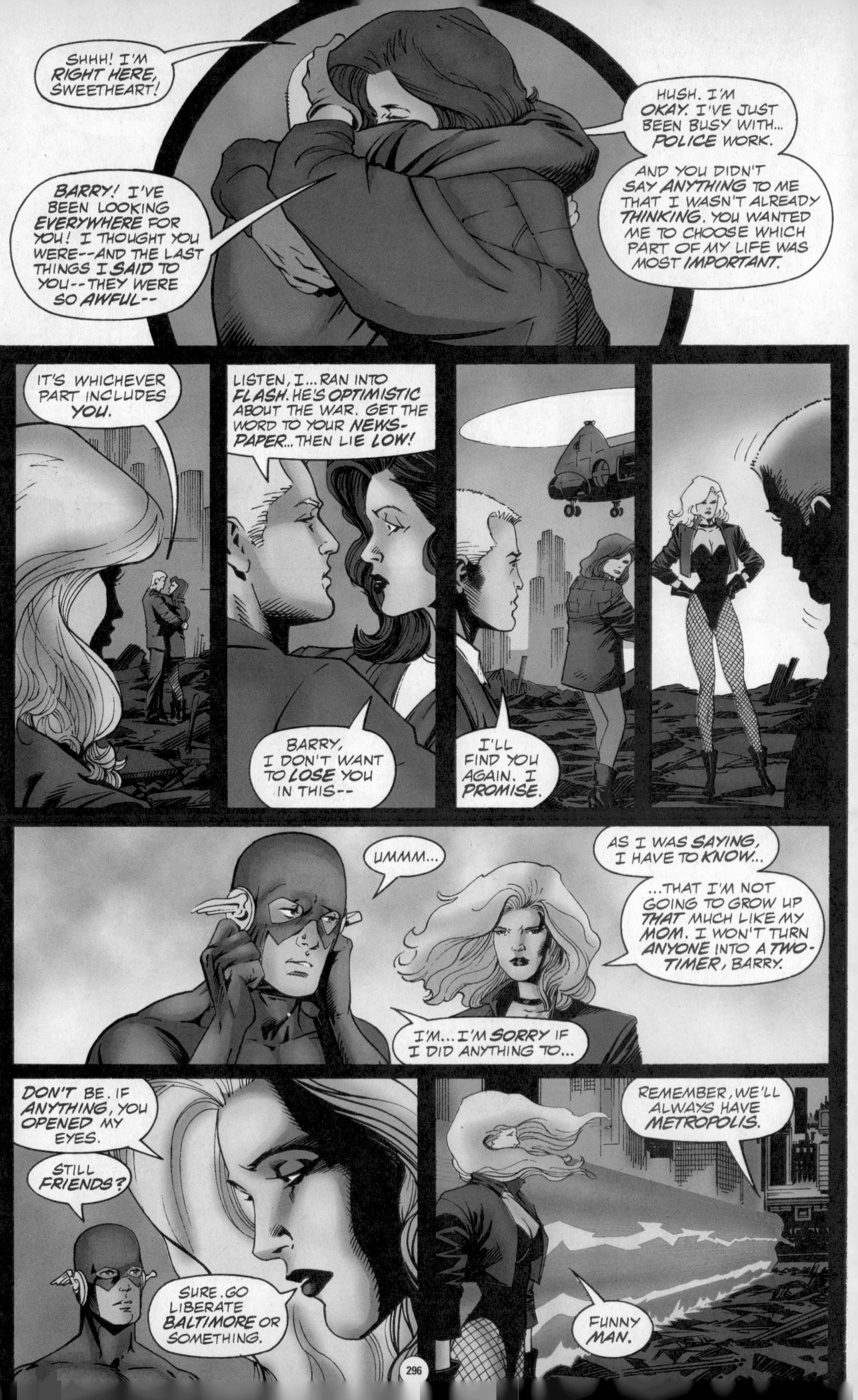
SHHH! I'M RIGHT HERE, SWEETHEART!
BARRY! I'VE BEEN LOOKING EVERYWHERE FOR YOU! I THOUGHT YOU WERE--AND THE LAST THINGS I SAID TO YOU--THEY WERE SO AWFUL--
HUSH. I'M OKAY. I'VE JUST BEEN BUSY WITH... POLICE WORK.
AND YOU DIDN'T SAY ANYTHING TO ME THAT I WASN'T ALREADY THINKING. YOU WANTED ME TO CHOOSE WHICH PART OF MY LIFE WAS MOST IMPORTANT.
IT'S WHICHEVER PART INCLUDES YOU.
LISTEN, I...RAN INTO FLASH. HE'S OPTIMISTIC ABOUT THE WAR. GET THE WORD TO YOUR NEWS-PAPER...THEN LIE LOW!
BARRY, I DON'T WANT TO LOSE YOU IN THIS--
I'LL FIND YOU AGAIN. I PROMISE.
UMMM...
AS I WAS SAYING, I HAVE TO KNOW...
...THAT I'M NOT GOING TO GROW UP THAT MUCH LIKE MY MOM. I WON'T TURN ANYONE INTO A TWO-TIMER, BARRY.
I'M...I'M SORRY IF I DID ANYTHING TO...
DON'T BE. IF ANYTHING, YOU OPENED MY EYES.
STILL FRIENDS?
SURE. GO LIBERATE BALTIMORE OR SOMETHING.
REMEMBER, WE'LL ALWAYS HAVE METROPOLIS.
FUNNY MAN.

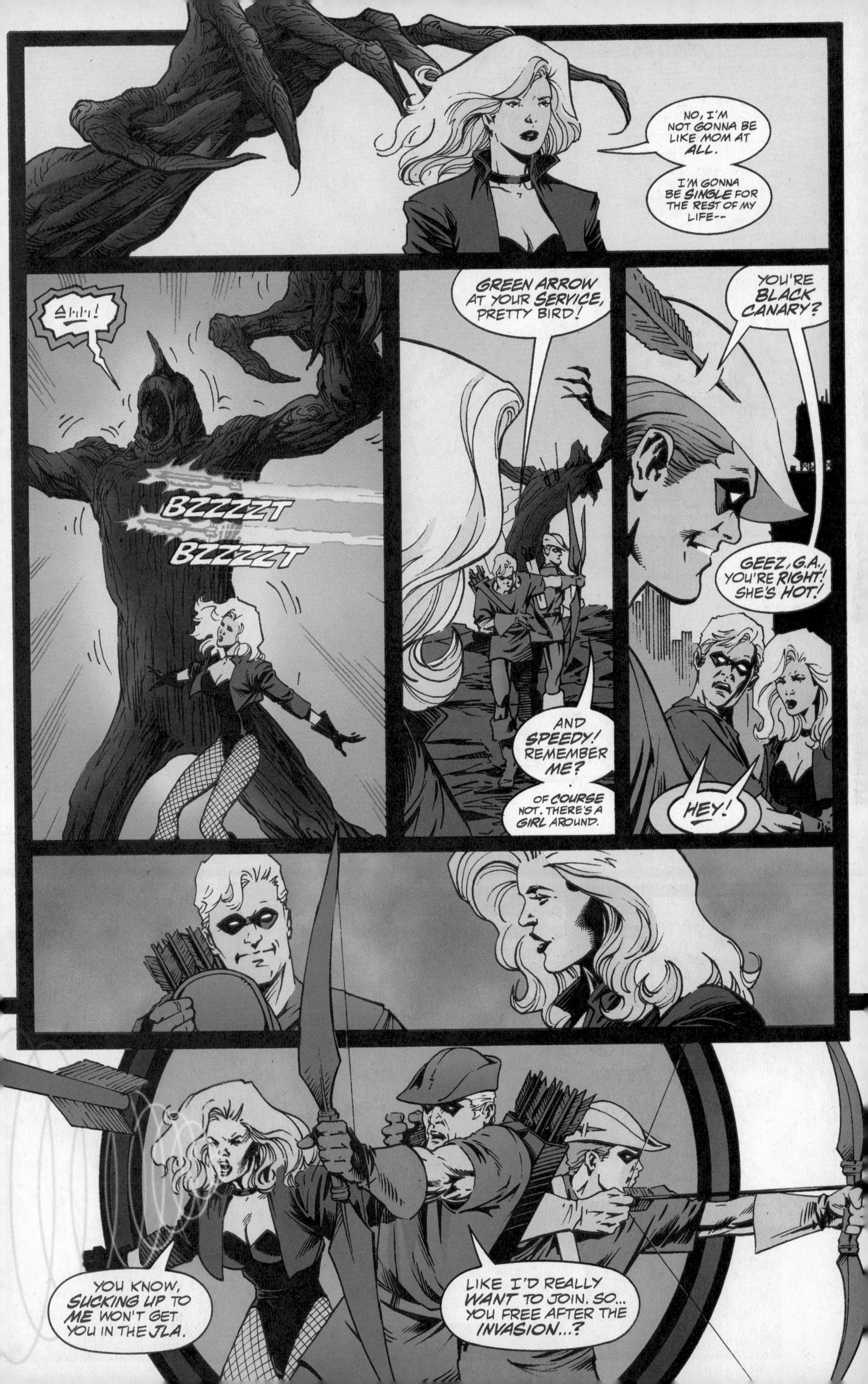
NO, I'M NOT GONNA BE LIKE MOM AT ALL.
I'M GONNA BE SINGLE FOR THE REST OF MY LIFE--
BZZZZZT
BZZZZZT
GREEN ARROW AT YOUR SERVICE, PRETTY BIRD!
AND SPEEDY! REMEMBER ME?
OF COURSE NOT. THERE'S A GIRL AROUND.
YOU'RE BLACK CANARY?
GEEZ, G.A., YOU'RE RIGHT! SHE'S HOT!
HEY!
YOU KNOW, SUCKING UP TO ME WON'T GET YOU IN THE JLA.
LIKE I'D REALLY WANT TO JOIN. SO... YOU FREE AFTER THE INVASION...?

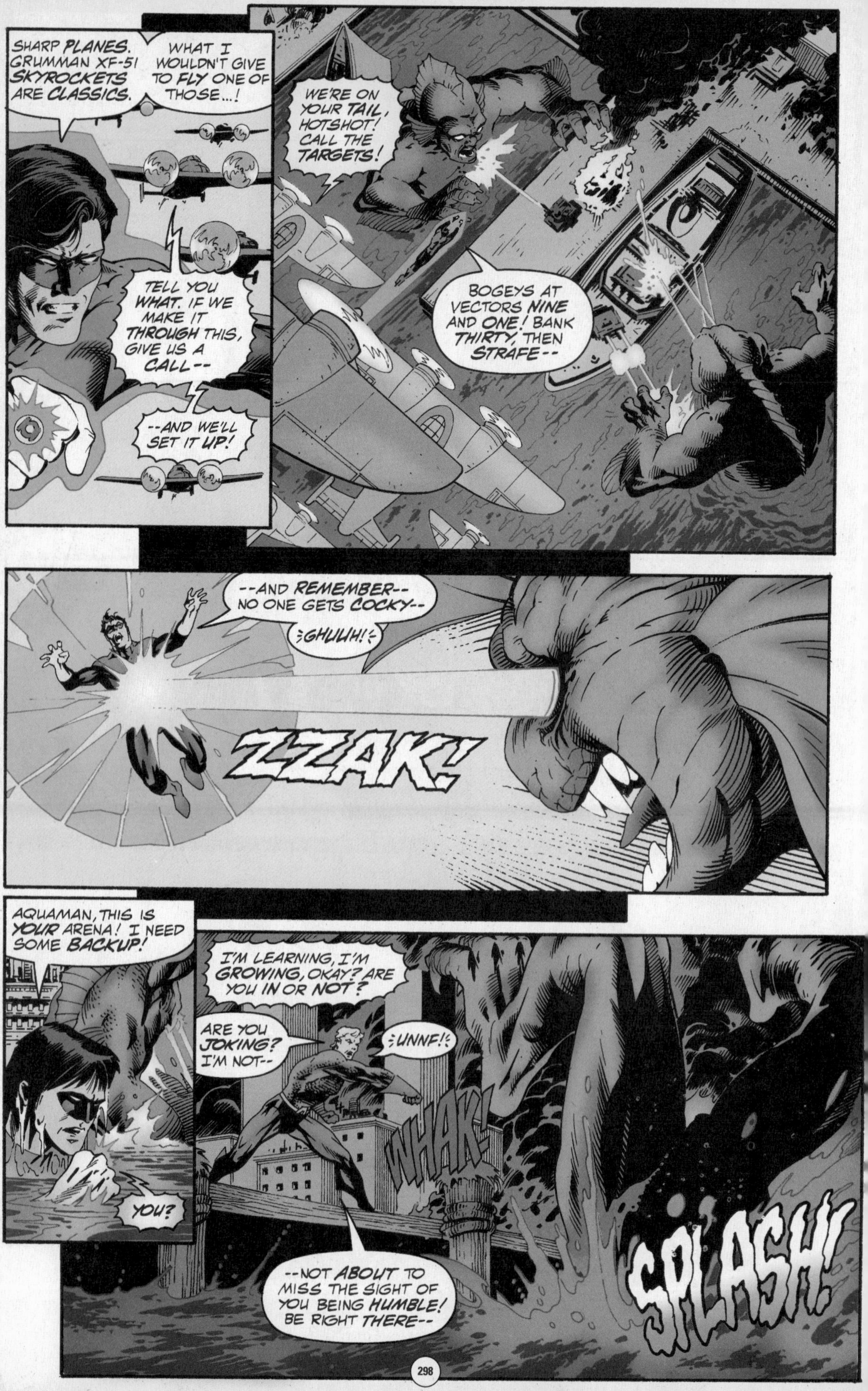
SHARP PLANES. GRUMMAN XF-51 SKYROCKETS ARE CLASSICS.
WHAT I WOULDN'T GIVE TO FLY ONE OF THOSE...!
WE'RE ON YOUR TAIL, HOTSHOT! CALL THE TARGETS!
TELL YOU WHAT. IF WE MAKE IT THROUGH THIS, GIVE US A CALL--
--AND WE'LL SET IT UP!
BOGEYS AT VECTORS NINE AND ONE! BANK THIRTY, THEN STRAFE--
--AND REMEMBER-- NO ONE GETS COCKY--
GHUUH!
ZZAK!
AQUAMAN, THIS IS YOUR ARENA! I NEED SOME BACKUP!
YOU?
I'M LEARNING, I'M GROWING, OKAY? ARE YOU IN OR NOT?
ARE YOU JOKING? I'M NOT--
UNNF!
WHAK!
--NOT ABOUT TO MISS THE SIGHT OF YOU BEING HUMBLE! BE RIGHT THERE--
SPLASH!

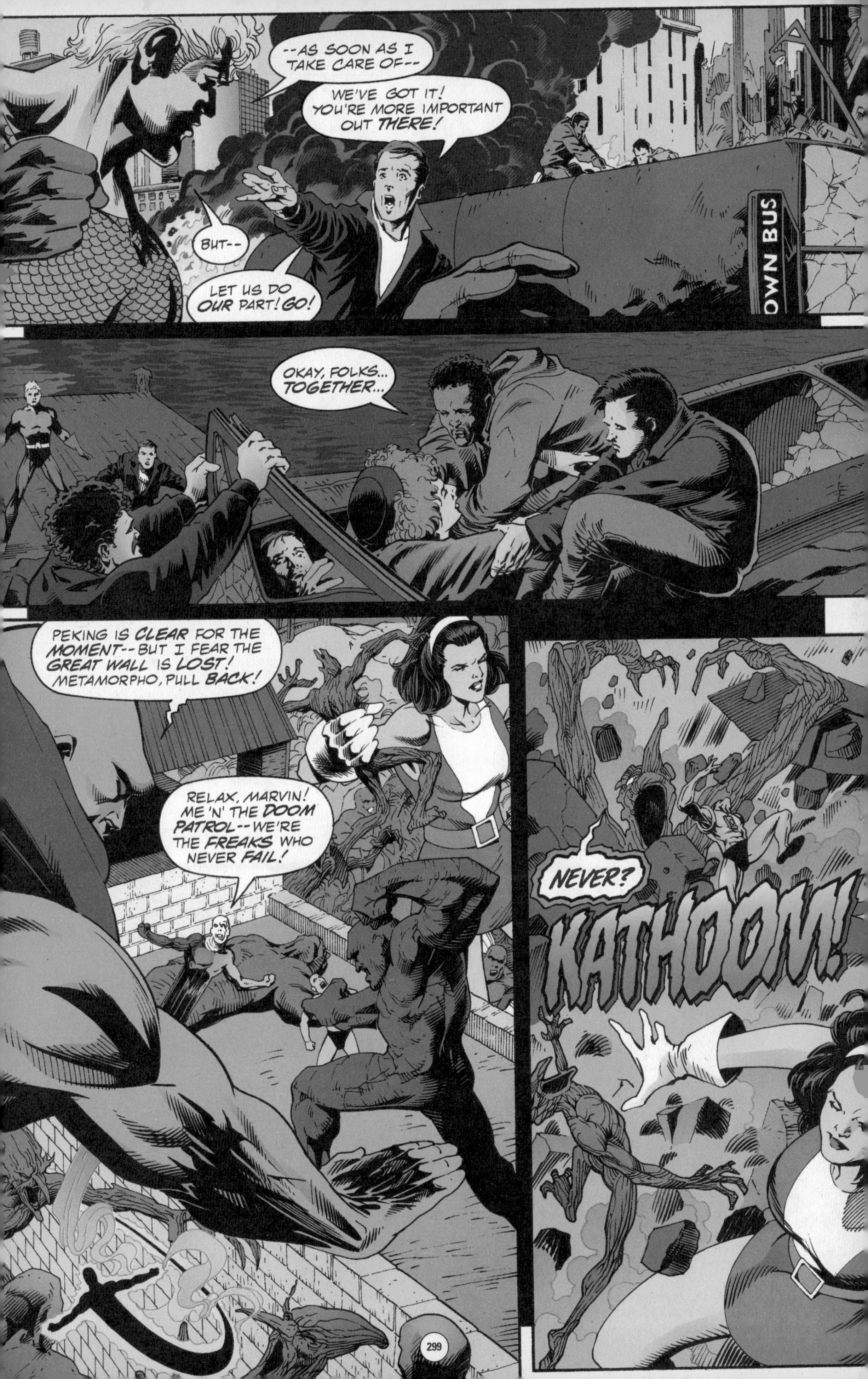
--AS SOON AS I TAKE CARE OF--
WE'VE GOT IT! YOU'RE MORE IMPORTANT OUT THERE!
BUT--
LET US DO OUR PART! GO!
OWN BUS
OKAY, FOLKS... TOGETHER...
PEKING IS CLEAR FOR THE MOMENT--BUT I FEAR THE GREAT WALL IS LOST! METAMORPHO, PULL BACK!
RELAX, MARVIN! ME 'N' THE DOOM PATROL--WE'RE THE FREAKS WHO NEVER FAIL!
NEVER?
KATHOOM!

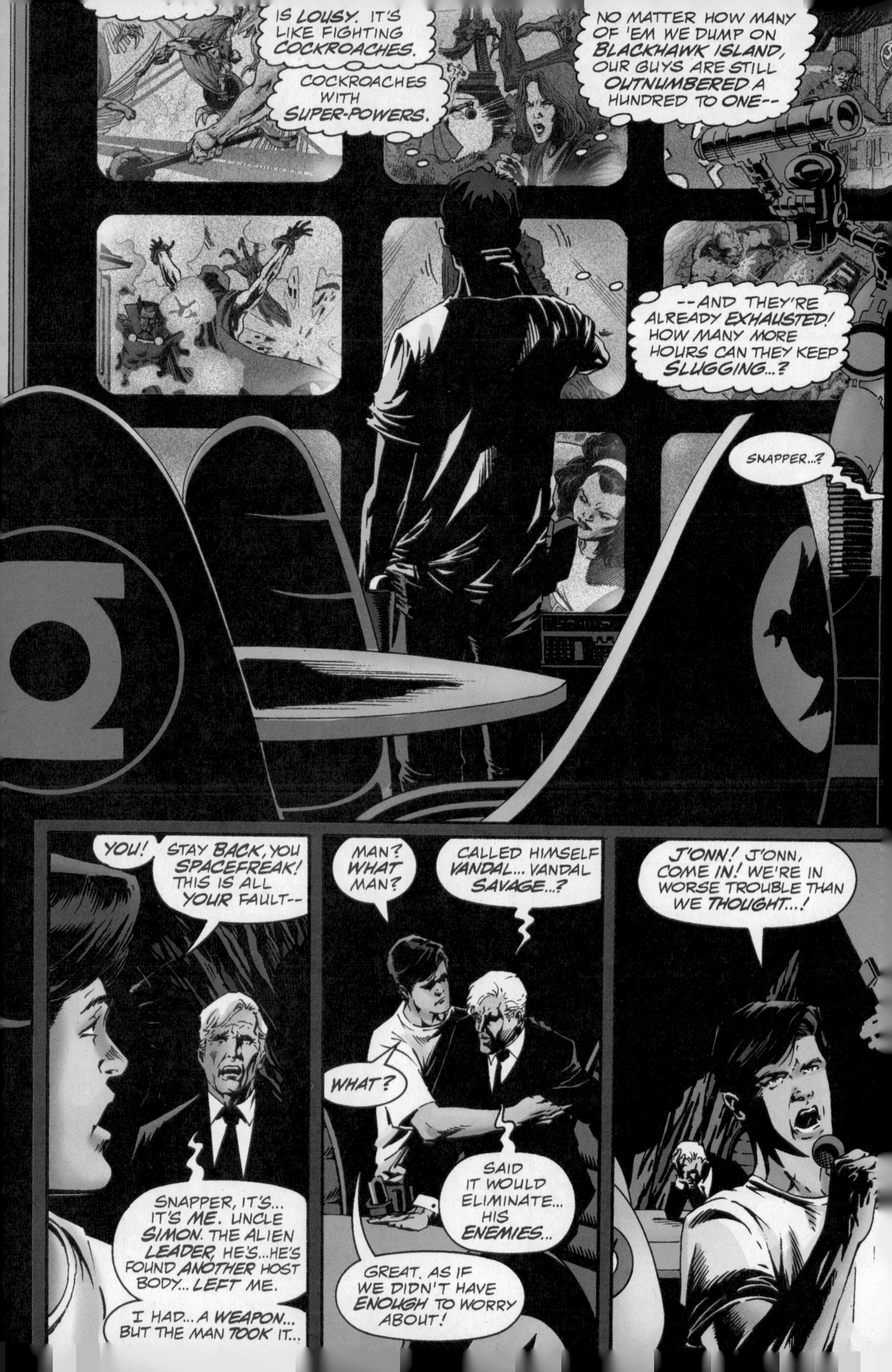

IS LOUSY. IT'S LIKE FIGHTING COCKROACHES.
COCKROACHES WITH SUPER-POWERS.
NO MATTER HOW MANY OF 'EM WE DUMP ON BLACKHAWK ISLAND, OUR GUYS ARE STILL OUTNUMBERED A HUNDRED TO ONE--
--AND THEY'RE ALREADY EXHAUSTED! HOW MANY MORE HOURS CAN THEY KEEP SLUGGING...?
SNAPPER...?
YOU!
STAY BACK, YOU SPACEFREAK! THIS IS ALL YOUR FAULT--
SNAPPER, IT'S... IT'S ME. UNCLE SIMON. THE ALIEN LEADER, HE'S...HE'S FOUND ANOTHER HOST BODY... LEFT ME.
I HAD... A WEAPON... BUT THE MAN TOOK IT...
MAN? WHAT MAN?
CALLED HIMSELF VANDAL... VANDAL SAVAGE...?
WHAT?
SAID IT WOULD ELIMINATE... HIS ENEMIES...
GREAT. AS IF WE DIDN'T HAVE ENOUGH TO WORRY ABOUT!
J'ONN! J'ONN, COME IN! WE'RE IN WORSE TROUBLE THAN WE THOUGHT...!

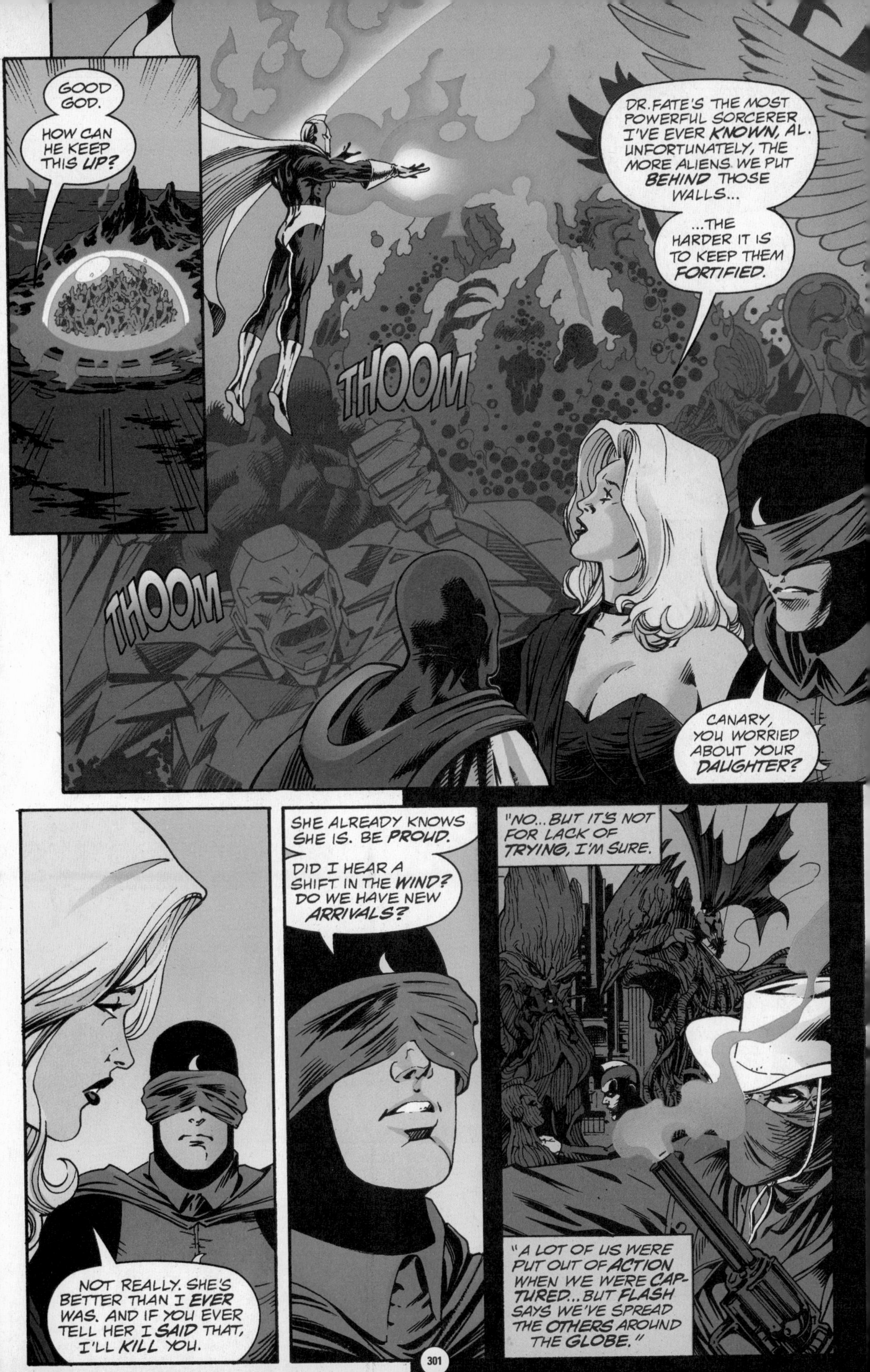
GOOD GOD.
HOW CAN HE KEEP THIS UP?
DR. FATE'S THE MOST POWERFUL SORCERER I'VE EVER KNOWN, AL. UNFORTUNATELY, THE MORE ALIENS WE PUT BEHIND THOSE WALLS...
...THE HARDER IT IS TO KEEP THEM FORTIFIED.
THOOM
THOOM
CANARY, YOU WORRIED ABOUT YOUR DAUGHTER?
NOT REALLY. SHE'S BETTER THAN I EVER WAS. AND IF YOU EVER TELL HER I SAID THAT, I'LL KILL YOU.
SHE ALREADY KNOWS SHE IS. BE PROUD.
DID I HEAR A SHIFT IN THE WIND? DO WE HAVE NEW ARRIVALS?
"NO... BUT IT'S NOT FOR LACK OF TRYING, I'M SURE.
"A LOT OF US WERE PUT OUT OF ACTION WHEN WE WERE CAPTURED... BUT FLASH SAYS WE'VE SPREAD THE OTHERS AROUND THE GLOBE."

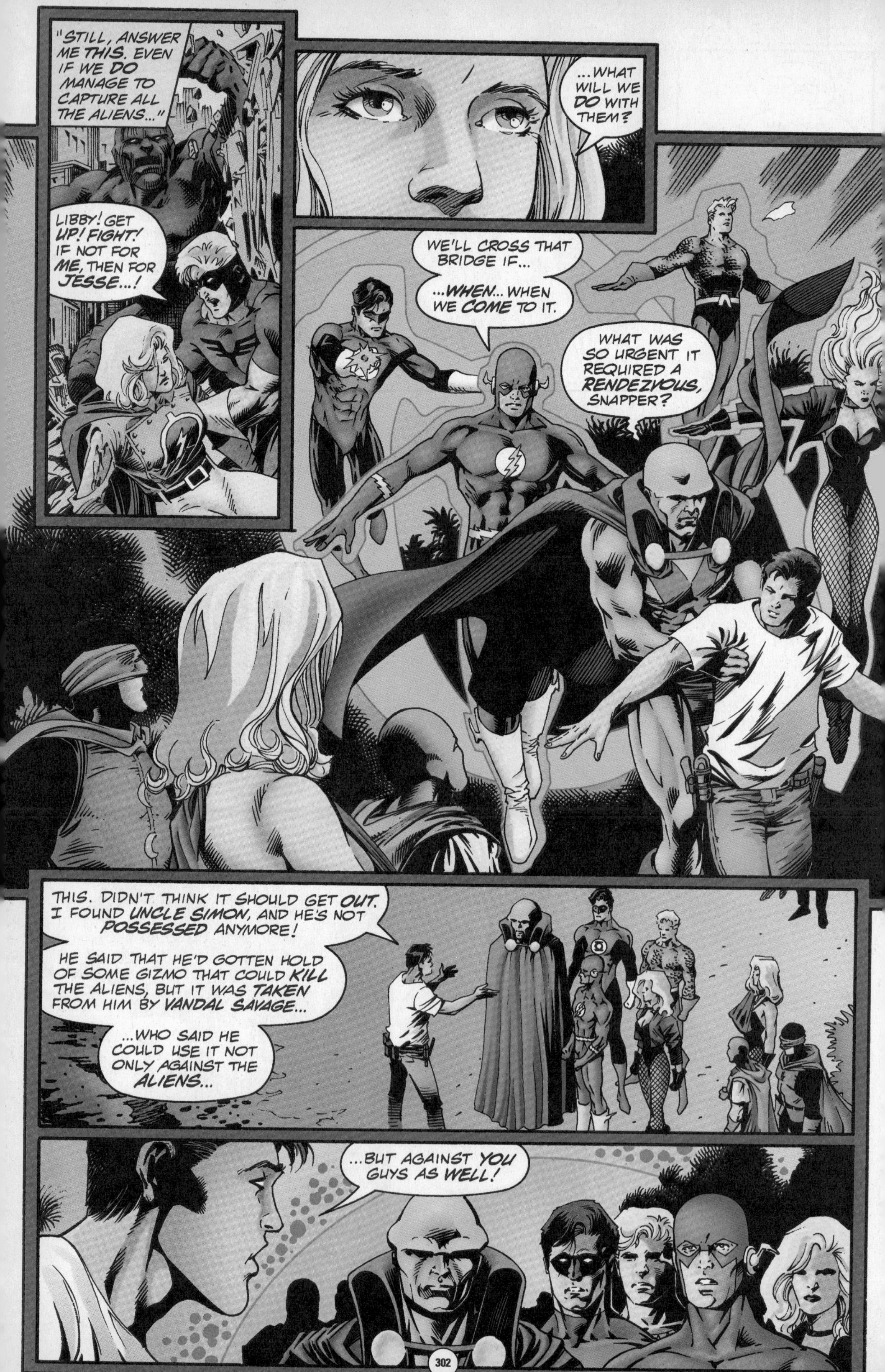
"STILL, ANSWER ME THIS. EVEN IF WE DO MANAGE TO CAPTURE ALL THE ALIENS..."
...WHAT WILL WE DO WITH THEM?
LIBBY! GET UP! FIGHT! IF NOT FOR ME, THEN FOR JESSE...!
WE'LL CROSS THAT BRIDGE IF...
...WHEN... WHEN WE COME TO IT.
WHAT WAS SO URGENT IT REQUIRED A RENDEZVOUS, SNAPPER?
THIS. DIDN'T THINK IT SHOULD GET OUT. I FOUND UNCLE SIMON, AND HE'S NOT POSSESSED ANYMORE!
HE SAID THAT HE'D GOTTEN HOLD OF SOME GIZMO THAT COULD KILL THE ALIENS, BUT IT WAS TAKEN FROM HIM BY VANDAL SAVAGE...
...WHO SAID HE COULD USE IT NOT ONLY AGAINST THE ALIENS...
...BUT AGAINST YOU GUYS AS WELL!

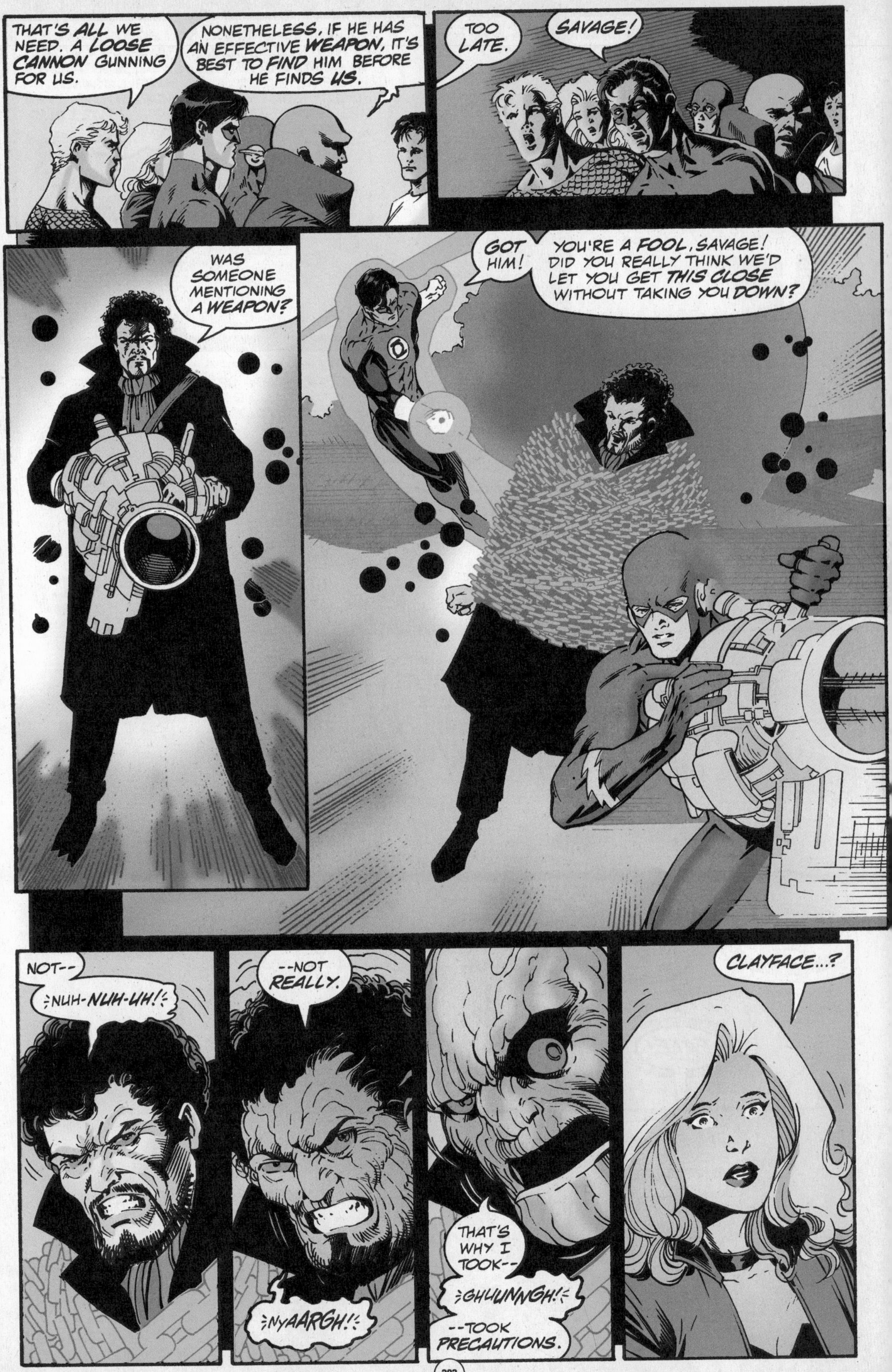
THAT'S ALL WE NEED. A LOOSE CANNON GUNNING FOR US.
NONETHELESS, IF HE HAS AN EFFECTIVE WEAPON, IT'S BEST TO FIND HIM BEFORE HE FINDS US.
TOO LATE.
SAVAGE!
WAS SOMEONE MENTIONING A WEAPON?
GOT HIM!
YOU'RE A FOOL, SAVAGE! DID YOU REALLY THINK WE'D LET YOU GET THIS CLOSE WITHOUT TAKING YOU DOWN?
NOT--
NUH-NUH-UH!
--NOT REALLY.
NyAARGH!
THAT'S WHY I TOOK--
GHUUNNGH!
--TOOK PRECAUTIONS.
CLAYFACE...?

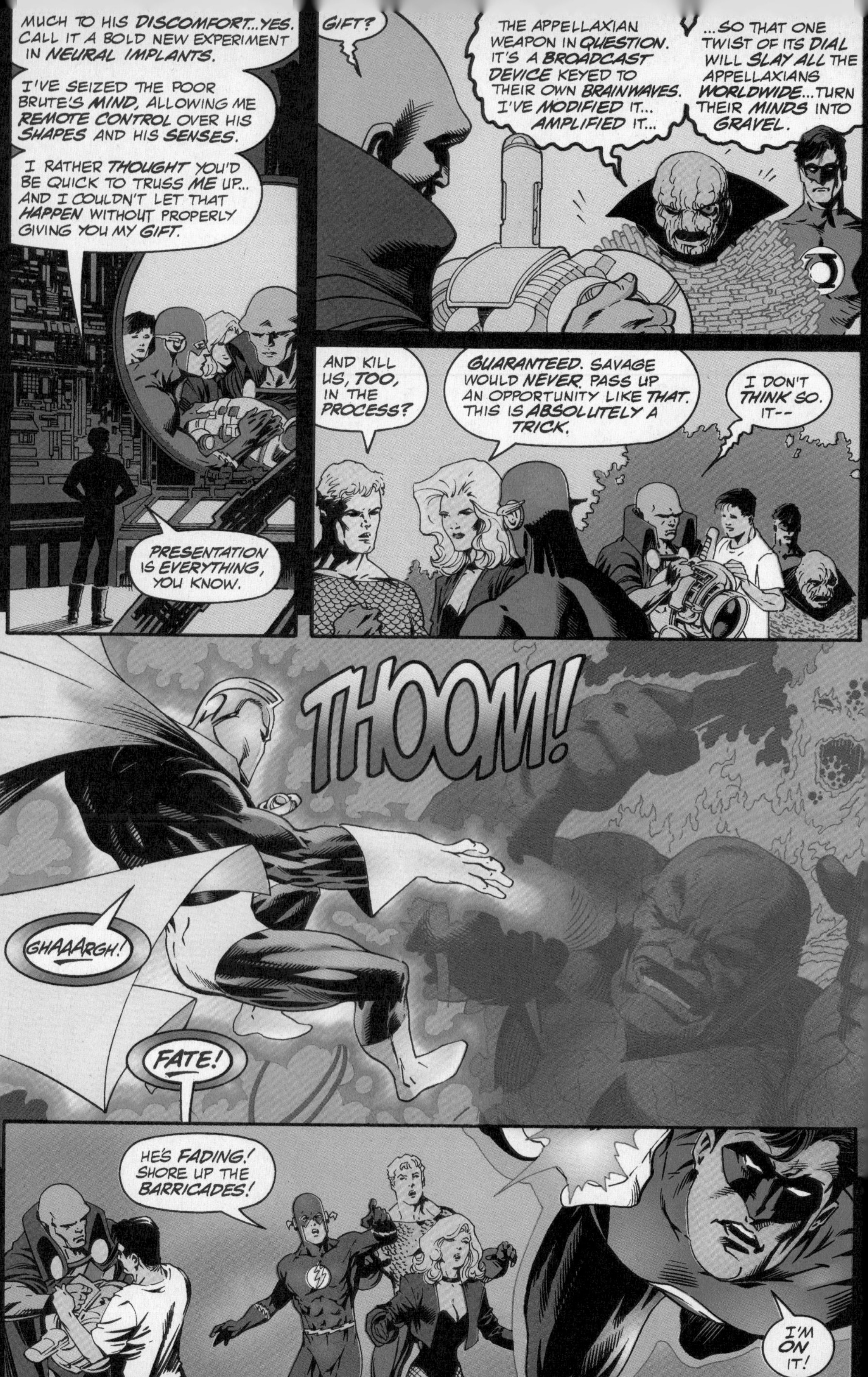
MUCH TO HIS DISCOMFORT...YES. CALL IT A BOLD NEW EXPERIMENT IN NEURAL IMPLANTS.
I'VE SEIZED THE POOR BRUTE'S MIND, ALLOWING ME REMOTE CONTROL OVER HIS SHAPES AND HIS SENSES.
I RATHER THOUGHT YOU'D BE QUICK TO TRUSS ME UP... AND I COULDN'T LET THAT HAPPEN WITHOUT PROPERLY GIVING YOU MY GIFT.
PRESENTATION IS EVERYTHING, YOU KNOW.
GIFT?
THE APPELLAXIAN WEAPON IN QUESTION. IT'S A BROADCAST DEVICE KEYED TO THEIR OWN BRAINWAVES. I'VE MODIFIED IT... AMPLIFIED IT...
...SO THAT ONE TWIST OF ITS DIAL WILL SLAY ALL THE APPELLAXIANS WORLDWIDE...TURN THEIR MINDS INTO GRAVEL.
AND KILL US, TOO, IN THE PROCESS?
GUARANTEED. SAVAGE WOULD NEVER PASS UP AN OPPORTUNITY LIKE THAT. THIS IS ABSOLUTELY A TRICK.
I DON'T THINK SO. IT--
THOOM!
GHAAARGH!
FATE!
HE'S FADING! SHORE UP THE BARRICADES!
I'M ON IT!

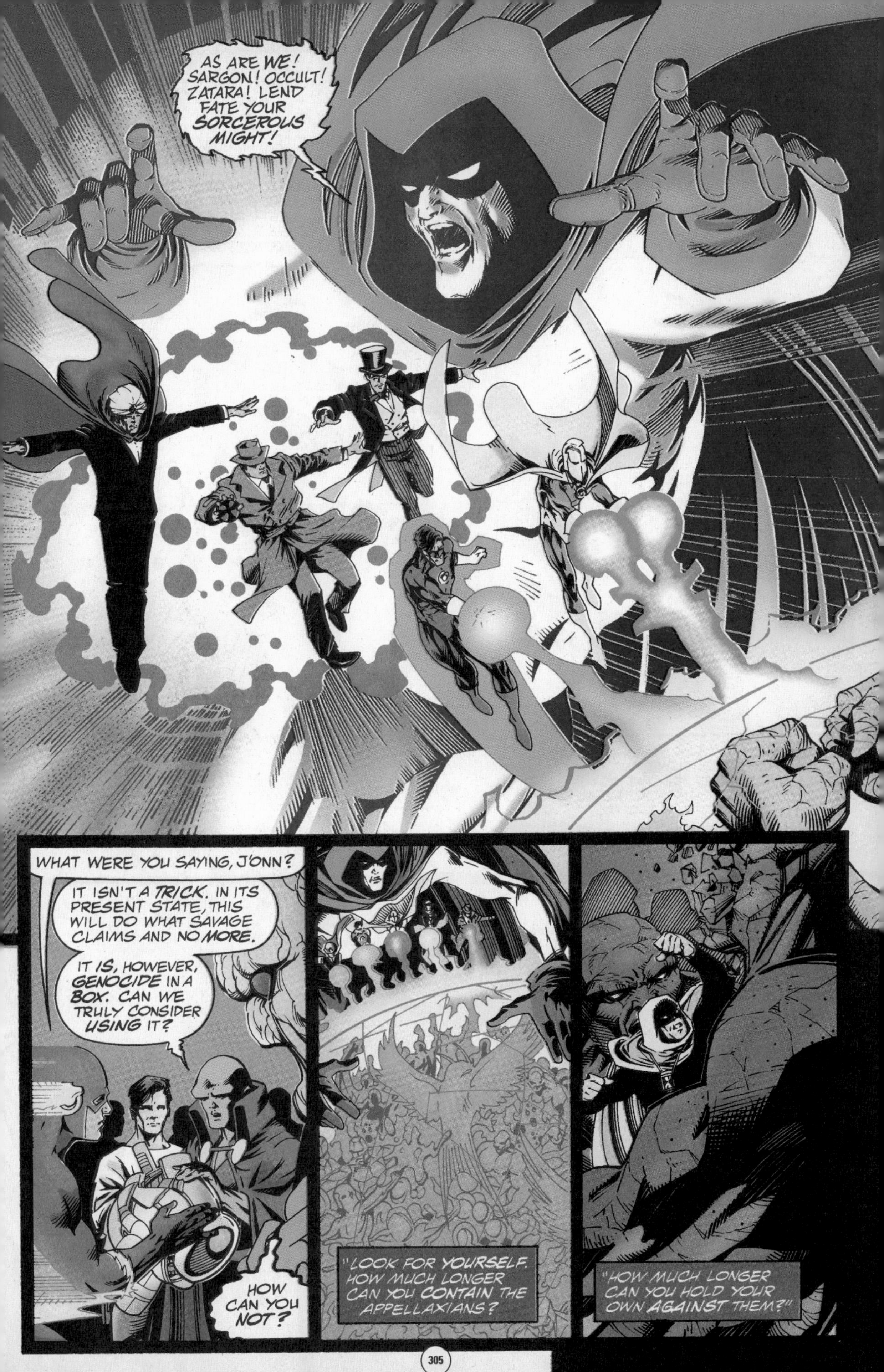
AS ARE WE! SARGON! OCCULT! ZATARA! LEND FATE YOUR SORCEROUS MIGHT!
WHAT WERE YOU SAYING, J'ONN?
IT ISN'T A TRICK. IN ITS PRESENT STATE, THIS WILL DO WHAT SAVAGE CLAIMS AND NO MORE.
IT IS, HOWEVER, GENOCIDE IN A BOX. CAN WE TRULY CONSIDER USING IT?
HOW CAN YOU NOT?
"LOOK FOR YOURSELF. HOW MUCH LONGER CAN YOU CONTAIN THE APPELLAXIANS?
"HOW MUCH LONGER CAN YOU HOLD YOUR OWN AGAINST THEM?"

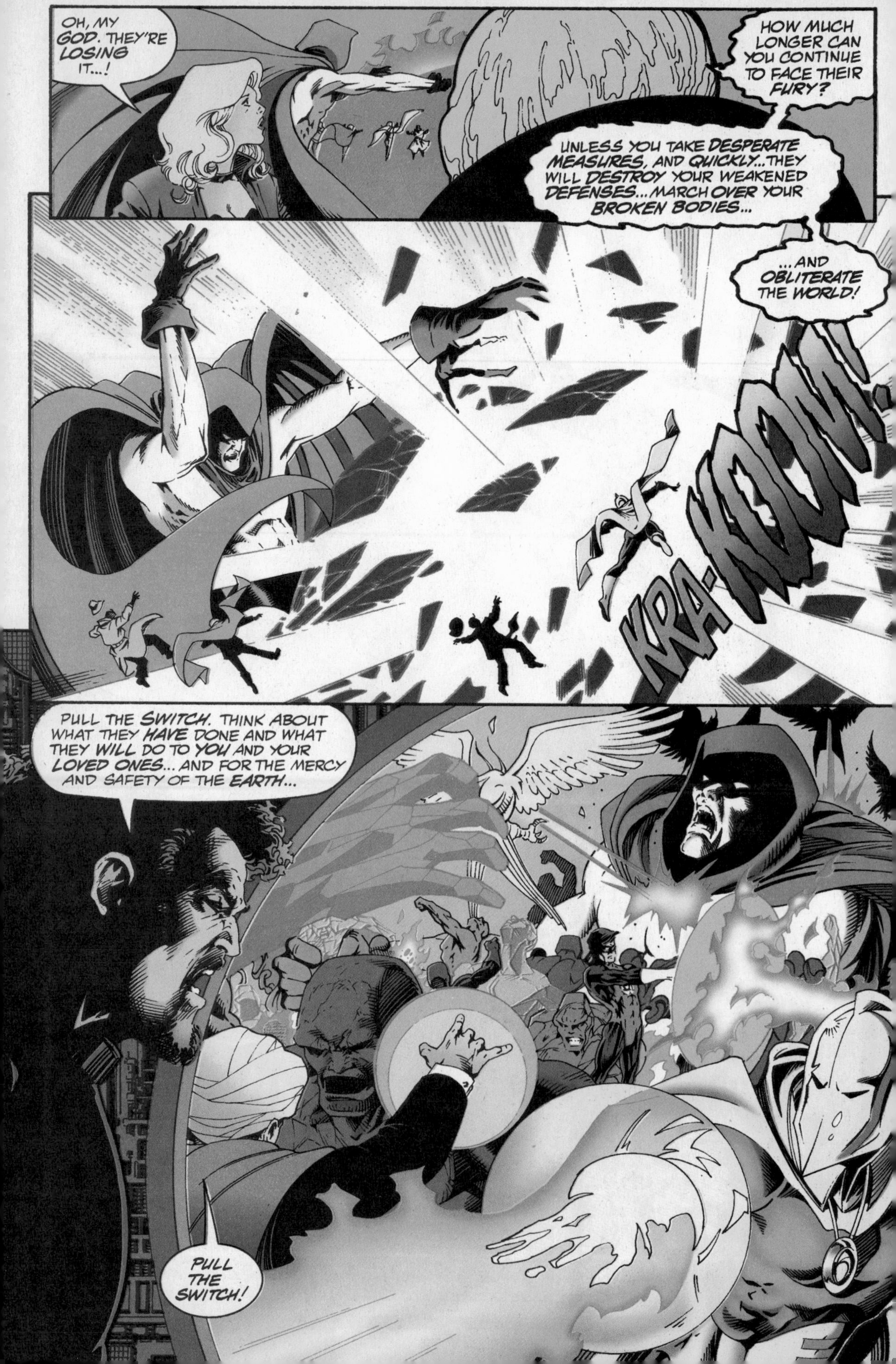
OH, MY GOD. THEY'RE LOSING IT...!
HOW MUCH LONGER CAN YOU CONTINUE TO FACE THEIR FURY?
UNLESS YOU TAKE DESPERATE MEASURES, AND QUICKLY...THEY WILL DESTROY YOUR WEAKENED DEFENSES...MARCH OVER YOUR BROKEN BODIES...
...AND OBLITERATE THE WORLD!
KRA-KOOM!
PULL THE SWITCH. THINK ABOUT WHAT THEY HAVE DONE AND WHAT THEY WILL DO TO YOU AND YOUR LOVED ONES... AND FOR THE MERCY AND SAFETY OF THE EARTH...
PULL THE SWITCH!

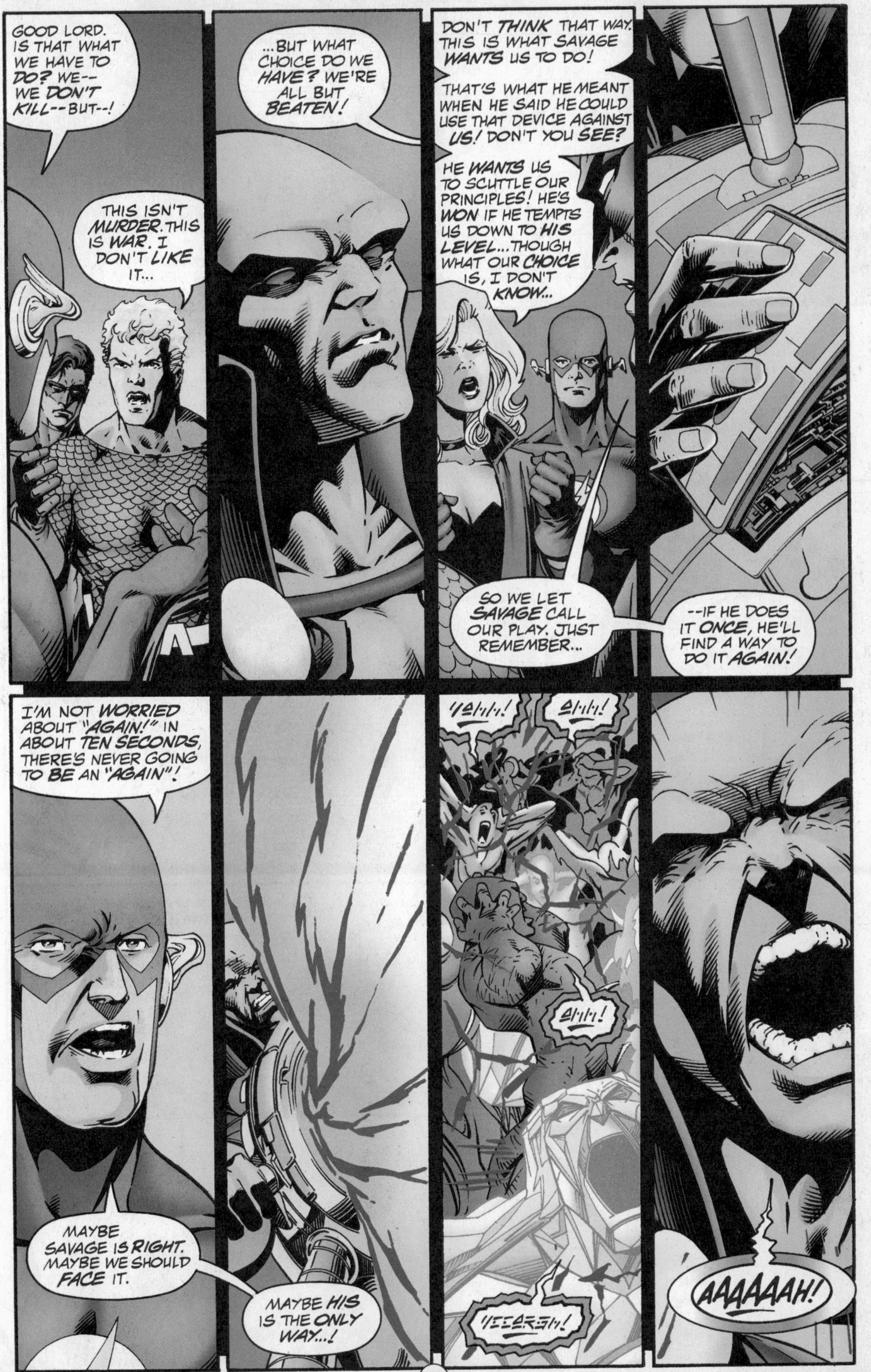
GOOD LORD. IS THAT WHAT WE HAVE TO DO? WE-- WE DON'T KILL--BUT--!
THIS ISN'T MURDER. THIS IS WAR. I DON'T LIKE IT...
...BUT WHAT CHOICE DO WE HAVE? WE'RE ALL BUT BEATEN!
DON'T THINK THAT WAY. THIS IS WHAT SAVAGE WANTS US TO DO!
THAT'S WHAT HE MEANT WHEN HE SAID HE COULD USE THAT DEVICE AGAINST US! DON'T YOU SEE?
HE WANTS US TO SCUTTLE OUR PRINCIPLES! HE'S WON IF HE TEMPTS US DOWN TO HIS LEVEL...THOUGH WHAT OUR CHOICE IS, I DON'T KNOW...
SO WE LET SAVAGE CALL OUR PLAY. JUST REMEMBER...
--IF HE DOES IT ONCE, HE'LL FIND A WAY TO DO IT AGAIN!
I'M NOT WORRIED ABOUT "AGAIN!" IN ABOUT TEN SECONDS, THERE'S NEVER GOING TO BE AN "AGAIN"!
MAYBE SAVAGE IS RIGHT. MAYBE WE SHOULD FACE IT.
MAYBE HIS IS THE ONLY WAY...!
AAAAAAH!

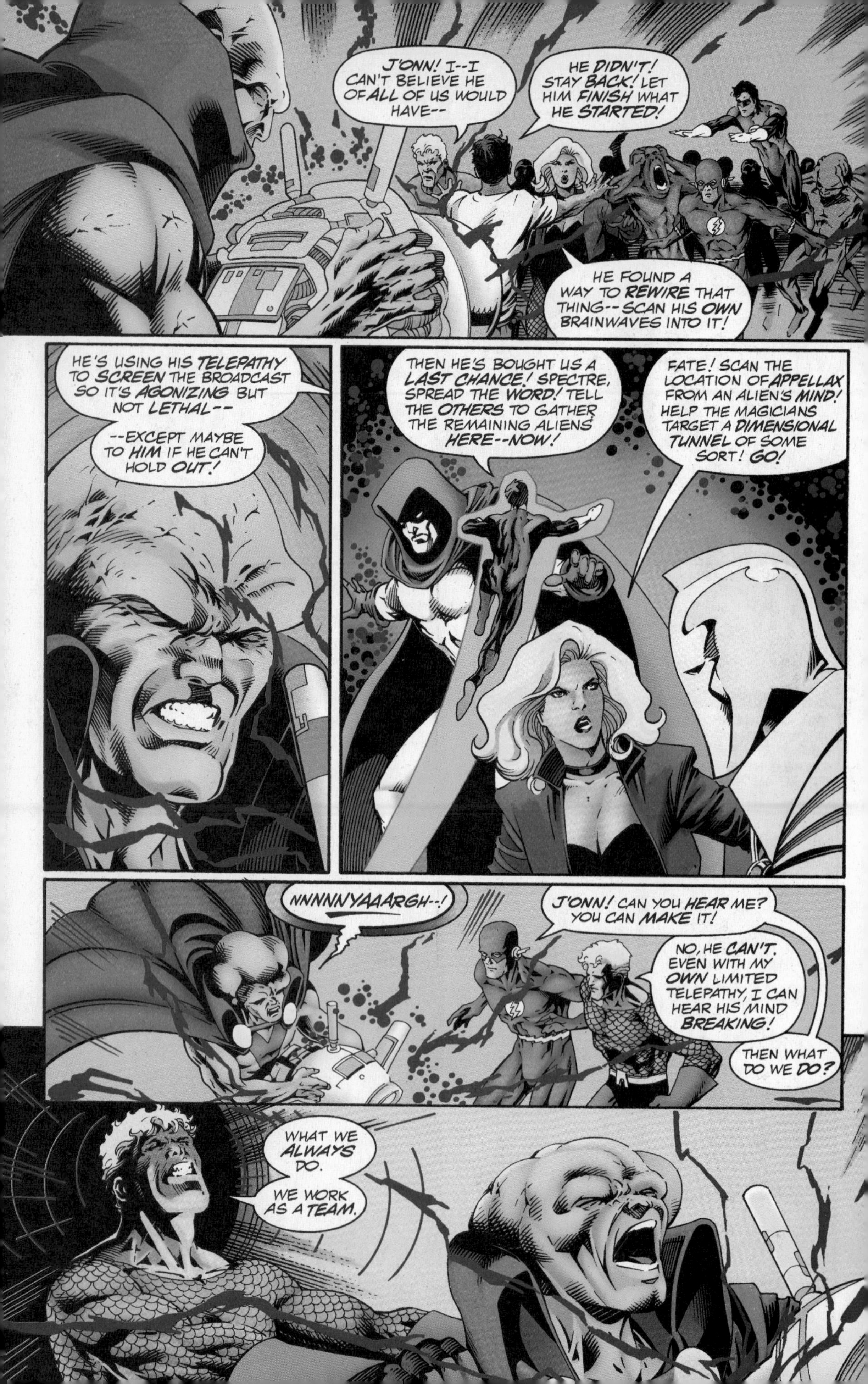
J'ONN! I--I CAN'T BELIEVE HE OF ALL OF US WOULD HAVE--
HE DIDN'T! STAY BACK! LET HIM FINISH WHAT HE STARTED!
HE FOUND A WAY TO REWIRE THAT THING--SCAN HIS OWN BRAINWAVES INTO IT!
HE'S USING HIS TELEPATHY TO SCREEN THE BROADCAST SO IT'S AGONIZING BUT NOT LETHAL--
--EXCEPT MAYBE TO HIM IF HE CAN'T HOLD OUT!
THEN HE'S BOUGHT US A LAST CHANCE! SPECTRE, SPREAD THE WORD! TELL THE OTHERS TO GATHER THE REMAINING ALIENS HERE--NOW!
FATE! SCAN THE LOCATION OF APPELLAX FROM AN ALIEN'S MIND! HELP THE MAGICIANS TARGET A DIMENSIONAL TUNNEL OF SOME SORT! GO!
NNNNNYAAARGH--!
J'ONN! CAN YOU HEAR ME? YOU CAN MAKE IT!
NO, HE CAN'T. EVEN WITH MY OWN LIMITED TELEPATHY, I CAN HEAR HIS MIND BREAKING!
THEN WHAT DO WE DO?
WHAT WE ALWAYS DO.
WE WORK AS A TEAM.

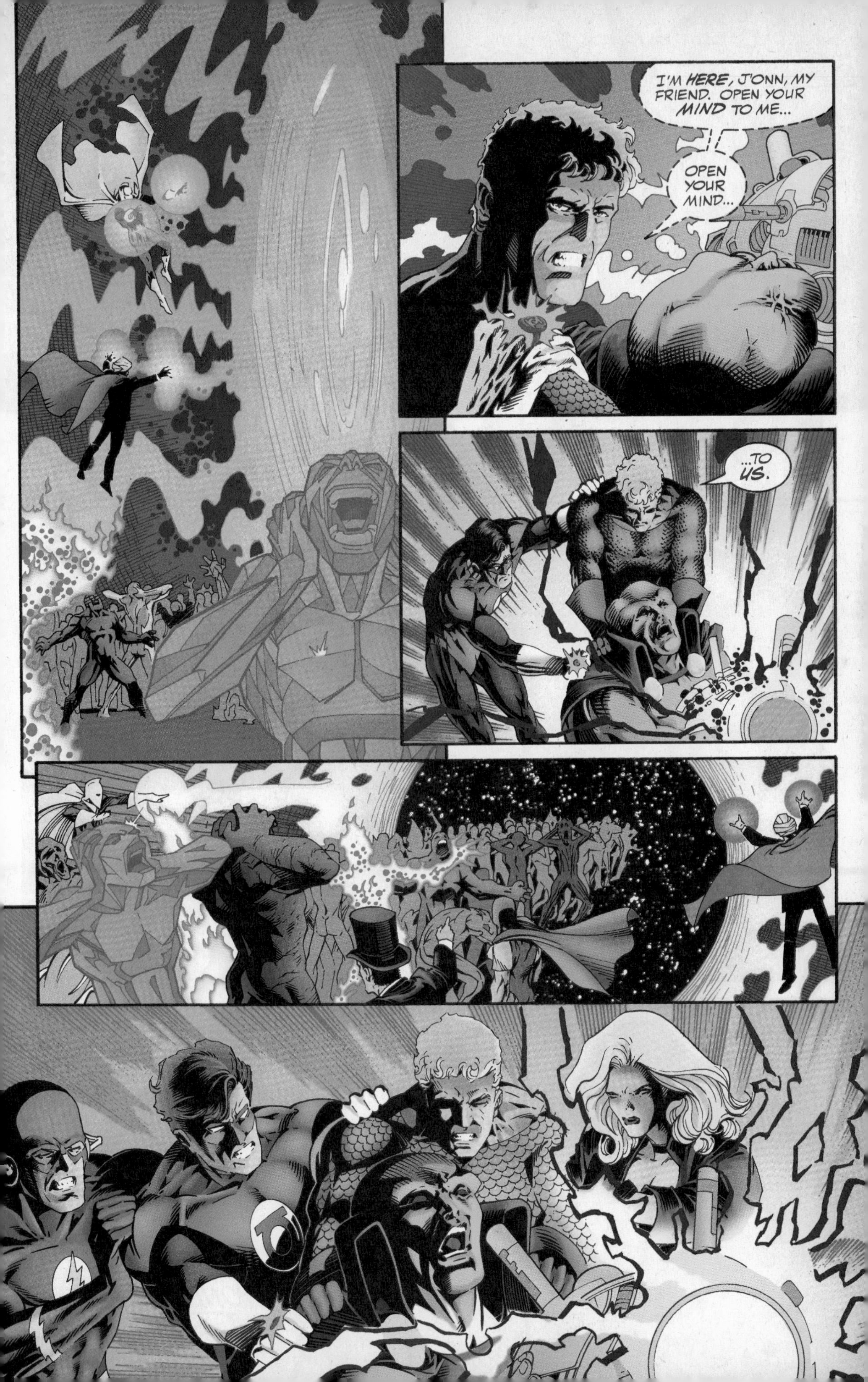
I'M HERE, J'ONN, MY FRIEND. OPEN YOUR MIND TO ME...
OPEN YOUR MIND...
...TO US.

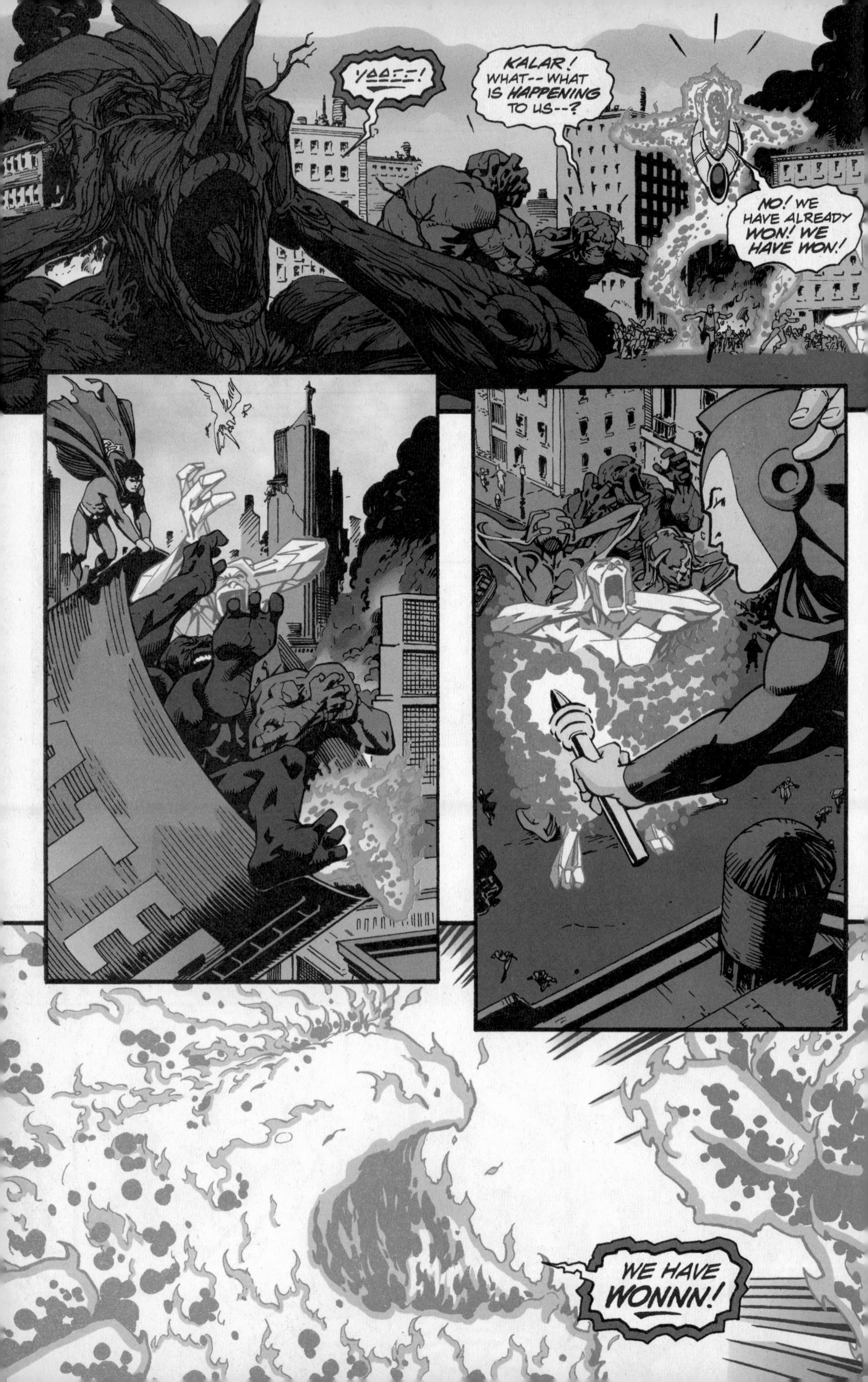
YAAEE!
KALAR! WHAT-- WHAT IS HAPPENING TO US--?
NO! WE HAVE ALREADY WON! WE HAVE WON!
WE HAVE WONNN!

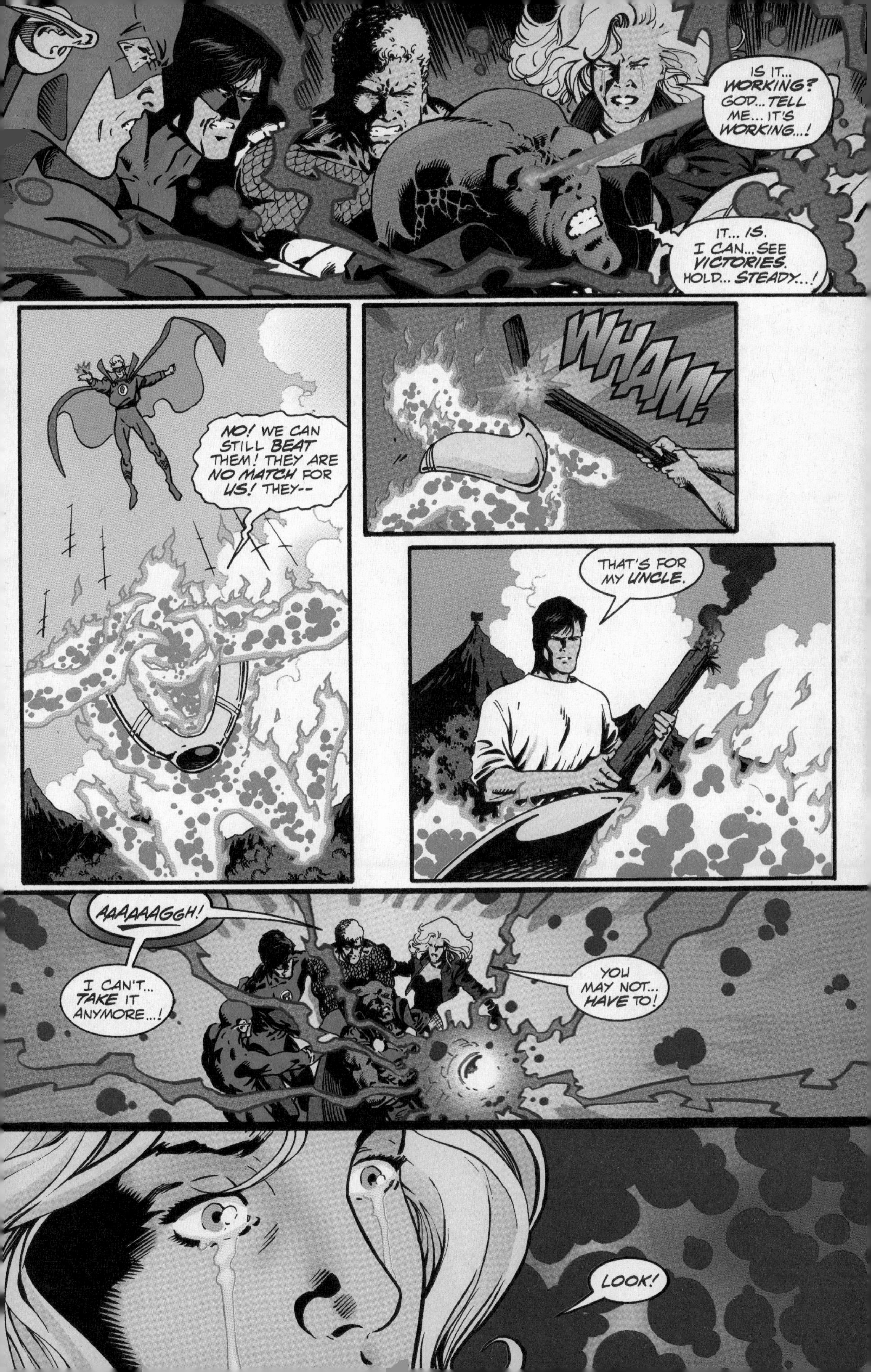
IS IT... WORKING? GOD... TELL ME... IT'S WORKING...!
IT... IS. I CAN... SEE VICTORIES. HOLD... STEADY...!
NO! WE CAN STILL BEAT THEM! THEY ARE NO MATCH FOR US! THEY--
WHAM!
THAT'S FOR MY UNCLE.
AAAAAAGGH!
I CAN'T... TAKE IT ANYMORE...!
YOU MAY NOT... HAVE TO!
LOOK!

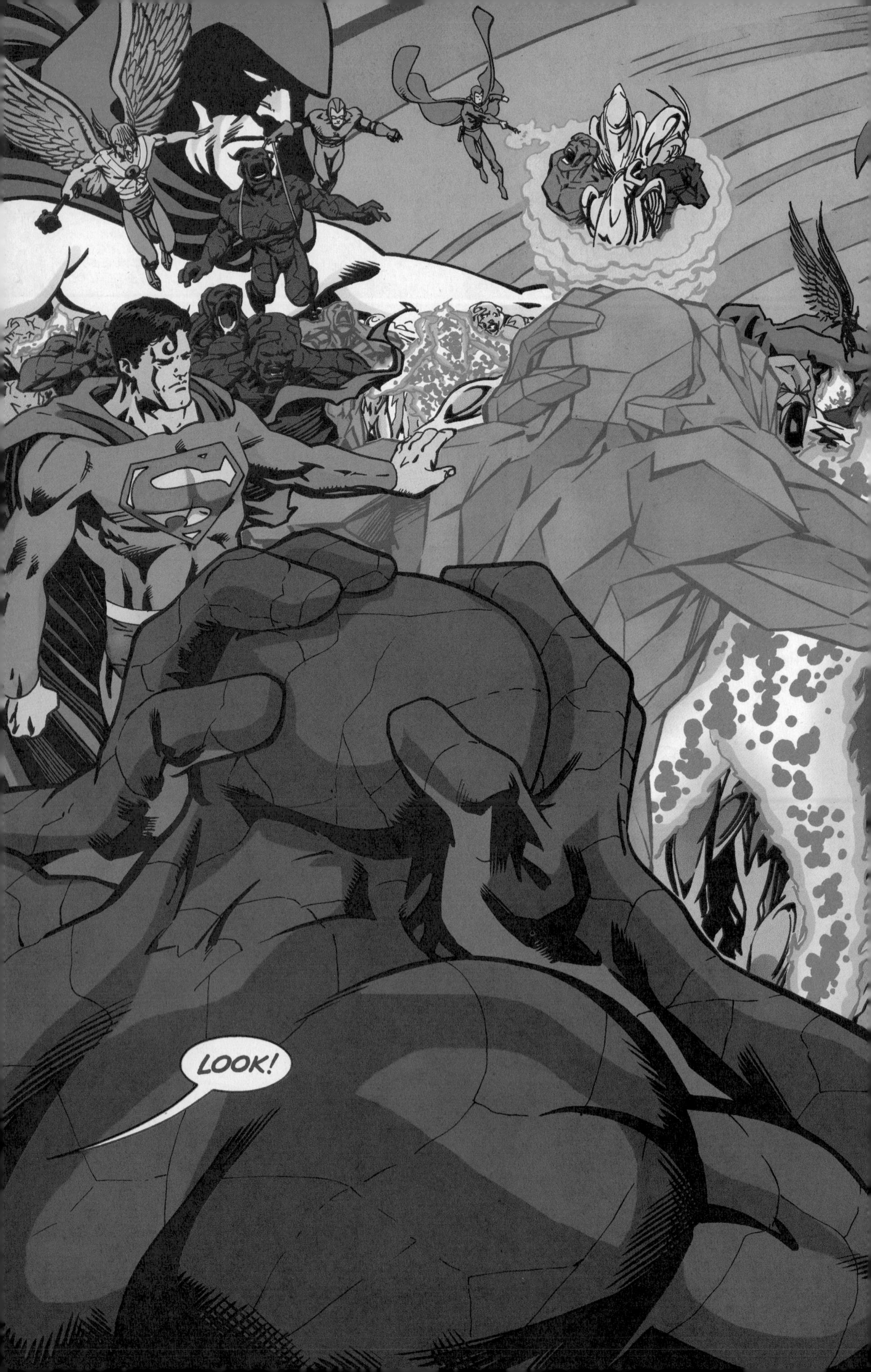
LOOK!

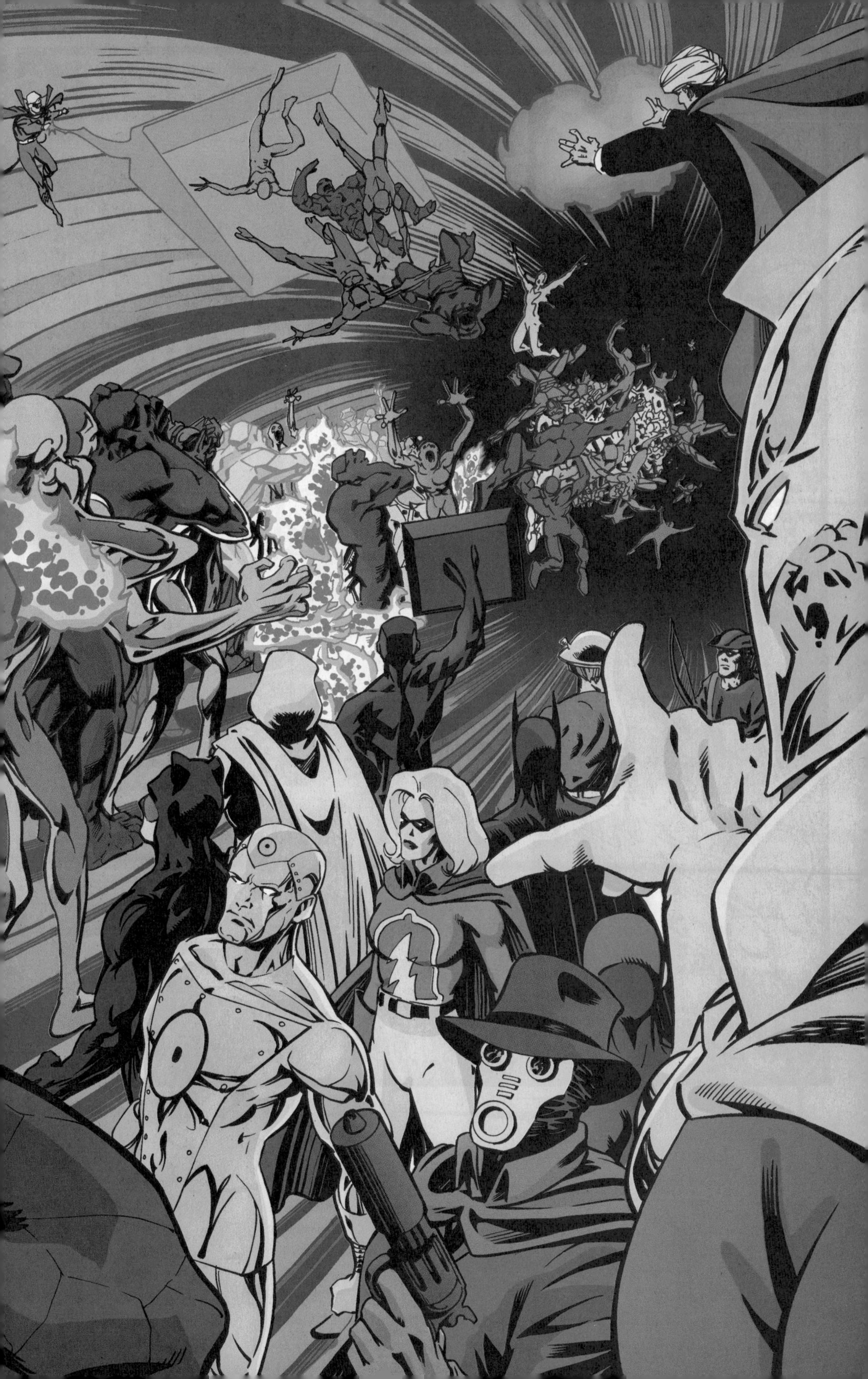

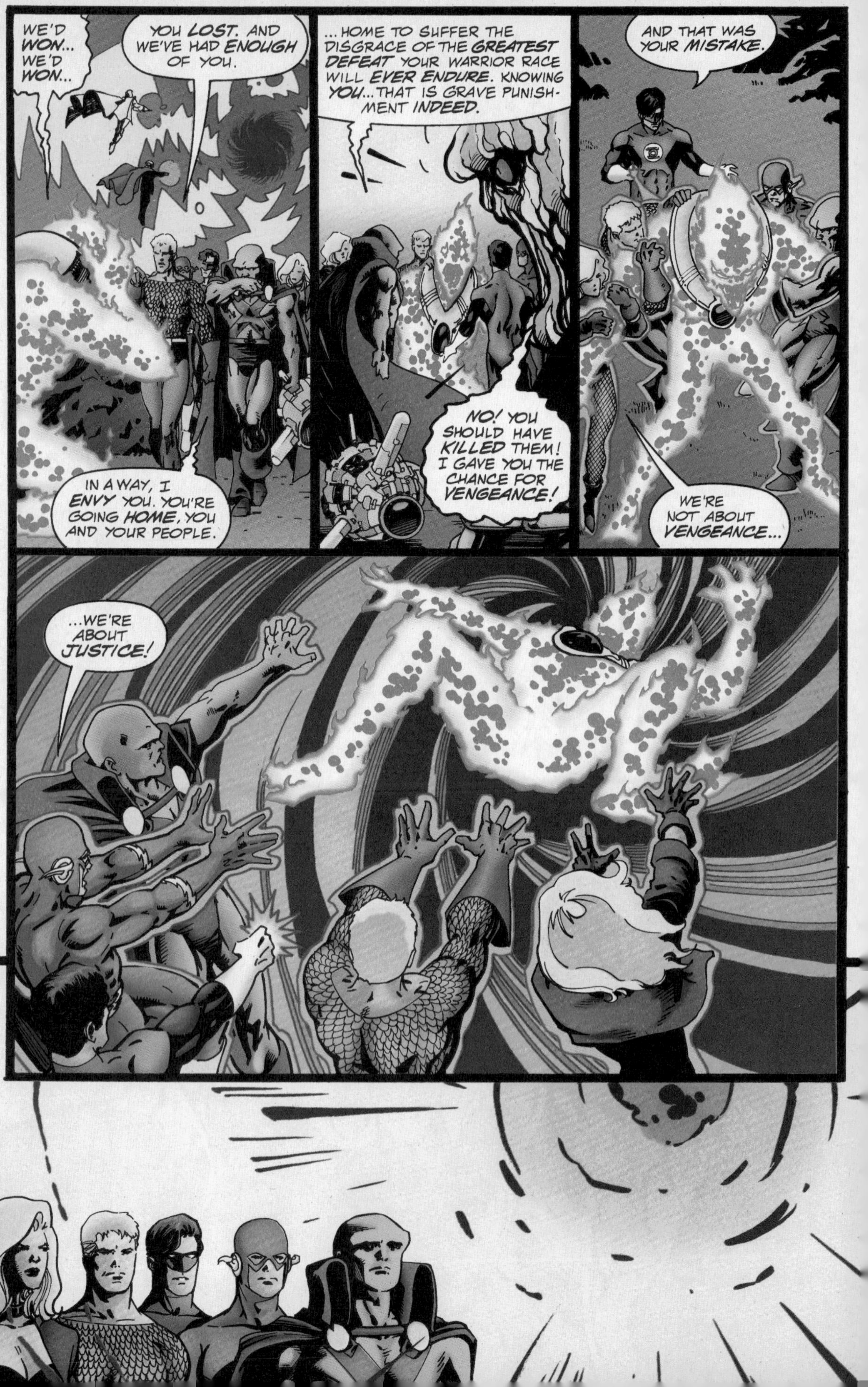
WE'D WON... WE'D WON...
YOU LOST. AND WE'VE HAD ENOUGH OF YOU.
IN A WAY, I ENVY YOU. YOU'RE GOING HOME, YOU AND YOUR PEOPLE.
... HOME TO SUFFER THE DISGRACE OF THE GREATEST DEFEAT YOUR WARRIOR RACE WILL EVER ENDURE. KNOWING YOU... THAT IS GRAVE PUNISHMENT INDEED.
NO! YOU SHOULD HAVE KILLED THEM! I GAVE YOU THE CHANCE FOR VENGEANCE!
AND THAT WAS YOUR MISTAKE.
WE'RE NOT ABOUT VENGEANCE...
...WE'RE ABOUT JUSTICE!

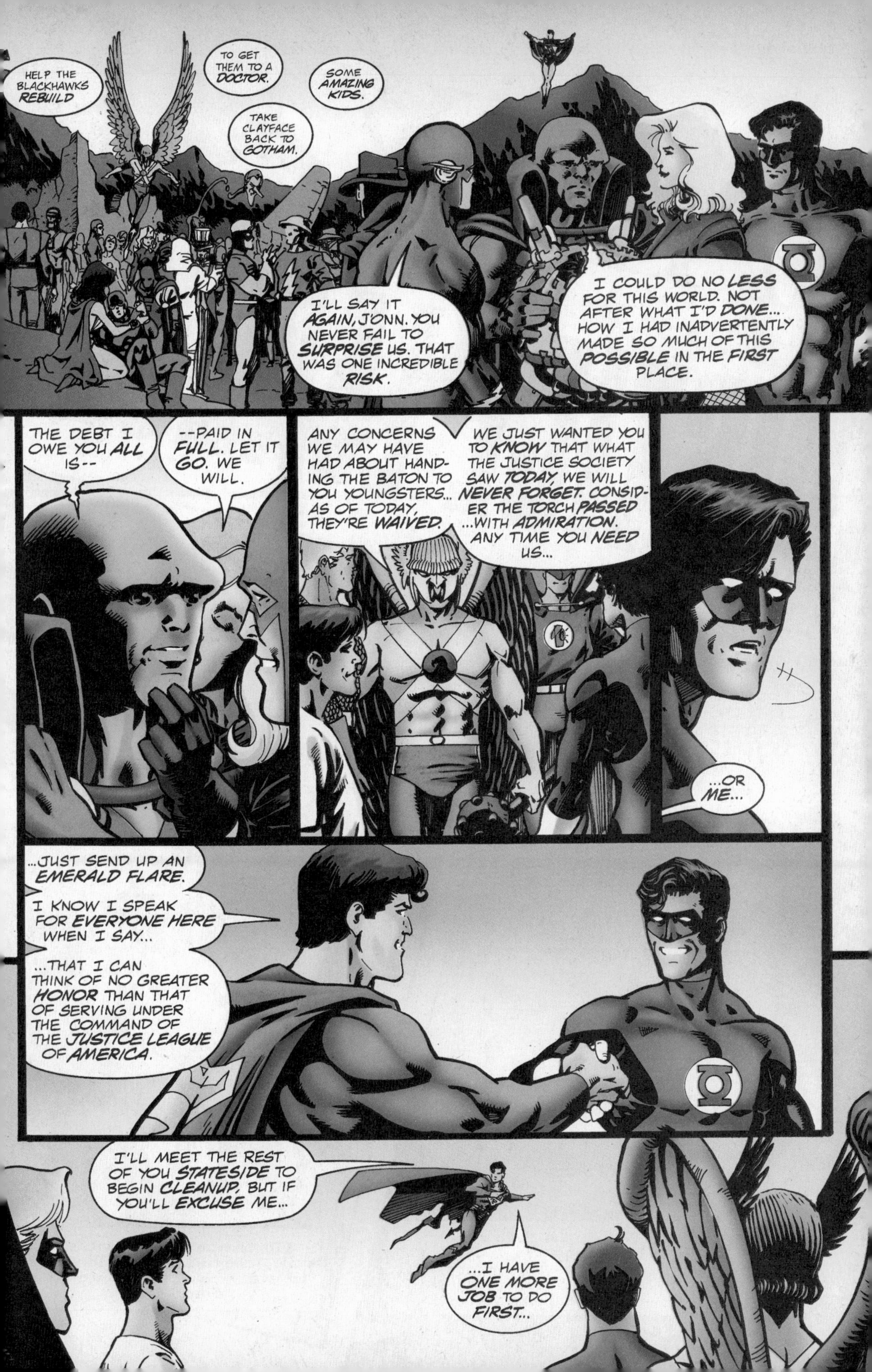

HELP THE BLACKHAWKS REBUILD
TO GET THEM TO A DOCTOR.
TAKE CLAYFACE BACK TO GOTHAM.
SOME AMAZING KIDS.
I'LL SAY IT AGAIN, J'ONN. YOU NEVER FAIL TO SURPRISE US. THAT WAS ONE INCREDIBLE RISK.
I COULD DO NO LESS FOR THIS WORLD. NOT AFTER WHAT I'D DONE... HOW I HAD INADVERTENTLY MADE SO MUCH OF THIS POSSIBLE IN THE FIRST PLACE.
THE DEBT I OWE YOU ALL IS--
--PAID IN FULL. LET IT GO. WE WILL.
ANY CONCERNS WE MAY HAVE HAD ABOUT HANDING THE BATON TO YOU YOUNGSTERS... AS OF TODAY, THEY'RE WAIVED.
WE JUST WANTED YOU TO KNOW THAT WHAT THE JUSTICE SOCIETY SAW TODAY, WE WILL NEVER FORGET. CONSIDER THE TORCH PASSED ...WITH ADMIRATION. ANY TIME YOU NEED US...
...OR ME...
...JUST SEND UP AN EMERALD FLARE.
I KNOW I SPEAK FOR EVERYONE HERE WHEN I SAY...
...THAT I CAN THINK OF NO GREATER HONOR THAN THAT OF SERVING UNDER THE COMMAND OF THE JUSTICE LEAGUE OF AMERICA.
I'LL MEET THE REST OF YOU STATESIDE TO BEGIN CLEANUP, BUT IF YOU'LL EXCUSE ME...
...I HAVE ONE MORE JOB TO DO FIRST...

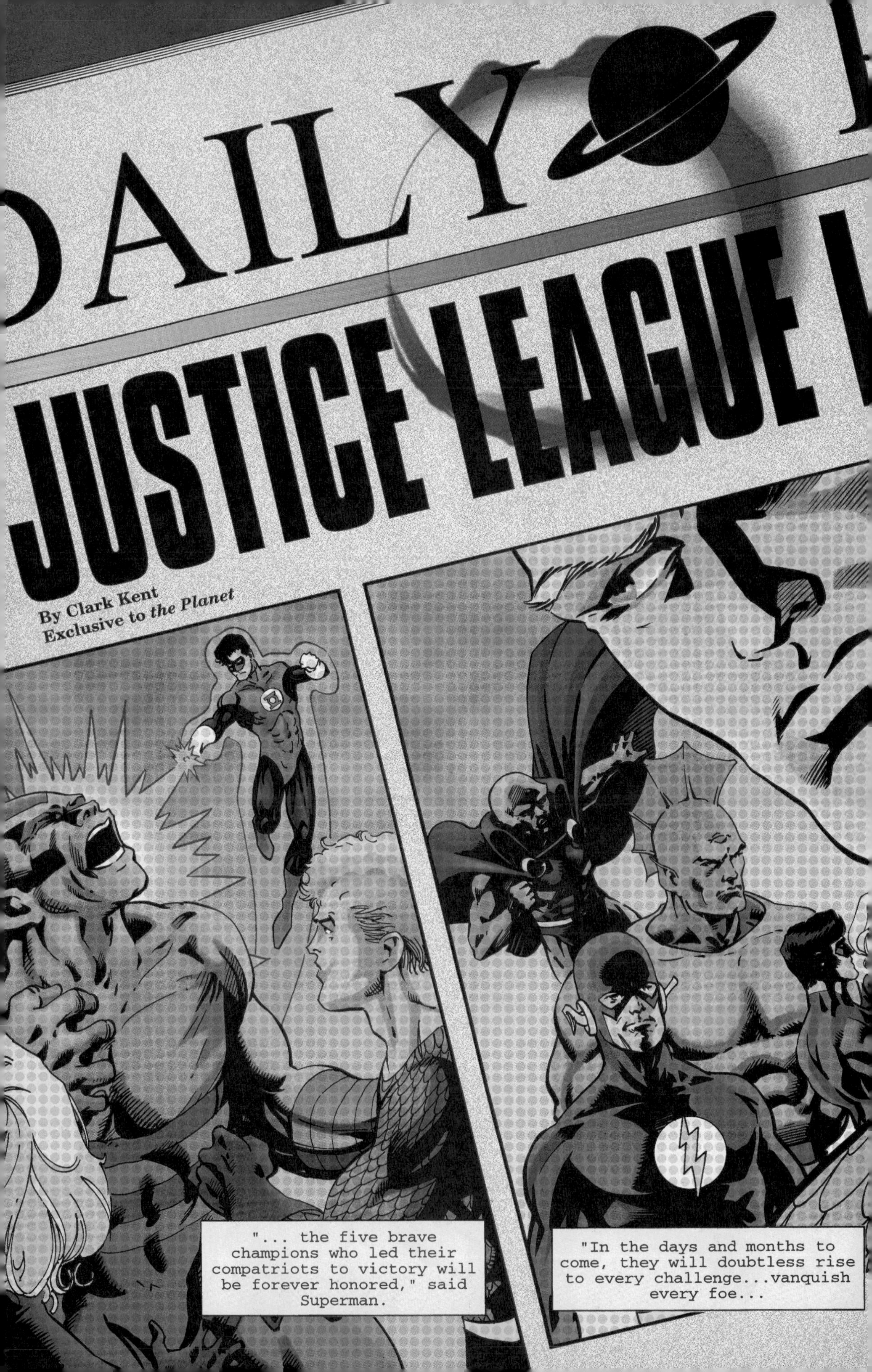
DAILY
JUSTICE LEAGUE
By Clark Kent
Exclusive to the Planet
"... the five brave champions who led their compatriots to victory will be forever honored," said Superman.
"In the days and months to come, they will doubtless rise to every challenge...vanquish every foe...

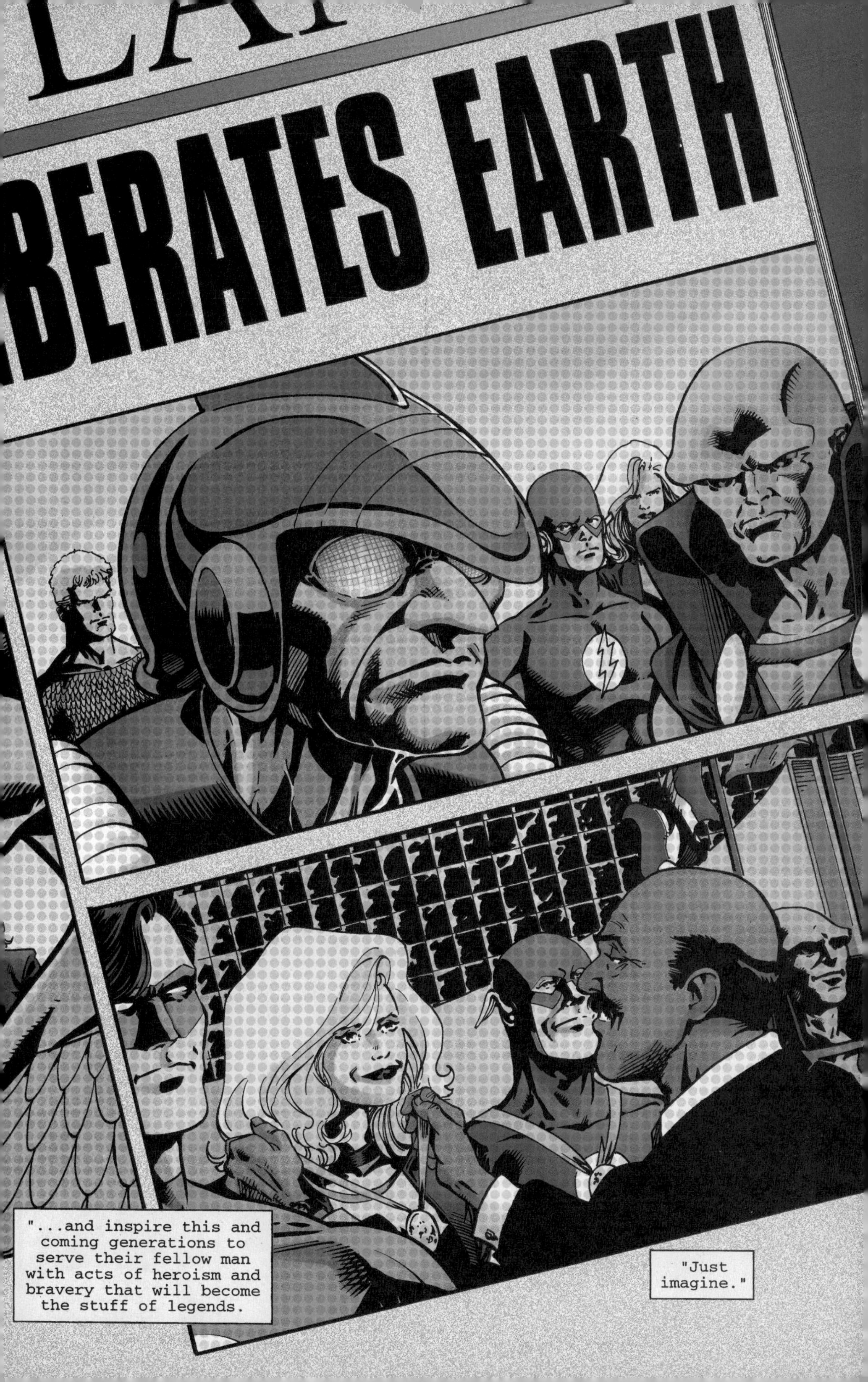
BERATES EARTH
"...and inspire this and coming generations to serve their fellow man with acts of heroism and bravery that will become the stuff of legends.
"Just imagine."

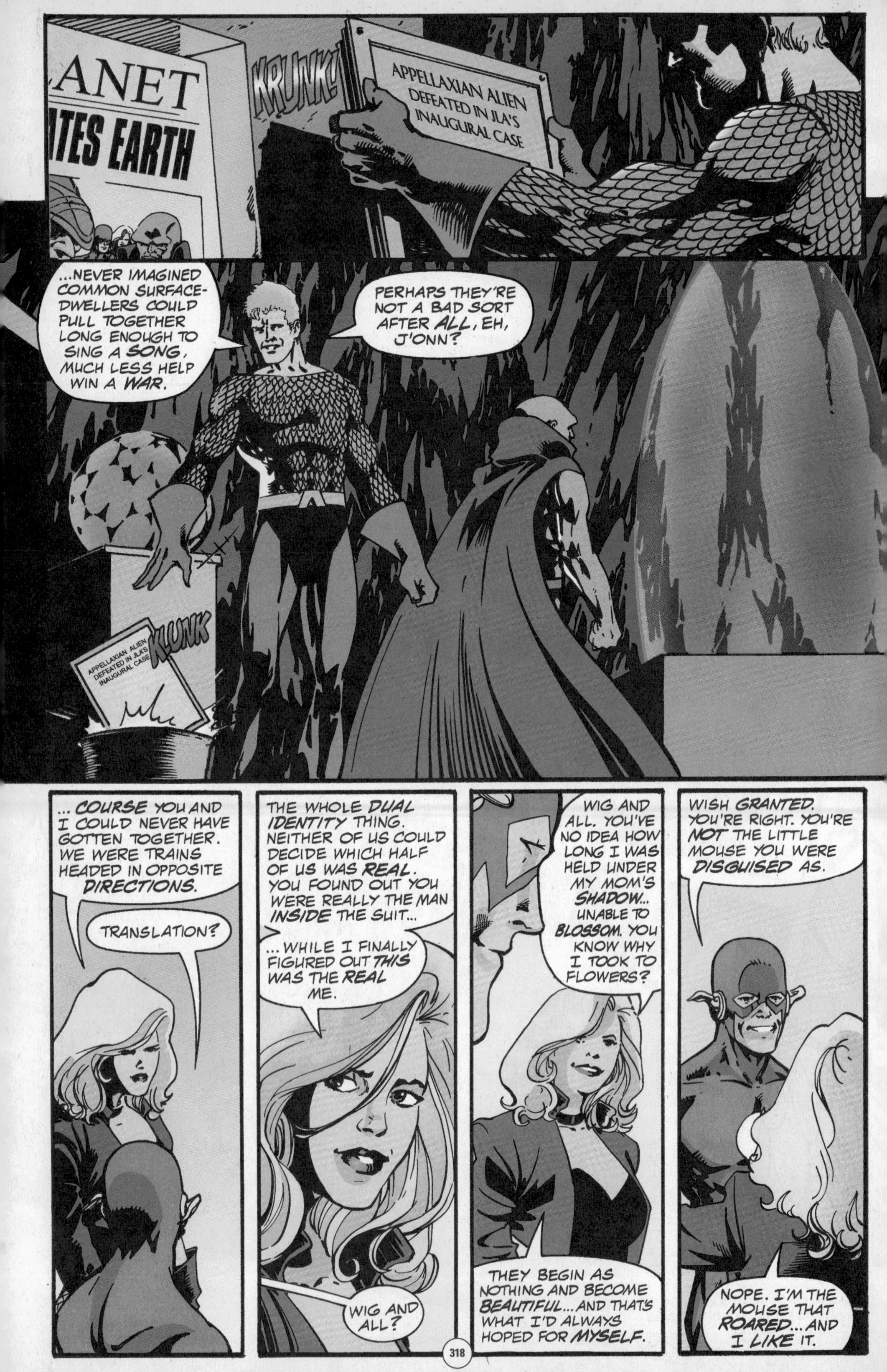
ANET
TES EARTH
KRUNK!
APPELLAXIAN ALIEN DEFEATED IN JLA'S INAUGURAL CASE
...NEVER IMAGINED COMMON SURFACE-DWELLERS COULD PULL TOGETHER LONG ENOUGH TO SING A SONG, MUCH LESS HELP WIN A WAR.
PERHAPS THEY'RE NOT A BAD SORT AFTER ALL, EH, J'ONN?
APPELLAXIAN ALIEN DEFEATED IN JLA'S INAUGURAL CASE
KLUNK
...COURSE YOU AND I COULD NEVER HAVE GOTTEN TOGETHER. WE WERE TRAINS HEADED IN OPPOSITE DIRECTIONS.
TRANSLATION?
THE WHOLE DUAL IDENTITY THING. NEITHER OF US COULD DECIDE WHICH HALF OF US WAS REAL. YOU FOUND OUT YOU WERE REALLY THE MAN INSIDE THE SUIT...
...WHILE I FINALLY FIGURED OUT THIS WAS THE REAL ME.
WIG AND ALL?
WIG AND ALL. YOU'VE NO IDEA HOW LONG I WAS HELD UNDER MY MOM'S SHADOW... UNABLE TO BLOSSOM. YOU KNOW WHY I TOOK TO FLOWERS?
THEY BEGIN AS NOTHING AND BECOME BEAUTIFUL... AND THAT'S WHAT I'D ALWAYS HOPED FOR MYSELF.
WISH GRANTED. YOU'RE RIGHT. YOU'RE NOT THE LITTLE MOUSE YOU WERE DISGUISED AS.
NOPE. I'M THE MOUSE THAT ROARED... AND I LIKE IT.

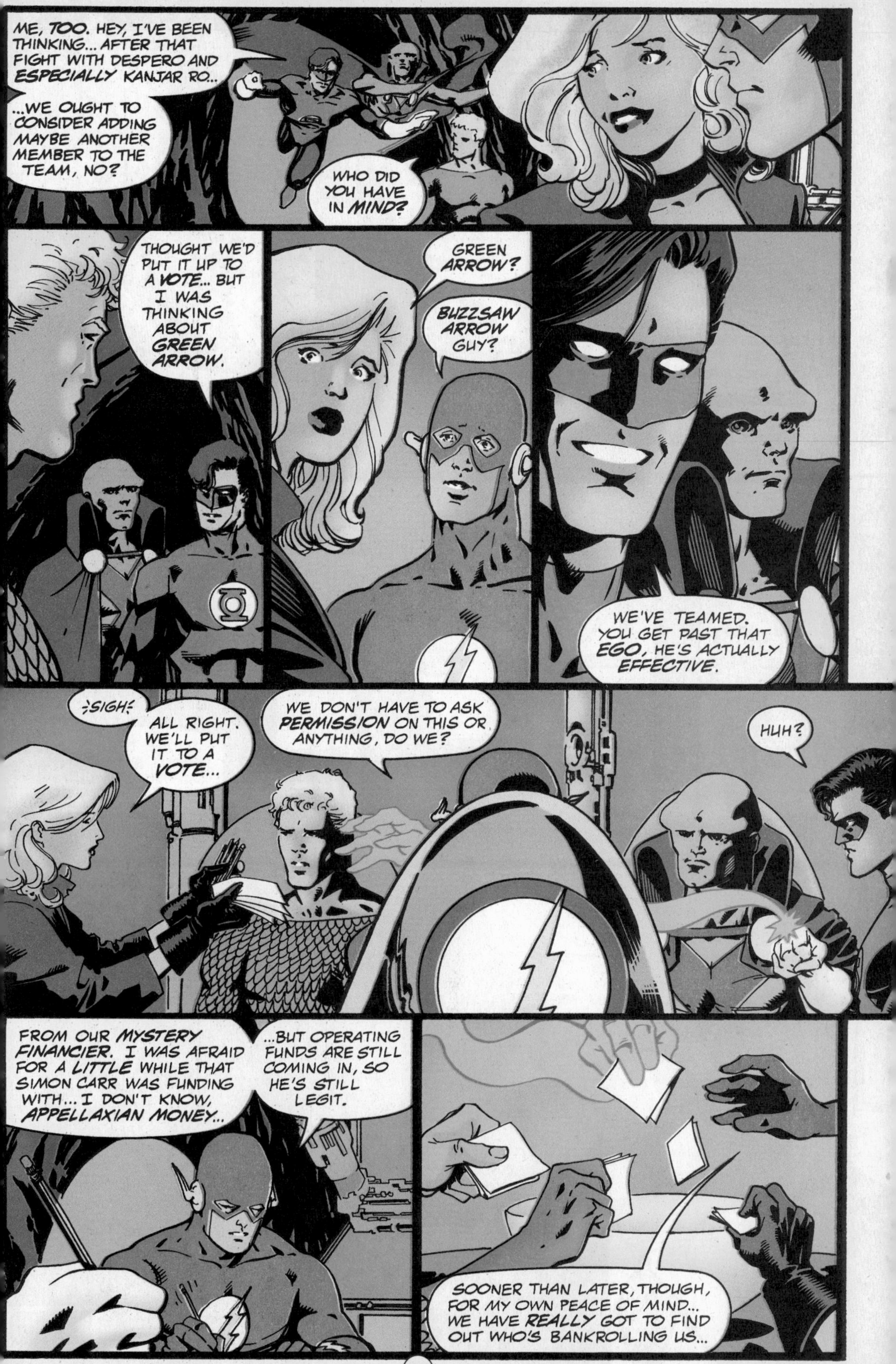

ME, TOO. HEY, I'VE BEEN THINKING... AFTER THAT FIGHT WITH DESPERO AND ESPECIALLY KANJAR RO...
...WE OUGHT TO CONSIDER ADDING MAYBE ANOTHER MEMBER TO THE TEAM, NO?
WHO DID YOU HAVE IN MIND?
THOUGHT WE'D PUT IT UP TO A VOTE... BUT I WAS THINKING ABOUT GREEN ARROW.
GREEN ARROW?
BUZZSAW ARROW GUY?
WE'VE TEAMED. YOU GET PAST THAT EGO, HE'S ACTUALLY EFFECTIVE.
:SIGH:
ALL RIGHT. WE'LL PUT IT TO A VOTE...
WE DON'T HAVE TO ASK PERMISSION ON THIS OR ANYTHING, DO WE?
HUH?
FROM OUR MYSTERY FINANCIER. I WAS AFRAID FOR A LITTLE WHILE THAT SIMON CARR WAS FUNDING WITH... I DON'T KNOW, APPELLAXIAN MONEY...
...BUT OPERATING FUNDS ARE STILL COMING IN, SO HE'S STILL LEGIT.
SOONER THAN LATER, THOUGH, FOR MY OWN PEACE OF MIND... WE HAVE REALLY GOT TO FIND OUT WHO'S BANKROLLING US...

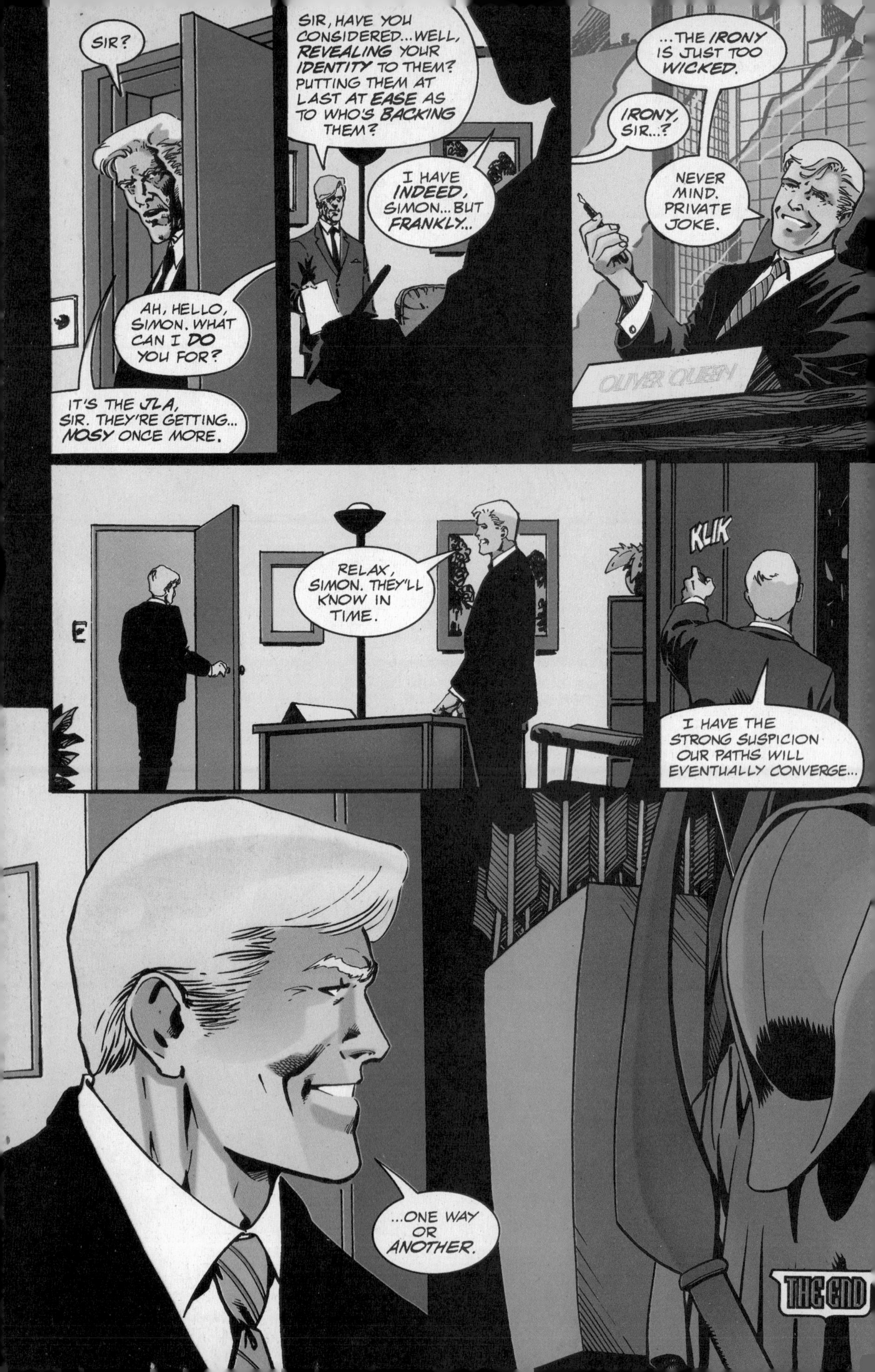
SIR?
AH, HELLO, SIMON. WHAT CAN I DO YOU FOR?
IT'S THE JLA, SIR. THEY'RE GETTING... NOSY ONCE MORE.
SIR, HAVE YOU CONSIDERED...WELL, REVEALING YOUR IDENTITY TO THEM? PUTTING THEM AT LAST AT EASE AS TO WHO'S BACKING THEM?
I HAVE INDEED, SIMON...BUT FRANKLY...
...THE IRONY IS JUST TOO WICKED.
IRONY, SIR...?
NEVER MIND. PRIVATE JOKE.
OLIVER QUEEN
RELAX, SIMON. THEY'LL KNOW IN TIME.
KLIK
I HAVE THE STRONG SUSPICION OUR PATHS WILL EVENTUALLY CONVERGE...
...ONE WAY OR ANOTHER.
THE END